LSAT
Problem-Type Drilling
Companion

A Comprehensive Drilling Reference for 82
Official LSAT PrepTests

Published by
Cambridge LSAT
303 E Elmwood Ave, Unit 304
Burbank, CA 91502-2695

Author: Morley Tatro

Manufactured in the United States
May 2016

ISBN-10: 0-692-70156-7
ISBN-13: 978-0-692-70156-0

Your first stop for all things LSAT.

www.cambridgelsat.com

If you're preparing for the LSAT (Law School Admission Test), chances are you understand the importance of this crucial admission test. In order to perform at your highest potential, quality preparation is critical. With so many prep courses and guides on the market, it's easy to become confused. The key to preparation is consistent and effective use of real LSAT questions. Our explanations help align your thought processes to those of the test makers, so you can navigate the tests efficiently and accurately. Our onsite bookstore groups the best LSAT prep materials by category, so you can get what you need quickly. The site also features a number of useful free resources, including a test tracking spreadsheet, a Logic Games tracker, advice, an LSAT FAQ, tutor listings, Logic Games practice, prep book excerpts/recommendations, and June 2007 LSAT explanations. Stop by today and download the materials you need instantly.

Why Cambridge LSAT?
o   You can download explanations and view/print them as needed.
o   No need to wait for books in the mail or go to the bookstore.
o   Eliminates the cost of shipping.
o   No need to tear out pages or flip through books to find particular explanations.
o   Gives you immediate access to detailed explanations for real test questions.
o   You can purchase only the materials needed for your study plan.
o   Our materials aren't course-specific; they can be used alongside other materials.

Have a question, comment, or concern? E-mail us at info@cambridgelsat.com.

TABLE OF CONTENTS

Introduction

The Importance of LSAT Problem-Types

Working through an LSAT section requires substantial mental agility. Although the LSAT is remarkably consistent from test to test, the composition of each section shows a great deal of variability. Your ability to smoothly transition between the different problem types within the three scored section types (Logic Games, Logical Reasoning, and Reading Comprehension) plays a significant part in your ultimate performance. However, before attempting to plough through sections which test both your understanding of the individual questions and your ability to transition between the problem types, it is important to develop mastery over the individual problem types themselves. Once you have a strong handle on the isolated concepts, then it makes sense to mix more complete section practice in with your prep work.

Reputable LSAT prep courses have been using problem-type classification systems to teach the exam for many years. When we conceived of Cambridge LSAT, the idea was to put such resources in the hands of those who choose to self study in lieu of taking expensive prep courses. Our problem set packets were a huge hit, but due to LSAC policy changes, we are no longer able to offer the packets for download. Without the efficient means to drill and perfect the question types, non-course students are at a serious disadvantage. The stumbling block isn't lack of content (LSAC distributes paperbacks which span upwards of 50 tests), but that the content isn't suitably organized for targeted practice. Thus, to drill from these books, you must seek out and identify problems of specific types.

That's where this book comes in. Instead of wasting time flipping through your books searching for problems, you can use our lists to go straight to them. The index portion of the book is split into two sections. In the first section, the different problem types are segregated and the individual problems are listed with their respective books and page numbers, where applicable. Many PrepTests are currently out-of-print, and since from a practical standpoint, you'd likely have to obtain prep course materials to get them, we have excluded the book and page information. The books and page numbers would vary depending on the company and prep course. In the second index, we list all the test sections with the respective problem types next to the individual problems. This way, you can use the index to either target and drill problems of a specific type or diagnose weak areas as you complete test sections and/or full-length tests. The following table maps shorthands used in this book to their respective publications.

Shorthand	Title
J07	June 2007 LSAT PrepTest
SP1	The Official LSAT SuperPrep
SP2	The Official LSAT SuperPrep II
V1	10 Actual, Official LSAT PrepTests
V2	10 More Actual, Official LSAT PrepTests
V3	The Next 10 Actual, Official LSAT PrepTests
V4	10 New Actual, Official LSAT PrepTests
V5	10 Actual, Official LSAT PrepTests Volume V

Logic Games Types

Using This Book

As you begin your preparation for the Logic Games portion of the LSAT, it is critical that you start to recognize recurring patterns and themes among the various games. Although most LSAT-prep companies have their own classification systems, there are many common threads which run through these various systems. The Cambridge LSAT system for classifying games was designed with simplicity in mind. It is easy to get caught up in the complexities of individual games and lose sight of the overall similarities. Although each individual game has its own quirks, there are overarching issues which appear in games of the same type. Our system is designed to exploit these similarities, so that visualizing the appropriate diagram for unseen games becomes second nature. Rigid application of these categorizations can be detrimental at times. The key is to use the categories as a guide for diagramming different games. Eventually, you will want to graduate from thinking about the categorizations, and simply pinpoint the driving forces at work in each game. Following a brief introduction of the different game types, I'll list several questions which you can use to distill a game down to its dominant components.

This book is not meant to be an introduction to the Logic Games section of the LSAT. We recommend that you purchase a book which covers games strategy extensively so that you have effective tools at your disposal with which to approach these games. If you need some guidance as to which Logic Games book to buy, visit https://www.cambridgelsat.com/bookstore/strategy-guides/. Within the bookstore, you can conveniently scroll through the various guides, and read the associated reviews.

Relative Ordering

Relative Ordering games hinge on ranking elements relative to each other. You will be given a list of elements along with some particular criteria by which the elements are to be ranked. Typically, the conditions can be combined to create an ordering map. Often, it is not necessary to create a slot diagram at the outset. Relative Ordering games test whether you can effectively translate relative rankings into fixed-position possibilities. The following is an example of a Relative Ordering game:

Six friends—Anne, Betty, Debbie, Jean, Katherine, and Margaret—are heading to Las Vegas for the weekend. Each one of the friends is bringing an amount of money with which to gamble. No two friends bring the same amount of money. The following information is known regarding the amounts:

   Anne brings more money than does either Debbie or Jean.
   Katherine brings less money than Margaret.
   If Anne brings more money than Margaret, then Jean brings less money than Betty.

Transcribing the conditions gives the following:

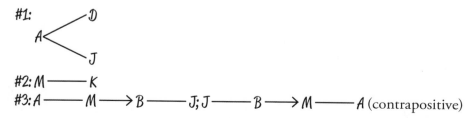

Since the third condition is a formal logic statement, we can use it to craft two ordering maps. When the third condition is triggered, we have the following:

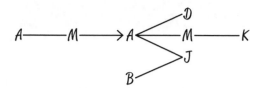

When the contrapositive of the third condition is triggered, we have the following:

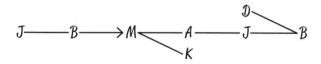

There is still one ordering map we haven't yet drawn. What if neither the third condition nor its contrapositive is triggered? We can create a third diagram to represent this scenario:

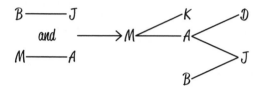

Notice that by drawing out these three ordering maps, we are properly prepared for any scenario which the questions may pose.

Simple Ordering

In contrast to Relative Ordering games, Simple Ordering games impose a much more rigid structure. To illustrate this difference, we're going to use the same elements, but alter the setup and conditions such that the game lends itself more to an ordered slot approach.

Six friends—Anne, Betty, Debbie, Jean, Katherine, and Margaret—are heading to Las Vegas for the weekend. Each one of the friends is bringing an amount of money with which to gamble. No two friends bring the same amount of money. Each friend will bring exactly one of six amounts—$300, $400, $500, $600, $700, and $800. The following information is known regarding the amounts:
  Anne brings exactly $100 more than Betty.
  Debbie does not bring the least amount of money.
  Exactly one of the friends brings less money than Katherine and more money than Margaret.

Transcribing the conditions gives the following:

#1: | BA |

#2: ~D_3

#3: | M _ K |

In this case, your diagram will consist of ordered slots. Since each one of the amounts is an increment of one hundred, you can leave out the zeros.

3	4	5	6	7	8
~D					

Because the MK piece is limited to four potential placements, you can create four scenarios with which to approach the questions.

#1	M	___	K	___	A/B	___
#2	J	M	D	K	B	A
#3	B	A	M	D/J	K	J/D
#4	___	A/B	___	M	___	K
	3	4	5	6	7	8

Note that you could also create scenarios using the BA piece instead. In the scenarios in which the MK piece leaves three open slots to either its left or its right (scenarios #1 and #4), we can infer from the first condition that one of A and B must fill the middle one of the three open slots. In scenario #2, we were able to create a complete solution due to the second condition.

Complex Ordering

Complex Ordering games are essentially Simple Ordering games stacked on top of each other. Instead of placing only one element per position, in Complex Ordering games, you will place two or more elements in each ordered position. Let's take a look at a sample Complex Ordering game:

Six families—the Blacks, the Johnsons, the Lakes, the Quails, the Smiths, and the Wileys—are moving over the course of six consecutive days—Monday, Tuesday, Wednesday, Thursday, Friday, and Saturday. Each family will rent a truck from exactly one of two companies—Penske and U-Haul—and each family will complete its move in one, two, or three trips. Each family will take exactly one complete day to move and no two families will move on the same day. The following conditions govern the six days:

    The Blacks complete their move in three trips.
    Exactly one family moves on the day in between the days on which the Johnsons and the Wileys move, and
       that family rents a Penske truck.
    The Quails, who rent a U-Haul truck, complete their move on either Wednesday or Thursday.
    The family which moves on Tuesday takes two trips.

Notice that, in addition to keeping track of which family moves on each particular day, you also must track what kind of truck that family rents along with how many trips the family takes to complete its move. Thus, this particular Complex Ordering game has three tiers, or levels. It is helpful to write the variable sets to the right of the slots as a reminder of their differentiation.

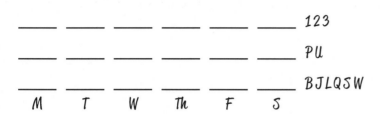

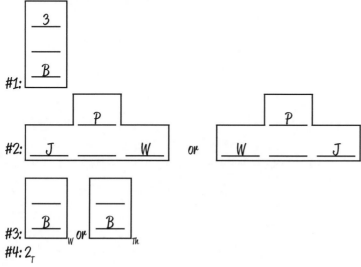

Because the pieces given by the second and third conditions cannot overlap due to the family names and the truck rentals, we can create two acceptable scenarios: one for Q_W, and one for Q_{Th}.

#1					
3/	2			/3	
		U		P	
B/		Q	J/W	/B	W/J
M	T	W	Th	F	S

#2					
	2			3/	/3
		P		U	
J/W		W/J		B/	/B
M	T	W	Th	F	S

B must occupy one of the three open family slots in each scenario. Due to the first and fourth conditions, B must occupy either the Monday or the Friday slot in scenario #1, and either the Friday or the Saturday slot in scenario #2.

In/Out Grouping

In/Out Grouping games are primarily characterized by placing elements into exactly one of two groups: the "in" group and the "out" group. In/Out Grouping games are typically dominated by formal logic statements which can often be chained together to create larger inferences. Although many In/Out games involve selecting a set of variables from a larger pool, this is not always the case. For instance, consider the following example game:

Eight private jets—an Airbus, a Boeing, a Cessna, a Dassault, an Embraer, a Gulfstream, a Hawker, and a Learjet—will be flying out of the airport on a Saturday afternoon. Each jet will take off from exactly one of two runways—1 and 2. Air traffic controllers have assigned the jets to the two runways according to the following conditions:

> If the Hawker takes off from runway 2, the Boeing takes off from runway 1.
> The Hawker does not take off from runway 1 unless the Airbus takes off from runway 1.
> The Boeing and the Cessna do not take off from the same runway.

Now, let's transcribe the conditions:

#1: $H_2 \longrightarrow B_1$; $B_2 \longrightarrow H_1$ (contrapositive)
#2: $H_1 \longrightarrow A_1$; $A_2 \longrightarrow H_2$ (contrapositive)
#3: $B_1 \longrightarrow C_2$; $C_1 \longrightarrow B_2$ (contrapositive)
    $B_2 \longrightarrow C_1$; $C_2 \longrightarrow B_1$ (contrapositive)

We can also transcribe the third condition using double, or biconditional, arrows:

$B_1 \longleftrightarrow C_2$
$B_2 \longleftrightarrow C_1$

Since a number of the conditions share like terms, we can combine them like so:

$A_2 \longrightarrow H_2 \longrightarrow B_1 \longleftrightarrow C_2$

To create the contrapositive of this chain, we only have to reverse the direction of the arrows and negate each of the included terms, like so:

$C_1 \longleftrightarrow B_2 \longrightarrow H_1 \longrightarrow A_1$

Another way to keep track of In/Out conditions is by using two columns: one for the "in" group, and one for the "out" group. For this particular game, the diagram would look like the following:

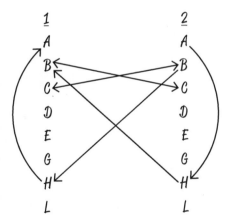

Note that this map shows the <u>exact</u> same information as does our previously-derived chain; it just does so in a more inclusive manner. The In/Out column approach helps to consolidate things into one diagram when there are two or more chains which are not interconnected.

Grouping (Distribution)

Grouping (Distribution) games require you to place each element into exactly one of a given number of groups. In contrast to In/Out Grouping games, which always have two groups, Grouping (Distribution) games typically have three or more groups. To illustrate the difference, I'm going to tweak the previous game:

Eight private jets—an Airbus, a Boeing, a Cessna, a Dassault, an Embraer, a Gulfstream, a Hawker, and a

Learjet—will be flying out of the airport on a Saturday afternoon. Each jet will take off from exactly one of three runways—1, 2, and 3. At least two jets take off from each one of the runways. Air traffic controllers have assigned the jets to the two runways according to the following conditions:

At least two other jets take off from the runway from which the Hawker takes off.
The Dassault takes off from runway 3.
Exactly two jets take off from runway 3.
The Boeing and the Cessna take off from the same runway.

We can make some deductions about the allocations of jets to runways. Since the number of jets which take off from runway 3 is fixed at two, we must allocate six jets among runways 1 and 2. Let's max out runway 1 and figure out the rest of the acceptable allocations. Since at least two jets must take off from runway 2, the greatest number of jets which can take off from runway 1 is four. Continuing this reasoning to its logical completion yields the following allocation table:

1	2	3
4	2	2
3	3	2
2	4	2

Let's transcribe these conditions:

#1: 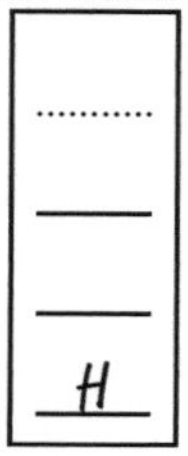

#2: D_3

#3: 

#4: 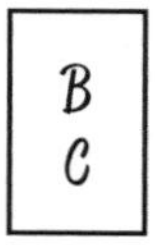

Combining all the conditions, we can deduce that none of B, C, and H can take off from runway 3.

```
.............  ..............

.............  ..............

_____  _____  _____

_____  _____  __D__
  1       2       3
                 ~B
                 ~C
                 ~H
```

We can also use the fourth condition to draw up two acceptable scenarios: one with the BC piece assigned to runway 1, and one with the BC piece assigned to runway 2.

```
#1  .............  ..............        #2  .............  ..............

   __H/_  _____                       _____  __/H__

   __B__   _____   _____                     _____   __B__   _____

   __C__   _/H__   __D__                     __H/_   __C__   __D__
    1       2       3                          1       2       3
```

Determined Assignment

Assignment games involve placing variables into structures. The structure for a particular Assignment game may be either ordered or unordered. Oftentimes Assignment games combine elements of both ordering and grouping. In a Determined Assignment game, the exact profile of the active variables—the variables which are to be assigned to positions in the structure—is completely determined by the setup paragraph and the conditions.

The following is an example of a Determined Assignment game.

An employee of a cable company will be doing installations in five different apartment buildings on a particular Friday. He will complete exactly two installations in each building—one cable Internet and one cable television. Once he completes both installations in one building, he will move on to another building, until he has completed all the installations. Ten families—the Bushes, the Damatos, the Easleys, the Funkhausers, the Gajardos, the Habibs, the McLarens, the Rosas, the Spencers, and the Turners—are scheduled to have their installations completed by this cable employee on this Friday. The employee's schedule must conform to the following:

The Funkhausers and the Habibs live in the same building.
The Easleys and the Rosas are both having cable Internet installed, and their buildings will be completed consecutively by the employee.
The Damatos live in the building which will be completed third in the schedule.
The McLarens are having cable Internet installed.

Here's how the conditions look transcribed:

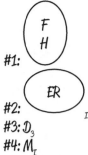

#1:

#2:

#3: D_3

#4: M_I

Let's see how these conditions can be combined. Because we have to place ten variables into the structure, and we know how many of each variable is to be placed (one), this Assignment game is determined. This game would be a Complex Ordering game if we were given which families were scheduled for each installation. Can we make any deductions about the installation types from the information that we do have? From the third condition, we know that D can be assigned to either kind of installation. If D is assigned to cable Internet, we will know with near certainty which families are scheduled for each kind of installation. The first condition makes this possible. Although we don't know which one of F and H is scheduled for cable Internet installation, we do know that one of them is. Therefore, if D is assigned to cable Internet, we have the following installation type assignments:

$D_I \longrightarrow$ I   F/H   D   E   R   M

           T   H/F   B   G   S   T

If we apply this to the ordered diagram, we can make additional deductions. With D placed in the center of the cable Internet slots, the ER piece must be placed either first and second, or fourth and fifth. Thus, we can draw up two scenarios for D being assigned to cable Internet:

$D_I \longrightarrow$ I E/R R/E D M/ /M   I M/ /M D E/R R/E

           T ___ ___ ___ ___ ___ or T ___ ___ ___ ___ ___

               1   2   3   4   5   1   2   3   4   5

Note that the FH piece must occupy one of the last two buildings in the first scenario and one of the first two buildings in the second scenario.

Undetermined Assignment

In contrast to Determined Assignment games, in an Undetermined Assignment game, there is uncertainty as to how many of each kind of variable are to be placed into the diagram. Consider the following sample game:

Each of the five starting players of the local high school basketball team—Aaron, Brett, Dwayne, Jamal, and Todd—can play at least one of the five positions—center, point guard, power forward, shooting guard, and small forward. The following information regarding their abilities is known:

> With the exception of Jamal, who can play four positions, none of the players can play more than three positions.
> Todd can play more positions than Brett.
> Dwayne can play fewer positions than Brett.
> Any player who can play shooting guard can also play small forward.

From the way the conditions are laid out, numbers are clearly a big factor in this game. Since we know more about the numbers of positions each player can play than we do about the number of players who can play any particular position, it makes sense to treat the players as the fixed variables. From the first, second, and third conditions, we can establish definite numbers for B, D, and T. Since we have T > B > D, and T cannot play more than three positions (first condition), the allocation of positions to players for these three is:

T	B	D
3	2	1

Since the number of positions A plays is open (other than the fact that it must be less than three), we can establish three overall allocations of positions to players:

A	B	D	J	T
1	2	1	4	3
2	2	1	4	3
3	2	1	4	3

From this allocation table we can create our diagram:

```
                    _____
............         _____  _____
............ _____   _____  _____
_____ _____  _____   _____  _____
  A     B      D       J      T
              -SG
```

As a consequence of the acceptable allocations and the fourth condition, D cannot play shooting guard; this is noted in the diagram underneath D's slot.

Miscellaneous

Miscellaneous games are those which are rare and/or have not appeared on an actual LSAT in a number of years. Often, games which fall in this category take elements of common game types and present them in a particularly challenging manner. Although Miscellaneous games should not be your main priority in mastering the section, exposing yourself to these "oddball" games can still be of benefit. The ability to handle the twists and turns that LSAC (the Law School Admission Council) builds into all the game types efficiently will ultimately determine your ability to successfully navigate the section on an actual test.

Let's take a look at a hypothetical Miscellaneous game:

Seven kindergarteners—Andrew, Ella, Kaitlin, Jocelyn, Matt, Nick, Trisha—are playing a game of musical chairs. The chairs are arranged in a circle and are consecutively numbered in a clockwise direction one through seven. Each chair is adjacent to two other chairs which are consecutively numbered with the exception of chairs one and seven, which are next to each other. Three rounds of the game will be played according to the following conditions.

 During each round, exactly one of the chairs numbered three, four, and five will be removed.
 Whenever a person lands on a removed chair, that person is out.
 Once a chair has been removed, each of the children must skip over it for the remainder of the game.

While diagramming this game is not particularly challenging, combining the conditions in any kind of meaningful way is. Since the number of chairs is odd, a spoke diagram would require you to erase one of the spokes. Alternatively, you could plot a standard slot ordering diagram and note that chairs numbered one and seven are adjacent.

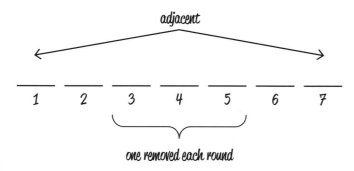

Limited Games

All LSAT Logic Games are limited to some degree. The setup paragraph and the conditions create the limitations. Some games are much more limited than others. We've touched on games which have Limited Allocations and games which have Limited Scenarios. There is a third type of limitation which, when used at the right time, can greatly accelerate your accurate completion of the associated questions: Limited Solutions. If a game has a limited number of solutions—generally between five and ten—by drawing them out at the outset, you will eliminate any uncertainty in the game and you should be able to breeze through the questions. The Index specifies these limitations where applicable.

What to Look For

As you progress through the chapters of this book, you will refine your technique and learn to make additional inferences in games of each type. You will also start to recognize many of the relevant clues which will help you determine the optimal diagram for each game. When reading through a game's setup and conditions for the first time, these are the kinds of questions you should be asking yourself:
o About which variable set do I have the most information?
o Is there an element of ordering to the game?
o Is each ordered position limited to one variable or can there be ties?
o Which variables should be fixed in place?

o   Which variables can change positions from question to question? These are the active variables.
o   Is each active variable limited to one assignment or can there be repeats?
o   Are any positions in the structure inherently limited?
o   Can I make any numerical deductions about the variables and/or the open positions?
o   Can I draw a few limited scenarios to keep better track of the information?
o   Is this game so limited that plotting out all the acceptable solutions is an efficient use of my time?

If you need help diagramming and solving the included games, you can purchase
LSAT Logic Games Solutions Manual through our bookstore or directly through Amazon.

Logical Reasoning Question Types

Logical Reasoning

Every LSAT is comprised of two scored Logical Reasoning sections. Each Logical Reasoning section contains 24-26 questions. Each passage, or stimulus, contains exactly one of three things: a one-sided argument, a multiple-sided argument, or a fact set. The question stems which accompany each passage will require you to analyze the information, make inferences, identify flaws, identify points of disagreement, identify underlying principles, etc. Fundamental to strong performance on LSAT Logical Reasoning questions is the ability to isolate argument conclusions and premises. The purpose of this book is to help you learn to recognize the patterns which LSAC (the Law School Admission Council) regularly draws upon in crafting these questions. Within this book, each Logical Reasoning question is classified according to its question stem—the question or statement which immediately follows the stimulus and immediately precedes the answer choices.

Using This Book

This is not an introductory book to the Logical Reasoning section. We recommend that you purchase a book which covers detailed strategies for the different question types that appear on the section. If you're unsure of what book to buy, visit https://www.cambridgelsat.com/bookstore/strategy-guides/. You will be able to conveniently scroll through the various offerings and read the associated reviews.

Inference

Inference questions test your ability to wade through a passage and determine one of four things: what must be true, what is likely to be true, what would best complete the passage, and what cannot be true.

Must Be True: Must Be True stimuli often contain conditional statements which can be linked to create chain inferences. The answer to a Must Be True question necessarily follows from the stimulus, if the information contained in the stimulus is true. From a formal logic standpoint, the correct answer to a Must Be True question is the necessary condition and the stimulus is the sufficient condition. Diagrammed, this looks like the following:

Statement 1 + Statement 2 + Statement 3… + Statement n ⟶ Correct Answer

The following are examples of Must Be True question stems:
Which one of the following conclusions can properly be drawn from the above statements?
If the statements above are true, which one of the following must on the basis of them also be true?
Which one of the following follows logically from the statements above?
Which one of the following is a proper inference from the passage?
If all the statements in the passage are true, each of the following must also be true EXCEPT:

Most Strongly Supported: Most Strongly Supported questions test your ability to make inferential leaps from the stimuli. Most Strongly Supported stimuli are typically not as couched in conditional reasoning as are Must Be True stimuli. Here are some example Most Strongly Supported question stems:
The statements above, if true, would provide the strongest support for which one of the following hypotheses?
The statements above most strongly support which one which one of the following conclusions?
The information above provides the most support for which one of the following conclusions?

Which one of the following inferences is most supported by the statements above?

If the view above is correct, it provides a reason for accepting which one of the following conclusions?

Complete the Passage: As the name implies, these questions ask you to fill in the blank with whatever information would logically complete the passage. That information may come in the form of the main conclusion or a premise. Here are some example question stems of this type:

Which one of the following best completes the passage?

Which one of the following best completes the argument?

Which one of the following most logically completes the commentator's argument?

Which one of the following, if true, most appropriately completes the explanation?

Which one of the following logically completes the argument?

Cannot Be True: Cannot Be True questions test your ability to pick out information which is incompatible. In other words, if the information in the stimulus is true, you must pick the answer choice which conflicts with it. The following are examples of Cannot Be True question stems:

Which one of the following conflicts with information in the passage?

Given the information in the passage, which one of the following must be false?

The statements above, if true, most seriously undermine which one of the following assertions?

According to the argument, each of the following could be true of teachers who have enabled their students to make their own decisions EXCEPT:

If the statements on which the conclusion above is based are all true, each of the following could be true EXCEPT:

Notice that the word "except" completely changes the meaning of the question. Because of its importance, LSAC always capitalizes the word "except" when it is used in a question of any section type.

Main Conclusion

Main Conclusion questions test your ability to isolate the main point which the argument supports. Often, Main Conclusion stimuli contain subsidiary points which are listed as attractive, but incorrect, answer choices. To test whether or not a particular piece of an argument is the main conclusion, you need to ask yourself if every other piece of the argument supports it. If not, it is not the main conclusion of the argument. The following are Main Conclusion question stems:

Which one of the following is the main point of the passage?

Which one of the following best expresses the main point of the passage?

Which one of the following is the main point of the passage as a whole?

Which one of the following best expresses the main point of the argument?

Which one of the following sentences best expresses the main point of the passage?

Point

Point questions are always associated with stimuli which contain two speakers. At the heart of the discussion is a disagreement. Sometimes the point of contention is easy to spot, and other times it can require a deeper analysis to isolate. On rare occasions, you may come across a dual-speaker stimulus and be asked to find a point on which the two speakers agree. These questions can be treated largely in the same fashion. In order to determine whether or not a person would agree or disagree with a particular point, you must use the evidence in the stimulus. The correct answer to a Point question is a statement with which one of the disputants would agree and the other disputant would disagree. Here are some Point question stems:

Which one of the following is a point at issue between the nutritionist and the consumer advocate?

The disagreement between the two paleontologists is over which one of the following?

Which one of the following is the main point at issue between Lola and Derek?

On the basis of their statements above, the consumer advocate and the manufacturer are committed to disagreeing about the truth of which one of the following statements?

The point at issue between Emile and Sabina is whether

Assumption

Learning to recognize underlying assumptions is critical to mastering the Logical Reasoning section. Assumption questions come in two varieties: Necessary Assumption and Sufficient Assumption.

Necessary: Necessary Assumption questions test your ability to find unstated assumptions which must be true in order for the arguments to be valid. Diagrammed, this looks like the following:

Valid Conclusion $\longrightarrow$ Necessary Assumption (Correct Answer) must be true

As with any conditional statement, the contrapositive is also valid. Thus, if the correct answer is negated, the conclusion is invalidated. This is an effective technique for narrowing down remaining answer choices to Necessary Assumption questions. The following are Necessary Assumption question stems:

The conclusion in the passage depends on the assumption that

Which one of the following is an assumption upon which the argument depends?

The argument requires the assumption that

Which one of the following is assumed in the passage?

The argument in the passage assumes which one of the following?

Sufficient: A sufficient assumption is information which, if added to the argument, ensures that the conclusion is valid. Diagrammed, this looks like so:

Premise(s) + Sufficient Assumption (Correct Answer) $\longrightarrow$ Valid Conclusion

Here's a typical Sufficient Assumption scenario:

Premise 1: If A, then B. (A $\longrightarrow$ B)

Premise 2: If C, then D. (C $\longrightarrow$ D)

Conclusion: Therefore, if A, then D. (A $\longrightarrow$ D)

To prove the conclusion, we only need to connect B and C like so: B $\longrightarrow$ C. Since the contrapositive is logically equivalent, if the answer were phrased as such ($\sim$C $\longrightarrow$ $\sim$B), it would also be correct.

The following are examples of Sufficient Assumption question stems:

Which one of the following is an assumption that would permit the conclusion above to be properly drawn?

The conclusion of the argument is properly drawn if which one of the following is assumed?

The conclusion follows logically from the premises if which one of the following is assumed?

The conclusion is properly drawn if which one of the following is assumed?

From which one of the following does the conclusion logically follow?

Impact

Impact questions test your understanding of how additional information affects the strength of argument conclusions. They come in three different varieties: Strengthen, Weaken, and Evaluate.

Strengthen: Strengthen questions ask you to select information which supports, or bolsters the strength of the conclusion. Here are some example Strengthen question stems:

> Which one of the following, if true, supports the conclusion in the passage?
> Each of the following, if true, would support the conclusion above EXCEPT:
> Which one of the following, if true, would most strengthen the argument?
> Each of the following, if true, provides support to the argument EXCEPT:
> Each of the following, if true, supports the claim above EXCEPT:

Note that three of the stems include the word "except." For questions like this, the correct answer will not necessarily weaken the argument. The correct answer can be one which doesn't affect the argument's conclusion at all.

Weaken: Weaken questions ask you to select information which undermines an argument's conclusion. Here are some example Weaken stems:

> Which one of the following, if true, most seriously weakens the argument?
> Which one of the following, if true, casts the most doubt on the author's hypothesis?
> Which one of the following, if true, would weaken the argument?
> Which one of the following, if true, would best challenge the conclusion of the passage?
> Which one of the following, if true, would cast doubt on the experimenters' conclusion?

Evaluate: Evaluate questions test your ability to pick out information which is most relevant to the argument at hand. They will ask you to either select a pertinent question or information which would be most helpful in determining the validity of the conclusion. The following are Evaluate question stem examples:

> Clarification of which one of the following issues would be most important to an evaluation of the skeptics' position?
> Which one of the following would it be most relevant to investigate in evaluating the conclusion of George's argument?
> Which one of the following issues would be LEAST important to resolve in evaluating the argument?
> The answer to which one of the following questions would be most useful in evaluating the truth of the conclusion drawn in the advertisement?
> Which one of the following would be most important to know in evaluating the hypothesis in the passage?

Method

Method questions test your ability to recognize argument structures. These questions are concerned with either the argument as a whole, or the function of a specific statement within the argument.

Argument: Method (Argument) questions ask you to analyze the argumentative strategy employed in the stimulus. The correct answer to a Method (Argument) question typically summarizes the argument in an abstract fashion. Here are some example question stems:

> In order to advance her point of view, the author does all of the following EXCEPT
> In the passage, the author

Which one of the following most accurately expresses the method used to counter the automakers' current position?

The passage employs which one of the following argumentative strategies?

Which one of the following argumentative strategies is used above?

Statement: Method (Statement) questions require you to analyze a piece of the argument in greater detail. Specifically, you must determine what role a particular plays in advancing the argument. The following are examples of Method (Statement) stems:

The statement that the car Peter took got damaged and the car Alicia took did not plays which one of the following roles in the argument?

The claim that a university should not be entitled to patent the inventions of its faculty members plays which one of the following roles in the argument?

The case of August Frenson plays which one of the following roles in the argument?

The statement that adolescents and adults are not the same plays which one of the following roles in the argument?

The proposition that the public is now more interested in reading and hearing about crime plays which one of the following roles in the argument?

Flaw

Flaw questions test your ability to spot and delineate logical fallacies in arguments. Flawed arguments tend to either overlook important information or make erroneous assumptions in presenting their conclusions. Here are some examples of Flaw question stems:

A flaw in the argument is that the author

Which one of the following indicates an error in the reasoning leading to the prediction above?

Which one of the following is a flaw in the argument?

The proposal mentioned above falls short of offering a complete solution to the problem it addresses because

Jack Jordan's remarks suggest that he is misinterpreting which one of the following words used by Mary Simms?

Parallel

Parallel questions test your ability to understand an argument's structure. Rather than simply asking you to delineate the structure, as do Method (Argument) questions, Parallel questions ask you to select the answer choice which illustrates a similar logical structure.

Reasoning: Parallel (Reasoning) question stems do not explicitly state whether or not the logic in the stimulus is flawed. Therefore, if you find fallacious reasoning in the stimulus, be on the lookout for similarly flawed reasoning when evaluating the answer choices. On the other hand, if the logic in the stimulus is valid, be sure to select an answer choice which is also logically sound. Parallel (Reasoning) questions often feature an incorrect distractor answer choice which addresses a similar topic as the stimulus, but does not have a comparable logical structure. Keep in mind that the contrapositive of a chain still represents a parallel method of reasoning. For instance, say that you are given an argument in the stimulus of the following form.

Premise: If A, then B. (A $\longrightarrow$ B)

Premise: If B, then C. (B $\longrightarrow$ C)

Conclusion: Therefore, if A, then C. (A $\longrightarrow$ C)

If an answer choice sets up a similar inference chain (A ⟶ B ⟶ C) and states that the contrapositive (~C ⟶ ~A) is true, then that answer is correct.

The following are examples of Parallel (Reasoning) question stems:

> Which one of the following most closely parallels the reasoning in the argument presented in the passage?
>
> The logical structure of the argument above is most similar to which one of the following?
>
> Which one of the following, in its logical features, most closely parallels the reasoning used in the passage?
>
> In which one of the following does the reasoning most closely parallel that employed in the passage?
>
> Which one of the following most closely parallels the reasoning used in the passage?

Flaw: In a Parallel (Flaw) stimulus, there is at least one error of reasoning. Your job is to select the answer choice which most closely parallels the error(s). A common flaw is confusing a necessary condition for a sufficient condition and vice versa. For instance, a premise may state "if A, then B" (A ⟶ B). If the conclusion states that B implies A, then the speaker has made a necessary/sufficient error. The correct answer to a question like this will similarly conflate the two types of conditions. Here are some example Parallel (Flaw) question stems:

> Which one of the following arguments contains an error of reasoning similar to that in the argument above?
>
> The flawed pattern of reasoning in the argument above is most similar to that in which one of the following?
>
> Which one of the following most closely parallels the flawed reasoning in the argument above?
>
> The flawed reasoning in the argument above most closely parallels that in which one of the following?
>
> The flawed reasoning in the advertisement most closely parallels that in which one of the following?

Paradox

Paradox questions ask you to explain facts, typically two, which are apparently at odds with each other. Your job is to select the answer choice which best reconciles the apparent discrepancy. Paradox questions may also ask you to explain a puzzling result. The following are example Paradox question stems:

> Which one of the following, if true, most helps to explain why treating deep wounds with sugar as described above is successful?
>
> Which one of the following, if true, best reconciles the discrepancy described above?
>
> Each of the following would, by itself, help to resolve the apparent paradox described in the passage EXCEPT:
>
> Which one of the following, if true, most helps to explain the difference in plant growth described above?
>
> Which one of the following, if true, establishes that the doctor's second reason does not cancel out the first?

Principle

Principle questions will ask you to do one of two things: select a principle which underlies an argument or course of action; apply an underlying principle in the stimulus to another situation.

Identify: Principle (Identify) questions ask you to identify a principle which could strengthen, or completely justify a position. Here are some example Principle (Identify) question stems:

> Which one of the following principles, if established, provides the strongest justification for the department chair's refusal, on the ground she gives, to sign the protest letter?
>
> Which one of the following principles, if accepted, would provide the most justification for the conclusion?
>
> Which one of the following principles, if accepted, would most help the citizens' group to justify drawing its conclusion that the mayor has in mind interests other than Plainsville's economy?

Mary's decision most closely accords with which one of the following principles?

If the voters' reactions are guided by a principle, which one of the following principles would best account for the contrast in reactions described above?

Apply: With Principle (Apply) questions, you will often have to identify a principle which underlies the stimulus and then apply that same principle to additional situations. The following are examples of Principle (Apply) question stems:

Which one of the following judgments conforms to the principle stated above?

Which one of the following, if true, can most logically serve as a premise for an argument that uses the principle to counter the claim?

In which one of the following situations is the principle expressed most clearly violated?

Which one of the following judgments conforms to the principles invoked above?

This principle, if accepted, would justify which one of the following judgments?

Dual-Question Stimuli

In previous years, some Logical Reasoning stimuli were followed by two discrete question stems. Thus, you will occasionally encounter duplicate stimuli as you work through the chapters. Wherever present, duplicate stimuli indicate that the particular passage was followed by two question stems. Although dual-question stimuli haven't appeared on scored Logical Reasoning sections in recent years, you should nevertheless be prepared for them.

Formal Logic

Formal Logic is a concept which can appear in Logical Reasoning questions of any type. Elements of Formal Logic include conditional reasoning, such as "if/then" statements, and quantifiers like "all," "most," "some," and "none." For instance, a passage with Formal Logic might contain statements like the following:

Most As are Bs.

All Bs are Cs.

If the example passage was followed by a Must Be True question stem, you could properly infer that most As are Cs.

Reading Comprehension Passage Types

Using This Book

The Reading Comprehension portion of the LSAT has earned the reputation of being the most difficult of the three section types in which to make gains. This is due to two reasons: (1) for many people, Reading Comprehension is the most familiar of the three section types initially, and (2) because students have been reading throughout their lives, it can be difficult to address poor habits in this area. Further, this portion of the exam does not lend itself to "gaming," or seeking to exploit patterns outside the realm of genuine comprehension. The LSAT is designed to exacting standards, and the psychometricians employed in its creation are extremely adept at determining your level of understanding of any given passage, whether it be comprehensive or cursory.

This book is not meant to serve as an introduction to LSAT Reading Comprehension. Rather, it is a practice workbook which you can use to implement and solidify concepts acquired from the strategy guide of your choice. Purchasing a guide for this section is certainly not as critical as it is for Logical Reasoning and Logic Games. However, exposing yourself to new approaches can help you navigate the sometimes murky waters of Reading Comprehension. For guidance on which book to purchase, visit https://www.cambridgelsat.com/bookstore/strategy-guides/. Within the store, you can browse the various guides and read the respective reviews. LSAC publishes The Official LSAT Handbook, which you can purchase through the store. It provides an excellent introduction to all three section types from the minds of the creators.

Anatomy of a Reading Comprehension Section

Each Reading Comprehension section features three long passages along with two comparative short passages. The comparative reading format was first introduced in June of 2007. The June 2007 test is available for download at www.lsac.org, and you can purchase the numbered PrepTests through our bookstore. Each passage, or comparative passage pair, is followed by five to eight questions. Argumentation is common to the majority of passages, and recent passages share many elements with Logical Reasoning stimuli, albeit on a larger scale. The questions can be loosely classified as either General or Specific, depending on the scope of the inquiry. General questions ask you to respond based on the passage as a whole while Specific questions draw your attention to particular portions of the text.

Here are some example General question stems:
    Which one of the following best expresses the main idea of the passage?
    Which one of the following best describes the organization of the material presented in the passage?
    The author's attitude toward the inquisitorial system can best be described as
    The primary purpose of the passage is to
    In the passage, the author is primarily concerned with

The following are examples of Specific question stems:
    The author quotes Fruton (lines 62–64) primarily in order to
    The author suggests that the "deceptive veil" (line 42) in Hughes's poetry obscures
    The author mentions laboratory experiments with adult water bugs (lines 63–66) in order to illustrate which one of the following?
    The author's discussion of the political significance of the "wage relationship" (line 48) serves to
    What is the main purpose of the third paragraph (lines 28–47)?

Active Reading

In order to master this section, you must learn to find an interest in any passage the test makers throw your way. Since the LSAT is an exercise in stratifying candidates for the convenience of law school admission committees, the passages are composed in such a way as to require a great attention to both the details and the global issues. By actively involving yourself in the reading process, you will be much better equipped to answer the subsequent questions. Here are some questions you should keep in the back of your mind as you read a passage for the first time:

o   Does this passage have a main point? If so…
o   What is the main point of the passage?
o   What was the author's purpose in writing the passage?
o   How is the passage structured?
o   What points of view are presented in the passage?
o   What evidence is used to support the viewpoint(s)?
o   If more than one point of view is present, how are they related to one another?
o   How persuasive are the arguments presented in favor of the viewpoint(s)?

Marking the Passages

While most people will do at least some diagramming in the Logical Reasoning and Logic Games portions of the exam, the decision of whether or not to mark Reading Comprehension passages is largely a personal one. For some, thinking about what to notate and how to notate it detracts from their overall comprehension of the passage. Clearly, this defeats the purpose. For others, not marking the passages ushers in a sense of complacency. The writers of the test frequently prey on such lackadaisical reading habits, and a lack of involvement in any passage can be deadly to your performance on the associated questions. Since you have a lot of passages with which to refine your technique, we recommend that you experiment with different markup strategies and find one which yields the most consistent and accurate results. In general, finding a happy medium between heavy markup styles and none at all will allow you to stay alert and involved in the passage without taking away from your understanding of the broader issues presented in the passage.

Whatever markup strategies you employ, if any, should enhance your ability to tackle not only the General questions, but also the Specific questions. You can use techniques like underlining, boxing, and circling to highlight important details. As you complete more and more passages, you will develop your intuition regarding which details are important and what you are likely to come across in the questions. Techniques like bracketing and writing notes next to the paragraphs can help you summarize key ideas and structural elements, and accurately answer General questions.

Passage Types

LSAT Reading Comprehension sections typically feature one passage, or passage set, in each of four broad areas. Correspondingly, the first four chapters of test content are as follows: Humanities, Law, Natural Sciences, and Social Sciences. If you are already an avid reader, you will have an edge on the competition prior to attempting your first LSAT passage. Reading news articles, including those found in such magazines as *The Economist*, can help prepare you for the rigors of this section. LSAC draws from a variety of sources in creating the passages, and the passages are generally written in a dense, academic style. Articles in academic and scientific journals provide excellent material with which to hone your critical reading skills. To obtain the greatest benefit from any such outside reading, be sure to practice your active reading and practice asking yourself the types of questions you might see on an actual LSAT Reading Comprehension passage. That being said, there is no substitute for practicing with actual LSAT passages, and that's where the value in this book lies.

Relative Ordering

SP1, Pg. 194 PTB-S2-G1

1 Ⓐ Ⓑ Ⓒ Ⓓ Ⓔ
2 Ⓐ Ⓑ Ⓒ Ⓓ Ⓔ
3 Ⓐ Ⓑ Ⓒ Ⓓ Ⓔ
4 Ⓐ Ⓑ Ⓒ Ⓓ Ⓔ
5 Ⓐ Ⓑ Ⓒ Ⓓ Ⓔ
6 Ⓐ Ⓑ Ⓒ Ⓓ Ⓔ

SP1, Pg. 297 PTC-S1-G2

6   Ⓐ Ⓑ Ⓒ Ⓓ Ⓔ
7   Ⓐ Ⓑ Ⓒ Ⓓ Ⓔ
8   Ⓐ Ⓑ Ⓒ Ⓓ Ⓔ
9   Ⓐ Ⓑ Ⓒ Ⓓ Ⓔ
10 Ⓐ Ⓑ Ⓒ Ⓓ Ⓔ
11 Ⓐ Ⓑ Ⓒ Ⓓ Ⓔ
12 Ⓐ Ⓑ Ⓒ Ⓓ Ⓔ

PT1-S2-G3

14 Ⓐ Ⓑ Ⓒ Ⓓ Ⓔ
15 Ⓐ Ⓑ Ⓒ Ⓓ Ⓔ
16 Ⓐ Ⓑ Ⓒ Ⓓ Ⓔ
17 Ⓐ Ⓑ Ⓒ Ⓓ Ⓔ
18 Ⓐ Ⓑ Ⓒ Ⓓ Ⓔ

PT2-S3-G1

1 Ⓐ Ⓑ Ⓒ Ⓓ Ⓔ
2 Ⓐ Ⓑ Ⓒ Ⓓ Ⓔ
3 Ⓐ Ⓑ Ⓒ Ⓓ Ⓔ
4 Ⓐ Ⓑ Ⓒ Ⓓ Ⓔ
5 Ⓐ Ⓑ Ⓒ Ⓓ Ⓔ

PT4-S3-G1

1 Ⓐ Ⓑ Ⓒ Ⓓ Ⓔ
2 Ⓐ Ⓑ Ⓒ Ⓓ Ⓔ
3 Ⓐ Ⓑ Ⓒ Ⓓ Ⓔ
4 Ⓐ Ⓑ Ⓒ Ⓓ Ⓔ
5 Ⓐ Ⓑ Ⓒ Ⓓ Ⓔ
6 Ⓐ Ⓑ Ⓒ Ⓓ Ⓔ

PT6-S4-G2

7   Ⓐ Ⓑ Ⓒ Ⓓ Ⓔ
8   Ⓐ Ⓑ Ⓒ Ⓓ Ⓔ
9   Ⓐ Ⓑ Ⓒ Ⓓ Ⓔ
10 Ⓐ Ⓑ Ⓒ Ⓓ Ⓔ
11 Ⓐ Ⓑ Ⓒ Ⓓ Ⓔ
12 Ⓐ Ⓑ Ⓒ Ⓓ Ⓔ

V1, Pg. 92   PT10-S2-G1

1 Ⓐ Ⓑ Ⓒ Ⓓ Ⓔ
2 Ⓐ Ⓑ Ⓒ Ⓓ Ⓔ
3 Ⓐ Ⓑ Ⓒ Ⓓ Ⓔ
4 Ⓐ Ⓑ Ⓒ Ⓓ Ⓔ
5 Ⓐ Ⓑ Ⓒ Ⓓ Ⓔ

V3, Pg. 176   PT33-S4-G1

1 Ⓐ Ⓑ Ⓒ Ⓓ Ⓔ
2 Ⓐ Ⓑ Ⓒ Ⓓ Ⓔ
3 Ⓐ Ⓑ Ⓒ Ⓓ Ⓔ
4 Ⓐ Ⓑ Ⓒ Ⓓ Ⓔ
5 Ⓐ Ⓑ Ⓒ Ⓓ Ⓔ

V3, Pg. 330   PT38-S2-G1

1 Ⓐ Ⓑ Ⓒ Ⓓ Ⓔ
2 Ⓐ Ⓑ Ⓒ Ⓓ Ⓔ
3 Ⓐ Ⓑ Ⓒ Ⓓ Ⓔ
4 Ⓐ Ⓑ Ⓒ Ⓓ Ⓔ
5 Ⓐ Ⓑ Ⓒ Ⓓ Ⓔ
6 Ⓐ Ⓑ Ⓒ Ⓓ Ⓔ
7 Ⓐ Ⓑ Ⓒ Ⓓ Ⓔ

PT42-S1-G2

6   Ⓐ Ⓑ Ⓒ Ⓓ Ⓔ
7   Ⓐ Ⓑ Ⓒ Ⓓ Ⓔ
8   Ⓐ Ⓑ Ⓒ Ⓓ Ⓔ
9   Ⓐ Ⓑ Ⓒ Ⓓ Ⓔ
10 Ⓐ Ⓑ Ⓒ Ⓓ Ⓔ
11 Ⓐ Ⓑ Ⓒ Ⓓ Ⓔ
12 Ⓐ Ⓑ Ⓒ Ⓓ Ⓔ

PT43-S4-G2

6   Ⓐ Ⓑ Ⓒ Ⓓ Ⓔ
7   Ⓐ Ⓑ Ⓒ Ⓓ Ⓔ
8   Ⓐ Ⓑ Ⓒ Ⓓ Ⓔ
9   Ⓐ Ⓑ Ⓒ Ⓓ Ⓔ
10 Ⓐ Ⓑ Ⓒ Ⓓ Ⓔ
11 Ⓐ Ⓑ Ⓒ Ⓓ Ⓔ
12 Ⓐ Ⓑ Ⓒ Ⓓ Ⓔ

PT48-S2-G2

7   Ⓐ Ⓑ Ⓒ Ⓓ Ⓔ
8   Ⓐ Ⓑ Ⓒ Ⓓ Ⓔ
9   Ⓐ Ⓑ Ⓒ Ⓓ Ⓔ
10 Ⓐ Ⓑ Ⓒ Ⓓ Ⓔ
11 Ⓐ Ⓑ Ⓒ Ⓓ Ⓔ
12 Ⓐ Ⓑ Ⓒ Ⓓ Ⓔ

PT51-S4-G2

6   Ⓐ Ⓑ Ⓒ Ⓓ Ⓔ
7   Ⓐ Ⓑ Ⓒ Ⓓ Ⓔ
8   Ⓐ Ⓑ Ⓒ Ⓓ Ⓔ
9   Ⓐ Ⓑ Ⓒ Ⓓ Ⓔ
10 Ⓐ Ⓑ Ⓒ Ⓓ Ⓔ

PT51-S4-G4

16 Ⓐ Ⓑ Ⓒ Ⓓ Ⓔ
17 Ⓐ Ⓑ Ⓒ Ⓓ Ⓔ
18 Ⓐ Ⓑ Ⓒ Ⓓ Ⓔ
19 Ⓐ Ⓑ Ⓒ Ⓓ Ⓔ
20 Ⓐ Ⓑ Ⓒ Ⓓ Ⓔ
21 Ⓐ Ⓑ Ⓒ Ⓓ Ⓔ
22 Ⓐ Ⓑ Ⓒ Ⓓ Ⓔ

V4, Pg. 16   PT52-S2-G1

1 Ⓐ Ⓑ Ⓒ Ⓓ Ⓔ
2 Ⓐ Ⓑ Ⓒ Ⓓ Ⓔ
3 Ⓐ Ⓑ Ⓒ Ⓓ Ⓔ
4 Ⓐ Ⓑ Ⓒ Ⓓ Ⓔ
5 Ⓐ Ⓑ Ⓒ Ⓓ Ⓔ
6 Ⓐ Ⓑ Ⓒ Ⓓ Ⓔ
7 Ⓐ Ⓑ Ⓒ Ⓓ Ⓔ

V4, Pg. 19   PT52-S2-G4

18 Ⓐ Ⓑ Ⓒ Ⓓ Ⓔ
19 Ⓐ Ⓑ Ⓒ Ⓓ Ⓔ
20 Ⓐ Ⓑ Ⓒ Ⓓ Ⓔ
21 Ⓐ Ⓑ Ⓒ Ⓓ Ⓔ
22 Ⓐ Ⓑ Ⓒ Ⓓ Ⓔ
23 Ⓐ Ⓑ Ⓒ Ⓓ Ⓔ

V4, Pg. 53   PT53-S2-G2

6   Ⓐ Ⓑ Ⓒ Ⓓ Ⓔ
7   Ⓐ Ⓑ Ⓒ Ⓓ Ⓔ
8   Ⓐ Ⓑ Ⓒ Ⓓ Ⓔ
9   Ⓐ Ⓑ Ⓒ Ⓓ Ⓔ
10 Ⓐ Ⓑ Ⓒ Ⓓ Ⓔ
11 Ⓐ Ⓑ Ⓒ Ⓓ Ⓔ

V4, Pg. 142   PT55-S4-G3

13 Ⓐ Ⓑ Ⓒ Ⓓ Ⓔ
14 Ⓐ Ⓑ Ⓒ Ⓓ Ⓔ
15 Ⓐ Ⓑ Ⓒ Ⓓ Ⓔ
16 Ⓐ Ⓑ Ⓒ Ⓓ Ⓔ
17 Ⓐ Ⓑ Ⓒ Ⓓ Ⓔ
18 Ⓐ Ⓑ Ⓒ Ⓓ Ⓔ

V4, Pg. 305   PT60-S2-G2

7 Ⓐ Ⓑ Ⓒ Ⓓ Ⓔ
8 Ⓐ Ⓑ Ⓒ Ⓓ Ⓔ
9 Ⓐ Ⓑ Ⓒ Ⓓ Ⓔ
10 Ⓐ Ⓑ Ⓒ Ⓓ Ⓔ
11 Ⓐ Ⓑ Ⓒ Ⓓ Ⓔ
12 Ⓐ Ⓑ Ⓒ Ⓓ Ⓔ

V4, Pg. 349   PT61-S3-G2

6 Ⓐ Ⓑ Ⓒ Ⓓ Ⓔ
7 Ⓐ Ⓑ Ⓒ Ⓓ Ⓔ
8 Ⓐ Ⓑ Ⓒ Ⓓ Ⓔ
9 Ⓐ Ⓑ Ⓒ Ⓓ Ⓔ
10 Ⓐ Ⓑ Ⓒ Ⓓ Ⓔ
11 Ⓐ Ⓑ Ⓒ Ⓓ Ⓔ

V5, Pg. 54   PT63-S2-G3

11 Ⓐ Ⓑ Ⓒ Ⓓ Ⓔ
12 Ⓐ Ⓑ Ⓒ Ⓓ Ⓔ
13 Ⓐ Ⓑ Ⓒ Ⓓ Ⓔ
14 Ⓐ Ⓑ Ⓒ Ⓓ Ⓔ
15 Ⓐ Ⓑ Ⓒ Ⓓ Ⓔ
16 Ⓐ Ⓑ Ⓒ Ⓓ Ⓔ
17 Ⓐ Ⓑ Ⓒ Ⓓ Ⓔ

V5, Pg. 124   PT65-S2-G1

1 Ⓐ Ⓑ Ⓒ Ⓓ Ⓔ
2 Ⓐ Ⓑ Ⓒ Ⓓ Ⓔ
3 Ⓐ Ⓑ Ⓒ Ⓓ Ⓔ
4 Ⓐ Ⓑ Ⓒ Ⓓ Ⓔ
5 Ⓐ Ⓑ Ⓒ Ⓓ Ⓔ

V5, Pg. 210   PT67-S3-G2

6 Ⓐ Ⓑ Ⓒ Ⓓ Ⓔ
7 Ⓐ Ⓑ Ⓒ Ⓓ Ⓔ
8 Ⓐ Ⓑ Ⓒ Ⓓ Ⓔ
9 Ⓐ Ⓑ Ⓒ Ⓓ Ⓔ
10 Ⓐ Ⓑ Ⓒ Ⓓ Ⓔ
11 Ⓐ Ⓑ Ⓒ Ⓓ Ⓔ
12 Ⓐ Ⓑ Ⓒ Ⓓ Ⓔ

V5, Pg. 360   PT71-S2-G1

1 Ⓐ Ⓑ Ⓒ Ⓓ Ⓔ
2 Ⓐ Ⓑ Ⓒ Ⓓ Ⓔ
3 Ⓐ Ⓑ Ⓒ Ⓓ Ⓔ
4 Ⓐ Ⓑ Ⓒ Ⓓ Ⓔ
5 Ⓐ Ⓑ Ⓒ Ⓓ Ⓔ

PT73, Pg. 26 PT73-S3-G1

1 Ⓐ Ⓑ Ⓒ Ⓓ Ⓔ
2 Ⓐ Ⓑ Ⓒ Ⓓ Ⓔ
3 Ⓐ Ⓑ Ⓒ Ⓓ Ⓔ
4 Ⓐ Ⓑ Ⓒ Ⓓ Ⓔ
5 Ⓐ Ⓑ Ⓒ Ⓓ Ⓔ
6 Ⓐ Ⓑ Ⓒ Ⓓ Ⓔ
7 Ⓐ Ⓑ Ⓒ Ⓓ Ⓔ

PT74, Pg. 18 PT74-S2-G1

1 Ⓐ Ⓑ Ⓒ Ⓓ Ⓔ
2 Ⓐ Ⓑ Ⓒ Ⓓ Ⓔ
3 Ⓐ Ⓑ Ⓒ Ⓓ Ⓔ
4 Ⓐ Ⓑ Ⓒ Ⓓ Ⓔ
5 Ⓐ Ⓑ Ⓒ Ⓓ Ⓔ

PT75, Pg. 38 PT75-S4-G3

12 Ⓐ Ⓑ Ⓒ Ⓓ Ⓔ
13 Ⓐ Ⓑ Ⓒ Ⓓ Ⓔ
14 Ⓐ Ⓑ Ⓒ Ⓓ Ⓔ
15 Ⓐ Ⓑ Ⓒ Ⓓ Ⓔ
16 Ⓐ Ⓑ Ⓒ Ⓓ Ⓔ
17 Ⓐ Ⓑ Ⓒ Ⓓ Ⓔ
18 Ⓐ Ⓑ Ⓒ Ⓓ Ⓔ

Simple Ordering

J07, Pg. 2   J07-S1-G1

1 Ⓐ Ⓑ Ⓒ Ⓓ Ⓔ
2 Ⓐ Ⓑ Ⓒ Ⓓ Ⓔ
3 Ⓐ Ⓑ Ⓒ Ⓓ Ⓔ
4 Ⓐ Ⓑ Ⓒ Ⓓ Ⓔ
5 Ⓐ Ⓑ Ⓒ Ⓓ Ⓔ

J07, Pg. 4   J07-S1-G3

11 Ⓐ Ⓑ Ⓒ Ⓓ Ⓔ
12 Ⓐ Ⓑ Ⓒ Ⓓ Ⓔ
13 Ⓐ Ⓑ Ⓒ Ⓓ Ⓔ
14 Ⓐ Ⓑ Ⓒ Ⓓ Ⓔ
15 Ⓐ Ⓑ Ⓒ Ⓓ Ⓔ
16 Ⓐ Ⓑ Ⓒ Ⓓ Ⓔ
17 Ⓐ Ⓑ Ⓒ Ⓓ Ⓔ

PTSP-S1-G1

1 Ⓐ Ⓑ Ⓒ Ⓓ Ⓔ
2 Ⓐ Ⓑ Ⓒ Ⓓ Ⓔ
3 Ⓐ Ⓑ Ⓒ Ⓓ Ⓔ
4 Ⓐ Ⓑ Ⓒ Ⓓ Ⓔ
5 Ⓐ Ⓑ Ⓒ Ⓓ Ⓔ

SP1, Pg. 84   PTA-S3-G1

1 Ⓐ Ⓑ Ⓒ Ⓓ Ⓔ
2 Ⓐ Ⓑ Ⓒ Ⓓ Ⓔ
3 Ⓐ Ⓑ Ⓒ Ⓓ Ⓔ
4 Ⓐ Ⓑ Ⓒ Ⓓ Ⓔ
5 Ⓐ Ⓑ Ⓒ Ⓓ Ⓔ

SP2, Pg. 348 PTC2-S1-G2

6 Ⓐ Ⓑ Ⓒ Ⓓ Ⓔ
7 Ⓐ Ⓑ Ⓒ Ⓓ Ⓔ
8 Ⓐ Ⓑ Ⓒ Ⓓ Ⓔ
9 Ⓐ Ⓑ Ⓒ Ⓓ Ⓔ
10 Ⓐ Ⓑ Ⓒ Ⓓ Ⓔ

PT3-S1-G2

8 Ⓐ Ⓑ Ⓒ Ⓓ Ⓔ
9 Ⓐ Ⓑ Ⓒ Ⓓ Ⓔ
10 Ⓐ Ⓑ Ⓒ Ⓓ Ⓔ
11 Ⓐ Ⓑ Ⓒ Ⓓ Ⓔ
12 Ⓐ Ⓑ Ⓒ Ⓓ Ⓔ
13 Ⓐ Ⓑ Ⓒ Ⓓ Ⓔ

V1, Pg. 24   PT7-S2-G1

1 Ⓐ Ⓑ Ⓒ Ⓓ Ⓔ
2 Ⓐ Ⓑ Ⓒ Ⓓ Ⓔ
3 Ⓐ Ⓑ Ⓒ Ⓓ Ⓔ
4 Ⓐ Ⓑ Ⓒ Ⓓ Ⓔ
5 Ⓐ Ⓑ Ⓒ Ⓓ Ⓔ
6 Ⓐ Ⓑ Ⓒ Ⓓ Ⓔ
7 Ⓐ Ⓑ Ⓒ Ⓓ Ⓔ

V1, Pg. 119   PT11-S1-G2

7 Ⓐ Ⓑ Ⓒ Ⓓ Ⓔ
8 Ⓐ Ⓑ Ⓒ Ⓓ Ⓔ
9 Ⓐ Ⓑ Ⓒ Ⓓ Ⓔ
10 Ⓐ Ⓑ Ⓒ Ⓓ Ⓔ
11 Ⓐ Ⓑ Ⓒ Ⓓ Ⓔ

V1, Pg. 160   PT12-S2-G1

1 Ⓐ Ⓑ Ⓒ Ⓓ Ⓔ
2 Ⓐ Ⓑ Ⓒ Ⓓ Ⓔ
3 Ⓐ Ⓑ Ⓒ Ⓓ Ⓔ
4 Ⓐ Ⓑ Ⓒ Ⓓ Ⓔ
5 Ⓐ Ⓑ Ⓒ Ⓓ Ⓔ
6 Ⓐ Ⓑ Ⓒ Ⓓ Ⓔ

V1, Pg. 187   PT13-S1-G2

7 Ⓐ Ⓑ Ⓒ Ⓓ Ⓔ
8 Ⓐ Ⓑ Ⓒ Ⓓ Ⓔ
9 Ⓐ Ⓑ Ⓒ Ⓓ Ⓔ
10 Ⓐ Ⓑ Ⓒ Ⓓ Ⓔ
11 Ⓐ Ⓑ Ⓒ Ⓓ Ⓔ

V1, Pg. 278   PT15-S4-G1

1 Ⓐ Ⓑ Ⓒ Ⓓ Ⓔ
2 Ⓐ Ⓑ Ⓒ Ⓓ Ⓔ
3 Ⓐ Ⓑ Ⓒ Ⓓ Ⓔ
4 Ⓐ Ⓑ Ⓒ Ⓓ Ⓔ
5 Ⓐ Ⓑ Ⓒ Ⓓ Ⓔ
6 Ⓐ Ⓑ Ⓒ Ⓓ Ⓔ

V1, Pg. 280   PT15-S4-G3

14 Ⓐ Ⓑ Ⓒ Ⓓ Ⓔ
15 Ⓐ Ⓑ Ⓒ Ⓓ Ⓔ
16 Ⓐ Ⓑ Ⓒ Ⓓ Ⓔ
17 Ⓐ Ⓑ Ⓒ Ⓓ Ⓔ
18 Ⓐ Ⓑ Ⓒ Ⓓ Ⓔ
19 Ⓐ Ⓑ Ⓒ Ⓓ Ⓔ

PT17-S1-G1

1 Ⓐ Ⓑ Ⓒ Ⓓ Ⓔ
2 Ⓐ Ⓑ Ⓒ Ⓓ Ⓔ
3 Ⓐ Ⓑ Ⓒ Ⓓ Ⓔ
4 Ⓐ Ⓑ Ⓒ Ⓓ Ⓔ
5 Ⓐ Ⓑ Ⓒ Ⓓ Ⓔ

V1, Pg. 323 PT18-S1-G2

7 Ⓐ Ⓑ Ⓒ Ⓓ Ⓔ
8 Ⓐ Ⓑ Ⓒ Ⓓ Ⓔ
9 Ⓐ Ⓑ Ⓒ Ⓓ Ⓔ
10 Ⓐ Ⓑ Ⓒ Ⓓ Ⓔ
11 Ⓐ Ⓑ Ⓒ Ⓓ Ⓔ
12 Ⓐ Ⓑ Ⓒ Ⓓ Ⓔ
13 Ⓐ Ⓑ Ⓒ Ⓓ Ⓔ

V2, Pg. 16 PT19-S1-G1

1 Ⓐ Ⓑ Ⓒ Ⓓ Ⓔ
2 Ⓐ Ⓑ Ⓒ Ⓓ Ⓔ
3 Ⓐ Ⓑ Ⓒ Ⓓ Ⓔ
4 Ⓐ Ⓑ Ⓒ Ⓓ Ⓔ
5 Ⓐ Ⓑ Ⓒ Ⓓ Ⓔ
6 Ⓐ Ⓑ Ⓒ Ⓓ Ⓔ
7 Ⓐ Ⓑ Ⓒ Ⓓ Ⓔ

V2, Pg. 152 PT23-S1-G1

1 Ⓐ Ⓑ Ⓒ Ⓓ Ⓔ
2 Ⓐ Ⓑ Ⓒ Ⓓ Ⓔ
3 Ⓐ Ⓑ Ⓒ Ⓓ Ⓔ
4 Ⓐ Ⓑ Ⓒ Ⓓ Ⓔ
5 Ⓐ Ⓑ Ⓒ Ⓓ Ⓔ

V2, Pg. 211 PT24-S4-G2

6 Ⓐ Ⓑ Ⓒ Ⓓ Ⓔ
7 Ⓐ Ⓑ Ⓒ Ⓓ Ⓔ
8 Ⓐ Ⓑ Ⓒ Ⓓ Ⓔ
9 Ⓐ Ⓑ Ⓒ Ⓓ Ⓔ
10 Ⓐ Ⓑ Ⓒ Ⓓ Ⓔ

V2, Pg. 255 PT26-S1-G2

8 Ⓐ Ⓑ Ⓒ Ⓓ Ⓔ
9 Ⓐ Ⓑ Ⓒ Ⓓ Ⓔ
10 Ⓐ Ⓑ Ⓒ Ⓓ Ⓔ
11 Ⓐ Ⓑ Ⓒ Ⓓ Ⓔ
12 Ⓐ Ⓑ Ⓒ Ⓓ Ⓔ

V2, Pg. 296 PT27-S2-G1

1 Ⓐ Ⓑ Ⓒ Ⓓ Ⓔ
2 Ⓐ Ⓑ Ⓒ Ⓓ Ⓔ
3 Ⓐ Ⓑ Ⓒ Ⓓ Ⓔ
4 Ⓐ Ⓑ Ⓒ Ⓓ Ⓔ
5 Ⓐ Ⓑ Ⓒ Ⓓ Ⓔ
6 Ⓐ Ⓑ Ⓒ Ⓓ Ⓔ

V2, Pg. 299 PT27-S2-G4

20 Ⓐ Ⓑ Ⓒ Ⓓ Ⓔ
21 Ⓐ Ⓑ Ⓒ Ⓓ Ⓔ
22 Ⓐ Ⓑ Ⓒ Ⓓ Ⓔ
23 Ⓐ Ⓑ Ⓒ Ⓓ Ⓔ
24 Ⓐ Ⓑ Ⓒ Ⓓ Ⓔ

V2, Pg. 330 PT28-S2-G1

1 Ⓐ Ⓑ Ⓒ Ⓓ Ⓔ
2 Ⓐ Ⓑ Ⓒ Ⓓ Ⓔ
3 Ⓐ Ⓑ Ⓒ Ⓓ Ⓔ
4 Ⓐ Ⓑ Ⓒ Ⓓ Ⓔ
5 Ⓐ Ⓑ Ⓒ Ⓓ Ⓔ

V3, Pg. 34 PT29-S3-G3

14 Ⓐ Ⓑ Ⓒ Ⓓ Ⓔ
15 Ⓐ Ⓑ Ⓒ Ⓓ Ⓔ
16 Ⓐ Ⓑ Ⓒ Ⓓ Ⓔ
17 Ⓐ Ⓑ Ⓒ Ⓓ Ⓔ
18 Ⓐ Ⓑ Ⓒ Ⓓ Ⓔ
19 Ⓐ Ⓑ Ⓒ Ⓓ Ⓔ

V3, Pg. 51 PT30-S1-G2

6 Ⓐ Ⓑ Ⓒ Ⓓ Ⓔ
7 Ⓐ Ⓑ Ⓒ Ⓓ Ⓔ
8 Ⓐ Ⓑ Ⓒ Ⓓ Ⓔ
9 Ⓐ Ⓑ Ⓒ Ⓓ Ⓔ
10 Ⓐ Ⓑ Ⓒ Ⓓ Ⓔ

V3, Pg. 53 PT30-S1-G4

17 Ⓐ Ⓑ Ⓒ Ⓓ Ⓔ
18 Ⓐ Ⓑ Ⓒ Ⓓ Ⓔ
19 Ⓐ Ⓑ Ⓒ Ⓓ Ⓔ
20 Ⓐ Ⓑ Ⓒ Ⓓ Ⓔ
21 Ⓐ Ⓑ Ⓒ Ⓓ Ⓔ
22 Ⓐ Ⓑ Ⓒ Ⓓ Ⓔ
23 Ⓐ Ⓑ Ⓒ Ⓓ Ⓔ

V3, Pg. 86 PT31-S1-G3

14 Ⓐ Ⓑ Ⓒ Ⓓ Ⓔ
15 Ⓐ Ⓑ Ⓒ Ⓓ Ⓔ
16 Ⓐ Ⓑ Ⓒ Ⓓ Ⓔ
17 Ⓐ Ⓑ Ⓒ Ⓓ Ⓔ
18 Ⓐ Ⓑ Ⓒ Ⓓ Ⓔ

V3, Pg. 136 PT32-S3-G3

12 Ⓐ Ⓑ Ⓒ Ⓓ Ⓔ
13 Ⓐ Ⓑ Ⓒ Ⓓ Ⓔ
14 Ⓐ Ⓑ Ⓒ Ⓓ Ⓔ
15 Ⓐ Ⓑ Ⓒ Ⓓ Ⓔ
16 Ⓐ Ⓑ Ⓒ Ⓓ Ⓔ
17 Ⓐ Ⓑ Ⓒ Ⓓ Ⓔ
18 Ⓐ Ⓑ Ⓒ Ⓓ Ⓔ

V3, Pg. 210 PT34-S4-G1

1 Ⓐ Ⓑ Ⓒ Ⓓ Ⓔ
2 Ⓐ Ⓑ Ⓒ Ⓓ Ⓔ
3 Ⓐ Ⓑ Ⓒ Ⓓ Ⓔ
4 Ⓐ Ⓑ Ⓒ Ⓓ Ⓔ
5 Ⓐ Ⓑ Ⓒ Ⓓ Ⓔ
6 Ⓐ Ⓑ Ⓒ Ⓓ Ⓔ
7 Ⓐ Ⓑ Ⓒ Ⓓ Ⓔ

V3, Pg. 211 PT34-S4-G2

8 Ⓐ Ⓑ Ⓒ Ⓓ Ⓔ
9 Ⓐ Ⓑ Ⓒ Ⓓ Ⓔ
10 Ⓐ Ⓑ Ⓒ Ⓓ Ⓔ
11 Ⓐ Ⓑ Ⓒ Ⓓ Ⓔ
12 Ⓐ Ⓑ Ⓒ Ⓓ Ⓔ

V3, Pg. 212 PT34-S4-G3

13 Ⓐ Ⓑ Ⓒ Ⓓ Ⓔ
14 Ⓐ Ⓑ Ⓒ Ⓓ Ⓔ
15 Ⓐ Ⓑ Ⓒ Ⓓ Ⓔ
16 Ⓐ Ⓑ Ⓒ Ⓓ Ⓔ
17 Ⓐ Ⓑ Ⓒ Ⓓ Ⓔ
18 Ⓐ Ⓑ Ⓒ Ⓓ Ⓔ

PT40-S2-G1

1 Ⓐ Ⓑ Ⓒ Ⓓ Ⓔ
2 Ⓐ Ⓑ Ⓒ Ⓓ Ⓔ
3 Ⓐ Ⓑ Ⓒ Ⓓ Ⓔ
4 Ⓐ Ⓑ Ⓒ Ⓓ Ⓔ
5 Ⓐ Ⓑ Ⓒ Ⓓ Ⓔ

PT40-S2-G2

6 Ⓐ Ⓑ Ⓒ Ⓓ Ⓔ
7 Ⓐ Ⓑ Ⓒ Ⓓ Ⓔ
8 Ⓐ Ⓑ Ⓒ Ⓓ Ⓔ
9 Ⓐ Ⓑ Ⓒ Ⓓ Ⓔ
10 Ⓐ Ⓑ Ⓒ Ⓓ Ⓔ

PT41-S2-G1

1 Ⓐ Ⓑ Ⓒ Ⓓ Ⓔ
2 Ⓐ Ⓑ Ⓒ Ⓓ Ⓔ
3 Ⓐ Ⓑ Ⓒ Ⓓ Ⓔ
4 Ⓐ Ⓑ Ⓒ Ⓓ Ⓔ
5 Ⓐ Ⓑ Ⓒ Ⓓ Ⓔ
6 Ⓐ Ⓑ Ⓒ Ⓓ Ⓔ
7 Ⓐ Ⓑ Ⓒ Ⓓ Ⓔ

PT43-S4-G1

1 Ⓐ Ⓑ Ⓒ Ⓓ Ⓔ
2 Ⓐ Ⓑ Ⓒ Ⓓ Ⓔ
3 Ⓐ Ⓑ Ⓒ Ⓓ Ⓔ
4 Ⓐ Ⓑ Ⓒ Ⓓ Ⓔ
5 Ⓐ Ⓑ Ⓒ Ⓓ Ⓔ

PT44-S3-G1

1 Ⓐ Ⓑ Ⓒ Ⓓ Ⓔ
2 Ⓐ Ⓑ Ⓒ Ⓓ Ⓔ
3 Ⓐ Ⓑ Ⓒ Ⓓ Ⓔ
4 Ⓐ Ⓑ Ⓒ Ⓓ Ⓔ
5 Ⓐ Ⓑ Ⓒ Ⓓ Ⓔ
6 Ⓐ Ⓑ Ⓒ Ⓓ Ⓔ

PT45-S3-G1

1 Ⓐ Ⓑ Ⓒ Ⓓ Ⓔ
2 Ⓐ Ⓑ Ⓒ Ⓓ Ⓔ
3 Ⓐ Ⓑ Ⓒ Ⓓ Ⓔ
4 Ⓐ Ⓑ Ⓒ Ⓓ Ⓔ
5 Ⓐ Ⓑ Ⓒ Ⓓ Ⓔ
6 Ⓐ Ⓑ Ⓒ Ⓓ Ⓔ

PT46-S4-G1

1 Ⓐ Ⓑ Ⓒ Ⓓ Ⓔ
2 Ⓐ Ⓑ Ⓒ Ⓓ Ⓔ
3 Ⓐ Ⓑ Ⓒ Ⓓ Ⓔ
4 Ⓐ Ⓑ Ⓒ Ⓓ Ⓔ
5 Ⓐ Ⓑ Ⓒ Ⓓ Ⓔ
6 Ⓐ Ⓑ Ⓒ Ⓓ Ⓔ

PT47-S4-G1

1 Ⓐ Ⓑ Ⓒ Ⓓ Ⓔ
2 Ⓐ Ⓑ Ⓒ Ⓓ Ⓔ
3 Ⓐ Ⓑ Ⓒ Ⓓ Ⓔ
4 Ⓐ Ⓑ Ⓒ Ⓓ Ⓔ
5 Ⓐ Ⓑ Ⓒ Ⓓ Ⓔ

PT49-S1-G1

1 Ⓐ Ⓑ Ⓒ Ⓓ Ⓔ
2 Ⓐ Ⓑ Ⓒ Ⓓ Ⓔ
3 Ⓐ Ⓑ Ⓒ Ⓓ Ⓔ
4 Ⓐ Ⓑ Ⓒ Ⓓ Ⓔ
5 Ⓐ Ⓑ Ⓒ Ⓓ Ⓔ
6 Ⓐ Ⓑ Ⓒ Ⓓ Ⓔ
7 Ⓐ Ⓑ Ⓒ Ⓓ Ⓔ

PT49-S1-G4

18 Ⓐ Ⓑ Ⓒ Ⓓ Ⓔ
19 Ⓐ Ⓑ Ⓒ Ⓓ Ⓔ
20 Ⓐ Ⓑ Ⓒ Ⓓ Ⓔ
21 Ⓐ Ⓑ Ⓒ Ⓓ Ⓔ
22 Ⓐ Ⓑ Ⓒ Ⓓ Ⓔ

PT50-S3-G1

1 Ⓐ Ⓑ Ⓒ Ⓓ Ⓔ
2 Ⓐ Ⓑ Ⓒ Ⓓ Ⓔ
3 Ⓐ Ⓑ Ⓒ Ⓓ Ⓔ
4 Ⓐ Ⓑ Ⓒ Ⓓ Ⓔ
5 Ⓐ Ⓑ Ⓒ Ⓓ Ⓔ

V4, Pg. 98   PT54-S3-G3

13 Ⓐ Ⓑ Ⓒ Ⓓ Ⓔ
14 Ⓐ Ⓑ Ⓒ Ⓓ Ⓔ
15 Ⓐ Ⓑ Ⓒ Ⓓ Ⓔ
16 Ⓐ Ⓑ Ⓒ Ⓓ Ⓔ
17 Ⓐ Ⓑ Ⓒ Ⓓ Ⓔ

V4, Pg. 99   PT54-S3-G4

18 Ⓐ Ⓑ Ⓒ Ⓓ Ⓔ
19 Ⓐ Ⓑ Ⓒ Ⓓ Ⓔ
20 Ⓐ Ⓑ Ⓒ Ⓓ Ⓔ
21 Ⓐ Ⓑ Ⓒ Ⓓ Ⓔ
22 Ⓐ Ⓑ Ⓒ Ⓓ Ⓔ
23 Ⓐ Ⓑ Ⓒ Ⓓ Ⓔ

V4, Pg. 141   PT55-S4-G2

7 Ⓐ Ⓑ Ⓒ Ⓓ Ⓔ
8 Ⓐ Ⓑ Ⓒ Ⓓ Ⓔ
9 Ⓐ Ⓑ Ⓒ Ⓓ Ⓔ
10 Ⓐ Ⓑ Ⓒ Ⓓ Ⓔ
11 Ⓐ Ⓑ Ⓒ Ⓓ Ⓔ
12 Ⓐ Ⓑ Ⓒ Ⓓ Ⓔ

V4, Pg. 152   PT56-S1-G1

1 Ⓐ Ⓑ Ⓒ Ⓓ Ⓔ
2 Ⓐ Ⓑ Ⓒ Ⓓ Ⓔ
3 Ⓐ Ⓑ Ⓒ Ⓓ Ⓔ
4 Ⓐ Ⓑ Ⓒ Ⓓ Ⓔ
5 Ⓐ Ⓑ Ⓒ Ⓓ Ⓔ
6 Ⓐ Ⓑ Ⓒ Ⓓ Ⓔ

V4, Pg. 188   PT57-S1-G1

1 Ⓐ Ⓑ Ⓒ Ⓓ Ⓔ
2 Ⓐ Ⓑ Ⓒ Ⓓ Ⓔ
3 Ⓐ Ⓑ Ⓒ Ⓓ Ⓔ
4 Ⓐ Ⓑ Ⓒ Ⓓ Ⓔ
5 Ⓐ Ⓑ Ⓒ Ⓓ Ⓔ

V4, Pg. 261   PT59-S1-G2

6 Ⓐ Ⓑ Ⓒ Ⓓ Ⓔ
7 Ⓐ Ⓑ Ⓒ Ⓓ Ⓔ
8 Ⓐ Ⓑ Ⓒ Ⓓ Ⓔ
9 Ⓐ Ⓑ Ⓒ Ⓓ Ⓔ
10 Ⓐ Ⓑ Ⓒ Ⓓ Ⓔ

V4, Pg. 263   PT59-S1-G4

17 Ⓐ Ⓑ Ⓒ Ⓓ Ⓔ
18 Ⓐ Ⓑ Ⓒ Ⓓ Ⓔ
19 Ⓐ Ⓑ Ⓒ Ⓓ Ⓔ
20 Ⓐ Ⓑ Ⓒ Ⓓ Ⓔ
21 Ⓐ Ⓑ Ⓒ Ⓓ Ⓔ
22 Ⓐ Ⓑ Ⓒ Ⓓ Ⓔ
23 Ⓐ Ⓑ Ⓒ Ⓓ Ⓔ

V4, Pg. 306   PT60-S2-G3

13 Ⓐ Ⓑ Ⓒ Ⓓ Ⓔ
14 Ⓐ Ⓑ Ⓒ Ⓓ Ⓔ
15 Ⓐ Ⓑ Ⓒ Ⓓ Ⓔ
16 Ⓐ Ⓑ Ⓒ Ⓓ Ⓔ
17 Ⓐ Ⓑ Ⓒ Ⓓ Ⓔ

V4, Pg. 350   PT61-S3-G3

12 Ⓐ Ⓑ Ⓒ Ⓓ Ⓔ
13 Ⓐ Ⓑ Ⓒ Ⓓ Ⓔ
14 Ⓐ Ⓑ Ⓒ Ⓓ Ⓔ
15 Ⓐ Ⓑ Ⓒ Ⓓ Ⓔ
16 Ⓐ Ⓑ Ⓒ Ⓓ Ⓔ
17 Ⓐ Ⓑ Ⓒ Ⓓ Ⓔ

V4, Pg. 351   PT61-S3-G4

18 Ⓐ Ⓑ Ⓒ Ⓓ Ⓔ
19 Ⓐ Ⓑ Ⓒ Ⓓ Ⓔ
20 Ⓐ Ⓑ Ⓒ Ⓓ Ⓔ
21 Ⓐ Ⓑ Ⓒ Ⓓ Ⓔ
22 Ⓐ Ⓑ Ⓒ Ⓓ Ⓔ
23 Ⓐ Ⓑ Ⓒ Ⓓ Ⓔ

V5, Pg. 24   PT62-S3-G1

1 Ⓐ Ⓑ Ⓒ Ⓓ Ⓔ
2 Ⓐ Ⓑ Ⓒ Ⓓ Ⓔ
3 Ⓐ Ⓑ Ⓒ Ⓓ Ⓔ
4 Ⓐ Ⓑ Ⓒ Ⓓ Ⓔ
5 Ⓐ Ⓑ Ⓒ Ⓓ Ⓔ
6 Ⓐ Ⓑ Ⓒ Ⓓ Ⓔ

V5, Pg. 27   PT62-S3-G4

19 Ⓐ Ⓑ Ⓒ Ⓓ Ⓔ
20 Ⓐ Ⓑ Ⓒ Ⓓ Ⓔ
21 Ⓐ Ⓑ Ⓒ Ⓓ Ⓔ
22 Ⓐ Ⓑ Ⓒ Ⓓ Ⓔ
23 Ⓐ Ⓑ Ⓒ Ⓓ Ⓔ

V5, Pg. 53   PT63-S2-G2

6 Ⓐ Ⓑ Ⓒ Ⓓ Ⓔ
7 Ⓐ Ⓑ Ⓒ Ⓓ Ⓔ
8 Ⓐ Ⓑ Ⓒ Ⓓ Ⓔ
9 Ⓐ Ⓑ Ⓒ Ⓓ Ⓔ
10 Ⓐ Ⓑ Ⓒ Ⓓ Ⓔ

V5, Pg. 55   PT63-S2-G4

18 Ⓐ Ⓑ Ⓒ Ⓓ Ⓔ
19 Ⓐ Ⓑ Ⓒ Ⓓ Ⓔ
20 Ⓐ Ⓑ Ⓒ Ⓓ Ⓔ
21 Ⓐ Ⓑ Ⓒ Ⓓ Ⓔ
22 Ⓐ Ⓑ Ⓒ Ⓓ Ⓔ
23 Ⓐ Ⓑ Ⓒ Ⓓ Ⓔ

V5, Pg. 88   PT64-S2-G1
1 Ⓐ Ⓑ Ⓒ Ⓓ Ⓔ
2 Ⓐ Ⓑ Ⓒ Ⓓ Ⓔ
3 Ⓐ Ⓑ Ⓒ Ⓓ Ⓔ
4 Ⓐ Ⓑ Ⓒ Ⓓ Ⓔ
5 Ⓐ Ⓑ Ⓒ Ⓓ Ⓔ
6 Ⓐ Ⓑ Ⓒ Ⓓ Ⓔ

V5, Pg. 127   PT65-S2-G4
17 Ⓐ Ⓑ Ⓒ Ⓓ Ⓔ
18 Ⓐ Ⓑ Ⓒ Ⓓ Ⓔ
19 Ⓐ Ⓑ Ⓒ Ⓓ Ⓔ
20 Ⓐ Ⓑ Ⓒ Ⓓ Ⓔ
21 Ⓐ Ⓑ Ⓒ Ⓓ Ⓔ
22 Ⓐ Ⓑ Ⓒ Ⓓ Ⓔ
23 Ⓐ Ⓑ Ⓒ Ⓓ Ⓔ

V5, Pg. 170   PT66-S3-G2
6 Ⓐ Ⓑ Ⓒ Ⓓ Ⓔ
7 Ⓐ Ⓑ Ⓒ Ⓓ Ⓔ
8 Ⓐ Ⓑ Ⓒ Ⓓ Ⓔ
9 Ⓐ Ⓑ Ⓒ Ⓓ Ⓔ
10 Ⓐ Ⓑ Ⓒ Ⓓ Ⓔ
11 Ⓐ Ⓑ Ⓒ Ⓓ Ⓔ

V5, Pg. 256   PT68-S4-G1
1 Ⓐ Ⓑ Ⓒ Ⓓ Ⓔ
2 Ⓐ Ⓑ Ⓒ Ⓓ Ⓔ
3 Ⓐ Ⓑ Ⓒ Ⓓ Ⓔ
4 Ⓐ Ⓑ Ⓒ Ⓓ Ⓔ
5 Ⓐ Ⓑ Ⓒ Ⓓ Ⓔ

V5, Pg. 280   PT69-S2-G1
1 Ⓐ Ⓑ Ⓒ Ⓓ Ⓔ
2 Ⓐ Ⓑ Ⓒ Ⓓ Ⓔ
3 Ⓐ Ⓑ Ⓒ Ⓓ Ⓔ
4 Ⓐ Ⓑ Ⓒ Ⓓ Ⓔ
5 Ⓐ Ⓑ Ⓒ Ⓓ Ⓔ

V5, Pg. 328   PT70-S3-G1
1 Ⓐ Ⓑ Ⓒ Ⓓ Ⓔ
2 Ⓐ Ⓑ Ⓒ Ⓓ Ⓔ
3 Ⓐ Ⓑ Ⓒ Ⓓ Ⓔ
4 Ⓐ Ⓑ Ⓒ Ⓓ Ⓔ
5 Ⓐ Ⓑ Ⓒ Ⓓ Ⓔ
6 Ⓐ Ⓑ Ⓒ Ⓓ Ⓔ
7 Ⓐ Ⓑ Ⓒ Ⓓ Ⓔ

V5, Pg. 366   PT71-S2-G4
17 Ⓐ Ⓑ Ⓒ Ⓓ Ⓔ
18 Ⓐ Ⓑ Ⓒ Ⓓ Ⓔ
19 Ⓐ Ⓑ Ⓒ Ⓓ Ⓔ
20 Ⓐ Ⓑ Ⓒ Ⓓ Ⓔ
21 Ⓐ Ⓑ Ⓒ Ⓓ Ⓔ
22 Ⓐ Ⓑ Ⓒ Ⓓ Ⓔ
23 Ⓐ Ⓑ Ⓒ Ⓓ Ⓔ

PT72, Pg. 36   PT72-S4-G2
7 Ⓐ Ⓑ Ⓒ Ⓓ Ⓔ
8 Ⓐ Ⓑ Ⓒ Ⓓ Ⓔ
9 Ⓐ Ⓑ Ⓒ Ⓓ Ⓔ
10 Ⓐ Ⓑ Ⓒ Ⓓ Ⓔ
11 Ⓐ Ⓑ Ⓒ Ⓓ Ⓔ
12 Ⓐ Ⓑ Ⓒ Ⓓ Ⓔ

PT75, Pg. 40   PT75-S4-G4
19 Ⓐ Ⓑ Ⓒ Ⓓ Ⓔ
20 Ⓐ Ⓑ Ⓒ Ⓓ Ⓔ
21 Ⓐ Ⓑ Ⓒ Ⓓ Ⓔ
22 Ⓐ Ⓑ Ⓒ Ⓓ Ⓔ
23 Ⓐ Ⓑ Ⓒ Ⓓ Ⓔ

PT76, Pg. 26   PT76-S3-G1
1 Ⓐ Ⓑ Ⓒ Ⓓ Ⓔ
2 Ⓐ Ⓑ Ⓒ Ⓓ Ⓔ
3 Ⓐ Ⓑ Ⓒ Ⓓ Ⓔ
4 Ⓐ Ⓑ Ⓒ Ⓓ Ⓔ
5 Ⓐ Ⓑ Ⓒ Ⓓ Ⓔ
6 Ⓐ Ⓑ Ⓒ Ⓓ Ⓔ

PT77, Pg. 26   PT77-S3-G1
1 Ⓐ Ⓑ Ⓒ Ⓓ Ⓔ
2 Ⓐ Ⓑ Ⓒ Ⓓ Ⓔ
3 Ⓐ Ⓑ Ⓒ Ⓓ Ⓔ
4 Ⓐ Ⓑ Ⓒ Ⓓ Ⓔ
5 Ⓐ Ⓑ Ⓒ Ⓓ Ⓔ

PT77, Pg. 28   PT77-S3-G2
6 Ⓐ Ⓑ Ⓒ Ⓓ Ⓔ
7 Ⓐ Ⓑ Ⓒ Ⓓ Ⓔ
8 Ⓐ Ⓑ Ⓒ Ⓓ Ⓔ
9 Ⓐ Ⓑ Ⓒ Ⓓ Ⓔ
10 Ⓐ Ⓑ Ⓒ Ⓓ Ⓔ
11 Ⓐ Ⓑ Ⓒ Ⓓ Ⓔ
12 Ⓐ Ⓑ Ⓒ Ⓓ Ⓔ

Complex Ordering

PTSP-S1-G4
18 Ⓐ Ⓑ Ⓒ Ⓓ Ⓔ
19 Ⓐ Ⓑ Ⓒ Ⓓ Ⓔ
20 Ⓐ Ⓑ Ⓒ Ⓓ Ⓔ
21 Ⓐ Ⓑ Ⓒ Ⓓ Ⓔ
22 Ⓐ Ⓑ Ⓒ Ⓓ Ⓔ

SP1, Pg. 86   PTA-S3-G3
11 Ⓐ Ⓑ Ⓒ Ⓓ Ⓔ
12 Ⓐ Ⓑ Ⓒ Ⓓ Ⓔ
13 Ⓐ Ⓑ Ⓒ Ⓓ Ⓔ
14 Ⓐ Ⓑ Ⓒ Ⓓ Ⓔ
15 Ⓐ Ⓑ Ⓒ Ⓓ Ⓔ
16 Ⓐ Ⓑ Ⓒ Ⓓ Ⓔ
17 Ⓐ Ⓑ Ⓒ Ⓓ Ⓔ

PT2-S3-G4
18 Ⓐ Ⓑ Ⓒ Ⓓ Ⓔ
19 Ⓐ Ⓑ Ⓒ Ⓓ Ⓔ
20 Ⓐ Ⓑ Ⓒ Ⓓ Ⓔ
21 Ⓐ Ⓑ Ⓒ Ⓓ Ⓔ
22 Ⓐ Ⓑ Ⓒ Ⓓ Ⓔ
23 Ⓐ Ⓑ Ⓒ Ⓓ Ⓔ
24 Ⓐ Ⓑ Ⓒ Ⓓ Ⓔ

PT5-S2-G4
18 Ⓐ Ⓑ Ⓒ Ⓓ Ⓔ
19 Ⓐ Ⓑ Ⓒ Ⓓ Ⓔ
20 Ⓐ Ⓑ Ⓒ Ⓓ Ⓔ
21 Ⓐ Ⓑ Ⓒ Ⓓ Ⓔ
22 Ⓐ Ⓑ Ⓒ Ⓓ Ⓔ
23 Ⓐ Ⓑ Ⓒ Ⓓ Ⓔ
24 Ⓐ Ⓑ Ⓒ Ⓓ Ⓔ

V1, Pg. 27   PT7-S2-G4
19 Ⓐ Ⓑ Ⓒ Ⓓ Ⓔ
20 Ⓐ Ⓑ Ⓒ Ⓓ Ⓔ
21 Ⓐ Ⓑ Ⓒ Ⓓ Ⓔ
22 Ⓐ Ⓑ Ⓒ Ⓓ Ⓔ
23 Ⓐ Ⓑ Ⓒ Ⓓ Ⓔ
24 Ⓐ Ⓑ Ⓒ Ⓓ Ⓔ

PT8-S2-G3
13 Ⓐ Ⓑ Ⓒ Ⓓ Ⓔ
14 Ⓐ Ⓑ Ⓒ Ⓓ Ⓔ
15 Ⓐ Ⓑ Ⓒ Ⓓ Ⓔ
16 Ⓐ Ⓑ Ⓒ Ⓓ Ⓔ
17 Ⓐ Ⓑ Ⓒ Ⓓ Ⓔ

V1, Pg. 221   PT14-S1-G2
7 Ⓐ Ⓑ Ⓒ Ⓓ Ⓔ
8 Ⓐ Ⓑ Ⓒ Ⓓ Ⓔ
9 Ⓐ Ⓑ Ⓒ Ⓓ Ⓔ
10 Ⓐ Ⓑ Ⓒ Ⓓ Ⓔ
11 Ⓐ Ⓑ Ⓒ Ⓓ Ⓔ
12 Ⓐ Ⓑ Ⓒ Ⓓ Ⓔ

V2, Pg. 69   PT20-S3-G4

19 Ⓐ Ⓑ Ⓒ Ⓓ Ⓔ
20 Ⓐ Ⓑ Ⓒ Ⓓ Ⓔ
21 Ⓐ Ⓑ Ⓒ Ⓓ Ⓔ
22 Ⓐ Ⓑ Ⓒ Ⓓ Ⓔ
23 Ⓐ Ⓑ Ⓒ Ⓓ Ⓔ
24 Ⓐ Ⓑ Ⓒ Ⓓ Ⓔ

V2, Pg. 135   PT22-S3-G2

8   Ⓐ Ⓑ Ⓒ Ⓓ Ⓔ
9   Ⓐ Ⓑ Ⓒ Ⓓ Ⓔ
10 Ⓐ Ⓑ Ⓒ Ⓓ Ⓔ
11 Ⓐ Ⓑ Ⓒ Ⓓ Ⓔ
12 Ⓐ Ⓑ Ⓒ Ⓓ Ⓔ
13 Ⓐ Ⓑ Ⓒ Ⓓ Ⓔ
14 Ⓐ Ⓑ Ⓒ Ⓓ Ⓔ

V2, Pg. 155   PT23-S1-G4

19 Ⓐ Ⓑ Ⓒ Ⓓ Ⓔ
20 Ⓐ Ⓑ Ⓒ Ⓓ Ⓔ
21 Ⓐ Ⓑ Ⓒ Ⓓ Ⓔ
22 Ⓐ Ⓑ Ⓒ Ⓓ Ⓔ
23 Ⓐ Ⓑ Ⓒ Ⓓ Ⓔ
24 Ⓐ Ⓑ Ⓒ Ⓓ Ⓔ

V2, Pg. 212   PT24-S4-G3

11 Ⓐ Ⓑ Ⓒ Ⓓ Ⓔ
12 Ⓐ Ⓑ Ⓒ Ⓓ Ⓔ
13 Ⓐ Ⓑ Ⓒ Ⓓ Ⓔ
14 Ⓐ Ⓑ Ⓒ Ⓓ Ⓔ
15 Ⓐ Ⓑ Ⓒ Ⓓ Ⓔ
16 Ⓐ Ⓑ Ⓒ Ⓓ Ⓔ
17 Ⓐ Ⓑ Ⓒ Ⓓ Ⓔ

V2, Pg. 239   PT25-S3-G4

19 Ⓐ Ⓑ Ⓒ Ⓓ Ⓔ
20 Ⓐ Ⓑ Ⓒ Ⓓ Ⓔ
21 Ⓐ Ⓑ Ⓒ Ⓓ Ⓔ
22 Ⓐ Ⓑ Ⓒ Ⓓ Ⓔ
23 Ⓐ Ⓑ Ⓒ Ⓓ Ⓔ
24 Ⓐ Ⓑ Ⓒ Ⓓ Ⓔ

V2, Pg. 254   PT26-S1-G1

1   Ⓐ Ⓑ Ⓒ Ⓓ Ⓔ
2   Ⓐ Ⓑ Ⓒ Ⓓ Ⓔ
3   Ⓐ Ⓑ Ⓒ Ⓓ Ⓔ
4   Ⓐ Ⓑ Ⓒ Ⓓ Ⓔ
5   Ⓐ Ⓑ Ⓒ Ⓓ Ⓔ
6   Ⓐ Ⓑ Ⓒ Ⓓ Ⓔ
7   Ⓐ Ⓑ Ⓒ Ⓓ Ⓔ

V3, Pg. 52   PT30-S1-G3

11 Ⓐ Ⓑ Ⓒ Ⓓ Ⓔ
12 Ⓐ Ⓑ Ⓒ Ⓓ Ⓔ
13 Ⓐ Ⓑ Ⓒ Ⓓ Ⓔ
14 Ⓐ Ⓑ Ⓒ Ⓓ Ⓔ
15 Ⓐ Ⓑ Ⓒ Ⓓ Ⓔ
16 Ⓐ Ⓑ Ⓒ Ⓓ Ⓔ

V3, Pg. 84   PT31-S1-G1

1   Ⓐ Ⓑ Ⓒ Ⓓ Ⓔ
2   Ⓐ Ⓑ Ⓒ Ⓓ Ⓔ
3   Ⓐ Ⓑ Ⓒ Ⓓ Ⓔ
4   Ⓐ Ⓑ Ⓒ Ⓓ Ⓔ
5   Ⓐ Ⓑ Ⓒ Ⓓ Ⓔ
6   Ⓐ Ⓑ Ⓒ Ⓓ Ⓔ

V3, Pg. 137   PT32-S3-G4

19 Ⓐ Ⓑ Ⓒ Ⓓ Ⓔ
20 Ⓐ Ⓑ Ⓒ Ⓓ Ⓔ
21 Ⓐ Ⓑ Ⓒ Ⓓ Ⓔ
22 Ⓐ Ⓑ Ⓒ Ⓓ Ⓔ
23 Ⓐ Ⓑ Ⓒ Ⓓ Ⓔ
24 Ⓐ Ⓑ Ⓒ Ⓓ Ⓔ

V3, Pg. 279   PT36-S4-G2

7   Ⓐ Ⓑ Ⓒ Ⓓ Ⓔ
8   Ⓐ Ⓑ Ⓒ Ⓓ Ⓔ
9   Ⓐ Ⓑ Ⓒ Ⓓ Ⓔ
10 Ⓐ Ⓑ Ⓒ Ⓓ Ⓔ
11 Ⓐ Ⓑ Ⓒ Ⓓ Ⓔ
12 Ⓐ Ⓑ Ⓒ Ⓓ Ⓔ
13 Ⓐ Ⓑ Ⓒ Ⓓ Ⓔ

V3, Pg. 281   PT36-S4-G4

19 Ⓐ Ⓑ Ⓒ Ⓓ Ⓔ
20 Ⓐ Ⓑ Ⓒ Ⓓ Ⓔ
21 Ⓐ Ⓑ Ⓒ Ⓓ Ⓔ
22 Ⓐ Ⓑ Ⓒ Ⓓ Ⓔ
23 Ⓐ Ⓑ Ⓒ Ⓓ Ⓔ

V3, Pg. 305   PT37-S3-G2

6   Ⓐ Ⓑ Ⓒ Ⓓ Ⓔ
7   Ⓐ Ⓑ Ⓒ Ⓓ Ⓔ
8   Ⓐ Ⓑ Ⓒ Ⓓ Ⓔ
9   Ⓐ Ⓑ Ⓒ Ⓓ Ⓔ
10 Ⓐ Ⓑ Ⓒ Ⓓ Ⓔ
11 Ⓐ Ⓑ Ⓒ Ⓓ Ⓔ

V3, Pg. 307   PT37-S3-G4

19 Ⓐ Ⓑ Ⓒ Ⓓ Ⓔ
20 Ⓐ Ⓑ Ⓒ Ⓓ Ⓔ
21 Ⓐ Ⓑ Ⓒ Ⓓ Ⓔ
22 Ⓐ Ⓑ Ⓒ Ⓓ Ⓔ
23 Ⓐ Ⓑ Ⓒ Ⓓ Ⓔ
24 Ⓐ Ⓑ Ⓒ Ⓓ Ⓔ

V3, Pg. 331   PT38-S2-G2

8   Ⓐ Ⓑ Ⓒ Ⓓ Ⓔ
9   Ⓐ Ⓑ Ⓒ Ⓓ Ⓔ
10 Ⓐ Ⓑ Ⓒ Ⓓ Ⓔ
11 Ⓐ Ⓑ Ⓒ Ⓓ Ⓔ
12 Ⓐ Ⓑ Ⓒ Ⓓ Ⓔ
13 Ⓐ Ⓑ Ⓒ Ⓓ Ⓔ

V3, Pg. 333   PT38-S2-G4

20 Ⓐ Ⓑ Ⓒ Ⓓ Ⓔ
21 Ⓐ Ⓑ Ⓒ Ⓓ Ⓔ
22 Ⓐ Ⓑ Ⓒ Ⓓ Ⓔ
23 Ⓐ Ⓑ Ⓒ Ⓓ Ⓔ
24 Ⓐ Ⓑ Ⓒ Ⓓ Ⓔ

PT39-S1-G1

1   Ⓐ Ⓑ Ⓒ Ⓓ Ⓔ
2   Ⓐ Ⓑ Ⓒ Ⓓ Ⓔ
3   Ⓐ Ⓑ Ⓒ Ⓓ Ⓔ
4   Ⓐ Ⓑ Ⓒ Ⓓ Ⓔ
5   Ⓐ Ⓑ Ⓒ Ⓓ Ⓔ

PT39-S1-G3

12 Ⓐ Ⓑ Ⓒ Ⓓ Ⓔ
13 Ⓐ Ⓑ Ⓒ Ⓓ Ⓔ
14 Ⓐ Ⓑ Ⓒ Ⓓ Ⓔ
15 Ⓐ Ⓑ Ⓒ Ⓓ Ⓔ
16 Ⓐ Ⓑ Ⓒ Ⓓ Ⓔ
17 Ⓐ Ⓑ Ⓒ Ⓓ Ⓔ
18 Ⓐ Ⓑ Ⓒ Ⓓ Ⓔ

PT41-S2-G2

8   Ⓐ Ⓑ Ⓒ Ⓓ Ⓔ
9   Ⓐ Ⓑ Ⓒ Ⓓ Ⓔ
10 Ⓐ Ⓑ Ⓒ Ⓓ Ⓔ
11 Ⓐ Ⓑ Ⓒ Ⓓ Ⓔ
12 Ⓐ Ⓑ Ⓒ Ⓓ Ⓔ

PT44-S3-G3

13 Ⓐ Ⓑ Ⓒ Ⓓ Ⓔ
14 Ⓐ Ⓑ Ⓒ Ⓓ Ⓔ
15 Ⓐ Ⓑ Ⓒ Ⓓ Ⓔ
16 Ⓐ Ⓑ Ⓒ Ⓓ Ⓔ
17 Ⓐ Ⓑ Ⓒ Ⓓ Ⓔ

PT44-S3-G4

18 Ⓐ Ⓑ Ⓒ Ⓓ Ⓔ
19 Ⓐ Ⓑ Ⓒ Ⓓ Ⓔ
20 Ⓐ Ⓑ Ⓒ Ⓓ Ⓔ
21 Ⓐ Ⓑ Ⓒ Ⓓ Ⓔ
22 Ⓐ Ⓑ Ⓒ Ⓓ Ⓔ

PT46-S4-G3

12 Ⓐ Ⓑ Ⓒ Ⓓ Ⓔ
13 Ⓐ Ⓑ Ⓒ Ⓓ Ⓔ
14 Ⓐ Ⓑ Ⓒ Ⓓ Ⓔ
15 Ⓐ Ⓑ Ⓒ Ⓓ Ⓔ
16 Ⓐ Ⓑ Ⓒ Ⓓ Ⓔ

PT51-S4-G3

11 Ⓐ Ⓑ Ⓒ Ⓓ Ⓔ
12 Ⓐ Ⓑ Ⓒ Ⓓ Ⓔ
13 Ⓐ Ⓑ Ⓒ Ⓓ Ⓔ
14 Ⓐ Ⓑ Ⓒ Ⓓ Ⓔ
15 Ⓐ Ⓑ Ⓒ Ⓓ Ⓔ

V4, Pg. 54   PT53-S2-G3

12 Ⓐ Ⓑ Ⓒ Ⓓ Ⓔ
13 Ⓐ Ⓑ Ⓒ Ⓓ Ⓔ
14 Ⓐ Ⓑ Ⓒ Ⓓ Ⓔ
15 Ⓐ Ⓑ Ⓒ Ⓓ Ⓔ
16 Ⓐ Ⓑ Ⓒ Ⓓ Ⓔ
17 Ⓐ Ⓑ Ⓒ Ⓓ Ⓔ

V4, Pg. 143   PT55-S4-G4

19 Ⓐ Ⓑ Ⓒ Ⓓ Ⓔ
20 Ⓐ Ⓑ Ⓒ Ⓓ Ⓔ
21 Ⓐ Ⓑ Ⓒ Ⓓ Ⓔ
22 Ⓐ Ⓑ Ⓒ Ⓓ Ⓔ
23 Ⓐ Ⓑ Ⓒ Ⓓ Ⓔ

V4, Pg. 242 PT58-S3-G3

13 Ⓐ Ⓑ Ⓒ Ⓓ Ⓔ
14 Ⓐ Ⓑ Ⓒ Ⓓ Ⓔ
15 Ⓐ Ⓑ Ⓒ Ⓓ Ⓔ
16 Ⓐ Ⓑ Ⓒ Ⓓ Ⓔ
17 Ⓐ Ⓑ Ⓒ Ⓓ Ⓔ

V5, Pg. 125 PT65-S2-G2

6 Ⓐ Ⓑ Ⓒ Ⓓ Ⓔ
7 Ⓐ Ⓑ Ⓒ Ⓓ Ⓔ
8 Ⓐ Ⓑ Ⓒ Ⓓ Ⓔ
9 Ⓐ Ⓑ Ⓒ Ⓓ Ⓔ
10 Ⓐ Ⓑ Ⓒ Ⓓ Ⓔ
11 Ⓐ Ⓑ Ⓒ Ⓓ Ⓔ

V5, Pg. 174 PT66-S3-G4

19 Ⓐ Ⓑ Ⓒ Ⓓ Ⓔ
20 Ⓐ Ⓑ Ⓒ Ⓓ Ⓔ
21 Ⓐ Ⓑ Ⓒ Ⓓ Ⓔ
22 Ⓐ Ⓑ Ⓒ Ⓓ Ⓔ
23 Ⓐ Ⓑ Ⓒ Ⓓ Ⓔ

V5, Pg. 262 PT68-S4-G4

17 Ⓐ Ⓑ Ⓒ Ⓓ Ⓔ
18 Ⓐ Ⓑ Ⓒ Ⓓ Ⓔ
19 Ⓐ Ⓑ Ⓒ Ⓓ Ⓔ
20 Ⓐ Ⓑ Ⓒ Ⓓ Ⓔ
21 Ⓐ Ⓑ Ⓒ Ⓓ Ⓔ
22 Ⓐ Ⓑ Ⓒ Ⓓ Ⓔ
23 Ⓐ Ⓑ Ⓒ Ⓓ Ⓔ

V5, Pg. 334 PT70-S3-G4

19 Ⓐ Ⓑ Ⓒ Ⓓ Ⓔ
20 Ⓐ Ⓑ Ⓒ Ⓓ Ⓔ
21 Ⓐ Ⓑ Ⓒ Ⓓ Ⓔ
22 Ⓐ Ⓑ Ⓒ Ⓓ Ⓔ
23 Ⓐ Ⓑ Ⓒ Ⓓ Ⓔ

V5, Pg. 364 PT71-S2-G3

12 Ⓐ Ⓑ Ⓒ Ⓓ Ⓔ
13 Ⓐ Ⓑ Ⓒ Ⓓ Ⓔ
14 Ⓐ Ⓑ Ⓒ Ⓓ Ⓔ
15 Ⓐ Ⓑ Ⓒ Ⓓ Ⓔ
16 Ⓐ Ⓑ Ⓒ Ⓓ Ⓔ

PT74, Pg. 20 PT74-S2-G2

6 Ⓐ Ⓑ Ⓒ Ⓓ Ⓔ
7 Ⓐ Ⓑ Ⓒ Ⓓ Ⓔ
8 Ⓐ Ⓑ Ⓒ Ⓓ Ⓔ
9 Ⓐ Ⓑ Ⓒ Ⓓ Ⓔ
10 Ⓐ Ⓑ Ⓒ Ⓓ Ⓔ

In-Out Grouping

PTSP-S1-G2

6 Ⓐ Ⓑ Ⓒ Ⓓ Ⓔ
7 Ⓐ Ⓑ Ⓒ Ⓓ Ⓔ
8 Ⓐ Ⓑ Ⓒ Ⓓ Ⓔ
9 Ⓐ Ⓑ Ⓒ Ⓓ Ⓔ
10 Ⓐ Ⓑ Ⓒ Ⓓ Ⓔ
11 Ⓐ Ⓑ Ⓒ Ⓓ Ⓔ

SP1, Pg. 195 PTB-S2-G2

7 Ⓐ Ⓑ Ⓒ Ⓓ Ⓔ
8 Ⓐ Ⓑ Ⓒ Ⓓ Ⓔ
9 Ⓐ Ⓑ Ⓒ Ⓓ Ⓔ
10 Ⓐ Ⓑ Ⓒ Ⓓ Ⓔ
11 Ⓐ Ⓑ Ⓒ Ⓓ Ⓔ
12 Ⓐ Ⓑ Ⓒ Ⓓ Ⓔ

PT5-S2-G3

12 Ⓐ Ⓑ Ⓒ Ⓓ Ⓔ
13 Ⓐ Ⓑ Ⓒ Ⓓ Ⓔ
14 Ⓐ Ⓑ Ⓒ Ⓓ Ⓔ
15 Ⓐ Ⓑ Ⓒ Ⓓ Ⓔ
16 Ⓐ Ⓑ Ⓒ Ⓓ Ⓔ
17 Ⓐ Ⓑ Ⓒ Ⓓ Ⓔ

V1, Pg. 67   PT9-S3-G2

8 Ⓐ Ⓑ Ⓒ Ⓓ Ⓔ
9 Ⓐ Ⓑ Ⓒ Ⓓ Ⓔ
10 Ⓐ Ⓑ Ⓒ Ⓓ Ⓔ
11 Ⓐ Ⓑ Ⓒ Ⓓ Ⓔ
12 Ⓐ Ⓑ Ⓒ Ⓓ Ⓔ
13 Ⓐ Ⓑ Ⓒ Ⓓ Ⓔ

V1, Pg. 95   PT10-S2-G4

19 Ⓐ Ⓑ Ⓒ Ⓓ Ⓔ
20 Ⓐ Ⓑ Ⓒ Ⓓ Ⓔ
21 Ⓐ Ⓑ Ⓒ Ⓓ Ⓔ
22 Ⓐ Ⓑ Ⓒ Ⓓ Ⓔ
23 Ⓐ Ⓑ Ⓒ Ⓓ Ⓔ
24 Ⓐ Ⓑ Ⓒ Ⓓ Ⓔ

V1, Pg. 120 PT11-S1-G3

12 Ⓐ Ⓑ Ⓒ Ⓓ Ⓔ
13 Ⓐ Ⓑ Ⓒ Ⓓ Ⓔ
14 Ⓐ Ⓑ Ⓒ Ⓓ Ⓔ
15 Ⓐ Ⓑ Ⓒ Ⓓ Ⓔ
16 Ⓐ Ⓑ Ⓒ Ⓓ Ⓔ
17 Ⓐ Ⓑ Ⓒ Ⓓ Ⓔ
18 Ⓐ Ⓑ Ⓒ Ⓓ Ⓔ
19 Ⓐ Ⓑ Ⓒ Ⓓ Ⓔ

V2, Pg. 67   PT20-S3-G2

6 Ⓐ Ⓑ Ⓒ Ⓓ Ⓔ
7 Ⓐ Ⓑ Ⓒ Ⓓ Ⓔ
8 Ⓐ Ⓑ Ⓒ Ⓓ Ⓔ
9 Ⓐ Ⓑ Ⓒ Ⓓ Ⓔ
10 Ⓐ Ⓑ Ⓒ Ⓓ Ⓔ
11 Ⓐ Ⓑ Ⓒ Ⓓ Ⓔ
12 Ⓐ Ⓑ Ⓒ Ⓓ Ⓔ

V2, Pg. 153 PT23-S1-G2

6 Ⓐ Ⓑ Ⓒ Ⓓ Ⓔ
7 Ⓐ Ⓑ Ⓒ Ⓓ Ⓔ
8 Ⓐ Ⓑ Ⓒ Ⓓ Ⓔ
9 Ⓐ Ⓑ Ⓒ Ⓓ Ⓔ
10 Ⓐ Ⓑ Ⓒ Ⓓ Ⓔ
11 Ⓐ Ⓑ Ⓒ Ⓓ Ⓔ

V2, Pg. 213 PT24-S4-G4

18 Ⓐ Ⓑ Ⓒ Ⓓ Ⓔ
19 Ⓐ Ⓑ Ⓒ Ⓓ Ⓔ
20 Ⓐ Ⓑ Ⓒ Ⓓ Ⓔ
21 Ⓐ Ⓑ Ⓒ Ⓓ Ⓔ
22 Ⓐ Ⓑ Ⓒ Ⓓ Ⓔ
23 Ⓐ Ⓑ Ⓒ Ⓓ Ⓔ

V2, Pg. 238   PT25-S3-G3

13 Ⓐ Ⓑ Ⓒ Ⓓ Ⓔ
14 Ⓐ Ⓑ Ⓒ Ⓓ Ⓔ
15 Ⓐ Ⓑ Ⓒ Ⓓ Ⓔ
16 Ⓐ Ⓑ Ⓒ Ⓓ Ⓔ
17 Ⓐ Ⓑ Ⓒ Ⓓ Ⓔ
18 Ⓐ Ⓑ Ⓒ Ⓓ Ⓔ

V3, Pg. 85   PT31-S1-G2

7 Ⓐ Ⓑ Ⓒ Ⓓ Ⓔ
8 Ⓐ Ⓑ Ⓒ Ⓓ Ⓔ
9 Ⓐ Ⓑ Ⓒ Ⓓ Ⓔ
10 Ⓐ Ⓑ Ⓒ Ⓓ Ⓔ
11 Ⓐ Ⓑ Ⓒ Ⓓ Ⓔ
12 Ⓐ Ⓑ Ⓒ Ⓓ Ⓔ
13 Ⓐ Ⓑ Ⓒ Ⓓ Ⓔ

V3, Pg. 177   PT33-S4-G2

6 Ⓐ Ⓑ Ⓒ Ⓓ Ⓔ
7 Ⓐ Ⓑ Ⓒ Ⓓ Ⓔ
8 Ⓐ Ⓑ Ⓒ Ⓓ Ⓔ
9 Ⓐ Ⓑ Ⓒ Ⓓ Ⓔ
10 Ⓐ Ⓑ Ⓒ Ⓓ Ⓔ
11 Ⓐ Ⓑ Ⓒ Ⓓ Ⓔ
12 Ⓐ Ⓑ Ⓒ Ⓓ Ⓔ

V3, Pg. 178   PT33-S4-G3

13 Ⓐ Ⓑ Ⓒ Ⓓ Ⓔ
14 Ⓐ Ⓑ Ⓒ Ⓓ Ⓔ
15 Ⓐ Ⓑ Ⓒ Ⓓ Ⓔ
16 Ⓐ Ⓑ Ⓒ Ⓓ Ⓔ
17 Ⓐ Ⓑ Ⓒ Ⓓ Ⓔ
18 Ⓐ Ⓑ Ⓒ Ⓓ Ⓔ

V3, Pg. 213   PT34-S4-G4

19 Ⓐ Ⓑ Ⓒ Ⓓ Ⓔ
20 Ⓐ Ⓑ Ⓒ Ⓓ Ⓔ
21 Ⓐ Ⓑ Ⓒ Ⓓ Ⓔ
22 Ⓐ Ⓑ Ⓒ Ⓓ Ⓔ
23 Ⓐ Ⓑ Ⓒ Ⓓ Ⓔ
24 Ⓐ Ⓑ Ⓒ Ⓓ Ⓔ

V3, Pg. 278   PT36-S4-G1

1 Ⓐ Ⓑ Ⓒ Ⓓ Ⓔ
2 Ⓐ Ⓑ Ⓒ Ⓓ Ⓔ
3 Ⓐ Ⓑ Ⓒ Ⓓ Ⓔ
4 Ⓐ Ⓑ Ⓒ Ⓓ Ⓔ
5 Ⓐ Ⓑ Ⓒ Ⓓ Ⓔ
6 Ⓐ Ⓑ Ⓒ Ⓓ Ⓔ

PT39-S1-G4

19 Ⓐ Ⓑ Ⓒ Ⓓ Ⓔ
20 Ⓐ Ⓑ Ⓒ Ⓓ Ⓔ
21 Ⓐ Ⓑ Ⓒ Ⓓ Ⓔ
22 Ⓐ Ⓑ Ⓒ Ⓓ Ⓔ
23 Ⓐ Ⓑ Ⓒ Ⓓ Ⓔ

PT40-S2-G4

18 Ⓐ Ⓑ Ⓒ Ⓓ Ⓔ
19 Ⓐ Ⓑ Ⓒ Ⓓ Ⓔ
20 Ⓐ Ⓑ Ⓒ Ⓓ Ⓔ
21 Ⓐ Ⓑ Ⓒ Ⓓ Ⓔ
22 Ⓐ Ⓑ Ⓒ Ⓓ Ⓔ
23 Ⓐ Ⓑ Ⓒ Ⓓ Ⓔ

PT41-S2-G3

13 Ⓐ Ⓑ Ⓒ Ⓓ Ⓔ
14 Ⓐ Ⓑ Ⓒ Ⓓ Ⓔ
15 Ⓐ Ⓑ Ⓒ Ⓓ Ⓔ
16 Ⓐ Ⓑ Ⓒ Ⓓ Ⓔ
17 Ⓐ Ⓑ Ⓒ Ⓓ Ⓔ

PT42-S1-G1

1 Ⓐ Ⓑ Ⓒ Ⓓ Ⓔ
2 Ⓐ Ⓑ Ⓒ Ⓓ Ⓔ
3 Ⓐ Ⓑ Ⓒ Ⓓ Ⓔ
4 Ⓐ Ⓑ Ⓒ Ⓓ Ⓔ
5 Ⓐ Ⓑ Ⓒ Ⓓ Ⓔ

PT45-S3-G3

13 Ⓐ Ⓑ Ⓒ Ⓓ Ⓔ
14 Ⓐ Ⓑ Ⓒ Ⓓ Ⓔ
15 Ⓐ Ⓑ Ⓒ Ⓓ Ⓔ
16 Ⓐ Ⓑ Ⓒ Ⓓ Ⓔ
17 Ⓐ Ⓑ Ⓒ Ⓓ Ⓔ

PT47-S4-G2

6 Ⓐ Ⓑ Ⓒ Ⓓ Ⓔ
7 Ⓐ Ⓑ Ⓒ Ⓓ Ⓔ
8 Ⓐ Ⓑ Ⓒ Ⓓ Ⓔ
9 Ⓐ Ⓑ Ⓒ Ⓓ Ⓔ
10 Ⓐ Ⓑ Ⓒ Ⓓ Ⓔ
11 Ⓐ Ⓑ Ⓒ Ⓓ Ⓔ

PT48-S2-G1

1 Ⓐ Ⓑ Ⓒ Ⓓ Ⓔ
2 Ⓐ Ⓑ Ⓒ Ⓓ Ⓔ
3 Ⓐ Ⓑ Ⓒ Ⓓ Ⓔ
4 Ⓐ Ⓑ Ⓒ Ⓓ Ⓔ
5 Ⓐ Ⓑ Ⓒ Ⓓ Ⓔ
6 Ⓐ Ⓑ Ⓒ Ⓓ Ⓔ

PT49-S1-G3

13 Ⓐ Ⓑ Ⓒ Ⓓ Ⓔ
14 Ⓐ Ⓑ Ⓒ Ⓓ Ⓔ
15 Ⓐ Ⓑ Ⓒ Ⓓ Ⓔ
16 Ⓐ Ⓑ Ⓒ Ⓓ Ⓔ
17 Ⓐ Ⓑ Ⓒ Ⓓ Ⓔ

PT50-S3-G2

6 Ⓐ Ⓑ Ⓒ Ⓓ Ⓔ
7 Ⓐ Ⓑ Ⓒ Ⓓ Ⓔ
8 Ⓐ Ⓑ Ⓒ Ⓓ Ⓔ
9 Ⓐ Ⓑ Ⓒ Ⓓ Ⓔ
10 Ⓐ Ⓑ Ⓒ Ⓓ Ⓔ
11 Ⓐ Ⓑ Ⓒ Ⓓ Ⓔ

V4, Pg. 96   PT54-S3-G1

1 Ⓐ Ⓑ Ⓒ Ⓓ Ⓔ
2 Ⓐ Ⓑ Ⓒ Ⓓ Ⓔ
3 Ⓐ Ⓑ Ⓒ Ⓓ Ⓔ
4 Ⓐ Ⓑ Ⓒ Ⓓ Ⓔ
5 Ⓐ Ⓑ Ⓒ Ⓓ Ⓔ

V4, Pg. 241   PT58-S3-G2

7 Ⓐ Ⓑ Ⓒ Ⓓ Ⓔ
8 Ⓐ Ⓑ Ⓒ Ⓓ Ⓔ
9 Ⓐ Ⓑ Ⓒ Ⓓ Ⓔ
10 Ⓐ Ⓑ Ⓒ Ⓓ Ⓔ
11 Ⓐ Ⓑ Ⓒ Ⓓ Ⓔ
12 Ⓐ Ⓑ Ⓒ Ⓓ Ⓔ

V4, Pg. 243   PT58-S3-G4

18 Ⓐ Ⓑ Ⓒ Ⓓ Ⓔ
19 Ⓐ Ⓑ Ⓒ Ⓓ Ⓔ
20 Ⓐ Ⓑ Ⓒ Ⓓ Ⓔ
21 Ⓐ Ⓑ Ⓒ Ⓓ Ⓔ
22 Ⓐ Ⓑ Ⓒ Ⓓ Ⓔ
23 Ⓐ Ⓑ Ⓒ Ⓓ Ⓔ

V4, Pg. 262   PT59-S1-G3

11 Ⓐ Ⓑ Ⓒ Ⓓ Ⓔ
12 Ⓐ Ⓑ Ⓒ Ⓓ Ⓔ
13 Ⓐ Ⓑ Ⓒ Ⓓ Ⓔ
14 Ⓐ Ⓑ Ⓒ Ⓓ Ⓔ
15 Ⓐ Ⓑ Ⓒ Ⓓ Ⓔ
16 Ⓐ Ⓑ Ⓒ Ⓓ Ⓔ

V5, Pg. 126   PT65-S2-G3

12 Ⓐ Ⓑ Ⓒ Ⓓ Ⓔ
13 Ⓐ Ⓑ Ⓒ Ⓓ Ⓔ
14 Ⓐ Ⓑ Ⓒ Ⓓ Ⓔ
15 Ⓐ Ⓑ Ⓒ Ⓓ Ⓔ
16 Ⓐ Ⓑ Ⓒ Ⓓ Ⓔ

V5, Pg. 330   PT70-S3-G2

8 Ⓐ Ⓑ Ⓒ Ⓓ Ⓔ
9 Ⓐ Ⓑ Ⓒ Ⓓ Ⓔ
10 Ⓐ Ⓑ Ⓒ Ⓓ Ⓔ
11 Ⓐ Ⓑ Ⓒ Ⓓ Ⓔ
12 Ⓐ Ⓑ Ⓒ Ⓓ Ⓔ

PT76, Pg. 32 PT76-S3-G4
19 Ⓐ Ⓑ Ⓒ Ⓓ Ⓔ
20 Ⓐ Ⓑ Ⓒ Ⓓ Ⓔ
21 Ⓐ Ⓑ Ⓒ Ⓓ Ⓔ
22 Ⓐ Ⓑ Ⓒ Ⓓ Ⓔ
23 Ⓐ Ⓑ Ⓒ Ⓓ Ⓔ

Grouping (Distribution)

SP1, Pg. 296 PTC-S1-G1
1 Ⓐ Ⓑ Ⓒ Ⓓ Ⓔ
2 Ⓐ Ⓑ Ⓒ Ⓓ Ⓔ
3 Ⓐ Ⓑ Ⓒ Ⓓ Ⓔ
4 Ⓐ Ⓑ Ⓒ Ⓓ Ⓔ
5 Ⓐ Ⓑ Ⓒ Ⓓ Ⓔ

PT6-S4-G1
1 Ⓐ Ⓑ Ⓒ Ⓓ Ⓔ
2 Ⓐ Ⓑ Ⓒ Ⓓ Ⓔ
3 Ⓐ Ⓑ Ⓒ Ⓓ Ⓔ
4 Ⓐ Ⓑ Ⓒ Ⓓ Ⓔ
5 Ⓐ Ⓑ Ⓒ Ⓓ Ⓔ
6 Ⓐ Ⓑ Ⓒ Ⓓ Ⓔ

V1, Pg. 26   PT7-S2-G3
13 Ⓐ Ⓑ Ⓒ Ⓓ Ⓔ
14 Ⓐ Ⓑ Ⓒ Ⓓ Ⓔ
15 Ⓐ Ⓑ Ⓒ Ⓓ Ⓔ
16 Ⓐ Ⓑ Ⓒ Ⓓ Ⓔ
17 Ⓐ Ⓑ Ⓒ Ⓓ Ⓔ
18 Ⓐ Ⓑ Ⓒ Ⓓ Ⓔ

V1, Pg. 93   PT10-S2-G2
6 Ⓐ Ⓑ Ⓒ Ⓓ Ⓔ
7 Ⓐ Ⓑ Ⓒ Ⓓ Ⓔ
8 Ⓐ Ⓑ Ⓒ Ⓓ Ⓔ
9 Ⓐ Ⓑ Ⓒ Ⓓ Ⓔ
10 Ⓐ Ⓑ Ⓒ Ⓓ Ⓔ
11 Ⓐ Ⓑ Ⓒ Ⓓ Ⓔ
12 Ⓐ Ⓑ Ⓒ Ⓓ Ⓔ

V1, Pg. 118 PT11-S1-G1
1 Ⓐ Ⓑ Ⓒ Ⓓ Ⓔ
2 Ⓐ Ⓑ Ⓒ Ⓓ Ⓔ
3 Ⓐ Ⓑ Ⓒ Ⓓ Ⓔ
4 Ⓐ Ⓑ Ⓒ Ⓓ Ⓔ
5 Ⓐ Ⓑ Ⓒ Ⓓ Ⓔ
6 Ⓐ Ⓑ Ⓒ Ⓓ Ⓔ

V1, Pg. 161 PT12-S2-G2
7 Ⓐ Ⓑ Ⓒ Ⓓ Ⓔ
8 Ⓐ Ⓑ Ⓒ Ⓓ Ⓔ
9 Ⓐ Ⓑ Ⓒ Ⓓ Ⓔ
10 Ⓐ Ⓑ Ⓒ Ⓓ Ⓔ
11 Ⓐ Ⓑ Ⓒ Ⓓ Ⓔ

V1, Pg. 186   PT13-S1-G1
1 Ⓐ Ⓑ Ⓒ Ⓓ Ⓔ
2 Ⓐ Ⓑ Ⓒ Ⓓ Ⓔ
3 Ⓐ Ⓑ Ⓒ Ⓓ Ⓔ
4 Ⓐ Ⓑ Ⓒ Ⓓ Ⓔ
5 Ⓐ Ⓑ Ⓒ Ⓓ Ⓔ
6 Ⓐ Ⓑ Ⓒ Ⓓ Ⓔ

V1, Pg. 222   PT14-S1-G3
13 Ⓐ Ⓑ Ⓒ Ⓓ Ⓔ
14 Ⓐ Ⓑ Ⓒ Ⓓ Ⓔ
15 Ⓐ Ⓑ Ⓒ Ⓓ Ⓔ
16 Ⓐ Ⓑ Ⓒ Ⓓ Ⓔ
17 Ⓐ Ⓑ Ⓒ Ⓓ Ⓔ
18 Ⓐ Ⓑ Ⓒ Ⓓ Ⓔ

V1, Pg. 288   PT16-S1-G1
1 Ⓐ Ⓑ Ⓒ Ⓓ Ⓔ
2 Ⓐ Ⓑ Ⓒ Ⓓ Ⓔ
3 Ⓐ Ⓑ Ⓒ Ⓓ Ⓔ
4 Ⓐ Ⓑ Ⓒ Ⓓ Ⓔ
5 Ⓐ Ⓑ Ⓒ Ⓓ Ⓔ
6 Ⓐ Ⓑ Ⓒ Ⓓ Ⓔ

V1, Pg. 322   PT18-S1-G1
1 Ⓐ Ⓑ Ⓒ Ⓓ Ⓔ
2 Ⓐ Ⓑ Ⓒ Ⓓ Ⓔ
3 Ⓐ Ⓑ Ⓒ Ⓓ Ⓔ
4 Ⓐ Ⓑ Ⓒ Ⓓ Ⓔ
5 Ⓐ Ⓑ Ⓒ Ⓓ Ⓔ
6 Ⓐ Ⓑ Ⓒ Ⓓ Ⓔ

V2, Pg. 18   PT19-S1-G3
13 Ⓐ Ⓑ Ⓒ Ⓓ Ⓔ
14 Ⓐ Ⓑ Ⓒ Ⓓ Ⓔ
15 Ⓐ Ⓑ Ⓒ Ⓓ Ⓔ
16 Ⓐ Ⓑ Ⓒ Ⓓ Ⓔ
17 Ⓐ Ⓑ Ⓒ Ⓓ Ⓔ
18 Ⓐ Ⓑ Ⓒ Ⓓ Ⓔ
19 Ⓐ Ⓑ Ⓒ Ⓓ Ⓔ

V2, Pg. 19   PT19-S1-G4
20 Ⓐ Ⓑ Ⓒ Ⓓ Ⓔ
21 Ⓐ Ⓑ Ⓒ Ⓓ Ⓔ
22 Ⓐ Ⓑ Ⓒ Ⓓ Ⓔ
23 Ⓐ Ⓑ Ⓒ Ⓓ Ⓔ
24 Ⓐ Ⓑ Ⓒ Ⓓ Ⓔ

V2, Pg. 134   PT22-S3-G1
1 Ⓐ Ⓑ Ⓒ Ⓓ Ⓔ
2 Ⓐ Ⓑ Ⓒ Ⓓ Ⓔ
3 Ⓐ Ⓑ Ⓒ Ⓓ Ⓔ
4 Ⓐ Ⓑ Ⓒ Ⓓ Ⓔ
5 Ⓐ Ⓑ Ⓒ Ⓓ Ⓔ
6 Ⓐ Ⓑ Ⓒ Ⓓ Ⓔ
7 Ⓐ Ⓑ Ⓒ Ⓓ Ⓔ

V2, Pg. 154   PT23-S1-G3
12 Ⓐ Ⓑ Ⓒ Ⓓ Ⓔ
13 Ⓐ Ⓑ Ⓒ Ⓓ Ⓔ
14 Ⓐ Ⓑ Ⓒ Ⓓ Ⓔ
15 Ⓐ Ⓑ Ⓒ Ⓓ Ⓔ
16 Ⓐ Ⓑ Ⓒ Ⓓ Ⓔ
17 Ⓐ Ⓑ Ⓒ Ⓓ Ⓔ
18 Ⓐ Ⓑ Ⓒ Ⓓ Ⓔ

V2, Pg. 210   PT24-S4-G1
1 Ⓐ Ⓑ Ⓒ Ⓓ Ⓔ
2 Ⓐ Ⓑ Ⓒ Ⓓ Ⓔ
3 Ⓐ Ⓑ Ⓒ Ⓓ Ⓔ
4 Ⓐ Ⓑ Ⓒ Ⓓ Ⓔ
5 Ⓐ Ⓑ Ⓒ Ⓓ Ⓔ

V2, Pg. 256   PT26-S1-G3
13 Ⓐ Ⓑ Ⓒ Ⓓ Ⓔ
14 Ⓐ Ⓑ Ⓒ Ⓓ Ⓔ
15 Ⓐ Ⓑ Ⓒ Ⓓ Ⓔ
16 Ⓐ Ⓑ Ⓒ Ⓓ Ⓔ
17 Ⓐ Ⓑ Ⓒ Ⓓ Ⓔ
18 Ⓐ Ⓑ Ⓒ Ⓓ Ⓔ

V2, Pg. 298   PT27-S2-G3
13 Ⓐ Ⓑ Ⓒ Ⓓ Ⓔ
14 Ⓐ Ⓑ Ⓒ Ⓓ Ⓔ
15 Ⓐ Ⓑ Ⓒ Ⓓ Ⓔ
16 Ⓐ Ⓑ Ⓒ Ⓓ Ⓔ
17 Ⓐ Ⓑ Ⓒ Ⓓ Ⓔ
18 Ⓐ Ⓑ Ⓒ Ⓓ Ⓔ
19 Ⓐ Ⓑ Ⓒ Ⓓ Ⓔ

V3, Pg. 32   PT29-S3-G1

1 Ⓐ Ⓑ Ⓒ Ⓓ Ⓔ
2 Ⓐ Ⓑ Ⓒ Ⓓ Ⓔ
3 Ⓐ Ⓑ Ⓒ Ⓓ Ⓔ
4 Ⓐ Ⓑ Ⓒ Ⓓ Ⓔ
5 Ⓐ Ⓑ Ⓒ Ⓓ Ⓔ
6 Ⓐ Ⓑ Ⓒ Ⓓ Ⓔ

V3, Pg. 306   PT37-S3-G3

12 Ⓐ Ⓑ Ⓒ Ⓓ Ⓔ
13 Ⓐ Ⓑ Ⓒ Ⓓ Ⓔ
14 Ⓐ Ⓑ Ⓒ Ⓓ Ⓔ
15 Ⓐ Ⓑ Ⓒ Ⓓ Ⓔ
16 Ⓐ Ⓑ Ⓒ Ⓓ Ⓔ
17 Ⓐ Ⓑ Ⓒ Ⓓ Ⓔ
18 Ⓐ Ⓑ Ⓒ Ⓓ Ⓔ

V3, Pg. 332   PT38-S2-G3

14 Ⓐ Ⓑ Ⓒ Ⓓ Ⓔ
15 Ⓐ Ⓑ Ⓒ Ⓓ Ⓔ
16 Ⓐ Ⓑ Ⓒ Ⓓ Ⓔ
17 Ⓐ Ⓑ Ⓒ Ⓓ Ⓔ
18 Ⓐ Ⓑ Ⓒ Ⓓ Ⓔ
19 Ⓐ Ⓑ Ⓒ Ⓓ Ⓔ

PT44-S3-G2

7   Ⓐ Ⓑ Ⓒ Ⓓ Ⓔ
8   Ⓐ Ⓑ Ⓒ Ⓓ Ⓔ
9   Ⓐ Ⓑ Ⓒ Ⓓ Ⓔ
10 Ⓐ Ⓑ Ⓒ Ⓓ Ⓔ
11 Ⓐ Ⓑ Ⓒ Ⓓ Ⓔ
12 Ⓐ Ⓑ Ⓒ Ⓓ Ⓔ

PT49-S1-G2

8   Ⓐ Ⓑ Ⓒ Ⓓ Ⓔ
9   Ⓐ Ⓑ Ⓒ Ⓓ Ⓔ
10 Ⓐ Ⓑ Ⓒ Ⓓ Ⓔ
11 Ⓐ Ⓑ Ⓒ Ⓓ Ⓔ
12 Ⓐ Ⓑ Ⓒ Ⓓ Ⓔ

V4, Pg. 17   PT52-S2-G2

8   Ⓐ Ⓑ Ⓒ Ⓓ Ⓔ
9   Ⓐ Ⓑ Ⓒ Ⓓ Ⓔ
10 Ⓐ Ⓑ Ⓒ Ⓓ Ⓔ
11 Ⓐ Ⓑ Ⓒ Ⓓ Ⓔ
12 Ⓐ Ⓑ Ⓒ Ⓓ Ⓔ

V4, Pg. 52   PT53-S2-G1

1 Ⓐ Ⓑ Ⓒ Ⓓ Ⓔ
2 Ⓐ Ⓑ Ⓒ Ⓓ Ⓔ
3 Ⓐ Ⓑ Ⓒ Ⓓ Ⓔ
4 Ⓐ Ⓑ Ⓒ Ⓓ Ⓔ
5 Ⓐ Ⓑ Ⓒ Ⓓ Ⓔ

V5, Pg. 52   PT63-S2-G1

1 Ⓐ Ⓑ Ⓒ Ⓓ Ⓔ
2 Ⓐ Ⓑ Ⓒ Ⓓ Ⓔ
3 Ⓐ Ⓑ Ⓒ Ⓓ Ⓔ
4 Ⓐ Ⓑ Ⓒ Ⓓ Ⓔ
5 Ⓐ Ⓑ Ⓒ Ⓓ Ⓔ

V5, Pg. 172   PT66-S3-G3

12 Ⓐ Ⓑ Ⓒ Ⓓ Ⓔ
13 Ⓐ Ⓑ Ⓒ Ⓓ Ⓔ
14 Ⓐ Ⓑ Ⓒ Ⓓ Ⓔ
15 Ⓐ Ⓑ Ⓒ Ⓓ Ⓔ
16 Ⓐ Ⓑ Ⓒ Ⓓ Ⓔ
17 Ⓐ Ⓑ Ⓒ Ⓓ Ⓔ
18 Ⓐ Ⓑ Ⓒ Ⓓ Ⓔ

V5, Pg. 258   PT68-S4-G2

6   Ⓐ Ⓑ Ⓒ Ⓓ Ⓔ
7   Ⓐ Ⓑ Ⓒ Ⓓ Ⓔ
8   Ⓐ Ⓑ Ⓒ Ⓓ Ⓔ
9   Ⓐ Ⓑ Ⓒ Ⓓ Ⓔ
10 Ⓐ Ⓑ Ⓒ Ⓓ Ⓔ

V5, Pg. 286   PT69-S2-G4

18 Ⓐ Ⓑ Ⓒ Ⓓ Ⓔ
19 Ⓐ Ⓑ Ⓒ Ⓓ Ⓔ
20 Ⓐ Ⓑ Ⓒ Ⓓ Ⓔ
21 Ⓐ Ⓑ Ⓒ Ⓓ Ⓔ
22 Ⓐ Ⓑ Ⓒ Ⓓ Ⓔ
23 Ⓐ Ⓑ Ⓒ Ⓓ Ⓔ

V5, Pg. 362   PT71-S2-G2

6   Ⓐ Ⓑ Ⓒ Ⓓ Ⓔ
7   Ⓐ Ⓑ Ⓒ Ⓓ Ⓔ
8   Ⓐ Ⓑ Ⓒ Ⓓ Ⓔ
9   Ⓐ Ⓑ Ⓒ Ⓓ Ⓔ
10 Ⓐ Ⓑ Ⓒ Ⓓ Ⓔ
11 Ⓐ Ⓑ Ⓒ Ⓓ Ⓔ

PT72, Pg. 38 PT72-S4-G3

13 Ⓐ Ⓑ Ⓒ Ⓓ Ⓔ
14 Ⓐ Ⓑ Ⓒ Ⓓ Ⓔ
15 Ⓐ Ⓑ Ⓒ Ⓓ Ⓔ
16 Ⓐ Ⓑ Ⓒ Ⓓ Ⓔ
17 Ⓐ Ⓑ Ⓒ Ⓓ Ⓔ
18 Ⓐ Ⓑ Ⓒ Ⓓ Ⓔ

PT73, Pg. 30 PT73-S3-G3

14 Ⓐ Ⓑ Ⓒ Ⓓ Ⓔ
15 Ⓐ Ⓑ Ⓒ Ⓓ Ⓔ
16 Ⓐ Ⓑ Ⓒ Ⓓ Ⓔ
17 Ⓐ Ⓑ Ⓒ Ⓓ Ⓔ
18 Ⓐ Ⓑ Ⓒ Ⓓ Ⓔ

PT74, Pg. 24 PT74-S2-G4

17 Ⓐ Ⓑ Ⓒ Ⓓ Ⓔ
18 Ⓐ Ⓑ Ⓒ Ⓓ Ⓔ
19 Ⓐ Ⓑ Ⓒ Ⓓ Ⓔ
20 Ⓐ Ⓑ Ⓒ Ⓓ Ⓔ
21 Ⓐ Ⓑ Ⓒ Ⓓ Ⓔ
22 Ⓐ Ⓑ Ⓒ Ⓓ Ⓔ
23 Ⓐ Ⓑ Ⓒ Ⓓ Ⓔ

PT75, Pg. 36 PT75-S4-G2

7   Ⓐ Ⓑ Ⓒ Ⓓ Ⓔ
8   Ⓐ Ⓑ Ⓒ Ⓓ Ⓔ
9   Ⓐ Ⓑ Ⓒ Ⓓ Ⓔ
10 Ⓐ Ⓑ Ⓒ Ⓓ Ⓔ
11 Ⓐ Ⓑ Ⓒ Ⓓ Ⓔ

Determined Assignment

PTSP-S1-G3

12 Ⓐ Ⓑ Ⓒ Ⓓ Ⓔ
13 Ⓐ Ⓑ Ⓒ Ⓓ Ⓔ
14 Ⓐ Ⓑ Ⓒ Ⓓ Ⓔ
15 Ⓐ Ⓑ Ⓒ Ⓓ Ⓔ
16 Ⓐ Ⓑ Ⓒ Ⓓ Ⓔ
17 Ⓐ Ⓑ Ⓒ Ⓓ Ⓔ

SP1, Pg. 85 PTA-S3-G2

6   Ⓐ Ⓑ Ⓒ Ⓓ Ⓔ
7   Ⓐ Ⓑ Ⓒ Ⓓ Ⓔ
8   Ⓐ Ⓑ Ⓒ Ⓓ Ⓔ
9   Ⓐ Ⓑ Ⓒ Ⓓ Ⓔ
10 Ⓐ Ⓑ Ⓒ Ⓓ Ⓔ

SP2, Pg. 346 PTC2-S1-G1

1 Ⓐ Ⓑ Ⓒ Ⓓ Ⓔ
2 Ⓐ Ⓑ Ⓒ Ⓓ Ⓔ
3 Ⓐ Ⓑ Ⓒ Ⓓ Ⓔ
4 Ⓐ Ⓑ Ⓒ Ⓓ Ⓔ
5 Ⓐ Ⓑ Ⓒ Ⓓ Ⓔ

SP2, Pg. 352 PTC2-S1-G4

18 Ⓐ Ⓑ Ⓒ Ⓓ Ⓔ
19 Ⓐ Ⓑ Ⓒ Ⓓ Ⓔ
20 Ⓐ Ⓑ Ⓒ Ⓓ Ⓔ
21 Ⓐ Ⓑ Ⓒ Ⓓ Ⓔ
22 Ⓐ Ⓑ Ⓒ Ⓓ Ⓔ
23 Ⓐ Ⓑ Ⓒ Ⓓ Ⓔ

PT2-S3-G2

6 Ⓐ Ⓑ Ⓒ Ⓓ Ⓔ
7 Ⓐ Ⓑ Ⓒ Ⓓ Ⓔ
8 Ⓐ Ⓑ Ⓒ Ⓓ Ⓔ
9 Ⓐ Ⓑ Ⓒ Ⓓ Ⓔ
10 Ⓐ Ⓑ Ⓒ Ⓓ Ⓔ
11 Ⓐ Ⓑ Ⓒ Ⓓ Ⓔ
12 Ⓐ Ⓑ Ⓒ Ⓓ Ⓔ

PT3-S1-G4

20 Ⓐ Ⓑ Ⓒ Ⓓ Ⓔ
21 Ⓐ Ⓑ Ⓒ Ⓓ Ⓔ
22 Ⓐ Ⓑ Ⓒ Ⓓ Ⓔ
23 Ⓐ Ⓑ Ⓒ Ⓓ Ⓔ
24 Ⓐ Ⓑ Ⓒ Ⓓ Ⓔ

PT4-S3-G3

12 Ⓐ Ⓑ Ⓒ Ⓓ Ⓔ
13 Ⓐ Ⓑ Ⓒ Ⓓ Ⓔ
14 Ⓐ Ⓑ Ⓒ Ⓓ Ⓔ
15 Ⓐ Ⓑ Ⓒ Ⓓ Ⓔ
16 Ⓐ Ⓑ Ⓒ Ⓓ Ⓔ
17 Ⓐ Ⓑ Ⓒ Ⓓ Ⓔ

PT5-S2-G1

1 Ⓐ Ⓑ Ⓒ Ⓓ Ⓔ
2 Ⓐ Ⓑ Ⓒ Ⓓ Ⓔ
3 Ⓐ Ⓑ Ⓒ Ⓓ Ⓔ
4 Ⓐ Ⓑ Ⓒ Ⓓ Ⓔ
5 Ⓐ Ⓑ Ⓒ Ⓓ Ⓔ
6 Ⓐ Ⓑ Ⓒ Ⓓ Ⓔ

V1, Pg. 25   PT7-S2-G2

8 Ⓐ Ⓑ Ⓒ Ⓓ Ⓔ
9 Ⓐ Ⓑ Ⓒ Ⓓ Ⓔ
10 Ⓐ Ⓑ Ⓒ Ⓓ Ⓔ
11 Ⓐ Ⓑ Ⓒ Ⓓ Ⓔ
12 Ⓐ Ⓑ Ⓒ Ⓓ Ⓔ

PT8-S2-G1

1 Ⓐ Ⓑ Ⓒ Ⓓ Ⓔ
2 Ⓐ Ⓑ Ⓒ Ⓓ Ⓔ
3 Ⓐ Ⓑ Ⓒ Ⓓ Ⓔ
4 Ⓐ Ⓑ Ⓒ Ⓓ Ⓔ
5 Ⓐ Ⓑ Ⓒ Ⓓ Ⓔ

V1, Pg. 68   PT9-S3-G3

14 Ⓐ Ⓑ Ⓒ Ⓓ Ⓔ
15 Ⓐ Ⓑ Ⓒ Ⓓ Ⓔ
16 Ⓐ Ⓑ Ⓒ Ⓓ Ⓔ
17 Ⓐ Ⓑ Ⓒ Ⓓ Ⓔ
18 Ⓐ Ⓑ Ⓒ Ⓓ Ⓔ

V1, Pg. 220   PT14-S1-G1

1 Ⓐ Ⓑ Ⓒ Ⓓ Ⓔ
2 Ⓐ Ⓑ Ⓒ Ⓓ Ⓔ
3 Ⓐ Ⓑ Ⓒ Ⓓ Ⓔ
4 Ⓐ Ⓑ Ⓒ Ⓓ Ⓔ
5 Ⓐ Ⓑ Ⓒ Ⓓ Ⓔ
6 Ⓐ Ⓑ Ⓒ Ⓓ Ⓔ

V1, Pg. 289   PT16-S1-G2

7 Ⓐ Ⓑ Ⓒ Ⓓ Ⓔ
8 Ⓐ Ⓑ Ⓒ Ⓓ Ⓔ
9 Ⓐ Ⓑ Ⓒ Ⓓ Ⓔ
10 Ⓐ Ⓑ Ⓒ Ⓓ Ⓔ
11 Ⓐ Ⓑ Ⓒ Ⓓ Ⓔ
12 Ⓐ Ⓑ Ⓒ Ⓓ Ⓔ

PT17-S1-G4

18 Ⓐ Ⓑ Ⓒ Ⓓ Ⓔ
19 Ⓐ Ⓑ Ⓒ Ⓓ Ⓔ
20 Ⓐ Ⓑ Ⓒ Ⓓ Ⓔ
21 Ⓐ Ⓑ Ⓒ Ⓓ Ⓔ
22 Ⓐ Ⓑ Ⓒ Ⓓ Ⓔ
23 Ⓐ Ⓑ Ⓒ Ⓓ Ⓔ
24 Ⓐ Ⓑ Ⓒ Ⓓ Ⓔ

V2, Pg. 17   PT19-S1-G2

8 Ⓐ Ⓑ Ⓒ Ⓓ Ⓔ
9 Ⓐ Ⓑ Ⓒ Ⓓ Ⓔ
10 Ⓐ Ⓑ Ⓒ Ⓓ Ⓔ
11 Ⓐ Ⓑ Ⓒ Ⓓ Ⓔ
12 Ⓐ Ⓑ Ⓒ Ⓓ Ⓔ

V2, Pg. 66   PT20-S3-G1

1 Ⓐ Ⓑ Ⓒ Ⓓ Ⓔ
2 Ⓐ Ⓑ Ⓒ Ⓓ Ⓔ
3 Ⓐ Ⓑ Ⓒ Ⓓ Ⓔ
4 Ⓐ Ⓑ Ⓒ Ⓓ Ⓔ
5 Ⓐ Ⓑ Ⓒ Ⓓ Ⓔ

V2, Pg. 84   PT21-S1-G1

1 Ⓐ Ⓑ Ⓒ Ⓓ Ⓔ
2 Ⓐ Ⓑ Ⓒ Ⓓ Ⓔ
3 Ⓐ Ⓑ Ⓒ Ⓓ Ⓔ
4 Ⓐ Ⓑ Ⓒ Ⓓ Ⓔ
5 Ⓐ Ⓑ Ⓒ Ⓓ Ⓔ
6 Ⓐ Ⓑ Ⓒ Ⓓ Ⓔ

V2, Pg. 86   PT21-S1-G3

12 Ⓐ Ⓑ Ⓒ Ⓓ Ⓔ
13 Ⓐ Ⓑ Ⓒ Ⓓ Ⓔ
14 Ⓐ Ⓑ Ⓒ Ⓓ Ⓔ
15 Ⓐ Ⓑ Ⓒ Ⓓ Ⓔ
16 Ⓐ Ⓑ Ⓒ Ⓓ Ⓔ
17 Ⓐ Ⓑ Ⓒ Ⓓ Ⓔ

V2, Pg. 237   PT25-S3-G2

6 Ⓐ Ⓑ Ⓒ Ⓓ Ⓔ
7 Ⓐ Ⓑ Ⓒ Ⓓ Ⓔ
8 Ⓐ Ⓑ Ⓒ Ⓓ Ⓔ
9 Ⓐ Ⓑ Ⓒ Ⓓ Ⓔ
10 Ⓐ Ⓑ Ⓒ Ⓓ Ⓔ
11 Ⓐ Ⓑ Ⓒ Ⓓ Ⓔ
12 Ⓐ Ⓑ Ⓒ Ⓓ Ⓔ

V2, Pg. 297   PT27-S2-G2

7 Ⓐ Ⓑ Ⓒ Ⓓ Ⓔ
8 Ⓐ Ⓑ Ⓒ Ⓓ Ⓔ
9 Ⓐ Ⓑ Ⓒ Ⓓ Ⓔ
10 Ⓐ Ⓑ Ⓒ Ⓓ Ⓔ
11 Ⓐ Ⓑ Ⓒ Ⓓ Ⓔ
12 Ⓐ Ⓑ Ⓒ Ⓓ Ⓔ

V2, Pg. 332   PT28-S2-G3

13 Ⓐ Ⓑ Ⓒ Ⓓ Ⓔ
14 Ⓐ Ⓑ Ⓒ Ⓓ Ⓔ
15 Ⓐ Ⓑ Ⓒ Ⓓ Ⓔ
16 Ⓐ Ⓑ Ⓒ Ⓓ Ⓔ
17 Ⓐ Ⓑ Ⓒ Ⓓ Ⓔ
18 Ⓐ Ⓑ Ⓒ Ⓓ Ⓔ

V2, Pg. 333   PT28-S2-G4

19 Ⓐ Ⓑ Ⓒ Ⓓ Ⓔ
20 Ⓐ Ⓑ Ⓒ Ⓓ Ⓔ
21 Ⓐ Ⓑ Ⓒ Ⓓ Ⓔ
22 Ⓐ Ⓑ Ⓒ Ⓓ Ⓔ
23 Ⓐ Ⓑ Ⓒ Ⓓ Ⓔ

V3, Pg. 35   PT29-S3-G4

20 Ⓐ Ⓑ Ⓒ Ⓓ Ⓔ
21 Ⓐ Ⓑ Ⓒ Ⓓ Ⓔ
22 Ⓐ Ⓑ Ⓒ Ⓓ Ⓔ
23 Ⓐ Ⓑ Ⓒ Ⓓ Ⓔ
24 Ⓐ Ⓑ Ⓒ Ⓓ Ⓔ

V3, Pg. 238   PT35-S3-G3

13 Ⓐ Ⓑ Ⓒ Ⓓ Ⓔ
14 Ⓐ Ⓑ Ⓒ Ⓓ Ⓔ
15 Ⓐ Ⓑ Ⓒ Ⓓ Ⓔ
16 Ⓐ Ⓑ Ⓒ Ⓓ Ⓔ
17 Ⓐ Ⓑ Ⓒ Ⓓ Ⓔ

V3, Pg. 239   PT35-S3-G4

18   Ⓐ Ⓑ Ⓒ Ⓓ Ⓔ
19   Ⓐ Ⓑ Ⓒ Ⓓ Ⓔ
20   Ⓐ Ⓑ Ⓒ Ⓓ Ⓔ
21   Ⓐ Ⓑ Ⓒ Ⓓ Ⓔ
22   Ⓐ Ⓑ Ⓒ Ⓓ Ⓔ
23   Ⓐ Ⓑ Ⓒ Ⓓ Ⓔ

V3, Pg. 280   PT36-S4-G3

14   Ⓐ Ⓑ Ⓒ Ⓓ Ⓔ
15   Ⓐ Ⓑ Ⓒ Ⓓ Ⓔ
16   Ⓐ Ⓑ Ⓒ Ⓓ Ⓔ
17   Ⓐ Ⓑ Ⓒ Ⓓ Ⓔ
18   Ⓐ Ⓑ Ⓒ Ⓓ Ⓔ

V3, Pg. 304   PT37-S3-G1

1   Ⓐ Ⓑ Ⓒ Ⓓ Ⓔ
2   Ⓐ Ⓑ Ⓒ Ⓓ Ⓔ
3   Ⓐ Ⓑ Ⓒ Ⓓ Ⓔ
4   Ⓐ Ⓑ Ⓒ Ⓓ Ⓔ
5   Ⓐ Ⓑ Ⓒ Ⓓ Ⓔ

PT39-S1-G2

6   Ⓐ Ⓑ Ⓒ Ⓓ Ⓔ
7   Ⓐ Ⓑ Ⓒ Ⓓ Ⓔ
8   Ⓐ Ⓑ Ⓒ Ⓓ Ⓔ
9   Ⓐ Ⓑ Ⓒ Ⓓ Ⓔ
10   Ⓐ Ⓑ Ⓒ Ⓓ Ⓔ
11   Ⓐ Ⓑ Ⓒ Ⓓ Ⓔ

PT42-S1-G3

13   Ⓐ Ⓑ Ⓒ Ⓓ Ⓔ
14   Ⓐ Ⓑ Ⓒ Ⓓ Ⓔ
15   Ⓐ Ⓑ Ⓒ Ⓓ Ⓔ
16   Ⓐ Ⓑ Ⓒ Ⓓ Ⓔ
17   Ⓐ Ⓑ Ⓒ Ⓓ Ⓔ
18   Ⓐ Ⓑ Ⓒ Ⓓ Ⓔ

PT43-S4-G3

13   Ⓐ Ⓑ Ⓒ Ⓓ Ⓔ
14   Ⓐ Ⓑ Ⓒ Ⓓ Ⓔ
15   Ⓐ Ⓑ Ⓒ Ⓓ Ⓔ
16   Ⓐ Ⓑ Ⓒ Ⓓ Ⓔ
17   Ⓐ Ⓑ Ⓒ Ⓓ Ⓔ

PT46-S4-G2

7   Ⓐ Ⓑ Ⓒ Ⓓ Ⓔ
8   Ⓐ Ⓑ Ⓒ Ⓓ Ⓔ
9   Ⓐ Ⓑ Ⓒ Ⓓ Ⓔ
10   Ⓐ Ⓑ Ⓒ Ⓓ Ⓔ
11   Ⓐ Ⓑ Ⓒ Ⓓ Ⓔ

PT48-S2-G4

18   Ⓐ Ⓑ Ⓒ Ⓓ Ⓔ
19   Ⓐ Ⓑ Ⓒ Ⓓ Ⓔ
20   Ⓐ Ⓑ Ⓒ Ⓓ Ⓔ
21   Ⓐ Ⓑ Ⓒ Ⓓ Ⓔ
22   Ⓐ Ⓑ Ⓒ Ⓓ Ⓔ

PT50-S3-G3

12   Ⓐ Ⓑ Ⓒ Ⓓ Ⓔ
13   Ⓐ Ⓑ Ⓒ Ⓓ Ⓔ
14   Ⓐ Ⓑ Ⓒ Ⓓ Ⓔ
15   Ⓐ Ⓑ Ⓒ Ⓓ Ⓔ
16   Ⓐ Ⓑ Ⓒ Ⓓ Ⓔ
17   Ⓐ Ⓑ Ⓒ Ⓓ Ⓔ

PT50-S3-G4

18   Ⓐ Ⓑ Ⓒ Ⓓ Ⓔ
19   Ⓐ Ⓑ Ⓒ Ⓓ Ⓔ
20   Ⓐ Ⓑ Ⓒ Ⓓ Ⓔ
21   Ⓐ Ⓑ Ⓒ Ⓓ Ⓔ
22   Ⓐ Ⓑ Ⓒ Ⓓ Ⓔ

V4, Pg. 18   PT52-S2-G3

13   Ⓐ Ⓑ Ⓒ Ⓓ Ⓔ
14   Ⓐ Ⓑ Ⓒ Ⓓ Ⓔ
15   Ⓐ Ⓑ Ⓒ Ⓓ Ⓔ
16   Ⓐ Ⓑ Ⓒ Ⓓ Ⓔ
17   Ⓐ Ⓑ Ⓒ Ⓓ Ⓔ

V4, Pg. 55   PT53-S2-G4

18   Ⓐ Ⓑ Ⓒ Ⓓ Ⓔ
19   Ⓐ Ⓑ Ⓒ Ⓓ Ⓔ
20   Ⓐ Ⓑ Ⓒ Ⓓ Ⓔ
21   Ⓐ Ⓑ Ⓒ Ⓓ Ⓔ
22   Ⓐ Ⓑ Ⓒ Ⓓ Ⓔ
23   Ⓐ Ⓑ Ⓒ Ⓓ Ⓔ

V4, Pg. 97   PT54-S3-G2

6   Ⓐ Ⓑ Ⓒ Ⓓ Ⓔ
7   Ⓐ Ⓑ Ⓒ Ⓓ Ⓔ
8   Ⓐ Ⓑ Ⓒ Ⓓ Ⓔ
9   Ⓐ Ⓑ Ⓒ Ⓓ Ⓔ
10   Ⓐ Ⓑ Ⓒ Ⓓ Ⓔ
11   Ⓐ Ⓑ Ⓒ Ⓓ Ⓔ
12   Ⓐ Ⓑ Ⓒ Ⓓ Ⓔ

V4, Pg. 140   PT55-S4-G1

1   Ⓐ Ⓑ Ⓒ Ⓓ Ⓔ
2   Ⓐ Ⓑ Ⓒ Ⓓ Ⓔ
3   Ⓐ Ⓑ Ⓒ Ⓓ Ⓔ
4   Ⓐ Ⓑ Ⓒ Ⓓ Ⓔ
5   Ⓐ Ⓑ Ⓒ Ⓓ Ⓔ
6   Ⓐ Ⓑ Ⓒ Ⓓ Ⓔ

V4, Pg. 155   PT56-S1-G4

17   Ⓐ Ⓑ Ⓒ Ⓓ Ⓔ
18   Ⓐ Ⓑ Ⓒ Ⓓ Ⓔ
19   Ⓐ Ⓑ Ⓒ Ⓓ Ⓔ
20   Ⓐ Ⓑ Ⓒ Ⓓ Ⓔ
21   Ⓐ Ⓑ Ⓒ Ⓓ Ⓔ
22   Ⓐ Ⓑ Ⓒ Ⓓ Ⓔ
23   Ⓐ Ⓑ Ⓒ Ⓓ Ⓔ

V4, Pg. 189   PT57-S1-G2

6   Ⓐ Ⓑ Ⓒ Ⓓ Ⓔ
7   Ⓐ Ⓑ Ⓒ Ⓓ Ⓔ
8   Ⓐ Ⓑ Ⓒ Ⓓ Ⓔ
9   Ⓐ Ⓑ Ⓒ Ⓓ Ⓔ
10   Ⓐ Ⓑ Ⓒ Ⓓ Ⓔ
11   Ⓐ Ⓑ Ⓒ Ⓓ Ⓔ

V4, Pg. 240   PT58-S3-G1

1   Ⓐ Ⓑ Ⓒ Ⓓ Ⓔ
2   Ⓐ Ⓑ Ⓒ Ⓓ Ⓔ
3   Ⓐ Ⓑ Ⓒ Ⓓ Ⓔ
4   Ⓐ Ⓑ Ⓒ Ⓓ Ⓔ
5   Ⓐ Ⓑ Ⓒ Ⓓ Ⓔ
6   Ⓐ Ⓑ Ⓒ Ⓓ Ⓔ

V4, Pg. 260   PT59-S1-G1

1   Ⓐ Ⓑ Ⓒ Ⓓ Ⓔ
2   Ⓐ Ⓑ Ⓒ Ⓓ Ⓔ
3   Ⓐ Ⓑ Ⓒ Ⓓ Ⓔ
4   Ⓐ Ⓑ Ⓒ Ⓓ Ⓔ
5   Ⓐ Ⓑ Ⓒ Ⓓ Ⓔ

V4, Pg. 304   PT60-S2-G1

1   Ⓐ Ⓑ Ⓒ Ⓓ Ⓔ
2   Ⓐ Ⓑ Ⓒ Ⓓ Ⓔ
3   Ⓐ Ⓑ Ⓒ Ⓓ Ⓔ
4   Ⓐ Ⓑ Ⓒ Ⓓ Ⓔ
5   Ⓐ Ⓑ Ⓒ Ⓓ Ⓔ
6   Ⓐ Ⓑ Ⓒ Ⓓ Ⓔ

V4, Pg. 307   PT60-S2-G4

18   Ⓐ Ⓑ Ⓒ Ⓓ Ⓔ
19   Ⓐ Ⓑ Ⓒ Ⓓ Ⓔ
20   Ⓐ Ⓑ Ⓒ Ⓓ Ⓔ
21   Ⓐ Ⓑ Ⓒ Ⓓ Ⓔ
22   Ⓐ Ⓑ Ⓒ Ⓓ Ⓔ
23   Ⓐ Ⓑ Ⓒ Ⓓ Ⓔ

V4, Pg. 348   PT61-S3-G1

1   Ⓐ Ⓑ Ⓒ Ⓓ Ⓔ
2   Ⓐ Ⓑ Ⓒ Ⓓ Ⓔ
3   Ⓐ Ⓑ Ⓒ Ⓓ Ⓔ
4   Ⓐ Ⓑ Ⓒ Ⓓ Ⓔ
5   Ⓐ Ⓑ Ⓒ Ⓓ Ⓔ

V5, Pg. 26   PT62-S3-G3

14 Ⓐ Ⓑ Ⓒ Ⓓ Ⓔ
15 Ⓐ Ⓑ Ⓒ Ⓓ Ⓔ
16 Ⓐ Ⓑ Ⓒ Ⓓ Ⓔ
17 Ⓐ Ⓑ Ⓒ Ⓓ Ⓔ
18 Ⓐ Ⓑ Ⓒ Ⓓ Ⓔ

V5, Pg. 90   PT64-S2-G3

13 Ⓐ Ⓑ Ⓒ Ⓓ Ⓔ
14 Ⓐ Ⓑ Ⓒ Ⓓ Ⓔ
15 Ⓐ Ⓑ Ⓒ Ⓓ Ⓔ
16 Ⓐ Ⓑ Ⓒ Ⓓ Ⓔ
17 Ⓐ Ⓑ Ⓒ Ⓓ Ⓔ
18 Ⓐ Ⓑ Ⓒ Ⓓ Ⓔ

V5, Pg. 91   PT64-S2-G4

19 Ⓐ Ⓑ Ⓒ Ⓓ Ⓔ
20 Ⓐ Ⓑ Ⓒ Ⓓ Ⓔ
21 Ⓐ Ⓑ Ⓒ Ⓓ Ⓔ
22 Ⓐ Ⓑ Ⓒ Ⓓ Ⓔ
23 Ⓐ Ⓑ Ⓒ Ⓓ Ⓔ

V5, Pg. 168   PT66-S3-G1

1 Ⓐ Ⓑ Ⓒ Ⓓ Ⓔ
2 Ⓐ Ⓑ Ⓒ Ⓓ Ⓔ
3 Ⓐ Ⓑ Ⓒ Ⓓ Ⓔ
4 Ⓐ Ⓑ Ⓒ Ⓓ Ⓔ
5 Ⓐ Ⓑ Ⓒ Ⓓ Ⓔ

V5, Pg. 208   PT67-S3-G1

1 Ⓐ Ⓑ Ⓒ Ⓓ Ⓔ
2 Ⓐ Ⓑ Ⓒ Ⓓ Ⓔ
3 Ⓐ Ⓑ Ⓒ Ⓓ Ⓔ
4 Ⓐ Ⓑ Ⓒ Ⓓ Ⓔ
5 Ⓐ Ⓑ Ⓒ Ⓓ Ⓔ

V5, Pg. 212   PT67-S3-G3

13 Ⓐ Ⓑ Ⓒ Ⓓ Ⓔ
14 Ⓐ Ⓑ Ⓒ Ⓓ Ⓔ
15 Ⓐ Ⓑ Ⓒ Ⓓ Ⓔ
16 Ⓐ Ⓑ Ⓒ Ⓓ Ⓔ
17 Ⓐ Ⓑ Ⓒ Ⓓ Ⓔ

V5, Pg. 282   PT69-S2-G2

6 Ⓐ Ⓑ Ⓒ Ⓓ Ⓔ
7 Ⓐ Ⓑ Ⓒ Ⓓ Ⓔ
8 Ⓐ Ⓑ Ⓒ Ⓓ Ⓔ
9 Ⓐ Ⓑ Ⓒ Ⓓ Ⓔ
10 Ⓐ Ⓑ Ⓒ Ⓓ Ⓔ
11 Ⓐ Ⓑ Ⓒ Ⓓ Ⓔ

V5, Pg. 284   PT69-S2-G3

12 Ⓐ Ⓑ Ⓒ Ⓓ Ⓔ
13 Ⓐ Ⓑ Ⓒ Ⓓ Ⓔ
14 Ⓐ Ⓑ Ⓒ Ⓓ Ⓔ
15 Ⓐ Ⓑ Ⓒ Ⓓ Ⓔ
16 Ⓐ Ⓑ Ⓒ Ⓓ Ⓔ
17 Ⓐ Ⓑ Ⓒ Ⓓ Ⓔ

V5, Pg. 332   PT70-S3-G3

13 Ⓐ Ⓑ Ⓒ Ⓓ Ⓔ
14 Ⓐ Ⓑ Ⓒ Ⓓ Ⓔ
15 Ⓐ Ⓑ Ⓒ Ⓓ Ⓔ
16 Ⓐ Ⓑ Ⓒ Ⓓ Ⓔ
17 Ⓐ Ⓑ Ⓒ Ⓓ Ⓔ
18 Ⓐ Ⓑ Ⓒ Ⓓ Ⓔ

PT72, Pg. 34 PT72-S4-G1

1 Ⓐ Ⓑ Ⓒ Ⓓ Ⓔ
2 Ⓐ Ⓑ Ⓒ Ⓓ Ⓔ
3 Ⓐ Ⓑ Ⓒ Ⓓ Ⓔ
4 Ⓐ Ⓑ Ⓒ Ⓓ Ⓔ
5 Ⓐ Ⓑ Ⓒ Ⓓ Ⓔ
6 Ⓐ Ⓑ Ⓒ Ⓓ Ⓔ

PT73, Pg. 28 PT73-S3-G2

8 Ⓐ Ⓑ Ⓒ Ⓓ Ⓔ
9 Ⓐ Ⓑ Ⓒ Ⓓ Ⓔ
10 Ⓐ Ⓑ Ⓒ Ⓓ Ⓔ
11 Ⓐ Ⓑ Ⓒ Ⓓ Ⓔ
12 Ⓐ Ⓑ Ⓒ Ⓓ Ⓔ
13 Ⓐ Ⓑ Ⓒ Ⓓ Ⓔ

PT75, Pg. 34 PT75-S4-G1

1 Ⓐ Ⓑ Ⓒ Ⓓ Ⓔ
2 Ⓐ Ⓑ Ⓒ Ⓓ Ⓔ
3 Ⓐ Ⓑ Ⓒ Ⓓ Ⓔ
4 Ⓐ Ⓑ Ⓒ Ⓓ Ⓔ
5 Ⓐ Ⓑ Ⓒ Ⓓ Ⓔ
6 Ⓐ Ⓑ Ⓒ Ⓓ Ⓔ

PT76, Pg. 30 PT76-S3-G3

14 Ⓐ Ⓑ Ⓒ Ⓓ Ⓔ
15 Ⓐ Ⓑ Ⓒ Ⓓ Ⓔ
16 Ⓐ Ⓑ Ⓒ Ⓓ Ⓔ
17 Ⓐ Ⓑ Ⓒ Ⓓ Ⓔ
18 Ⓐ Ⓑ Ⓒ Ⓓ Ⓔ

Undetermined Assignment

J07, Pg. 3   J07-S1-G2

6 Ⓐ Ⓑ Ⓒ Ⓓ Ⓔ
7 Ⓐ Ⓑ Ⓒ Ⓓ Ⓔ
8 Ⓐ Ⓑ Ⓒ Ⓓ Ⓔ
9 Ⓐ Ⓑ Ⓒ Ⓓ Ⓔ
10 Ⓐ Ⓑ Ⓒ Ⓓ Ⓔ

J07, Pg. 5   J07-S1-G4

18 Ⓐ Ⓑ Ⓒ Ⓓ Ⓔ
19 Ⓐ Ⓑ Ⓒ Ⓓ Ⓔ
20 Ⓐ Ⓑ Ⓒ Ⓓ Ⓔ
21 Ⓐ Ⓑ Ⓒ Ⓓ Ⓔ
22 Ⓐ Ⓑ Ⓒ Ⓓ Ⓔ
23 Ⓐ Ⓑ Ⓒ Ⓓ Ⓔ

SP1, Pg. 87   PTA-S3-G4

18 Ⓐ Ⓑ Ⓒ Ⓓ Ⓔ
19 Ⓐ Ⓑ Ⓒ Ⓓ Ⓔ
20 Ⓐ Ⓑ Ⓒ Ⓓ Ⓔ
21 Ⓐ Ⓑ Ⓒ Ⓓ Ⓔ
22 Ⓐ Ⓑ Ⓒ Ⓓ Ⓔ
23 Ⓐ Ⓑ Ⓒ Ⓓ Ⓔ
24 Ⓐ Ⓑ Ⓒ Ⓓ Ⓔ

SP1, Pg. 197 PTB-S2-G4

19 Ⓐ Ⓑ Ⓒ Ⓓ Ⓔ
20 Ⓐ Ⓑ Ⓒ Ⓓ Ⓔ
21 Ⓐ Ⓑ Ⓒ Ⓓ Ⓔ
22 Ⓐ Ⓑ Ⓒ Ⓓ Ⓔ
23 Ⓐ Ⓑ Ⓒ Ⓓ Ⓔ
24 Ⓐ Ⓑ Ⓒ Ⓓ Ⓔ

SP1, Pg. 298 PTC-S1-G3

13 Ⓐ Ⓑ Ⓒ Ⓓ Ⓔ
14 Ⓐ Ⓑ Ⓒ Ⓓ Ⓔ
15 Ⓐ Ⓑ Ⓒ Ⓓ Ⓔ
16 Ⓐ Ⓑ Ⓒ Ⓓ Ⓔ
17 Ⓐ Ⓑ Ⓒ Ⓓ Ⓔ
18 Ⓐ Ⓑ Ⓒ Ⓓ Ⓔ
19 Ⓐ Ⓑ Ⓒ Ⓓ Ⓔ

SP1, Pg. 299 PTC-S1-G4

20 Ⓐ Ⓑ Ⓒ Ⓓ Ⓔ
21 Ⓐ Ⓑ Ⓒ Ⓓ Ⓔ
22 Ⓐ Ⓑ Ⓒ Ⓓ Ⓔ
23 Ⓐ Ⓑ Ⓒ Ⓓ Ⓔ
24 Ⓐ Ⓑ Ⓒ Ⓓ Ⓔ

SP2, Pg. 350 PTC2-S1-G3

11 Ⓐ Ⓑ Ⓒ Ⓓ Ⓔ
12 Ⓐ Ⓑ Ⓒ Ⓓ Ⓔ
13 Ⓐ Ⓑ Ⓒ Ⓓ Ⓔ
14 Ⓐ Ⓑ Ⓒ Ⓓ Ⓔ
15 Ⓐ Ⓑ Ⓒ Ⓓ Ⓔ
16 Ⓐ Ⓑ Ⓒ Ⓓ Ⓔ
17 Ⓐ Ⓑ Ⓒ Ⓓ Ⓔ

PT1-S2-G2

8 Ⓐ Ⓑ Ⓒ Ⓓ Ⓔ
9 Ⓐ Ⓑ Ⓒ Ⓓ Ⓔ
10 Ⓐ Ⓑ Ⓒ Ⓓ Ⓔ
11 Ⓐ Ⓑ Ⓒ Ⓓ Ⓔ
12 Ⓐ Ⓑ Ⓒ Ⓓ Ⓔ
13 Ⓐ Ⓑ Ⓒ Ⓓ Ⓔ

PT1-S2-G4

19 Ⓐ Ⓑ Ⓒ Ⓓ Ⓔ
20 Ⓐ Ⓑ Ⓒ Ⓓ Ⓔ
21 Ⓐ Ⓑ Ⓒ Ⓓ Ⓔ
22 Ⓐ Ⓑ Ⓒ Ⓓ Ⓔ
23 Ⓐ Ⓑ Ⓒ Ⓓ Ⓔ
24 Ⓐ Ⓑ Ⓒ Ⓓ Ⓔ

PT3-S1-G1

1 Ⓐ Ⓑ Ⓒ Ⓓ Ⓔ
2 Ⓐ Ⓑ Ⓒ Ⓓ Ⓔ
3 Ⓐ Ⓑ Ⓒ Ⓓ Ⓔ
4 Ⓐ Ⓑ Ⓒ Ⓓ Ⓔ
5 Ⓐ Ⓑ Ⓒ Ⓓ Ⓔ
6 Ⓐ Ⓑ Ⓒ Ⓓ Ⓔ
7 Ⓐ Ⓑ Ⓒ Ⓓ Ⓔ

PT3-S1-G3

14 Ⓐ Ⓑ Ⓒ Ⓓ Ⓔ
15 Ⓐ Ⓑ Ⓒ Ⓓ Ⓔ
16 Ⓐ Ⓑ Ⓒ Ⓓ Ⓔ
17 Ⓐ Ⓑ Ⓒ Ⓓ Ⓔ
18 Ⓐ Ⓑ Ⓒ Ⓓ Ⓔ
19 Ⓐ Ⓑ Ⓒ Ⓓ Ⓔ

PT4-S3-G2

7 Ⓐ Ⓑ Ⓒ Ⓓ Ⓔ
8 Ⓐ Ⓑ Ⓒ Ⓓ Ⓔ
9 Ⓐ Ⓑ Ⓒ Ⓓ Ⓔ
10 Ⓐ Ⓑ Ⓒ Ⓓ Ⓔ
11 Ⓐ Ⓑ Ⓒ Ⓓ Ⓔ

PT5-S2-G2

7 Ⓐ Ⓑ Ⓒ Ⓓ Ⓔ
8 Ⓐ Ⓑ Ⓒ Ⓓ Ⓔ
9 Ⓐ Ⓑ Ⓒ Ⓓ Ⓔ
10 Ⓐ Ⓑ Ⓒ Ⓓ Ⓔ
11 Ⓐ Ⓑ Ⓒ Ⓓ Ⓔ

PT8-S2-G4

18 Ⓐ Ⓑ Ⓒ Ⓓ Ⓔ
19 Ⓐ Ⓑ Ⓒ Ⓓ Ⓔ
20 Ⓐ Ⓑ Ⓒ Ⓓ Ⓔ
21 Ⓐ Ⓑ Ⓒ Ⓓ Ⓔ
22 Ⓐ Ⓑ Ⓒ Ⓓ Ⓔ
23 Ⓐ Ⓑ Ⓒ Ⓓ Ⓔ
24 Ⓐ Ⓑ Ⓒ Ⓓ Ⓔ

V1, Pg. 66 PT9-S3-G1

1 Ⓐ Ⓑ Ⓒ Ⓓ Ⓔ
2 Ⓐ Ⓑ Ⓒ Ⓓ Ⓔ
3 Ⓐ Ⓑ Ⓒ Ⓓ Ⓔ
4 Ⓐ Ⓑ Ⓒ Ⓓ Ⓔ
5 Ⓐ Ⓑ Ⓒ Ⓓ Ⓔ
6 Ⓐ Ⓑ Ⓒ Ⓓ Ⓔ
7 Ⓐ Ⓑ Ⓒ Ⓓ Ⓔ

V1, Pg. 162 PT12-S2-G3

12 Ⓐ Ⓑ Ⓒ Ⓓ Ⓔ
13 Ⓐ Ⓑ Ⓒ Ⓓ Ⓔ
14 Ⓐ Ⓑ Ⓒ Ⓓ Ⓔ
15 Ⓐ Ⓑ Ⓒ Ⓓ Ⓔ
16 Ⓐ Ⓑ Ⓒ Ⓓ Ⓔ
17 Ⓐ Ⓑ Ⓒ Ⓓ Ⓔ

V1, Pg. 188 PT13-S1-G3

12 Ⓐ Ⓑ Ⓒ Ⓓ Ⓔ
13 Ⓐ Ⓑ Ⓒ Ⓓ Ⓔ
14 Ⓐ Ⓑ Ⓒ Ⓓ Ⓔ
15 Ⓐ Ⓑ Ⓒ Ⓓ Ⓔ
16 Ⓐ Ⓑ Ⓒ Ⓓ Ⓔ
17 Ⓐ Ⓑ Ⓒ Ⓓ Ⓔ

V1, Pg. 223 PT14-S1-G4

19 Ⓐ Ⓑ Ⓒ Ⓓ Ⓔ
20 Ⓐ Ⓑ Ⓒ Ⓓ Ⓔ
21 Ⓐ Ⓑ Ⓒ Ⓓ Ⓔ
22 Ⓐ Ⓑ Ⓒ Ⓓ Ⓔ
23 Ⓐ Ⓑ Ⓒ Ⓓ Ⓔ
24 Ⓐ Ⓑ Ⓒ Ⓓ Ⓔ

V1, Pg. 281 PT15-S4-G4

20 Ⓐ Ⓑ Ⓒ Ⓓ Ⓔ
21 Ⓐ Ⓑ Ⓒ Ⓓ Ⓔ
22 Ⓐ Ⓑ Ⓒ Ⓓ Ⓔ
23 Ⓐ Ⓑ Ⓒ Ⓓ Ⓔ
24 Ⓐ Ⓑ Ⓒ Ⓓ Ⓔ

V1, Pg. 290 PT16-S1-G3

13 Ⓐ Ⓑ Ⓒ Ⓓ Ⓔ
14 Ⓐ Ⓑ Ⓒ Ⓓ Ⓔ
15 Ⓐ Ⓑ Ⓒ Ⓓ Ⓔ
16 Ⓐ Ⓑ Ⓒ Ⓓ Ⓔ
17 Ⓐ Ⓑ Ⓒ Ⓓ Ⓔ
18 Ⓐ Ⓑ Ⓒ Ⓓ Ⓔ

PT17-S1-G2

6 Ⓐ Ⓑ Ⓒ Ⓓ Ⓔ
7 Ⓐ Ⓑ Ⓒ Ⓓ Ⓔ
8 Ⓐ Ⓑ Ⓒ Ⓓ Ⓔ
9 Ⓐ Ⓑ Ⓒ Ⓓ Ⓔ
10 Ⓐ Ⓑ Ⓒ Ⓓ Ⓔ
11 Ⓐ Ⓑ Ⓒ Ⓓ Ⓔ
12 Ⓐ Ⓑ Ⓒ Ⓓ Ⓔ

PT17-S1-G3

13 Ⓐ Ⓑ Ⓒ Ⓓ Ⓔ
14 Ⓐ Ⓑ Ⓒ Ⓓ Ⓔ
15 Ⓐ Ⓑ Ⓒ Ⓓ Ⓔ
16 Ⓐ Ⓑ Ⓒ Ⓓ Ⓔ
17 Ⓐ Ⓑ Ⓒ Ⓓ Ⓔ

V2, Pg. 87 PT21-S1-G4

18 Ⓐ Ⓑ Ⓒ Ⓓ Ⓔ
19 Ⓐ Ⓑ Ⓒ Ⓓ Ⓔ
20 Ⓐ Ⓑ Ⓒ Ⓓ Ⓔ
21 Ⓐ Ⓑ Ⓒ Ⓓ Ⓔ
22 Ⓐ Ⓑ Ⓒ Ⓓ Ⓔ
23 Ⓐ Ⓑ Ⓒ Ⓓ Ⓔ
24 Ⓐ Ⓑ Ⓒ Ⓓ Ⓔ

V2, Pg. 136 PT22-S3-G3

15 Ⓐ Ⓑ Ⓒ Ⓓ Ⓔ
16 Ⓐ Ⓑ Ⓒ Ⓓ Ⓔ
17 Ⓐ Ⓑ Ⓒ Ⓓ Ⓔ
18 Ⓐ Ⓑ Ⓒ Ⓓ Ⓔ
19 Ⓐ Ⓑ Ⓒ Ⓓ Ⓔ

V2, Pg. 137 PT22-S3-G4

20 Ⓐ Ⓑ Ⓒ Ⓓ Ⓔ
21 Ⓐ Ⓑ Ⓒ Ⓓ Ⓔ
22 Ⓐ Ⓑ Ⓒ Ⓓ Ⓔ
23 Ⓐ Ⓑ Ⓒ Ⓓ Ⓔ
24 Ⓐ Ⓑ Ⓒ Ⓓ Ⓔ

V2, Pg. 236 PT25-S3-G1

1 Ⓐ Ⓑ Ⓒ Ⓓ Ⓔ
2 Ⓐ Ⓑ Ⓒ Ⓓ Ⓔ
3 Ⓐ Ⓑ Ⓒ Ⓓ Ⓔ
4 Ⓐ Ⓑ Ⓒ Ⓓ Ⓔ
5 Ⓐ Ⓑ Ⓒ Ⓓ Ⓔ

V2, Pg. 257 PT26-S1-G4

19 Ⓐ Ⓑ Ⓒ Ⓓ Ⓔ
20 Ⓐ Ⓑ Ⓒ Ⓓ Ⓔ
21 Ⓐ Ⓑ Ⓒ Ⓓ Ⓔ
22 Ⓐ Ⓑ Ⓒ Ⓓ Ⓔ
23 Ⓐ Ⓑ Ⓒ Ⓓ Ⓔ
24 Ⓐ Ⓑ Ⓒ Ⓓ Ⓔ

V2, Pg. 331 PT28-S2-G2

6 Ⓐ Ⓑ Ⓒ Ⓓ Ⓔ
7 Ⓐ Ⓑ Ⓒ Ⓓ Ⓔ
8 Ⓐ Ⓑ Ⓒ Ⓓ Ⓔ
9 Ⓐ Ⓑ Ⓒ Ⓓ Ⓔ
10 Ⓐ Ⓑ Ⓒ Ⓓ Ⓔ
11 Ⓐ Ⓑ Ⓒ Ⓓ Ⓔ
12 Ⓐ Ⓑ Ⓒ Ⓓ Ⓔ

V3, Pg. 33 PT29-S3-G2

7 Ⓐ Ⓑ Ⓒ Ⓓ Ⓔ
8 Ⓐ Ⓑ Ⓒ Ⓓ Ⓔ
9 Ⓐ Ⓑ Ⓒ Ⓓ Ⓔ
10 Ⓐ Ⓑ Ⓒ Ⓓ Ⓔ
11 Ⓐ Ⓑ Ⓒ Ⓓ Ⓔ
12 Ⓐ Ⓑ Ⓒ Ⓓ Ⓔ
13 Ⓐ Ⓑ Ⓒ Ⓓ Ⓔ

V3, Pg. 87 PT31-S1-G4

19 Ⓐ Ⓑ Ⓒ Ⓓ Ⓔ
20 Ⓐ Ⓑ Ⓒ Ⓓ Ⓔ
21 Ⓐ Ⓑ Ⓒ Ⓓ Ⓔ
22 Ⓐ Ⓑ Ⓒ Ⓓ Ⓔ
23 Ⓐ Ⓑ Ⓒ Ⓓ Ⓔ

V3, Pg. 134 PT32-S3-G1

1 Ⓐ Ⓑ Ⓒ Ⓓ Ⓔ
2 Ⓐ Ⓑ Ⓒ Ⓓ Ⓔ
3 Ⓐ Ⓑ Ⓒ Ⓓ Ⓔ
4 Ⓐ Ⓑ Ⓒ Ⓓ Ⓔ
5 Ⓐ Ⓑ Ⓒ Ⓓ Ⓔ
6 Ⓐ Ⓑ Ⓒ Ⓓ Ⓔ

V3, Pg. 135 PT32-S3-G2

7 Ⓐ Ⓑ Ⓒ Ⓓ Ⓔ
8 Ⓐ Ⓑ Ⓒ Ⓓ Ⓔ
9 Ⓐ Ⓑ Ⓒ Ⓓ Ⓔ
10 Ⓐ Ⓑ Ⓒ Ⓓ Ⓔ
11 Ⓐ Ⓑ Ⓒ Ⓓ Ⓔ

V3, Pg. 179 PT33-S4-G4

19 Ⓐ Ⓑ Ⓒ Ⓓ Ⓔ
20 Ⓐ Ⓑ Ⓒ Ⓓ Ⓔ
21 Ⓐ Ⓑ Ⓒ Ⓓ Ⓔ
22 Ⓐ Ⓑ Ⓒ Ⓓ Ⓔ
23 Ⓐ Ⓑ Ⓒ Ⓓ Ⓔ

V3, Pg. 236 PT35-S3-G1

1 Ⓐ Ⓑ Ⓒ Ⓓ Ⓔ
2 Ⓐ Ⓑ Ⓒ Ⓓ Ⓔ
3 Ⓐ Ⓑ Ⓒ Ⓓ Ⓔ
4 Ⓐ Ⓑ Ⓒ Ⓓ Ⓔ
5 Ⓐ Ⓑ Ⓒ Ⓓ Ⓔ

V3, Pg. 237 PT35-S3-G2

6 Ⓐ Ⓑ Ⓒ Ⓓ Ⓔ
7 Ⓐ Ⓑ Ⓒ Ⓓ Ⓔ
8 Ⓐ Ⓑ Ⓒ Ⓓ Ⓔ
9 Ⓐ Ⓑ Ⓒ Ⓓ Ⓔ
10 Ⓐ Ⓑ Ⓒ Ⓓ Ⓔ
11 Ⓐ Ⓑ Ⓒ Ⓓ Ⓔ
12 Ⓐ Ⓑ Ⓒ Ⓓ Ⓔ

PT42-S1-G4

19 Ⓐ Ⓑ Ⓒ Ⓓ Ⓔ
20 Ⓐ Ⓑ Ⓒ Ⓓ Ⓔ
21 Ⓐ Ⓑ Ⓒ Ⓓ Ⓔ
22 Ⓐ Ⓑ Ⓒ Ⓓ Ⓔ
23 Ⓐ Ⓑ Ⓒ Ⓓ Ⓔ

PT43-S4-G4

18 Ⓐ Ⓑ Ⓒ Ⓓ Ⓔ
19 Ⓐ Ⓑ Ⓒ Ⓓ Ⓔ
20 Ⓐ Ⓑ Ⓒ Ⓓ Ⓔ
21 Ⓐ Ⓑ Ⓒ Ⓓ Ⓔ
22 Ⓐ Ⓑ Ⓒ Ⓓ Ⓔ

PT45-S3-G2

7 Ⓐ Ⓑ Ⓒ Ⓓ Ⓔ
8 Ⓐ Ⓑ Ⓒ Ⓓ Ⓔ
9 Ⓐ Ⓑ Ⓒ Ⓓ Ⓔ
10 Ⓐ Ⓑ Ⓒ Ⓓ Ⓔ
11 Ⓐ Ⓑ Ⓒ Ⓓ Ⓔ
12 Ⓐ Ⓑ Ⓒ Ⓓ Ⓔ

PT45-S3-G4

18 Ⓐ Ⓑ Ⓒ Ⓓ Ⓔ
19 Ⓐ Ⓑ Ⓒ Ⓓ Ⓔ
20 Ⓐ Ⓑ Ⓒ Ⓓ Ⓔ
21 Ⓐ Ⓑ Ⓒ Ⓓ Ⓔ
22 Ⓐ Ⓑ Ⓒ Ⓓ Ⓔ

PT46-S4-G4

17 Ⓐ Ⓑ Ⓒ Ⓓ Ⓔ
18 Ⓐ Ⓑ Ⓒ Ⓓ Ⓔ
19 Ⓐ Ⓑ Ⓒ Ⓓ Ⓔ
20 Ⓐ Ⓑ Ⓒ Ⓓ Ⓔ
21 Ⓐ Ⓑ Ⓒ Ⓓ Ⓔ
22 Ⓐ Ⓑ Ⓒ Ⓓ Ⓔ

PT47-S4-G3

12 Ⓐ Ⓑ Ⓒ Ⓓ Ⓔ
13 Ⓐ Ⓑ Ⓒ Ⓓ Ⓔ
14 Ⓐ Ⓑ Ⓒ Ⓓ Ⓔ
15 Ⓐ Ⓑ Ⓒ Ⓓ Ⓔ
16 Ⓐ Ⓑ Ⓒ Ⓓ Ⓔ
17 Ⓐ Ⓑ Ⓒ Ⓓ Ⓔ

PT47-S4-G4

18 Ⓐ Ⓑ Ⓒ Ⓓ Ⓔ
19 Ⓐ Ⓑ Ⓒ Ⓓ Ⓔ
20 Ⓐ Ⓑ Ⓒ Ⓓ Ⓔ
21 Ⓐ Ⓑ Ⓒ Ⓓ Ⓔ
22 Ⓐ Ⓑ Ⓒ Ⓓ Ⓔ

PT48-S2-G3

13 Ⓐ Ⓑ Ⓒ Ⓓ Ⓔ
14 Ⓐ Ⓑ Ⓒ Ⓓ Ⓔ
15 Ⓐ Ⓑ Ⓒ Ⓓ Ⓔ
16 Ⓐ Ⓑ Ⓒ Ⓓ Ⓔ
17 Ⓐ Ⓑ Ⓒ Ⓓ Ⓔ

PT51-S4-G1

1 Ⓐ Ⓑ Ⓒ Ⓓ Ⓔ
2 Ⓐ Ⓑ Ⓒ Ⓓ Ⓔ
3 Ⓐ Ⓑ Ⓒ Ⓓ Ⓔ
4 Ⓐ Ⓑ Ⓒ Ⓓ Ⓔ
5 Ⓐ Ⓑ Ⓒ Ⓓ Ⓔ

V4, Pg. 153 PT56-S1-G2

7 Ⓐ Ⓑ Ⓒ Ⓓ Ⓔ
8 Ⓐ Ⓑ Ⓒ Ⓓ Ⓔ
9 Ⓐ Ⓑ Ⓒ Ⓓ Ⓔ
10 Ⓐ Ⓑ Ⓒ Ⓓ Ⓔ
11 Ⓐ Ⓑ Ⓒ Ⓓ Ⓔ

V4, Pg. 154 PT56-S1-G3

12 Ⓐ Ⓑ Ⓒ Ⓓ Ⓔ
13 Ⓐ Ⓑ Ⓒ Ⓓ Ⓔ
14 Ⓐ Ⓑ Ⓒ Ⓓ Ⓔ
15 Ⓐ Ⓑ Ⓒ Ⓓ Ⓔ
16 Ⓐ Ⓑ Ⓒ Ⓓ Ⓔ

V4, Pg. 190 PT57-S1-G3

12 Ⓐ Ⓑ Ⓒ Ⓓ Ⓔ
13 Ⓐ Ⓑ Ⓒ Ⓓ Ⓔ
14 Ⓐ Ⓑ Ⓒ Ⓓ Ⓔ
15 Ⓐ Ⓑ Ⓒ Ⓓ Ⓔ
16 Ⓐ Ⓑ Ⓒ Ⓓ Ⓔ
17 Ⓐ Ⓑ Ⓒ Ⓓ Ⓔ

V4, Pg. 191 PT57-S1-G4

18 Ⓐ Ⓑ Ⓒ Ⓓ Ⓔ
19 Ⓐ Ⓑ Ⓒ Ⓓ Ⓔ
20 Ⓐ Ⓑ Ⓒ Ⓓ Ⓔ
21 Ⓐ Ⓑ Ⓒ Ⓓ Ⓔ
22 Ⓐ Ⓑ Ⓒ Ⓓ Ⓔ
23 Ⓐ Ⓑ Ⓒ Ⓓ Ⓔ

V5, Pg. 25   PT62-S3-G2
7   Ⓐ Ⓑ Ⓒ Ⓓ Ⓔ
8   Ⓐ Ⓑ Ⓒ Ⓓ Ⓔ
9   Ⓐ Ⓑ Ⓒ Ⓓ Ⓔ
10 Ⓐ Ⓑ Ⓒ Ⓓ Ⓔ
11 Ⓐ Ⓑ Ⓒ Ⓓ Ⓔ
12 Ⓐ Ⓑ Ⓒ Ⓓ Ⓔ
13 Ⓐ Ⓑ Ⓒ Ⓓ Ⓔ

V5, Pg. 89   PT64-S2-G2
7   Ⓐ Ⓑ Ⓒ Ⓓ Ⓔ
8   Ⓐ Ⓑ Ⓒ Ⓓ Ⓔ
9   Ⓐ Ⓑ Ⓒ Ⓓ Ⓔ
10 Ⓐ Ⓑ Ⓒ Ⓓ Ⓔ
11 Ⓐ Ⓑ Ⓒ Ⓓ Ⓔ
12 Ⓐ Ⓑ Ⓒ Ⓓ Ⓔ

V5, Pg. 214   PT67-S3-G4
18 Ⓐ Ⓑ Ⓒ Ⓓ Ⓔ
19 Ⓐ Ⓑ Ⓒ Ⓓ Ⓔ
20 Ⓐ Ⓑ Ⓒ Ⓓ Ⓔ
21 Ⓐ Ⓑ Ⓒ Ⓓ Ⓔ
22 Ⓐ Ⓑ Ⓒ Ⓓ Ⓔ
23 Ⓐ Ⓑ Ⓒ Ⓓ Ⓔ

V5, Pg. 260   PT68-S4-G3
11 Ⓐ Ⓑ Ⓒ Ⓓ Ⓔ
12 Ⓐ Ⓑ Ⓒ Ⓓ Ⓔ
13 Ⓐ Ⓑ Ⓒ Ⓓ Ⓔ
14 Ⓐ Ⓑ Ⓒ Ⓓ Ⓔ
15 Ⓐ Ⓑ Ⓒ Ⓓ Ⓔ
16 Ⓐ Ⓑ Ⓒ Ⓓ Ⓔ

PT73, Pg. 32 PT73-S3-G4
19 Ⓐ Ⓑ Ⓒ Ⓓ Ⓔ
20 Ⓐ Ⓑ Ⓒ Ⓓ Ⓔ
21 Ⓐ Ⓑ Ⓒ Ⓓ Ⓔ
22 Ⓐ Ⓑ Ⓒ Ⓓ Ⓔ
23 Ⓐ Ⓑ Ⓒ Ⓓ Ⓔ

PT74, Pg. 22 PT74-S2-G3
11 Ⓐ Ⓑ Ⓒ Ⓓ Ⓔ
12 Ⓐ Ⓑ Ⓒ Ⓓ Ⓔ
13 Ⓐ Ⓑ Ⓒ Ⓓ Ⓔ
14 Ⓐ Ⓑ Ⓒ Ⓓ Ⓔ
15 Ⓐ Ⓑ Ⓒ Ⓓ Ⓔ
16 Ⓐ Ⓑ Ⓒ Ⓓ Ⓔ

PT76, Pg. 28 PT76-S3-G2
7   Ⓐ Ⓑ Ⓒ Ⓓ Ⓔ
8   Ⓐ Ⓑ Ⓒ Ⓓ Ⓔ
9   Ⓐ Ⓑ Ⓒ Ⓓ Ⓔ
10 Ⓐ Ⓑ Ⓒ Ⓓ Ⓔ
11 Ⓐ Ⓑ Ⓒ Ⓓ Ⓔ
12 Ⓐ Ⓑ Ⓒ Ⓓ Ⓔ
13 Ⓐ Ⓑ Ⓒ Ⓓ Ⓔ

PT77, Pg. 32 PT77-S3-G4
18 Ⓐ Ⓑ Ⓒ Ⓓ Ⓔ
19 Ⓐ Ⓑ Ⓒ Ⓓ Ⓔ
20 Ⓐ Ⓑ Ⓒ Ⓓ Ⓔ
21 Ⓐ Ⓑ Ⓒ Ⓓ Ⓔ
22 Ⓐ Ⓑ Ⓒ Ⓓ Ⓔ
23 Ⓐ Ⓑ Ⓒ Ⓓ Ⓔ

Miscellaneous

SP1, Pg. 196 PTB-S2-G3
13 Ⓐ Ⓑ Ⓒ Ⓓ Ⓔ
14 Ⓐ Ⓑ Ⓒ Ⓓ Ⓔ
15 Ⓐ Ⓑ Ⓒ Ⓓ Ⓔ
16 Ⓐ Ⓑ Ⓒ Ⓓ Ⓔ
17 Ⓐ Ⓑ Ⓒ Ⓓ Ⓔ
18 Ⓐ Ⓑ Ⓒ Ⓓ Ⓔ

PT1-S2-G1
1   Ⓐ Ⓑ Ⓒ Ⓓ Ⓔ
2   Ⓐ Ⓑ Ⓒ Ⓓ Ⓔ
3   Ⓐ Ⓑ Ⓒ Ⓓ Ⓔ
4   Ⓐ Ⓑ Ⓒ Ⓓ Ⓔ
5   Ⓐ Ⓑ Ⓒ Ⓓ Ⓔ
6   Ⓐ Ⓑ Ⓒ Ⓓ Ⓔ
7   Ⓐ Ⓑ Ⓒ Ⓓ Ⓔ

PT2-S3-G3
13 Ⓐ Ⓑ Ⓒ Ⓓ Ⓔ
14 Ⓐ Ⓑ Ⓒ Ⓓ Ⓔ
15 Ⓐ Ⓑ Ⓒ Ⓓ Ⓔ
16 Ⓐ Ⓑ Ⓒ Ⓓ Ⓔ
17 Ⓐ Ⓑ Ⓒ Ⓓ Ⓔ

PT4-S3-G4
18 Ⓐ Ⓑ Ⓒ Ⓓ Ⓔ
19 Ⓐ Ⓑ Ⓒ Ⓓ Ⓔ
20 Ⓐ Ⓑ Ⓒ Ⓓ Ⓔ
21 Ⓐ Ⓑ Ⓒ Ⓓ Ⓔ
22 Ⓐ Ⓑ Ⓒ Ⓓ Ⓔ
23 Ⓐ Ⓑ Ⓒ Ⓓ Ⓔ
24 Ⓐ Ⓑ Ⓒ Ⓓ Ⓔ

PT6-S4-G3
13 Ⓐ Ⓑ Ⓒ Ⓓ Ⓔ
14 Ⓐ Ⓑ Ⓒ Ⓓ Ⓔ
15 Ⓐ Ⓑ Ⓒ Ⓓ Ⓔ
16 Ⓐ Ⓑ Ⓒ Ⓓ Ⓔ
17 Ⓐ Ⓑ Ⓒ Ⓓ Ⓔ
18 Ⓐ Ⓑ Ⓒ Ⓓ Ⓔ
19 Ⓐ Ⓑ Ⓒ Ⓓ Ⓔ

PT6-S4-G4
20 Ⓐ Ⓑ Ⓒ Ⓓ Ⓔ
21 Ⓐ Ⓑ Ⓒ Ⓓ Ⓔ
22 Ⓐ Ⓑ Ⓒ Ⓓ Ⓔ
23 Ⓐ Ⓑ Ⓒ Ⓓ Ⓔ
24 Ⓐ Ⓑ Ⓒ Ⓓ Ⓔ

PT8-S2-G2
6   Ⓐ Ⓑ Ⓒ Ⓓ Ⓔ
7   Ⓐ Ⓑ Ⓒ Ⓓ Ⓔ
8   Ⓐ Ⓑ Ⓒ Ⓓ Ⓔ
9   Ⓐ Ⓑ Ⓒ Ⓓ Ⓔ
10 Ⓐ Ⓑ Ⓒ Ⓓ Ⓔ
11 Ⓐ Ⓑ Ⓒ Ⓓ Ⓔ
12 Ⓐ Ⓑ Ⓒ Ⓓ Ⓔ

V1, Pg. 69   PT9-S3-G4
19 Ⓐ Ⓑ Ⓒ Ⓓ Ⓔ
20 Ⓐ Ⓑ Ⓒ Ⓓ Ⓔ
21 Ⓐ Ⓑ Ⓒ Ⓓ Ⓔ
22 Ⓐ Ⓑ Ⓒ Ⓓ Ⓔ
23 Ⓐ Ⓑ Ⓒ Ⓓ Ⓔ
24 Ⓐ Ⓑ Ⓒ Ⓓ Ⓔ

V1, Pg. 94   PT10-S2-G3
13 Ⓐ Ⓑ Ⓒ Ⓓ Ⓔ
14 Ⓐ Ⓑ Ⓒ Ⓓ Ⓔ
15 Ⓐ Ⓑ Ⓒ Ⓓ Ⓔ
16 Ⓐ Ⓑ Ⓒ Ⓓ Ⓔ
17 Ⓐ Ⓑ Ⓒ Ⓓ Ⓔ
18 Ⓐ Ⓑ Ⓒ Ⓓ Ⓔ

V1, Pg. 121   PT11-S1-G4

20 Ⓐ Ⓑ Ⓒ Ⓓ Ⓔ
21 Ⓐ Ⓑ Ⓒ Ⓓ Ⓔ
22 Ⓐ Ⓑ Ⓒ Ⓓ Ⓔ
23 Ⓐ Ⓑ Ⓒ Ⓓ Ⓔ
24 Ⓐ Ⓑ Ⓒ Ⓓ Ⓔ

V1, Pg. 163   PT12-S2-G4

18 Ⓐ Ⓑ Ⓒ Ⓓ Ⓔ
19 Ⓐ Ⓑ Ⓒ Ⓓ Ⓔ
20 Ⓐ Ⓑ Ⓒ Ⓓ Ⓔ
21 Ⓐ Ⓑ Ⓒ Ⓓ Ⓔ
22 Ⓐ Ⓑ Ⓒ Ⓓ Ⓔ
23 Ⓐ Ⓑ Ⓒ Ⓓ Ⓔ
24 Ⓐ Ⓑ Ⓒ Ⓓ Ⓔ

V1, Pg. 189   PT13-S1-G4

18 Ⓐ Ⓑ Ⓒ Ⓓ Ⓔ
19 Ⓐ Ⓑ Ⓒ Ⓓ Ⓔ
20 Ⓐ Ⓑ Ⓒ Ⓓ Ⓔ
21 Ⓐ Ⓑ Ⓒ Ⓓ Ⓔ
22 Ⓐ Ⓑ Ⓒ Ⓓ Ⓔ
23 Ⓐ Ⓑ Ⓒ Ⓓ Ⓔ
24 Ⓐ Ⓑ Ⓒ Ⓓ Ⓔ

V1, Pg. 279   PT15-S4-G2

7   Ⓐ Ⓑ Ⓒ Ⓓ Ⓔ
8   Ⓐ Ⓑ Ⓒ Ⓓ Ⓔ
9   Ⓐ Ⓑ Ⓒ Ⓓ Ⓔ
10 Ⓐ Ⓑ Ⓒ Ⓓ Ⓔ
11 Ⓐ Ⓑ Ⓒ Ⓓ Ⓔ
12 Ⓐ Ⓑ Ⓒ Ⓓ Ⓔ
13 Ⓐ Ⓑ Ⓒ Ⓓ Ⓔ

V1, Pg. 291   PT16-S1-G4

19 Ⓐ Ⓑ Ⓒ Ⓓ Ⓔ
20 Ⓐ Ⓑ Ⓒ Ⓓ Ⓔ
21 Ⓐ Ⓑ Ⓒ Ⓓ Ⓔ
22 Ⓐ Ⓑ Ⓒ Ⓓ Ⓔ
23 Ⓐ Ⓑ Ⓒ Ⓓ Ⓔ
24 Ⓐ Ⓑ Ⓒ Ⓓ Ⓔ

V1, Pg. 324   PT18-S1-G3

14 Ⓐ Ⓑ Ⓒ Ⓓ Ⓔ
15 Ⓐ Ⓑ Ⓒ Ⓓ Ⓔ
16 Ⓐ Ⓑ Ⓒ Ⓓ Ⓔ
17 Ⓐ Ⓑ Ⓒ Ⓓ Ⓔ
18 Ⓐ Ⓑ Ⓒ Ⓓ Ⓔ
19 Ⓐ Ⓑ Ⓒ Ⓓ Ⓔ

V1, Pg. 325   PT18-S1-G4

20 Ⓐ Ⓑ Ⓒ Ⓓ Ⓔ
21 Ⓐ Ⓑ Ⓒ Ⓓ Ⓔ
22 Ⓐ Ⓑ Ⓒ Ⓓ Ⓔ
23 Ⓐ Ⓑ Ⓒ Ⓓ Ⓔ
24 Ⓐ Ⓑ Ⓒ Ⓓ Ⓔ

V2, Pg. 68   PT20-S3-G3

13 Ⓐ Ⓑ Ⓒ Ⓓ Ⓔ
14 Ⓐ Ⓑ Ⓒ Ⓓ Ⓔ
15 Ⓐ Ⓑ Ⓒ Ⓓ Ⓔ
16 Ⓐ Ⓑ Ⓒ Ⓓ Ⓔ
17 Ⓐ Ⓑ Ⓒ Ⓓ Ⓔ
18 Ⓐ Ⓑ Ⓒ Ⓓ Ⓔ

V2, Pg. 85   PT21-S1-G2

7   Ⓐ Ⓑ Ⓒ Ⓓ Ⓔ
8   Ⓐ Ⓑ Ⓒ Ⓓ Ⓔ
9   Ⓐ Ⓑ Ⓒ Ⓓ Ⓔ
10 Ⓐ Ⓑ Ⓒ Ⓓ Ⓔ
11 Ⓐ Ⓑ Ⓒ Ⓓ Ⓔ

V3, Pg. 50   PT30-S1-G1

1 Ⓐ Ⓑ Ⓒ Ⓓ Ⓔ
2 Ⓐ Ⓑ Ⓒ Ⓓ Ⓔ
3 Ⓐ Ⓑ Ⓒ Ⓓ Ⓔ
4 Ⓐ Ⓑ Ⓒ Ⓓ Ⓔ
5 Ⓐ Ⓑ Ⓒ Ⓓ Ⓔ

PT40-S2-G3

11 Ⓐ Ⓑ Ⓒ Ⓓ Ⓔ
12 Ⓐ Ⓑ Ⓒ Ⓓ Ⓔ
13 Ⓐ Ⓑ Ⓒ Ⓓ Ⓔ
14 Ⓐ Ⓑ Ⓒ Ⓓ Ⓔ
15 Ⓐ Ⓑ Ⓒ Ⓓ Ⓔ
16 Ⓐ Ⓑ Ⓒ Ⓓ Ⓔ
17 Ⓐ Ⓑ Ⓒ Ⓓ Ⓔ

PT41-S2-G4

18 Ⓐ Ⓑ Ⓒ Ⓓ Ⓔ
19 Ⓐ Ⓑ Ⓒ Ⓓ Ⓔ
20 Ⓐ Ⓑ Ⓒ Ⓓ Ⓔ
21 Ⓐ Ⓑ Ⓒ Ⓓ Ⓔ
22 Ⓐ Ⓑ Ⓒ Ⓓ Ⓔ
23 Ⓐ Ⓑ Ⓒ Ⓓ Ⓔ
24 Ⓐ Ⓑ Ⓒ Ⓓ Ⓔ

PT72, Pg. 40 PT72-S4-G4

19 Ⓐ Ⓑ Ⓒ Ⓓ Ⓔ
20 Ⓐ Ⓑ Ⓒ Ⓓ Ⓔ
21 Ⓐ Ⓑ Ⓒ Ⓓ Ⓔ
22 Ⓐ Ⓑ Ⓒ Ⓓ Ⓔ
23 Ⓐ Ⓑ Ⓒ Ⓓ Ⓔ

PT77, Pg. 30 PT77-S3-G3

13 Ⓐ Ⓑ Ⓒ Ⓓ Ⓔ
14 Ⓐ Ⓑ Ⓒ Ⓓ Ⓔ
15 Ⓐ Ⓑ Ⓒ Ⓓ Ⓔ
16 Ⓐ Ⓑ Ⓒ Ⓓ Ⓔ
17 Ⓐ Ⓑ Ⓒ Ⓓ Ⓔ

Limited Allocations

J07, Pg. 4   J07-S1-G3

11 Ⓐ Ⓑ Ⓒ Ⓓ Ⓔ
12 Ⓐ Ⓑ Ⓒ Ⓓ Ⓔ
13 Ⓐ Ⓑ Ⓒ Ⓓ Ⓔ
14 Ⓐ Ⓑ Ⓒ Ⓓ Ⓔ
15 Ⓐ Ⓑ Ⓒ Ⓓ Ⓔ
16 Ⓐ Ⓑ Ⓒ Ⓓ Ⓔ
17 Ⓐ Ⓑ Ⓒ Ⓓ Ⓔ

PT2-S3-G3

13 Ⓐ Ⓑ Ⓒ Ⓓ Ⓔ
14 Ⓐ Ⓑ Ⓒ Ⓓ Ⓔ
15 Ⓐ Ⓑ Ⓒ Ⓓ Ⓔ
16 Ⓐ Ⓑ Ⓒ Ⓓ Ⓔ
17 Ⓐ Ⓑ Ⓒ Ⓓ Ⓔ

PT6-S4-G1

1 Ⓐ Ⓑ Ⓒ Ⓓ Ⓔ
2 Ⓐ Ⓑ Ⓒ Ⓓ Ⓔ
3 Ⓐ Ⓑ Ⓒ Ⓓ Ⓔ
4 Ⓐ Ⓑ Ⓒ Ⓓ Ⓔ
5 Ⓐ Ⓑ Ⓒ Ⓓ Ⓔ
6 Ⓐ Ⓑ Ⓒ Ⓓ Ⓔ

V1, Pg. 26   PT7-S2-G3

13 Ⓐ Ⓑ Ⓒ Ⓓ Ⓔ
14 Ⓐ Ⓑ Ⓒ Ⓓ Ⓔ
15 Ⓐ Ⓑ Ⓒ Ⓓ Ⓔ
16 Ⓐ Ⓑ Ⓒ Ⓓ Ⓔ
17 Ⓐ Ⓑ Ⓒ Ⓓ Ⓔ
18 Ⓐ Ⓑ Ⓒ Ⓓ Ⓔ

V1, Pg. 66   PT9-S3-G1

1 Ⓐ Ⓑ Ⓒ Ⓓ Ⓔ
2 Ⓐ Ⓑ Ⓒ Ⓓ Ⓔ
3 Ⓐ Ⓑ Ⓒ Ⓓ Ⓔ
4 Ⓐ Ⓑ Ⓒ Ⓓ Ⓔ
5 Ⓐ Ⓑ Ⓒ Ⓓ Ⓔ
6 Ⓐ Ⓑ Ⓒ Ⓓ Ⓔ
7 Ⓐ Ⓑ Ⓒ Ⓓ Ⓔ

V1, Pg. 119   PT11-S1-G2

7   Ⓐ Ⓑ Ⓒ Ⓓ Ⓔ
8   Ⓐ Ⓑ Ⓒ Ⓓ Ⓔ
9   Ⓐ Ⓑ Ⓒ Ⓓ Ⓔ
10 Ⓐ Ⓑ Ⓒ Ⓓ Ⓔ
11 Ⓐ Ⓑ Ⓒ Ⓓ Ⓔ

V1, Pg. 280   PT15-S4-G3

14 Ⓐ Ⓑ Ⓒ Ⓓ Ⓔ
15 Ⓐ Ⓑ Ⓒ Ⓓ Ⓔ
16 Ⓐ Ⓑ Ⓒ Ⓓ Ⓔ
17 Ⓐ Ⓑ Ⓒ Ⓓ Ⓔ
18 Ⓐ Ⓑ Ⓒ Ⓓ Ⓔ
19 Ⓐ Ⓑ Ⓒ Ⓓ Ⓔ

V3, Pg. 35   PT29-S3-G4

20 Ⓐ Ⓑ Ⓒ Ⓓ Ⓔ
21 Ⓐ Ⓑ Ⓒ Ⓓ Ⓔ
22 Ⓐ Ⓑ Ⓒ Ⓓ Ⓔ
23 Ⓐ Ⓑ Ⓒ Ⓓ Ⓔ
24 Ⓐ Ⓑ Ⓒ Ⓓ Ⓔ

V3, Pg. 51   PT30-S1-G2

6   Ⓐ Ⓑ Ⓒ Ⓓ Ⓔ
7   Ⓐ Ⓑ Ⓒ Ⓓ Ⓔ
8   Ⓐ Ⓑ Ⓒ Ⓓ Ⓔ
9   Ⓐ Ⓑ Ⓒ Ⓓ Ⓔ
10 Ⓐ Ⓑ Ⓒ Ⓓ Ⓔ

V3, Pg. 178   PT33-S4-G3

13 Ⓐ Ⓑ Ⓒ Ⓓ Ⓔ
14 Ⓐ Ⓑ Ⓒ Ⓓ Ⓔ
15 Ⓐ Ⓑ Ⓒ Ⓓ Ⓔ
16 Ⓐ Ⓑ Ⓒ Ⓓ Ⓔ
17 Ⓐ Ⓑ Ⓒ Ⓓ Ⓔ
18 Ⓐ Ⓑ Ⓒ Ⓓ Ⓔ

V3, Pg. 237   PT35-S3-G2

6   Ⓐ Ⓑ Ⓒ Ⓓ Ⓔ
7   Ⓐ Ⓑ Ⓒ Ⓓ Ⓔ
8   Ⓐ Ⓑ Ⓒ Ⓓ Ⓔ
9   Ⓐ Ⓑ Ⓒ Ⓓ Ⓔ
10 Ⓐ Ⓑ Ⓒ Ⓓ Ⓔ
11 Ⓐ Ⓑ Ⓒ Ⓓ Ⓔ
12 Ⓐ Ⓑ Ⓒ Ⓓ Ⓔ

PT41-S2-G3

13 Ⓐ Ⓑ Ⓒ Ⓓ Ⓔ
14 Ⓐ Ⓑ Ⓒ Ⓓ Ⓔ
15 Ⓐ Ⓑ Ⓒ Ⓓ Ⓔ
16 Ⓐ Ⓑ Ⓒ Ⓓ Ⓔ
17 Ⓐ Ⓑ Ⓒ Ⓓ Ⓔ

PT42-S1-G4

19 Ⓐ Ⓑ Ⓒ Ⓓ Ⓔ
20 Ⓐ Ⓑ Ⓒ Ⓓ Ⓔ
21 Ⓐ Ⓑ Ⓒ Ⓓ Ⓔ
22 Ⓐ Ⓑ Ⓒ Ⓓ Ⓔ
23 Ⓐ Ⓑ Ⓒ Ⓓ Ⓔ

PT43-S4-G4

18 Ⓐ Ⓑ Ⓒ Ⓓ Ⓔ
19 Ⓐ Ⓑ Ⓒ Ⓓ Ⓔ
20 Ⓐ Ⓑ Ⓒ Ⓓ Ⓔ
21 Ⓐ Ⓑ Ⓒ Ⓓ Ⓔ
22 Ⓐ Ⓑ Ⓒ Ⓓ Ⓔ

PT44-S3-G1

1   Ⓐ Ⓑ Ⓒ Ⓓ Ⓔ
2   Ⓐ Ⓑ Ⓒ Ⓓ Ⓔ
3   Ⓐ Ⓑ Ⓒ Ⓓ Ⓔ
4   Ⓐ Ⓑ Ⓒ Ⓓ Ⓔ
5   Ⓐ Ⓑ Ⓒ Ⓓ Ⓔ
6   Ⓐ Ⓑ Ⓒ Ⓓ Ⓔ

PT44-S3-G4

18 Ⓐ Ⓑ Ⓒ Ⓓ Ⓔ
19 Ⓐ Ⓑ Ⓒ Ⓓ Ⓔ
20 Ⓐ Ⓑ Ⓒ Ⓓ Ⓔ
21 Ⓐ Ⓑ Ⓒ Ⓓ Ⓔ
22 Ⓐ Ⓑ Ⓒ Ⓓ Ⓔ

PT45-S3-G4

18 Ⓐ Ⓑ Ⓒ Ⓓ Ⓔ
19 Ⓐ Ⓑ Ⓒ Ⓓ Ⓔ
20 Ⓐ Ⓑ Ⓒ Ⓓ Ⓔ
21 Ⓐ Ⓑ Ⓒ Ⓓ Ⓔ
22 Ⓐ Ⓑ Ⓒ Ⓓ Ⓔ

PT46-S4-G4

17 Ⓐ Ⓑ Ⓒ Ⓓ Ⓔ
18 Ⓐ Ⓑ Ⓒ Ⓓ Ⓔ
19 Ⓐ Ⓑ Ⓒ Ⓓ Ⓔ
20 Ⓐ Ⓑ Ⓒ Ⓓ Ⓔ
21 Ⓐ Ⓑ Ⓒ Ⓓ Ⓔ
22 Ⓐ Ⓑ Ⓒ Ⓓ Ⓔ

PT47-S4-G3

12 Ⓐ Ⓑ Ⓒ Ⓓ Ⓔ
13 Ⓐ Ⓑ Ⓒ Ⓓ Ⓔ
14 Ⓐ Ⓑ Ⓒ Ⓓ Ⓔ
15 Ⓐ Ⓑ Ⓒ Ⓓ Ⓔ
16 Ⓐ Ⓑ Ⓒ Ⓓ Ⓔ
17 Ⓐ Ⓑ Ⓒ Ⓓ Ⓔ

PT48-S2-G3

13 Ⓐ Ⓑ Ⓒ Ⓓ Ⓔ
14 Ⓐ Ⓑ Ⓒ Ⓓ Ⓔ
15 Ⓐ Ⓑ Ⓒ Ⓓ Ⓔ
16 Ⓐ Ⓑ Ⓒ Ⓓ Ⓔ
17 Ⓐ Ⓑ Ⓒ Ⓓ Ⓔ

PT49-S1-G2

8   Ⓐ Ⓑ Ⓒ Ⓓ Ⓔ
9   Ⓐ Ⓑ Ⓒ Ⓓ Ⓔ
10 Ⓐ Ⓑ Ⓒ Ⓓ Ⓔ
11 Ⓐ Ⓑ Ⓒ Ⓓ Ⓔ
12 Ⓐ Ⓑ Ⓒ Ⓓ Ⓔ

PT50-S3-G2

6   Ⓐ Ⓑ Ⓒ Ⓓ Ⓔ
7   Ⓐ Ⓑ Ⓒ Ⓓ Ⓔ
8   Ⓐ Ⓑ Ⓒ Ⓓ Ⓔ
9   Ⓐ Ⓑ Ⓒ Ⓓ Ⓔ
10 Ⓐ Ⓑ Ⓒ Ⓓ Ⓔ
11 Ⓐ Ⓑ Ⓒ Ⓓ Ⓔ

V4, Pg. 97   PT54-S3-G2

6   Ⓐ Ⓑ Ⓒ Ⓓ Ⓔ
7   Ⓐ Ⓑ Ⓒ Ⓓ Ⓔ
8   Ⓐ Ⓑ Ⓒ Ⓓ Ⓔ
9   Ⓐ Ⓑ Ⓒ Ⓓ Ⓔ
10 Ⓐ Ⓑ Ⓒ Ⓓ Ⓔ
11 Ⓐ Ⓑ Ⓒ Ⓓ Ⓔ
12 Ⓐ Ⓑ Ⓒ Ⓓ Ⓔ

V4, Pg. 153   PT56-S1-G2

7   Ⓐ Ⓑ Ⓒ Ⓓ Ⓔ
8   Ⓐ Ⓑ Ⓒ Ⓓ Ⓔ
9   Ⓐ Ⓑ Ⓒ Ⓓ Ⓔ
10 Ⓐ Ⓑ Ⓒ Ⓓ Ⓔ
11 Ⓐ Ⓑ Ⓒ Ⓓ Ⓔ

V4, Pg. 155   PT56-S1-G4

17 Ⓐ Ⓑ Ⓒ Ⓓ Ⓔ
18 Ⓐ Ⓑ Ⓒ Ⓓ Ⓔ
19 Ⓐ Ⓑ Ⓒ Ⓓ Ⓔ
20 Ⓐ Ⓑ Ⓒ Ⓓ Ⓔ
21 Ⓐ Ⓑ Ⓒ Ⓓ Ⓔ
22 Ⓐ Ⓑ Ⓒ Ⓓ Ⓔ
23 Ⓐ Ⓑ Ⓒ Ⓓ Ⓔ

V4, Pg. 189   PT57-S1-G2

6   Ⓐ Ⓑ Ⓒ Ⓓ Ⓔ
7   Ⓐ Ⓑ Ⓒ Ⓓ Ⓔ
8   Ⓐ Ⓑ Ⓒ Ⓓ Ⓔ
9   Ⓐ Ⓑ Ⓒ Ⓓ Ⓔ
10 Ⓐ Ⓑ Ⓒ Ⓓ Ⓔ
11 Ⓐ Ⓑ Ⓒ Ⓓ Ⓔ

V5, Pg. 52   PT63-S2-G1

1   Ⓐ Ⓑ Ⓒ Ⓓ Ⓔ
2   Ⓐ Ⓑ Ⓒ Ⓓ Ⓔ
3   Ⓐ Ⓑ Ⓒ Ⓓ Ⓔ
4   Ⓐ Ⓑ Ⓒ Ⓓ Ⓔ
5   Ⓐ Ⓑ Ⓒ Ⓓ Ⓔ

V5, Pg. 55   PT63-S2-G4
18 Ⓐ Ⓑ Ⓒ Ⓓ Ⓔ
19 Ⓐ Ⓑ Ⓒ Ⓓ Ⓔ
20 Ⓐ Ⓑ Ⓒ Ⓓ Ⓔ
21 Ⓐ Ⓑ Ⓒ Ⓓ Ⓔ
22 Ⓐ Ⓑ Ⓒ Ⓓ Ⓔ
23 Ⓐ Ⓑ Ⓒ Ⓓ Ⓔ

V5, Pg. 286   PT69-S2-G4
18 Ⓐ Ⓑ Ⓒ Ⓓ Ⓔ
19 Ⓐ Ⓑ Ⓒ Ⓓ Ⓔ
20 Ⓐ Ⓑ Ⓒ Ⓓ Ⓔ
21 Ⓐ Ⓑ Ⓒ Ⓓ Ⓔ
22 Ⓐ Ⓑ Ⓒ Ⓓ Ⓔ
23 Ⓐ Ⓑ Ⓒ Ⓓ Ⓔ

PT74, Pg. 22   PT74-S2-G3
11 Ⓐ Ⓑ Ⓒ Ⓓ Ⓔ
12 Ⓐ Ⓑ Ⓒ Ⓓ Ⓔ
13 Ⓐ Ⓑ Ⓒ Ⓓ Ⓔ
14 Ⓐ Ⓑ Ⓒ Ⓓ Ⓔ
15 Ⓐ Ⓑ Ⓒ Ⓓ Ⓔ
16 Ⓐ Ⓑ Ⓒ Ⓓ Ⓔ

V5, Pg. 282   PT69-S2-G2
6 Ⓐ Ⓑ Ⓒ Ⓓ Ⓔ
7 Ⓐ Ⓑ Ⓒ Ⓓ Ⓔ
8 Ⓐ Ⓑ Ⓒ Ⓓ Ⓔ
9 Ⓐ Ⓑ Ⓒ Ⓓ Ⓔ
10 Ⓐ Ⓑ Ⓒ Ⓓ Ⓔ
11 Ⓐ Ⓑ Ⓒ Ⓓ Ⓔ

V5, Pg. 362   PT71-S2-G2
6 Ⓐ Ⓑ Ⓒ Ⓓ Ⓔ
7 Ⓐ Ⓑ Ⓒ Ⓓ Ⓔ
8 Ⓐ Ⓑ Ⓒ Ⓓ Ⓔ
9 Ⓐ Ⓑ Ⓒ Ⓓ Ⓔ
10 Ⓐ Ⓑ Ⓒ Ⓓ Ⓔ
11 Ⓐ Ⓑ Ⓒ Ⓓ Ⓔ

PT77, Pg. 32   PT77-S3-G4
18 Ⓐ Ⓑ Ⓒ Ⓓ Ⓔ
19 Ⓐ Ⓑ Ⓒ Ⓓ Ⓔ
20 Ⓐ Ⓑ Ⓒ Ⓓ Ⓔ
21 Ⓐ Ⓑ Ⓒ Ⓓ Ⓔ
22 Ⓐ Ⓑ Ⓒ Ⓓ Ⓔ
23 Ⓐ Ⓑ Ⓒ Ⓓ Ⓔ

Limited Scenarios

SP1, Pg. 297   PTC-S1-G2
6 Ⓐ Ⓑ Ⓒ Ⓓ Ⓔ
7 Ⓐ Ⓑ Ⓒ Ⓓ Ⓔ
8 Ⓐ Ⓑ Ⓒ Ⓓ Ⓔ
9 Ⓐ Ⓑ Ⓒ Ⓓ Ⓔ
10 Ⓐ Ⓑ Ⓒ Ⓓ Ⓔ
11 Ⓐ Ⓑ Ⓒ Ⓓ Ⓔ
12 Ⓐ Ⓑ Ⓒ Ⓓ Ⓔ

V1, Pg. 27   PT7-S2-G4
19 Ⓐ Ⓑ Ⓒ Ⓓ Ⓔ
20 Ⓐ Ⓑ Ⓒ Ⓓ Ⓔ
21 Ⓐ Ⓑ Ⓒ Ⓓ Ⓔ
22 Ⓐ Ⓑ Ⓒ Ⓓ Ⓔ
23 Ⓐ Ⓑ Ⓒ Ⓓ Ⓔ
24 Ⓐ Ⓑ Ⓒ Ⓓ Ⓔ

V1, Pg. 221   PT14-S1-G2
7 Ⓐ Ⓑ Ⓒ Ⓓ Ⓔ
8 Ⓐ Ⓑ Ⓒ Ⓓ Ⓔ
9 Ⓐ Ⓑ Ⓒ Ⓓ Ⓔ
10 Ⓐ Ⓑ Ⓒ Ⓓ Ⓔ
11 Ⓐ Ⓑ Ⓒ Ⓓ Ⓔ
12 Ⓐ Ⓑ Ⓒ Ⓓ Ⓔ

SP2, Pg. 346   PTC2-S1-G1
1 Ⓐ Ⓑ Ⓒ Ⓓ Ⓔ
2 Ⓐ Ⓑ Ⓒ Ⓓ Ⓔ
3 Ⓐ Ⓑ Ⓒ Ⓓ Ⓔ
4 Ⓐ Ⓑ Ⓒ Ⓓ Ⓔ
5 Ⓐ Ⓑ Ⓒ Ⓓ Ⓔ

V1, Pg. 93   PT10-S2-G2
6 Ⓐ Ⓑ Ⓒ Ⓓ Ⓔ
7 Ⓐ Ⓑ Ⓒ Ⓓ Ⓔ
8 Ⓐ Ⓑ Ⓒ Ⓓ Ⓔ
9 Ⓐ Ⓑ Ⓒ Ⓓ Ⓔ
10 Ⓐ Ⓑ Ⓒ Ⓓ Ⓔ
11 Ⓐ Ⓑ Ⓒ Ⓓ Ⓔ
12 Ⓐ Ⓑ Ⓒ Ⓓ Ⓔ

V1, Pg. 289   PT16-S1-G2
7 Ⓐ Ⓑ Ⓒ Ⓓ Ⓔ
8 Ⓐ Ⓑ Ⓒ Ⓓ Ⓔ
9 Ⓐ Ⓑ Ⓒ Ⓓ Ⓔ
10 Ⓐ Ⓑ Ⓒ Ⓓ Ⓔ
11 Ⓐ Ⓑ Ⓒ Ⓓ Ⓔ
12 Ⓐ Ⓑ Ⓒ Ⓓ Ⓔ

SP2, Pg. 348   PTC2-S1-G2
6 Ⓐ Ⓑ Ⓒ Ⓓ Ⓔ
7 Ⓐ Ⓑ Ⓒ Ⓓ Ⓔ
8 Ⓐ Ⓑ Ⓒ Ⓓ Ⓔ
9 Ⓐ Ⓑ Ⓒ Ⓓ Ⓔ
10 Ⓐ Ⓑ Ⓒ Ⓓ Ⓔ

V1, Pg. 160   PT12-S2-G1
1 Ⓐ Ⓑ Ⓒ Ⓓ Ⓔ
2 Ⓐ Ⓑ Ⓒ Ⓓ Ⓔ
3 Ⓐ Ⓑ Ⓒ Ⓓ Ⓔ
4 Ⓐ Ⓑ Ⓒ Ⓓ Ⓔ
5 Ⓐ Ⓑ Ⓒ Ⓓ Ⓔ
6 Ⓐ Ⓑ Ⓒ Ⓓ Ⓔ

V1, Pg. 322   PT18-S1-G1
1 Ⓐ Ⓑ Ⓒ Ⓓ Ⓔ
2 Ⓐ Ⓑ Ⓒ Ⓓ Ⓔ
3 Ⓐ Ⓑ Ⓒ Ⓓ Ⓔ
4 Ⓐ Ⓑ Ⓒ Ⓓ Ⓔ
5 Ⓐ Ⓑ Ⓒ Ⓓ Ⓔ
6 Ⓐ Ⓑ Ⓒ Ⓓ Ⓔ

SP2, Pg. 350   PTC2-S1-G3
11 Ⓐ Ⓑ Ⓒ Ⓓ Ⓔ
12 Ⓐ Ⓑ Ⓒ Ⓓ Ⓔ
13 Ⓐ Ⓑ Ⓒ Ⓓ Ⓔ
14 Ⓐ Ⓑ Ⓒ Ⓓ Ⓔ
15 Ⓐ Ⓑ Ⓒ Ⓓ Ⓔ
16 Ⓐ Ⓑ Ⓒ Ⓓ Ⓔ
17 Ⓐ Ⓑ Ⓒ Ⓓ Ⓔ

V1, Pg. 220   PT14-S1-G1
1 Ⓐ Ⓑ Ⓒ Ⓓ Ⓔ
2 Ⓐ Ⓑ Ⓒ Ⓓ Ⓔ
3 Ⓐ Ⓑ Ⓒ Ⓓ Ⓔ
4 Ⓐ Ⓑ Ⓒ Ⓓ Ⓔ
5 Ⓐ Ⓑ Ⓒ Ⓓ Ⓔ
6 Ⓐ Ⓑ Ⓒ Ⓓ Ⓔ

V1, Pg. 323   PT18-S1-G2
7 Ⓐ Ⓑ Ⓒ Ⓓ Ⓔ
8 Ⓐ Ⓑ Ⓒ Ⓓ Ⓔ
9 Ⓐ Ⓑ Ⓒ Ⓓ Ⓔ
10 Ⓐ Ⓑ Ⓒ Ⓓ Ⓔ
11 Ⓐ Ⓑ Ⓒ Ⓓ Ⓔ
12 Ⓐ Ⓑ Ⓒ Ⓓ Ⓔ
13 Ⓐ Ⓑ Ⓒ Ⓓ Ⓔ

PT1-S2-G2
8 Ⓐ Ⓑ Ⓒ Ⓓ Ⓔ
9 Ⓐ Ⓑ Ⓒ Ⓓ Ⓔ
10 Ⓐ Ⓑ Ⓒ Ⓓ Ⓔ
11 Ⓐ Ⓑ Ⓒ Ⓓ Ⓔ
12 Ⓐ Ⓑ Ⓒ Ⓓ Ⓔ
13 Ⓐ Ⓑ Ⓒ Ⓓ Ⓔ

V2, Pg. 17   PT19-S1-G2
8 Ⓐ Ⓑ Ⓒ Ⓓ Ⓔ
9 Ⓐ Ⓑ Ⓒ Ⓓ Ⓔ
10 Ⓐ Ⓑ Ⓒ Ⓓ Ⓔ
11 Ⓐ Ⓑ Ⓒ Ⓓ Ⓔ
12 Ⓐ Ⓑ Ⓒ Ⓓ Ⓔ

V2, Pg. 84   PT21-S1-G1

1 Ⓐ Ⓑ Ⓒ Ⓓ Ⓔ
2 Ⓐ Ⓑ Ⓒ Ⓓ Ⓔ
3 Ⓐ Ⓑ Ⓒ Ⓓ Ⓔ
4 Ⓐ Ⓑ Ⓒ Ⓓ Ⓔ
5 Ⓐ Ⓑ Ⓒ Ⓓ Ⓔ
6 Ⓐ Ⓑ Ⓒ Ⓓ Ⓔ

V2, Pg. 86   PT21-S1-G3

12 Ⓐ Ⓑ Ⓒ Ⓓ Ⓔ
13 Ⓐ Ⓑ Ⓒ Ⓓ Ⓔ
14 Ⓐ Ⓑ Ⓒ Ⓓ Ⓔ
15 Ⓐ Ⓑ Ⓒ Ⓓ Ⓔ
16 Ⓐ Ⓑ Ⓒ Ⓓ Ⓔ
17 Ⓐ Ⓑ Ⓒ Ⓓ Ⓔ

V2, Pg. 135   PT22-S3-G2

8 Ⓐ Ⓑ Ⓒ Ⓓ Ⓔ
9 Ⓐ Ⓑ Ⓒ Ⓓ Ⓔ
10 Ⓐ Ⓑ Ⓒ Ⓓ Ⓔ
11 Ⓐ Ⓑ Ⓒ Ⓓ Ⓔ
12 Ⓐ Ⓑ Ⓒ Ⓓ Ⓔ
13 Ⓐ Ⓑ Ⓒ Ⓓ Ⓔ
14 Ⓐ Ⓑ Ⓒ Ⓓ Ⓔ

V2, Pg. 212   PT24-S4-G3

11 Ⓐ Ⓑ Ⓒ Ⓓ Ⓔ
12 Ⓐ Ⓑ Ⓒ Ⓓ Ⓔ
13 Ⓐ Ⓑ Ⓒ Ⓓ Ⓔ
14 Ⓐ Ⓑ Ⓒ Ⓓ Ⓔ
15 Ⓐ Ⓑ Ⓒ Ⓓ Ⓔ
16 Ⓐ Ⓑ Ⓒ Ⓓ Ⓔ
17 Ⓐ Ⓑ Ⓒ Ⓓ Ⓔ

V2, Pg. 237   PT25-S3-G2

6 Ⓐ Ⓑ Ⓒ Ⓓ Ⓔ
7 Ⓐ Ⓑ Ⓒ Ⓓ Ⓔ
8 Ⓐ Ⓑ Ⓒ Ⓓ Ⓔ
9 Ⓐ Ⓑ Ⓒ Ⓓ Ⓔ
10 Ⓐ Ⓑ Ⓒ Ⓓ Ⓔ
11 Ⓐ Ⓑ Ⓒ Ⓓ Ⓔ
12 Ⓐ Ⓑ Ⓒ Ⓓ Ⓔ

V2, Pg. 238   PT25-S3-G3

13 Ⓐ Ⓑ Ⓒ Ⓓ Ⓔ
14 Ⓐ Ⓑ Ⓒ Ⓓ Ⓔ
15 Ⓐ Ⓑ Ⓒ Ⓓ Ⓔ
16 Ⓐ Ⓑ Ⓒ Ⓓ Ⓔ
17 Ⓐ Ⓑ Ⓒ Ⓓ Ⓔ
18 Ⓐ Ⓑ Ⓒ Ⓓ Ⓔ

V2, Pg. 256   PT26-S1-G3

13 Ⓐ Ⓑ Ⓒ Ⓓ Ⓔ
14 Ⓐ Ⓑ Ⓒ Ⓓ Ⓔ
15 Ⓐ Ⓑ Ⓒ Ⓓ Ⓔ
16 Ⓐ Ⓑ Ⓒ Ⓓ Ⓔ
17 Ⓐ Ⓑ Ⓒ Ⓓ Ⓔ
18 Ⓐ Ⓑ Ⓒ Ⓓ Ⓔ

V2, Pg. 297   PT27-S2-G2

7 Ⓐ Ⓑ Ⓒ Ⓓ Ⓔ
8 Ⓐ Ⓑ Ⓒ Ⓓ Ⓔ
9 Ⓐ Ⓑ Ⓒ Ⓓ Ⓔ
10 Ⓐ Ⓑ Ⓒ Ⓓ Ⓔ
11 Ⓐ Ⓑ Ⓒ Ⓓ Ⓔ
12 Ⓐ Ⓑ Ⓒ Ⓓ Ⓔ

V2, Pg. 298   PT27-S2-G3

13 Ⓐ Ⓑ Ⓒ Ⓓ Ⓔ
14 Ⓐ Ⓑ Ⓒ Ⓓ Ⓔ
15 Ⓐ Ⓑ Ⓒ Ⓓ Ⓔ
16 Ⓐ Ⓑ Ⓒ Ⓓ Ⓔ
17 Ⓐ Ⓑ Ⓒ Ⓓ Ⓔ
18 Ⓐ Ⓑ Ⓒ Ⓓ Ⓔ
19 Ⓐ Ⓑ Ⓒ Ⓓ Ⓔ

V2, Pg. 330   PT28-S2-G1

1 Ⓐ Ⓑ Ⓒ Ⓓ Ⓔ
2 Ⓐ Ⓑ Ⓒ Ⓓ Ⓔ
3 Ⓐ Ⓑ Ⓒ Ⓓ Ⓔ
4 Ⓐ Ⓑ Ⓒ Ⓓ Ⓔ
5 Ⓐ Ⓑ Ⓒ Ⓓ Ⓔ

V3, Pg. 32   PT29-S3-G1

1 Ⓐ Ⓑ Ⓒ Ⓓ Ⓔ
2 Ⓐ Ⓑ Ⓒ Ⓓ Ⓔ
3 Ⓐ Ⓑ Ⓒ Ⓓ Ⓔ
4 Ⓐ Ⓑ Ⓒ Ⓓ Ⓔ
5 Ⓐ Ⓑ Ⓒ Ⓓ Ⓔ
6 Ⓐ Ⓑ Ⓒ Ⓓ Ⓔ

V3, Pg. 33   PT29-S3-G2

7 Ⓐ Ⓑ Ⓒ Ⓓ Ⓔ
8 Ⓐ Ⓑ Ⓒ Ⓓ Ⓔ
9 Ⓐ Ⓑ Ⓒ Ⓓ Ⓔ
10 Ⓐ Ⓑ Ⓒ Ⓓ Ⓔ
11 Ⓐ Ⓑ Ⓒ Ⓓ Ⓔ
12 Ⓐ Ⓑ Ⓒ Ⓓ Ⓔ
13 Ⓐ Ⓑ Ⓒ Ⓓ Ⓔ

V3, Pg. 52   PT30-S1-G3

11 Ⓐ Ⓑ Ⓒ Ⓓ Ⓔ
12 Ⓐ Ⓑ Ⓒ Ⓓ Ⓔ
13 Ⓐ Ⓑ Ⓒ Ⓓ Ⓔ
14 Ⓐ Ⓑ Ⓒ Ⓓ Ⓔ
15 Ⓐ Ⓑ Ⓒ Ⓓ Ⓔ
16 Ⓐ Ⓑ Ⓒ Ⓓ Ⓔ

V3, Pg. 86   PT31-S1-G3

14 Ⓐ Ⓑ Ⓒ Ⓓ Ⓔ
15 Ⓐ Ⓑ Ⓒ Ⓓ Ⓔ
16 Ⓐ Ⓑ Ⓒ Ⓓ Ⓔ
17 Ⓐ Ⓑ Ⓒ Ⓓ Ⓔ
18 Ⓐ Ⓑ Ⓒ Ⓓ Ⓔ

V3, Pg. 137   PT32-S3-G4

19 Ⓐ Ⓑ Ⓒ Ⓓ Ⓔ
20 Ⓐ Ⓑ Ⓒ Ⓓ Ⓔ
21 Ⓐ Ⓑ Ⓒ Ⓓ Ⓔ
22 Ⓐ Ⓑ Ⓒ Ⓓ Ⓔ
23 Ⓐ Ⓑ Ⓒ Ⓓ Ⓔ
24 Ⓐ Ⓑ Ⓒ Ⓓ Ⓔ

V3, Pg. 210   PT34-S4-G1

1 Ⓐ Ⓑ Ⓒ Ⓓ Ⓔ
2 Ⓐ Ⓑ Ⓒ Ⓓ Ⓔ
3 Ⓐ Ⓑ Ⓒ Ⓓ Ⓔ
4 Ⓐ Ⓑ Ⓒ Ⓓ Ⓔ
5 Ⓐ Ⓑ Ⓒ Ⓓ Ⓔ
6 Ⓐ Ⓑ Ⓒ Ⓓ Ⓔ
7 Ⓐ Ⓑ Ⓒ Ⓓ Ⓔ

V3, Pg. 212   PT34-S4-G3

13 Ⓐ Ⓑ Ⓒ Ⓓ Ⓔ
14 Ⓐ Ⓑ Ⓒ Ⓓ Ⓔ
15 Ⓐ Ⓑ Ⓒ Ⓓ Ⓔ
16 Ⓐ Ⓑ Ⓒ Ⓓ Ⓔ
17 Ⓐ Ⓑ Ⓒ Ⓓ Ⓔ
18 Ⓐ Ⓑ Ⓒ Ⓓ Ⓔ

V3, Pg. 238   PT35-S3-G3

13 Ⓐ Ⓑ Ⓒ Ⓓ Ⓔ
14 Ⓐ Ⓑ Ⓒ Ⓓ Ⓔ
15 Ⓐ Ⓑ Ⓒ Ⓓ Ⓔ
16 Ⓐ Ⓑ Ⓒ Ⓓ Ⓔ
17 Ⓐ Ⓑ Ⓒ Ⓓ Ⓔ

V3, Pg. 279   PT36-S4-G2

7 Ⓐ Ⓑ Ⓒ Ⓓ Ⓔ
8 Ⓐ Ⓑ Ⓒ Ⓓ Ⓔ
9 Ⓐ Ⓑ Ⓒ Ⓓ Ⓔ
10 Ⓐ Ⓑ Ⓒ Ⓓ Ⓔ
11 Ⓐ Ⓑ Ⓒ Ⓓ Ⓔ
12 Ⓐ Ⓑ Ⓒ Ⓓ Ⓔ
13 Ⓐ Ⓑ Ⓒ Ⓓ Ⓔ

V3, Pg. 281   PT36-S4-G4

19 Ⓐ Ⓑ Ⓒ Ⓓ Ⓔ
20 Ⓐ Ⓑ Ⓒ Ⓓ Ⓔ
21 Ⓐ Ⓑ Ⓒ Ⓓ Ⓔ
22 Ⓐ Ⓑ Ⓒ Ⓓ Ⓔ
23 Ⓐ Ⓑ Ⓒ Ⓓ Ⓔ

V3, Pg. 306   PT37-S3-G3

12 Ⓐ Ⓑ Ⓒ Ⓓ Ⓔ
13 Ⓐ Ⓑ Ⓒ Ⓓ Ⓔ
14 Ⓐ Ⓑ Ⓒ Ⓓ Ⓔ
15 Ⓐ Ⓑ Ⓒ Ⓓ Ⓔ
16 Ⓐ Ⓑ Ⓒ Ⓓ Ⓔ
17 Ⓐ Ⓑ Ⓒ Ⓓ Ⓔ
18 Ⓐ Ⓑ Ⓒ Ⓓ Ⓔ

V3, Pg. 307   PT37-S3-G4

19 Ⓐ Ⓑ Ⓒ Ⓓ Ⓔ
20 Ⓐ Ⓑ Ⓒ Ⓓ Ⓔ
21 Ⓐ Ⓑ Ⓒ Ⓓ Ⓔ
22 Ⓐ Ⓑ Ⓒ Ⓓ Ⓔ
23 Ⓐ Ⓑ Ⓒ Ⓓ Ⓔ
24 Ⓐ Ⓑ Ⓒ Ⓓ Ⓔ

V3, Pg. 332   PT38-S2-G3

14 Ⓐ Ⓑ Ⓒ Ⓓ Ⓔ
15 Ⓐ Ⓑ Ⓒ Ⓓ Ⓔ
16 Ⓐ Ⓑ Ⓒ Ⓓ Ⓔ
17 Ⓐ Ⓑ Ⓒ Ⓓ Ⓔ
18 Ⓐ Ⓑ Ⓒ Ⓓ Ⓔ
19 Ⓐ Ⓑ Ⓒ Ⓓ Ⓔ

V3, Pg. 333   PT38-S2-G4

20 Ⓐ Ⓑ Ⓒ Ⓓ Ⓔ
21 Ⓐ Ⓑ Ⓒ Ⓓ Ⓔ
22 Ⓐ Ⓑ Ⓒ Ⓓ Ⓔ
23 Ⓐ Ⓑ Ⓒ Ⓓ Ⓔ
24 Ⓐ Ⓑ Ⓒ Ⓓ Ⓔ

PT39-S1-G3

12 Ⓐ Ⓑ Ⓒ Ⓓ Ⓔ
13 Ⓐ Ⓑ Ⓒ Ⓓ Ⓔ
14 Ⓐ Ⓑ Ⓒ Ⓓ Ⓔ
15 Ⓐ Ⓑ Ⓒ Ⓓ Ⓔ
16 Ⓐ Ⓑ Ⓒ Ⓓ Ⓔ
17 Ⓐ Ⓑ Ⓒ Ⓓ Ⓔ
18 Ⓐ Ⓑ Ⓒ Ⓓ Ⓔ

PT41-S2-G1

1 Ⓐ Ⓑ Ⓒ Ⓓ Ⓔ
2 Ⓐ Ⓑ Ⓒ Ⓓ Ⓔ
3 Ⓐ Ⓑ Ⓒ Ⓓ Ⓔ
4 Ⓐ Ⓑ Ⓒ Ⓓ Ⓔ
5 Ⓐ Ⓑ Ⓒ Ⓓ Ⓔ
6 Ⓐ Ⓑ Ⓒ Ⓓ Ⓔ
7 Ⓐ Ⓑ Ⓒ Ⓓ Ⓔ

PT41-S2-G2

8 Ⓐ Ⓑ Ⓒ Ⓓ Ⓔ
9 Ⓐ Ⓑ Ⓒ Ⓓ Ⓔ
10 Ⓐ Ⓑ Ⓒ Ⓓ Ⓔ
11 Ⓐ Ⓑ Ⓒ Ⓓ Ⓔ
12 Ⓐ Ⓑ Ⓒ Ⓓ Ⓔ

PT42-S1-G3

13 Ⓐ Ⓑ Ⓒ Ⓓ Ⓔ
14 Ⓐ Ⓑ Ⓒ Ⓓ Ⓔ
15 Ⓐ Ⓑ Ⓒ Ⓓ Ⓔ
16 Ⓐ Ⓑ Ⓒ Ⓓ Ⓔ
17 Ⓐ Ⓑ Ⓒ Ⓓ Ⓔ
18 Ⓐ Ⓑ Ⓒ Ⓓ Ⓔ

PT43-S4-G1

1 Ⓐ Ⓑ Ⓒ Ⓓ Ⓔ
2 Ⓐ Ⓑ Ⓒ Ⓓ Ⓔ
3 Ⓐ Ⓑ Ⓒ Ⓓ Ⓔ
4 Ⓐ Ⓑ Ⓒ Ⓓ Ⓔ
5 Ⓐ Ⓑ Ⓒ Ⓓ Ⓔ

PT44-S3-G2

7 Ⓐ Ⓑ Ⓒ Ⓓ Ⓔ
8 Ⓐ Ⓑ Ⓒ Ⓓ Ⓔ
9 Ⓐ Ⓑ Ⓒ Ⓓ Ⓔ
10 Ⓐ Ⓑ Ⓒ Ⓓ Ⓔ
11 Ⓐ Ⓑ Ⓒ Ⓓ Ⓔ
12 Ⓐ Ⓑ Ⓒ Ⓓ Ⓔ

PT45-S3-G2

7 Ⓐ Ⓑ Ⓒ Ⓓ Ⓔ
8 Ⓐ Ⓑ Ⓒ Ⓓ Ⓔ
9 Ⓐ Ⓑ Ⓒ Ⓓ Ⓔ
10 Ⓐ Ⓑ Ⓒ Ⓓ Ⓔ
11 Ⓐ Ⓑ Ⓒ Ⓓ Ⓔ
12 Ⓐ Ⓑ Ⓒ Ⓓ Ⓔ

PT46-S4-G3

12 Ⓐ Ⓑ Ⓒ Ⓓ Ⓔ
13 Ⓐ Ⓑ Ⓒ Ⓓ Ⓔ
14 Ⓐ Ⓑ Ⓒ Ⓓ Ⓔ
15 Ⓐ Ⓑ Ⓒ Ⓓ Ⓔ
16 Ⓐ Ⓑ Ⓒ Ⓓ Ⓔ

PT48-S2-G4

18 Ⓐ Ⓑ Ⓒ Ⓓ Ⓔ
19 Ⓐ Ⓑ Ⓒ Ⓓ Ⓔ
20 Ⓐ Ⓑ Ⓒ Ⓓ Ⓔ
21 Ⓐ Ⓑ Ⓒ Ⓓ Ⓔ
22 Ⓐ Ⓑ Ⓒ Ⓓ Ⓔ

PT49-S1-G4

18 Ⓐ Ⓑ Ⓒ Ⓓ Ⓔ
19 Ⓐ Ⓑ Ⓒ Ⓓ Ⓔ
20 Ⓐ Ⓑ Ⓒ Ⓓ Ⓔ
21 Ⓐ Ⓑ Ⓒ Ⓓ Ⓔ
22 Ⓐ Ⓑ Ⓒ Ⓓ Ⓔ

PT51-S4-G1

1 Ⓐ Ⓑ Ⓒ Ⓓ Ⓔ
2 Ⓐ Ⓑ Ⓒ Ⓓ Ⓔ
3 Ⓐ Ⓑ Ⓒ Ⓓ Ⓔ
4 Ⓐ Ⓑ Ⓒ Ⓓ Ⓔ
5 Ⓐ Ⓑ Ⓒ Ⓓ Ⓔ

PT51-S4-G2

6 Ⓐ Ⓑ Ⓒ Ⓓ Ⓔ
7 Ⓐ Ⓑ Ⓒ Ⓓ Ⓔ
8 Ⓐ Ⓑ Ⓒ Ⓓ Ⓔ
9 Ⓐ Ⓑ Ⓒ Ⓓ Ⓔ
10 Ⓐ Ⓑ Ⓒ Ⓓ Ⓔ

V4, Pg. 19   PT52-S2-G4

18 Ⓐ Ⓑ Ⓒ Ⓓ Ⓔ
19 Ⓐ Ⓑ Ⓒ Ⓓ Ⓔ
20 Ⓐ Ⓑ Ⓒ Ⓓ Ⓔ
21 Ⓐ Ⓑ Ⓒ Ⓓ Ⓔ
22 Ⓐ Ⓑ Ⓒ Ⓓ Ⓔ
23 Ⓐ Ⓑ Ⓒ Ⓓ Ⓔ

V4, Pg. 52   PT53-S2-G1

1 Ⓐ Ⓑ Ⓒ Ⓓ Ⓔ
2 Ⓐ Ⓑ Ⓒ Ⓓ Ⓔ
3 Ⓐ Ⓑ Ⓒ Ⓓ Ⓔ
4 Ⓐ Ⓑ Ⓒ Ⓓ Ⓔ
5 Ⓐ Ⓑ Ⓒ Ⓓ Ⓔ

V4, Pg. 55   PT53-S2-G4

18 Ⓐ Ⓑ Ⓒ Ⓓ Ⓔ
19 Ⓐ Ⓑ Ⓒ Ⓓ Ⓔ
20 Ⓐ Ⓑ Ⓒ Ⓓ Ⓔ
21 Ⓐ Ⓑ Ⓒ Ⓓ Ⓔ
22 Ⓐ Ⓑ Ⓒ Ⓓ Ⓔ
23 Ⓐ Ⓑ Ⓒ Ⓓ Ⓔ

V4, Pg. 99   PT54-S3-G4

18 Ⓐ Ⓑ Ⓒ Ⓓ Ⓔ
19 Ⓐ Ⓑ Ⓒ Ⓓ Ⓔ
20 Ⓐ Ⓑ Ⓒ Ⓓ Ⓔ
21 Ⓐ Ⓑ Ⓒ Ⓓ Ⓔ
22 Ⓐ Ⓑ Ⓒ Ⓓ Ⓔ
23 Ⓐ Ⓑ Ⓒ Ⓓ Ⓔ

V4, Pg. 141   PT55-S4-G2

7 Ⓐ Ⓑ Ⓒ Ⓓ Ⓔ
8 Ⓐ Ⓑ Ⓒ Ⓓ Ⓔ
9 Ⓐ Ⓑ Ⓒ Ⓓ Ⓔ
10 Ⓐ Ⓑ Ⓒ Ⓓ Ⓔ
11 Ⓐ Ⓑ Ⓒ Ⓓ Ⓔ
12 Ⓐ Ⓑ Ⓒ Ⓓ Ⓔ

V4, Pg. 152   PT56-S1-G1

1 Ⓐ Ⓑ Ⓒ Ⓓ Ⓔ
2 Ⓐ Ⓑ Ⓒ Ⓓ Ⓔ
3 Ⓐ Ⓑ Ⓒ Ⓓ Ⓔ
4 Ⓐ Ⓑ Ⓒ Ⓓ Ⓔ
5 Ⓐ Ⓑ Ⓒ Ⓓ Ⓔ
6 Ⓐ Ⓑ Ⓒ Ⓓ Ⓔ

V4, Pg. 191   PT57-S1-G4

18 Ⓐ Ⓑ Ⓒ Ⓓ Ⓔ
19 Ⓐ Ⓑ Ⓒ Ⓓ Ⓔ
20 Ⓐ Ⓑ Ⓒ Ⓓ Ⓔ
21 Ⓐ Ⓑ Ⓒ Ⓓ Ⓔ
22 Ⓐ Ⓑ Ⓒ Ⓓ Ⓔ
23 Ⓐ Ⓑ Ⓒ Ⓓ Ⓔ

V4, Pg. 260   PT59-S1-G1

1 Ⓐ Ⓑ Ⓒ Ⓓ Ⓔ
2 Ⓐ Ⓑ Ⓒ Ⓓ Ⓔ
3 Ⓐ Ⓑ Ⓒ Ⓓ Ⓔ
4 Ⓐ Ⓑ Ⓒ Ⓓ Ⓔ
5 Ⓐ Ⓑ Ⓒ Ⓓ Ⓔ

V4, Pg. 263   PT59-S1-G4

17 Ⓐ Ⓑ Ⓒ Ⓓ Ⓔ
18 Ⓐ Ⓑ Ⓒ Ⓓ Ⓔ
19 Ⓐ Ⓑ Ⓒ Ⓓ Ⓔ
20 Ⓐ Ⓑ Ⓒ Ⓓ Ⓔ
21 Ⓐ Ⓑ Ⓒ Ⓓ Ⓔ
22 Ⓐ Ⓑ Ⓒ Ⓓ Ⓔ
23 Ⓐ Ⓑ Ⓒ Ⓓ Ⓔ

V4, Pg. 307   PT60-S2-G4

18 Ⓐ Ⓑ Ⓒ Ⓓ Ⓔ
19 Ⓐ Ⓑ Ⓒ Ⓓ Ⓔ
20 Ⓐ Ⓑ Ⓒ Ⓓ Ⓔ
21 Ⓐ Ⓑ Ⓒ Ⓓ Ⓔ
22 Ⓐ Ⓑ Ⓒ Ⓓ Ⓔ
23 Ⓐ Ⓑ Ⓒ Ⓓ Ⓔ

V4, Pg. 348   PT61-S3-G1

1 Ⓐ Ⓑ Ⓒ Ⓓ Ⓔ
2 Ⓐ Ⓑ Ⓒ Ⓓ Ⓔ
3 Ⓐ Ⓑ Ⓒ Ⓓ Ⓔ
4 Ⓐ Ⓑ Ⓒ Ⓓ Ⓔ
5 Ⓐ Ⓑ Ⓒ Ⓓ Ⓔ

V4, Pg. 349   PT61-S3-G2

6 Ⓐ Ⓑ Ⓒ Ⓓ Ⓔ
7 Ⓐ Ⓑ Ⓒ Ⓓ Ⓔ
8 Ⓐ Ⓑ Ⓒ Ⓓ Ⓔ
9 Ⓐ Ⓑ Ⓒ Ⓓ Ⓔ
10 Ⓐ Ⓑ Ⓒ Ⓓ Ⓔ
11 Ⓐ Ⓑ Ⓒ Ⓓ Ⓔ

V4, Pg. 350   PT61-S3-G3

12 Ⓐ Ⓑ Ⓒ Ⓓ Ⓔ
13 Ⓐ Ⓑ Ⓒ Ⓓ Ⓔ
14 Ⓐ Ⓑ Ⓒ Ⓓ Ⓔ
15 Ⓐ Ⓑ Ⓒ Ⓓ Ⓔ
16 Ⓐ Ⓑ Ⓒ Ⓓ Ⓔ
17 Ⓐ Ⓑ Ⓒ Ⓓ Ⓔ

V5, Pg. 24   PT62-S3-G1

1 Ⓐ Ⓑ Ⓒ Ⓓ Ⓔ
2 Ⓐ Ⓑ Ⓒ Ⓓ Ⓔ
3 Ⓐ Ⓑ Ⓒ Ⓓ Ⓔ
4 Ⓐ Ⓑ Ⓒ Ⓓ Ⓔ
5 Ⓐ Ⓑ Ⓒ Ⓓ Ⓔ
6 Ⓐ Ⓑ Ⓒ Ⓓ Ⓔ

V5, Pg. 25   PT62-S3-G2

7 Ⓐ Ⓑ Ⓒ Ⓓ Ⓔ
8 Ⓐ Ⓑ Ⓒ Ⓓ Ⓔ
9 Ⓐ Ⓑ Ⓒ Ⓓ Ⓔ
10 Ⓐ Ⓑ Ⓒ Ⓓ Ⓔ
11 Ⓐ Ⓑ Ⓒ Ⓓ Ⓔ
12 Ⓐ Ⓑ Ⓒ Ⓓ Ⓔ
13 Ⓐ Ⓑ Ⓒ Ⓓ Ⓔ

V5, Pg. 26   PT62-S3-G3

14 Ⓐ Ⓑ Ⓒ Ⓓ Ⓔ
15 Ⓐ Ⓑ Ⓒ Ⓓ Ⓔ
16 Ⓐ Ⓑ Ⓒ Ⓓ Ⓔ
17 Ⓐ Ⓑ Ⓒ Ⓓ Ⓔ
18 Ⓐ Ⓑ Ⓒ Ⓓ Ⓔ

V5, Pg. 54   PT63-S2-G3

11 Ⓐ Ⓑ Ⓒ Ⓓ Ⓔ
12 Ⓐ Ⓑ Ⓒ Ⓓ Ⓔ
13 Ⓐ Ⓑ Ⓒ Ⓓ Ⓔ
14 Ⓐ Ⓑ Ⓒ Ⓓ Ⓔ
15 Ⓐ Ⓑ Ⓒ Ⓓ Ⓔ
16 Ⓐ Ⓑ Ⓒ Ⓓ Ⓔ
17 Ⓐ Ⓑ Ⓒ Ⓓ Ⓔ

V5, Pg. 88   PT64-S2-G1

1 Ⓐ Ⓑ Ⓒ Ⓓ Ⓔ
2 Ⓐ Ⓑ Ⓒ Ⓓ Ⓔ
3 Ⓐ Ⓑ Ⓒ Ⓓ Ⓔ
4 Ⓐ Ⓑ Ⓒ Ⓓ Ⓔ
5 Ⓐ Ⓑ Ⓒ Ⓓ Ⓔ
6 Ⓐ Ⓑ Ⓒ Ⓓ Ⓔ

V5, Pg. 89   PT64-S2-G2

7 Ⓐ Ⓑ Ⓒ Ⓓ Ⓔ
8 Ⓐ Ⓑ Ⓒ Ⓓ Ⓔ
9 Ⓐ Ⓑ Ⓒ Ⓓ Ⓔ
10 Ⓐ Ⓑ Ⓒ Ⓓ Ⓔ
11 Ⓐ Ⓑ Ⓒ Ⓓ Ⓔ
12 Ⓐ Ⓑ Ⓒ Ⓓ Ⓔ

V5, Pg. 90   PT64-S2-G3

13 Ⓐ Ⓑ Ⓒ Ⓓ Ⓔ
14 Ⓐ Ⓑ Ⓒ Ⓓ Ⓔ
15 Ⓐ Ⓑ Ⓒ Ⓓ Ⓔ
16 Ⓐ Ⓑ Ⓒ Ⓓ Ⓔ
17 Ⓐ Ⓑ Ⓒ Ⓓ Ⓔ
18 Ⓐ Ⓑ Ⓒ Ⓓ Ⓔ

V5, Pg. 91   PT64-S2-G4

19 Ⓐ Ⓑ Ⓒ Ⓓ Ⓔ
20 Ⓐ Ⓑ Ⓒ Ⓓ Ⓔ
21 Ⓐ Ⓑ Ⓒ Ⓓ Ⓔ
22 Ⓐ Ⓑ Ⓒ Ⓓ Ⓔ
23 Ⓐ Ⓑ Ⓒ Ⓓ Ⓔ

V5, Pg. 125   PT65-S2-G2

6 Ⓐ Ⓑ Ⓒ Ⓓ Ⓔ
7 Ⓐ Ⓑ Ⓒ Ⓓ Ⓔ
8 Ⓐ Ⓑ Ⓒ Ⓓ Ⓔ
9 Ⓐ Ⓑ Ⓒ Ⓓ Ⓔ
10 Ⓐ Ⓑ Ⓒ Ⓓ Ⓔ
11 Ⓐ Ⓑ Ⓒ Ⓓ Ⓔ

V5, Pg. 127   PT65-S2-G4

17 Ⓐ Ⓑ Ⓒ Ⓓ Ⓔ
18 Ⓐ Ⓑ Ⓒ Ⓓ Ⓔ
19 Ⓐ Ⓑ Ⓒ Ⓓ Ⓔ
20 Ⓐ Ⓑ Ⓒ Ⓓ Ⓔ
21 Ⓐ Ⓑ Ⓒ Ⓓ Ⓔ
22 Ⓐ Ⓑ Ⓒ Ⓓ Ⓔ
23 Ⓐ Ⓑ Ⓒ Ⓓ Ⓔ

V5, Pg. 168   PT66-S3-G1

1 Ⓐ Ⓑ Ⓒ Ⓓ Ⓔ
2 Ⓐ Ⓑ Ⓒ Ⓓ Ⓔ
3 Ⓐ Ⓑ Ⓒ Ⓓ Ⓔ
4 Ⓐ Ⓑ Ⓒ Ⓓ Ⓔ
5 Ⓐ Ⓑ Ⓒ Ⓓ Ⓔ

V5, Pg. 170   PT66-S3-G2

6 Ⓐ Ⓑ Ⓒ Ⓓ Ⓔ
7 Ⓐ Ⓑ Ⓒ Ⓓ Ⓔ
8 Ⓐ Ⓑ Ⓒ Ⓓ Ⓔ
9 Ⓐ Ⓑ Ⓒ Ⓓ Ⓔ
10 Ⓐ Ⓑ Ⓒ Ⓓ Ⓔ
11 Ⓐ Ⓑ Ⓒ Ⓓ Ⓔ

V5, Pg. 172   PT66-S3-G3

12 Ⓐ Ⓑ Ⓒ Ⓓ Ⓔ
13 Ⓐ Ⓑ Ⓒ Ⓓ Ⓔ
14 Ⓐ Ⓑ Ⓒ Ⓓ Ⓔ
15 Ⓐ Ⓑ Ⓒ Ⓓ Ⓔ
16 Ⓐ Ⓑ Ⓒ Ⓓ Ⓔ
17 Ⓐ Ⓑ Ⓒ Ⓓ Ⓔ
18 Ⓐ Ⓑ Ⓒ Ⓓ Ⓔ

V5, Pg. 174   PT66-S3-G4

19 Ⓐ Ⓑ Ⓒ Ⓓ Ⓔ
20 Ⓐ Ⓑ Ⓒ Ⓓ Ⓔ
21 Ⓐ Ⓑ Ⓒ Ⓓ Ⓔ
22 Ⓐ Ⓑ Ⓒ Ⓓ Ⓔ
23 Ⓐ Ⓑ Ⓒ Ⓓ Ⓔ

V5, Pg. 210   PT67-S3-G2

6   Ⓐ Ⓑ Ⓒ Ⓓ Ⓔ
7   Ⓐ Ⓑ Ⓒ Ⓓ Ⓔ
8   Ⓐ Ⓑ Ⓒ Ⓓ Ⓔ
9   Ⓐ Ⓑ Ⓒ Ⓓ Ⓔ
10 Ⓐ Ⓑ Ⓒ Ⓓ Ⓔ
11 Ⓐ Ⓑ Ⓒ Ⓓ Ⓔ
12 Ⓐ Ⓑ Ⓒ Ⓓ Ⓔ

V5, Pg. 212   PT67-S3-G3

13 Ⓐ Ⓑ Ⓒ Ⓓ Ⓔ
14 Ⓐ Ⓑ Ⓒ Ⓓ Ⓔ
15 Ⓐ Ⓑ Ⓒ Ⓓ Ⓔ
16 Ⓐ Ⓑ Ⓒ Ⓓ Ⓔ
17 Ⓐ Ⓑ Ⓒ Ⓓ Ⓔ

V5, Pg. 284   PT69-S2-G3

12 Ⓐ Ⓑ Ⓒ Ⓓ Ⓔ
13 Ⓐ Ⓑ Ⓒ Ⓓ Ⓔ
14 Ⓐ Ⓑ Ⓒ Ⓓ Ⓔ
15 Ⓐ Ⓑ Ⓒ Ⓓ Ⓔ
16 Ⓐ Ⓑ Ⓒ Ⓓ Ⓔ
17 Ⓐ Ⓑ Ⓒ Ⓓ Ⓔ

PT72, Pg. 36 PT72-S4-G2

7   Ⓐ Ⓑ Ⓒ Ⓓ Ⓔ
8   Ⓐ Ⓑ Ⓒ Ⓓ Ⓔ
9   Ⓐ Ⓑ Ⓒ Ⓓ Ⓔ
10 Ⓐ Ⓑ Ⓒ Ⓓ Ⓔ
11 Ⓐ Ⓑ Ⓒ Ⓓ Ⓔ
12 Ⓐ Ⓑ Ⓒ Ⓓ Ⓔ

PT72, Pg. 40 PT72-S4-G4

19 Ⓐ Ⓑ Ⓒ Ⓓ Ⓔ
20 Ⓐ Ⓑ Ⓒ Ⓓ Ⓔ
21 Ⓐ Ⓑ Ⓒ Ⓓ Ⓔ
22 Ⓐ Ⓑ Ⓒ Ⓓ Ⓔ
23 Ⓐ Ⓑ Ⓒ Ⓓ Ⓔ

PT73, Pg. 26 PT73-S3-G1

1   Ⓐ Ⓑ Ⓒ Ⓓ Ⓔ
2   Ⓐ Ⓑ Ⓒ Ⓓ Ⓔ
3   Ⓐ Ⓑ Ⓒ Ⓓ Ⓔ
4   Ⓐ Ⓑ Ⓒ Ⓓ Ⓔ
5   Ⓐ Ⓑ Ⓒ Ⓓ Ⓔ
6   Ⓐ Ⓑ Ⓒ Ⓓ Ⓔ
7   Ⓐ Ⓑ Ⓒ Ⓓ Ⓔ

PT73, Pg. 30 PT73-S3-G3

14 Ⓐ Ⓑ Ⓒ Ⓓ Ⓔ
15 Ⓐ Ⓑ Ⓒ Ⓓ Ⓔ
16 Ⓐ Ⓑ Ⓒ Ⓓ Ⓔ
17 Ⓐ Ⓑ Ⓒ Ⓓ Ⓔ
18 Ⓐ Ⓑ Ⓒ Ⓓ Ⓔ

PT74, Pg. 18 PT74-S2-G1

1   Ⓐ Ⓑ Ⓒ Ⓓ Ⓔ
2   Ⓐ Ⓑ Ⓒ Ⓓ Ⓔ
3   Ⓐ Ⓑ Ⓒ Ⓓ Ⓔ
4   Ⓐ Ⓑ Ⓒ Ⓓ Ⓔ
5   Ⓐ Ⓑ Ⓒ Ⓓ Ⓔ

PT74, Pg. 20 PT74-S2-G2

6   Ⓐ Ⓑ Ⓒ Ⓓ Ⓔ
7   Ⓐ Ⓑ Ⓒ Ⓓ Ⓔ
8   Ⓐ Ⓑ Ⓒ Ⓓ Ⓔ
9   Ⓐ Ⓑ Ⓒ Ⓓ Ⓔ
10 Ⓐ Ⓑ Ⓒ Ⓓ Ⓔ

PT75, Pg. 36 PT75-S4-G2

7   Ⓐ Ⓑ Ⓒ Ⓓ Ⓔ
8   Ⓐ Ⓑ Ⓒ Ⓓ Ⓔ
9   Ⓐ Ⓑ Ⓒ Ⓓ Ⓔ
10 Ⓐ Ⓑ Ⓒ Ⓓ Ⓔ
11 Ⓐ Ⓑ Ⓒ Ⓓ Ⓔ

PT76, Pg. 26 PT76-S3-G1

1   Ⓐ Ⓑ Ⓒ Ⓓ Ⓔ
2   Ⓐ Ⓑ Ⓒ Ⓓ Ⓔ
3   Ⓐ Ⓑ Ⓒ Ⓓ Ⓔ
4   Ⓐ Ⓑ Ⓒ Ⓓ Ⓔ
5   Ⓐ Ⓑ Ⓒ Ⓓ Ⓔ
6   Ⓐ Ⓑ Ⓒ Ⓓ Ⓔ

PT76, Pg. 28 PT76-S3-G2

7   Ⓐ Ⓑ Ⓒ Ⓓ Ⓔ
8   Ⓐ Ⓑ Ⓒ Ⓓ Ⓔ
9   Ⓐ Ⓑ Ⓒ Ⓓ Ⓔ
10 Ⓐ Ⓑ Ⓒ Ⓓ Ⓔ
11 Ⓐ Ⓑ Ⓒ Ⓓ Ⓔ
12 Ⓐ Ⓑ Ⓒ Ⓓ Ⓔ
13 Ⓐ Ⓑ Ⓒ Ⓓ Ⓔ

PT76, Pg. 30 PT76-S3-G3

14 Ⓐ Ⓑ Ⓒ Ⓓ Ⓔ
15 Ⓐ Ⓑ Ⓒ Ⓓ Ⓔ
16 Ⓐ Ⓑ Ⓒ Ⓓ Ⓔ
17 Ⓐ Ⓑ Ⓒ Ⓓ Ⓔ
18 Ⓐ Ⓑ Ⓒ Ⓓ Ⓔ

Limited Solutions

J07, Pg. 2   J07-S1-G1

1   Ⓐ Ⓑ Ⓒ Ⓓ Ⓔ
2   Ⓐ Ⓑ Ⓒ Ⓓ Ⓔ
3   Ⓐ Ⓑ Ⓒ Ⓓ Ⓔ
4   Ⓐ Ⓑ Ⓒ Ⓓ Ⓔ
5   Ⓐ Ⓑ Ⓒ Ⓓ Ⓔ

PT4-S3-G2

7   Ⓐ Ⓑ Ⓒ Ⓓ Ⓔ
8   Ⓐ Ⓑ Ⓒ Ⓓ Ⓔ
9   Ⓐ Ⓑ Ⓒ Ⓓ Ⓔ
10 Ⓐ Ⓑ Ⓒ Ⓓ Ⓔ
11 Ⓐ Ⓑ Ⓒ Ⓓ Ⓔ

PT4-S3-G4

18 Ⓐ Ⓑ Ⓒ Ⓓ Ⓔ
19 Ⓐ Ⓑ Ⓒ Ⓓ Ⓔ
20 Ⓐ Ⓑ Ⓒ Ⓓ Ⓔ
21 Ⓐ Ⓑ Ⓒ Ⓓ Ⓔ
22 Ⓐ Ⓑ Ⓒ Ⓓ Ⓔ
23 Ⓐ Ⓑ Ⓒ Ⓓ Ⓔ
24 Ⓐ Ⓑ Ⓒ Ⓓ Ⓔ

PT8-S2-G2

6   Ⓐ Ⓑ Ⓒ Ⓓ Ⓔ
7   Ⓐ Ⓑ Ⓒ Ⓓ Ⓔ
8   Ⓐ Ⓑ Ⓒ Ⓓ Ⓔ
9   Ⓐ Ⓑ Ⓒ Ⓓ Ⓔ
10 Ⓐ Ⓑ Ⓒ Ⓓ Ⓔ
11 Ⓐ Ⓑ Ⓒ Ⓓ Ⓔ
12 Ⓐ Ⓑ Ⓒ Ⓓ Ⓔ

V1, Pg. 68   PT9-S3-G3

14 Ⓐ Ⓑ Ⓒ Ⓓ Ⓔ
15 Ⓐ Ⓑ Ⓒ Ⓓ Ⓔ
16 Ⓐ Ⓑ Ⓒ Ⓓ Ⓔ
17 Ⓐ Ⓑ Ⓒ Ⓓ Ⓔ
18 Ⓐ Ⓑ Ⓒ Ⓓ Ⓔ

V1, Pg. 121 PT11-S1-G4

20 Ⓐ Ⓑ Ⓒ Ⓓ Ⓔ
21 Ⓐ Ⓑ Ⓒ Ⓓ Ⓔ
22 Ⓐ Ⓑ Ⓒ Ⓓ Ⓔ
23 Ⓐ Ⓑ Ⓒ Ⓓ Ⓔ
24 Ⓐ Ⓑ Ⓒ Ⓓ Ⓔ

V1, Pg. 163 PT12-S2-G4

18 Ⓐ Ⓑ Ⓒ Ⓓ Ⓔ
19 Ⓐ Ⓑ Ⓒ Ⓓ Ⓔ
20 Ⓐ Ⓑ Ⓒ Ⓓ Ⓔ
21 Ⓐ Ⓑ Ⓒ Ⓓ Ⓔ
22 Ⓐ Ⓑ Ⓒ Ⓓ Ⓔ
23 Ⓐ Ⓑ Ⓒ Ⓓ Ⓔ
24 Ⓐ Ⓑ Ⓒ Ⓓ Ⓔ

PT17-S1-G4

18 Ⓐ Ⓑ Ⓒ Ⓓ Ⓔ
19 Ⓐ Ⓑ Ⓒ Ⓓ Ⓔ
20 Ⓐ Ⓑ Ⓒ Ⓓ Ⓔ
21 Ⓐ Ⓑ Ⓒ Ⓓ Ⓔ
22 Ⓐ Ⓑ Ⓒ Ⓓ Ⓔ
23 Ⓐ Ⓑ Ⓒ Ⓓ Ⓔ
24 Ⓐ Ⓑ Ⓒ Ⓓ Ⓔ

V2, Pg. 210 PT24-S4-G1

1 Ⓐ Ⓑ Ⓒ Ⓓ Ⓔ
2 Ⓐ Ⓑ Ⓒ Ⓓ Ⓔ
3 Ⓐ Ⓑ Ⓒ Ⓓ Ⓔ
4 Ⓐ Ⓑ Ⓒ Ⓓ Ⓔ
5 Ⓐ Ⓑ Ⓒ Ⓓ Ⓔ

V2, Pg. 213 PT24-S4-G4

18 Ⓐ Ⓑ Ⓒ Ⓓ Ⓔ
19 Ⓐ Ⓑ Ⓒ Ⓓ Ⓔ
20 Ⓐ Ⓑ Ⓒ Ⓓ Ⓔ
21 Ⓐ Ⓑ Ⓒ Ⓓ Ⓔ
22 Ⓐ Ⓑ Ⓒ Ⓓ Ⓔ
23 Ⓐ Ⓑ Ⓒ Ⓓ Ⓔ

V2, Pg. 257 PT26-S1-G4

19 Ⓐ Ⓑ Ⓒ Ⓓ Ⓔ
20 Ⓐ Ⓑ Ⓒ Ⓓ Ⓔ
21 Ⓐ Ⓑ Ⓒ Ⓓ Ⓔ
22 Ⓐ Ⓑ Ⓒ Ⓓ Ⓔ
23 Ⓐ Ⓑ Ⓒ Ⓓ Ⓔ
24 Ⓐ Ⓑ Ⓒ Ⓓ Ⓔ

V2, Pg. 299 PT27-S2-G4

20 Ⓐ Ⓑ Ⓒ Ⓓ Ⓔ
21 Ⓐ Ⓑ Ⓒ Ⓓ Ⓔ
22 Ⓐ Ⓑ Ⓒ Ⓓ Ⓔ
23 Ⓐ Ⓑ Ⓒ Ⓓ Ⓔ
24 Ⓐ Ⓑ Ⓒ Ⓓ Ⓔ

V2, Pg. 333 PT28-S2-G4

19 Ⓐ Ⓑ Ⓒ Ⓓ Ⓔ
20 Ⓐ Ⓑ Ⓒ Ⓓ Ⓔ
21 Ⓐ Ⓑ Ⓒ Ⓓ Ⓔ
22 Ⓐ Ⓑ Ⓒ Ⓓ Ⓔ
23 Ⓐ Ⓑ Ⓒ Ⓓ Ⓔ

V3, Pg. 211 PT34-S4-G2

8   Ⓐ Ⓑ Ⓒ Ⓓ Ⓔ
9   Ⓐ Ⓑ Ⓒ Ⓓ Ⓔ
10 Ⓐ Ⓑ Ⓒ Ⓓ Ⓔ
11 Ⓐ Ⓑ Ⓒ Ⓓ Ⓔ
12 Ⓐ Ⓑ Ⓒ Ⓓ Ⓔ

V3, Pg. 239 PT35-S3-G4

18 Ⓐ Ⓑ Ⓒ Ⓓ Ⓔ
19 Ⓐ Ⓑ Ⓒ Ⓓ Ⓔ
20 Ⓐ Ⓑ Ⓒ Ⓓ Ⓔ
21 Ⓐ Ⓑ Ⓒ Ⓓ Ⓔ
22 Ⓐ Ⓑ Ⓒ Ⓓ Ⓔ
23 Ⓐ Ⓑ Ⓒ Ⓓ Ⓔ

V4, Pg. 154 PT56-S1-G3

12 Ⓐ Ⓑ Ⓒ Ⓓ Ⓔ
13 Ⓐ Ⓑ Ⓒ Ⓓ Ⓔ
14 Ⓐ Ⓑ Ⓒ Ⓓ Ⓔ
15 Ⓐ Ⓑ Ⓒ Ⓓ Ⓔ
16 Ⓐ Ⓑ Ⓒ Ⓓ Ⓔ

V4, Pg. 306 PT60-S2-G3

13 Ⓐ Ⓑ Ⓒ Ⓓ Ⓔ
14 Ⓐ Ⓑ Ⓒ Ⓓ Ⓔ
15 Ⓐ Ⓑ Ⓒ Ⓓ Ⓔ
16 Ⓐ Ⓑ Ⓒ Ⓓ Ⓔ
17 Ⓐ Ⓑ Ⓒ Ⓓ Ⓔ

PT77, Pg. 26 PT77-S3-G1

1 Ⓐ Ⓑ Ⓒ Ⓓ Ⓔ
2 Ⓐ Ⓑ Ⓒ Ⓓ Ⓔ
3 Ⓐ Ⓑ Ⓒ Ⓓ Ⓔ
4 Ⓐ Ⓑ Ⓒ Ⓓ Ⓔ
5 Ⓐ Ⓑ Ⓒ Ⓓ Ⓔ

Must Be True

J07, Pg. 21	J07-S3-Q22	Ⓐ Ⓑ Ⓒ Ⓓ Ⓔ		PT4-S1-Q12	Ⓐ Ⓑ Ⓒ Ⓓ Ⓔ
SP1, Pg. 73	PTA-S1-Q19	Ⓐ Ⓑ Ⓒ Ⓓ Ⓔ		PT4-S1-Q15	Ⓐ Ⓑ Ⓒ Ⓓ Ⓔ
SP1, Pg. 94	PTA-S4-Q22	Ⓐ Ⓑ Ⓒ Ⓓ Ⓔ		PT4-S4-Q5	Ⓐ Ⓑ Ⓒ Ⓓ Ⓔ
SP1, Pg. 95	PTA-S4-Q24	Ⓐ Ⓑ Ⓒ Ⓓ Ⓔ		PT4-S4-Q7	Ⓐ Ⓑ Ⓒ Ⓓ Ⓔ
SP1, Pg. 187	PTB-S1-Q6	Ⓐ Ⓑ Ⓒ Ⓓ Ⓔ		PT4-S4-Q9	Ⓐ Ⓑ Ⓒ Ⓓ Ⓔ
SP1, Pg. 210	PTB-S4-Q17	Ⓐ Ⓑ Ⓒ Ⓓ Ⓔ		PT4-S4-Q17	Ⓐ Ⓑ Ⓒ Ⓓ Ⓔ
SP2, Pg. 365	PTC2-S3-Q13	Ⓐ Ⓑ Ⓒ Ⓓ Ⓔ		PT4-S4-Q21	Ⓐ Ⓑ Ⓒ Ⓓ Ⓔ
	PT1-S3-Q4	Ⓐ Ⓑ Ⓒ Ⓓ Ⓔ		PT5-S1-Q25	Ⓐ Ⓑ Ⓒ Ⓓ Ⓔ
	PT1-S3-Q7	Ⓐ Ⓑ Ⓒ Ⓓ Ⓔ		PT5-S3-Q12	Ⓐ Ⓑ Ⓒ Ⓓ Ⓔ
	PT1-S3-Q14	Ⓐ Ⓑ Ⓒ Ⓓ Ⓔ		PT5-S3-Q22	Ⓐ Ⓑ Ⓒ Ⓓ Ⓔ
	PT1-S3-Q16	Ⓐ Ⓑ Ⓒ Ⓓ Ⓔ		PT5-S3-Q23	Ⓐ Ⓑ Ⓒ Ⓓ Ⓔ
	PT1-S4-Q2	Ⓐ Ⓑ Ⓒ Ⓓ Ⓔ		PT6-S2-Q3	Ⓐ Ⓑ Ⓒ Ⓓ Ⓔ
	PT1-S4-Q6	Ⓐ Ⓑ Ⓒ Ⓓ Ⓔ		PT6-S2-Q6	Ⓐ Ⓑ Ⓒ Ⓓ Ⓔ
	PT1-S4-Q9	Ⓐ Ⓑ Ⓒ Ⓓ Ⓔ		PT6-S2-Q10	Ⓐ Ⓑ Ⓒ Ⓓ Ⓔ
	PT1-S4-Q11	Ⓐ Ⓑ Ⓒ Ⓓ Ⓔ		PT6-S2-Q11	Ⓐ Ⓑ Ⓒ Ⓓ Ⓔ
	PT1-S4-Q14	Ⓐ Ⓑ Ⓒ Ⓓ Ⓔ		PT6-S2-Q13	Ⓐ Ⓑ Ⓒ Ⓓ Ⓔ
	PT1-S4-Q21	Ⓐ Ⓑ Ⓒ Ⓓ Ⓔ		PT6-S2-Q23	Ⓐ Ⓑ Ⓒ Ⓓ Ⓔ
	PT2-S2-Q9	Ⓐ Ⓑ Ⓒ Ⓓ Ⓔ		PT6-S3-Q1	Ⓐ Ⓑ Ⓒ Ⓓ Ⓔ
	PT2-S2-Q11	Ⓐ Ⓑ Ⓒ Ⓓ Ⓔ		PT6-S3-Q11	Ⓐ Ⓑ Ⓒ Ⓓ Ⓔ
	PT2-S2-Q13	Ⓐ Ⓑ Ⓒ Ⓓ Ⓔ	V1, Pg. 16	PT7-S1-Q3	Ⓐ Ⓑ Ⓒ Ⓓ Ⓔ
	PT2-S2-Q16	Ⓐ Ⓑ Ⓒ Ⓓ Ⓔ	V1, Pg. 19	PT7-S1-Q12	Ⓐ Ⓑ Ⓒ Ⓓ Ⓔ
	PT2-S2-Q21	Ⓐ Ⓑ Ⓒ Ⓓ Ⓔ	V1, Pg. 38	PT7-S4-Q7	Ⓐ Ⓑ Ⓒ Ⓓ Ⓔ
	PT2-S2-Q24	Ⓐ Ⓑ Ⓒ Ⓓ Ⓔ	V1, Pg. 40	PT7-S4-Q15	Ⓐ Ⓑ Ⓒ Ⓓ Ⓔ
	PT2-S4-Q18	Ⓐ Ⓑ Ⓒ Ⓓ Ⓔ		PT8-S1-Q9	Ⓐ Ⓑ Ⓒ Ⓓ Ⓔ
	PT2-S4-Q21	Ⓐ Ⓑ Ⓒ Ⓓ Ⓔ		PT8-S1-Q19	Ⓐ Ⓑ Ⓒ Ⓓ Ⓔ
	PT2-S4-Q23	Ⓐ Ⓑ Ⓒ Ⓓ Ⓔ		PT8-S1-Q24	Ⓐ Ⓑ Ⓒ Ⓓ Ⓔ
	PT3-S2-Q4	Ⓐ Ⓑ Ⓒ Ⓓ Ⓔ		PT8-S4-Q5	Ⓐ Ⓑ Ⓒ Ⓓ Ⓔ
	PT3-S2-Q7	Ⓐ Ⓑ Ⓒ Ⓓ Ⓔ	V1, Pg. 61	PT9-S2-Q13	Ⓐ Ⓑ Ⓒ Ⓓ Ⓔ
	PT3-S2-Q10	Ⓐ Ⓑ Ⓒ Ⓓ Ⓔ	V1, Pg. 62	PT9-S2-Q16	Ⓐ Ⓑ Ⓒ Ⓓ Ⓔ
	PT3-S2-Q22	Ⓐ Ⓑ Ⓒ Ⓓ Ⓔ	V1, Pg. 70	PT9-S4-Q4	Ⓐ Ⓑ Ⓒ Ⓓ Ⓔ
	PT3-S4-Q10	Ⓐ Ⓑ Ⓒ Ⓓ Ⓔ	V1, Pg. 73	PT9-S4-Q13	Ⓐ Ⓑ Ⓒ Ⓓ Ⓔ
	PT3-S4-Q13	Ⓐ Ⓑ Ⓒ Ⓓ Ⓔ	V1, Pg. 74	PT9-S4-Q16	Ⓐ Ⓑ Ⓒ Ⓓ Ⓔ
	PT3-S4-Q22	Ⓐ Ⓑ Ⓒ Ⓓ Ⓔ	V1, Pg. 76	PT9-S4-Q23	Ⓐ Ⓑ Ⓒ Ⓓ Ⓔ
	PT4-S1-Q7	Ⓐ Ⓑ Ⓒ Ⓓ Ⓔ	V1, Pg. 88	PT10-S1-Q18	Ⓐ Ⓑ Ⓒ Ⓓ Ⓔ

V1, Pg. 110	PT10-S4-Q22	Ⓐ Ⓑ Ⓒ Ⓓ Ⓔ	V2, Pg. 25	PT19-S2-Q17	Ⓐ Ⓑ Ⓒ Ⓓ Ⓔ
V1, Pg. 123	PT11-S2-Q7	Ⓐ Ⓑ Ⓒ Ⓓ Ⓔ	V2, Pg. 51	PT20-S1-Q7	Ⓐ Ⓑ Ⓒ Ⓓ Ⓔ
V1, Pg. 125	PT11-S2-Q12	Ⓐ Ⓑ Ⓒ Ⓓ Ⓔ	V2, Pg. 57	PT20-S1-Q24	Ⓐ Ⓑ Ⓒ Ⓓ Ⓔ
V1, Pg. 126	PT11-S2-Q16	Ⓐ Ⓑ Ⓒ Ⓓ Ⓔ	V2, Pg. 71	PT20-S4-Q6	Ⓐ Ⓑ Ⓒ Ⓓ Ⓔ
V1, Pg. 142	PT11-S4-Q16	Ⓐ Ⓑ Ⓒ Ⓓ Ⓔ	V2, Pg. 75	PT20-S4-Q19	Ⓐ Ⓑ Ⓒ Ⓓ Ⓔ
V1, Pg. 154	PT12-S1-Q8	Ⓐ Ⓑ Ⓒ Ⓓ Ⓔ	V2, Pg. 90	PT21-S2-Q8	Ⓐ Ⓑ Ⓒ Ⓓ Ⓔ
V1, Pg. 157	PT12-S1-Q21	Ⓐ Ⓑ Ⓒ Ⓓ Ⓔ	V2, Pg. 90	PT21-S2-Q10	Ⓐ Ⓑ Ⓒ Ⓓ Ⓔ
V1, Pg. 159	PT12-S1-Q25	Ⓐ Ⓑ Ⓒ Ⓓ Ⓔ	V2, Pg. 93	PT21-S2-Q18	Ⓐ Ⓑ Ⓒ Ⓓ Ⓔ
V1, Pg. 192	PT13-S2-Q10	Ⓐ Ⓑ Ⓒ Ⓓ Ⓔ	V2, Pg. 96	PT21-S3-Q1	Ⓐ Ⓑ Ⓒ Ⓓ Ⓔ
V1, Pg. 197	PT13-S2-Q25	Ⓐ Ⓑ Ⓒ Ⓓ Ⓔ	V2, Pg. 103	PT21-S3-Q24	Ⓐ Ⓑ Ⓒ Ⓓ Ⓔ
V1, Pg. 207	PT13-S4-Q5	Ⓐ Ⓑ Ⓒ Ⓓ Ⓔ	V2, Pg. 139	PT22-S4-Q4	Ⓐ Ⓑ Ⓒ Ⓓ Ⓔ
V1, Pg. 207	PT13-S4-Q7	Ⓐ Ⓑ Ⓒ Ⓓ Ⓔ	V2, Pg. 145	PT22-S4-Q25	Ⓐ Ⓑ Ⓒ Ⓓ Ⓔ
V1, Pg. 209	PT13-S4-Q14	Ⓐ Ⓑ Ⓒ Ⓓ Ⓔ	V2, Pg. 158	PT23-S2-Q10	Ⓐ Ⓑ Ⓒ Ⓓ Ⓔ
V1, Pg. 211	PT13-S4-Q18	Ⓐ Ⓑ Ⓒ Ⓓ Ⓔ	V2, Pg. 159	PT23-S2-Q12	Ⓐ Ⓑ Ⓒ Ⓓ Ⓔ
V1, Pg. 212	PT13-S4-Q21	Ⓐ Ⓑ Ⓒ Ⓓ Ⓔ	V2, Pg. 161	PT23-S2-Q20	Ⓐ Ⓑ Ⓒ Ⓓ Ⓔ
V1, Pg. 227	PT14-S2-Q11	Ⓐ Ⓑ Ⓒ Ⓓ Ⓔ	V2, Pg. 196	PT24-S2-Q11	Ⓐ Ⓑ Ⓒ Ⓓ Ⓔ
V1, Pg. 228	PT14-S2-Q16	Ⓐ Ⓑ Ⓒ Ⓓ Ⓔ	V2, Pg. 204	PT24-S3-Q8	Ⓐ Ⓑ Ⓒ Ⓓ Ⓔ
V1, Pg. 245	PT14-S4-Q17	Ⓐ Ⓑ Ⓒ Ⓓ Ⓔ	V2, Pg. 204	PT24-S3-Q11	Ⓐ Ⓑ Ⓒ Ⓓ Ⓔ
V1, Pg. 265	PT15-S2-Q12	Ⓐ Ⓑ Ⓒ Ⓓ Ⓔ	V2, Pg. 205	PT24-S3-Q15	Ⓐ Ⓑ Ⓒ Ⓓ Ⓔ
V1, Pg. 271	PT15-S3-Q5	Ⓐ Ⓑ Ⓒ Ⓓ Ⓔ	V2, Pg. 234	PT25-S2-Q21	Ⓐ Ⓑ Ⓒ Ⓓ Ⓔ
V1, Pg. 271	PT15-S3-Q7	Ⓐ Ⓑ Ⓒ Ⓓ Ⓔ	V2, Pg. 240	PT25-S4-Q2	Ⓐ Ⓑ Ⓒ Ⓓ Ⓔ
V1, Pg. 277	PT15-S3-Q26	Ⓐ Ⓑ Ⓒ Ⓓ Ⓔ	V2, Pg. 259	PT26-S2-Q6	Ⓐ Ⓑ Ⓒ Ⓓ Ⓔ
V1, Pg. 293	PT16-S2-Q3	Ⓐ Ⓑ Ⓒ Ⓓ Ⓔ	V2, Pg. 263	PT26-S2-Q19	Ⓐ Ⓑ Ⓒ Ⓓ Ⓔ
V1, Pg. 294	PT16-S2-Q9	Ⓐ Ⓑ Ⓒ Ⓓ Ⓔ	V2, Pg. 272	PT26-S3-Q22	Ⓐ Ⓑ Ⓒ Ⓓ Ⓔ
V1, Pg. 298	PT16-S2-Q20	Ⓐ Ⓑ Ⓒ Ⓓ Ⓔ	V2, Pg. 291	PT27-S1-Q9	Ⓐ Ⓑ Ⓒ Ⓓ Ⓔ
V1, Pg. 302	PT16-S3-Q8	Ⓐ Ⓑ Ⓒ Ⓓ Ⓔ	V2, Pg. 293	PT27-S1-Q19	Ⓐ Ⓑ Ⓒ Ⓓ Ⓔ
V1, Pg. 304	PT16-S3-Q16	Ⓐ Ⓑ Ⓒ Ⓓ Ⓔ	V2, Pg. 294	PT27-S1-Q22	Ⓐ Ⓑ Ⓒ Ⓓ Ⓔ
V1, Pg. 305	PT16-S3-Q21	Ⓐ Ⓑ Ⓒ Ⓓ Ⓔ	V2, Pg. 309	PT27-S4-Q5	Ⓐ Ⓑ Ⓒ Ⓓ Ⓔ
	PT17-S2-Q1	Ⓐ Ⓑ Ⓒ Ⓓ Ⓔ	V2, Pg. 312	PT27-S4-Q14	Ⓐ Ⓑ Ⓒ Ⓓ Ⓔ
	PT17-S2-Q9	Ⓐ Ⓑ Ⓒ Ⓓ Ⓔ	V2, Pg. 313	PT27-S4-Q17	Ⓐ Ⓑ Ⓒ Ⓓ Ⓔ
	PT17-S2-Q20	Ⓐ Ⓑ Ⓒ Ⓓ Ⓔ	V2, Pg. 314	PT27-S4-Q22	Ⓐ Ⓑ Ⓒ Ⓓ Ⓔ
	PT17-S3-Q1	Ⓐ Ⓑ Ⓒ Ⓓ Ⓔ	V2, Pg. 325	PT28-S1-Q14	Ⓐ Ⓑ Ⓒ Ⓓ Ⓔ
	PT17-S3-Q11	Ⓐ Ⓑ Ⓒ Ⓓ Ⓔ	V2, Pg. 334	PT28-S3-Q1	Ⓐ Ⓑ Ⓒ Ⓓ Ⓔ
	PT17-S3-Q24	Ⓐ Ⓑ Ⓒ Ⓓ Ⓔ	V2, Pg. 335	PT28-S3-Q8	Ⓐ Ⓑ Ⓒ Ⓓ Ⓔ
V1, Pg. 326	PT18-S2-Q3	Ⓐ Ⓑ Ⓒ Ⓓ Ⓔ	V3, Pg. 17	PT29-S1-Q6	Ⓐ Ⓑ Ⓒ Ⓓ Ⓔ
V1, Pg. 343	PT18-S4-Q6	Ⓐ Ⓑ Ⓒ Ⓓ Ⓔ	V3, Pg. 21	PT29-S1-Q18	Ⓐ Ⓑ Ⓒ Ⓓ Ⓔ
V1, Pg. 344	PT18-S4-Q10	Ⓐ Ⓑ Ⓒ Ⓓ Ⓔ	V3, Pg. 22	PT29-S1-Q21	Ⓐ Ⓑ Ⓒ Ⓓ Ⓔ

V3, Pg. 42	PT29-S4-Q23	Ⓐ Ⓑ Ⓒ Ⓓ Ⓔ		PT43-S3-Q21	Ⓐ Ⓑ Ⓒ Ⓓ Ⓔ
V3, Pg. 59	PT30-S2-Q18	Ⓐ Ⓑ Ⓒ Ⓓ Ⓔ		PT43-S3-Q24	Ⓐ Ⓑ Ⓒ Ⓓ Ⓔ
V3, Pg. 59	PT30-S2-Q20	Ⓐ Ⓑ Ⓒ Ⓓ Ⓔ		PT44-S4-Q15	Ⓐ Ⓑ Ⓒ Ⓓ Ⓔ
V3, Pg. 60	PT30-S2-Q23	Ⓐ Ⓑ Ⓒ Ⓓ Ⓔ		PT45-S1-Q8	Ⓐ Ⓑ Ⓒ Ⓓ Ⓔ
V3, Pg. 71	PT30-S4-Q4	Ⓐ Ⓑ Ⓒ Ⓓ Ⓔ		PT45-S1-Q22	Ⓐ Ⓑ Ⓒ Ⓓ Ⓔ
V3, Pg. 93	PT31-S2-Q17	Ⓐ Ⓑ Ⓒ Ⓓ Ⓔ		PT46-S2-Q2	Ⓐ Ⓑ Ⓒ Ⓓ Ⓔ
V3, Pg. 98	PT31-S3-Q10	Ⓐ Ⓑ Ⓒ Ⓓ Ⓔ		PT46-S2-Q7	Ⓐ Ⓑ Ⓒ Ⓓ Ⓔ
V3, Pg. 120	PT32-S1-Q7	Ⓐ Ⓑ Ⓒ Ⓓ Ⓔ		PT46-S3-Q11	Ⓐ Ⓑ Ⓒ Ⓓ Ⓔ
V3, Pg. 121	PT32-S1-Q11	Ⓐ Ⓑ Ⓒ Ⓓ Ⓔ		PT46-S3-Q25	Ⓐ Ⓑ Ⓒ Ⓓ Ⓔ
V3, Pg. 145	PT32-S4-Q24	Ⓐ Ⓑ Ⓒ Ⓓ Ⓔ		PT47-S1-Q18	Ⓐ Ⓑ Ⓒ Ⓓ Ⓔ
V3, Pg. 155	PT33-S1-Q11	Ⓐ Ⓑ Ⓒ Ⓓ Ⓔ		PT48-S1-Q14	Ⓐ Ⓑ Ⓒ Ⓓ Ⓔ
V3, Pg. 170	PT33-S3-Q8	Ⓐ Ⓑ Ⓒ Ⓓ Ⓔ		PT48-S1-Q26	Ⓐ Ⓑ Ⓒ Ⓓ Ⓔ
V3, Pg. 200	PT34-S2-Q23	Ⓐ Ⓑ Ⓒ Ⓓ Ⓔ		PT48-S4-Q14	Ⓐ Ⓑ Ⓒ Ⓓ Ⓔ
V3, Pg. 205	PT34-S3-Q13	Ⓐ Ⓑ Ⓒ Ⓓ Ⓔ		PT49-S4-Q3	Ⓐ Ⓑ Ⓒ Ⓓ Ⓔ
V3, Pg. 257	PT36-S1-Q11	Ⓐ Ⓑ Ⓒ Ⓓ Ⓔ		PT49-S4-Q10	Ⓐ Ⓑ Ⓒ Ⓓ Ⓔ
V3, Pg. 258	PT36-S1-Q14	Ⓐ Ⓑ Ⓒ Ⓓ Ⓔ		PT50-S2-Q9	Ⓐ Ⓑ Ⓒ Ⓓ Ⓔ
V3, Pg. 296	PT37-S2-Q2	Ⓐ Ⓑ Ⓒ Ⓓ Ⓔ		PT50-S4-Q10	Ⓐ Ⓑ Ⓒ Ⓓ Ⓔ
V3, Pg. 297	PT37-S2-Q7	Ⓐ Ⓑ Ⓒ Ⓓ Ⓔ		PT51-S1-Q11	Ⓐ Ⓑ Ⓒ Ⓓ Ⓔ
V3, Pg. 299	PT37-S2-Q12	Ⓐ Ⓑ Ⓒ Ⓓ Ⓔ		PT51-S3-Q14	Ⓐ Ⓑ Ⓒ Ⓓ Ⓔ
V3, Pg. 342	PT38-S4-Q1	Ⓐ Ⓑ Ⓒ Ⓓ Ⓔ		PT51-S3-Q19	Ⓐ Ⓑ Ⓒ Ⓓ Ⓔ
	PT39-S2-Q7	Ⓐ Ⓑ Ⓒ Ⓓ Ⓔ	V4, Pg. 9	PT52-S1-Q5	Ⓐ Ⓑ Ⓒ Ⓓ Ⓔ
	PT39-S2-Q12	Ⓐ Ⓑ Ⓒ Ⓓ Ⓔ	V4, Pg. 45	PT53-S1-Q7	Ⓐ Ⓑ Ⓒ Ⓓ Ⓔ
	PT39-S4-Q6	Ⓐ Ⓑ Ⓒ Ⓓ Ⓔ	V4, Pg. 48	PT53-S1-Q16	Ⓐ Ⓑ Ⓒ Ⓓ Ⓔ
	PT39-S4-Q10	Ⓐ Ⓑ Ⓒ Ⓓ Ⓔ	V4, Pg. 61	PT53-S3-Q19	Ⓐ Ⓑ Ⓒ Ⓓ Ⓔ
	PT40-S1-Q3	Ⓐ Ⓑ Ⓒ Ⓓ Ⓔ	V4, Pg. 91	PT54-S2-Q16	Ⓐ Ⓑ Ⓒ Ⓓ Ⓔ
	PT40-S1-Q22	Ⓐ Ⓑ Ⓒ Ⓓ Ⓔ	V4, Pg. 95	PT54-S2-Q25	Ⓐ Ⓑ Ⓒ Ⓓ Ⓔ
	PT40-S1-Q24	Ⓐ Ⓑ Ⓒ Ⓓ Ⓔ	V4, Pg. 106	PT54-S4-Q23	Ⓐ Ⓑ Ⓒ Ⓓ Ⓔ
	PT40-S3-Q11	Ⓐ Ⓑ Ⓒ Ⓓ Ⓔ	V4, Pg. 120	PT55-S1-Q15	Ⓐ Ⓑ Ⓒ Ⓓ Ⓔ
	PT41-S1-Q21	Ⓐ Ⓑ Ⓒ Ⓓ Ⓔ	V4, Pg. 123	PT55-S1-Q25	Ⓐ Ⓑ Ⓒ Ⓓ Ⓔ
	PT41-S3-Q25	Ⓐ Ⓑ Ⓒ Ⓓ Ⓔ	V4, Pg. 157	PT56-S2-Q5	Ⓐ Ⓑ Ⓒ Ⓓ Ⓔ
	PT42-S2-Q16	Ⓐ Ⓑ Ⓒ Ⓓ Ⓔ	V4, Pg. 161	PT56-S2-Q19	Ⓐ Ⓑ Ⓒ Ⓓ Ⓔ
	PT42-S4-Q17	Ⓐ Ⓑ Ⓒ Ⓓ Ⓔ	V4, Pg. 162	PT56-S2-Q23	Ⓐ Ⓑ Ⓒ Ⓓ Ⓔ
	PT42-S4-Q26	Ⓐ Ⓑ Ⓒ Ⓓ Ⓔ	V4, Pg. 199	PT57-S2-Q25	Ⓐ Ⓑ Ⓒ Ⓓ Ⓔ
	PT43-S2-Q7	Ⓐ Ⓑ Ⓒ Ⓓ Ⓔ	V4, Pg. 228	PT58-S1-Q15	Ⓐ Ⓑ Ⓒ Ⓓ Ⓔ
	PT43-S2-Q17	Ⓐ Ⓑ Ⓒ Ⓓ Ⓔ	V4, Pg. 229	PT58-S1-Q20	Ⓐ Ⓑ Ⓒ Ⓓ Ⓔ
	PT43-S2-Q22	Ⓐ Ⓑ Ⓒ Ⓓ Ⓔ	V4, Pg. 246	PT58-S4-Q9	Ⓐ Ⓑ Ⓒ Ⓓ Ⓔ
	PT43-S3-Q9	Ⓐ Ⓑ Ⓒ Ⓓ Ⓔ	V4, Pg. 269	PT59-S2-Q19	Ⓐ Ⓑ Ⓒ Ⓓ Ⓔ

V4, Pg. 277	PT59-S3-Q19	Ⓐ Ⓑ Ⓒ Ⓓ Ⓔ		V5, Pg. 240	PT68-S2-Q1	Ⓐ Ⓑ Ⓒ Ⓓ Ⓔ
V4, Pg. 296	PT60-S1-Q3	Ⓐ Ⓑ Ⓒ Ⓓ Ⓔ		V5, Pg. 244	PT68-S2-Q18	Ⓐ Ⓑ Ⓒ Ⓓ Ⓔ
V4, Pg. 311	PT60-S3-Q12	Ⓐ Ⓑ Ⓒ Ⓓ Ⓔ		V5, Pg. 249	PT68-S3-Q4	Ⓐ Ⓑ Ⓒ Ⓓ Ⓔ
V4, Pg. 312	PT60-S3-Q17	Ⓐ Ⓑ Ⓒ Ⓓ Ⓔ		V5, Pg. 278	PT69-S1-Q21	Ⓐ Ⓑ Ⓒ Ⓓ Ⓔ
V4, Pg. 341	PT61-S2-Q3	Ⓐ Ⓑ Ⓒ Ⓓ Ⓔ		V5, Pg. 302	PT69-S4-Q20	Ⓐ Ⓑ Ⓒ Ⓓ Ⓔ
V4, Pg. 342	PT61-S2-Q10	Ⓐ Ⓑ Ⓒ Ⓓ Ⓔ		V5, Pg. 314	PT70-S1-Q8	Ⓐ Ⓑ Ⓒ Ⓓ Ⓔ
V4, Pg. 344	PT61-S2-Q17	Ⓐ Ⓑ Ⓒ Ⓓ Ⓔ		V5, Pg. 318	PT70-S1-Q22	Ⓐ Ⓑ Ⓒ Ⓓ Ⓔ
V5, Pg. 17	PT62-S2-Q6	Ⓐ Ⓑ Ⓒ Ⓓ Ⓔ		V5, Pg. 319	PT70-S1-Q24	Ⓐ Ⓑ Ⓒ Ⓓ Ⓔ
V5, Pg. 21	PT62-S2-Q19	Ⓐ Ⓑ Ⓒ Ⓓ Ⓔ		V5, Pg. 339	PT70-S4-Q14	Ⓐ Ⓑ Ⓒ Ⓓ Ⓔ
V5, Pg. 29	PT62-S4-Q6	Ⓐ Ⓑ Ⓒ Ⓓ Ⓔ		V5, Pg. 341	PT70-S4-Q21	Ⓐ Ⓑ Ⓒ Ⓓ Ⓔ
V5, Pg. 45	PT63-S1-Q6	Ⓐ Ⓑ Ⓒ Ⓓ Ⓔ		V5, Pg. 357	PT71-S1-Q17	Ⓐ Ⓑ Ⓒ Ⓓ Ⓔ
V5, Pg. 46	PT63-S1-Q9	Ⓐ Ⓑ Ⓒ Ⓓ Ⓔ		V5, Pg. 370	PT71-S3-Q10	Ⓐ Ⓑ Ⓒ Ⓓ Ⓔ
V5, Pg. 49	PT63-S1-Q20	Ⓐ Ⓑ Ⓒ Ⓓ Ⓔ		PT72, Pg. 24	PT72-S2-Q24	Ⓐ Ⓑ Ⓒ Ⓓ Ⓔ
V5, Pg. 57	PT63-S3-Q5	Ⓐ Ⓑ Ⓒ Ⓓ Ⓔ		PT72, Pg. 33	PT72-S3-Q24	Ⓐ Ⓑ Ⓒ Ⓓ Ⓔ
V5, Pg. 80	PT64-S1-Q2	Ⓐ Ⓑ Ⓒ Ⓓ Ⓔ		PT73, Pg. 24	PT73-S2-Q21	Ⓐ Ⓑ Ⓒ Ⓓ Ⓔ
V5, Pg. 85	PT64-S1-Q18	Ⓐ Ⓑ Ⓒ Ⓓ Ⓔ		PT74, Pg. 17	PT74-S1-Q24	Ⓐ Ⓑ Ⓒ Ⓓ Ⓔ
V5, Pg. 85	PT64-S1-Q20	Ⓐ Ⓑ Ⓒ Ⓓ Ⓔ		PT74, Pg. 37	PT74-S4-Q13	Ⓐ Ⓑ Ⓒ Ⓓ Ⓔ
V5, Pg. 123	PT65-S1-Q25	Ⓐ Ⓑ Ⓒ Ⓓ Ⓔ		PT76, Pg. 21	PT76-S2-Q13	Ⓐ Ⓑ Ⓒ Ⓓ Ⓔ
V5, Pg. 137	PT65-S4-Q6	Ⓐ Ⓑ Ⓒ Ⓓ Ⓔ		PT76, Pg. 38	PT76-S4-Q19	Ⓐ Ⓑ Ⓒ Ⓓ Ⓔ
V5, Pg. 163	PT66-S2-Q14	Ⓐ Ⓑ Ⓒ Ⓓ Ⓔ		PT77, Pg. 24	PT77-S2-Q23	Ⓐ Ⓑ Ⓒ Ⓓ Ⓔ
V5, Pg. 182	PT66-S4-Q21	Ⓐ Ⓑ Ⓒ Ⓓ Ⓔ		PT77, Pg. 37	PT77-S4-Q13	Ⓐ Ⓑ Ⓒ Ⓓ Ⓔ
V5, Pg. 221	PT67-S4-Q17	Ⓐ Ⓑ Ⓒ Ⓓ Ⓔ		PT77, Pg. 39	PT77-S4-Q18	Ⓐ Ⓑ Ⓒ Ⓓ Ⓔ

Most Strongly Supported

J07, Pg. 11	J07-S2-Q18	Ⓐ Ⓑ Ⓒ Ⓓ Ⓔ		SP1, Pg. 305	PTC-S2-Q17	Ⓐ Ⓑ Ⓒ Ⓓ Ⓔ
J07, Pg. 12	J07-S2-Q22	Ⓐ Ⓑ Ⓒ Ⓓ Ⓔ		SP1, Pg. 314	PTC-S3-Q23	Ⓐ Ⓑ Ⓒ Ⓓ Ⓔ
SP1, Pg. 68	PTA-S1-Q1	Ⓐ Ⓑ Ⓒ Ⓓ Ⓔ		SP2, Pg. 354	PTC2-S2-Q2	Ⓐ Ⓑ Ⓒ Ⓓ Ⓔ
SP1, Pg. 69	PTA-S1-Q3	Ⓐ Ⓑ Ⓒ Ⓓ Ⓔ		SP2, Pg. 360	PTC2-S2-Q21	Ⓐ Ⓑ Ⓒ Ⓓ Ⓔ
SP1, Pg. 70	PTA-S1-Q8	Ⓐ Ⓑ Ⓒ Ⓓ Ⓔ		SP2, Pg. 367	PTC2-S3-Q21	Ⓐ Ⓑ Ⓒ Ⓓ Ⓔ
SP1, Pg. 90	PTA-S4-Q6	Ⓐ Ⓑ Ⓒ Ⓓ Ⓔ			PT1-S3-Q11	Ⓐ Ⓑ Ⓒ Ⓓ Ⓔ
SP1, Pg. 93	PTA-S4-Q16	Ⓐ Ⓑ Ⓒ Ⓓ Ⓔ			PT1-S3-Q20	Ⓐ Ⓑ Ⓒ Ⓓ Ⓔ
SP1, Pg. 190	PTB-S1-Q17	Ⓐ Ⓑ Ⓒ Ⓓ Ⓔ			PT1-S4-Q18	Ⓐ Ⓑ Ⓒ Ⓓ Ⓔ
SP1, Pg. 191	PTB-S1-Q20	Ⓐ Ⓑ Ⓒ Ⓓ Ⓔ			PT2-S4-Q2	Ⓐ Ⓑ Ⓒ Ⓓ Ⓔ
SP1, Pg. 206	PTB-S4-Q1	Ⓐ Ⓑ Ⓒ Ⓓ Ⓔ			PT2-S4-Q8	Ⓐ Ⓑ Ⓒ Ⓓ Ⓔ
SP1, Pg. 207	PTB-S4-Q3	Ⓐ Ⓑ Ⓒ Ⓓ Ⓔ			PT3-S4-Q1	Ⓐ Ⓑ Ⓒ Ⓓ Ⓔ
SP1, Pg. 210	PTB-S4-Q15	Ⓐ Ⓑ Ⓒ Ⓓ Ⓔ			PT3-S4-Q4	Ⓐ Ⓑ Ⓒ Ⓓ Ⓔ
SP1, Pg. 301	PTC-S2-Q7	Ⓐ Ⓑ Ⓒ Ⓓ Ⓔ			PT3-S4-Q9	Ⓐ Ⓑ Ⓒ Ⓓ Ⓔ

	PT3-S4-Q16	Ⓐ Ⓑ Ⓒ Ⓓ Ⓔ	V1, Pg. 332	PT18-S2-Q20	Ⓐ Ⓑ Ⓒ Ⓓ Ⓔ
	PT4-S1-Q17	Ⓐ Ⓑ Ⓒ Ⓓ Ⓔ	V1, Pg. 349	PT18-S4-Q24	Ⓐ Ⓑ Ⓒ Ⓓ Ⓔ
	PT4-S1-Q19	Ⓐ Ⓑ Ⓒ Ⓓ Ⓔ	V2, Pg. 20	PT19-S2-Q3	Ⓐ Ⓑ Ⓒ Ⓓ Ⓔ
	PT4-S1-Q22	Ⓐ Ⓑ Ⓒ Ⓓ Ⓔ	V2, Pg. 27	PT19-S2-Q24	Ⓐ Ⓑ Ⓒ Ⓓ Ⓔ
	PT5-S1-Q1	Ⓐ Ⓑ Ⓒ Ⓓ Ⓔ	V2, Pg. 39	PT19-S4-Q12	Ⓐ Ⓑ Ⓒ Ⓓ Ⓔ
	PT6-S3-Q5	Ⓐ Ⓑ Ⓒ Ⓓ Ⓔ	V2, Pg. 41	PT19-S4-Q19	Ⓐ Ⓑ Ⓒ Ⓓ Ⓔ
V1, Pg. 18	PT7-S1-Q8	Ⓐ Ⓑ Ⓒ Ⓓ Ⓔ	V2, Pg. 50	PT20-S1-Q1	Ⓐ Ⓑ Ⓒ Ⓓ Ⓔ
V1, Pg. 18	PT7-S1-Q9	Ⓐ Ⓑ Ⓒ Ⓓ Ⓔ	V2, Pg. 51	PT20-S1-Q6	Ⓐ Ⓑ Ⓒ Ⓓ Ⓔ
V1, Pg. 20	PT7-S1-Q16	Ⓐ Ⓑ Ⓒ Ⓓ Ⓔ	V2, Pg. 57	PT20-S1-Q23	Ⓐ Ⓑ Ⓒ Ⓓ Ⓔ
V1, Pg. 22	PT7-S1-Q21	Ⓐ Ⓑ Ⓒ Ⓓ Ⓔ	V2, Pg. 72	PT20-S4-Q10	Ⓐ Ⓑ Ⓒ Ⓓ Ⓔ
V1, Pg. 38	PT7-S4-Q10	Ⓐ Ⓑ Ⓒ Ⓓ Ⓔ	V2, Pg. 91	PT21-S2-Q13	Ⓐ Ⓑ Ⓒ Ⓓ Ⓔ
V1, Pg. 41	PT7-S4-Q19	Ⓐ Ⓑ Ⓒ Ⓓ Ⓔ	V2, Pg. 99	PT21-S3-Q12	Ⓐ Ⓑ Ⓒ Ⓓ Ⓔ
	PT8-S1-Q14	Ⓐ Ⓑ Ⓒ Ⓓ Ⓔ	V2, Pg. 100	PT21-S3-Q16	Ⓐ Ⓑ Ⓒ Ⓓ Ⓔ
	PT8-S1-Q22	Ⓐ Ⓑ Ⓒ Ⓓ Ⓔ	V2, Pg. 101	PT21-S3-Q18	Ⓐ Ⓑ Ⓒ Ⓓ Ⓔ
V1, Pg. 71	PT9-S4-Q7	Ⓐ Ⓑ Ⓒ Ⓓ Ⓔ	V2, Pg. 127	PT22-S2-Q5	Ⓐ Ⓑ Ⓒ Ⓓ Ⓔ
V1, Pg. 90	PT10-S1-Q22	Ⓐ Ⓑ Ⓒ Ⓓ Ⓔ	V2, Pg. 130	PT22-S2-Q15	Ⓐ Ⓑ Ⓒ Ⓓ Ⓔ
V1, Pg. 91	PT10-S1-Q24	Ⓐ Ⓑ Ⓒ Ⓓ Ⓔ	V2, Pg. 130	PT22-S2-Q17	Ⓐ Ⓑ Ⓒ Ⓓ Ⓔ
V1, Pg. 104	PT10-S4-Q3	Ⓐ Ⓑ Ⓒ Ⓓ Ⓔ	V2, Pg. 132	PT22-S2-Q22	Ⓐ Ⓑ Ⓒ Ⓓ Ⓔ
V1, Pg. 106	PT10-S4-Q10	Ⓐ Ⓑ Ⓒ Ⓓ Ⓔ	V2, Pg. 141	PT22-S4-Q12	Ⓐ Ⓑ Ⓒ Ⓓ Ⓔ
V1, Pg. 109	PT10-S4-Q16	Ⓐ Ⓑ Ⓒ Ⓓ Ⓔ	V2, Pg. 141	PT22-S4-Q14	Ⓐ Ⓑ Ⓒ Ⓓ Ⓔ
V1, Pg. 110	PT10-S4-Q20	Ⓐ Ⓑ Ⓒ Ⓓ Ⓔ	V2, Pg. 157	PT23-S2-Q7	Ⓐ Ⓑ Ⓒ Ⓓ Ⓔ
V1, Pg. 138	PT11-S4-Q4	Ⓐ Ⓑ Ⓒ Ⓓ Ⓔ	V2, Pg. 162	PT23-S2-Q24	Ⓐ Ⓑ Ⓒ Ⓓ Ⓔ
V1, Pg. 142	PT11-S4-Q14	Ⓐ Ⓑ Ⓒ Ⓓ Ⓔ	V2, Pg. 165	PT23-S3-Q4	Ⓐ Ⓑ Ⓒ Ⓓ Ⓔ
V1, Pg. 172	PT12-S4-Q1	Ⓐ Ⓑ Ⓒ Ⓓ Ⓔ	V2, Pg. 165	PT23-S3-Q6	Ⓐ Ⓑ Ⓒ Ⓓ Ⓔ
V1, Pg. 173	PT12-S4-Q3	Ⓐ Ⓑ Ⓒ Ⓓ Ⓔ	V2, Pg. 167	PT23-S3-Q12	Ⓐ Ⓑ Ⓒ Ⓓ Ⓔ
V1, Pg. 177	PT12-S4-Q16	Ⓐ Ⓑ Ⓒ Ⓓ Ⓔ	V2, Pg. 169	PT23-S3-Q20	Ⓐ Ⓑ Ⓒ Ⓓ Ⓔ
V1, Pg. 191	PT13-S2-Q4	Ⓐ Ⓑ Ⓒ Ⓓ Ⓔ	V2, Pg. 194	PT24-S2-Q2	Ⓐ Ⓑ Ⓒ Ⓓ Ⓔ
V1, Pg. 191	PT13-S2-Q6	Ⓐ Ⓑ Ⓒ Ⓓ Ⓔ	V2, Pg. 204	PT24-S3-Q7	Ⓐ Ⓑ Ⓒ Ⓓ Ⓔ
V1, Pg. 195	PT13-S2-Q18	Ⓐ Ⓑ Ⓒ Ⓓ Ⓔ	V2, Pg. 232	PT25-S2-Q13	Ⓐ Ⓑ Ⓒ Ⓓ Ⓔ
V1, Pg. 230	PT14-S2-Q23	Ⓐ Ⓑ Ⓒ Ⓓ Ⓔ	V2, Pg. 234	PT25-S2-Q19	Ⓐ Ⓑ Ⓒ Ⓓ Ⓔ
V1, Pg. 241	PT14-S4-Q5	Ⓐ Ⓑ Ⓒ Ⓓ Ⓔ	V2, Pg. 260	PT26-S2-Q9	Ⓐ Ⓑ Ⓒ Ⓓ Ⓔ
V1, Pg. 243	PT14-S4-Q12	Ⓐ Ⓑ Ⓒ Ⓓ Ⓔ	V2, Pg. 270	PT26-S3-Q15	Ⓐ Ⓑ Ⓒ Ⓓ Ⓔ
V1, Pg. 246	PT14-S4-Q21	Ⓐ Ⓑ Ⓒ Ⓓ Ⓔ	V2, Pg. 272	PT26-S3-Q20	Ⓐ Ⓑ Ⓒ Ⓓ Ⓔ
V1, Pg. 264	PT15-S2-Q9	Ⓐ Ⓑ Ⓒ Ⓓ Ⓔ	V2, Pg. 289	PT27-S1-Q3	Ⓐ Ⓑ Ⓒ Ⓓ Ⓔ
V1, Pg. 266	PT15-S2-Q15	Ⓐ Ⓑ Ⓒ Ⓓ Ⓔ	V2, Pg. 292	PT27-S1-Q12	Ⓐ Ⓑ Ⓒ Ⓓ Ⓔ
V1, Pg. 295	PT16-S2-Q11	Ⓐ Ⓑ Ⓒ Ⓓ Ⓔ	V2, Pg. 294	PT27-S1-Q20	Ⓐ Ⓑ Ⓒ Ⓓ Ⓔ
V1, Pg. 301	PT16-S3-Q5	Ⓐ Ⓑ Ⓒ Ⓓ Ⓔ	V2, Pg. 314	PT27-S4-Q23	Ⓐ Ⓑ Ⓒ Ⓓ Ⓔ

V2, Pg. 326	PT28-S1-Q16	Ⓐ Ⓑ Ⓒ Ⓓ Ⓔ		V3, Pg. 325	PT38-S1-Q13	Ⓐ Ⓑ Ⓒ Ⓓ Ⓔ
V2, Pg. 328	PT28-S1-Q22	Ⓐ Ⓑ Ⓒ Ⓓ Ⓔ		V3, Pg. 326	PT38-S1-Q15	Ⓐ Ⓑ Ⓒ Ⓓ Ⓔ
V2, Pg. 334	PT28-S3-Q4	Ⓐ Ⓑ Ⓒ Ⓓ Ⓔ		V3, Pg. 327	PT38-S1-Q20	Ⓐ Ⓑ Ⓒ Ⓓ Ⓔ
V3, Pg. 18	PT29-S1-Q8	Ⓐ Ⓑ Ⓒ Ⓓ Ⓔ		V3, Pg. 328	PT38-S1-Q21	Ⓐ Ⓑ Ⓒ Ⓓ Ⓔ
V3, Pg. 36	PT29-S4-Q3	Ⓐ Ⓑ Ⓒ Ⓓ Ⓔ		V3, Pg. 348	PT38-S4-Q24	Ⓐ Ⓑ Ⓒ Ⓓ Ⓔ
V3, Pg. 39	PT29-S4-Q12	Ⓐ Ⓑ Ⓒ Ⓓ Ⓔ			PT39-S4-Q16	Ⓐ Ⓑ Ⓒ Ⓓ Ⓔ
V3, Pg. 58	PT30-S2-Q16	Ⓐ Ⓑ Ⓒ Ⓓ Ⓔ			PT40-S3-Q3	Ⓐ Ⓑ Ⓒ Ⓓ Ⓔ
V3, Pg. 72	PT30-S4-Q10	Ⓐ Ⓑ Ⓒ Ⓓ Ⓔ			PT41-S1-Q9	Ⓐ Ⓑ Ⓒ Ⓓ Ⓔ
V3, Pg. 76	PT30-S4-Q22	Ⓐ Ⓑ Ⓒ Ⓓ Ⓔ			PT41-S1-Q11	Ⓐ Ⓑ Ⓒ Ⓓ Ⓔ
V3, Pg. 90	PT31-S2-Q7	Ⓐ Ⓑ Ⓒ Ⓓ Ⓔ			PT41-S3-Q3	Ⓐ Ⓑ Ⓒ Ⓓ Ⓔ
V3, Pg. 94	PT31-S2-Q20	Ⓐ Ⓑ Ⓒ Ⓓ Ⓔ			PT41-S3-Q6	Ⓐ Ⓑ Ⓒ Ⓓ Ⓔ
V3, Pg. 96	PT31-S3-Q3	Ⓐ Ⓑ Ⓒ Ⓓ Ⓔ			PT42-S2-Q7	Ⓐ Ⓑ Ⓒ Ⓓ Ⓔ
V3, Pg. 97	PT31-S3-Q6	Ⓐ Ⓑ Ⓒ Ⓓ Ⓔ			PT42-S2-Q11	Ⓐ Ⓑ Ⓒ Ⓓ Ⓔ
V3, Pg. 101	PT31-S3-Q22	Ⓐ Ⓑ Ⓒ Ⓓ Ⓔ			PT42-S4-Q7	Ⓐ Ⓑ Ⓒ Ⓓ Ⓔ
V3, Pg. 120	PT32-S1-Q9	Ⓐ Ⓑ Ⓒ Ⓓ Ⓔ			PT43-S2-Q4	Ⓐ Ⓑ Ⓒ Ⓓ Ⓔ
V3, Pg. 124	PT32-S1-Q18	Ⓐ Ⓑ Ⓒ Ⓓ Ⓔ			PT44-S2-Q2	Ⓐ Ⓑ Ⓒ Ⓓ Ⓔ
V3, Pg. 125	PT32-S1-Q24	Ⓐ Ⓑ Ⓒ Ⓓ Ⓔ			PT44-S2-Q11	Ⓐ Ⓑ Ⓒ Ⓓ Ⓔ
V3, Pg. 140	PT32-S4-Q10	Ⓐ Ⓑ Ⓒ Ⓓ Ⓔ			PT44-S2-Q14	Ⓐ Ⓑ Ⓒ Ⓓ Ⓔ
V3, Pg. 142	PT32-S4-Q14	Ⓐ Ⓑ Ⓒ Ⓓ Ⓔ			PT44-S4-Q3	Ⓐ Ⓑ Ⓒ Ⓓ Ⓔ
V3, Pg. 154	PT33-S1-Q7	Ⓐ Ⓑ Ⓒ Ⓓ Ⓔ			PT44-S4-Q12	Ⓐ Ⓑ Ⓒ Ⓓ Ⓔ
V3, Pg. 154	PT33-S1-Q9	Ⓐ Ⓑ Ⓒ Ⓓ Ⓔ			PT45-S4-Q16	Ⓐ Ⓑ Ⓒ Ⓓ Ⓔ
V3, Pg. 170	PT33-S3-Q10	Ⓐ Ⓑ Ⓒ Ⓓ Ⓔ			PT45-S4-Q18	Ⓐ Ⓑ Ⓒ Ⓓ Ⓔ
V3, Pg. 171	PT33-S3-Q13	Ⓐ Ⓑ Ⓒ Ⓓ Ⓔ			PT46-S2-Q12	Ⓐ Ⓑ Ⓒ Ⓓ Ⓔ
V3, Pg. 195	PT34-S2-Q4	Ⓐ Ⓑ Ⓒ Ⓓ Ⓔ			PT46-S3-Q9	Ⓐ Ⓑ Ⓒ Ⓓ Ⓔ
V3, Pg. 199	PT34-S2-Q19	Ⓐ Ⓑ Ⓒ Ⓓ Ⓔ			PT47-S1-Q16	Ⓐ Ⓑ Ⓒ Ⓓ Ⓔ
V3, Pg. 207	PT34-S3-Q19	Ⓐ Ⓑ Ⓒ Ⓓ Ⓔ			PT47-S3-Q1	Ⓐ Ⓑ Ⓒ Ⓓ Ⓔ
V3, Pg. 223	PT35-S1-Q12	Ⓐ Ⓑ Ⓒ Ⓓ Ⓔ			PT47-S3-Q3	Ⓐ Ⓑ Ⓒ Ⓓ Ⓔ
V3, Pg. 225	PT35-S1-Q19	Ⓐ Ⓑ Ⓒ Ⓓ Ⓔ			PT47-S3-Q10	Ⓐ Ⓑ Ⓒ Ⓓ Ⓔ
V3, Pg. 240	PT35-S4-Q1	Ⓐ Ⓑ Ⓒ Ⓓ Ⓔ			PT48-S4-Q3	Ⓐ Ⓑ Ⓒ Ⓓ Ⓔ
V3, Pg. 240	PT35-S4-Q3	Ⓐ Ⓑ Ⓒ Ⓓ Ⓔ			PT49-S2-Q9	Ⓐ Ⓑ Ⓒ Ⓓ Ⓔ
V3, Pg. 246	PT35-S4-Q21	Ⓐ Ⓑ Ⓒ Ⓓ Ⓔ			PT49-S2-Q20	Ⓐ Ⓑ Ⓒ Ⓓ Ⓔ
V3, Pg. 247	PT35-S4-Q26	Ⓐ Ⓑ Ⓒ Ⓓ Ⓔ			PT49-S4-Q14	Ⓐ Ⓑ Ⓒ Ⓓ Ⓔ
V3, Pg. 255	PT36-S1-Q4	Ⓐ Ⓑ Ⓒ Ⓓ Ⓔ			PT49-S4-Q19	Ⓐ Ⓑ Ⓒ Ⓓ Ⓔ
V3, Pg. 258	PT36-S1-Q16	Ⓐ Ⓑ Ⓒ Ⓓ Ⓔ			PT50-S2-Q18	Ⓐ Ⓑ Ⓒ Ⓓ Ⓔ
V3, Pg. 275	PT36-S3-Q17	Ⓐ Ⓑ Ⓒ Ⓓ Ⓔ			PT50-S4-Q1	Ⓐ Ⓑ Ⓒ Ⓓ Ⓔ
V3, Pg. 308	PT37-S4-Q3	Ⓐ Ⓑ Ⓒ Ⓓ Ⓔ			PT50-S4-Q15	Ⓐ Ⓑ Ⓒ Ⓓ Ⓔ
V3, Pg. 309	PT37-S4-Q6	Ⓐ Ⓑ Ⓒ Ⓓ Ⓔ			PT51-S1-Q21	Ⓐ Ⓑ Ⓒ Ⓓ Ⓔ

	PT51-S3-Q12	Ⓐ Ⓑ Ⓒ Ⓓ Ⓔ	V5, Pg. 30	PT62-S4-Q8	Ⓐ Ⓑ Ⓒ Ⓓ Ⓔ
	PT51-S3-Q21	Ⓐ Ⓑ Ⓒ Ⓓ Ⓔ	V5, Pg. 31	PT62-S4-Q11	Ⓐ Ⓑ Ⓒ Ⓓ Ⓔ
V4, Pg. 10	PT52-S1-Q7	Ⓐ Ⓑ Ⓒ Ⓓ Ⓔ	V5, Pg. 47	PT63-S1-Q12	Ⓐ Ⓑ Ⓒ Ⓓ Ⓔ
V4, Pg. 12	PT52-S1-Q15	Ⓐ Ⓑ Ⓒ Ⓓ Ⓔ	V5, Pg. 57	PT63-S3-Q7	Ⓐ Ⓑ Ⓒ Ⓓ Ⓔ
V4, Pg. 15	PT52-S1-Q24	Ⓐ Ⓑ Ⓒ Ⓓ Ⓔ	V5, Pg. 59	PT63-S3-Q13	Ⓐ Ⓑ Ⓒ Ⓓ Ⓔ
V4, Pg. 23	PT52-S3-Q14	Ⓐ Ⓑ Ⓒ Ⓓ Ⓔ	V5, Pg. 98	PT64-S3-Q22	Ⓐ Ⓑ Ⓒ Ⓓ Ⓔ
V4, Pg. 26	PT52-S3-Q23	Ⓐ Ⓑ Ⓒ Ⓓ Ⓔ	V5, Pg. 138	PT65-S4-Q9	Ⓐ Ⓑ Ⓒ Ⓓ Ⓔ
V4, Pg. 61	PT53-S3-Q21	Ⓐ Ⓑ Ⓒ Ⓓ Ⓔ	V5, Pg. 166	PT66-S2-Q22	Ⓐ Ⓑ Ⓒ Ⓓ Ⓔ
V4, Pg. 90	PT54-S2-Q12	Ⓐ Ⓑ Ⓒ Ⓓ Ⓔ	V5, Pg. 201	PT67-S2-Q7	Ⓐ Ⓑ Ⓒ Ⓓ Ⓔ
V4, Pg. 93	PT54-S2-Q20	Ⓐ Ⓑ Ⓒ Ⓓ Ⓔ	V5, Pg. 202	PT67-S2-Q11	Ⓐ Ⓑ Ⓒ Ⓓ Ⓔ
V4, Pg. 101	PT54-S4-Q5	Ⓐ Ⓑ Ⓒ Ⓓ Ⓔ	V5, Pg. 217	PT67-S4-Q5	Ⓐ Ⓑ Ⓒ Ⓓ Ⓔ
V4, Pg. 103	PT54-S4-Q12	Ⓐ Ⓑ Ⓒ Ⓓ Ⓔ	V5, Pg. 220	PT67-S4-Q15	Ⓐ Ⓑ Ⓒ Ⓓ Ⓔ
V4, Pg. 117	PT55-S1-Q5	Ⓐ Ⓑ Ⓒ Ⓓ Ⓔ	V5, Pg. 241	PT68-S2-Q8	Ⓐ Ⓑ Ⓒ Ⓓ Ⓔ
V4, Pg. 118	PT55-S1-Q8	Ⓐ Ⓑ Ⓒ Ⓓ Ⓔ	V5, Pg. 242	PT68-S2-Q10	Ⓐ Ⓑ Ⓒ Ⓓ Ⓔ
V4, Pg. 133	PT55-S3-Q5	Ⓐ Ⓑ Ⓒ Ⓓ Ⓔ	V5, Pg. 248	PT68-S3-Q2	Ⓐ Ⓑ Ⓒ Ⓓ Ⓔ
V4, Pg. 135	PT55-S3-Q12	Ⓐ Ⓑ Ⓒ Ⓓ Ⓔ	V5, Pg. 251	PT68-S3-Q10	Ⓐ Ⓑ Ⓒ Ⓓ Ⓔ
V4, Pg. 136	PT55-S3-Q16	Ⓐ Ⓑ Ⓒ Ⓓ Ⓔ	V5, Pg. 252	PT68-S3-Q13	Ⓐ Ⓑ Ⓒ Ⓓ Ⓔ
V4, Pg. 164	PT56-S3-Q2	Ⓐ Ⓑ Ⓒ Ⓓ Ⓔ	V5, Pg. 275	PT69-S1-Q10	Ⓐ Ⓑ Ⓒ Ⓓ Ⓔ
V4, Pg. 166	PT56-S3-Q11	Ⓐ Ⓑ Ⓒ Ⓓ Ⓔ	V5, Pg. 275	PT69-S1-Q12	Ⓐ Ⓑ Ⓒ Ⓓ Ⓔ
V4, Pg. 168	PT56-S3-Q15	Ⓐ Ⓑ Ⓒ Ⓓ Ⓔ	V5, Pg. 296	PT69-S4-Q2	Ⓐ Ⓑ Ⓒ Ⓓ Ⓔ
V4, Pg. 203	PT57-S3-Q13	Ⓐ Ⓑ Ⓒ Ⓓ Ⓔ	V5, Pg. 298	PT69-S4-Q9	Ⓐ Ⓑ Ⓒ Ⓓ Ⓔ
V4, Pg. 207	PT57-S3-Q23	Ⓐ Ⓑ Ⓒ Ⓓ Ⓔ	V5, Pg. 336	PT70-S4-Q2	Ⓐ Ⓑ Ⓒ Ⓓ Ⓔ
V4, Pg. 207	PT57-S3-Q25	Ⓐ Ⓑ Ⓒ Ⓓ Ⓔ	V5, Pg. 340	PT70-S4-Q18	Ⓐ Ⓑ Ⓒ Ⓓ Ⓔ
V4, Pg. 226	PT58-S1-Q10	Ⓐ Ⓑ Ⓒ Ⓓ Ⓔ	V5, Pg. 354	PT71-S1-Q8	Ⓐ Ⓑ Ⓒ Ⓓ Ⓔ
V4, Pg. 245	PT58-S4-Q6	Ⓐ Ⓑ Ⓒ Ⓓ Ⓔ	V5, Pg. 356	PT71-S1-Q15	Ⓐ Ⓑ Ⓒ Ⓓ Ⓔ
V4, Pg. 247	PT58-S4-Q13	Ⓐ Ⓑ Ⓒ Ⓓ Ⓔ	V5, Pg. 373	PT71-S3-Q17	Ⓐ Ⓑ Ⓒ Ⓓ Ⓔ
V4, Pg. 247	PT58-S4-Q15	Ⓐ Ⓑ Ⓒ Ⓓ Ⓔ	V5, Pg. 374	PT71-S3-Q23	Ⓐ Ⓑ Ⓒ Ⓓ Ⓔ
V4, Pg. 273	PT59-S3-Q3	Ⓐ Ⓑ Ⓒ Ⓓ Ⓔ	PT72, Pg. 22	PT72-S2-Q17	Ⓐ Ⓑ Ⓒ Ⓓ Ⓔ
V4, Pg. 274	PT59-S3-Q7	Ⓐ Ⓑ Ⓒ Ⓓ Ⓔ	PT72, Pg. 32	PT72-S3-Q20	Ⓐ Ⓑ Ⓒ Ⓓ Ⓔ
V4, Pg. 278	PT59-S3-Q21	Ⓐ Ⓑ Ⓒ Ⓓ Ⓔ	PT73, Pg. 24	PT73-S2-Q23	Ⓐ Ⓑ Ⓒ Ⓓ Ⓔ
V4, Pg. 303	PT60-S1-Q24	Ⓐ Ⓑ Ⓒ Ⓓ Ⓔ	PT73, Pg. 36	PT73-S4-Q8	Ⓐ Ⓑ Ⓒ Ⓓ Ⓔ
V4, Pg. 310	PT60-S3-Q10	Ⓐ Ⓑ Ⓒ Ⓓ Ⓔ	PT73, Pg. 37	PT73-S4-Q12	Ⓐ Ⓑ Ⓒ Ⓓ Ⓔ
V4, Pg. 352	PT61-S4-Q3	Ⓐ Ⓑ Ⓒ Ⓓ Ⓔ	PT73, Pg. 37	PT73-S4-Q14	Ⓐ Ⓑ Ⓒ Ⓓ Ⓔ
V4, Pg. 353	PT61-S4-Q5	Ⓐ Ⓑ Ⓒ Ⓓ Ⓔ	PT73, Pg. 38	PT73-S4-Q16	Ⓐ Ⓑ Ⓒ Ⓓ Ⓔ
V4, Pg. 353	PT61-S4-Q7	Ⓐ Ⓑ Ⓒ Ⓓ Ⓔ	PT74, Pg. 13	PT74-S1-Q11	Ⓐ Ⓑ Ⓒ Ⓓ Ⓔ
V4, Pg. 355	PT61-S4-Q10	Ⓐ Ⓑ Ⓒ Ⓓ Ⓔ	PT74, Pg. 16	PT74-S1-Q22	Ⓐ Ⓑ Ⓒ Ⓓ Ⓔ
V5, Pg. 22	PT62-S2-Q21	Ⓐ Ⓑ Ⓒ Ⓓ Ⓔ	PT74, Pg. 34	PT74-S4-Q1	Ⓐ Ⓑ Ⓒ Ⓓ Ⓔ

PT74, Pg. 36	PT74-S4-Q11	Ⓐ Ⓑ Ⓒ Ⓓ Ⓔ	PT75, Pg. 33	PT75-S3-Q24	Ⓐ Ⓑ Ⓒ Ⓓ Ⓔ
PT75, Pg. 13	PT75-S1-Q13	Ⓐ Ⓑ Ⓒ Ⓓ Ⓔ	PT76, Pg. 23	PT76-S2-Q17	Ⓐ Ⓑ Ⓒ Ⓓ Ⓔ
PT75, Pg. 14	PT75-S1-Q17	Ⓐ Ⓑ Ⓒ Ⓓ Ⓔ	PT76, Pg. 38	PT76-S4-Q17	Ⓐ Ⓑ Ⓒ Ⓓ Ⓔ
PT75, Pg. 15	PT75-S1-Q20	Ⓐ Ⓑ Ⓒ Ⓓ Ⓔ	PT77, Pg. 38	PT77-S4-Q15	Ⓐ Ⓑ Ⓒ Ⓓ Ⓔ
PT75, Pg. 26	PT75-S3-Q4	Ⓐ Ⓑ Ⓒ Ⓓ Ⓔ			

Complete the Passage

J07, Pg. 7	J07-S2-Q3	Ⓐ Ⓑ Ⓒ Ⓓ Ⓔ		PT48-S1-Q6	Ⓐ Ⓑ Ⓒ Ⓓ Ⓔ
J07, Pg. 8	J07-S2-Q8	Ⓐ Ⓑ Ⓒ Ⓓ Ⓔ	V4, Pg. 11	PT52-S1-Q13	Ⓐ Ⓑ Ⓒ Ⓓ Ⓔ
J07, Pg. 16	J07-S3-Q10	Ⓐ Ⓑ Ⓒ Ⓓ Ⓔ	V4, Pg. 58	PT53-S3-Q7	Ⓐ Ⓑ Ⓒ Ⓓ Ⓔ
J07, Pg. 18	J07-S3-Q16	Ⓐ Ⓑ Ⓒ Ⓓ Ⓔ	V4, Pg. 89	PT54-S2-Q7	Ⓐ Ⓑ Ⓒ Ⓓ Ⓔ
SP2, Pg. 355	PTC2-S2-Q5	Ⓐ Ⓑ Ⓒ Ⓓ Ⓔ	V4, Pg. 132	PT55-S3-Q3	Ⓐ Ⓑ Ⓒ Ⓓ Ⓔ
	PT3-S2-Q24	Ⓐ Ⓑ Ⓒ Ⓓ Ⓔ	V4, Pg. 192	PT57-S2-Q2	Ⓐ Ⓑ Ⓒ Ⓓ Ⓔ
	PT5-S1-Q9	Ⓐ Ⓑ Ⓒ Ⓓ Ⓔ	V4, Pg. 197	PT57-S2-Q18	Ⓐ Ⓑ Ⓒ Ⓓ Ⓔ
V1, Pg. 17	PT7-S1-Q5	Ⓐ Ⓑ Ⓒ Ⓓ Ⓔ	V4, Pg. 267	PT59-S2-Q12	Ⓐ Ⓑ Ⓒ Ⓓ Ⓔ
V1, Pg. 41	PT7-S4-Q18	Ⓐ Ⓑ Ⓒ Ⓓ Ⓔ	V4, Pg. 270	PT59-S2-Q24	Ⓐ Ⓑ Ⓒ Ⓓ Ⓔ
V1, Pg. 111	PT10-S4-Q24	Ⓐ Ⓑ Ⓒ Ⓓ Ⓔ	V4, Pg. 311	PT60-S3-Q14	Ⓐ Ⓑ Ⓒ Ⓓ Ⓔ
V1, Pg. 192	PT13-S2-Q9	Ⓐ Ⓑ Ⓒ Ⓓ Ⓔ	V4, Pg. 344	PT61-S2-Q15	Ⓐ Ⓑ Ⓒ Ⓓ Ⓔ
V1, Pg. 275	PT15-S3-Q21	Ⓐ Ⓑ Ⓒ Ⓓ Ⓔ	V5, Pg. 34	PT62-S4-Q24	Ⓐ Ⓑ Ⓒ Ⓓ Ⓔ
V1, Pg. 331	PT18-S2-Q18	Ⓐ Ⓑ Ⓒ Ⓓ Ⓔ	V5, Pg. 44	PT63-S1-Q1	Ⓐ Ⓑ Ⓒ Ⓓ Ⓔ
V1, Pg. 343	PT18-S4-Q4	Ⓐ Ⓑ Ⓒ Ⓓ Ⓔ	V5, Pg. 92	PT64-S3-Q1	Ⓐ Ⓑ Ⓒ Ⓓ Ⓔ
V2, Pg. 25	PT19-S2-Q19	Ⓐ Ⓑ Ⓒ Ⓓ Ⓔ	V5, Pg. 92	PT64-S3-Q3	Ⓐ Ⓑ Ⓒ Ⓓ Ⓔ
V2, Pg. 73	PT20-S4-Q13	Ⓐ Ⓑ Ⓒ Ⓓ Ⓔ	V5, Pg. 117	PT65-S1-Q4	Ⓐ Ⓑ Ⓒ Ⓓ Ⓔ
V2, Pg. 229	PT25-S2-Q3	Ⓐ Ⓑ Ⓒ Ⓓ Ⓔ	V5, Pg. 118	PT65-S1-Q7	Ⓐ Ⓑ Ⓒ Ⓓ Ⓔ
V2, Pg. 267	PT26-S3-Q7	Ⓐ Ⓑ Ⓒ Ⓓ Ⓔ	V5, Pg. 140	PT65-S4-Q15	Ⓐ Ⓑ Ⓒ Ⓓ Ⓔ
V3, Pg. 205	PT34-S3-Q12	Ⓐ Ⓑ Ⓒ Ⓓ Ⓔ	V5, Pg. 201	PT67-S2-Q5	Ⓐ Ⓑ Ⓒ Ⓓ Ⓔ
V3, Pg. 298	PT37-S2-Q9	Ⓐ Ⓑ Ⓒ Ⓓ Ⓔ	V5, Pg. 207	PT67-S2-Q24	Ⓐ Ⓑ Ⓒ Ⓓ Ⓔ
V3, Pg. 308	PT37-S4-Q1	Ⓐ Ⓑ Ⓒ Ⓓ Ⓔ	V5, Pg. 222	PT67-S4-Q20	Ⓐ Ⓑ Ⓒ Ⓓ Ⓔ
V3, Pg. 310	PT37-S4-Q8	Ⓐ Ⓑ Ⓒ Ⓓ Ⓔ	V5, Pg. 253	PT68-S3-Q19	Ⓐ Ⓑ Ⓒ Ⓓ Ⓔ
V3, Pg. 327	PT38-S1-Q19	Ⓐ Ⓑ Ⓒ Ⓓ Ⓔ	V5, Pg. 276	PT69-S1-Q16	Ⓐ Ⓑ Ⓒ Ⓓ Ⓔ
V3, Pg. 344	PT38-S4-Q10	Ⓐ Ⓑ Ⓒ Ⓓ Ⓔ	V5, Pg. 312	PT70-S1-Q1	Ⓐ Ⓑ Ⓒ Ⓓ Ⓔ
	PT39-S2-Q6	Ⓐ Ⓑ Ⓒ Ⓓ Ⓔ	V5, Pg. 353	PT71-S1-Q4	Ⓐ Ⓑ Ⓒ Ⓓ Ⓔ
	PT40-S1-Q7	Ⓐ Ⓑ Ⓒ Ⓓ Ⓔ	V5, Pg. 369	PT71-S3-Q5	Ⓐ Ⓑ Ⓒ Ⓓ Ⓔ
	PT44-S4-Q8	Ⓐ Ⓑ Ⓒ Ⓓ Ⓔ	PT72, Pg. 30	PT72-S3-Q16	Ⓐ Ⓑ Ⓒ Ⓓ Ⓔ
	PT44-S4-Q23	Ⓐ Ⓑ Ⓒ Ⓓ Ⓔ	PT73, Pg. 25	PT73-S2-Q25	Ⓐ Ⓑ Ⓒ Ⓓ Ⓔ
	PT47-S1-Q13	Ⓐ Ⓑ Ⓒ Ⓓ Ⓔ	PT74, Pg. 10	PT74-S1-Q1	Ⓐ Ⓑ Ⓒ Ⓓ Ⓔ
	PT47-S3-Q12	Ⓐ Ⓑ Ⓒ Ⓓ Ⓔ	PT74, Pg. 35	PT74-S4-Q7	Ⓐ Ⓑ Ⓒ Ⓓ Ⓔ

PT75, Pg. 26	PT75-S3-Q1	Ⓐ Ⓑ Ⓒ Ⓓ Ⓔ	PT77, Pg. 22	PT77-S2-Q13	Ⓐ Ⓑ Ⓒ Ⓓ Ⓔ
PT76, Pg. 18	PT76-S2-Q2	Ⓐ Ⓑ Ⓒ Ⓓ Ⓔ	PT77, Pg. 35	PT77-S4-Q5	Ⓐ Ⓑ Ⓒ Ⓓ Ⓔ
PT76, Pg. 22	PT76-S2-Q15	Ⓐ Ⓑ Ⓒ Ⓓ Ⓔ			

Cannot Be True

SP1, Pg. 75	PTA-S1-Q23	Ⓐ Ⓑ Ⓒ Ⓓ Ⓔ	V3, Pg. 71	PT30-S4-Q7	Ⓐ Ⓑ Ⓒ Ⓓ Ⓔ
SP1, Pg. 211	PTB-S4-Q21	Ⓐ Ⓑ Ⓒ Ⓓ Ⓔ	V3, Pg. 90	PT31-S2-Q8	Ⓐ Ⓑ Ⓒ Ⓓ Ⓔ
SP1, Pg. 312	PTC-S3-Q18	Ⓐ Ⓑ Ⓒ Ⓓ Ⓔ	V3, Pg. 92	PT31-S2-Q15	Ⓐ Ⓑ Ⓒ Ⓓ Ⓔ
	PT2-S2-Q17	Ⓐ Ⓑ Ⓒ Ⓓ Ⓔ	V3, Pg. 207	PT34-S3-Q22	Ⓐ Ⓑ Ⓒ Ⓓ Ⓔ
	PT3-S4-Q14	Ⓐ Ⓑ Ⓒ Ⓓ Ⓔ	V3, Pg. 246	PT35-S4-Q22	Ⓐ Ⓑ Ⓒ Ⓓ Ⓔ
	PT4-S4-Q24	Ⓐ Ⓑ Ⓒ Ⓓ Ⓔ	V3, Pg. 349	PT38-S4-Q25	Ⓐ Ⓑ Ⓒ Ⓓ Ⓔ
	PT5-S1-Q15	Ⓐ Ⓑ Ⓒ Ⓓ Ⓔ		PT39-S2-Q24	Ⓐ Ⓑ Ⓒ Ⓓ Ⓔ
	PT6-S3-Q19	Ⓐ Ⓑ Ⓒ Ⓓ Ⓔ		PT41-S1-Q7	Ⓐ Ⓑ Ⓒ Ⓓ Ⓔ
V1, Pg. 21	PT7-S1-Q19	Ⓐ Ⓑ Ⓒ Ⓓ Ⓔ		PT41-S3-Q2	Ⓐ Ⓑ Ⓒ Ⓓ Ⓔ
V1, Pg. 39	PT7-S4-Q12	Ⓐ Ⓑ Ⓒ Ⓓ Ⓔ		PT41-S3-Q10	Ⓐ Ⓑ Ⓒ Ⓓ Ⓔ
	PT8-S1-Q8	Ⓐ Ⓑ Ⓒ Ⓓ Ⓔ		PT42-S4-Q25	Ⓐ Ⓑ Ⓒ Ⓓ Ⓔ
V1, Pg. 62	PT9-S2-Q17	Ⓐ Ⓑ Ⓒ Ⓓ Ⓔ		PT43-S3-Q17	Ⓐ Ⓑ Ⓒ Ⓓ Ⓔ
V1, Pg. 224	PT14-S2-Q2	Ⓐ Ⓑ Ⓒ Ⓓ Ⓔ		PT44-S4-Q18	Ⓐ Ⓑ Ⓒ Ⓓ Ⓔ
	PT17-S3-Q15	Ⓐ Ⓑ Ⓒ Ⓓ Ⓔ		PT48-S4-Q18	Ⓐ Ⓑ Ⓒ Ⓓ Ⓔ
V1, Pg. 333	PT18-S2-Q23	Ⓐ Ⓑ Ⓒ Ⓓ Ⓔ		PT49-S2-Q16	Ⓐ Ⓑ Ⓒ Ⓓ Ⓔ
V2, Pg. 39	PT19-S4-Q13	Ⓐ Ⓑ Ⓒ Ⓓ Ⓔ		PT49-S2-Q21	Ⓐ Ⓑ Ⓒ Ⓓ Ⓔ
V2, Pg. 244	PT25-S4-Q15	Ⓐ Ⓑ Ⓒ Ⓓ Ⓔ		PT49-S4-Q5	Ⓐ Ⓑ Ⓒ Ⓓ Ⓔ
V2, Pg. 244	PT25-S4-Q16	Ⓐ Ⓑ Ⓒ Ⓓ Ⓔ	V4, Pg. 13	PT52-S1-Q18	Ⓐ Ⓑ Ⓒ Ⓓ Ⓔ
V2, Pg. 247	PT25-S4-Q26	Ⓐ Ⓑ Ⓒ Ⓓ Ⓔ	V4, Pg. 170	PT56-S3-Q22	Ⓐ Ⓑ Ⓒ Ⓓ Ⓔ
V2, Pg. 269	PT26-S3-Q12	Ⓐ Ⓑ Ⓒ Ⓓ Ⓔ	V4, Pg. 199	PT57-S2-Q23	Ⓐ Ⓑ Ⓒ Ⓓ Ⓔ
V2, Pg. 324	PT28-S1-Q11	Ⓐ Ⓑ Ⓒ Ⓓ Ⓔ	V5, Pg. 22	PT62-S2-Q24	Ⓐ Ⓑ Ⓒ Ⓓ Ⓔ
V2, Pg. 327	PT28-S1-Q20	Ⓐ Ⓑ Ⓒ Ⓓ Ⓔ	PT77, Pg. 25	PT77-S2-Q25	Ⓐ Ⓑ Ⓒ Ⓓ Ⓔ
V2, Pg. 336	PT28-S3-Q12	Ⓐ Ⓑ Ⓒ Ⓓ Ⓔ	PT77, Pg. 36	PT77-S4-Q10	Ⓐ Ⓑ Ⓒ Ⓓ Ⓔ
V3, Pg. 42	PT29-S4-Q22	Ⓐ Ⓑ Ⓒ Ⓓ Ⓔ			

Main Conclusion

J07, Pg. 6	J07-S2-Q1	Ⓐ Ⓑ Ⓒ Ⓓ Ⓔ	SP1, Pg. 213	PTB-S4-Q25	Ⓐ Ⓑ Ⓒ Ⓓ Ⓔ
J07, Pg. 8	J07-S2-Q10	Ⓐ Ⓑ Ⓒ Ⓓ Ⓔ	SP1, Pg. 310	PTC-S3-Q8	Ⓐ Ⓑ Ⓒ Ⓓ Ⓔ
J07, Pg. 17	J07-S3-Q12	Ⓐ Ⓑ Ⓒ Ⓓ Ⓔ	SP2, Pg. 357	PTC2-S2-Q13	Ⓐ Ⓑ Ⓒ Ⓓ Ⓔ
SP1, Pg. 71	PTA-S1-Q9	Ⓐ Ⓑ Ⓒ Ⓓ Ⓔ	SP2, Pg. 362	PTC2-S3-Q2	Ⓐ Ⓑ Ⓒ Ⓓ Ⓔ
SP1, Pg. 88	PTA-S4-Q2	Ⓐ Ⓑ Ⓒ Ⓓ Ⓔ	SP2, Pg. 366	PTC2-S3-Q16	Ⓐ Ⓑ Ⓒ Ⓓ Ⓔ
SP1, Pg. 186	PTB-S1-Q1	Ⓐ Ⓑ Ⓒ Ⓓ Ⓔ		PT1-S3-Q13	Ⓐ Ⓑ Ⓒ Ⓓ Ⓔ
SP1, Pg. 208	PTB-S4-Q6	Ⓐ Ⓑ Ⓒ Ⓓ Ⓔ		PT1-S4-Q19	Ⓐ Ⓑ Ⓒ Ⓓ Ⓔ

	PT2-S2-Q6	Ⓐ Ⓑ Ⓒ Ⓓ Ⓔ	V2, Pg. 197	PT24-S2-Q12	Ⓐ Ⓑ Ⓒ Ⓓ Ⓔ
	PT2-S4-Q19	Ⓐ Ⓑ Ⓒ Ⓓ Ⓔ	V2, Pg. 198	PT24-S2-Q15	Ⓐ Ⓑ Ⓒ Ⓓ Ⓔ
	PT3-S2-Q18	Ⓐ Ⓑ Ⓒ Ⓓ Ⓔ	V2, Pg. 228	PT25-S2-Q1	Ⓐ Ⓑ Ⓒ Ⓓ Ⓔ
	PT5-S3-Q3	Ⓐ Ⓑ Ⓒ Ⓓ Ⓔ	V2, Pg. 230	PT25-S2-Q7	Ⓐ Ⓑ Ⓒ Ⓓ Ⓔ
	PT6-S2-Q1	Ⓐ Ⓑ Ⓒ Ⓓ Ⓔ	V2, Pg. 240	PT25-S4-Q1	Ⓐ Ⓑ Ⓒ Ⓓ Ⓔ
	PT6-S2-Q18	Ⓐ Ⓑ Ⓒ Ⓓ Ⓔ	V2, Pg. 259	PT26-S2-Q8	Ⓐ Ⓑ Ⓒ Ⓓ Ⓔ
	PT6-S3-Q12	Ⓐ Ⓑ Ⓒ Ⓓ Ⓔ	V2, Pg. 327	PT28-S1-Q18	Ⓐ Ⓑ Ⓒ Ⓓ Ⓔ
V1, Pg. 36	PT7-S4-Q2	Ⓐ Ⓑ Ⓒ Ⓓ Ⓔ	V2, Pg. 337	PT28-S3-Q14	Ⓐ Ⓑ Ⓒ Ⓓ Ⓔ
V1, Pg. 59	PT9-S2-Q3	Ⓐ Ⓑ Ⓒ Ⓓ Ⓔ	V3, Pg. 19	PT29-S1-Q11	Ⓐ Ⓑ Ⓒ Ⓓ Ⓔ
V1, Pg. 74	PT9-S4-Q18	Ⓐ Ⓑ Ⓒ Ⓓ Ⓔ	V3, Pg. 37	PT29-S4-Q6	Ⓐ Ⓑ Ⓒ Ⓓ Ⓔ
V1, Pg. 86	PT10-S1-Q11	Ⓐ Ⓑ Ⓒ Ⓓ Ⓔ	V3, Pg. 70	PT30-S4-Q2	Ⓐ Ⓑ Ⓒ Ⓓ Ⓔ
V1, Pg. 123	PT11-S2-Q4	Ⓐ Ⓑ Ⓒ Ⓓ Ⓔ	V3, Pg. 89	PT31-S2-Q4	Ⓐ Ⓑ Ⓒ Ⓓ Ⓔ
V1, Pg. 127	PT11-S2-Q20	Ⓐ Ⓑ Ⓒ Ⓓ Ⓔ	V3, Pg. 99	PT31-S3-Q14	Ⓐ Ⓑ Ⓒ Ⓓ Ⓔ
V1, Pg. 140	PT11-S4-Q8	Ⓐ Ⓑ Ⓒ Ⓓ Ⓔ	V3, Pg. 122	PT32-S1-Q13	Ⓐ Ⓑ Ⓒ Ⓓ Ⓔ
V1, Pg. 152	PT12-S1-Q1	Ⓐ Ⓑ Ⓒ Ⓓ Ⓔ	V3, Pg. 141	PT32-S4-Q12	Ⓐ Ⓑ Ⓒ Ⓓ Ⓔ
V1, Pg. 154	PT12-S1-Q9	Ⓐ Ⓑ Ⓒ Ⓓ Ⓔ	V3, Pg. 153	PT33-S1-Q5	Ⓐ Ⓑ Ⓒ Ⓓ Ⓔ
V1, Pg. 175	PT12-S4-Q10	Ⓐ Ⓑ Ⓒ Ⓓ Ⓔ	V3, Pg. 198	PT34-S2-Q15	Ⓐ Ⓑ Ⓒ Ⓓ Ⓔ
V1, Pg. 206	PT13-S4-Q3	Ⓐ Ⓑ Ⓒ Ⓓ Ⓔ	V3, Pg. 199	PT34-S2-Q18	Ⓐ Ⓑ Ⓒ Ⓓ Ⓔ
V1, Pg. 228	PT14-S2-Q14	Ⓐ Ⓑ Ⓒ Ⓓ Ⓔ	V3, Pg. 221	PT35-S1-Q3	Ⓐ Ⓑ Ⓒ Ⓓ Ⓔ
V1, Pg. 229	PT14-S2-Q19	Ⓐ Ⓑ Ⓒ Ⓓ Ⓔ	V3, Pg. 224	PT35-S1-Q16	Ⓐ Ⓑ Ⓒ Ⓓ Ⓔ
V1, Pg. 264	PT15-S2-Q8	Ⓐ Ⓑ Ⓒ Ⓓ Ⓔ	V3, Pg. 242	PT35-S4-Q9	Ⓐ Ⓑ Ⓒ Ⓓ Ⓔ
V1, Pg. 265	PT15-S2-Q11	Ⓐ Ⓑ Ⓒ Ⓓ Ⓔ	V3, Pg. 256	PT36-S1-Q6	Ⓐ Ⓑ Ⓒ Ⓓ Ⓔ
V1, Pg. 270	PT15-S3-Q1	Ⓐ Ⓑ Ⓒ Ⓓ Ⓔ	V3, Pg. 271	PT36-S3-Q3	Ⓐ Ⓑ Ⓒ Ⓓ Ⓔ
V1, Pg. 271	PT15-S3-Q4	Ⓐ Ⓑ Ⓒ Ⓓ Ⓔ	V3, Pg. 272	PT36-S3-Q9	Ⓐ Ⓑ Ⓒ Ⓓ Ⓔ
V1, Pg. 305	PT16-S3-Q19	Ⓐ Ⓑ Ⓒ Ⓓ Ⓔ	V3, Pg. 277	PT36-S3-Q23	Ⓐ Ⓑ Ⓒ Ⓓ Ⓔ
	PT17-S2-Q6	Ⓐ Ⓑ Ⓒ Ⓓ Ⓔ	V3, Pg. 322	PT38-S1-Q2	Ⓐ Ⓑ Ⓒ Ⓓ Ⓔ
	PT17-S2-Q19	Ⓐ Ⓑ Ⓒ Ⓓ Ⓔ	V3, Pg. 342	PT38-S4-Q3	Ⓐ Ⓑ Ⓒ Ⓓ Ⓔ
V1, Pg. 329	PT18-S2-Q10	Ⓐ Ⓑ Ⓒ Ⓓ Ⓔ	V3, Pg. 344	PT38-S4-Q11	Ⓐ Ⓑ Ⓒ Ⓓ Ⓔ
V1, Pg. 342	PT18-S4-Q2	Ⓐ Ⓑ Ⓒ Ⓓ Ⓔ		PT39-S2-Q1	Ⓐ Ⓑ Ⓒ Ⓓ Ⓔ
V2, Pg. 88	PT21-S2-Q1	Ⓐ Ⓑ Ⓒ Ⓓ Ⓔ		PT40-S1-Q9	Ⓐ Ⓑ Ⓒ Ⓓ Ⓔ
V2, Pg. 92	PT21-S2-Q14	Ⓐ Ⓑ Ⓒ Ⓓ Ⓔ		PT40-S3-Q4	Ⓐ Ⓑ Ⓒ Ⓓ Ⓔ
V2, Pg. 96	PT21-S3-Q2	Ⓐ Ⓑ Ⓒ Ⓓ Ⓔ		PT41-S1-Q5	Ⓐ Ⓑ Ⓒ Ⓓ Ⓔ
V2, Pg. 98	PT21-S3-Q10	Ⓐ Ⓑ Ⓒ Ⓓ Ⓔ		PT41-S3-Q18	Ⓐ Ⓑ Ⓒ Ⓓ Ⓔ
V2, Pg. 126	PT22-S2-Q2	Ⓐ Ⓑ Ⓒ Ⓓ Ⓔ		PT42-S4-Q10	Ⓐ Ⓑ Ⓒ Ⓓ Ⓔ
V2, Pg. 156	PT23-S2-Q2	Ⓐ Ⓑ Ⓒ Ⓓ Ⓔ		PT43-S3-Q14	Ⓐ Ⓑ Ⓒ Ⓓ Ⓔ
V2, Pg. 169	PT23-S3-Q21	Ⓐ Ⓑ Ⓒ Ⓓ Ⓔ		PT43-S3-Q23	Ⓐ Ⓑ Ⓒ Ⓓ Ⓔ
V2, Pg. 171	PT23-S3-Q25	Ⓐ Ⓑ Ⓒ Ⓓ Ⓔ		PT44-S2-Q16	Ⓐ Ⓑ Ⓒ Ⓓ Ⓔ

	PT45-S1-Q1	Ⓐ Ⓑ Ⓒ Ⓓ Ⓔ	V4, Pg. 342	PT61-S2-Q9	Ⓐ Ⓑ Ⓒ Ⓓ Ⓔ
	PT45-S1-Q17	Ⓐ Ⓑ Ⓒ Ⓓ Ⓔ	V4, Pg. 353	PT61-S4-Q6	Ⓐ Ⓑ Ⓒ Ⓓ Ⓔ
	PT45-S4-Q1	Ⓐ Ⓑ Ⓒ Ⓓ Ⓔ	V4, Pg. 356	PT61-S4-Q16	Ⓐ Ⓑ Ⓒ Ⓓ Ⓔ
	PT45-S4-Q9	Ⓐ Ⓑ Ⓒ Ⓓ Ⓔ	V5, Pg. 19	PT62-S2-Q10	Ⓐ Ⓑ Ⓒ Ⓓ Ⓔ
	PT46-S3-Q5	Ⓐ Ⓑ Ⓒ Ⓓ Ⓔ	V5, Pg. 28	PT62-S4-Q1	Ⓐ Ⓑ Ⓒ Ⓓ Ⓔ
	PT46-S3-Q21	Ⓐ Ⓑ Ⓒ Ⓓ Ⓔ	V5, Pg. 31	PT62-S4-Q12	Ⓐ Ⓑ Ⓒ Ⓓ Ⓔ
	PT47-S3-Q6	Ⓐ Ⓑ Ⓒ Ⓓ Ⓔ	V5, Pg. 46	PT63-S1-Q8	Ⓐ Ⓑ Ⓒ Ⓓ Ⓔ
	PT48-S1-Q5	Ⓐ Ⓑ Ⓒ Ⓓ Ⓔ	V5, Pg. 47	PT63-S1-Q13	Ⓐ Ⓑ Ⓒ Ⓓ Ⓔ
	PT48-S1-Q8	Ⓐ Ⓑ Ⓒ Ⓓ Ⓔ	V5, Pg. 58	PT63-S3-Q10	Ⓐ Ⓑ Ⓒ Ⓓ Ⓔ
	PT48-S4-Q1	Ⓐ Ⓑ Ⓒ Ⓓ Ⓔ	V5, Pg. 80	PT64-S1-Q1	Ⓐ Ⓑ Ⓒ Ⓓ Ⓔ
	PT48-S4-Q12	Ⓐ Ⓑ Ⓒ Ⓓ Ⓔ	V5, Pg. 116	PT65-S1-Q2	Ⓐ Ⓑ Ⓒ Ⓓ Ⓔ
	PT49-S4-Q7	Ⓐ Ⓑ Ⓒ Ⓓ Ⓔ	V5, Pg. 118	PT65-S1-Q9	Ⓐ Ⓑ Ⓒ Ⓓ Ⓔ
	PT50-S2-Q4	Ⓐ Ⓑ Ⓒ Ⓓ Ⓔ	V5, Pg. 139	PT65-S4-Q14	Ⓐ Ⓑ Ⓒ Ⓓ Ⓔ
	PT50-S2-Q20	Ⓐ Ⓑ Ⓒ Ⓓ Ⓔ	V5, Pg. 165	PT66-S2-Q18	Ⓐ Ⓑ Ⓒ Ⓓ Ⓔ
	PT50-S4-Q25	Ⓐ Ⓑ Ⓒ Ⓓ Ⓔ	V5, Pg. 177	PT66-S4-Q5	Ⓐ Ⓑ Ⓒ Ⓓ Ⓔ
	PT51-S1-Q1	Ⓐ Ⓑ Ⓒ Ⓓ Ⓔ	V5, Pg. 178	PT66-S4-Q9	Ⓐ Ⓑ Ⓒ Ⓓ Ⓔ
	PT51-S1-Q13	Ⓐ Ⓑ Ⓒ Ⓓ Ⓔ	V5, Pg. 183	PT66-S4-Q26	Ⓐ Ⓑ Ⓒ Ⓓ Ⓔ
	PT51-S3-Q16	Ⓐ Ⓑ Ⓒ Ⓓ Ⓔ	V5, Pg. 216	PT67-S4-Q1	Ⓐ Ⓑ Ⓒ Ⓓ Ⓔ
V4, Pg. 8	PT52-S1-Q1	Ⓐ Ⓑ Ⓒ Ⓓ Ⓔ	V5, Pg. 244	PT68-S2-Q17	Ⓐ Ⓑ Ⓒ Ⓓ Ⓔ
V4, Pg. 20	PT52-S3-Q2	Ⓐ Ⓑ Ⓒ Ⓓ Ⓔ	V5, Pg. 245	PT68-S2-Q19	Ⓐ Ⓑ Ⓒ Ⓓ Ⓔ
V4, Pg. 44	PT53-S1-Q4	Ⓐ Ⓑ Ⓒ Ⓓ Ⓔ	V5, Pg. 250	PT68-S3-Q8	Ⓐ Ⓑ Ⓒ Ⓓ Ⓔ
V4, Pg. 57	PT53-S3-Q3	Ⓐ Ⓑ Ⓒ Ⓓ Ⓔ	V5, Pg. 251	PT68-S3-Q11	Ⓐ Ⓑ Ⓒ Ⓓ Ⓔ
V4, Pg. 57	PT53-S3-Q5	Ⓐ Ⓑ Ⓒ Ⓓ Ⓔ	V5, Pg. 275	PT69-S1-Q9	Ⓐ Ⓑ Ⓒ Ⓓ Ⓔ
V4, Pg. 90	PT54-S2-Q11	Ⓐ Ⓑ Ⓒ Ⓓ Ⓔ	V5, Pg. 296	PT69-S4-Q1	Ⓐ Ⓑ Ⓒ Ⓓ Ⓔ
V4, Pg. 103	PT54-S4-Q11	Ⓐ Ⓑ Ⓒ Ⓓ Ⓔ	V5, Pg. 303	PT69-S4-Q24	Ⓐ Ⓑ Ⓒ Ⓓ Ⓔ
V4, Pg. 120	PT55-S1-Q18	Ⓐ Ⓑ Ⓒ Ⓓ Ⓔ	V5, Pg. 316	PT70-S1-Q18	Ⓐ Ⓑ Ⓒ Ⓓ Ⓔ
V4, Pg. 135	PT55-S3-Q13	Ⓐ Ⓑ Ⓒ Ⓓ Ⓔ	V5, Pg. 340	PT70-S4-Q16	Ⓐ Ⓑ Ⓒ Ⓓ Ⓔ
V4, Pg. 138	PT55-S3-Q20	Ⓐ Ⓑ Ⓒ Ⓓ Ⓔ	V5, Pg. 353	PT71-S1-Q5	Ⓐ Ⓑ Ⓒ Ⓓ Ⓔ
V4, Pg. 165	PT56-S3-Q5	Ⓐ Ⓑ Ⓒ Ⓓ Ⓔ	V5, Pg. 354	PT71-S1-Q7	Ⓐ Ⓑ Ⓒ Ⓓ Ⓔ
V4, Pg. 169	PT56-S3-Q19	Ⓐ Ⓑ Ⓒ Ⓓ Ⓔ	V5, Pg. 371	PT71-S3-Q12	Ⓐ Ⓑ Ⓒ Ⓓ Ⓔ
V4, Pg. 200	PT57-S3-Q3	Ⓐ Ⓑ Ⓒ Ⓓ Ⓔ	PT72, Pg. 19	PT72-S2-Q4	Ⓐ Ⓑ Ⓒ Ⓓ Ⓔ
V4, Pg. 227	PT58-S1-Q13	Ⓐ Ⓑ Ⓒ Ⓓ Ⓔ	PT72, Pg. 27	PT72-S3-Q3	Ⓐ Ⓑ Ⓒ Ⓓ Ⓔ
V4, Pg. 244	PT58-S4-Q3	Ⓐ Ⓑ Ⓒ Ⓓ Ⓔ	PT72, Pg. 28	PT72-S3-Q9	Ⓐ Ⓑ Ⓒ Ⓓ Ⓔ
V4, Pg. 266	PT59-S2-Q10	Ⓐ Ⓑ Ⓒ Ⓓ Ⓔ	PT73, Pg. 21	PT73-S2-Q11	Ⓐ Ⓑ Ⓒ Ⓓ Ⓔ
V4, Pg. 274	PT59-S3-Q9	Ⓐ Ⓑ Ⓒ Ⓓ Ⓔ	PT73, Pg. 35	PT73-S4-Q5	Ⓐ Ⓑ Ⓒ Ⓓ Ⓔ
V4, Pg. 298	PT60-S1-Q8	Ⓐ Ⓑ Ⓒ Ⓓ Ⓔ	PT73, Pg. 37	PT73-S4-Q11	Ⓐ Ⓑ Ⓒ Ⓓ Ⓔ
V4, Pg. 312	PT60-S3-Q15	Ⓐ Ⓑ Ⓒ Ⓓ Ⓔ	PT74, Pg. 13	PT74-S1-Q13	Ⓐ Ⓑ Ⓒ Ⓓ Ⓔ

PT74, Pg. 34	PT74-S4-Q2	Ⓐ Ⓑ Ⓒ Ⓓ Ⓔ		PT77, Pg. 21	PT77-S2-Q11	Ⓐ Ⓑ Ⓒ Ⓓ Ⓔ
PT75, Pg. 12	PT75-S1-Q8	Ⓐ Ⓑ Ⓒ Ⓓ Ⓔ		PT77, Pg. 36	PT77-S4-Q8	Ⓐ Ⓑ Ⓒ Ⓓ Ⓔ
PT75, Pg. 27	PT75-S3-Q8	Ⓐ Ⓑ Ⓒ Ⓓ Ⓔ				

Point

J07, Pg. 11	J07-S2-Q16	Ⓐ Ⓑ Ⓒ Ⓓ Ⓔ		V2, Pg. 53	PT20-S1-Q13	Ⓐ Ⓑ Ⓒ Ⓓ Ⓔ
J07, Pg. 14	J07-S3-Q3	Ⓐ Ⓑ Ⓒ Ⓓ Ⓔ		V2, Pg. 76	PT20-S4-Q21	Ⓐ Ⓑ Ⓒ Ⓓ Ⓔ
J07, Pg. 15	J07-S3-Q7	Ⓐ Ⓑ Ⓒ Ⓓ Ⓔ		V2, Pg. 139	PT22-S4-Q3	Ⓐ Ⓑ Ⓒ Ⓓ Ⓔ
SP1, Pg. 70	PTA-S1-Q6	Ⓐ Ⓑ Ⓒ Ⓓ Ⓔ		V2, Pg. 140	PT22-S4-Q10	Ⓐ Ⓑ Ⓒ Ⓓ Ⓔ
SP1, Pg. 93	PTA-S4-Q18	Ⓐ Ⓑ Ⓒ Ⓓ Ⓔ		V2, Pg. 198	PT24-S2-Q14	Ⓐ Ⓑ Ⓒ Ⓓ Ⓔ
SP1, Pg. 190	PTB-S1-Q15	Ⓐ Ⓑ Ⓒ Ⓓ Ⓔ		V2, Pg. 202	PT24-S3-Q1	Ⓐ Ⓑ Ⓒ Ⓓ Ⓔ
SP1, Pg. 300	PTC-S2-Q1	Ⓐ Ⓑ Ⓒ Ⓓ Ⓔ		V2, Pg. 246	PT25-S4-Q22	Ⓐ Ⓑ Ⓒ Ⓓ Ⓔ
SP1, Pg. 302	PTC-S2-Q11	Ⓐ Ⓑ Ⓒ Ⓓ Ⓔ		V2, Pg. 258	PT26-S2-Q3	Ⓐ Ⓑ Ⓒ Ⓓ Ⓔ
SP1, Pg. 303	PTC-S2-Q13	Ⓐ Ⓑ Ⓒ Ⓓ Ⓔ		V2, Pg. 265	PT26-S2-Q24	Ⓐ Ⓑ Ⓒ Ⓓ Ⓔ
SP1, Pg. 313	PTC-S3-Q20	Ⓐ Ⓑ Ⓒ Ⓓ Ⓔ		V2, Pg. 288	PT27-S1-Q1	Ⓐ Ⓑ Ⓒ Ⓓ Ⓔ
SP1, Pg. 315	PTC-S3-Q26	Ⓐ Ⓑ Ⓒ Ⓓ Ⓔ		V2, Pg. 311	PT27-S4-Q11	Ⓐ Ⓑ Ⓒ Ⓓ Ⓔ
SP2, Pg. 358	PTC2-S2-Q16	Ⓐ Ⓑ Ⓒ Ⓓ Ⓔ		V2, Pg. 323	PT28-S1-Q6	Ⓐ Ⓑ Ⓒ Ⓓ Ⓔ
SP2, Pg. 361	PTC2-S2-Q24	Ⓐ Ⓑ Ⓒ Ⓓ Ⓔ		V3, Pg. 16	PT29-S1-Q1	Ⓐ Ⓑ Ⓒ Ⓓ Ⓔ
SP2, Pg. 363	PTC2-S3-Q4	Ⓐ Ⓑ Ⓒ Ⓓ Ⓔ		V3, Pg. 18	PT29-S1-Q9	Ⓐ Ⓑ Ⓒ Ⓓ Ⓔ
	PT1-S3-Q25	Ⓐ Ⓑ Ⓒ Ⓓ Ⓔ		V3, Pg. 39	PT29-S4-Q13	Ⓐ Ⓑ Ⓒ Ⓓ Ⓔ
	PT2-S4-Q13	Ⓐ Ⓑ Ⓒ Ⓓ Ⓔ		V3, Pg. 40	PT29-S4-Q16	Ⓐ Ⓑ Ⓒ Ⓓ Ⓔ
	PT4-S4-Q14	Ⓐ Ⓑ Ⓒ Ⓓ Ⓔ		V3, Pg. 56	PT30-S2-Q10	Ⓐ Ⓑ Ⓒ Ⓓ Ⓔ
	PT5-S1-Q7	Ⓐ Ⓑ Ⓒ Ⓓ Ⓔ		V3, Pg. 76	PT30-S4-Q21	Ⓐ Ⓑ Ⓒ Ⓓ Ⓔ
	PT5-S3-Q18	Ⓐ Ⓑ Ⓒ Ⓓ Ⓔ		V3, Pg. 88	PT31-S2-Q1	Ⓐ Ⓑ Ⓒ Ⓓ Ⓔ
	PT8-S1-Q17	Ⓐ Ⓑ Ⓒ Ⓓ Ⓔ		V3, Pg. 101	PT31-S3-Q19	Ⓐ Ⓑ Ⓒ Ⓓ Ⓔ
	PT8-S4-Q6	Ⓐ Ⓑ Ⓒ Ⓓ Ⓔ		V3, Pg. 143	PT32-S4-Q20	Ⓐ Ⓑ Ⓒ Ⓓ Ⓔ
	PT8-S4-Q15	Ⓐ Ⓑ Ⓒ Ⓓ Ⓔ		V3, Pg. 153	PT33-S1-Q3	Ⓐ Ⓑ Ⓒ Ⓓ Ⓔ
	PT8-S4-Q23	Ⓐ Ⓑ Ⓒ Ⓓ Ⓔ		V3, Pg. 173	PT33-S3-Q19	Ⓐ Ⓑ Ⓒ Ⓓ Ⓔ
V1, Pg. 106	PT10-S4-Q7	Ⓐ Ⓑ Ⓒ Ⓓ Ⓔ		V3, Pg. 204	PT34-S3-Q7	Ⓐ Ⓑ Ⓒ Ⓓ Ⓔ
V1, Pg. 138	PT11-S4-Q2	Ⓐ Ⓑ Ⓒ Ⓓ Ⓔ		V3, Pg. 206	PT34-S3-Q15	Ⓐ Ⓑ Ⓒ Ⓓ Ⓔ
V1, Pg. 193	PT13-S2-Q11	Ⓐ Ⓑ Ⓒ Ⓓ Ⓔ		V3, Pg. 227	PT35-S1-Q26	Ⓐ Ⓑ Ⓒ Ⓓ Ⓔ
V1, Pg. 243	PT14-S4-Q11	Ⓐ Ⓑ Ⓒ Ⓓ Ⓔ		V3, Pg. 271	PT36-S3-Q4	Ⓐ Ⓑ Ⓒ Ⓓ Ⓔ
V1, Pg. 295	PT16-S2-Q13	Ⓐ Ⓑ Ⓒ Ⓓ Ⓔ		V3, Pg. 298	PT37-S2-Q11	Ⓐ Ⓑ Ⓒ Ⓓ Ⓔ
V1, Pg. 301	PT16-S3-Q4	Ⓐ Ⓑ Ⓒ Ⓓ Ⓔ		V3, Pg. 302	PT37-S2-Q23	Ⓐ Ⓑ Ⓒ Ⓓ Ⓔ
	PT17-S3-Q5	Ⓐ Ⓑ Ⓒ Ⓓ Ⓔ		V3, Pg. 309	PT37-S4-Q7	Ⓐ Ⓑ Ⓒ Ⓓ Ⓔ
V2, Pg. 24	PT19-S2-Q16	Ⓐ Ⓑ Ⓒ Ⓓ Ⓔ		V3, Pg. 323	PT38-S1-Q5	Ⓐ Ⓑ Ⓒ Ⓓ Ⓔ
V2, Pg. 40	PT19-S4-Q16	Ⓐ Ⓑ Ⓒ Ⓓ Ⓔ		V3, Pg. 349	PT38-S4-Q26	Ⓐ Ⓑ Ⓒ Ⓓ Ⓔ

	PT39-S2-Q13	Ⓐ Ⓑ Ⓒ Ⓓ Ⓔ	V4, Pg. 162	PT56-S2-Q21	Ⓐ Ⓑ Ⓒ Ⓓ Ⓔ
	PT39-S2-Q23	Ⓐ Ⓑ Ⓒ Ⓓ Ⓔ	V4, Pg. 195	PT57-S2-Q11	Ⓐ Ⓑ Ⓒ Ⓓ Ⓔ
	PT39-S4-Q2	Ⓐ Ⓑ Ⓒ Ⓓ Ⓔ	V4, Pg. 264	PT59-S2-Q2	Ⓐ Ⓑ Ⓒ Ⓓ Ⓔ
	PT39-S4-Q7	Ⓐ Ⓑ Ⓒ Ⓓ Ⓔ	V4, Pg. 315	PT60-S3-Q25	Ⓐ Ⓑ Ⓒ Ⓓ Ⓔ
	PT40-S3-Q16	Ⓐ Ⓑ Ⓒ Ⓓ Ⓔ	V4, Pg. 342	PT61-S2-Q7	Ⓐ Ⓑ Ⓒ Ⓓ Ⓔ
	PT42-S2-Q8	Ⓐ Ⓑ Ⓒ Ⓓ Ⓔ	V4, Pg. 357	PT61-S4-Q18	Ⓐ Ⓑ Ⓒ Ⓓ Ⓔ
	PT42-S2-Q13	Ⓐ Ⓑ Ⓒ Ⓓ Ⓔ	V5, Pg. 48	PT63-S1-Q14	Ⓐ Ⓑ Ⓒ Ⓓ Ⓔ
	PT43-S2-Q1	Ⓐ Ⓑ Ⓒ Ⓓ Ⓔ	V5, Pg. 57	PT63-S3-Q4	Ⓐ Ⓑ Ⓒ Ⓓ Ⓔ
	PT43-S2-Q13	Ⓐ Ⓑ Ⓒ Ⓓ Ⓔ	V5, Pg. 93	PT64-S3-Q5	Ⓐ Ⓑ Ⓒ Ⓓ Ⓔ
	PT43-S2-Q19	Ⓐ Ⓑ Ⓒ Ⓓ Ⓔ	V5, Pg. 93	PT64-S3-Q7	Ⓐ Ⓑ Ⓒ Ⓓ Ⓔ
	PT43-S3-Q6	Ⓐ Ⓑ Ⓒ Ⓓ Ⓔ	V5, Pg. 123	PT65-S1-Q23	Ⓐ Ⓑ Ⓒ Ⓓ Ⓔ
	PT44-S2-Q6	Ⓐ Ⓑ Ⓒ Ⓓ Ⓔ	V5, Pg. 137	PT65-S4-Q4	Ⓐ Ⓑ Ⓒ Ⓓ Ⓔ
	PT44-S4-Q10	Ⓐ Ⓑ Ⓒ Ⓓ Ⓔ	V5, Pg. 143	PT65-S4-Q25	Ⓐ Ⓑ Ⓒ Ⓓ Ⓔ
	PT45-S1-Q6	Ⓐ Ⓑ Ⓒ Ⓓ Ⓔ	V5, Pg. 165	PT66-S2-Q20	Ⓐ Ⓑ Ⓒ Ⓓ Ⓔ
	PT45-S1-Q10	Ⓐ Ⓑ Ⓒ Ⓓ Ⓔ	V5, Pg. 181	PT66-S4-Q19	Ⓐ Ⓑ Ⓒ Ⓓ Ⓔ
	PT45-S4-Q8	Ⓐ Ⓑ Ⓒ Ⓓ Ⓔ	V5, Pg. 182	PT66-S4-Q23	Ⓐ Ⓑ Ⓒ Ⓓ Ⓔ
	PT46-S2-Q1	Ⓐ Ⓑ Ⓒ Ⓓ Ⓔ	V5, Pg. 202	PT67-S2-Q10	Ⓐ Ⓑ Ⓒ Ⓓ Ⓔ
	PT46-S2-Q9	Ⓐ Ⓑ Ⓒ Ⓓ Ⓔ	V5, Pg. 204	PT67-S2-Q16	Ⓐ Ⓑ Ⓒ Ⓓ Ⓔ
	PT47-S1-Q4	Ⓐ Ⓑ Ⓒ Ⓓ Ⓔ	V5, Pg. 246	PT68-S2-Q21	Ⓐ Ⓑ Ⓒ Ⓓ Ⓔ
	PT47-S1-Q25	Ⓐ Ⓑ Ⓒ Ⓓ Ⓔ	V5, Pg. 255	PT68-S3-Q25	Ⓐ Ⓑ Ⓒ Ⓓ Ⓔ
	PT47-S3-Q5	Ⓐ Ⓑ Ⓒ Ⓓ Ⓔ	V5, Pg. 272	PT69-S1-Q2	Ⓐ Ⓑ Ⓒ Ⓓ Ⓔ
	PT47-S3-Q9	Ⓐ Ⓑ Ⓒ Ⓓ Ⓔ	V5, Pg. 303	PT69-S4-Q25	Ⓐ Ⓑ Ⓒ Ⓓ Ⓔ
	PT49-S2-Q1	Ⓐ Ⓑ Ⓒ Ⓓ Ⓔ	V5, Pg. 313	PT70-S1-Q4	Ⓐ Ⓑ Ⓒ Ⓓ Ⓔ
	PT49-S2-Q10	Ⓐ Ⓑ Ⓒ Ⓓ Ⓔ	V5, Pg. 337	PT70-S4-Q5	Ⓐ Ⓑ Ⓒ Ⓓ Ⓔ
	PT50-S2-Q11	Ⓐ Ⓑ Ⓒ Ⓓ Ⓔ	V5, Pg. 354	PT71-S1-Q10	Ⓐ Ⓑ Ⓒ Ⓓ Ⓔ
	PT50-S4-Q8	Ⓐ Ⓑ Ⓒ Ⓓ Ⓔ	V5, Pg. 368	PT71-S3-Q2	Ⓐ Ⓑ Ⓒ Ⓓ Ⓔ
	PT51-S1-Q23	Ⓐ Ⓑ Ⓒ Ⓓ Ⓔ	PT72, Pg. 23	PT72-S2-Q19	Ⓐ Ⓑ Ⓒ Ⓓ Ⓔ
V4, Pg. 22	PT52-S3-Q10	Ⓐ Ⓑ Ⓒ Ⓓ Ⓔ	PT76, Pg. 19	PT76-S2-Q3	Ⓐ Ⓑ Ⓒ Ⓓ Ⓔ
V4, Pg. 44	PT53-S1-Q2	Ⓐ Ⓑ Ⓒ Ⓓ Ⓔ	PT76, Pg. 34	PT76-S4-Q4	Ⓐ Ⓑ Ⓒ Ⓓ Ⓔ
V4, Pg. 156	PT56-S2-Q2	Ⓐ Ⓑ Ⓒ Ⓓ Ⓔ	PT76, Pg. 36	PT76-S4-Q10	Ⓐ Ⓑ Ⓒ Ⓓ Ⓔ
V4, Pg. 160	PT56-S2-Q17	Ⓐ Ⓑ Ⓒ Ⓓ Ⓔ	PT77, Pg. 34	PT77-S4-Q2	Ⓐ Ⓑ Ⓒ Ⓓ Ⓔ

Necessary Assumption

J07, Pg. 16	J07-S3-Q9	Ⓐ Ⓑ Ⓒ Ⓓ Ⓔ	SP1, Pg. 71	PTA-S1-Q11	Ⓐ Ⓑ Ⓒ Ⓓ Ⓔ
J07, Pg. 16	J07-S3-Q11	Ⓐ Ⓑ Ⓒ Ⓓ Ⓔ	SP1, Pg. 90	PTA-S4-Q8	Ⓐ Ⓑ Ⓒ Ⓓ Ⓔ
J07, Pg. 19	J07-S3-Q17	Ⓐ Ⓑ Ⓒ Ⓓ Ⓔ	SP1, Pg. 93	PTA-S4-Q17	Ⓐ Ⓑ Ⓒ Ⓓ Ⓔ
SP1, Pg. 69	PTA-S1-Q5	Ⓐ Ⓑ Ⓒ Ⓓ Ⓔ	SP1, Pg. 93	PTA-S4-Q19	Ⓐ Ⓑ Ⓒ Ⓓ Ⓔ

SP1, Pg. 188	PTB-S1-Q8	Ⓐ Ⓑ Ⓒ Ⓓ Ⓔ		PT4-S4-Q3	Ⓐ Ⓑ Ⓒ Ⓓ Ⓔ
SP1, Pg. 190	PTB-S1-Q18	Ⓐ Ⓑ Ⓒ Ⓓ Ⓔ		PT4-S4-Q10	Ⓐ Ⓑ Ⓒ Ⓓ Ⓔ
SP1, Pg. 191	PTB-S1-Q21	Ⓐ Ⓑ Ⓒ Ⓓ Ⓔ		PT4-S4-Q23	Ⓐ Ⓑ Ⓒ Ⓓ Ⓔ
SP1, Pg. 192	PTB-S1-Q23	Ⓐ Ⓑ Ⓒ Ⓓ Ⓔ		PT5-S1-Q3	Ⓐ Ⓑ Ⓒ Ⓓ Ⓔ
SP1, Pg. 207	PTB-S4-Q4	Ⓐ Ⓑ Ⓒ Ⓓ Ⓔ		PT5-S3-Q5	Ⓐ Ⓑ Ⓒ Ⓓ Ⓔ
SP1, Pg. 210	PTB-S4-Q14	Ⓐ Ⓑ Ⓒ Ⓓ Ⓔ		PT5-S3-Q7	Ⓐ Ⓑ Ⓒ Ⓓ Ⓔ
SP1, Pg. 301	PTC-S2-Q5	Ⓐ Ⓑ Ⓒ Ⓓ Ⓔ		PT5-S3-Q10	Ⓐ Ⓑ Ⓒ Ⓓ Ⓔ
SP1, Pg. 304	PTC-S2-Q15	Ⓐ Ⓑ Ⓒ Ⓓ Ⓔ		PT5-S3-Q14	Ⓐ Ⓑ Ⓒ Ⓓ Ⓔ
SP1, Pg. 306	PTC-S2-Q20	Ⓐ Ⓑ Ⓒ Ⓓ Ⓔ		PT5-S3-Q17	Ⓐ Ⓑ Ⓒ Ⓓ Ⓔ
SP1, Pg. 307	PTC-S2-Q23	Ⓐ Ⓑ Ⓒ Ⓓ Ⓔ		PT6-S2-Q2	Ⓐ Ⓑ Ⓒ Ⓓ Ⓔ
SP1, Pg. 308	PTC-S3-Q1	Ⓐ Ⓑ Ⓒ Ⓓ Ⓔ		PT6-S2-Q9	Ⓐ Ⓑ Ⓒ Ⓓ Ⓔ
SP1, Pg. 311	PTC-S3-Q11	Ⓐ Ⓑ Ⓒ Ⓓ Ⓔ		PT6-S2-Q15	Ⓐ Ⓑ Ⓒ Ⓓ Ⓔ
SP2, Pg. 356	PTC2-S2-Q10	Ⓐ Ⓑ Ⓒ Ⓓ Ⓔ		PT6-S3-Q3	Ⓐ Ⓑ Ⓒ Ⓓ Ⓔ
SP2, Pg. 366	PTC2-S3-Q17	Ⓐ Ⓑ Ⓒ Ⓓ Ⓔ		PT6-S3-Q7	Ⓐ Ⓑ Ⓒ Ⓓ Ⓔ
SP2, Pg. 367	PTC2-S3-Q20	Ⓐ Ⓑ Ⓒ Ⓓ Ⓔ		PT6-S3-Q9	Ⓐ Ⓑ Ⓒ Ⓓ Ⓔ
SP2, Pg. 368	PTC2-S3-Q22	Ⓐ Ⓑ Ⓒ Ⓓ Ⓔ		PT6-S3-Q15	Ⓐ Ⓑ Ⓒ Ⓓ Ⓔ
SP2, Pg. 369	PTC2-S3-Q25	Ⓐ Ⓑ Ⓒ Ⓓ Ⓔ	V1, Pg. 16	PT7-S1-Q2	Ⓐ Ⓑ Ⓒ Ⓓ Ⓔ
	PT1-S3-Q10	Ⓐ Ⓑ Ⓒ Ⓓ Ⓔ	V1, Pg. 19	PT7-S1-Q14	Ⓐ Ⓑ Ⓒ Ⓓ Ⓔ
	PT1-S3-Q17	Ⓐ Ⓑ Ⓒ Ⓓ Ⓔ	V1, Pg. 23	PT7-S1-Q24	Ⓐ Ⓑ Ⓒ Ⓓ Ⓔ
	PT1-S3-Q19	Ⓐ Ⓑ Ⓒ Ⓓ Ⓔ	V1, Pg. 37	PT7-S4-Q6	Ⓐ Ⓑ Ⓒ Ⓓ Ⓔ
	PT1-S3-Q21	Ⓐ Ⓑ Ⓒ Ⓓ Ⓔ	V1, Pg. 39	PT7-S4-Q13	Ⓐ Ⓑ Ⓒ Ⓓ Ⓔ
	PT1-S4-Q3	Ⓐ Ⓑ Ⓒ Ⓓ Ⓔ	V1, Pg. 43	PT7-S4-Q24	Ⓐ Ⓑ Ⓒ Ⓓ Ⓔ
	PT1-S4-Q7	Ⓐ Ⓑ Ⓒ Ⓓ Ⓔ		PT8-S1-Q2	Ⓐ Ⓑ Ⓒ Ⓓ Ⓔ
	PT1-S4-Q13	Ⓐ Ⓑ Ⓒ Ⓓ Ⓔ		PT8-S1-Q6	Ⓐ Ⓑ Ⓒ Ⓓ Ⓔ
	PT1-S4-Q22	Ⓐ Ⓑ Ⓒ Ⓓ Ⓔ		PT8-S1-Q12	Ⓐ Ⓑ Ⓒ Ⓓ Ⓔ
	PT2-S2-Q3	Ⓐ Ⓑ Ⓒ Ⓓ Ⓔ		PT8-S4-Q10	Ⓐ Ⓑ Ⓒ Ⓓ Ⓔ
	PT2-S2-Q19	Ⓐ Ⓑ Ⓒ Ⓓ Ⓔ		PT8-S4-Q13	Ⓐ Ⓑ Ⓒ Ⓓ Ⓔ
	PT2-S2-Q23	Ⓐ Ⓑ Ⓒ Ⓓ Ⓔ		PT8-S4-Q18	Ⓐ Ⓑ Ⓒ Ⓓ Ⓔ
	PT2-S4-Q9	Ⓐ Ⓑ Ⓒ Ⓓ Ⓔ		PT8-S4-Q21	Ⓐ Ⓑ Ⓒ Ⓓ Ⓔ
	PT2-S4-Q15	Ⓐ Ⓑ Ⓒ Ⓓ Ⓔ	V1, Pg. 63	PT9-S2-Q19	Ⓐ Ⓑ Ⓒ Ⓓ Ⓔ
	PT3-S2-Q3	Ⓐ Ⓑ Ⓒ Ⓓ Ⓔ	V1, Pg. 64	PT9-S2-Q21	Ⓐ Ⓑ Ⓒ Ⓓ Ⓔ
	PT3-S2-Q15	Ⓐ Ⓑ Ⓒ Ⓓ Ⓔ	V1, Pg. 65	PT9-S2-Q25	Ⓐ Ⓑ Ⓒ Ⓓ Ⓔ
	PT3-S2-Q21	Ⓐ Ⓑ Ⓒ Ⓓ Ⓔ	V1, Pg. 71	PT9-S4-Q6	Ⓐ Ⓑ Ⓒ Ⓓ Ⓔ
	PT3-S4-Q12	Ⓐ Ⓑ Ⓒ Ⓓ Ⓔ	V1, Pg. 72	PT9-S4-Q10	Ⓐ Ⓑ Ⓒ Ⓓ Ⓔ
	PT3-S4-Q19	Ⓐ Ⓑ Ⓒ Ⓓ Ⓔ	V1, Pg. 74	PT9-S4-Q19	Ⓐ Ⓑ Ⓒ Ⓓ Ⓔ
	PT4-S1-Q5	Ⓐ Ⓑ Ⓒ Ⓓ Ⓔ	V1, Pg. 77	PT9-S4-Q25	Ⓐ Ⓑ Ⓒ Ⓓ Ⓔ
	PT4-S1-Q10	Ⓐ Ⓑ Ⓒ Ⓓ Ⓔ	V1, Pg. 84	PT10-S1-Q1	Ⓐ Ⓑ Ⓒ Ⓓ Ⓔ

V1, Pg. 84	PT10-S1-Q3	Ⓐ Ⓑ Ⓒ Ⓓ Ⓔ	V1, Pg. 301	PT16-S3-Q3	Ⓐ Ⓑ Ⓒ Ⓓ Ⓔ
V1, Pg. 85	PT10-S1-Q7	Ⓐ Ⓑ Ⓒ Ⓓ Ⓔ	V1, Pg. 303	PT16-S3-Q12	Ⓐ Ⓑ Ⓒ Ⓓ Ⓔ
V1, Pg. 87	PT10-S1-Q15	Ⓐ Ⓑ Ⓒ Ⓓ Ⓔ	V1, Pg. 303	PT16-S3-Q14	Ⓐ Ⓑ Ⓒ Ⓓ Ⓔ
V1, Pg. 104	PT10-S4-Q4	Ⓐ Ⓑ Ⓒ Ⓓ Ⓔ		PT17-S2-Q10	Ⓐ Ⓑ Ⓒ Ⓓ Ⓔ
V1, Pg. 106	PT10-S4-Q8	Ⓐ Ⓑ Ⓒ Ⓓ Ⓔ		PT17-S2-Q12	Ⓐ Ⓑ Ⓒ Ⓓ Ⓔ
V1, Pg. 109	PT10-S4-Q18	Ⓐ Ⓑ Ⓒ Ⓓ Ⓔ		PT17-S2-Q21	Ⓐ Ⓑ Ⓒ Ⓓ Ⓔ
V1, Pg. 123	PT11-S2-Q5	Ⓐ Ⓑ Ⓒ Ⓓ Ⓔ		PT17-S2-Q23	Ⓐ Ⓑ Ⓒ Ⓓ Ⓔ
V1, Pg. 125	PT11-S2-Q13	Ⓐ Ⓑ Ⓒ Ⓓ Ⓔ		PT17-S3-Q3	Ⓐ Ⓑ Ⓒ Ⓓ Ⓔ
V1, Pg. 127	PT11-S2-Q18	Ⓐ Ⓑ Ⓒ Ⓓ Ⓔ		PT17-S3-Q21	Ⓐ Ⓑ Ⓒ Ⓓ Ⓔ
V1, Pg. 128	PT11-S2-Q24	Ⓐ Ⓑ Ⓒ Ⓓ Ⓔ		PT17-S3-Q25	Ⓐ Ⓑ Ⓒ Ⓓ Ⓔ
V1, Pg. 140	PT11-S4-Q7	Ⓐ Ⓑ Ⓒ Ⓓ Ⓔ	V1, Pg. 328	PT18-S2-Q9	Ⓐ Ⓑ Ⓒ Ⓓ Ⓔ
V1, Pg. 141	PT11-S4-Q13	Ⓐ Ⓑ Ⓒ Ⓓ Ⓔ	V1, Pg. 330	PT18-S2-Q15	Ⓐ Ⓑ Ⓒ Ⓓ Ⓔ
V1, Pg. 142	PT11-S4-Q15	Ⓐ Ⓑ Ⓒ Ⓓ Ⓔ	V1, Pg. 344	PT18-S4-Q8	Ⓐ Ⓑ Ⓒ Ⓓ Ⓔ
V1, Pg. 152	PT12-S1-Q2	Ⓐ Ⓑ Ⓒ Ⓓ Ⓔ	V1, Pg. 347	PT18-S4-Q18	Ⓐ Ⓑ Ⓒ Ⓓ Ⓔ
V1, Pg. 154	PT12-S1-Q10	Ⓐ Ⓑ Ⓒ Ⓓ Ⓔ	V1, Pg. 348	PT18-S4-Q22	Ⓐ Ⓑ Ⓒ Ⓓ Ⓔ
V1, Pg. 155	PT12-S1-Q13	Ⓐ Ⓑ Ⓒ Ⓓ Ⓔ	V2, Pg. 20	PT19-S2-Q2	Ⓐ Ⓑ Ⓒ Ⓓ Ⓔ
V1, Pg. 172	PT12-S4-Q2	Ⓐ Ⓑ Ⓒ Ⓓ Ⓔ	V2, Pg. 22	PT19-S2-Q9	Ⓐ Ⓑ Ⓒ Ⓓ Ⓔ
V1, Pg. 173	PT12-S4-Q6	Ⓐ Ⓑ Ⓒ Ⓓ Ⓔ	V2, Pg. 23	PT19-S2-Q13	Ⓐ Ⓑ Ⓒ Ⓓ Ⓔ
V1, Pg. 174	PT12-S4-Q8	Ⓐ Ⓑ Ⓒ Ⓓ Ⓔ	V2, Pg. 24	PT19-S2-Q15	Ⓐ Ⓑ Ⓒ Ⓓ Ⓔ
V1, Pg. 193	PT13-S2-Q12	Ⓐ Ⓑ Ⓒ Ⓓ Ⓔ	V2, Pg. 36	PT19-S4-Q4	Ⓐ Ⓑ Ⓒ Ⓓ Ⓔ
V1, Pg. 193	PT13-S2-Q14	Ⓐ Ⓑ Ⓒ Ⓓ Ⓔ	V2, Pg. 38	PT19-S4-Q8	Ⓐ Ⓑ Ⓒ Ⓓ Ⓔ
V1, Pg. 206	PT13-S4-Q4	Ⓐ Ⓑ Ⓒ Ⓓ Ⓔ	V2, Pg. 39	PT19-S4-Q14	Ⓐ Ⓑ Ⓒ Ⓓ Ⓔ
V1, Pg. 208	PT13-S4-Q8	Ⓐ Ⓑ Ⓒ Ⓓ Ⓔ	V2, Pg. 50	PT20-S1-Q3	Ⓐ Ⓑ Ⓒ Ⓓ Ⓔ
V1, Pg. 209	PT13-S4-Q11	Ⓐ Ⓑ Ⓒ Ⓓ Ⓔ	V2, Pg. 52	PT20-S1-Q11	Ⓐ Ⓑ Ⓒ Ⓓ Ⓔ
V1, Pg. 229	PT14-S2-Q17	Ⓐ Ⓑ Ⓒ Ⓓ Ⓔ	V2, Pg. 54	PT20-S1-Q16	Ⓐ Ⓑ Ⓒ Ⓓ Ⓔ
V1, Pg. 229	PT14-S2-Q18	Ⓐ Ⓑ Ⓒ Ⓓ Ⓔ	V2, Pg. 56	PT20-S1-Q20	Ⓐ Ⓑ Ⓒ Ⓓ Ⓔ
V1, Pg. 230	PT14-S2-Q20	Ⓐ Ⓑ Ⓒ Ⓓ Ⓔ	V2, Pg. 70	PT20-S4-Q1	Ⓐ Ⓑ Ⓒ Ⓓ Ⓔ
V1, Pg. 244	PT14-S4-Q13	Ⓐ Ⓑ Ⓒ Ⓓ Ⓔ	V2, Pg. 71	PT20-S4-Q8	Ⓐ Ⓑ Ⓒ Ⓓ Ⓔ
V1, Pg. 245	PT14-S4-Q19	Ⓐ Ⓑ Ⓒ Ⓓ Ⓔ	V2, Pg. 72	PT20-S4-Q11	Ⓐ Ⓑ Ⓒ Ⓓ Ⓔ
V1, Pg. 263	PT15-S2-Q6	Ⓐ Ⓑ Ⓒ Ⓓ Ⓔ	V2, Pg. 74	PT20-S4-Q16	Ⓐ Ⓑ Ⓒ Ⓓ Ⓔ
V1, Pg. 266	PT15-S2-Q16	Ⓐ Ⓑ Ⓒ Ⓓ Ⓔ	V2, Pg. 89	PT21-S2-Q3	Ⓐ Ⓑ Ⓒ Ⓓ Ⓔ
V1, Pg. 269	PT15-S2-Q23	Ⓐ Ⓑ Ⓒ Ⓓ Ⓔ	V2, Pg. 89	PT21-S2-Q6	Ⓐ Ⓑ Ⓒ Ⓓ Ⓔ
V1, Pg. 270	PT15-S3-Q3	Ⓐ Ⓑ Ⓒ Ⓓ Ⓔ	V2, Pg. 91	PT21-S2-Q11	Ⓐ Ⓑ Ⓒ Ⓓ Ⓔ
V1, Pg. 273	PT15-S3-Q12	Ⓐ Ⓑ Ⓒ Ⓓ Ⓔ	V2, Pg. 93	PT21-S2-Q19	Ⓐ Ⓑ Ⓒ Ⓓ Ⓔ
V1, Pg. 277	PT15-S3-Q24	Ⓐ Ⓑ Ⓒ Ⓓ Ⓔ	V2, Pg. 97	PT21-S3-Q4	Ⓐ Ⓑ Ⓒ Ⓓ Ⓔ
V1, Pg. 293	PT16-S2-Q6	Ⓐ Ⓑ Ⓒ Ⓓ Ⓔ	V2, Pg. 97	PT21-S3-Q6	Ⓐ Ⓑ Ⓒ Ⓓ Ⓔ
V1, Pg. 296	PT16-S2-Q14	Ⓐ Ⓑ Ⓒ Ⓓ Ⓔ	V2, Pg. 98	PT21-S3-Q8	Ⓐ Ⓑ Ⓒ Ⓓ Ⓔ

V2, Pg. 99	PT21-S3-Q13	Ⓐ Ⓑ Ⓒ Ⓓ Ⓔ	V2, Pg. 327	PT28-S1-Q21	Ⓐ Ⓑ Ⓒ Ⓓ Ⓔ
V2, Pg. 126	PT22-S2-Q1	Ⓐ Ⓑ Ⓒ Ⓓ Ⓔ	V2, Pg. 337	PT28-S3-Q16	Ⓐ Ⓑ Ⓒ Ⓓ Ⓔ
V2, Pg. 129	PT22-S2-Q14	Ⓐ Ⓑ Ⓒ Ⓓ Ⓔ	V2, Pg. 338	PT28-S3-Q19	Ⓐ Ⓑ Ⓒ Ⓓ Ⓔ
V2, Pg. 131	PT22-S2-Q19	Ⓐ Ⓑ Ⓒ Ⓓ Ⓔ	V2, Pg. 339	PT28-S3-Q22	Ⓐ Ⓑ Ⓒ Ⓓ Ⓔ
V2, Pg. 141	PT22-S4-Q11	Ⓐ Ⓑ Ⓒ Ⓓ Ⓔ	V3, Pg. 17	PT29-S1-Q5	Ⓐ Ⓑ Ⓒ Ⓓ Ⓔ
V2, Pg. 142	PT22-S4-Q16	Ⓐ Ⓑ Ⓒ Ⓓ Ⓔ	V3, Pg. 20	PT29-S1-Q15	Ⓐ Ⓑ Ⓒ Ⓓ Ⓔ
V2, Pg. 144	PT22-S4-Q22	Ⓐ Ⓑ Ⓒ Ⓓ Ⓔ	V3, Pg. 37	PT29-S4-Q4	Ⓐ Ⓑ Ⓒ Ⓓ Ⓔ
V2, Pg. 157	PT23-S2-Q6	Ⓐ Ⓑ Ⓒ Ⓓ Ⓔ	V3, Pg. 37	PT29-S4-Q5	Ⓐ Ⓑ Ⓒ Ⓓ Ⓔ
V2, Pg. 158	PT23-S2-Q9	Ⓐ Ⓑ Ⓒ Ⓓ Ⓔ	V3, Pg. 38	PT29-S4-Q8	Ⓐ Ⓑ Ⓒ Ⓓ Ⓔ
V2, Pg. 160	PT23-S2-Q17	Ⓐ Ⓑ Ⓒ Ⓓ Ⓔ	V3, Pg. 57	PT30-S2-Q11	Ⓐ Ⓑ Ⓒ Ⓓ Ⓔ
V2, Pg. 164	PT23-S3-Q3	Ⓐ Ⓑ Ⓒ Ⓓ Ⓔ	V3, Pg. 58	PT30-S2-Q15	Ⓐ Ⓑ Ⓒ Ⓓ Ⓔ
V2, Pg. 166	PT23-S3-Q9	Ⓐ Ⓑ Ⓒ Ⓓ Ⓔ	V3, Pg. 60	PT30-S2-Q22	Ⓐ Ⓑ Ⓒ Ⓓ Ⓔ
V2, Pg. 167	PT23-S3-Q11	Ⓐ Ⓑ Ⓒ Ⓓ Ⓔ	V3, Pg. 75	PT30-S4-Q19	Ⓐ Ⓑ Ⓒ Ⓓ Ⓔ
V2, Pg. 199	PT24-S2-Q17	Ⓐ Ⓑ Ⓒ Ⓓ Ⓔ	V3, Pg. 88	PT31-S2-Q2	Ⓐ Ⓑ Ⓒ Ⓓ Ⓔ
V2, Pg. 203	PT24-S3-Q5	Ⓐ Ⓑ Ⓒ Ⓓ Ⓔ	V3, Pg. 92	PT31-S2-Q14	Ⓐ Ⓑ Ⓒ Ⓓ Ⓔ
V2, Pg. 205	PT24-S3-Q13	Ⓐ Ⓑ Ⓒ Ⓓ Ⓔ	V3, Pg. 98	PT31-S3-Q11	Ⓐ Ⓑ Ⓒ Ⓓ Ⓔ
V2, Pg. 206	PT24-S3-Q18	Ⓐ Ⓑ Ⓒ Ⓓ Ⓔ	V3, Pg. 99	PT31-S3-Q13	Ⓐ Ⓑ Ⓒ Ⓓ Ⓔ
V2, Pg. 230	PT25-S2-Q6	Ⓐ Ⓑ Ⓒ Ⓓ Ⓔ	V3, Pg. 100	PT31-S3-Q17	Ⓐ Ⓑ Ⓒ Ⓓ Ⓔ
V2, Pg. 232	PT25-S2-Q12	Ⓐ Ⓑ Ⓒ Ⓓ Ⓔ	V3, Pg. 101	PT31-S3-Q21	Ⓐ Ⓑ Ⓒ Ⓓ Ⓔ
V2, Pg. 233	PT25-S2-Q16	Ⓐ Ⓑ Ⓒ Ⓓ Ⓔ	V3, Pg. 118	PT32-S1-Q1	Ⓐ Ⓑ Ⓒ Ⓓ Ⓔ
V2, Pg. 242	PT25-S4-Q9	Ⓐ Ⓑ Ⓒ Ⓓ Ⓔ	V3, Pg. 124	PT32-S1-Q21	Ⓐ Ⓑ Ⓒ Ⓓ Ⓔ
V2, Pg. 247	PT25-S4-Q25	Ⓐ Ⓑ Ⓒ Ⓓ Ⓔ	V3, Pg. 125	PT32-S1-Q23	Ⓐ Ⓑ Ⓒ Ⓓ Ⓔ
V2, Pg. 259	PT26-S2-Q7	Ⓐ Ⓑ Ⓒ Ⓓ Ⓔ	V3, Pg. 125	PT32-S1-Q25	Ⓐ Ⓑ Ⓒ Ⓓ Ⓔ
V2, Pg. 260	PT26-S2-Q10	Ⓐ Ⓑ Ⓒ Ⓓ Ⓔ	V3, Pg. 140	PT32-S4-Q7	Ⓐ Ⓑ Ⓒ Ⓓ Ⓔ
V2, Pg. 261	PT26-S2-Q13	Ⓐ Ⓑ Ⓒ Ⓓ Ⓔ	V3, Pg. 142	PT32-S4-Q16	Ⓐ Ⓑ Ⓒ Ⓓ Ⓔ
V2, Pg. 264	PT26-S2-Q22	Ⓐ Ⓑ Ⓒ Ⓓ Ⓔ	V3, Pg. 143	PT32-S4-Q19	Ⓐ Ⓑ Ⓒ Ⓓ Ⓔ
V2, Pg. 265	PT26-S2-Q25	Ⓐ Ⓑ Ⓒ Ⓓ Ⓔ	V3, Pg. 154	PT33-S1-Q10	Ⓐ Ⓑ Ⓒ Ⓓ Ⓔ
V2, Pg. 268	PT26-S3-Q9	Ⓐ Ⓑ Ⓒ Ⓓ Ⓔ	V3, Pg. 155	PT33-S1-Q13	Ⓐ Ⓑ Ⓒ Ⓓ Ⓔ
V2, Pg. 268	PT26-S3-Q11	Ⓐ Ⓑ Ⓒ Ⓓ Ⓔ	V3, Pg. 157	PT33-S1-Q19	Ⓐ Ⓑ Ⓒ Ⓓ Ⓔ
V2, Pg. 292	PT27-S1-Q13	Ⓐ Ⓑ Ⓒ Ⓓ Ⓔ	V3, Pg. 171	PT33-S3-Q11	Ⓐ Ⓑ Ⓒ Ⓓ Ⓔ
V2, Pg. 294	PT27-S1-Q21	Ⓐ Ⓑ Ⓒ Ⓓ Ⓔ	V3, Pg. 172	PT33-S3-Q16	Ⓐ Ⓑ Ⓒ Ⓓ Ⓔ
V2, Pg. 309	PT27-S4-Q4	Ⓐ Ⓑ Ⓒ Ⓓ Ⓔ	V3, Pg. 175	PT33-S3-Q25	Ⓐ Ⓑ Ⓒ Ⓓ Ⓔ
V2, Pg. 310	PT27-S4-Q9	Ⓐ Ⓑ Ⓒ Ⓓ Ⓔ	V3, Pg. 197	PT34-S2-Q13	Ⓐ Ⓑ Ⓒ Ⓓ Ⓔ
V2, Pg. 313	PT27-S4-Q19	Ⓐ Ⓑ Ⓒ Ⓓ Ⓔ	V3, Pg. 198	PT34-S2-Q16	Ⓐ Ⓑ Ⓒ Ⓓ Ⓔ
V2, Pg. 313	PT27-S4-Q20	Ⓐ Ⓑ Ⓒ Ⓓ Ⓔ	V3, Pg. 199	PT34-S2-Q21	Ⓐ Ⓑ Ⓒ Ⓓ Ⓔ
V2, Pg. 322	PT28-S1-Q2	Ⓐ Ⓑ Ⓒ Ⓓ Ⓔ	V3, Pg. 202	PT34-S3-Q3	Ⓐ Ⓑ Ⓒ Ⓓ Ⓔ
V2, Pg. 325	PT28-S1-Q12	Ⓐ Ⓑ Ⓒ Ⓓ Ⓔ	V3, Pg. 203	PT34-S3-Q5	Ⓐ Ⓑ Ⓒ Ⓓ Ⓔ

V3, Pg. 204	PT34-S3-Q9	Ⓐ Ⓑ Ⓒ Ⓓ Ⓔ	PT42-S4-Q2	Ⓐ Ⓑ Ⓒ Ⓓ Ⓔ
V3, Pg. 205	PT34-S3-Q11	Ⓐ Ⓑ Ⓒ Ⓓ Ⓔ	PT42-S4-Q13	Ⓐ Ⓑ Ⓒ Ⓓ Ⓔ
V3, Pg. 206	PT34-S3-Q17	Ⓐ Ⓑ Ⓒ Ⓓ Ⓔ	PT42-S4-Q19	Ⓐ Ⓑ Ⓒ Ⓓ Ⓔ
V3, Pg. 224	PT35-S1-Q14	Ⓐ Ⓑ Ⓒ Ⓓ Ⓔ	PT43-S2-Q10	Ⓐ Ⓑ Ⓒ Ⓓ Ⓔ
V3, Pg. 225	PT35-S1-Q18	Ⓐ Ⓑ Ⓒ Ⓓ Ⓔ	PT43-S2-Q16	Ⓐ Ⓑ Ⓒ Ⓓ Ⓔ
V3, Pg. 244	PT35-S4-Q16	Ⓐ Ⓑ Ⓒ Ⓓ Ⓔ	PT43-S3-Q1	Ⓐ Ⓑ Ⓒ Ⓓ Ⓔ
V3, Pg. 255	PT36-S1-Q3	Ⓐ Ⓑ Ⓒ Ⓓ Ⓔ	PT43-S3-Q12	Ⓐ Ⓑ Ⓒ Ⓓ Ⓔ
V3, Pg. 259	PT36-S1-Q20	Ⓐ Ⓑ Ⓒ Ⓓ Ⓔ	PT43-S3-Q16	Ⓐ Ⓑ Ⓒ Ⓓ Ⓔ
V3, Pg. 274	PT36-S3-Q14	Ⓐ Ⓑ Ⓒ Ⓓ Ⓔ	PT44-S2-Q5	Ⓐ Ⓑ Ⓒ Ⓓ Ⓔ
V3, Pg. 275	PT36-S3-Q16	Ⓐ Ⓑ Ⓒ Ⓓ Ⓔ	PT44-S2-Q9	Ⓐ Ⓑ Ⓒ Ⓓ Ⓔ
V3, Pg. 275	PT36-S3-Q18	Ⓐ Ⓑ Ⓒ Ⓓ Ⓔ	PT44-S2-Q18	Ⓐ Ⓑ Ⓒ Ⓓ Ⓔ
V3, Pg. 276	PT36-S3-Q22	Ⓐ Ⓑ Ⓒ Ⓓ Ⓔ	PT44-S2-Q23	Ⓐ Ⓑ Ⓒ Ⓓ Ⓔ
V3, Pg. 300	PT37-S2-Q15	Ⓐ Ⓑ Ⓒ Ⓓ Ⓔ	PT44-S4-Q7	Ⓐ Ⓑ Ⓒ Ⓓ Ⓔ
V3, Pg. 301	PT37-S2-Q19	Ⓐ Ⓑ Ⓒ Ⓓ Ⓔ	PT44-S4-Q16	Ⓐ Ⓑ Ⓒ Ⓓ Ⓔ
V3, Pg. 312	PT37-S4-Q15	Ⓐ Ⓑ Ⓒ Ⓓ Ⓔ	PT45-S1-Q3	Ⓐ Ⓑ Ⓒ Ⓓ Ⓔ
V3, Pg. 313	PT37-S4-Q19	Ⓐ Ⓑ Ⓒ Ⓓ Ⓔ	PT45-S4-Q6	Ⓐ Ⓑ Ⓒ Ⓓ Ⓔ
V3, Pg. 315	PT37-S4-Q23	Ⓐ Ⓑ Ⓒ Ⓓ Ⓔ	PT45-S4-Q13	Ⓐ Ⓑ Ⓒ Ⓓ Ⓔ
V3, Pg. 325	PT38-S1-Q12	Ⓐ Ⓑ Ⓒ Ⓓ Ⓔ	PT46-S2-Q10	Ⓐ Ⓑ Ⓒ Ⓓ Ⓔ
V3, Pg. 325	PT38-S1-Q14	Ⓐ Ⓑ Ⓒ Ⓓ Ⓔ	PT46-S2-Q13	Ⓐ Ⓑ Ⓒ Ⓓ Ⓔ
V3, Pg. 329	PT38-S1-Q24	Ⓐ Ⓑ Ⓒ Ⓓ Ⓔ	PT46-S3-Q15	Ⓐ Ⓑ Ⓒ Ⓓ Ⓔ
V3, Pg. 343	PT38-S4-Q6	Ⓐ Ⓑ Ⓒ Ⓓ Ⓔ	PT46-S3-Q17	Ⓐ Ⓑ Ⓒ Ⓓ Ⓔ
V3, Pg. 347	PT38-S4-Q20	Ⓐ Ⓑ Ⓒ Ⓓ Ⓔ	PT46-S3-Q20	Ⓐ Ⓑ Ⓒ Ⓓ Ⓔ
V3, Pg. 347	PT38-S4-Q22	Ⓐ Ⓑ Ⓒ Ⓓ Ⓔ	PT46-S3-Q26	Ⓐ Ⓑ Ⓒ Ⓓ Ⓔ
	PT39-S2-Q17	Ⓐ Ⓑ Ⓒ Ⓓ Ⓔ	PT47-S1-Q14	Ⓐ Ⓑ Ⓒ Ⓓ Ⓔ
	PT39-S4-Q4	Ⓐ Ⓑ Ⓒ Ⓓ Ⓔ	PT47-S1-Q17	Ⓐ Ⓑ Ⓒ Ⓓ Ⓔ
	PT39-S4-Q19	Ⓐ Ⓑ Ⓒ Ⓓ Ⓔ	PT47-S1-Q20	Ⓐ Ⓑ Ⓒ Ⓓ Ⓔ
	PT39-S4-Q25	Ⓐ Ⓑ Ⓒ Ⓓ Ⓔ	PT47-S3-Q13	Ⓐ Ⓑ Ⓒ Ⓓ Ⓔ
	PT40-S1-Q5	Ⓐ Ⓑ Ⓒ Ⓓ Ⓔ	PT47-S3-Q17	Ⓐ Ⓑ Ⓒ Ⓓ Ⓔ
	PT40-S1-Q16	Ⓐ Ⓑ Ⓒ Ⓓ Ⓔ	PT48-S1-Q15	Ⓐ Ⓑ Ⓒ Ⓓ Ⓔ
	PT40-S3-Q20	Ⓐ Ⓑ Ⓒ Ⓓ Ⓔ	PT48-S1-Q20	Ⓐ Ⓑ Ⓒ Ⓓ Ⓔ
	PT40-S3-Q22	Ⓐ Ⓑ Ⓒ Ⓓ Ⓔ	PT48-S4-Q10	Ⓐ Ⓑ Ⓒ Ⓓ Ⓔ
	PT41-S1-Q6	Ⓐ Ⓑ Ⓒ Ⓓ Ⓔ	PT49-S2-Q17	Ⓐ Ⓑ Ⓒ Ⓓ Ⓔ
	PT41-S1-Q10	Ⓐ Ⓑ Ⓒ Ⓓ Ⓔ	PT49-S2-Q22	Ⓐ Ⓑ Ⓒ Ⓓ Ⓔ
	PT41-S1-Q24	Ⓐ Ⓑ Ⓒ Ⓓ Ⓔ	PT49-S4-Q13	Ⓐ Ⓑ Ⓒ Ⓓ Ⓔ
	PT41-S3-Q7	Ⓐ Ⓑ Ⓒ Ⓓ Ⓔ	PT49-S4-Q16	Ⓐ Ⓑ Ⓒ Ⓓ Ⓔ
	PT41-S3-Q17	Ⓐ Ⓑ Ⓒ Ⓓ Ⓔ	PT49-S4-Q20	Ⓐ Ⓑ Ⓒ Ⓓ Ⓔ
	PT42-S2-Q14	Ⓐ Ⓑ Ⓒ Ⓓ Ⓔ	PT50-S2-Q14	Ⓐ Ⓑ Ⓒ Ⓓ Ⓔ

	PT50-S2-Q16	Ⓐ Ⓑ Ⓒ Ⓓ Ⓔ	V4, Pg. 199	PT57-S2-Q24	Ⓐ Ⓑ Ⓒ Ⓓ Ⓔ
	PT50-S4-Q11	Ⓐ Ⓑ Ⓒ Ⓓ Ⓔ	V4, Pg. 203	PT57-S3-Q12	Ⓐ Ⓑ Ⓒ Ⓓ Ⓔ
	PT50-S4-Q21	Ⓐ Ⓑ Ⓒ Ⓓ Ⓔ	V4, Pg. 204	PT57-S3-Q17	Ⓐ Ⓑ Ⓒ Ⓓ Ⓔ
	PT51-S1-Q7	Ⓐ Ⓑ Ⓒ Ⓓ Ⓔ	V4, Pg. 224	PT58-S1-Q1	Ⓐ Ⓑ Ⓒ Ⓓ Ⓔ
	PT51-S3-Q2	Ⓐ Ⓑ Ⓒ Ⓓ Ⓔ	V4, Pg. 227	PT58-S1-Q14	Ⓐ Ⓑ Ⓒ Ⓓ Ⓔ
	PT51-S3-Q15	Ⓐ Ⓑ Ⓒ Ⓓ Ⓔ	V4, Pg. 228	PT58-S1-Q16	Ⓐ Ⓑ Ⓒ Ⓓ Ⓔ
	PT51-S3-Q18	Ⓐ Ⓑ Ⓒ Ⓓ Ⓔ	V4, Pg. 229	PT58-S1-Q19	Ⓐ Ⓑ Ⓒ Ⓓ Ⓔ
V4, Pg. 11	PT52-S1-Q10	Ⓐ Ⓑ Ⓒ Ⓓ Ⓔ	V4, Pg. 230	PT58-S1-Q22	Ⓐ Ⓑ Ⓒ Ⓓ Ⓔ
V4, Pg. 15	PT52-S1-Q25	Ⓐ Ⓑ Ⓒ Ⓓ Ⓔ	V4, Pg. 246	PT58-S4-Q11	Ⓐ Ⓑ Ⓒ Ⓓ Ⓔ
V4, Pg. 22	PT52-S3-Q7	Ⓐ Ⓑ Ⓒ Ⓓ Ⓔ	V4, Pg. 248	PT58-S4-Q17	Ⓐ Ⓑ Ⓒ Ⓓ Ⓔ
V4, Pg. 22	PT52-S3-Q9	Ⓐ Ⓑ Ⓒ Ⓓ Ⓔ	V4, Pg. 249	PT58-S4-Q21	Ⓐ Ⓑ Ⓒ Ⓓ Ⓔ
V4, Pg. 23	PT52-S3-Q13	Ⓐ Ⓑ Ⓒ Ⓓ Ⓔ	V4, Pg. 267	PT59-S2-Q14	Ⓐ Ⓑ Ⓒ Ⓓ Ⓔ
V4, Pg. 46	PT53-S1-Q9	Ⓐ Ⓑ Ⓒ Ⓓ Ⓔ	V4, Pg. 275	PT59-S3-Q12	Ⓐ Ⓑ Ⓒ Ⓓ Ⓔ
V4, Pg. 47	PT53-S1-Q13	Ⓐ Ⓑ Ⓒ Ⓓ Ⓔ	V4, Pg. 276	PT59-S3-Q16	Ⓐ Ⓑ Ⓒ Ⓓ Ⓔ
V4, Pg. 48	PT53-S1-Q15	Ⓐ Ⓑ Ⓒ Ⓓ Ⓔ	V4, Pg. 279	PT59-S3-Q25	Ⓐ Ⓑ Ⓒ Ⓓ Ⓔ
V4, Pg. 51	PT53-S1-Q23	Ⓐ Ⓑ Ⓒ Ⓓ Ⓔ	V4, Pg. 297	PT60-S1-Q7	Ⓐ Ⓑ Ⓒ Ⓓ Ⓔ
V4, Pg. 58	PT53-S3-Q8	Ⓐ Ⓑ Ⓒ Ⓓ Ⓔ	V4, Pg. 299	PT60-S1-Q14	Ⓐ Ⓑ Ⓒ Ⓓ Ⓔ
V4, Pg. 60	PT53-S3-Q15	Ⓐ Ⓑ Ⓒ Ⓓ Ⓔ	V4, Pg. 301	PT60-S1-Q20	Ⓐ Ⓑ Ⓒ Ⓓ Ⓔ
V4, Pg. 61	PT53-S3-Q20	Ⓐ Ⓑ Ⓒ Ⓓ Ⓔ	V4, Pg. 311	PT60-S3-Q11	Ⓐ Ⓑ Ⓒ Ⓓ Ⓔ
V4, Pg. 88	PT54-S2-Q2	Ⓐ Ⓑ Ⓒ Ⓓ Ⓔ	V4, Pg. 314	PT60-S3-Q22	Ⓐ Ⓑ Ⓒ Ⓓ Ⓔ
V4, Pg. 89	PT54-S2-Q6	Ⓐ Ⓑ Ⓒ Ⓓ Ⓔ	V4, Pg. 344	PT61-S2-Q16	Ⓐ Ⓑ Ⓒ Ⓓ Ⓔ
V4, Pg. 90	PT54-S2-Q9	Ⓐ Ⓑ Ⓒ Ⓓ Ⓔ	V4, Pg. 357	PT61-S4-Q20	Ⓐ Ⓑ Ⓒ Ⓓ Ⓔ
V4, Pg. 101	PT54-S4-Q3	Ⓐ Ⓑ Ⓒ Ⓓ Ⓔ	V5, Pg. 19	PT62-S2-Q12	Ⓐ Ⓑ Ⓒ Ⓓ Ⓔ
V4, Pg. 102	PT54-S4-Q7	Ⓐ Ⓑ Ⓒ Ⓓ Ⓔ	V5, Pg. 23	PT62-S2-Q25	Ⓐ Ⓑ Ⓒ Ⓓ Ⓔ
V4, Pg. 105	PT54-S4-Q18	Ⓐ Ⓑ Ⓒ Ⓓ Ⓔ	V5, Pg. 34	PT62-S4-Q23	Ⓐ Ⓑ Ⓒ Ⓓ Ⓔ
V4, Pg. 107	PT54-S4-Q24	Ⓐ Ⓑ Ⓒ Ⓓ Ⓔ	V5, Pg. 45	PT63-S1-Q5	Ⓐ Ⓑ Ⓒ Ⓓ Ⓔ
V4, Pg. 116	PT55-S1-Q2	Ⓐ Ⓑ Ⓒ Ⓓ Ⓔ	V5, Pg. 49	PT63-S1-Q19	Ⓐ Ⓑ Ⓒ Ⓓ Ⓔ
V4, Pg. 119	PT55-S1-Q12	Ⓐ Ⓑ Ⓒ Ⓓ Ⓔ	V5, Pg. 57	PT63-S3-Q6	Ⓐ Ⓑ Ⓒ Ⓓ Ⓔ
V4, Pg. 120	PT55-S1-Q17	Ⓐ Ⓑ Ⓒ Ⓓ Ⓔ	V5, Pg. 58	PT63-S3-Q11	Ⓐ Ⓑ Ⓒ Ⓓ Ⓔ
V4, Pg. 134	PT55-S3-Q8	Ⓐ Ⓑ Ⓒ Ⓓ Ⓔ	V5, Pg. 59	PT63-S3-Q15	Ⓐ Ⓑ Ⓒ Ⓓ Ⓔ
V4, Pg. 137	PT55-S3-Q19	Ⓐ Ⓑ Ⓒ Ⓓ Ⓔ	V5, Pg. 84	PT64-S1-Q15	Ⓐ Ⓑ Ⓒ Ⓓ Ⓔ
V4, Pg. 139	PT55-S3-Q24	Ⓐ Ⓑ Ⓒ Ⓓ Ⓔ	V5, Pg. 95	PT64-S3-Q12	Ⓐ Ⓑ Ⓒ Ⓓ Ⓔ
V4, Pg. 157	PT56-S2-Q4	Ⓐ Ⓑ Ⓒ Ⓓ Ⓔ	V5, Pg. 97	PT64-S3-Q19	Ⓐ Ⓑ Ⓒ Ⓓ Ⓔ
V4, Pg. 157	PT56-S2-Q6	Ⓐ Ⓑ Ⓒ Ⓓ Ⓔ	V5, Pg. 122	PT65-S1-Q18	Ⓐ Ⓑ Ⓒ Ⓓ Ⓔ
V4, Pg. 166	PT56-S3-Q9	Ⓐ Ⓑ Ⓒ Ⓓ Ⓔ	V5, Pg. 122	PT65-S1-Q21	Ⓐ Ⓑ Ⓒ Ⓓ Ⓔ
V4, Pg. 168	PT56-S3-Q18	Ⓐ Ⓑ Ⓒ Ⓓ Ⓔ	V5, Pg. 136	PT65-S4-Q2	Ⓐ Ⓑ Ⓒ Ⓓ Ⓔ
V4, Pg. 171	PT56-S3-Q25	Ⓐ Ⓑ Ⓒ Ⓓ Ⓔ	V5, Pg. 139	PT65-S4-Q13	Ⓐ Ⓑ Ⓒ Ⓓ Ⓔ

V5, Pg. 141	PT65-S4-Q20	Ⓐ Ⓑ Ⓒ Ⓓ Ⓔ	PT72, Pg. 27	PT72-S3-Q4	Ⓐ Ⓑ Ⓒ Ⓓ Ⓔ
V5, Pg. 160	PT66-S2-Q2	Ⓐ Ⓑ Ⓒ Ⓓ Ⓔ	PT72, Pg. 31	PT72-S3-Q18	Ⓐ Ⓑ Ⓒ Ⓓ Ⓔ
V5, Pg. 161	PT66-S2-Q4	Ⓐ Ⓑ Ⓒ Ⓓ Ⓔ	PT73, Pg. 18	PT73-S2-Q1	Ⓐ Ⓑ Ⓒ Ⓓ Ⓔ
V5, Pg. 162	PT66-S2-Q10	Ⓐ Ⓑ Ⓒ Ⓓ Ⓔ	PT73, Pg. 20	PT73-S2-Q8	Ⓐ Ⓑ Ⓒ Ⓓ Ⓔ
V5, Pg. 176	PT66-S4-Q3	Ⓐ Ⓑ Ⓒ Ⓓ Ⓔ	PT73, Pg. 23	PT73-S2-Q20	Ⓐ Ⓑ Ⓒ Ⓓ Ⓔ
V5, Pg. 177	PT66-S4-Q7	Ⓐ Ⓑ Ⓒ Ⓓ Ⓔ	PT73, Pg. 37	PT73-S4-Q13	Ⓐ Ⓑ Ⓒ Ⓓ Ⓔ
V5, Pg. 201	PT67-S2-Q6	Ⓐ Ⓑ Ⓒ Ⓓ Ⓔ	PT73, Pg. 39	PT73-S4-Q19	Ⓐ Ⓑ Ⓒ Ⓓ Ⓔ
V5, Pg. 204	PT67-S2-Q14	Ⓐ Ⓑ Ⓒ Ⓓ Ⓔ	PT73, Pg. 41	PT73-S4-Q26	Ⓐ Ⓑ Ⓒ Ⓓ Ⓔ
V5, Pg. 216	PT67-S4-Q2	Ⓐ Ⓑ Ⓒ Ⓓ Ⓔ	PT74, Pg. 12	PT74-S1-Q8	Ⓐ Ⓑ Ⓒ Ⓓ Ⓔ
V5, Pg. 219	PT67-S4-Q11	Ⓐ Ⓑ Ⓒ Ⓓ Ⓔ	PT74, Pg. 35	PT74-S4-Q4	Ⓐ Ⓑ Ⓒ Ⓓ Ⓔ
V5, Pg. 220	PT67-S4-Q16	Ⓐ Ⓑ Ⓒ Ⓓ Ⓔ	PT74, Pg. 35	PT74-S4-Q6	Ⓐ Ⓑ Ⓒ Ⓓ Ⓔ
V5, Pg. 221	PT67-S4-Q18	Ⓐ Ⓑ Ⓒ Ⓓ Ⓔ	PT75, Pg. 10	PT75-S1-Q1	Ⓐ Ⓑ Ⓒ Ⓓ Ⓔ
V5, Pg. 244	PT68-S2-Q15	Ⓐ Ⓑ Ⓒ Ⓓ Ⓔ	PT75, Pg. 11	PT75-S1-Q3	Ⓐ Ⓑ Ⓒ Ⓓ Ⓔ
V5, Pg. 253	PT68-S3-Q18	Ⓐ Ⓑ Ⓒ Ⓓ Ⓔ	PT75, Pg. 26	PT75-S3-Q2	Ⓐ Ⓑ Ⓒ Ⓓ Ⓔ
V5, Pg. 255	PT68-S3-Q23	Ⓐ Ⓑ Ⓒ Ⓓ Ⓔ	PT75, Pg. 30	PT75-S3-Q17	Ⓐ Ⓑ Ⓒ Ⓓ Ⓔ
V5, Pg. 273	PT69-S1-Q4	Ⓐ Ⓑ Ⓒ Ⓓ Ⓔ	PT75, Pg. 31	PT75-S3-Q19	Ⓐ Ⓑ Ⓒ Ⓓ Ⓔ
V5, Pg. 274	PT69-S1-Q7	Ⓐ Ⓑ Ⓒ Ⓓ Ⓔ	PT75, Pg. 32	PT75-S3-Q23	Ⓐ Ⓑ Ⓒ Ⓓ Ⓔ
V5, Pg. 278	PT69-S1-Q19	Ⓐ Ⓑ Ⓒ Ⓓ Ⓔ	PT75, Pg. 33	PT75-S3-Q25	Ⓐ Ⓑ Ⓒ Ⓓ Ⓔ
V5, Pg. 298	PT69-S4-Q8	Ⓐ Ⓑ Ⓒ Ⓓ Ⓔ	PT76, Pg. 19	PT76-S2-Q5	Ⓐ Ⓑ Ⓒ Ⓓ Ⓔ
V5, Pg. 315	PT70-S1-Q13	Ⓐ Ⓑ Ⓒ Ⓓ Ⓔ	PT76, Pg. 23	PT76-S2-Q18	Ⓐ Ⓑ Ⓒ Ⓓ Ⓔ
V5, Pg. 318	PT70-S1-Q21	Ⓐ Ⓑ Ⓒ Ⓓ Ⓔ	PT76, Pg. 25	PT76-S2-Q24	Ⓐ Ⓑ Ⓒ Ⓓ Ⓔ
V5, Pg. 337	PT70-S4-Q6	Ⓐ Ⓑ Ⓒ Ⓓ Ⓔ	PT76, Pg. 37	PT76-S4-Q12	Ⓐ Ⓑ Ⓒ Ⓓ Ⓔ
V5, Pg. 338	PT70-S4-Q10	Ⓐ Ⓑ Ⓒ Ⓓ Ⓔ	PT76, Pg. 38	PT76-S4-Q16	Ⓐ Ⓑ Ⓒ Ⓓ Ⓔ
V5, Pg. 341	PT70-S4-Q20	Ⓐ Ⓑ Ⓒ Ⓓ Ⓔ	PT76, Pg. 38	PT76-S4-Q18	Ⓐ Ⓑ Ⓒ Ⓓ Ⓔ
V5, Pg. 343	PT70-S4-Q25	Ⓐ Ⓑ Ⓒ Ⓓ Ⓔ	PT76, Pg. 39	PT76-S4-Q20	Ⓐ Ⓑ Ⓒ Ⓓ Ⓔ
V5, Pg. 357	PT71-S1-Q16	Ⓐ Ⓑ Ⓒ Ⓓ Ⓔ	PT76, Pg. 41	PT76-S4-Q24	Ⓐ Ⓑ Ⓒ Ⓓ Ⓔ
V5, Pg. 358	PT71-S1-Q22	Ⓐ Ⓑ Ⓒ Ⓓ Ⓔ	PT77, Pg. 19	PT77-S2-Q3	Ⓐ Ⓑ Ⓒ Ⓓ Ⓔ
V5, Pg. 373	PT71-S3-Q19	Ⓐ Ⓑ Ⓒ Ⓓ Ⓔ	PT77, Pg. 20	PT77-S2-Q6	Ⓐ Ⓑ Ⓒ Ⓓ Ⓔ
PT72, Pg. 21	PT72-S2-Q12	Ⓐ Ⓑ Ⓒ Ⓓ Ⓔ	PT77, Pg. 25	PT77-S2-Q24	Ⓐ Ⓑ Ⓒ Ⓓ Ⓔ
PT72, Pg. 22	PT72-S2-Q15	Ⓐ Ⓑ Ⓒ Ⓓ Ⓔ	PT77, Pg. 41	PT77-S4-Q26	Ⓐ Ⓑ Ⓒ Ⓓ Ⓔ
PT72, Pg. 23	PT72-S2-Q21	Ⓐ Ⓑ Ⓒ Ⓓ Ⓔ			

Sufficient Assumption

J07, Pg. 7	J07-S2-Q6	Ⓐ Ⓑ Ⓒ Ⓓ Ⓔ	J07, Pg. 15	J07-S3-Q5	Ⓐ Ⓑ Ⓒ Ⓓ Ⓔ
J07, Pg. 10	J07-S2-Q13	Ⓐ Ⓑ Ⓒ Ⓓ Ⓔ	SP1, Pg. 75	PTA-S1-Q24	Ⓐ Ⓑ Ⓒ Ⓓ Ⓔ
J07, Pg. 10	J07-S2-Q15	Ⓐ Ⓑ Ⓒ Ⓓ Ⓔ	SP1, Pg. 188	PTB-S1-Q9	Ⓐ Ⓑ Ⓒ Ⓓ Ⓔ
J07, Pg. 12	J07-S2-Q23	Ⓐ Ⓑ Ⓒ Ⓓ Ⓔ	SP1, Pg. 212	PTB-S4-Q22	Ⓐ Ⓑ Ⓒ Ⓓ Ⓔ

SP1, Pg. 309	PTC-S3-Q4	Ⓐ Ⓑ Ⓒ Ⓓ Ⓔ	V2, Pg. 272	PT26-S3-Q21	Ⓐ Ⓑ Ⓒ Ⓓ Ⓔ
SP2, Pg. 358	PTC2-S2-Q15	Ⓐ Ⓑ Ⓒ Ⓓ Ⓔ	V2, Pg. 293	PT27-S1-Q16	Ⓐ Ⓑ Ⓒ Ⓓ Ⓔ
SP2, Pg. 359	PTC2-S2-Q20	Ⓐ Ⓑ Ⓒ Ⓓ Ⓔ	V2, Pg. 328	PT28-S1-Q24	Ⓐ Ⓑ Ⓒ Ⓓ Ⓔ
SP2, Pg. 364	PTC2-S3-Q11	Ⓐ Ⓑ Ⓒ Ⓓ Ⓔ	V3, Pg. 21	PT29-S1-Q20	Ⓐ Ⓑ Ⓒ Ⓓ Ⓔ
	PT2-S4-Q17	Ⓐ Ⓑ Ⓒ Ⓓ Ⓔ	V3, Pg. 70	PT30-S4-Q1	Ⓐ Ⓑ Ⓒ Ⓓ Ⓔ
	PT3-S2-Q12	Ⓐ Ⓑ Ⓒ Ⓓ Ⓔ	V3, Pg. 91	PT31-S2-Q10	Ⓐ Ⓑ Ⓒ Ⓓ Ⓔ
	PT3-S4-Q17	Ⓐ Ⓑ Ⓒ Ⓓ Ⓔ	V3, Pg. 119	PT32-S1-Q5	Ⓐ Ⓑ Ⓒ Ⓓ Ⓔ
	PT4-S1-Q2	Ⓐ Ⓑ Ⓒ Ⓓ Ⓔ	V3, Pg. 139	PT32-S4-Q4	Ⓐ Ⓑ Ⓒ Ⓓ Ⓔ
	PT5-S1-Q12	Ⓐ Ⓑ Ⓒ Ⓓ Ⓔ	V3, Pg. 173	PT33-S3-Q21	Ⓐ Ⓑ Ⓒ Ⓓ Ⓔ
	PT5-S1-Q16	Ⓐ Ⓑ Ⓒ Ⓓ Ⓔ	V3, Pg. 174	PT33-S3-Q23	Ⓐ Ⓑ Ⓒ Ⓓ Ⓔ
V1, Pg. 43	PT7-S4-Q23	Ⓐ Ⓑ Ⓒ Ⓓ Ⓔ	V3, Pg. 194	PT34-S2-Q2	Ⓐ Ⓑ Ⓒ Ⓓ Ⓔ
	PT8-S1-Q5	Ⓐ Ⓑ Ⓒ Ⓓ Ⓔ	V3, Pg. 196	PT34-S2-Q10	Ⓐ Ⓑ Ⓒ Ⓓ Ⓔ
	PT8-S4-Q9	Ⓐ Ⓑ Ⓒ Ⓓ Ⓔ	V3, Pg. 225	PT35-S1-Q20	Ⓐ Ⓑ Ⓒ Ⓓ Ⓔ
V1, Pg. 64	PT9-S2-Q23	Ⓐ Ⓑ Ⓒ Ⓓ Ⓔ	V3, Pg. 226	PT35-S1-Q22	Ⓐ Ⓑ Ⓒ Ⓓ Ⓔ
V1, Pg. 72	PT9-S4-Q12	Ⓐ Ⓑ Ⓒ Ⓓ Ⓔ	V3, Pg. 244	PT35-S4-Q14	Ⓐ Ⓑ Ⓒ Ⓓ Ⓔ
V1, Pg. 128	PT11-S2-Q22	Ⓐ Ⓑ Ⓒ Ⓓ Ⓔ	V3, Pg. 245	PT35-S4-Q19	Ⓐ Ⓑ Ⓒ Ⓓ Ⓔ
V1, Pg. 158	PT12-S1-Q22	Ⓐ Ⓑ Ⓒ Ⓓ Ⓔ	V3, Pg. 259	PT36-S1-Q18	Ⓐ Ⓑ Ⓒ Ⓓ Ⓔ
V1, Pg. 178	PT12-S4-Q20	Ⓐ Ⓑ Ⓒ Ⓓ Ⓔ	V3, Pg. 260	PT36-S1-Q22	Ⓐ Ⓑ Ⓒ Ⓓ Ⓔ
V1, Pg. 227	PT14-S2-Q13	Ⓐ Ⓑ Ⓒ Ⓓ Ⓔ	V3, Pg. 261	PT36-S1-Q26	Ⓐ Ⓑ Ⓒ Ⓓ Ⓔ
V1, Pg. 242	PT14-S4-Q7	Ⓐ Ⓑ Ⓒ Ⓓ Ⓔ	V3, Pg. 273	PT36-S3-Q12	Ⓐ Ⓑ Ⓒ Ⓓ Ⓔ
V1, Pg. 246	PT14-S4-Q23	Ⓐ Ⓑ Ⓒ Ⓓ Ⓔ	V3, Pg. 297	PT37-S2-Q5	Ⓐ Ⓑ Ⓒ Ⓓ Ⓔ
V1, Pg. 274	PT15-S3-Q18	Ⓐ Ⓑ Ⓒ Ⓓ Ⓔ	V3, Pg. 310	PT37-S4-Q9	Ⓐ Ⓑ Ⓒ Ⓓ Ⓔ
	PT17-S3-Q14	Ⓐ Ⓑ Ⓒ Ⓓ Ⓔ	V3, Pg. 313	PT37-S4-Q20	Ⓐ Ⓑ Ⓒ Ⓓ Ⓔ
V1, Pg. 345	PT18-S4-Q12	Ⓐ Ⓑ Ⓒ Ⓓ Ⓔ	V3, Pg. 322	PT38-S1-Q1	Ⓐ Ⓑ Ⓒ Ⓓ Ⓔ
V2, Pg. 25	PT19-S2-Q18	Ⓐ Ⓑ Ⓒ Ⓓ Ⓔ	V3, Pg. 346	PT38-S4-Q16	Ⓐ Ⓑ Ⓒ Ⓓ Ⓔ
V2, Pg. 38	PT19-S4-Q11	Ⓐ Ⓑ Ⓒ Ⓓ Ⓔ		PT39-S2-Q21	Ⓐ Ⓑ Ⓒ Ⓓ Ⓔ
V2, Pg. 94	PT21-S2-Q20	Ⓐ Ⓑ Ⓒ Ⓓ Ⓔ		PT39-S4-Q17	Ⓐ Ⓑ Ⓒ Ⓓ Ⓔ
V2, Pg. 138	PT22-S4-Q2	Ⓐ Ⓑ Ⓒ Ⓓ Ⓔ		PT40-S1-Q8	Ⓐ Ⓑ Ⓒ Ⓓ Ⓔ
V2, Pg. 139	PT22-S4-Q5	Ⓐ Ⓑ Ⓒ Ⓓ Ⓔ		PT40-S1-Q19	Ⓐ Ⓑ Ⓒ Ⓓ Ⓔ
V2, Pg. 141	PT22-S4-Q13	Ⓐ Ⓑ Ⓒ Ⓓ Ⓔ		PT40-S1-Q21	Ⓐ Ⓑ Ⓒ Ⓓ Ⓔ
V2, Pg. 157	PT23-S2-Q5	Ⓐ Ⓑ Ⓒ Ⓓ Ⓔ		PT40-S3-Q15	Ⓐ Ⓑ Ⓒ Ⓓ Ⓔ
V2, Pg. 167	PT23-S3-Q14	Ⓐ Ⓑ Ⓒ Ⓓ Ⓔ		PT41-S3-Q22	Ⓐ Ⓑ Ⓒ Ⓓ Ⓔ
V2, Pg. 200	PT24-S2-Q21	Ⓐ Ⓑ Ⓒ Ⓓ Ⓔ		PT42-S2-Q19	Ⓐ Ⓑ Ⓒ Ⓓ Ⓔ
V2, Pg. 201	PT24-S2-Q24	Ⓐ Ⓑ Ⓒ Ⓓ Ⓔ		PT42-S2-Q23	Ⓐ Ⓑ Ⓒ Ⓓ Ⓔ
V2, Pg. 204	PT24-S3-Q10	Ⓐ Ⓑ Ⓒ Ⓓ Ⓔ		PT43-S2-Q18	Ⓐ Ⓑ Ⓒ Ⓓ Ⓔ
V2, Pg. 207	PT24-S3-Q19	Ⓐ Ⓑ Ⓒ Ⓓ Ⓔ		PT44-S2-Q13	Ⓐ Ⓑ Ⓒ Ⓓ Ⓔ
V2, Pg. 245	PT25-S4-Q18	Ⓐ Ⓑ Ⓒ Ⓓ Ⓔ		PT44-S4-Q26	Ⓐ Ⓑ Ⓒ Ⓓ Ⓔ

	PT45-S1-Q21	Ⓐ Ⓑ © Ⓓ Ⓔ	V4, Pg. 207	PT57-S3-Q24	Ⓐ Ⓑ © Ⓓ Ⓔ
	PT45-S1-Q23	Ⓐ Ⓑ © Ⓓ Ⓔ	V4, Pg. 227	PT58-S1-Q12	Ⓐ Ⓑ © Ⓓ Ⓔ
	PT45-S4-Q22	Ⓐ Ⓑ © Ⓓ Ⓔ	V4, Pg. 231	PT58-S1-Q25	Ⓐ Ⓑ © Ⓓ Ⓔ
	PT46-S2-Q4	Ⓐ Ⓑ © Ⓓ Ⓔ	V4, Pg. 248	PT58-S4-Q19	Ⓐ Ⓑ © Ⓓ Ⓔ
	PT46-S2-Q23	Ⓐ Ⓑ © Ⓓ Ⓔ	V4, Pg. 251	PT58-S4-Q24	Ⓐ Ⓑ © Ⓓ Ⓔ
	PT46-S3-Q24	Ⓐ Ⓑ © Ⓓ Ⓔ	V4, Pg. 268	PT59-S2-Q17	Ⓐ Ⓑ © Ⓓ Ⓔ
	PT47-S1-Q9	Ⓐ Ⓑ © Ⓓ Ⓔ	V4, Pg. 271	PT59-S2-Q26	Ⓐ Ⓑ © Ⓓ Ⓔ
	PT47-S1-Q12	Ⓐ Ⓑ © Ⓓ Ⓔ	V4, Pg. 275	PT59-S3-Q10	Ⓐ Ⓑ © Ⓓ Ⓔ
	PT47-S3-Q21	Ⓐ Ⓑ © Ⓓ Ⓔ	V4, Pg. 302	PT60-S1-Q22	Ⓐ Ⓑ © Ⓓ Ⓔ
	PT48-S1-Q25	Ⓐ Ⓑ © Ⓓ Ⓔ	V4, Pg. 309	PT60-S3-Q3	Ⓐ Ⓑ © Ⓓ Ⓔ
	PT48-S4-Q8	Ⓐ Ⓑ © Ⓓ Ⓔ	V4, Pg. 343	PT61-S2-Q13	Ⓐ Ⓑ © Ⓓ Ⓔ
	PT48-S4-Q21	Ⓐ Ⓑ © Ⓓ Ⓔ	V4, Pg. 347	PT61-S2-Q24	Ⓐ Ⓑ © Ⓓ Ⓔ
	PT49-S2-Q7	Ⓐ Ⓑ © Ⓓ Ⓔ	V4, Pg. 355	PT61-S4-Q13	Ⓐ Ⓑ © Ⓓ Ⓔ
	PT49-S2-Q19	Ⓐ Ⓑ © Ⓓ Ⓔ	V4, Pg. 359	PT61-S4-Q25	Ⓐ Ⓑ © Ⓓ Ⓔ
	PT49-S2-Q25	Ⓐ Ⓑ © Ⓓ Ⓔ	V5, Pg. 18	PT62-S2-Q9	Ⓐ Ⓑ © Ⓓ Ⓔ
	PT49-S4-Q18	Ⓐ Ⓑ © Ⓓ Ⓔ	V5, Pg. 20	PT62-S2-Q15	Ⓐ Ⓑ © Ⓓ Ⓔ
	PT49-S4-Q22	Ⓐ Ⓑ © Ⓓ Ⓔ	V5, Pg. 21	PT62-S2-Q17	Ⓐ Ⓑ © Ⓓ Ⓔ
	PT50-S2-Q7	Ⓐ Ⓑ © Ⓓ Ⓔ	V5, Pg. 32	PT62-S4-Q16	Ⓐ Ⓑ © Ⓓ Ⓔ
	PT50-S2-Q22	Ⓐ Ⓑ © Ⓓ Ⓔ	V5, Pg. 33	PT62-S4-Q18	Ⓐ Ⓑ © Ⓓ Ⓔ
	PT50-S4-Q13	Ⓐ Ⓑ © Ⓓ Ⓔ	V5, Pg. 47	PT63-S1-Q10	Ⓐ Ⓑ © Ⓓ Ⓔ
	PT51-S1-Q16	Ⓐ Ⓑ © Ⓓ Ⓔ	V5, Pg. 60	PT63-S3-Q17	Ⓐ Ⓑ © Ⓓ Ⓔ
	PT51-S1-Q19	Ⓐ Ⓑ © Ⓓ Ⓔ	V5, Pg. 62	PT63-S3-Q24	Ⓐ Ⓑ © Ⓓ Ⓔ
	PT51-S3-Q20	Ⓐ Ⓑ © Ⓓ Ⓔ	V5, Pg. 83	PT64-S1-Q11	Ⓐ Ⓑ © Ⓓ Ⓔ
V4, Pg. 12	PT52-S1-Q17	Ⓐ Ⓑ © Ⓓ Ⓔ	V5, Pg. 86	PT64-S1-Q23	Ⓐ Ⓑ © Ⓓ Ⓔ
V4, Pg. 14	PT52-S1-Q20	Ⓐ Ⓑ © Ⓓ Ⓔ	V5, Pg. 97	PT64-S3-Q21	Ⓐ Ⓑ © Ⓓ Ⓔ
V4, Pg. 24	PT52-S3-Q15	Ⓐ Ⓑ © Ⓓ Ⓔ	V5, Pg. 99	PT64-S3-Q26	Ⓐ Ⓑ © Ⓓ Ⓔ
V4, Pg. 50	PT53-S1-Q20	Ⓐ Ⓑ © Ⓓ Ⓔ	V5, Pg. 121	PT65-S1-Q16	Ⓐ Ⓑ © Ⓓ Ⓔ
V4, Pg. 91	PT54-S2-Q13	Ⓐ Ⓑ © Ⓓ Ⓔ	V5, Pg. 161	PT66-S2-Q6	Ⓐ Ⓑ © Ⓓ Ⓔ
V4, Pg. 95	PT54-S2-Q26	Ⓐ Ⓑ © Ⓓ Ⓔ	V5, Pg. 165	PT66-S2-Q19	Ⓐ Ⓑ © Ⓓ Ⓔ
V4, Pg. 106	PT54-S4-Q22	Ⓐ Ⓑ © Ⓓ Ⓔ	V5, Pg. 181	PT66-S4-Q17	Ⓐ Ⓑ © Ⓓ Ⓔ
V4, Pg. 117	PT55-S1-Q4	Ⓐ Ⓑ © Ⓓ Ⓔ	V5, Pg. 181	PT66-S4-Q20	Ⓐ Ⓑ © Ⓓ Ⓔ
V4, Pg. 134	PT55-S3-Q10	Ⓐ Ⓑ © Ⓓ Ⓔ	V5, Pg. 219	PT67-S4-Q13	Ⓐ Ⓑ © Ⓓ Ⓔ
V4, Pg. 138	PT55-S3-Q21	Ⓐ Ⓑ © Ⓓ Ⓔ	V5, Pg. 246	PT68-S2-Q23	Ⓐ Ⓑ © Ⓓ Ⓔ
V4, Pg. 158	PT56-S2-Q10	Ⓐ Ⓑ © Ⓓ Ⓔ	V5, Pg. 252	PT68-S3-Q15	Ⓐ Ⓑ © Ⓓ Ⓔ
V4, Pg. 168	PT56-S3-Q16	Ⓐ Ⓑ © Ⓓ Ⓔ	V5, Pg. 279	PT69-S1-Q25	Ⓐ Ⓑ © Ⓓ Ⓔ
V4, Pg. 194	PT57-S2-Q7	Ⓐ Ⓑ © Ⓓ Ⓔ	V5, Pg. 299	PT69-S4-Q13	Ⓐ Ⓑ © Ⓓ Ⓔ
V4, Pg. 195	PT57-S2-Q12	Ⓐ Ⓑ © Ⓓ Ⓔ	V5, Pg. 302	PT69-S4-Q21	Ⓐ Ⓑ © Ⓓ Ⓔ

V5, Pg. 313	PT70-S1-Q7	Ⓐ Ⓑ Ⓒ Ⓓ Ⓔ	PT74, Pg. 38	PT74-S4-Q16	Ⓐ Ⓑ Ⓒ Ⓓ Ⓔ
V5, Pg. 342	PT70-S4-Q22	Ⓐ Ⓑ Ⓒ Ⓓ Ⓔ	PT75, Pg. 16	PT75-S1-Q23	Ⓐ Ⓑ Ⓒ Ⓓ Ⓔ
V5, Pg. 352	PT71-S1-Q1	Ⓐ Ⓑ Ⓒ Ⓓ Ⓔ	PT75, Pg. 30	PT75-S3-Q15	Ⓐ Ⓑ Ⓒ Ⓓ Ⓔ
V5, Pg. 370	PT71-S3-Q11	Ⓐ Ⓑ Ⓒ Ⓓ Ⓔ	PT76, Pg. 20	PT76-S2-Q10	Ⓐ Ⓑ Ⓒ Ⓓ Ⓔ
V5, Pg. 371	PT71-S3-Q14	Ⓐ Ⓑ Ⓒ Ⓓ Ⓔ	PT76, Pg. 24	PT76-S2-Q22	Ⓐ Ⓑ Ⓒ Ⓓ Ⓔ
PT72, Pg. 20	PT72-S2-Q8	Ⓐ Ⓑ Ⓒ Ⓓ Ⓔ	PT76, Pg. 34	PT76-S4-Q1	Ⓐ Ⓑ Ⓒ Ⓓ Ⓔ
PT73, Pg. 21	PT73-S2-Q10	Ⓐ Ⓑ Ⓒ Ⓓ Ⓔ	PT76, Pg. 37	PT76-S4-Q14	Ⓐ Ⓑ Ⓒ Ⓓ Ⓔ
PT73, Pg. 21	PT73-S2-Q12	Ⓐ Ⓑ Ⓒ Ⓓ Ⓔ	PT77, Pg. 20	PT77-S2-Q9	Ⓐ Ⓑ Ⓒ Ⓓ Ⓔ
PT73, Pg. 40	PT73-S4-Q24	Ⓐ Ⓑ Ⓒ Ⓓ Ⓔ	PT77, Pg. 22	PT77-S2-Q15	Ⓐ Ⓑ Ⓒ Ⓓ Ⓔ
PT74, Pg. 13	PT74-S1-Q12	Ⓐ Ⓑ Ⓒ Ⓓ Ⓔ	PT77, Pg. 39	PT77-S4-Q20	Ⓐ Ⓑ Ⓒ Ⓓ Ⓔ
PT74, Pg. 16	PT74-S1-Q20	Ⓐ Ⓑ Ⓒ Ⓓ Ⓔ	PT77, Pg. 41	PT77-S4-Q24	Ⓐ Ⓑ Ⓒ Ⓓ Ⓔ

Strengthen

J07, Pg. 11	J07-S2-Q19	Ⓐ Ⓑ Ⓒ Ⓓ Ⓔ		PT2-S2-Q22	Ⓐ Ⓑ Ⓒ Ⓓ Ⓔ
J07, Pg. 17	J07-S3-Q13	Ⓐ Ⓑ Ⓒ Ⓓ Ⓔ		PT2-S4-Q7	Ⓐ Ⓑ Ⓒ Ⓓ Ⓔ
J07, Pg. 19	J07-S3-Q19	Ⓐ Ⓑ Ⓒ Ⓓ Ⓔ		PT2-S4-Q10	Ⓐ Ⓑ Ⓒ Ⓓ Ⓔ
SP1, Pg. 73	PTA-S1-Q17	Ⓐ Ⓑ Ⓒ Ⓓ Ⓔ		PT2-S4-Q14	Ⓐ Ⓑ Ⓒ Ⓓ Ⓔ
SP1, Pg. 89	PTA-S4-Q3	Ⓐ Ⓑ Ⓒ Ⓓ Ⓔ		PT2-S4-Q25	Ⓐ Ⓑ Ⓒ Ⓓ Ⓔ
SP1, Pg. 89	PTA-S4-Q5	Ⓐ Ⓑ Ⓒ Ⓓ Ⓔ		PT3-S2-Q9	Ⓐ Ⓑ Ⓒ Ⓓ Ⓔ
SP1, Pg. 90	PTA-S4-Q7	Ⓐ Ⓑ Ⓒ Ⓓ Ⓔ		PT3-S2-Q17	Ⓐ Ⓑ Ⓒ Ⓓ Ⓔ
SP1, Pg. 186	PTB-S1-Q3	Ⓐ Ⓑ Ⓒ Ⓓ Ⓔ		PT3-S4-Q21	Ⓐ Ⓑ Ⓒ Ⓓ Ⓔ
SP1, Pg. 187	PTB-S1-Q7	Ⓐ Ⓑ Ⓒ Ⓓ Ⓔ		PT5-S1-Q23	Ⓐ Ⓑ Ⓒ Ⓓ Ⓔ
SP1, Pg. 191	PTB-S1-Q19	Ⓐ Ⓑ Ⓒ Ⓓ Ⓔ		PT5-S3-Q6	Ⓐ Ⓑ Ⓒ Ⓓ Ⓔ
SP1, Pg. 209	PTB-S4-Q11	Ⓐ Ⓑ Ⓒ Ⓓ Ⓔ		PT6-S2-Q21	Ⓐ Ⓑ Ⓒ Ⓓ Ⓔ
SP1, Pg. 210	PTB-S4-Q16	Ⓐ Ⓑ Ⓒ Ⓓ Ⓔ	V1, Pg. 20	PT7-S1-Q15	Ⓐ Ⓑ Ⓒ Ⓓ Ⓔ
SP1, Pg. 303	PTC-S2-Q14	Ⓐ Ⓑ Ⓒ Ⓓ Ⓔ	V1, Pg. 22	PT7-S1-Q23	Ⓐ Ⓑ Ⓒ Ⓓ Ⓔ
SP1, Pg. 305	PTC-S2-Q19	Ⓐ Ⓑ Ⓒ Ⓓ Ⓔ	V1, Pg. 36	PT7-S4-Q1	Ⓐ Ⓑ Ⓒ Ⓓ Ⓔ
SP1, Pg. 310	PTC-S3-Q7	Ⓐ Ⓑ Ⓒ Ⓓ Ⓔ		PT8-S1-Q10	Ⓐ Ⓑ Ⓒ Ⓓ Ⓔ
SP1, Pg. 311	PTC-S3-Q12	Ⓐ Ⓑ Ⓒ Ⓓ Ⓔ		PT8-S4-Q11	Ⓐ Ⓑ Ⓒ Ⓓ Ⓔ
SP2, Pg. 354	PTC2-S2-Q1	Ⓐ Ⓑ Ⓒ Ⓓ Ⓔ	V1, Pg. 60	PT9-S2-Q9	Ⓐ Ⓑ Ⓒ Ⓓ Ⓔ
SP2, Pg. 356	PTC2-S2-Q11	Ⓐ Ⓑ Ⓒ Ⓓ Ⓔ	V1, Pg. 60	PT9-S2-Q10	Ⓐ Ⓑ Ⓒ Ⓓ Ⓔ
SP2, Pg. 362	PTC2-S3-Q1	Ⓐ Ⓑ Ⓒ Ⓓ Ⓔ	V1, Pg. 74	PT9-S4-Q17	Ⓐ Ⓑ Ⓒ Ⓓ Ⓔ
	PT1-S3-Q15	Ⓐ Ⓑ Ⓒ Ⓓ Ⓔ	V1, Pg. 86	PT10-S1-Q9	Ⓐ Ⓑ Ⓒ Ⓓ Ⓔ
	PT1-S3-Q23	Ⓐ Ⓑ Ⓒ Ⓓ Ⓔ	V1, Pg. 104	PT10-S4-Q2	Ⓐ Ⓑ Ⓒ Ⓓ Ⓔ
	PT1-S4-Q4	Ⓐ Ⓑ Ⓒ Ⓓ Ⓔ	V1, Pg. 107	PT10-S4-Q11	Ⓐ Ⓑ Ⓒ Ⓓ Ⓔ
	PT1-S4-Q23	Ⓐ Ⓑ Ⓒ Ⓓ Ⓔ	V1, Pg. 143	PT11-S4-Q18	Ⓐ Ⓑ Ⓒ Ⓓ Ⓔ
	PT2-S2-Q10	Ⓐ Ⓑ Ⓒ Ⓓ Ⓔ	V1, Pg. 155	PT12-S1-Q11	Ⓐ Ⓑ Ⓒ Ⓓ Ⓔ

V1, Pg. 156	PT12-S1-Q15	Ⓐ Ⓑ Ⓒ Ⓓ Ⓔ	V2, Pg. 229	PT25-S2-Q4	Ⓐ Ⓑ Ⓒ Ⓓ Ⓔ
V1, Pg. 157	PT12-S1-Q19	Ⓐ Ⓑ Ⓒ Ⓓ Ⓔ	V2, Pg. 231	PT25-S2-Q10	Ⓐ Ⓑ Ⓒ Ⓓ Ⓔ
V1, Pg. 191	PT13-S2-Q5	Ⓐ Ⓑ Ⓒ Ⓓ Ⓔ	V2, Pg. 241	PT25-S4-Q6	Ⓐ Ⓑ Ⓒ Ⓓ Ⓔ
V1, Pg. 213	PT13-S4-Q23	Ⓐ Ⓑ Ⓒ Ⓓ Ⓔ	V2, Pg. 242	PT25-S4-Q7	Ⓐ Ⓑ Ⓒ Ⓓ Ⓔ
V1, Pg. 225	PT14-S2-Q6	Ⓐ Ⓑ Ⓒ Ⓓ Ⓔ	V2, Pg. 260	PT26-S2-Q11	Ⓐ Ⓑ Ⓒ Ⓓ Ⓔ
V1, Pg. 226	PT14-S2-Q7	Ⓐ Ⓑ Ⓒ Ⓓ Ⓔ	V2, Pg. 266	PT26-S3-Q3	Ⓐ Ⓑ Ⓒ Ⓓ Ⓔ
V1, Pg. 262	PT15-S2-Q3	Ⓐ Ⓑ Ⓒ Ⓓ Ⓔ	V2, Pg. 289	PT27-S1-Q5	Ⓐ Ⓑ Ⓒ Ⓓ Ⓔ
V1, Pg. 272	PT15-S3-Q8	Ⓐ Ⓑ Ⓒ Ⓓ Ⓔ	V2, Pg. 293	PT27-S1-Q18	Ⓐ Ⓑ Ⓒ Ⓓ Ⓔ
V1, Pg. 272	PT15-S3-Q10	Ⓐ Ⓑ Ⓒ Ⓓ Ⓔ	V2, Pg. 308	PT27-S4-Q2	Ⓐ Ⓑ Ⓒ Ⓓ Ⓔ
V1, Pg. 276	PT15-S3-Q23	Ⓐ Ⓑ Ⓒ Ⓓ Ⓔ	V2, Pg. 312	PT27-S4-Q16	Ⓐ Ⓑ Ⓒ Ⓓ Ⓔ
V1, Pg. 297	PT16-S2-Q18	Ⓐ Ⓑ Ⓒ Ⓓ Ⓔ	V2, Pg. 322	PT28-S1-Q1	Ⓐ Ⓑ Ⓒ Ⓓ Ⓔ
V1, Pg. 298	PT16-S2-Q21	Ⓐ Ⓑ Ⓒ Ⓓ Ⓔ	V2, Pg. 326	PT28-S1-Q15	Ⓐ Ⓑ Ⓒ Ⓓ Ⓔ
V1, Pg. 303	PT16-S3-Q13	Ⓐ Ⓑ Ⓒ Ⓓ Ⓔ	V2, Pg. 329	PT28-S1-Q26	Ⓐ Ⓑ Ⓒ Ⓓ Ⓔ
	PT17-S2-Q7	Ⓐ Ⓑ Ⓒ Ⓓ Ⓔ	V2, Pg. 335	PT28-S3-Q6	Ⓐ Ⓑ Ⓒ Ⓓ Ⓔ
	PT17-S3-Q6	Ⓐ Ⓑ Ⓒ Ⓓ Ⓔ	V2, Pg. 336	PT28-S3-Q9	Ⓐ Ⓑ Ⓒ Ⓓ Ⓔ
	PT17-S3-Q12	Ⓐ Ⓑ Ⓒ Ⓓ Ⓔ	V2, Pg. 337	PT28-S3-Q13	Ⓐ Ⓑ Ⓒ Ⓓ Ⓔ
	PT17-S3-Q18	Ⓐ Ⓑ Ⓒ Ⓓ Ⓔ	V2, Pg. 340	PT28-S3-Q24	Ⓐ Ⓑ Ⓒ Ⓓ Ⓔ
V1, Pg. 326	PT18-S2-Q2	Ⓐ Ⓑ Ⓒ Ⓓ Ⓔ	V3, Pg. 16	PT29-S1-Q3	Ⓐ Ⓑ Ⓒ Ⓓ Ⓔ
V1, Pg. 330	PT18-S2-Q16	Ⓐ Ⓑ Ⓒ Ⓓ Ⓔ	V3, Pg. 36	PT29-S4-Q1	Ⓐ Ⓑ Ⓒ Ⓓ Ⓔ
V1, Pg. 332	PT18-S2-Q21	Ⓐ Ⓑ Ⓒ Ⓓ Ⓔ	V3, Pg. 39	PT29-S4-Q11	Ⓐ Ⓑ Ⓒ Ⓓ Ⓔ
V2, Pg. 26	PT19-S2-Q21	Ⓐ Ⓑ Ⓒ Ⓓ Ⓔ	V3, Pg. 41	PT29-S4-Q20	Ⓐ Ⓑ Ⓒ Ⓓ Ⓔ
V2, Pg. 37	PT19-S4-Q7	Ⓐ Ⓑ Ⓒ Ⓓ Ⓔ	V3, Pg. 55	PT30-S2-Q3	Ⓐ Ⓑ Ⓒ Ⓓ Ⓔ
V2, Pg. 39	PT19-S4-Q15	Ⓐ Ⓑ Ⓒ Ⓓ Ⓔ	V3, Pg. 55	PT30-S2-Q4	Ⓐ Ⓑ Ⓒ Ⓓ Ⓔ
V2, Pg. 52	PT20-S1-Q9	Ⓐ Ⓑ Ⓒ Ⓓ Ⓔ	V3, Pg. 60	PT30-S2-Q21	Ⓐ Ⓑ Ⓒ Ⓓ Ⓔ
V2, Pg. 71	PT20-S4-Q5	Ⓐ Ⓑ Ⓒ Ⓓ Ⓔ	V3, Pg. 60	PT30-S2-Q24	Ⓐ Ⓑ Ⓒ Ⓓ Ⓔ
V2, Pg. 95	PT21-S2-Q23	Ⓐ Ⓑ Ⓒ Ⓓ Ⓔ	V3, Pg. 73	PT30-S4-Q12	Ⓐ Ⓑ Ⓒ Ⓓ Ⓔ
V2, Pg. 98	PT21-S3-Q9	Ⓐ Ⓑ Ⓒ Ⓓ Ⓔ	V3, Pg. 74	PT30-S4-Q15	Ⓐ Ⓑ Ⓒ Ⓓ Ⓔ
V2, Pg. 128	PT22-S2-Q9	Ⓐ Ⓑ Ⓒ Ⓓ Ⓔ	V3, Pg. 75	PT30-S4-Q18	Ⓐ Ⓑ Ⓒ Ⓓ Ⓔ
V2, Pg. 140	PT22-S4-Q8	Ⓐ Ⓑ Ⓒ Ⓓ Ⓔ	V3, Pg. 75	PT30-S4-Q20	Ⓐ Ⓑ Ⓒ Ⓓ Ⓔ
V2, Pg. 159	PT23-S2-Q14	Ⓐ Ⓑ Ⓒ Ⓓ Ⓔ	V3, Pg. 89	PT31-S2-Q5	Ⓐ Ⓑ Ⓒ Ⓓ Ⓔ
V2, Pg. 160	PT23-S2-Q16	Ⓐ Ⓑ Ⓒ Ⓓ Ⓔ	V3, Pg. 98	PT31-S3-Q9	Ⓐ Ⓑ Ⓒ Ⓓ Ⓔ
V2, Pg. 160	PT23-S2-Q18	Ⓐ Ⓑ Ⓒ Ⓓ Ⓔ	V3, Pg. 124	PT32-S1-Q20	Ⓐ Ⓑ Ⓒ Ⓓ Ⓔ
V2, Pg. 166	PT23-S3-Q10	Ⓐ Ⓑ Ⓒ Ⓓ Ⓔ	V3, Pg. 140	PT32-S4-Q9	Ⓐ Ⓑ Ⓒ Ⓓ Ⓔ
V2, Pg. 167	PT23-S3-Q13	Ⓐ Ⓑ Ⓒ Ⓓ Ⓔ	V3, Pg. 141	PT32-S4-Q11	Ⓐ Ⓑ Ⓒ Ⓓ Ⓔ
V2, Pg. 168	PT23-S3-Q15	Ⓐ Ⓑ Ⓒ Ⓓ Ⓔ	V3, Pg. 152	PT33-S1-Q1	Ⓐ Ⓑ Ⓒ Ⓓ Ⓔ
V2, Pg. 194	PT24-S2-Q4	Ⓐ Ⓑ Ⓒ Ⓓ Ⓔ	V3, Pg. 153	PT33-S1-Q6	Ⓐ Ⓑ Ⓒ Ⓓ Ⓔ
V2, Pg. 208	PT24-S3-Q23	Ⓐ Ⓑ Ⓒ Ⓓ Ⓔ	V3, Pg. 169	PT33-S3-Q4	Ⓐ Ⓑ Ⓒ Ⓓ Ⓔ

V3, Pg. 170	PT33-S3-Q9	Ⓐ Ⓑ Ⓒ Ⓓ Ⓔ		PT43-S2-Q14	Ⓐ Ⓑ Ⓒ Ⓓ Ⓔ
V3, Pg. 173	PT33-S3-Q20	Ⓐ Ⓑ Ⓒ Ⓓ Ⓔ		PT43-S3-Q2	Ⓐ Ⓑ Ⓒ Ⓓ Ⓔ
V3, Pg. 197	PT34-S2-Q14	Ⓐ Ⓑ Ⓒ Ⓓ Ⓔ		PT43-S3-Q10	Ⓐ Ⓑ Ⓒ Ⓓ Ⓔ
V3, Pg. 207	PT34-S3-Q21	Ⓐ Ⓑ Ⓒ Ⓓ Ⓔ		PT44-S2-Q7	Ⓐ Ⓑ Ⓒ Ⓓ Ⓔ
V3, Pg. 208	PT34-S3-Q24	Ⓐ Ⓑ Ⓒ Ⓓ Ⓔ		PT44-S2-Q15	Ⓐ Ⓑ Ⓒ Ⓓ Ⓔ
V3, Pg. 224	PT35-S1-Q15	Ⓐ Ⓑ Ⓒ Ⓓ Ⓔ		PT44-S4-Q14	Ⓐ Ⓑ Ⓒ Ⓓ Ⓔ
V3, Pg. 242	PT35-S4-Q10	Ⓐ Ⓑ Ⓒ Ⓓ Ⓔ		PT44-S4-Q17	Ⓐ Ⓑ Ⓒ Ⓓ Ⓔ
V3, Pg. 272	PT36-S3-Q7	Ⓐ Ⓑ Ⓒ Ⓓ Ⓔ		PT45-S1-Q14	Ⓐ Ⓑ Ⓒ Ⓓ Ⓔ
V3, Pg. 273	PT36-S3-Q11	Ⓐ Ⓑ Ⓒ Ⓓ Ⓔ		PT45-S1-Q19	Ⓐ Ⓑ Ⓒ Ⓓ Ⓔ
V3, Pg. 277	PT36-S3-Q26	Ⓐ Ⓑ Ⓒ Ⓓ Ⓔ		PT45-S1-Q26	Ⓐ Ⓑ Ⓒ Ⓓ Ⓔ
V3, Pg. 296	PT37-S2-Q1	Ⓐ Ⓑ Ⓒ Ⓓ Ⓔ		PT45-S4-Q7	Ⓐ Ⓑ Ⓒ Ⓓ Ⓔ
V3, Pg. 297	PT37-S2-Q6	Ⓐ Ⓑ Ⓒ Ⓓ Ⓔ		PT45-S4-Q25	Ⓐ Ⓑ Ⓒ Ⓓ Ⓔ
V3, Pg. 301	PT37-S2-Q20	Ⓐ Ⓑ Ⓒ Ⓓ Ⓔ		PT46-S2-Q16	Ⓐ Ⓑ Ⓒ Ⓓ Ⓔ
V3, Pg. 311	PT37-S4-Q13	Ⓐ Ⓑ Ⓒ Ⓓ Ⓔ		PT46-S2-Q19	Ⓐ Ⓑ Ⓒ Ⓓ Ⓔ
V3, Pg. 315	PT37-S4-Q25	Ⓐ Ⓑ Ⓒ Ⓓ Ⓔ		PT46-S3-Q22	Ⓐ Ⓑ Ⓒ Ⓓ Ⓔ
V3, Pg. 322	PT38-S1-Q4	Ⓐ Ⓑ Ⓒ Ⓓ Ⓔ		PT47-S1-Q11	Ⓐ Ⓑ Ⓒ Ⓓ Ⓔ
V3, Pg. 343	PT38-S4-Q5	Ⓐ Ⓑ Ⓒ Ⓓ Ⓔ		PT47-S1-Q26	Ⓐ Ⓑ Ⓒ Ⓓ Ⓔ
	PT39-S2-Q10	Ⓐ Ⓑ Ⓒ Ⓓ Ⓔ		PT47-S3-Q2	Ⓐ Ⓑ Ⓒ Ⓓ Ⓔ
	PT39-S2-Q15	Ⓐ Ⓑ Ⓒ Ⓓ Ⓔ		PT48-S1-Q3	Ⓐ Ⓑ Ⓒ Ⓓ Ⓔ
	PT39-S4-Q13	Ⓐ Ⓑ Ⓒ Ⓓ Ⓔ		PT48-S1-Q7	Ⓐ Ⓑ Ⓒ Ⓓ Ⓔ
	PT39-S4-Q18	Ⓐ Ⓑ Ⓒ Ⓓ Ⓔ		PT48-S1-Q10	Ⓐ Ⓑ Ⓒ Ⓓ Ⓔ
	PT40-S1-Q6	Ⓐ Ⓑ Ⓒ Ⓓ Ⓔ		PT48-S1-Q16	Ⓐ Ⓑ Ⓒ Ⓓ Ⓔ
	PT40-S1-Q11	Ⓐ Ⓑ Ⓒ Ⓓ Ⓔ		PT48-S4-Q2	Ⓐ Ⓑ Ⓒ Ⓓ Ⓔ
	PT40-S1-Q13	Ⓐ Ⓑ Ⓒ Ⓓ Ⓔ		PT49-S2-Q4	Ⓐ Ⓑ Ⓒ Ⓓ Ⓔ
	PT40-S3-Q2	Ⓐ Ⓑ Ⓒ Ⓓ Ⓔ		PT49-S2-Q11	Ⓐ Ⓑ Ⓒ Ⓓ Ⓔ
	PT40-S3-Q8	Ⓐ Ⓑ Ⓒ Ⓓ Ⓔ		PT49-S4-Q4	Ⓐ Ⓑ Ⓒ Ⓓ Ⓔ
	PT40-S3-Q18	Ⓐ Ⓑ Ⓒ Ⓓ Ⓔ		PT50-S2-Q13	Ⓐ Ⓑ Ⓒ Ⓓ Ⓔ
	PT40-S3-Q24	Ⓐ Ⓑ Ⓒ Ⓓ Ⓔ		PT50-S4-Q9	Ⓐ Ⓑ Ⓒ Ⓓ Ⓔ
	PT41-S1-Q12	Ⓐ Ⓑ Ⓒ Ⓓ Ⓔ		PT50-S4-Q23	Ⓐ Ⓑ Ⓒ Ⓓ Ⓔ
	PT41-S3-Q15	Ⓐ Ⓑ Ⓒ Ⓓ Ⓔ		PT51-S1-Q24	Ⓐ Ⓑ Ⓒ Ⓓ Ⓔ
	PT41-S3-Q19	Ⓐ Ⓑ Ⓒ Ⓓ Ⓔ		PT51-S3-Q3	Ⓐ Ⓑ Ⓒ Ⓓ Ⓔ
	PT42-S2-Q10	Ⓐ Ⓑ Ⓒ Ⓓ Ⓔ		PT51-S3-Q25	Ⓐ Ⓑ Ⓒ Ⓓ Ⓔ
	PT42-S2-Q18	Ⓐ Ⓑ Ⓒ Ⓓ Ⓔ	V4, Pg. 9	PT52-S1-Q4	Ⓐ Ⓑ Ⓒ Ⓓ Ⓔ
	PT42-S4-Q1	Ⓐ Ⓑ Ⓒ Ⓓ Ⓔ	V4, Pg. 20	PT52-S3-Q3	Ⓐ Ⓑ Ⓒ Ⓓ Ⓔ
	PT42-S4-Q9	Ⓐ Ⓑ Ⓒ Ⓓ Ⓔ	V4, Pg. 44	PT53-S1-Q1	Ⓐ Ⓑ Ⓒ Ⓓ Ⓔ
	PT42-S4-Q23	Ⓐ Ⓑ Ⓒ Ⓓ Ⓔ	V4, Pg. 45	PT53-S1-Q6	Ⓐ Ⓑ Ⓒ Ⓓ Ⓔ
	PT43-S2-Q8	Ⓐ Ⓑ Ⓒ Ⓓ Ⓔ	V4, Pg. 46	PT53-S1-Q10	Ⓐ Ⓑ Ⓒ Ⓓ Ⓔ

V4, Pg. 56	PT53-S3-Q1	Ⓐ Ⓑ Ⓒ Ⓓ Ⓔ
V4, Pg. 59	PT53-S3-Q11	Ⓐ Ⓑ Ⓒ Ⓓ Ⓔ
V4, Pg. 95	PT54-S2-Q24	Ⓐ Ⓑ Ⓒ Ⓓ Ⓔ
V4, Pg. 100	PT54-S4-Q1	Ⓐ Ⓑ Ⓒ Ⓓ Ⓔ
V4, Pg. 105	PT54-S4-Q20	Ⓐ Ⓑ Ⓒ Ⓓ Ⓔ
V4, Pg. 122	PT55-S1-Q23	Ⓐ Ⓑ Ⓒ Ⓓ Ⓔ
V4, Pg. 135	PT55-S3-Q14	Ⓐ Ⓑ Ⓒ Ⓓ Ⓔ
V4, Pg. 159	PT56-S2-Q14	Ⓐ Ⓑ Ⓒ Ⓓ Ⓔ
V4, Pg. 163	PT56-S2-Q24	Ⓐ Ⓑ Ⓒ Ⓓ Ⓔ
V4, Pg. 166	PT56-S3-Q8	Ⓐ Ⓑ Ⓒ Ⓓ Ⓔ
V4, Pg. 167	PT56-S3-Q13	Ⓐ Ⓑ Ⓒ Ⓓ Ⓔ
V4, Pg. 193	PT57-S2-Q5	Ⓐ Ⓑ Ⓒ Ⓓ Ⓔ
V4, Pg. 198	PT57-S2-Q22	Ⓐ Ⓑ Ⓒ Ⓓ Ⓔ
V4, Pg. 202	PT57-S3-Q9	Ⓐ Ⓑ Ⓒ Ⓓ Ⓔ
V4, Pg. 225	PT58-S1-Q3	Ⓐ Ⓑ Ⓒ Ⓓ Ⓔ
V4, Pg. 250	PT58-S4-Q23	Ⓐ Ⓑ Ⓒ Ⓓ Ⓔ
V4, Pg. 264	PT59-S2-Q1	Ⓐ Ⓑ Ⓒ Ⓓ Ⓔ
V4, Pg. 265	PT59-S2-Q3	Ⓐ Ⓑ Ⓒ Ⓓ Ⓔ
V4, Pg. 265	PT59-S2-Q5	Ⓐ Ⓑ Ⓒ Ⓓ Ⓔ
V4, Pg. 269	PT59-S2-Q22	Ⓐ Ⓑ Ⓒ Ⓓ Ⓔ
V4, Pg. 275	PT59-S3-Q11	Ⓐ Ⓑ Ⓒ Ⓓ Ⓔ
V4, Pg. 299	PT60-S1-Q11	Ⓐ Ⓑ Ⓒ Ⓓ Ⓔ
V4, Pg. 308	PT60-S3-Q2	Ⓐ Ⓑ Ⓒ Ⓓ Ⓔ
V4, Pg. 313	PT60-S3-Q21	Ⓐ Ⓑ Ⓒ Ⓓ Ⓔ
V4, Pg. 341	PT61-S2-Q6	Ⓐ Ⓑ Ⓒ Ⓓ Ⓔ
V4, Pg. 346	PT61-S2-Q22	Ⓐ Ⓑ Ⓒ Ⓓ Ⓔ
V4, Pg. 352	PT61-S4-Q4	Ⓐ Ⓑ Ⓒ Ⓓ Ⓔ
V5, Pg. 16	PT62-S2-Q2	Ⓐ Ⓑ Ⓒ Ⓓ Ⓔ
V5, Pg. 16	PT62-S2-Q3	Ⓐ Ⓑ Ⓒ Ⓓ Ⓔ
V5, Pg. 17	PT62-S2-Q4	Ⓐ Ⓑ Ⓒ Ⓓ Ⓔ
V5, Pg. 20	PT62-S2-Q16	Ⓐ Ⓑ Ⓒ Ⓓ Ⓔ
V5, Pg. 29	PT62-S4-Q3	Ⓐ Ⓑ Ⓒ Ⓓ Ⓔ
V5, Pg. 33	PT62-S4-Q20	Ⓐ Ⓑ Ⓒ Ⓓ Ⓔ
V5, Pg. 34	PT62-S4-Q22	Ⓐ Ⓑ Ⓒ Ⓓ Ⓔ
V5, Pg. 47	PT63-S1-Q11	Ⓐ Ⓑ Ⓒ Ⓓ Ⓔ
V5, Pg. 48	PT63-S1-Q15	Ⓐ Ⓑ Ⓒ Ⓓ Ⓔ
V5, Pg. 48	PT63-S1-Q16	Ⓐ Ⓑ Ⓒ Ⓓ Ⓔ

V5, Pg. 50	PT63-S1-Q22	Ⓐ Ⓑ Ⓒ Ⓓ Ⓔ
V5, Pg. 61	PT63-S3-Q21	Ⓐ Ⓑ Ⓒ Ⓓ Ⓔ
V5, Pg. 84	PT64-S1-Q17	Ⓐ Ⓑ Ⓒ Ⓓ Ⓔ
V5, Pg. 86	PT64-S1-Q22	Ⓐ Ⓑ Ⓒ Ⓓ Ⓔ
V5, Pg. 94	PT64-S3-Q9	Ⓐ Ⓑ Ⓒ Ⓓ Ⓔ
V5, Pg. 96	PT64-S3-Q17	Ⓐ Ⓑ Ⓒ Ⓓ Ⓔ
V5, Pg. 98	PT64-S3-Q24	Ⓐ Ⓑ Ⓒ Ⓓ Ⓔ
V5, Pg. 116	PT65-S1-Q1	Ⓐ Ⓑ Ⓒ Ⓓ Ⓔ
V5, Pg. 120	PT65-S1-Q13	Ⓐ Ⓑ Ⓒ Ⓓ Ⓔ
V5, Pg. 122	PT65-S1-Q19	Ⓐ Ⓑ Ⓒ Ⓓ Ⓔ
V5, Pg. 141	PT65-S4-Q22	Ⓐ Ⓑ Ⓒ Ⓓ Ⓔ
V5, Pg. 165	PT66-S2-Q17	Ⓐ Ⓑ Ⓒ Ⓓ Ⓔ
V5, Pg. 178	PT66-S4-Q12	Ⓐ Ⓑ Ⓒ Ⓓ Ⓔ
V5, Pg. 200	PT67-S2-Q3	Ⓐ Ⓑ Ⓒ Ⓓ Ⓔ
V5, Pg. 217	PT67-S4-Q4	Ⓐ Ⓑ Ⓒ Ⓓ Ⓔ
V5, Pg. 243	PT68-S2-Q13	Ⓐ Ⓑ Ⓒ Ⓓ Ⓔ
V5, Pg. 250	PT68-S3-Q7	Ⓐ Ⓑ Ⓒ Ⓓ Ⓔ
V5, Pg. 253	PT68-S3-Q17	Ⓐ Ⓑ Ⓒ Ⓓ Ⓔ
V5, Pg. 272	PT69-S1-Q1	Ⓐ Ⓑ Ⓒ Ⓓ Ⓔ
V5, Pg. 276	PT69-S1-Q13	Ⓐ Ⓑ Ⓒ Ⓓ Ⓔ
V5, Pg. 303	PT69-S4-Q23	Ⓐ Ⓑ Ⓒ Ⓓ Ⓔ
V5, Pg. 312	PT70-S1-Q3	Ⓐ Ⓑ Ⓒ Ⓓ Ⓔ
V5, Pg. 319	PT70-S1-Q25	Ⓐ Ⓑ Ⓒ Ⓓ Ⓔ
V5, Pg. 337	PT70-S4-Q4	Ⓐ Ⓑ Ⓒ Ⓓ Ⓔ
V5, Pg. 353	PT71-S1-Q6	Ⓐ Ⓑ Ⓒ Ⓓ Ⓔ
V5, Pg. 355	PT71-S1-Q12	Ⓐ Ⓑ Ⓒ Ⓓ Ⓔ
V5, Pg. 369	PT71-S3-Q4	Ⓐ Ⓑ Ⓒ Ⓓ Ⓔ
V5, Pg. 370	PT71-S3-Q8	Ⓐ Ⓑ Ⓒ Ⓓ Ⓔ
V5, Pg. 372	PT71-S3-Q16	Ⓐ Ⓑ Ⓒ Ⓓ Ⓔ
V5, Pg. 375	PT71-S3-Q25	Ⓐ Ⓑ Ⓒ Ⓓ Ⓔ
PT72, Pg. 18	PT72-S2-Q3	Ⓐ Ⓑ Ⓒ Ⓓ Ⓔ
PT72, Pg. 19	PT72-S2-Q7	Ⓐ Ⓑ Ⓒ Ⓓ Ⓔ
PT72, Pg. 24	PT72-S2-Q23	Ⓐ Ⓑ Ⓒ Ⓓ Ⓔ
PT72, Pg. 25	PT72-S2-Q25	Ⓐ Ⓑ Ⓒ Ⓓ Ⓔ
PT72, Pg. 27	PT72-S3-Q6	Ⓐ Ⓑ Ⓒ Ⓓ Ⓔ
PT72, Pg. 28	PT72-S3-Q8	Ⓐ Ⓑ Ⓒ Ⓓ Ⓔ
PT72, Pg. 29	PT72-S3-Q12	Ⓐ Ⓑ Ⓒ Ⓓ Ⓔ

PT73, Pg. 24	PT73-S2-Q22	Ⓐ Ⓑ Ⓒ Ⓓ Ⓔ		PT75, Pg. 15	PT75-S1-Q21	Ⓐ Ⓑ Ⓒ Ⓓ Ⓔ
PT73, Pg. 39	PT73-S4-Q20	Ⓐ Ⓑ Ⓒ Ⓓ Ⓔ		PT75, Pg. 27	PT75-S3-Q6	Ⓐ Ⓑ Ⓒ Ⓓ Ⓔ
PT74, Pg. 10	PT74-S1-Q2	Ⓐ Ⓑ Ⓒ Ⓓ Ⓔ		PT75, Pg. 32	PT75-S3-Q21	Ⓐ Ⓑ Ⓒ Ⓓ Ⓔ
PT74, Pg. 11	PT74-S1-Q4	Ⓐ Ⓑ Ⓒ Ⓓ Ⓔ		PT76, Pg. 25	PT76-S2-Q25	Ⓐ Ⓑ Ⓒ Ⓓ Ⓔ
PT74, Pg. 14	PT74-S1-Q17	Ⓐ Ⓑ Ⓒ Ⓓ Ⓔ		PT76, Pg. 35	PT76-S4-Q8	Ⓐ Ⓑ Ⓒ Ⓓ Ⓔ
PT74, Pg. 34	PT74-S4-Q3	Ⓐ Ⓑ Ⓒ Ⓓ Ⓔ		PT77, Pg. 18	PT77-S2-Q1	Ⓐ Ⓑ Ⓒ Ⓓ Ⓔ
PT74, Pg. 41	PT74-S4-Q26	Ⓐ Ⓑ Ⓒ Ⓓ Ⓔ		PT77, Pg. 18	PT77-S2-Q2	Ⓐ Ⓑ Ⓒ Ⓓ Ⓔ
PT75, Pg. 12	PT75-S1-Q9	Ⓐ Ⓑ Ⓒ Ⓓ Ⓔ		PT77, Pg. 20	PT77-S2-Q7	Ⓐ Ⓑ Ⓒ Ⓓ Ⓔ
PT75, Pg. 14	PT75-S1-Q15	Ⓐ Ⓑ Ⓒ Ⓓ Ⓔ		PT77, Pg. 35	PT77-S4-Q4	Ⓐ Ⓑ Ⓒ Ⓓ Ⓔ

Weaken

J07, Pg. 7	J07-S2-Q5	Ⓐ Ⓑ Ⓒ Ⓓ Ⓔ			PT2-S2-Q18	Ⓐ Ⓑ Ⓒ Ⓓ Ⓔ
J07, Pg. 8	J07-S2-Q9	Ⓐ Ⓑ Ⓒ Ⓓ Ⓔ			PT2-S4-Q5	Ⓐ Ⓑ Ⓒ Ⓓ Ⓔ
J07, Pg. 10	J07-S2-Q14	Ⓐ Ⓑ Ⓒ Ⓓ Ⓔ			PT2-S4-Q16	Ⓐ Ⓑ Ⓒ Ⓓ Ⓔ
J07, Pg. 18	J07-S3-Q15	Ⓐ Ⓑ Ⓒ Ⓓ Ⓔ			PT3-S2-Q14	Ⓐ Ⓑ Ⓒ Ⓓ Ⓔ
J07, Pg. 20	J07-S3-Q21	Ⓐ Ⓑ Ⓒ Ⓓ Ⓔ			PT3-S2-Q16	Ⓐ Ⓑ Ⓒ Ⓓ Ⓔ
SP1, Pg. 73	PTA-S1-Q16	Ⓐ Ⓑ Ⓒ Ⓓ Ⓔ			PT3-S2-Q20	Ⓐ Ⓑ Ⓒ Ⓓ Ⓔ
SP1, Pg. 91	PTA-S4-Q10	Ⓐ Ⓑ Ⓒ Ⓓ Ⓔ			PT3-S2-Q23	Ⓐ Ⓑ Ⓒ Ⓓ Ⓔ
SP1, Pg. 187	PTB-S1-Q4	Ⓐ Ⓑ Ⓒ Ⓓ Ⓔ			PT3-S4-Q2	Ⓐ Ⓑ Ⓒ Ⓓ Ⓔ
SP1, Pg. 190	PTB-S1-Q16	Ⓐ Ⓑ Ⓒ Ⓓ Ⓔ			PT3-S4-Q5	Ⓐ Ⓑ Ⓒ Ⓓ Ⓔ
SP1, Pg. 207	PTB-S4-Q5	Ⓐ Ⓑ Ⓒ Ⓓ Ⓔ			PT3-S4-Q11	Ⓐ Ⓑ Ⓒ Ⓓ Ⓔ
SP1, Pg. 208	PTB-S4-Q9	Ⓐ Ⓑ Ⓒ Ⓓ Ⓔ			PT4-S1-Q1	Ⓐ Ⓑ Ⓒ Ⓓ Ⓔ
SP1, Pg. 211	PTB-S4-Q18	Ⓐ Ⓑ Ⓒ Ⓓ Ⓔ			PT4-S1-Q3	Ⓐ Ⓑ Ⓒ Ⓓ Ⓔ
SP1, Pg. 300	PTC-S2-Q3	Ⓐ Ⓑ Ⓒ Ⓓ Ⓔ			PT4-S1-Q4	Ⓐ Ⓑ Ⓒ Ⓓ Ⓔ
SP1, Pg. 308	PTC-S3-Q2	Ⓐ Ⓑ Ⓒ Ⓓ Ⓔ			PT4-S1-Q9	Ⓐ Ⓑ Ⓒ Ⓓ Ⓔ
SP1, Pg. 310	PTC-S3-Q10	Ⓐ Ⓑ Ⓒ Ⓓ Ⓔ			PT4-S1-Q13	Ⓐ Ⓑ Ⓒ Ⓓ Ⓔ
SP1, Pg. 313	PTC-S3-Q21	Ⓐ Ⓑ Ⓒ Ⓓ Ⓔ			PT4-S4-Q1	Ⓐ Ⓑ Ⓒ Ⓓ Ⓔ
SP2, Pg. 355	PTC2-S2-Q7	Ⓐ Ⓑ Ⓒ Ⓓ Ⓔ			PT4-S4-Q6	Ⓐ Ⓑ Ⓒ Ⓓ Ⓔ
SP2, Pg. 358	PTC2-S2-Q17	Ⓐ Ⓑ Ⓒ Ⓓ Ⓔ			PT4-S4-Q8	Ⓐ Ⓑ Ⓒ Ⓓ Ⓔ
SP2, Pg. 363	PTC2-S3-Q5	Ⓐ Ⓑ Ⓒ Ⓓ Ⓔ			PT4-S4-Q11	Ⓐ Ⓑ Ⓒ Ⓓ Ⓔ
SP2, Pg. 363	PTC2-S3-Q7	Ⓐ Ⓑ Ⓒ Ⓓ Ⓔ			PT5-S1-Q5	Ⓐ Ⓑ Ⓒ Ⓓ Ⓔ
	PT1-S3-Q5	Ⓐ Ⓑ Ⓒ Ⓓ Ⓔ			PT5-S1-Q8	Ⓐ Ⓑ Ⓒ Ⓓ Ⓔ
	PT1-S3-Q9	Ⓐ Ⓑ Ⓒ Ⓓ Ⓔ			PT5-S1-Q10	Ⓐ Ⓑ Ⓒ Ⓓ Ⓔ
	PT1-S4-Q12	Ⓐ Ⓑ Ⓒ Ⓓ Ⓔ			PT5-S1-Q17	Ⓐ Ⓑ Ⓒ Ⓓ Ⓔ
	PT1-S4-Q15	Ⓐ Ⓑ Ⓒ Ⓓ Ⓔ			PT5-S3-Q2	Ⓐ Ⓑ Ⓒ Ⓓ Ⓔ
	PT2-S2-Q7	Ⓐ Ⓑ Ⓒ Ⓓ Ⓔ			PT5-S3-Q8	Ⓐ Ⓑ Ⓒ Ⓓ Ⓔ
	PT2-S2-Q14	Ⓐ Ⓑ Ⓒ Ⓓ Ⓔ			PT5-S3-Q24	Ⓐ Ⓑ Ⓒ Ⓓ Ⓔ

	PT6-S2-Q7	Ⓐ Ⓑ Ⓒ Ⓓ Ⓔ	V1, Pg. 196	PT13-S2-Q21	Ⓐ Ⓑ Ⓒ Ⓓ Ⓔ
	PT6-S2-Q19	Ⓐ Ⓑ Ⓒ Ⓓ Ⓔ	V1, Pg. 209	PT13-S4-Q12	Ⓐ Ⓑ Ⓒ Ⓓ Ⓔ
	PT6-S3-Q2	Ⓐ Ⓑ Ⓒ Ⓓ Ⓔ	V1, Pg. 211	PT13-S4-Q17	Ⓐ Ⓑ Ⓒ Ⓓ Ⓔ
	PT6-S3-Q4	Ⓐ Ⓑ Ⓒ Ⓓ Ⓔ	V1, Pg. 211	PT13-S4-Q19	Ⓐ Ⓑ Ⓒ Ⓓ Ⓔ
	PT6-S3-Q13	Ⓐ Ⓑ Ⓒ Ⓓ Ⓔ	V1, Pg. 227	PT14-S2-Q12	Ⓐ Ⓑ Ⓒ Ⓓ Ⓔ
	PT6-S3-Q17	Ⓐ Ⓑ Ⓒ Ⓓ Ⓔ	V1, Pg. 230	PT14-S2-Q21	Ⓐ Ⓑ Ⓒ Ⓓ Ⓔ
V1, Pg. 16	PT7-S1-Q1	Ⓐ Ⓑ Ⓒ Ⓓ Ⓔ	V1, Pg. 231	PT14-S2-Q24	Ⓐ Ⓑ Ⓒ Ⓓ Ⓔ
V1, Pg. 17	PT7-S1-Q4	Ⓐ Ⓑ Ⓒ Ⓓ Ⓔ	V1, Pg. 241	PT14-S4-Q4	Ⓐ Ⓑ Ⓒ Ⓓ Ⓔ
V1, Pg. 37	PT7-S4-Q4	Ⓐ Ⓑ Ⓒ Ⓓ Ⓔ	V1, Pg. 242	PT14-S4-Q6	Ⓐ Ⓑ Ⓒ Ⓓ Ⓔ
	PT8-S1-Q7	Ⓐ Ⓑ Ⓒ Ⓓ Ⓔ	V1, Pg. 246	PT14-S4-Q22	Ⓐ Ⓑ Ⓒ Ⓓ Ⓔ
	PT8-S1-Q11	Ⓐ Ⓑ Ⓒ Ⓓ Ⓔ	V1, Pg. 247	PT14-S4-Q25	Ⓐ Ⓑ Ⓒ Ⓓ Ⓔ
	PT8-S1-Q13	Ⓐ Ⓑ Ⓒ Ⓓ Ⓔ	V1, Pg. 264	PT15-S2-Q7	Ⓐ Ⓑ Ⓒ Ⓓ Ⓔ
	PT8-S4-Q14	Ⓐ Ⓑ Ⓒ Ⓓ Ⓔ	V1, Pg. 277	PT15-S3-Q25	Ⓐ Ⓑ Ⓒ Ⓓ Ⓔ
	PT8-S4-Q24	Ⓐ Ⓑ Ⓒ Ⓓ Ⓔ	V1, Pg. 292	PT16-S2-Q2	Ⓐ Ⓑ Ⓒ Ⓓ Ⓔ
	PT8-S4-Q25	Ⓐ Ⓑ Ⓒ Ⓓ Ⓔ	V1, Pg. 293	PT16-S2-Q5	Ⓐ Ⓑ Ⓒ Ⓓ Ⓔ
V1, Pg. 59	PT9-S2-Q4	Ⓐ Ⓑ Ⓒ Ⓓ Ⓔ	V1, Pg. 296	PT16-S2-Q16	Ⓐ Ⓑ Ⓒ Ⓓ Ⓔ
V1, Pg. 60	PT9-S2-Q7	Ⓐ Ⓑ Ⓒ Ⓓ Ⓔ	V1, Pg. 300	PT16-S3-Q1	Ⓐ Ⓑ Ⓒ Ⓓ Ⓔ
V1, Pg. 61	PT9-S2-Q12	Ⓐ Ⓑ Ⓒ Ⓓ Ⓔ	V1, Pg. 301	PT16-S3-Q6	Ⓐ Ⓑ Ⓒ Ⓓ Ⓔ
V1, Pg. 70	PT9-S4-Q2	Ⓐ Ⓑ Ⓒ Ⓓ Ⓔ	V1, Pg. 304	PT16-S3-Q18	Ⓐ Ⓑ Ⓒ Ⓓ Ⓔ
V1, Pg. 76	PT9-S4-Q22	Ⓐ Ⓑ Ⓒ Ⓓ Ⓔ		PT17-S2-Q8	Ⓐ Ⓑ Ⓒ Ⓓ Ⓔ
V1, Pg. 87	PT10-S1-Q16	Ⓐ Ⓑ Ⓒ Ⓓ Ⓔ		PT17-S2-Q13	Ⓐ Ⓑ Ⓒ Ⓓ Ⓔ
V1, Pg. 88	PT10-S1-Q19	Ⓐ Ⓑ Ⓒ Ⓓ Ⓔ		PT17-S3-Q17	Ⓐ Ⓑ Ⓒ Ⓓ Ⓔ
V1, Pg. 104	PT10-S4-Q1	Ⓐ Ⓑ Ⓒ Ⓓ Ⓔ	V1, Pg. 327	PT18-S2-Q6	Ⓐ Ⓑ Ⓒ Ⓓ Ⓔ
V1, Pg. 106	PT10-S4-Q9	Ⓐ Ⓑ Ⓒ Ⓓ Ⓔ	V1, Pg. 333	PT18-S2-Q24	Ⓐ Ⓑ Ⓒ Ⓓ Ⓔ
V1, Pg. 122	PT11-S2-Q1	Ⓐ Ⓑ Ⓒ Ⓓ Ⓔ	V1, Pg. 344	PT18-S4-Q7	Ⓐ Ⓑ Ⓒ Ⓓ Ⓔ
V1, Pg. 124	PT11-S2-Q11	Ⓐ Ⓑ Ⓒ Ⓓ Ⓔ	V1, Pg. 345	PT18-S4-Q14	Ⓐ Ⓑ Ⓒ Ⓓ Ⓔ
V1, Pg. 127	PT11-S2-Q19	Ⓐ Ⓑ Ⓒ Ⓓ Ⓔ	V1, Pg. 348	PT18-S4-Q23	Ⓐ Ⓑ Ⓒ Ⓓ Ⓔ
V1, Pg. 127	PT11-S2-Q21	Ⓐ Ⓑ Ⓒ Ⓓ Ⓔ	V2, Pg. 21	PT19-S2-Q4	Ⓐ Ⓑ Ⓒ Ⓓ Ⓔ
V1, Pg. 139	PT11-S4-Q5	Ⓐ Ⓑ Ⓒ Ⓓ Ⓔ	V2, Pg. 23	PT19-S2-Q12	Ⓐ Ⓑ Ⓒ Ⓓ Ⓔ
V1, Pg. 141	PT11-S4-Q11	Ⓐ Ⓑ Ⓒ Ⓓ Ⓔ	V2, Pg. 38	PT19-S4-Q9	Ⓐ Ⓑ Ⓒ Ⓓ Ⓔ
V1, Pg. 144	PT11-S4-Q21	Ⓐ Ⓑ Ⓒ Ⓓ Ⓔ	V2, Pg. 38	PT19-S4-Q10	Ⓐ Ⓑ Ⓒ Ⓓ Ⓔ
V1, Pg. 156	PT12-S1-Q16	Ⓐ Ⓑ Ⓒ Ⓓ Ⓔ	V2, Pg. 43	PT19-S4-Q26	Ⓐ Ⓑ Ⓒ Ⓓ Ⓔ
V1, Pg. 173	PT12-S4-Q4	Ⓐ Ⓑ Ⓒ Ⓓ Ⓔ	V2, Pg. 50	PT20-S1-Q2	Ⓐ Ⓑ Ⓒ Ⓓ Ⓔ
V1, Pg. 175	PT12-S4-Q11	Ⓐ Ⓑ Ⓒ Ⓓ Ⓔ	V2, Pg. 51	PT20-S1-Q4	Ⓐ Ⓑ Ⓒ Ⓓ Ⓔ
V1, Pg. 178	PT12-S4-Q21	Ⓐ Ⓑ Ⓒ Ⓓ Ⓔ	V2, Pg. 53	PT20-S1-Q12	Ⓐ Ⓑ Ⓒ Ⓓ Ⓔ
V1, Pg. 190	PT13-S2-Q1	Ⓐ Ⓑ Ⓒ Ⓓ Ⓔ	V2, Pg. 70	PT20-S4-Q3	Ⓐ Ⓑ Ⓒ Ⓓ Ⓔ
V1, Pg. 193	PT13-S2-Q13	Ⓐ Ⓑ Ⓒ Ⓓ Ⓔ	V2, Pg. 74	PT20-S4-Q17	Ⓐ Ⓑ Ⓒ Ⓓ Ⓔ

V2, Pg. 76	PT20-S4-Q23	Ⓐ Ⓑ Ⓒ Ⓓ Ⓔ	V2, Pg. 328	PT28-S1-Q23	Ⓐ Ⓑ Ⓒ Ⓓ Ⓔ
V2, Pg. 77	PT20-S4-Q25	Ⓐ Ⓑ Ⓒ Ⓓ Ⓔ	V2, Pg. 336	PT28-S3-Q11	Ⓐ Ⓑ Ⓒ Ⓓ Ⓔ
V2, Pg. 90	PT21-S2-Q7	Ⓐ Ⓑ Ⓒ Ⓓ Ⓔ	V2, Pg. 337	PT28-S3-Q15	Ⓐ Ⓑ Ⓒ Ⓓ Ⓔ
V2, Pg. 93	PT21-S2-Q17	Ⓐ Ⓑ Ⓒ Ⓓ Ⓔ	V2, Pg. 338	PT28-S3-Q17	Ⓐ Ⓑ Ⓒ Ⓓ Ⓔ
V2, Pg. 101	PT21-S3-Q21	Ⓐ Ⓑ Ⓒ Ⓓ Ⓔ	V2, Pg. 341	PT28-S3-Q25	Ⓐ Ⓑ Ⓒ Ⓓ Ⓔ
V2, Pg. 102	PT21-S3-Q23	Ⓐ Ⓑ Ⓒ Ⓓ Ⓔ	V3, Pg. 20	PT29-S1-Q16	Ⓐ Ⓑ Ⓒ Ⓓ Ⓔ
V2, Pg. 127	PT22-S2-Q4	Ⓐ Ⓑ Ⓒ Ⓓ Ⓔ	V3, Pg. 23	PT29-S1-Q24	Ⓐ Ⓑ Ⓒ Ⓓ Ⓔ
V2, Pg. 128	PT22-S2-Q8	Ⓐ Ⓑ Ⓒ Ⓓ Ⓔ	V3, Pg. 38	PT29-S4-Q9	Ⓐ Ⓑ Ⓒ Ⓓ Ⓔ
V2, Pg. 143	PT22-S4-Q19	Ⓐ Ⓑ Ⓒ Ⓓ Ⓔ	V3, Pg. 43	PT29-S4-Q24	Ⓐ Ⓑ Ⓒ Ⓓ Ⓔ
V2, Pg. 144	PT22-S4-Q24	Ⓐ Ⓑ Ⓒ Ⓓ Ⓔ	V3, Pg. 54	PT30-S2-Q1	Ⓐ Ⓑ Ⓒ Ⓓ Ⓔ
V2, Pg. 145	PT22-S4-Q26	Ⓐ Ⓑ Ⓒ Ⓓ Ⓔ	V3, Pg. 56	PT30-S2-Q8	Ⓐ Ⓑ Ⓒ Ⓓ Ⓔ
V2, Pg. 158	PT23-S2-Q8	Ⓐ Ⓑ Ⓒ Ⓓ Ⓔ	V3, Pg. 56	PT30-S2-Q9	Ⓐ Ⓑ Ⓒ Ⓓ Ⓔ
V2, Pg. 163	PT23-S2-Q26	Ⓐ Ⓑ Ⓒ Ⓓ Ⓔ	V3, Pg. 73	PT30-S4-Q11	Ⓐ Ⓑ Ⓒ Ⓓ Ⓔ
V2, Pg. 169	PT23-S3-Q19	Ⓐ Ⓑ Ⓒ Ⓓ Ⓔ	V3, Pg. 74	PT30-S4-Q17	Ⓐ Ⓑ Ⓒ Ⓓ Ⓔ
V2, Pg. 195	PT24-S2-Q7	Ⓐ Ⓑ Ⓒ Ⓓ Ⓔ	V3, Pg. 77	PT30-S4-Q24	Ⓐ Ⓑ Ⓒ Ⓓ Ⓔ
V2, Pg. 200	PT24-S2-Q19	Ⓐ Ⓑ Ⓒ Ⓓ Ⓔ	V3, Pg. 89	PT31-S2-Q6	Ⓐ Ⓑ Ⓒ Ⓓ Ⓔ
V2, Pg. 200	PT24-S2-Q20	Ⓐ Ⓑ Ⓒ Ⓓ Ⓔ	V3, Pg. 93	PT31-S2-Q16	Ⓐ Ⓑ Ⓒ Ⓓ Ⓔ
V2, Pg. 203	PT24-S3-Q6	Ⓐ Ⓑ Ⓒ Ⓓ Ⓔ	V3, Pg. 93	PT31-S2-Q19	Ⓐ Ⓑ Ⓒ Ⓓ Ⓔ
V2, Pg. 204	PT24-S3-Q9	Ⓐ Ⓑ Ⓒ Ⓓ Ⓔ	V3, Pg. 99	PT31-S3-Q12	Ⓐ Ⓑ Ⓒ Ⓓ Ⓔ
V2, Pg. 208	PT24-S3-Q22	Ⓐ Ⓑ Ⓒ Ⓓ Ⓔ	V3, Pg. 102	PT31-S3-Q24	Ⓐ Ⓑ Ⓒ Ⓓ Ⓔ
V2, Pg. 229	PT25-S2-Q5	Ⓐ Ⓑ Ⓒ Ⓓ Ⓔ	V3, Pg. 121	PT32-S1-Q12	Ⓐ Ⓑ Ⓒ Ⓓ Ⓔ
V2, Pg. 233	PT25-S2-Q15	Ⓐ Ⓑ Ⓒ Ⓓ Ⓔ	V3, Pg. 123	PT32-S1-Q17	Ⓐ Ⓑ Ⓒ Ⓓ Ⓔ
V2, Pg. 241	PT25-S4-Q3	Ⓐ Ⓑ Ⓒ Ⓓ Ⓔ	V3, Pg. 138	PT32-S4-Q2	Ⓐ Ⓑ Ⓒ Ⓓ Ⓔ
V2, Pg. 242	PT25-S4-Q10	Ⓐ Ⓑ Ⓒ Ⓓ Ⓔ	V3, Pg. 153	PT33-S1-Q4	Ⓐ Ⓑ Ⓒ Ⓓ Ⓔ
V2, Pg. 243	PT25-S4-Q11	Ⓐ Ⓑ Ⓒ Ⓓ Ⓔ	V3, Pg. 157	PT33-S1-Q17	Ⓐ Ⓑ Ⓒ Ⓓ Ⓔ
V2, Pg. 246	PT25-S4-Q24	Ⓐ Ⓑ Ⓒ Ⓓ Ⓔ	V3, Pg. 157	PT33-S1-Q20	Ⓐ Ⓑ Ⓒ Ⓓ Ⓔ
V2, Pg. 259	PT26-S2-Q5	Ⓐ Ⓑ Ⓒ Ⓓ Ⓔ	V3, Pg. 159	PT33-S1-Q25	Ⓐ Ⓑ Ⓒ Ⓓ Ⓔ
V2, Pg. 261	PT26-S2-Q12	Ⓐ Ⓑ Ⓒ Ⓓ Ⓔ	V3, Pg. 170	PT33-S3-Q7	Ⓐ Ⓑ Ⓒ Ⓓ Ⓔ
V2, Pg. 267	PT26-S3-Q6	Ⓐ Ⓑ Ⓒ Ⓓ Ⓔ	V3, Pg. 175	PT33-S3-Q24	Ⓐ Ⓑ Ⓒ Ⓓ Ⓔ
V2, Pg. 270	PT26-S3-Q14	Ⓐ Ⓑ Ⓒ Ⓓ Ⓔ	V3, Pg. 197	PT34-S2-Q12	Ⓐ Ⓑ Ⓒ Ⓓ Ⓔ
V2, Pg. 273	PT26-S3-Q24	Ⓐ Ⓑ Ⓒ Ⓓ Ⓔ	V3, Pg. 198	PT34-S2-Q17	Ⓐ Ⓑ Ⓒ Ⓓ Ⓔ
V2, Pg. 289	PT27-S1-Q4	Ⓐ Ⓑ Ⓒ Ⓓ Ⓔ	V3, Pg. 201	PT34-S2-Q25	Ⓐ Ⓑ Ⓒ Ⓓ Ⓔ
V2, Pg. 290	PT27-S1-Q8	Ⓐ Ⓑ Ⓒ Ⓓ Ⓔ	V3, Pg. 203	PT34-S3-Q6	Ⓐ Ⓑ Ⓒ Ⓓ Ⓔ
V2, Pg. 291	PT27-S1-Q10	Ⓐ Ⓑ Ⓒ Ⓓ Ⓔ	V3, Pg. 206	PT34-S3-Q18	Ⓐ Ⓑ Ⓒ Ⓓ Ⓔ
V2, Pg. 312	PT27-S4-Q15	Ⓐ Ⓑ Ⓒ Ⓓ Ⓔ	V3, Pg. 207	PT34-S3-Q20	Ⓐ Ⓑ Ⓒ Ⓓ Ⓔ
V2, Pg. 313	PT27-S4-Q18	Ⓐ Ⓑ Ⓒ Ⓓ Ⓔ	V3, Pg. 221	PT35-S1-Q4	Ⓐ Ⓑ Ⓒ Ⓓ Ⓔ
V2, Pg. 323	PT28-S1-Q5	Ⓐ Ⓑ Ⓒ Ⓓ Ⓔ	V3, Pg. 222	PT35-S1-Q8	Ⓐ Ⓑ Ⓒ Ⓓ Ⓔ

V3, Pg. 223	PT35-S1-Q13	Ⓐ Ⓑ Ⓒ Ⓓ Ⓔ	PT44-S2-Q4	Ⓐ Ⓑ Ⓒ Ⓓ Ⓔ
V3, Pg. 241	PT35-S4-Q5	Ⓐ Ⓑ Ⓒ Ⓓ Ⓔ	PT44-S2-Q8	Ⓐ Ⓑ Ⓒ Ⓓ Ⓔ
V3, Pg. 244	PT35-S4-Q17	Ⓐ Ⓑ Ⓒ Ⓓ Ⓔ	PT44-S2-Q20	Ⓐ Ⓑ Ⓒ Ⓓ Ⓔ
V3, Pg. 245	PT35-S4-Q20	Ⓐ Ⓑ Ⓒ Ⓓ Ⓔ	PT44-S4-Q1	Ⓐ Ⓑ Ⓒ Ⓓ Ⓔ
V3, Pg. 254	PT36-S1-Q2	Ⓐ Ⓑ Ⓒ Ⓓ Ⓔ	PT44-S4-Q5	Ⓐ Ⓑ Ⓒ Ⓓ Ⓔ
V3, Pg. 256	PT36-S1-Q8	Ⓐ Ⓑ Ⓒ Ⓓ Ⓔ	PT45-S1-Q2	Ⓐ Ⓑ Ⓒ Ⓓ Ⓔ
V3, Pg. 261	PT36-S1-Q25	Ⓐ Ⓑ Ⓒ Ⓓ Ⓔ	PT45-S1-Q12	Ⓐ Ⓑ Ⓒ Ⓓ Ⓔ
V3, Pg. 270	PT36-S3-Q2	Ⓐ Ⓑ Ⓒ Ⓓ Ⓔ	PT45-S1-Q16	Ⓐ Ⓑ Ⓒ Ⓓ Ⓔ
V3, Pg. 271	PT36-S3-Q5	Ⓐ Ⓑ Ⓒ Ⓓ Ⓔ	PT45-S1-Q18	Ⓐ Ⓑ Ⓒ Ⓓ Ⓔ
V3, Pg. 297	PT37-S2-Q4	Ⓐ Ⓑ Ⓒ Ⓓ Ⓔ	PT45-S4-Q4	Ⓐ Ⓑ Ⓒ Ⓓ Ⓔ
V3, Pg. 299	PT37-S2-Q14	Ⓐ Ⓑ Ⓒ Ⓓ Ⓔ	PT46-S2-Q8	Ⓐ Ⓑ Ⓒ Ⓓ Ⓔ
V3, Pg. 308	PT37-S4-Q2	Ⓐ Ⓑ Ⓒ Ⓓ Ⓔ	PT46-S2-Q22	Ⓐ Ⓑ Ⓒ Ⓓ Ⓔ
V3, Pg. 311	PT37-S4-Q11	Ⓐ Ⓑ Ⓒ Ⓓ Ⓔ	PT46-S2-Q25	Ⓐ Ⓑ Ⓒ Ⓓ Ⓔ
V3, Pg. 313	PT37-S4-Q18	Ⓐ Ⓑ Ⓒ Ⓓ Ⓔ	PT46-S3-Q6	Ⓐ Ⓑ Ⓒ Ⓓ Ⓔ
V3, Pg. 324	PT38-S1-Q10	Ⓐ Ⓑ Ⓒ Ⓓ Ⓔ	PT47-S1-Q2	Ⓐ Ⓑ Ⓒ Ⓓ Ⓔ
V3, Pg. 327	PT38-S1-Q17	Ⓐ Ⓑ Ⓒ Ⓓ Ⓔ	PT47-S1-Q19	Ⓐ Ⓑ Ⓒ Ⓓ Ⓔ
V3, Pg. 345	PT38-S4-Q13	Ⓐ Ⓑ Ⓒ Ⓓ Ⓔ	PT47-S1-Q22	Ⓐ Ⓑ Ⓒ Ⓓ Ⓔ
V3, Pg. 345	PT38-S4-Q15	Ⓐ Ⓑ Ⓒ Ⓓ Ⓔ	PT47-S3-Q4	Ⓐ Ⓑ Ⓒ Ⓓ Ⓔ
	PT39-S2-Q9	Ⓐ Ⓑ Ⓒ Ⓓ Ⓔ	PT47-S3-Q7	Ⓐ Ⓑ Ⓒ Ⓓ Ⓔ
	PT39-S4-Q1	Ⓐ Ⓑ Ⓒ Ⓓ Ⓔ	PT47-S3-Q14	Ⓐ Ⓑ Ⓒ Ⓓ Ⓔ
	PT39-S4-Q22	Ⓐ Ⓑ Ⓒ Ⓓ Ⓔ	PT47-S3-Q24	Ⓐ Ⓑ Ⓒ Ⓓ Ⓔ
	PT40-S1-Q17	Ⓐ Ⓑ Ⓒ Ⓓ Ⓔ	PT48-S1-Q1	Ⓐ Ⓑ Ⓒ Ⓓ Ⓔ
	PT40-S3-Q5	Ⓐ Ⓑ Ⓒ Ⓓ Ⓔ	PT48-S1-Q19	Ⓐ Ⓑ Ⓒ Ⓓ Ⓔ
	PT40-S3-Q26	Ⓐ Ⓑ Ⓒ Ⓓ Ⓔ	PT48-S4-Q9	Ⓐ Ⓑ Ⓒ Ⓓ Ⓔ
	PT41-S1-Q13	Ⓐ Ⓑ Ⓒ Ⓓ Ⓔ	PT48-S4-Q20	Ⓐ Ⓑ Ⓒ Ⓓ Ⓔ
	PT41-S1-Q16	Ⓐ Ⓑ Ⓒ Ⓓ Ⓔ	PT48-S4-Q23	Ⓐ Ⓑ Ⓒ Ⓓ Ⓔ
	PT41-S3-Q16	Ⓐ Ⓑ Ⓒ Ⓓ Ⓔ	PT48-S4-Q26	Ⓐ Ⓑ Ⓒ Ⓓ Ⓔ
	PT41-S3-Q26	Ⓐ Ⓑ Ⓒ Ⓓ Ⓔ	PT49-S2-Q6	Ⓐ Ⓑ Ⓒ Ⓓ Ⓔ
	PT42-S2-Q1	Ⓐ Ⓑ Ⓒ Ⓓ Ⓔ	PT49-S2-Q8	Ⓐ Ⓑ Ⓒ Ⓓ Ⓔ
	PT42-S2-Q4	Ⓐ Ⓑ Ⓒ Ⓓ Ⓔ	PT49-S2-Q14	Ⓐ Ⓑ Ⓒ Ⓓ Ⓔ
	PT42-S2-Q6	Ⓐ Ⓑ Ⓒ Ⓓ Ⓔ	PT49-S4-Q8	Ⓐ Ⓑ Ⓒ Ⓓ Ⓔ
	PT42-S2-Q20	Ⓐ Ⓑ Ⓒ Ⓓ Ⓔ	PT50-S2-Q2	Ⓐ Ⓑ Ⓒ Ⓓ Ⓔ
	PT42-S2-Q25	Ⓐ Ⓑ Ⓒ Ⓓ Ⓔ	PT50-S2-Q24	Ⓐ Ⓑ Ⓒ Ⓓ Ⓔ
	PT42-S4-Q6	Ⓐ Ⓑ Ⓒ Ⓓ Ⓔ	PT50-S4-Q5	Ⓐ Ⓑ Ⓒ Ⓓ Ⓔ
	PT43-S2-Q6	Ⓐ Ⓑ Ⓒ Ⓓ Ⓔ	PT50-S4-Q12	Ⓐ Ⓑ Ⓒ Ⓓ Ⓔ
	PT43-S3-Q8	Ⓐ Ⓑ Ⓒ Ⓓ Ⓔ	PT51-S1-Q8	Ⓐ Ⓑ Ⓒ Ⓓ Ⓔ
	PT43-S3-Q19	Ⓐ Ⓑ Ⓒ Ⓓ Ⓔ	PT51-S1-Q25	Ⓐ Ⓑ Ⓒ Ⓓ Ⓔ

	PT51-S3-Q1	Ⓐ Ⓑ Ⓒ Ⓓ Ⓔ	V4, Pg. 275	PT59-S3-Q13	Ⓐ Ⓑ Ⓒ Ⓓ Ⓔ
V4, Pg. 10	PT52-S1-Q9	Ⓐ Ⓑ Ⓒ Ⓓ Ⓔ	V4, Pg. 297	PT60-S1-Q6	Ⓐ Ⓑ Ⓒ Ⓓ Ⓔ
V4, Pg. 11	PT52-S1-Q12	Ⓐ Ⓑ Ⓒ Ⓓ Ⓔ	V4, Pg. 299	PT60-S1-Q13	Ⓐ Ⓑ Ⓒ Ⓓ Ⓔ
V4, Pg. 14	PT52-S1-Q21	Ⓐ Ⓑ Ⓒ Ⓓ Ⓔ	V4, Pg. 300	PT60-S1-Q16	Ⓐ Ⓑ Ⓒ Ⓓ Ⓔ
V4, Pg. 21	PT52-S3-Q6	Ⓐ Ⓑ Ⓒ Ⓓ Ⓔ	V4, Pg. 309	PT60-S3-Q4	Ⓐ Ⓑ Ⓒ Ⓓ Ⓔ
V4, Pg. 25	PT52-S3-Q19	Ⓐ Ⓑ Ⓒ Ⓓ Ⓔ	V4, Pg. 311	PT60-S3-Q13	Ⓐ Ⓑ Ⓒ Ⓓ Ⓔ
V4, Pg. 44	PT53-S1-Q3	Ⓐ Ⓑ Ⓒ Ⓓ Ⓔ	V4, Pg. 343	PT61-S2-Q11	Ⓐ Ⓑ Ⓒ Ⓓ Ⓔ
V4, Pg. 45	PT53-S1-Q8	Ⓐ Ⓑ Ⓒ Ⓓ Ⓔ	V4, Pg. 343	PT61-S2-Q14	Ⓐ Ⓑ Ⓒ Ⓓ Ⓔ
V4, Pg. 57	PT53-S3-Q4	Ⓐ Ⓑ Ⓒ Ⓓ Ⓔ	V4, Pg. 345	PT61-S2-Q20	Ⓐ Ⓑ Ⓒ Ⓓ Ⓔ
V4, Pg. 58	PT53-S3-Q9	Ⓐ Ⓑ Ⓒ Ⓓ Ⓔ	V4, Pg. 354	PT61-S4-Q8	Ⓐ Ⓑ Ⓒ Ⓓ Ⓔ
V4, Pg. 60	PT53-S3-Q14	Ⓐ Ⓑ Ⓒ Ⓓ Ⓔ	V4, Pg. 358	PT61-S4-Q21	Ⓐ Ⓑ Ⓒ Ⓓ Ⓔ
V4, Pg. 60	PT53-S3-Q16	Ⓐ Ⓑ Ⓒ Ⓓ Ⓔ	V5, Pg. 22	PT62-S2-Q22	Ⓐ Ⓑ Ⓒ Ⓓ Ⓔ
V4, Pg. 88	PT54-S2-Q3	Ⓐ Ⓑ Ⓒ Ⓓ Ⓔ	V5, Pg. 29	PT62-S4-Q5	Ⓐ Ⓑ Ⓒ Ⓓ Ⓔ
V4, Pg. 91	PT54-S2-Q14	Ⓐ Ⓑ Ⓒ Ⓓ Ⓔ	V5, Pg. 31	PT62-S4-Q14	Ⓐ Ⓑ Ⓒ Ⓓ Ⓔ
V4, Pg. 103	PT54-S4-Q10	Ⓐ Ⓑ Ⓒ Ⓓ Ⓔ	V5, Pg. 44	PT63-S1-Q2	Ⓐ Ⓑ Ⓒ Ⓓ Ⓔ
V4, Pg. 118	PT55-S1-Q7	Ⓐ Ⓑ Ⓒ Ⓓ Ⓔ	V5, Pg. 45	PT63-S1-Q7	Ⓐ Ⓑ Ⓒ Ⓓ Ⓔ
V4, Pg. 118	PT55-S1-Q9	Ⓐ Ⓑ Ⓒ Ⓓ Ⓔ	V5, Pg. 58	PT63-S3-Q9	Ⓐ Ⓑ Ⓒ Ⓓ Ⓔ
V4, Pg. 122	PT55-S1-Q22	Ⓐ Ⓑ Ⓒ Ⓓ Ⓔ	V5, Pg. 60	PT63-S3-Q16	Ⓐ Ⓑ Ⓒ Ⓓ Ⓔ
V4, Pg. 133	PT55-S3-Q4	Ⓐ Ⓑ Ⓒ Ⓓ Ⓔ	V5, Pg. 81	PT64-S1-Q4	Ⓐ Ⓑ Ⓒ Ⓓ Ⓔ
V4, Pg. 134	PT55-S3-Q9	Ⓐ Ⓑ Ⓒ Ⓓ Ⓔ	V5, Pg. 82	PT64-S1-Q8	Ⓐ Ⓑ Ⓒ Ⓓ Ⓔ
V4, Pg. 138	PT55-S3-Q22	Ⓐ Ⓑ Ⓒ Ⓓ Ⓔ	V5, Pg. 82	PT64-S1-Q10	Ⓐ Ⓑ Ⓒ Ⓓ Ⓔ
V4, Pg. 156	PT56-S2-Q3	Ⓐ Ⓑ Ⓒ Ⓓ Ⓔ	V5, Pg. 83	PT64-S1-Q13	Ⓐ Ⓑ Ⓒ Ⓓ Ⓔ
V4, Pg. 158	PT56-S2-Q8	Ⓐ Ⓑ Ⓒ Ⓓ Ⓔ	V5, Pg. 95	PT64-S3-Q15	Ⓐ Ⓑ Ⓒ Ⓓ Ⓔ
V4, Pg. 169	PT56-S3-Q20	Ⓐ Ⓑ Ⓒ Ⓓ Ⓔ	V5, Pg. 117	PT65-S1-Q5	Ⓐ Ⓑ Ⓒ Ⓓ Ⓔ
V4, Pg. 194	PT57-S2-Q9	Ⓐ Ⓑ Ⓒ Ⓓ Ⓔ	V5, Pg. 137	PT65-S4-Q3	Ⓐ Ⓑ Ⓒ Ⓓ Ⓔ
V4, Pg. 196	PT57-S2-Q14	Ⓐ Ⓑ Ⓒ Ⓓ Ⓔ	V5, Pg. 141	PT65-S4-Q19	Ⓐ Ⓑ Ⓒ Ⓓ Ⓔ
V4, Pg. 197	PT57-S2-Q17	Ⓐ Ⓑ Ⓒ Ⓓ Ⓔ	V5, Pg. 161	PT66-S2-Q5	Ⓐ Ⓑ Ⓒ Ⓓ Ⓔ
V4, Pg. 198	PT57-S2-Q20	Ⓐ Ⓑ Ⓒ Ⓓ Ⓔ	V5, Pg. 176	PT66-S4-Q4	Ⓐ Ⓑ Ⓒ Ⓓ Ⓔ
V4, Pg. 201	PT57-S3-Q6	Ⓐ Ⓑ Ⓒ Ⓓ Ⓔ	V5, Pg. 177	PT66-S4-Q6	Ⓐ Ⓑ Ⓒ Ⓓ Ⓔ
V4, Pg. 202	PT57-S3-Q11	Ⓐ Ⓑ Ⓒ Ⓓ Ⓔ	V5, Pg. 177	PT66-S4-Q8	Ⓐ Ⓑ Ⓒ Ⓓ Ⓔ
V4, Pg. 225	PT58-S1-Q5	Ⓐ Ⓑ Ⓒ Ⓓ Ⓔ	V5, Pg. 200	PT67-S2-Q1	Ⓐ Ⓑ Ⓒ Ⓓ Ⓔ
V4, Pg. 230	PT58-S1-Q24	Ⓐ Ⓑ Ⓒ Ⓓ Ⓔ	V5, Pg. 204	PT67-S2-Q17	Ⓐ Ⓑ Ⓒ Ⓓ Ⓔ
V4, Pg. 244	PT58-S4-Q2	Ⓐ Ⓑ Ⓒ Ⓓ Ⓔ	V5, Pg. 217	PT67-S4-Q6	Ⓐ Ⓑ Ⓒ Ⓓ Ⓔ
V4, Pg. 246	PT58-S4-Q10	Ⓐ Ⓑ Ⓒ Ⓓ Ⓔ	V5, Pg. 218	PT67-S4-Q10	Ⓐ Ⓑ Ⓒ Ⓓ Ⓔ
V4, Pg. 269	PT59-S2-Q21	Ⓐ Ⓑ Ⓒ Ⓓ Ⓔ	V5, Pg. 223	PT67-S4-Q24	Ⓐ Ⓑ Ⓒ Ⓓ Ⓔ
V4, Pg. 271	PT59-S2-Q25	Ⓐ Ⓑ Ⓒ Ⓓ Ⓔ	V5, Pg. 240	PT68-S2-Q4	Ⓐ Ⓑ Ⓒ Ⓓ Ⓔ
V4, Pg. 272	PT59-S3-Q2	Ⓐ Ⓑ Ⓒ Ⓓ Ⓔ	V5, Pg. 251	PT68-S3-Q9	Ⓐ Ⓑ Ⓒ Ⓓ Ⓔ

V5, Pg. 277	PT69-S1-Q17	Ⓐ Ⓑ Ⓒ Ⓓ Ⓔ	PT73, Pg. 34	PT73-S4-Q1	Ⓐ Ⓑ Ⓒ Ⓓ Ⓔ
V5, Pg. 278	PT69-S1-Q22	Ⓐ Ⓑ Ⓒ Ⓓ Ⓔ	PT73, Pg. 38	PT73-S4-Q17	Ⓐ Ⓑ Ⓒ Ⓓ Ⓔ
V5, Pg. 297	PT69-S4-Q7	Ⓐ Ⓑ Ⓒ Ⓓ Ⓔ	PT74, Pg. 11	PT74-S1-Q6	Ⓐ Ⓑ Ⓒ Ⓓ Ⓔ
V5, Pg. 300	PT69-S4-Q15	Ⓐ Ⓑ Ⓒ Ⓓ Ⓔ	PT74, Pg. 16	PT74-S1-Q23	Ⓐ Ⓑ Ⓒ Ⓓ Ⓔ
V5, Pg. 302	PT69-S4-Q19	Ⓐ Ⓑ Ⓒ Ⓓ Ⓔ	PT74, Pg. 40	PT74-S4-Q24	Ⓐ Ⓑ Ⓒ Ⓓ Ⓔ
V5, Pg. 316	PT70-S1-Q16	Ⓐ Ⓑ Ⓒ Ⓓ Ⓔ	PT75, Pg. 11	PT75-S1-Q5	Ⓐ Ⓑ Ⓒ Ⓓ Ⓔ
V5, Pg. 339	PT70-S4-Q12	Ⓐ Ⓑ Ⓒ Ⓓ Ⓔ	PT75, Pg. 13	PT75-S1-Q11	Ⓐ Ⓑ Ⓒ Ⓓ Ⓔ
V5, Pg. 341	PT70-S4-Q19	Ⓐ Ⓑ Ⓒ Ⓓ Ⓔ	PT75, Pg. 29	PT75-S3-Q13	Ⓐ Ⓑ Ⓒ Ⓓ Ⓔ
V5, Pg. 355	PT71-S1-Q13	Ⓐ Ⓑ Ⓒ Ⓓ Ⓔ	PT75, Pg. 32	PT75-S3-Q22	Ⓐ Ⓑ Ⓒ Ⓓ Ⓔ
V5, Pg. 374	PT71-S3-Q21	Ⓐ Ⓑ Ⓒ Ⓓ Ⓔ	PT76, Pg. 20	PT76-S2-Q9	Ⓐ Ⓑ Ⓒ Ⓓ Ⓔ
PT72, Pg. 18	PT72-S2-Q2	Ⓐ Ⓑ Ⓒ Ⓓ Ⓔ	PT76, Pg. 21	PT76-S2-Q12	Ⓐ Ⓑ Ⓒ Ⓓ Ⓔ
PT72, Pg. 20	PT72-S2-Q10	Ⓐ Ⓑ Ⓒ Ⓓ Ⓔ	PT76, Pg. 39	PT76-S4-Q21	Ⓐ Ⓑ Ⓒ Ⓓ Ⓔ
PT72, Pg. 26	PT72-S3-Q2	Ⓐ Ⓑ Ⓒ Ⓓ Ⓔ	PT76, Pg. 40	PT76-S4-Q23	Ⓐ Ⓑ Ⓒ Ⓓ Ⓔ
PT72, Pg. 29	PT72-S3-Q10	Ⓐ Ⓑ Ⓒ Ⓓ Ⓔ	PT77, Pg. 19	PT77-S2-Q4	Ⓐ Ⓑ Ⓒ Ⓓ Ⓔ
PT73, Pg. 20	PT73-S2-Q9	Ⓐ Ⓑ Ⓒ Ⓓ Ⓔ	PT77, Pg. 37	PT77-S4-Q11	Ⓐ Ⓑ Ⓒ Ⓓ Ⓔ
PT73, Pg. 23	PT73-S2-Q19	Ⓐ Ⓑ Ⓒ Ⓓ Ⓔ	PT77, Pg. 39	PT77-S4-Q19	Ⓐ Ⓑ Ⓒ Ⓓ Ⓔ

Evaluate

SP1, Pg. 302	PTC-S2-Q9	Ⓐ Ⓑ Ⓒ Ⓓ Ⓔ	V3, Pg. 346	PT38-S4-Q19	Ⓐ Ⓑ Ⓒ Ⓓ Ⓔ
	PT3-S4-Q23	Ⓐ Ⓑ Ⓒ Ⓓ Ⓔ		PT45-S4-Q11	Ⓐ Ⓑ Ⓒ Ⓓ Ⓔ
V1, Pg. 22	PT7-S1-Q22	Ⓐ Ⓑ Ⓒ Ⓓ Ⓔ		PT46-S3-Q3	Ⓐ Ⓑ Ⓒ Ⓓ Ⓔ
V1, Pg. 38	PT7-S4-Q8	Ⓐ Ⓑ Ⓒ Ⓓ Ⓔ		PT49-S4-Q2	Ⓐ Ⓑ Ⓒ Ⓓ Ⓔ
V1, Pg. 71	PT9-S4-Q8	Ⓐ Ⓑ Ⓒ Ⓓ Ⓔ		PT51-S1-Q2	Ⓐ Ⓑ Ⓒ Ⓓ Ⓔ
V1, Pg. 85	PT10-S1-Q6	Ⓐ Ⓑ Ⓒ Ⓓ Ⓔ	V4, Pg. 352	PT61-S4-Q2	Ⓐ Ⓑ Ⓒ Ⓓ Ⓔ
V1, Pg. 122	PT11-S2-Q2	Ⓐ Ⓑ Ⓒ Ⓓ Ⓔ	V5, Pg. 116	PT65-S1-Q3	Ⓐ Ⓑ Ⓒ Ⓓ Ⓔ
V1, Pg. 196	PT13-S2-Q22	Ⓐ Ⓑ Ⓒ Ⓓ Ⓔ	V5, Pg. 138	PT65-S4-Q7	Ⓐ Ⓑ Ⓒ Ⓓ Ⓔ
V1, Pg. 268	PT15-S2-Q22	Ⓐ Ⓑ Ⓒ Ⓓ Ⓔ	V5, Pg. 240	PT68-S2-Q2	Ⓐ Ⓑ Ⓒ Ⓓ Ⓔ
V1, Pg. 274	PT15-S3-Q16	Ⓐ Ⓑ Ⓒ Ⓓ Ⓔ	V5, Pg. 243	PT68-S2-Q14	Ⓐ Ⓑ Ⓒ Ⓓ Ⓔ
V2, Pg. 42	PT19-S4-Q22	Ⓐ Ⓑ Ⓒ Ⓓ Ⓔ	V5, Pg. 273	PT69-S1-Q5	Ⓐ Ⓑ Ⓒ Ⓓ Ⓔ
V2, Pg. 71	PT20-S4-Q7	Ⓐ Ⓑ Ⓒ Ⓓ Ⓔ	PT73, Pg. 35	PT73-S4-Q6	Ⓐ Ⓑ Ⓒ Ⓓ Ⓔ
V2, Pg. 98	PT21-S3-Q11	Ⓐ Ⓑ Ⓒ Ⓓ Ⓔ	PT74, Pg. 16	PT74-S1-Q21	Ⓐ Ⓑ Ⓒ Ⓓ Ⓔ
V2, Pg. 198	PT24-S2-Q16	Ⓐ Ⓑ Ⓒ Ⓓ Ⓔ	PT74, Pg. 36	PT74-S4-Q10	Ⓐ Ⓑ Ⓒ Ⓓ Ⓔ
V2, Pg. 309	PT27-S4-Q6	Ⓐ Ⓑ Ⓒ Ⓓ Ⓔ	PT77, Pg. 21	PT77-S2-Q10	Ⓐ Ⓑ Ⓒ Ⓓ Ⓔ
V3, Pg. 260	PT36-S1-Q24	Ⓐ Ⓑ Ⓒ Ⓓ Ⓔ			

Method (Argument)

J07, Pg. 12	J07-S2-Q20	Ⓐ Ⓑ Ⓒ Ⓓ Ⓔ	SP1, Pg. 71	PTA-S1-Q13	Ⓐ Ⓑ Ⓒ Ⓓ Ⓔ
SP1, Pg. 70	PTA-S1-Q7	Ⓐ Ⓑ Ⓒ Ⓓ Ⓔ	SP1, Pg. 73	PTA-S1-Q18	Ⓐ Ⓑ Ⓒ Ⓓ Ⓔ

SP1, Pg. 89	PTA-S4-Q4	Ⓐ Ⓑ Ⓒ Ⓓ Ⓔ	V1, Pg. 61	PT9-S2-Q11	Ⓐ Ⓑ Ⓒ Ⓓ Ⓔ
SP1, Pg. 189	PTB-S1-Q13	Ⓐ Ⓑ Ⓒ Ⓓ Ⓔ	V1, Pg. 62	PT9-S2-Q15	Ⓐ Ⓑ Ⓒ Ⓓ Ⓔ
SP1, Pg. 211	PTB-S4-Q20	Ⓐ Ⓑ Ⓒ Ⓓ Ⓔ	V1, Pg. 72	PT9-S4-Q9	Ⓐ Ⓑ Ⓒ Ⓓ Ⓔ
SP1, Pg. 302	PTC-S2-Q10	Ⓐ Ⓑ Ⓒ Ⓓ Ⓔ	V1, Pg. 84	PT10-S1-Q4	Ⓐ Ⓑ Ⓒ Ⓓ Ⓔ
SP1, Pg. 311	PTC-S3-Q13	Ⓐ Ⓑ Ⓒ Ⓓ Ⓔ	V1, Pg. 86	PT10-S1-Q12	Ⓐ Ⓑ Ⓒ Ⓓ Ⓔ
SP1, Pg. 315	PTC-S3-Q25	Ⓐ Ⓑ Ⓒ Ⓓ Ⓔ	V1, Pg. 111	PT10-S4-Q25	Ⓐ Ⓑ Ⓒ Ⓓ Ⓔ
SP2, Pg. 364	PTC2-S3-Q8	Ⓐ Ⓑ Ⓒ Ⓓ Ⓔ	V1, Pg. 122	PT11-S2-Q3	Ⓐ Ⓑ Ⓒ Ⓓ Ⓔ
	PT1-S4-Q5	Ⓐ Ⓑ Ⓒ Ⓓ Ⓔ	V1, Pg. 124	PT11-S2-Q8	Ⓐ Ⓑ Ⓒ Ⓓ Ⓔ
	PT1-S4-Q20	Ⓐ Ⓑ Ⓒ Ⓓ Ⓔ	V1, Pg. 125	PT11-S2-Q14	Ⓐ Ⓑ Ⓒ Ⓓ Ⓔ
	PT2-S2-Q8	Ⓐ Ⓑ Ⓒ Ⓓ Ⓔ	V1, Pg. 141	PT11-S4-Q10	Ⓐ Ⓑ Ⓒ Ⓓ Ⓔ
	PT2-S2-Q12	Ⓐ Ⓑ Ⓒ Ⓓ Ⓔ	V1, Pg. 141	PT11-S4-Q12	Ⓐ Ⓑ Ⓒ Ⓓ Ⓔ
	PT2-S4-Q3	Ⓐ Ⓑ Ⓒ Ⓓ Ⓔ	V1, Pg. 153	PT12-S1-Q6	Ⓐ Ⓑ Ⓒ Ⓓ Ⓔ
	PT2-S4-Q24	Ⓐ Ⓑ Ⓒ Ⓓ Ⓔ	V1, Pg. 176	PT12-S4-Q14	Ⓐ Ⓑ Ⓒ Ⓓ Ⓔ
	PT3-S2-Q6	Ⓐ Ⓑ Ⓒ Ⓓ Ⓔ	V1, Pg. 190	PT13-S2-Q2	Ⓐ Ⓑ Ⓒ Ⓓ Ⓔ
	PT3-S2-Q11	Ⓐ Ⓑ Ⓒ Ⓓ Ⓔ	V1, Pg. 194	PT13-S2-Q17	Ⓐ Ⓑ Ⓒ Ⓓ Ⓔ
	PT3-S2-Q19	Ⓐ Ⓑ Ⓒ Ⓓ Ⓔ	V1, Pg. 206	PT13-S4-Q1	Ⓐ Ⓑ Ⓒ Ⓓ Ⓔ
	PT4-S1-Q6	Ⓐ Ⓑ Ⓒ Ⓓ Ⓔ	V1, Pg. 207	PT13-S4-Q6	Ⓐ Ⓑ Ⓒ Ⓓ Ⓔ
	PT4-S1-Q18	Ⓐ Ⓑ Ⓒ Ⓓ Ⓔ	V1, Pg. 226	PT14-S2-Q8	Ⓐ Ⓑ Ⓒ Ⓓ Ⓔ
	PT4-S1-Q21	Ⓐ Ⓑ Ⓒ Ⓓ Ⓔ	V1, Pg. 244	PT14-S4-Q16	Ⓐ Ⓑ Ⓒ Ⓓ Ⓔ
	PT4-S4-Q16	Ⓐ Ⓑ Ⓒ Ⓓ Ⓔ	V1, Pg. 247	PT14-S4-Q24	Ⓐ Ⓑ Ⓒ Ⓓ Ⓔ
	PT4-S4-Q18	Ⓐ Ⓑ Ⓒ Ⓓ Ⓔ	V1, Pg. 269	PT15-S2-Q24	Ⓐ Ⓑ Ⓒ Ⓓ Ⓔ
	PT5-S1-Q6	Ⓐ Ⓑ Ⓒ Ⓓ Ⓔ	V1, Pg. 274	PT15-S3-Q15	Ⓐ Ⓑ Ⓒ Ⓓ Ⓔ
	PT5-S3-Q4	Ⓐ Ⓑ Ⓒ Ⓓ Ⓔ	V1, Pg. 274	PT15-S3-Q17	Ⓐ Ⓑ Ⓒ Ⓓ Ⓔ
	PT5-S3-Q19	Ⓐ Ⓑ Ⓒ Ⓓ Ⓔ	V1, Pg. 297	PT16-S2-Q17	Ⓐ Ⓑ Ⓒ Ⓓ Ⓔ
	PT6-S2-Q20	Ⓐ Ⓑ Ⓒ Ⓓ Ⓔ	V1, Pg. 299	PT16-S2-Q23	Ⓐ Ⓑ Ⓒ Ⓓ Ⓔ
	PT6-S3-Q21	Ⓐ Ⓑ Ⓒ Ⓓ Ⓔ	V1, Pg. 302	PT16-S3-Q7	Ⓐ Ⓑ Ⓒ Ⓓ Ⓔ
	PT6-S3-Q23	Ⓐ Ⓑ Ⓒ Ⓓ Ⓔ	V1, Pg. 305	PT16-S3-Q20	Ⓐ Ⓑ Ⓒ Ⓓ Ⓔ
	PT6-S3-Q26	Ⓐ Ⓑ Ⓒ Ⓓ Ⓔ	V1, Pg. 307	PT16-S3-Q25	Ⓐ Ⓑ Ⓒ Ⓓ Ⓔ
V1, Pg. 17	PT7-S1-Q6	Ⓐ Ⓑ Ⓒ Ⓓ Ⓔ		PT17-S2-Q4	Ⓐ Ⓑ Ⓒ Ⓓ Ⓔ
V1, Pg. 18	PT7-S1-Q7	Ⓐ Ⓑ Ⓒ Ⓓ Ⓔ		PT17-S2-Q18	Ⓐ Ⓑ Ⓒ Ⓓ Ⓔ
V1, Pg. 40	PT7-S4-Q16	Ⓐ Ⓑ Ⓒ Ⓓ Ⓔ		PT17-S2-Q25	Ⓐ Ⓑ Ⓒ Ⓓ Ⓔ
V1, Pg. 42	PT7-S4-Q20	Ⓐ Ⓑ Ⓒ Ⓓ Ⓔ		PT17-S3-Q4	Ⓐ Ⓑ Ⓒ Ⓓ Ⓔ
V1, Pg. 42	PT7-S4-Q21	Ⓐ Ⓑ Ⓒ Ⓓ Ⓔ		PT17-S3-Q10	Ⓐ Ⓑ Ⓒ Ⓓ Ⓔ
	PT8-S1-Q4	Ⓐ Ⓑ Ⓒ Ⓓ Ⓔ	V1, Pg. 326	PT18-S2-Q1	Ⓐ Ⓑ Ⓒ Ⓓ Ⓔ
	PT8-S1-Q15	Ⓐ Ⓑ Ⓒ Ⓓ Ⓔ	V1, Pg. 327	PT18-S2-Q5	Ⓐ Ⓑ Ⓒ Ⓓ Ⓔ
	PT8-S1-Q18	Ⓐ Ⓑ Ⓒ Ⓓ Ⓔ	V1, Pg. 328	PT18-S2-Q7	Ⓐ Ⓑ Ⓒ Ⓓ Ⓔ
	PT8-S4-Q17	Ⓐ Ⓑ Ⓒ Ⓓ Ⓔ	V1, Pg. 329	PT18-S2-Q12	Ⓐ Ⓑ Ⓒ Ⓓ Ⓔ

V1, Pg. 348	PT18-S4-Q21	Ⓐ Ⓑ Ⓒ Ⓓ Ⓔ	V2, Pg. 336	PT28-S3-Q10	Ⓐ Ⓑ Ⓒ Ⓓ Ⓔ
V2, Pg. 21	PT19-S2-Q6	Ⓐ Ⓑ Ⓒ Ⓓ Ⓔ	V3, Pg. 16	PT29-S1-Q2	Ⓐ Ⓑ Ⓒ Ⓓ Ⓔ
V2, Pg. 22	PT19-S2-Q8	Ⓐ Ⓑ Ⓒ Ⓓ Ⓔ	V3, Pg. 19	PT29-S1-Q12	Ⓐ Ⓑ Ⓒ Ⓓ Ⓔ
V2, Pg. 23	PT19-S2-Q11	Ⓐ Ⓑ Ⓒ Ⓓ Ⓔ	V3, Pg. 56	PT30-S2-Q7	Ⓐ Ⓑ Ⓒ Ⓓ Ⓔ
V2, Pg. 36	PT19-S4-Q2	Ⓐ Ⓑ Ⓒ Ⓓ Ⓔ	V3, Pg. 74	PT30-S4-Q16	Ⓐ Ⓑ Ⓒ Ⓓ Ⓔ
V2, Pg. 40	PT19-S4-Q18	Ⓐ Ⓑ Ⓒ Ⓓ Ⓔ	V3, Pg. 101	PT31-S3-Q20	Ⓐ Ⓑ Ⓒ Ⓓ Ⓔ
V2, Pg. 43	PT19-S4-Q25	Ⓐ Ⓑ Ⓒ Ⓓ Ⓔ	V3, Pg. 120	PT32-S1-Q8	Ⓐ Ⓑ Ⓒ Ⓓ Ⓔ
V2, Pg. 52	PT20-S1-Q8	Ⓐ Ⓑ Ⓒ Ⓓ Ⓔ	V3, Pg. 138	PT32-S4-Q1	Ⓐ Ⓑ Ⓒ Ⓓ Ⓔ
V2, Pg. 56	PT20-S1-Q21	Ⓐ Ⓑ Ⓒ Ⓓ Ⓔ	V3, Pg. 152	PT33-S1-Q2	Ⓐ Ⓑ Ⓒ Ⓓ Ⓔ
V2, Pg. 57	PT20-S1-Q25	Ⓐ Ⓑ Ⓒ Ⓓ Ⓔ	V3, Pg. 171	PT33-S3-Q12	Ⓐ Ⓑ Ⓒ Ⓓ Ⓔ
V2, Pg. 70	PT20-S4-Q4	Ⓐ Ⓑ Ⓒ Ⓓ Ⓔ	V3, Pg. 196	PT34-S2-Q8	Ⓐ Ⓑ Ⓒ Ⓓ Ⓔ
V2, Pg. 90	PT21-S2-Q9	Ⓐ Ⓑ Ⓒ Ⓓ Ⓔ	V3, Pg. 204	PT34-S3-Q8	Ⓐ Ⓑ Ⓒ Ⓓ Ⓔ
V2, Pg. 91	PT21-S2-Q12	Ⓐ Ⓑ Ⓒ Ⓓ Ⓔ	V3, Pg. 221	PT35-S1-Q5	Ⓐ Ⓑ Ⓒ Ⓓ Ⓔ
V2, Pg. 95	PT21-S2-Q24	Ⓐ Ⓑ Ⓒ Ⓓ Ⓔ	V3, Pg. 223	PT35-S1-Q11	Ⓐ Ⓑ Ⓒ Ⓓ Ⓔ
V2, Pg. 99	PT21-S3-Q14	Ⓐ Ⓑ Ⓒ Ⓓ Ⓔ	V3, Pg. 247	PT35-S4-Q25	Ⓐ Ⓑ Ⓒ Ⓓ Ⓔ
V2, Pg. 101	PT21-S3-Q20	Ⓐ Ⓑ Ⓒ Ⓓ Ⓔ	V3, Pg. 254	PT36-S1-Q1	Ⓐ Ⓑ Ⓒ Ⓓ Ⓔ
V2, Pg. 126	PT22-S2-Q3	Ⓐ Ⓑ Ⓒ Ⓓ Ⓔ	V3, Pg. 256	PT36-S1-Q7	Ⓐ Ⓑ Ⓒ Ⓓ Ⓔ
V2, Pg. 128	PT22-S2-Q11	Ⓐ Ⓑ Ⓒ Ⓓ Ⓔ	V3, Pg. 272	PT36-S3-Q8	Ⓐ Ⓑ Ⓒ Ⓓ Ⓔ
V2, Pg. 129	PT22-S2-Q13	Ⓐ Ⓑ Ⓒ Ⓓ Ⓔ	V3, Pg. 273	PT36-S3-Q10	Ⓐ Ⓑ Ⓒ Ⓓ Ⓔ
V2, Pg. 144	PT22-S4-Q23	Ⓐ Ⓑ Ⓒ Ⓓ Ⓔ	V3, Pg. 277	PT36-S3-Q24	Ⓐ Ⓑ Ⓒ Ⓓ Ⓔ
V2, Pg. 156	PT23-S2-Q1	Ⓐ Ⓑ Ⓒ Ⓓ Ⓔ	V3, Pg. 298	PT37-S2-Q10	Ⓐ Ⓑ Ⓒ Ⓓ Ⓔ
V2, Pg. 156	PT23-S2-Q3	Ⓐ Ⓑ Ⓒ Ⓓ Ⓔ	V3, Pg. 299	PT37-S2-Q13	Ⓐ Ⓑ Ⓒ Ⓓ Ⓔ
V2, Pg. 159	PT23-S2-Q15	Ⓐ Ⓑ Ⓒ Ⓓ Ⓔ	V3, Pg. 311	PT37-S4-Q10	Ⓐ Ⓑ Ⓒ Ⓓ Ⓔ
V2, Pg. 166	PT23-S3-Q8	Ⓐ Ⓑ Ⓒ Ⓓ Ⓔ	V3, Pg. 315	PT37-S4-Q24	Ⓐ Ⓑ Ⓒ Ⓓ Ⓔ
V2, Pg. 194	PT24-S2-Q3	Ⓐ Ⓑ Ⓒ Ⓓ Ⓔ		PT39-S2-Q4	Ⓐ Ⓑ Ⓒ Ⓓ Ⓔ
V2, Pg. 203	PT24-S3-Q3	Ⓐ Ⓑ Ⓒ Ⓓ Ⓔ		PT39-S4-Q3	Ⓐ Ⓑ Ⓒ Ⓓ Ⓔ
V2, Pg. 206	PT24-S3-Q17	Ⓐ Ⓑ Ⓒ Ⓓ Ⓔ		PT39-S4-Q8	Ⓐ Ⓑ Ⓒ Ⓓ Ⓔ
V2, Pg. 245	PT25-S4-Q19	Ⓐ Ⓑ Ⓒ Ⓓ Ⓔ		PT40-S1-Q2	Ⓐ Ⓑ Ⓒ Ⓓ Ⓔ
V2, Pg. 246	PT25-S4-Q21	Ⓐ Ⓑ Ⓒ Ⓓ Ⓔ		PT40-S1-Q4	Ⓐ Ⓑ Ⓒ Ⓓ Ⓔ
V2, Pg. 266	PT26-S3-Q2	Ⓐ Ⓑ Ⓒ Ⓓ Ⓔ		PT40-S3-Q13	Ⓐ Ⓑ Ⓒ Ⓓ Ⓔ
V2, Pg. 270	PT26-S3-Q16	Ⓐ Ⓑ Ⓒ Ⓓ Ⓔ		PT41-S1-Q3	Ⓐ Ⓑ Ⓒ Ⓓ Ⓔ
V2, Pg. 290	PT27-S1-Q6	Ⓐ Ⓑ Ⓒ Ⓓ Ⓔ		PT41-S3-Q9	Ⓐ Ⓑ Ⓒ Ⓓ Ⓔ
V2, Pg. 292	PT27-S1-Q15	Ⓐ Ⓑ Ⓒ Ⓓ Ⓔ		PT41-S3-Q12	Ⓐ Ⓑ Ⓒ Ⓓ Ⓔ
V2, Pg. 311	PT27-S4-Q12	Ⓐ Ⓑ Ⓒ Ⓓ Ⓔ		PT45-S1-Q4	Ⓐ Ⓑ Ⓒ Ⓓ Ⓔ
V2, Pg. 314	PT27-S4-Q21	Ⓐ Ⓑ Ⓒ Ⓓ Ⓔ		PT45-S1-Q7	Ⓐ Ⓑ Ⓒ Ⓓ Ⓔ
V2, Pg. 323	PT28-S1-Q7	Ⓐ Ⓑ Ⓒ Ⓓ Ⓔ		PT45-S4-Q12	Ⓐ Ⓑ Ⓒ Ⓓ Ⓔ
V2, Pg. 335	PT28-S3-Q7	Ⓐ Ⓑ Ⓒ Ⓓ Ⓔ		PT46-S2-Q17	Ⓐ Ⓑ Ⓒ Ⓓ Ⓔ

	PT46-S3-Q10	Ⓐ Ⓑ Ⓒ Ⓓ Ⓔ	V5, Pg. 60	PT63-S3-Q19	Ⓐ Ⓑ Ⓒ Ⓓ Ⓔ
	PT47-S1-Q10	Ⓐ Ⓑ Ⓒ Ⓓ Ⓔ	V5, Pg. 80	PT64-S1-Q3	Ⓐ Ⓑ Ⓒ Ⓓ Ⓔ
	PT47-S3-Q20	Ⓐ Ⓑ Ⓒ Ⓓ Ⓔ	V5, Pg. 140	PT65-S4-Q16	Ⓐ Ⓑ Ⓒ Ⓓ Ⓔ
	PT49-S4-Q15	Ⓐ Ⓑ Ⓒ Ⓓ Ⓔ	V5, Pg. 167	PT66-S2-Q25	Ⓐ Ⓑ Ⓒ Ⓓ Ⓔ
	PT50-S4-Q6	Ⓐ Ⓑ Ⓒ Ⓓ Ⓔ	V5, Pg. 203	PT67-S2-Q12	Ⓐ Ⓑ Ⓒ Ⓓ Ⓔ
V4, Pg. 21	PT52-S3-Q5	Ⓐ Ⓑ Ⓒ Ⓓ Ⓔ	V5, Pg. 219	PT67-S4-Q12	Ⓐ Ⓑ Ⓒ Ⓓ Ⓔ
V4, Pg. 63	PT53-S3-Q24	Ⓐ Ⓑ Ⓒ Ⓓ Ⓔ	V5, Pg. 247	PT68-S2-Q26	Ⓐ Ⓑ Ⓒ Ⓓ Ⓔ
V4, Pg. 90	PT54-S2-Q10	Ⓐ Ⓑ Ⓒ Ⓓ Ⓔ	V5, Pg. 254	PT68-S3-Q20	Ⓐ Ⓑ Ⓒ Ⓓ Ⓔ
V4, Pg. 100	PT54-S4-Q2	Ⓐ Ⓑ Ⓒ Ⓓ Ⓔ	V5, Pg. 279	PT69-S1-Q23	Ⓐ Ⓑ Ⓒ Ⓓ Ⓔ
V4, Pg. 116	PT55-S1-Q3	Ⓐ Ⓑ Ⓒ Ⓓ Ⓔ	V5, Pg. 297	PT69-S4-Q4	Ⓐ Ⓑ Ⓒ Ⓓ Ⓔ
V4, Pg. 158	PT56-S2-Q11	Ⓐ Ⓑ Ⓒ Ⓓ Ⓔ	V5, Pg. 338	PT70-S4-Q8	Ⓐ Ⓑ Ⓒ Ⓓ Ⓔ
V4, Pg. 165	PT56-S3-Q6	Ⓐ Ⓑ Ⓒ Ⓓ Ⓔ	V5, Pg. 343	PT70-S4-Q26	Ⓐ Ⓑ Ⓒ Ⓓ Ⓔ
V4, Pg. 201	PT57-S3-Q5	Ⓐ Ⓑ Ⓒ Ⓓ Ⓔ	V5, Pg. 352	PT71-S1-Q2	Ⓐ Ⓑ Ⓒ Ⓓ Ⓔ
V4, Pg. 225	PT58-S1-Q6	Ⓐ Ⓑ Ⓒ Ⓓ Ⓔ	V5, Pg. 354	PT71-S1-Q9	Ⓐ Ⓑ Ⓒ Ⓓ Ⓔ
V4, Pg. 231	PT58-S1-Q26	Ⓐ Ⓑ Ⓒ Ⓓ Ⓔ	PT73, Pg. 22	PT73-S2-Q14	Ⓐ Ⓑ Ⓒ Ⓓ Ⓔ
V4, Pg. 247	PT58-S4-Q12	Ⓐ Ⓑ Ⓒ Ⓓ Ⓔ	PT73, Pg. 22	PT73-S2-Q16	Ⓐ Ⓑ Ⓒ Ⓓ Ⓔ
V4, Pg. 276	PT59-S3-Q14	Ⓐ Ⓑ Ⓒ Ⓓ Ⓔ	PT73, Pg. 35	PT73-S4-Q4	Ⓐ Ⓑ Ⓒ Ⓓ Ⓔ
V4, Pg. 278	PT59-S3-Q23	Ⓐ Ⓑ Ⓒ Ⓓ Ⓔ	PT74, Pg. 37	PT74-S4-Q14	Ⓐ Ⓑ Ⓒ Ⓓ Ⓔ
V4, Pg. 296	PT60-S1-Q2	Ⓐ Ⓑ Ⓒ Ⓓ Ⓔ	PT74, Pg. 38	PT74-S4-Q17	Ⓐ Ⓑ Ⓒ Ⓓ Ⓔ
V4, Pg. 303	PT60-S1-Q25	Ⓐ Ⓑ Ⓒ Ⓓ Ⓔ	PT75, Pg. 11	PT75-S1-Q4	Ⓐ Ⓑ Ⓒ Ⓓ Ⓔ
V4, Pg. 341	PT61-S2-Q4	Ⓐ Ⓑ Ⓒ Ⓓ Ⓔ	PT75, Pg. 28	PT75-S3-Q11	Ⓐ Ⓑ Ⓒ Ⓓ Ⓔ
V5, Pg. 20	PT62-S2-Q14	Ⓐ Ⓑ Ⓒ Ⓓ Ⓔ	PT76, Pg. 20	PT76-S2-Q8	Ⓐ Ⓑ Ⓒ Ⓓ Ⓔ
V5, Pg. 33	PT62-S4-Q21	Ⓐ Ⓑ Ⓒ Ⓓ Ⓔ	PT77, Pg. 23	PT77-S2-Q17	Ⓐ Ⓑ Ⓒ Ⓓ Ⓔ
V5, Pg. 48	PT63-S1-Q17	Ⓐ Ⓑ Ⓒ Ⓓ Ⓔ			

Method (Statement)

J07, Pg. 9	J07-S2-Q11	Ⓐ Ⓑ Ⓒ Ⓓ Ⓔ	V1, Pg. 63	PT9-S2-Q20	Ⓐ Ⓑ Ⓒ Ⓓ Ⓔ
SP1, Pg. 90	PTA-S4-Q9	Ⓐ Ⓑ Ⓒ Ⓓ Ⓔ	V1, Pg. 75	PT9-S4-Q20	Ⓐ Ⓑ Ⓒ Ⓓ Ⓔ
SP1, Pg. 92	PTA-S4-Q15	Ⓐ Ⓑ Ⓒ Ⓓ Ⓔ	V1, Pg. 108	PT10-S4-Q13	Ⓐ Ⓑ Ⓒ Ⓓ Ⓔ
SP1, Pg. 94	PTA-S4-Q21	Ⓐ Ⓑ Ⓒ Ⓓ Ⓔ	V1, Pg. 145	PT11-S4-Q24	Ⓐ Ⓑ Ⓒ Ⓓ Ⓔ
SP1, Pg. 186	PTB-S1-Q2	Ⓐ Ⓑ Ⓒ Ⓓ Ⓔ	V1, Pg. 152	PT12-S1-Q3	Ⓐ Ⓑ Ⓒ Ⓓ Ⓔ
SP1, Pg. 188	PTB-S1-Q11	Ⓐ Ⓑ Ⓒ Ⓓ Ⓔ	V1, Pg. 226	PT14-S2-Q9	Ⓐ Ⓑ Ⓒ Ⓓ Ⓔ
SP1, Pg. 307	PTC-S2-Q22	Ⓐ Ⓑ Ⓒ Ⓓ Ⓔ	V1, Pg. 266	PT15-S2-Q14	Ⓐ Ⓑ Ⓒ Ⓓ Ⓔ
SP2, Pg. 356	PTC2-S2-Q8	Ⓐ Ⓑ Ⓒ Ⓓ Ⓔ	V1, Pg. 272	PT15-S3-Q11	Ⓐ Ⓑ Ⓒ Ⓓ Ⓔ
SP2, Pg. 364	PTC2-S3-Q10	Ⓐ Ⓑ Ⓒ Ⓓ Ⓔ	V1, Pg. 343	PT18-S4-Q5	Ⓐ Ⓑ Ⓒ Ⓓ Ⓔ
	PT3-S4-Q20	Ⓐ Ⓑ Ⓒ Ⓓ Ⓔ	V2, Pg. 40	PT19-S4-Q17	Ⓐ Ⓑ Ⓒ Ⓓ Ⓔ
V1, Pg. 21	PT7-S1-Q18	Ⓐ Ⓑ Ⓒ Ⓓ Ⓔ	V2, Pg. 72	PT20-S4-Q9	Ⓐ Ⓑ Ⓒ Ⓓ Ⓔ

V2, Pg. 158	PT23-S2-Q11	Ⓐ Ⓑ Ⓒ Ⓓ Ⓔ
V2, Pg. 196	PT24-S2-Q10	Ⓐ Ⓑ Ⓒ Ⓓ Ⓔ
V2, Pg. 267	PT26-S3-Q4	Ⓐ Ⓑ Ⓒ Ⓓ Ⓔ
V2, Pg. 292	PT27-S1-Q14	Ⓐ Ⓑ Ⓒ Ⓓ Ⓔ
V2, Pg. 293	PT27-S1-Q17	Ⓐ Ⓑ Ⓒ Ⓓ Ⓔ
V2, Pg. 315	PT27-S4-Q24	Ⓐ Ⓑ Ⓒ Ⓓ Ⓔ
V3, Pg. 36	PT29-S4-Q2	Ⓐ Ⓑ Ⓒ Ⓓ Ⓔ
V3, Pg. 40	PT29-S4-Q15	Ⓐ Ⓑ Ⓒ Ⓓ Ⓔ
V3, Pg. 70	PT30-S4-Q3	Ⓐ Ⓑ Ⓒ Ⓓ Ⓔ
V3, Pg. 73	PT30-S4-Q13	Ⓐ Ⓑ Ⓒ Ⓓ Ⓔ
V3, Pg. 91	PT31-S2-Q12	Ⓐ Ⓑ Ⓒ Ⓓ Ⓔ
V3, Pg. 100	PT31-S3-Q16	Ⓐ Ⓑ Ⓒ Ⓓ Ⓔ
V3, Pg. 122	PT32-S1-Q15	Ⓐ Ⓑ Ⓒ Ⓓ Ⓔ
V3, Pg. 145	PT32-S4-Q23	Ⓐ Ⓑ Ⓒ Ⓓ Ⓔ
V3, Pg. 171	PT33-S3-Q14	Ⓐ Ⓑ Ⓒ Ⓓ Ⓔ
V3, Pg. 200	PT34-S2-Q22	Ⓐ Ⓑ Ⓒ Ⓓ Ⓔ
V3, Pg. 205	PT34-S3-Q14	Ⓐ Ⓑ Ⓒ Ⓓ Ⓔ
V3, Pg. 209	PT34-S3-Q26	Ⓐ Ⓑ Ⓒ Ⓓ Ⓔ
V3, Pg. 220	PT35-S1-Q1	Ⓐ Ⓑ Ⓒ Ⓓ Ⓔ
V3, Pg. 222	PT35-S1-Q9	Ⓐ Ⓑ Ⓒ Ⓓ Ⓔ
V3, Pg. 240	PT35-S4-Q2	Ⓐ Ⓑ Ⓒ Ⓓ Ⓔ
V3, Pg. 244	PT35-S4-Q15	Ⓐ Ⓑ Ⓒ Ⓓ Ⓔ
V3, Pg. 271	PT36-S3-Q6	Ⓐ Ⓑ Ⓒ Ⓓ Ⓔ
V3, Pg. 327	PT38-S1-Q18	Ⓐ Ⓑ Ⓒ Ⓓ Ⓔ
V3, Pg. 346	PT38-S4-Q18	Ⓐ Ⓑ Ⓒ Ⓓ Ⓔ
	PT39-S2-Q16	Ⓐ Ⓑ Ⓒ Ⓓ Ⓔ
	PT39-S2-Q22	Ⓐ Ⓑ Ⓒ Ⓓ Ⓔ
	PT40-S1-Q25	Ⓐ Ⓑ Ⓒ Ⓓ Ⓔ
	PT40-S3-Q6	Ⓐ Ⓑ Ⓒ Ⓓ Ⓔ
	PT42-S2-Q2	Ⓐ Ⓑ Ⓒ Ⓓ Ⓔ
	PT42-S4-Q3	Ⓐ Ⓑ Ⓒ Ⓓ Ⓔ
	PT42-S4-Q16	Ⓐ Ⓑ Ⓒ Ⓓ Ⓔ
	PT42-S4-Q18	Ⓐ Ⓑ Ⓒ Ⓓ Ⓔ
	PT42-S4-Q21	Ⓐ Ⓑ Ⓒ Ⓓ Ⓔ
	PT43-S2-Q2	Ⓐ Ⓑ Ⓒ Ⓓ Ⓔ
	PT43-S2-Q23	Ⓐ Ⓑ Ⓒ Ⓓ Ⓔ
	PT44-S2-Q19	Ⓐ Ⓑ Ⓒ Ⓓ Ⓔ

	PT44-S2-Q24	Ⓐ Ⓑ Ⓒ Ⓓ Ⓔ
	PT44-S4-Q6	Ⓐ Ⓑ Ⓒ Ⓓ Ⓔ
	PT44-S4-Q24	Ⓐ Ⓑ Ⓒ Ⓓ Ⓔ
	PT45-S4-Q23	Ⓐ Ⓑ Ⓒ Ⓓ Ⓔ
	PT46-S3-Q16	Ⓐ Ⓑ Ⓒ Ⓓ Ⓔ
	PT46-S3-Q18	Ⓐ Ⓑ Ⓒ Ⓓ Ⓔ
	PT48-S4-Q5	Ⓐ Ⓑ Ⓒ Ⓓ Ⓔ
	PT49-S2-Q12	Ⓐ Ⓑ Ⓒ Ⓓ Ⓔ
	PT50-S2-Q15	Ⓐ Ⓑ Ⓒ Ⓓ Ⓔ
	PT50-S2-Q19	Ⓐ Ⓑ Ⓒ Ⓓ Ⓔ
	PT51-S1-Q14	Ⓐ Ⓑ Ⓒ Ⓓ Ⓔ
	PT51-S3-Q11	Ⓐ Ⓑ Ⓒ Ⓓ Ⓔ
	PT51-S3-Q23	Ⓐ Ⓑ Ⓒ Ⓓ Ⓔ
V4, Pg. 24	PT52-S3-Q17	Ⓐ Ⓑ Ⓒ Ⓓ Ⓔ
V4, Pg. 46	PT53-S1-Q11	Ⓐ Ⓑ Ⓒ Ⓓ Ⓔ
V4, Pg. 47	PT53-S1-Q14	Ⓐ Ⓑ Ⓒ Ⓓ Ⓔ
V4, Pg. 59	PT53-S3-Q10	Ⓐ Ⓑ Ⓒ Ⓓ Ⓔ
V4, Pg. 92	PT54-S2-Q17	Ⓐ Ⓑ Ⓒ Ⓓ Ⓔ
V4, Pg. 104	PT54-S4-Q15	Ⓐ Ⓑ Ⓒ Ⓓ Ⓔ
V4, Pg. 121	PT55-S1-Q19	Ⓐ Ⓑ Ⓒ Ⓓ Ⓔ
V4, Pg. 133	PT55-S3-Q7	Ⓐ Ⓑ Ⓒ Ⓓ Ⓔ
V4, Pg. 158	PT56-S2-Q9	Ⓐ Ⓑ Ⓒ Ⓓ Ⓔ
V4, Pg. 163	PT56-S2-Q25	Ⓐ Ⓑ Ⓒ Ⓓ Ⓔ
V4, Pg. 195	PT57-S2-Q13	Ⓐ Ⓑ Ⓒ Ⓓ Ⓔ
V4, Pg. 196	PT57-S2-Q16	Ⓐ Ⓑ Ⓒ Ⓓ Ⓔ
V4, Pg. 198	PT57-S2-Q21	Ⓐ Ⓑ Ⓒ Ⓓ Ⓔ
V4, Pg. 206	PT57-S3-Q21	Ⓐ Ⓑ Ⓒ Ⓓ Ⓔ
V4, Pg. 266	PT59-S2-Q7	Ⓐ Ⓑ Ⓒ Ⓓ Ⓔ
V4, Pg. 268	PT59-S2-Q18	Ⓐ Ⓑ Ⓒ Ⓓ Ⓔ
V4, Pg. 297	PT60-S1-Q4	Ⓐ Ⓑ Ⓒ Ⓓ Ⓔ
V4, Pg. 309	PT60-S3-Q5	Ⓐ Ⓑ Ⓒ Ⓓ Ⓔ
V4, Pg. 310	PT60-S3-Q7	Ⓐ Ⓑ Ⓒ Ⓓ Ⓔ
V4, Pg. 356	PT61-S4-Q17	Ⓐ Ⓑ Ⓒ Ⓓ Ⓔ
V4, Pg. 358	PT61-S4-Q22	Ⓐ Ⓑ Ⓒ Ⓓ Ⓔ
V5, Pg. 29	PT62-S4-Q4	Ⓐ Ⓑ Ⓒ Ⓓ Ⓔ
V5, Pg. 56	PT63-S3-Q1	Ⓐ Ⓑ Ⓒ Ⓓ Ⓔ
V5, Pg. 84	PT64-S1-Q14	Ⓐ Ⓑ Ⓒ Ⓓ Ⓔ

V5, Pg. 87	PT64-S1-Q25	Ⓐ Ⓑ Ⓒ Ⓓ Ⓔ	V5, Pg. 343	PT70-S4-Q24	Ⓐ Ⓑ Ⓒ Ⓓ Ⓔ
V5, Pg. 94	PT64-S3-Q10	Ⓐ Ⓑ Ⓒ Ⓓ Ⓔ	V5, Pg. 355	PT71-S1-Q11	Ⓐ Ⓑ Ⓒ Ⓓ Ⓔ
V5, Pg. 96	PT64-S3-Q16	Ⓐ Ⓑ Ⓒ Ⓓ Ⓔ	PT72, Pg. 21	PT72-S2-Q13	Ⓐ Ⓑ Ⓒ Ⓓ Ⓔ
V5, Pg. 118	PT65-S1-Q10	Ⓐ Ⓑ Ⓒ Ⓓ Ⓔ	PT72, Pg. 30	PT72-S3-Q15	Ⓐ Ⓑ Ⓒ Ⓓ Ⓔ
V5, Pg. 123	PT65-S1-Q22	Ⓐ Ⓑ Ⓒ Ⓓ Ⓔ	PT73, Pg. 36	PT73-S4-Q9	Ⓐ Ⓑ Ⓒ Ⓓ Ⓔ
V5, Pg. 139	PT65-S4-Q12	Ⓐ Ⓑ Ⓒ Ⓓ Ⓔ	PT74, Pg. 13	PT74-S1-Q14	Ⓐ Ⓑ Ⓒ Ⓓ Ⓔ
V5, Pg. 141	PT65-S4-Q21	Ⓐ Ⓑ Ⓒ Ⓓ Ⓔ	PT75, Pg. 13	PT75-S1-Q14	Ⓐ Ⓑ Ⓒ Ⓓ Ⓔ
V5, Pg. 206	PT67-S2-Q20	Ⓐ Ⓑ Ⓒ Ⓓ Ⓔ	PT75, Pg. 14	PT75-S1-Q16	Ⓐ Ⓑ Ⓒ Ⓓ Ⓔ
V5, Pg. 206	PT67-S2-Q22	Ⓐ Ⓑ Ⓒ Ⓓ Ⓔ	PT75, Pg. 31	PT75-S3-Q20	Ⓐ Ⓑ Ⓒ Ⓓ Ⓔ
V5, Pg. 222	PT67-S4-Q22	Ⓐ Ⓑ Ⓒ Ⓓ Ⓔ	PT76, Pg. 35	PT76-S4-Q7	Ⓐ Ⓑ Ⓒ Ⓓ Ⓔ
V5, Pg. 242	PT68-S2-Q11	Ⓐ Ⓑ Ⓒ Ⓓ Ⓔ	PT77, Pg. 24	PT77-S2-Q20	Ⓐ Ⓑ Ⓒ Ⓓ Ⓔ
V5, Pg. 246	PT68-S2-Q22	Ⓐ Ⓑ Ⓒ Ⓓ Ⓔ	PT77, Pg. 35	PT77-S4-Q7	Ⓐ Ⓑ Ⓒ Ⓓ Ⓔ
V5, Pg. 275	PT69-S1-Q11	Ⓐ Ⓑ Ⓒ Ⓓ Ⓔ	PT77, Pg. 37	PT77-S4-Q14	Ⓐ Ⓑ Ⓒ Ⓓ Ⓔ
V5, Pg. 299	PT69-S4-Q12	Ⓐ Ⓑ Ⓒ Ⓓ Ⓔ	PT77, Pg. 38	PT77-S4-Q16	Ⓐ Ⓑ Ⓒ Ⓓ Ⓔ
V5, Pg. 316	PT70-S1-Q17	Ⓐ Ⓑ Ⓒ Ⓓ Ⓔ	PT77, Pg. 40	PT77-S4-Q22	Ⓐ Ⓑ Ⓒ Ⓓ Ⓔ

Flaw

J07, Pg. 7	J07-S2-Q4	Ⓐ Ⓑ Ⓒ Ⓓ Ⓔ	SP1, Pg. 211	PTB-S4-Q19	Ⓐ Ⓑ Ⓒ Ⓓ Ⓔ
J07, Pg. 11	J07-S2-Q17	Ⓐ Ⓑ Ⓒ Ⓓ Ⓔ	SP1, Pg. 300	PTC-S2-Q2	Ⓐ Ⓑ Ⓒ Ⓓ Ⓔ
J07, Pg. 12	J07-S2-Q21	Ⓐ Ⓑ Ⓒ Ⓓ Ⓔ	SP1, Pg. 301	PTC-S2-Q6	Ⓐ Ⓑ Ⓒ Ⓓ Ⓔ
J07, Pg. 15	J07-S3-Q4	Ⓐ Ⓑ Ⓒ Ⓓ Ⓔ	SP1, Pg. 303	PTC-S2-Q12	Ⓐ Ⓑ Ⓒ Ⓓ Ⓔ
J07, Pg. 16	J07-S3-Q8	Ⓐ Ⓑ Ⓒ Ⓓ Ⓔ	SP1, Pg. 305	PTC-S2-Q18	Ⓐ Ⓑ Ⓒ Ⓓ Ⓔ
J07, Pg. 19	J07-S3-Q18	Ⓐ Ⓑ Ⓒ Ⓓ Ⓔ	SP1, Pg. 309	PTC-S3-Q5	Ⓐ Ⓑ Ⓒ Ⓓ Ⓔ
J07, Pg. 21	J07-S3-Q23	Ⓐ Ⓑ Ⓒ Ⓓ Ⓔ	SP1, Pg. 310	PTC-S3-Q9	Ⓐ Ⓑ Ⓒ Ⓓ Ⓔ
J07, Pg. 21	J07-S3-Q25	Ⓐ Ⓑ Ⓒ Ⓓ Ⓔ	SP1, Pg. 312	PTC-S3-Q15	Ⓐ Ⓑ Ⓒ Ⓓ Ⓔ
SP1, Pg. 68	PTA-S1-Q2	Ⓐ Ⓑ Ⓒ Ⓓ Ⓔ	SP1, Pg. 313	PTC-S3-Q19	Ⓐ Ⓑ Ⓒ Ⓓ Ⓔ
SP1, Pg. 69	PTA-S1-Q4	Ⓐ Ⓑ Ⓒ Ⓓ Ⓔ	SP2, Pg. 354	PTC2-S2-Q3	Ⓐ Ⓑ Ⓒ Ⓓ Ⓔ
SP1, Pg. 71	PTA-S1-Q10	Ⓐ Ⓑ Ⓒ Ⓓ Ⓔ	SP2, Pg. 356	PTC2-S2-Q9	Ⓐ Ⓑ Ⓒ Ⓓ Ⓔ
SP1, Pg. 74	PTA-S1-Q21	Ⓐ Ⓑ Ⓒ Ⓓ Ⓔ	SP2, Pg. 360	PTC2-S2-Q22	Ⓐ Ⓑ Ⓒ Ⓓ Ⓔ
SP1, Pg. 91	PTA-S4-Q11	Ⓐ Ⓑ Ⓒ Ⓓ Ⓔ	SP2, Pg. 361	PTC2-S2-Q25	Ⓐ Ⓑ Ⓒ Ⓓ Ⓔ
SP1, Pg. 94	PTA-S4-Q20	Ⓐ Ⓑ Ⓒ Ⓓ Ⓔ	SP2, Pg. 363	PTC2-S3-Q6	Ⓐ Ⓑ Ⓒ Ⓓ Ⓔ
SP1, Pg. 95	PTA-S4-Q25	Ⓐ Ⓑ Ⓒ Ⓓ Ⓔ	SP2, Pg. 364	PTC2-S3-Q9	Ⓐ Ⓑ Ⓒ Ⓓ Ⓔ
SP1, Pg. 187	PTB-S1-Q5	Ⓐ Ⓑ Ⓒ Ⓓ Ⓔ	SP2, Pg. 365	PTC2-S3-Q12	Ⓐ Ⓑ Ⓒ Ⓓ Ⓔ
SP1, Pg. 188	PTB-S1-Q10	Ⓐ Ⓑ Ⓒ Ⓓ Ⓔ	SP2, Pg. 365	PTC2-S3-Q14	Ⓐ Ⓑ Ⓒ Ⓓ Ⓔ
SP1, Pg. 193	PTB-S1-Q26	Ⓐ Ⓑ Ⓒ Ⓓ Ⓔ	SP2, Pg. 366	PTC2-S3-Q18	Ⓐ Ⓑ Ⓒ Ⓓ Ⓔ
SP1, Pg. 208	PTB-S4-Q8	Ⓐ Ⓑ Ⓒ Ⓓ Ⓔ	SP2, Pg. 369	PTC2-S3-Q24	Ⓐ Ⓑ Ⓒ Ⓓ Ⓔ
SP1, Pg. 209	PTB-S4-Q13	Ⓐ Ⓑ Ⓒ Ⓓ Ⓔ		PT1-S3-Q8	Ⓐ Ⓑ Ⓒ Ⓓ Ⓔ

PT1-S3-Q12	Ⓐ Ⓑ Ⓒ Ⓓ Ⓔ		PT6-S3-Q20	Ⓐ Ⓑ Ⓒ Ⓓ Ⓔ
PT1-S3-Q22	Ⓐ Ⓑ Ⓒ Ⓓ Ⓔ		PT6-S3-Q22	Ⓐ Ⓑ Ⓒ Ⓓ Ⓔ
PT1-S4-Q1	Ⓐ Ⓑ Ⓒ Ⓓ Ⓔ		PT6-S3-Q24	Ⓐ Ⓑ Ⓒ Ⓓ Ⓔ
PT1-S4-Q8	Ⓐ Ⓑ Ⓒ Ⓓ Ⓔ	V1, Pg. 18	PT7-S1-Q10	Ⓐ Ⓑ Ⓒ Ⓓ Ⓔ
PT1-S4-Q16	Ⓐ Ⓑ Ⓒ Ⓓ Ⓔ	V1, Pg. 20	PT7-S1-Q17	Ⓐ Ⓑ Ⓒ Ⓓ Ⓔ
PT2-S2-Q2	Ⓐ Ⓑ Ⓒ Ⓓ Ⓔ	V1, Pg. 37	PT7-S4-Q3	Ⓐ Ⓑ Ⓒ Ⓓ Ⓔ
PT2-S2-Q5	Ⓐ Ⓑ Ⓒ Ⓓ Ⓔ	V1, Pg. 38	PT7-S4-Q9	Ⓐ Ⓑ Ⓒ Ⓓ Ⓔ
PT2-S4-Q4	Ⓐ Ⓑ Ⓒ Ⓓ Ⓔ	V1, Pg. 39	PT7-S4-Q11	Ⓐ Ⓑ Ⓒ Ⓓ Ⓔ
PT2-S4-Q6	Ⓐ Ⓑ Ⓒ Ⓓ Ⓔ	V1, Pg. 42	PT7-S4-Q22	Ⓐ Ⓑ Ⓒ Ⓓ Ⓔ
PT2-S4-Q11	Ⓐ Ⓑ Ⓒ Ⓓ Ⓔ		PT8-S1-Q3	Ⓐ Ⓑ Ⓒ Ⓓ Ⓔ
PT3-S2-Q2	Ⓐ Ⓑ Ⓒ Ⓓ Ⓔ		PT8-S1-Q21	Ⓐ Ⓑ Ⓒ Ⓓ Ⓔ
PT3-S2-Q5	Ⓐ Ⓑ Ⓒ Ⓓ Ⓔ		PT8-S1-Q23	Ⓐ Ⓑ Ⓒ Ⓓ Ⓔ
PT3-S2-Q25	Ⓐ Ⓑ Ⓒ Ⓓ Ⓔ		PT8-S4-Q1	Ⓐ Ⓑ Ⓒ Ⓓ Ⓔ
PT3-S4-Q7	Ⓐ Ⓑ Ⓒ Ⓓ Ⓔ		PT8-S4-Q8	Ⓐ Ⓑ Ⓒ Ⓓ Ⓔ
PT3-S4-Q15	Ⓐ Ⓑ Ⓒ Ⓓ Ⓔ		PT8-S4-Q20	Ⓐ Ⓑ Ⓒ Ⓓ Ⓔ
PT3-S4-Q18	Ⓐ Ⓑ Ⓒ Ⓓ Ⓔ	V1, Pg. 58	PT9-S2-Q2	Ⓐ Ⓑ Ⓒ Ⓓ Ⓔ
PT4-S1-Q8	Ⓐ Ⓑ Ⓒ Ⓓ Ⓔ	V1, Pg. 59	PT9-S2-Q5	Ⓐ Ⓑ Ⓒ Ⓓ Ⓔ
PT4-S1-Q16	Ⓐ Ⓑ Ⓒ Ⓓ Ⓔ	V1, Pg. 62	PT9-S2-Q14	Ⓐ Ⓑ Ⓒ Ⓓ Ⓔ
PT4-S1-Q23	Ⓐ Ⓑ Ⓒ Ⓓ Ⓔ	V1, Pg. 64	PT9-S2-Q22	Ⓐ Ⓑ Ⓒ Ⓓ Ⓔ
PT4-S4-Q4	Ⓐ Ⓑ Ⓒ Ⓓ Ⓔ	V1, Pg. 70	PT9-S4-Q1	Ⓐ Ⓑ Ⓒ Ⓓ Ⓔ
PT4-S4-Q12	Ⓐ Ⓑ Ⓒ Ⓓ Ⓔ	V1, Pg. 71	PT9-S4-Q5	Ⓐ Ⓑ Ⓒ Ⓓ Ⓔ
PT4-S4-Q19	Ⓐ Ⓑ Ⓒ Ⓓ Ⓔ	V1, Pg. 73	PT9-S4-Q14	Ⓐ Ⓑ Ⓒ Ⓓ Ⓔ
PT5-S1-Q2	Ⓐ Ⓑ Ⓒ Ⓓ Ⓔ	V1, Pg. 85	PT10-S1-Q5	Ⓐ Ⓑ Ⓒ Ⓓ Ⓔ
PT5-S1-Q11	Ⓐ Ⓑ Ⓒ Ⓓ Ⓔ	V1, Pg. 85	PT10-S1-Q8	Ⓐ Ⓑ Ⓒ Ⓓ Ⓔ
PT5-S1-Q13	Ⓐ Ⓑ Ⓒ Ⓓ Ⓔ	V1, Pg. 86	PT10-S1-Q10	Ⓐ Ⓑ Ⓒ Ⓓ Ⓔ
PT5-S1-Q24	Ⓐ Ⓑ Ⓒ Ⓓ Ⓔ	V1, Pg. 87	PT10-S1-Q13	Ⓐ Ⓑ Ⓒ Ⓓ Ⓔ
PT5-S3-Q1	Ⓐ Ⓑ Ⓒ Ⓓ Ⓔ	V1, Pg. 88	PT10-S1-Q17	Ⓐ Ⓑ Ⓒ Ⓓ Ⓔ
PT5-S3-Q9	Ⓐ Ⓑ Ⓒ Ⓓ Ⓔ	V1, Pg. 89	PT10-S1-Q21	Ⓐ Ⓑ Ⓒ Ⓓ Ⓔ
PT5-S3-Q11	Ⓐ Ⓑ Ⓒ Ⓓ Ⓔ	V1, Pg. 108	PT10-S4-Q14	Ⓐ Ⓑ Ⓒ Ⓓ Ⓔ
PT5-S3-Q16	Ⓐ Ⓑ Ⓒ Ⓓ Ⓔ	V1, Pg. 110	PT10-S4-Q19	Ⓐ Ⓑ Ⓒ Ⓓ Ⓔ
PT6-S2-Q4	Ⓐ Ⓑ Ⓒ Ⓓ Ⓔ	V1, Pg. 110	PT10-S4-Q21	Ⓐ Ⓑ Ⓒ Ⓓ Ⓔ
PT6-S2-Q14	Ⓐ Ⓑ Ⓒ Ⓓ Ⓔ	V1, Pg. 124	PT11-S2-Q9	Ⓐ Ⓑ Ⓒ Ⓓ Ⓔ
PT6-S2-Q17	Ⓐ Ⓑ Ⓒ Ⓓ Ⓔ	V1, Pg. 125	PT11-S2-Q15	Ⓐ Ⓑ Ⓒ Ⓓ Ⓔ
PT6-S2-Q22	Ⓐ Ⓑ Ⓒ Ⓓ Ⓔ	V1, Pg. 129	PT11-S2-Q26	Ⓐ Ⓑ Ⓒ Ⓓ Ⓔ
PT6-S3-Q8	Ⓐ Ⓑ Ⓒ Ⓓ Ⓔ	V1, Pg. 138	PT11-S4-Q3	Ⓐ Ⓑ Ⓒ Ⓓ Ⓔ
PT6-S3-Q16	Ⓐ Ⓑ Ⓒ Ⓓ Ⓔ	V1, Pg. 140	PT11-S4-Q9	Ⓐ Ⓑ Ⓒ Ⓓ Ⓔ
PT6-S3-Q18	Ⓐ Ⓑ Ⓒ Ⓓ Ⓔ	V1, Pg. 143	PT11-S4-Q17	Ⓐ Ⓑ Ⓒ Ⓓ Ⓔ

V1, Pg. 143	PT11-S4-Q19	Ⓐ Ⓑ Ⓒ Ⓓ Ⓔ	V1, Pg. 299	PT16-S2-Q24	Ⓐ Ⓑ Ⓒ Ⓓ Ⓔ
V1, Pg. 145	PT11-S4-Q23	Ⓐ Ⓑ Ⓒ Ⓓ Ⓔ	V1, Pg. 300	PT16-S3-Q2	Ⓐ Ⓑ Ⓒ Ⓓ Ⓔ
V1, Pg. 155	PT12-S1-Q14	Ⓐ Ⓑ Ⓒ Ⓓ Ⓔ	V1, Pg. 302	PT16-S3-Q9	Ⓐ Ⓑ Ⓒ Ⓓ Ⓔ
V1, Pg. 157	PT12-S1-Q18	Ⓐ Ⓑ Ⓒ Ⓓ Ⓔ	V1, Pg. 302	PT16-S3-Q11	Ⓐ Ⓑ Ⓒ Ⓓ Ⓔ
V1, Pg. 157	PT12-S1-Q20	Ⓐ Ⓑ Ⓒ Ⓓ Ⓔ	V1, Pg. 307	PT16-S3-Q24	Ⓐ Ⓑ Ⓒ Ⓓ Ⓔ
V1, Pg. 159	PT12-S1-Q24	Ⓐ Ⓑ Ⓒ Ⓓ Ⓔ	V1, Pg. 307	PT16-S3-Q26	Ⓐ Ⓑ Ⓒ Ⓓ Ⓔ
V1, Pg. 159	PT12-S1-Q26	Ⓐ Ⓑ Ⓒ Ⓓ Ⓔ		PT17-S2-Q2	Ⓐ Ⓑ Ⓒ Ⓓ Ⓔ
V1, Pg. 173	PT12-S4-Q5	Ⓐ Ⓑ Ⓒ Ⓓ Ⓔ		PT17-S2-Q5	Ⓐ Ⓑ Ⓒ Ⓓ Ⓔ
V1, Pg. 174	PT12-S4-Q7	Ⓐ Ⓑ Ⓒ Ⓓ Ⓔ		PT17-S2-Q11	Ⓐ Ⓑ Ⓒ Ⓓ Ⓔ
V1, Pg. 176	PT12-S4-Q15	Ⓐ Ⓑ Ⓒ Ⓓ Ⓔ		PT17-S2-Q17	Ⓐ Ⓑ Ⓒ Ⓓ Ⓔ
V1, Pg. 177	PT12-S4-Q17	Ⓐ Ⓑ Ⓒ Ⓓ Ⓔ		PT17-S2-Q22	Ⓐ Ⓑ Ⓒ Ⓓ Ⓔ
V1, Pg. 178	PT12-S4-Q19	Ⓐ Ⓑ Ⓒ Ⓓ Ⓔ		PT17-S3-Q7	Ⓐ Ⓑ Ⓒ Ⓓ Ⓔ
V1, Pg. 179	PT12-S4-Q24	Ⓐ Ⓑ Ⓒ Ⓓ Ⓔ		PT17-S3-Q9	Ⓐ Ⓑ Ⓒ Ⓓ Ⓔ
V1, Pg. 191	PT13-S2-Q7	Ⓐ Ⓑ Ⓒ Ⓓ Ⓔ		PT17-S3-Q16	Ⓐ Ⓑ Ⓒ Ⓓ Ⓔ
V1, Pg. 195	PT13-S2-Q20	Ⓐ Ⓑ Ⓒ Ⓓ Ⓔ		PT17-S3-Q20	Ⓐ Ⓑ Ⓒ Ⓓ Ⓔ
V1, Pg. 197	PT13-S2-Q24	Ⓐ Ⓑ Ⓒ Ⓓ Ⓔ		PT17-S3-Q22	Ⓐ Ⓑ Ⓒ Ⓓ Ⓔ
V1, Pg. 197	PT13-S2-Q26	Ⓐ Ⓑ Ⓒ Ⓓ Ⓔ	V1, Pg. 327	PT18-S2-Q4	Ⓐ Ⓑ Ⓒ Ⓓ Ⓔ
V1, Pg. 208	PT13-S4-Q9	Ⓐ Ⓑ Ⓒ Ⓓ Ⓔ	V1, Pg. 328	PT18-S2-Q8	Ⓐ Ⓑ Ⓒ Ⓓ Ⓔ
V1, Pg. 212	PT13-S4-Q20	Ⓐ Ⓑ Ⓒ Ⓓ Ⓔ	V1, Pg. 330	PT18-S2-Q14	Ⓐ Ⓑ Ⓒ Ⓓ Ⓔ
V1, Pg. 225	PT14-S2-Q4	Ⓐ Ⓑ Ⓒ Ⓓ Ⓔ	V1, Pg. 344	PT18-S4-Q9	Ⓐ Ⓑ Ⓒ Ⓓ Ⓔ
V1, Pg. 227	PT14-S2-Q10	Ⓐ Ⓑ Ⓒ Ⓓ Ⓔ	V1, Pg. 345	PT18-S4-Q11	Ⓐ Ⓑ Ⓒ Ⓓ Ⓔ
V1, Pg. 230	PT14-S2-Q22	Ⓐ Ⓑ Ⓒ Ⓓ Ⓔ	V1, Pg. 346	PT18-S4-Q17	Ⓐ Ⓑ Ⓒ Ⓓ Ⓔ
V1, Pg. 243	PT14-S4-Q9	Ⓐ Ⓑ Ⓒ Ⓓ Ⓔ	V1, Pg. 349	PT18-S4-Q25	Ⓐ Ⓑ Ⓒ Ⓓ Ⓔ
V1, Pg. 243	PT14-S4-Q10	Ⓐ Ⓑ Ⓒ Ⓓ Ⓔ	V2, Pg. 20	PT19-S2-Q1	Ⓐ Ⓑ Ⓒ Ⓓ Ⓔ
V1, Pg. 244	PT14-S4-Q15	Ⓐ Ⓑ Ⓒ Ⓓ Ⓔ	V2, Pg. 21	PT19-S2-Q7	Ⓐ Ⓑ Ⓒ Ⓓ Ⓔ
V1, Pg. 245	PT14-S4-Q18	Ⓐ Ⓑ Ⓒ Ⓓ Ⓔ	V2, Pg. 24	PT19-S2-Q14	Ⓐ Ⓑ Ⓒ Ⓓ Ⓔ
V1, Pg. 246	PT14-S4-Q20	Ⓐ Ⓑ Ⓒ Ⓓ Ⓔ	V2, Pg. 27	PT19-S2-Q23	Ⓐ Ⓑ Ⓒ Ⓓ Ⓔ
V1, Pg. 262	PT15-S2-Q2	Ⓐ Ⓑ Ⓒ Ⓓ Ⓔ	V2, Pg. 36	PT19-S4-Q1	Ⓐ Ⓑ Ⓒ Ⓓ Ⓔ
V1, Pg. 267	PT15-S2-Q17	Ⓐ Ⓑ Ⓒ Ⓓ Ⓔ	V2, Pg. 36	PT19-S4-Q3	Ⓐ Ⓑ Ⓒ Ⓓ Ⓔ
V1, Pg. 267	PT15-S2-Q19	Ⓐ Ⓑ Ⓒ Ⓓ Ⓔ	V2, Pg. 37	PT19-S4-Q5	Ⓐ Ⓑ Ⓒ Ⓓ Ⓔ
V1, Pg. 268	PT15-S2-Q20	Ⓐ Ⓑ Ⓒ Ⓓ Ⓔ	V2, Pg. 37	PT19-S4-Q6	Ⓐ Ⓑ Ⓒ Ⓓ Ⓔ
V1, Pg. 270	PT15-S3-Q2	Ⓐ Ⓑ Ⓒ Ⓓ Ⓔ	V2, Pg. 52	PT20-S1-Q10	Ⓐ Ⓑ Ⓒ Ⓓ Ⓔ
V1, Pg. 272	PT15-S3-Q9	Ⓐ Ⓑ Ⓒ Ⓓ Ⓔ	V2, Pg. 53	PT20-S1-Q14	Ⓐ Ⓑ Ⓒ Ⓓ Ⓔ
V1, Pg. 273	PT15-S3-Q14	Ⓐ Ⓑ Ⓒ Ⓓ Ⓔ	V2, Pg. 54	PT20-S1-Q15	Ⓐ Ⓑ Ⓒ Ⓓ Ⓔ
V1, Pg. 275	PT15-S3-Q19	Ⓐ Ⓑ Ⓒ Ⓓ Ⓔ	V2, Pg. 56	PT20-S1-Q22	Ⓐ Ⓑ Ⓒ Ⓓ Ⓔ
V1, Pg. 294	PT16-S2-Q10	Ⓐ Ⓑ Ⓒ Ⓓ Ⓔ	V2, Pg. 70	PT20-S4-Q2	Ⓐ Ⓑ Ⓒ Ⓓ Ⓔ
V1, Pg. 298	PT16-S2-Q22	Ⓐ Ⓑ Ⓒ Ⓓ Ⓔ	V2, Pg. 73	PT20-S4-Q14	Ⓐ Ⓑ Ⓒ Ⓓ Ⓔ

V2, Pg. 75	PT20-S4-Q18	Ⓐ Ⓑ Ⓒ Ⓓ Ⓔ	V2, Pg. 242	PT25-S4-Q8	Ⓐ Ⓑ Ⓒ Ⓓ Ⓔ
V2, Pg. 76	PT20-S4-Q22	Ⓐ Ⓑ Ⓒ Ⓓ Ⓔ	V2, Pg. 245	PT25-S4-Q17	Ⓐ Ⓑ Ⓒ Ⓓ Ⓔ
V2, Pg. 89	PT21-S2-Q5	Ⓐ Ⓑ Ⓒ Ⓓ Ⓔ	V2, Pg. 246	PT25-S4-Q23	Ⓐ Ⓑ Ⓒ Ⓓ Ⓔ
V2, Pg. 95	PT21-S2-Q22	Ⓐ Ⓑ Ⓒ Ⓓ Ⓔ	V2, Pg. 258	PT26-S2-Q1	Ⓐ Ⓑ Ⓒ Ⓓ Ⓔ
V2, Pg. 95	PT21-S2-Q25	Ⓐ Ⓑ Ⓒ Ⓓ Ⓔ	V2, Pg. 258	PT26-S2-Q4	Ⓐ Ⓑ Ⓒ Ⓓ Ⓔ
V2, Pg. 97	PT21-S3-Q5	Ⓐ Ⓑ Ⓒ Ⓓ Ⓔ	V2, Pg. 262	PT26-S2-Q15	Ⓐ Ⓑ Ⓒ Ⓓ Ⓔ
V2, Pg. 101	PT21-S3-Q19	Ⓐ Ⓑ Ⓒ Ⓓ Ⓔ	V2, Pg. 262	PT26-S2-Q17	Ⓐ Ⓑ Ⓒ Ⓓ Ⓔ
V2, Pg. 127	PT22-S2-Q6	Ⓐ Ⓑ Ⓒ Ⓓ Ⓔ	V2, Pg. 264	PT26-S2-Q21	Ⓐ Ⓑ Ⓒ Ⓓ Ⓔ
V2, Pg. 127	PT22-S2-Q7	Ⓐ Ⓑ Ⓒ Ⓓ Ⓔ	V2, Pg. 267	PT26-S3-Q5	Ⓐ Ⓑ Ⓒ Ⓓ Ⓔ
V2, Pg. 128	PT22-S2-Q10	Ⓐ Ⓑ Ⓒ Ⓓ Ⓔ	V2, Pg. 268	PT26-S3-Q8	Ⓐ Ⓑ Ⓒ Ⓓ Ⓔ
V2, Pg. 129	PT22-S2-Q12	Ⓐ Ⓑ Ⓒ Ⓓ Ⓔ	V2, Pg. 268	PT26-S3-Q10	Ⓐ Ⓑ Ⓒ Ⓓ Ⓔ
V2, Pg. 131	PT22-S2-Q20	Ⓐ Ⓑ Ⓒ Ⓓ Ⓔ	V2, Pg. 271	PT26-S3-Q17	Ⓐ Ⓑ Ⓒ Ⓓ Ⓔ
V2, Pg. 133	PT22-S2-Q24	Ⓐ Ⓑ Ⓒ Ⓓ Ⓔ	V2, Pg. 271	PT26-S3-Q19	Ⓐ Ⓑ Ⓒ Ⓓ Ⓔ
V2, Pg. 133	PT22-S2-Q25	Ⓐ Ⓑ Ⓒ Ⓓ Ⓔ	V2, Pg. 288	PT27-S1-Q2	Ⓐ Ⓑ Ⓒ Ⓓ Ⓔ
V2, Pg. 138	PT22-S4-Q1	Ⓐ Ⓑ Ⓒ Ⓓ Ⓔ	V2, Pg. 294	PT27-S1-Q23	Ⓐ Ⓑ Ⓒ Ⓓ Ⓔ
V2, Pg. 140	PT22-S4-Q9	Ⓐ Ⓑ Ⓒ Ⓓ Ⓔ	V2, Pg. 295	PT27-S1-Q25	Ⓐ Ⓑ Ⓒ Ⓓ Ⓔ
V2, Pg. 142	PT22-S4-Q18	Ⓐ Ⓑ Ⓒ Ⓓ Ⓔ	V2, Pg. 310	PT27-S4-Q7	Ⓐ Ⓑ Ⓒ Ⓓ Ⓔ
V2, Pg. 144	PT22-S4-Q21	Ⓐ Ⓑ Ⓒ Ⓓ Ⓔ	V2, Pg. 310	PT27-S4-Q10	Ⓐ Ⓑ Ⓒ Ⓓ Ⓔ
V2, Pg. 157	PT23-S2-Q4	Ⓐ Ⓑ Ⓒ Ⓓ Ⓔ	V2, Pg. 315	PT27-S4-Q25	Ⓐ Ⓑ Ⓒ Ⓓ Ⓔ
V2, Pg. 160	PT23-S2-Q19	Ⓐ Ⓑ Ⓒ Ⓓ Ⓔ	V2, Pg. 324	PT28-S1-Q9	Ⓐ Ⓑ Ⓒ Ⓓ Ⓔ
V2, Pg. 161	PT23-S2-Q21	Ⓐ Ⓑ Ⓒ Ⓓ Ⓔ	V2, Pg. 327	PT28-S1-Q19	Ⓐ Ⓑ Ⓒ Ⓓ Ⓔ
V2, Pg. 165	PT23-S3-Q7	Ⓐ Ⓑ Ⓒ Ⓓ Ⓔ	V2, Pg. 329	PT28-S1-Q25	Ⓐ Ⓑ Ⓒ Ⓓ Ⓔ
V2, Pg. 168	PT23-S3-Q16	Ⓐ Ⓑ Ⓒ Ⓓ Ⓔ	V2, Pg. 334	PT28-S3-Q2	Ⓐ Ⓑ Ⓒ Ⓓ Ⓔ
V2, Pg. 168	PT23-S3-Q17	Ⓐ Ⓑ Ⓒ Ⓓ Ⓔ	V2, Pg. 335	PT28-S3-Q5	Ⓐ Ⓑ Ⓒ Ⓓ Ⓔ
V2, Pg. 169	PT23-S3-Q22	Ⓐ Ⓑ Ⓒ Ⓓ Ⓔ	V2, Pg. 339	PT28-S3-Q20	Ⓐ Ⓑ Ⓒ Ⓓ Ⓔ
V2, Pg. 194	PT24-S2-Q1	Ⓐ Ⓑ Ⓒ Ⓓ Ⓔ	V3, Pg. 17	PT29-S1-Q7	Ⓐ Ⓑ Ⓒ Ⓓ Ⓔ
V2, Pg. 195	PT24-S2-Q6	Ⓐ Ⓑ Ⓒ Ⓓ Ⓔ	V3, Pg. 20	PT29-S1-Q14	Ⓐ Ⓑ Ⓒ Ⓓ Ⓔ
V2, Pg. 196	PT24-S2-Q8	Ⓐ Ⓑ Ⓒ Ⓓ Ⓔ	V3, Pg. 20	PT29-S1-Q17	Ⓐ Ⓑ Ⓒ Ⓓ Ⓔ
V2, Pg. 201	PT24-S2-Q23	Ⓐ Ⓑ Ⓒ Ⓓ Ⓔ	V3, Pg. 39	PT29-S4-Q14	Ⓐ Ⓑ Ⓒ Ⓓ Ⓔ
V2, Pg. 202	PT24-S3-Q2	Ⓐ Ⓑ Ⓒ Ⓓ Ⓔ	V3, Pg. 41	PT29-S4-Q18	Ⓐ Ⓑ Ⓒ Ⓓ Ⓔ
V2, Pg. 203	PT24-S3-Q4	Ⓐ Ⓑ Ⓒ Ⓓ Ⓔ	V3, Pg. 43	PT29-S4-Q25	Ⓐ Ⓑ Ⓒ Ⓓ Ⓔ
V2, Pg. 205	PT24-S3-Q12	Ⓐ Ⓑ Ⓒ Ⓓ Ⓔ	V3, Pg. 54	PT30-S2-Q2	Ⓐ Ⓑ Ⓒ Ⓓ Ⓔ
V2, Pg. 209	PT24-S3-Q25	Ⓐ Ⓑ Ⓒ Ⓓ Ⓔ	V3, Pg. 57	PT30-S2-Q13	Ⓐ Ⓑ Ⓒ Ⓓ Ⓔ
V2, Pg. 231	PT25-S2-Q9	Ⓐ Ⓑ Ⓒ Ⓓ Ⓔ	V3, Pg. 59	PT30-S2-Q17	Ⓐ Ⓑ Ⓒ Ⓓ Ⓔ
V2, Pg. 234	PT25-S2-Q18	Ⓐ Ⓑ Ⓒ Ⓓ Ⓔ	V3, Pg. 61	PT30-S2-Q25	Ⓐ Ⓑ Ⓒ Ⓓ Ⓔ
V2, Pg. 234	PT25-S2-Q20	Ⓐ Ⓑ Ⓒ Ⓓ Ⓔ	V3, Pg. 61	PT30-S2-Q26	Ⓐ Ⓑ Ⓒ Ⓓ Ⓔ
V2, Pg. 241	PT25-S4-Q4	Ⓐ Ⓑ Ⓒ Ⓓ Ⓔ	V3, Pg. 71	PT30-S4-Q6	Ⓐ Ⓑ Ⓒ Ⓓ Ⓔ

V3, Pg. 72	PT30-S4-Q8	Ⓐ Ⓑ Ⓒ Ⓓ Ⓔ	V3, Pg. 243	PT35-S4-Q13	Ⓐ Ⓑ Ⓒ Ⓓ Ⓔ
V3, Pg. 73	PT30-S4-Q14	Ⓐ Ⓑ Ⓒ Ⓓ Ⓔ	V3, Pg. 245	PT35-S4-Q18	Ⓐ Ⓑ Ⓒ Ⓓ Ⓔ
V3, Pg. 88	PT31-S2-Q3	Ⓐ Ⓑ Ⓒ Ⓓ Ⓔ	V3, Pg. 246	PT35-S4-Q24	Ⓐ Ⓑ Ⓒ Ⓓ Ⓔ
V3, Pg. 90	PT31-S2-Q9	Ⓐ Ⓑ Ⓒ Ⓓ Ⓔ	V3, Pg. 257	PT36-S1-Q10	Ⓐ Ⓑ Ⓒ Ⓓ Ⓔ
V3, Pg. 93	PT31-S2-Q18	Ⓐ Ⓑ Ⓒ Ⓓ Ⓔ	V3, Pg. 257	PT36-S1-Q12	Ⓐ Ⓑ Ⓒ Ⓓ Ⓔ
V3, Pg. 96	PT31-S3-Q1	Ⓐ Ⓑ Ⓒ Ⓓ Ⓔ	V3, Pg. 259	PT36-S1-Q19	Ⓐ Ⓑ Ⓒ Ⓓ Ⓔ
V3, Pg. 97	PT31-S3-Q5	Ⓐ Ⓑ Ⓒ Ⓓ Ⓔ	V3, Pg. 273	PT36-S3-Q13	Ⓐ Ⓑ Ⓒ Ⓓ Ⓔ
V3, Pg. 98	PT31-S3-Q8	Ⓐ Ⓑ Ⓒ Ⓓ Ⓔ	V3, Pg. 276	PT36-S3-Q21	Ⓐ Ⓑ Ⓒ Ⓓ Ⓔ
V3, Pg. 99	PT31-S3-Q15	Ⓐ Ⓑ Ⓒ Ⓓ Ⓔ	V3, Pg. 277	PT36-S3-Q25	Ⓐ Ⓑ Ⓒ Ⓓ Ⓔ
V3, Pg. 103	PT31-S3-Q25	Ⓐ Ⓑ Ⓒ Ⓓ Ⓔ	V3, Pg. 296	PT37-S2-Q3	Ⓐ Ⓑ Ⓒ Ⓓ Ⓔ
V3, Pg. 119	PT32-S1-Q4	Ⓐ Ⓑ Ⓒ Ⓓ Ⓔ	V3, Pg. 300	PT37-S2-Q16	Ⓐ Ⓑ Ⓒ Ⓓ Ⓔ
V3, Pg. 120	PT32-S1-Q6	Ⓐ Ⓑ Ⓒ Ⓓ Ⓔ	V3, Pg. 303	PT37-S2-Q25	Ⓐ Ⓑ Ⓒ Ⓓ Ⓔ
V3, Pg. 121	PT32-S1-Q10	Ⓐ Ⓑ Ⓒ Ⓓ Ⓔ	V3, Pg. 311	PT37-S4-Q12	Ⓐ Ⓑ Ⓒ Ⓓ Ⓔ
V3, Pg. 122	PT32-S1-Q14	Ⓐ Ⓑ Ⓒ Ⓓ Ⓔ	V3, Pg. 312	PT37-S4-Q16	Ⓐ Ⓑ Ⓒ Ⓓ Ⓔ
V3, Pg. 124	PT32-S1-Q19	Ⓐ Ⓑ Ⓒ Ⓓ Ⓔ	V3, Pg. 312	PT37-S4-Q17	Ⓐ Ⓑ Ⓒ Ⓓ Ⓔ
V3, Pg. 139	PT32-S4-Q6	Ⓐ Ⓑ Ⓒ Ⓓ Ⓔ	V3, Pg. 314	PT37-S4-Q22	Ⓐ Ⓑ Ⓒ Ⓓ Ⓔ
V3, Pg. 141	PT32-S4-Q13	Ⓐ Ⓑ Ⓒ Ⓓ Ⓔ	V3, Pg. 323	PT38-S1-Q6	Ⓐ Ⓑ Ⓒ Ⓓ Ⓔ
V3, Pg. 142	PT32-S4-Q15	Ⓐ Ⓑ Ⓒ Ⓓ Ⓔ	V3, Pg. 323	PT38-S1-Q8	Ⓐ Ⓑ Ⓒ Ⓓ Ⓔ
V3, Pg. 145	PT32-S4-Q25	Ⓐ Ⓑ Ⓒ Ⓓ Ⓔ	V3, Pg. 325	PT38-S1-Q11	Ⓐ Ⓑ Ⓒ Ⓓ Ⓔ
V3, Pg. 155	PT33-S1-Q12	Ⓐ Ⓑ Ⓒ Ⓓ Ⓔ	V3, Pg. 329	PT38-S1-Q23	Ⓐ Ⓑ Ⓒ Ⓓ Ⓔ
V3, Pg. 158	PT33-S1-Q22	Ⓐ Ⓑ Ⓒ Ⓓ Ⓔ	V3, Pg. 342	PT38-S4-Q2	Ⓐ Ⓑ Ⓒ Ⓓ Ⓔ
V3, Pg. 159	PT33-S1-Q24	Ⓐ Ⓑ Ⓒ Ⓓ Ⓔ	V3, Pg. 344	PT38-S4-Q8	Ⓐ Ⓑ Ⓒ Ⓓ Ⓔ
V3, Pg. 168	PT33-S3-Q2	Ⓐ Ⓑ Ⓒ Ⓓ Ⓔ	V3, Pg. 345	PT38-S4-Q14	Ⓐ Ⓑ Ⓒ Ⓓ Ⓔ
V3, Pg. 169	PT33-S3-Q5	Ⓐ Ⓑ Ⓒ Ⓓ Ⓔ	V3, Pg. 347	PT38-S4-Q21	Ⓐ Ⓑ Ⓒ Ⓓ Ⓔ
V3, Pg. 172	PT33-S3-Q15	Ⓐ Ⓑ Ⓒ Ⓓ Ⓔ		PT39-S2-Q2	Ⓐ Ⓑ Ⓒ Ⓓ Ⓔ
V3, Pg. 172	PT33-S3-Q17	Ⓐ Ⓑ Ⓒ Ⓓ Ⓔ		PT39-S2-Q14	Ⓐ Ⓑ Ⓒ Ⓓ Ⓔ
V3, Pg. 194	PT34-S2-Q1	Ⓐ Ⓑ Ⓒ Ⓓ Ⓔ		PT39-S2-Q20	Ⓐ Ⓑ Ⓒ Ⓓ Ⓔ
V3, Pg. 194	PT34-S2-Q3	Ⓐ Ⓑ Ⓒ Ⓓ Ⓔ		PT39-S4-Q11	Ⓐ Ⓑ Ⓒ Ⓓ Ⓔ
V3, Pg. 196	PT34-S2-Q9	Ⓐ Ⓑ Ⓒ Ⓓ Ⓔ		PT39-S4-Q15	Ⓐ Ⓑ Ⓒ Ⓓ Ⓔ
V3, Pg. 197	PT34-S2-Q11	Ⓐ Ⓑ Ⓒ Ⓓ Ⓔ		PT39-S4-Q20	Ⓐ Ⓑ Ⓒ Ⓓ Ⓔ
V3, Pg. 203	PT34-S3-Q4	Ⓐ Ⓑ Ⓒ Ⓓ Ⓔ		PT39-S4-Q21	Ⓐ Ⓑ Ⓒ Ⓓ Ⓔ
V3, Pg. 204	PT34-S3-Q10	Ⓐ Ⓑ Ⓒ Ⓓ Ⓔ		PT39-S4-Q23	Ⓐ Ⓑ Ⓒ Ⓓ Ⓔ
V3, Pg. 221	PT35-S1-Q6	Ⓐ Ⓑ Ⓒ Ⓓ Ⓔ		PT40-S1-Q10	Ⓐ Ⓑ Ⓒ Ⓓ Ⓔ
V3, Pg. 224	PT35-S1-Q17	Ⓐ Ⓑ Ⓒ Ⓓ Ⓔ		PT40-S1-Q12	Ⓐ Ⓑ Ⓒ Ⓓ Ⓔ
V3, Pg. 226	PT35-S1-Q23	Ⓐ Ⓑ Ⓒ Ⓓ Ⓔ		PT40-S1-Q14	Ⓐ Ⓑ Ⓒ Ⓓ Ⓔ
V3, Pg. 242	PT35-S4-Q7	Ⓐ Ⓑ Ⓒ Ⓓ Ⓔ		PT40-S1-Q15	Ⓐ Ⓑ Ⓒ Ⓓ Ⓔ
V3, Pg. 242	PT35-S4-Q8	Ⓐ Ⓑ Ⓒ Ⓓ Ⓔ		PT40-S3-Q10	Ⓐ Ⓑ Ⓒ Ⓓ Ⓔ

PT40-S3-Q12	Ⓐ Ⓑ Ⓒ Ⓓ Ⓔ		PT44-S4-Q22	Ⓐ Ⓑ Ⓒ Ⓓ Ⓔ
PT40-S3-Q14	Ⓐ Ⓑ Ⓒ Ⓓ Ⓔ		PT45-S1-Q13	Ⓐ Ⓑ Ⓒ Ⓓ Ⓔ
PT40-S3-Q19	Ⓐ Ⓑ Ⓒ Ⓓ Ⓔ		PT45-S1-Q15	Ⓐ Ⓑ Ⓒ Ⓓ Ⓔ
PT40-S3-Q21	Ⓐ Ⓑ Ⓒ Ⓓ Ⓔ		PT45-S1-Q20	Ⓐ Ⓑ Ⓒ Ⓓ Ⓔ
PT40-S3-Q23	Ⓐ Ⓑ Ⓒ Ⓓ Ⓔ		PT45-S1-Q24	Ⓐ Ⓑ Ⓒ Ⓓ Ⓔ
PT41-S1-Q1	Ⓐ Ⓑ Ⓒ Ⓓ Ⓔ		PT45-S4-Q10	Ⓐ Ⓑ Ⓒ Ⓓ Ⓔ
PT41-S1-Q18	Ⓐ Ⓑ Ⓒ Ⓓ Ⓔ		PT45-S4-Q14	Ⓐ Ⓑ Ⓒ Ⓓ Ⓔ
PT41-S1-Q20	Ⓐ Ⓑ Ⓒ Ⓓ Ⓔ		PT45-S4-Q17	Ⓐ Ⓑ Ⓒ Ⓓ Ⓔ
PT41-S1-Q22	Ⓐ Ⓑ Ⓒ Ⓓ Ⓔ		PT45-S4-Q19	Ⓐ Ⓑ Ⓒ Ⓓ Ⓔ
PT41-S1-Q25	Ⓐ Ⓑ Ⓒ Ⓓ Ⓔ		PT45-S4-Q24	Ⓐ Ⓑ Ⓒ Ⓓ Ⓔ
PT41-S3-Q4	Ⓐ Ⓑ Ⓒ Ⓓ Ⓔ		PT46-S2-Q11	Ⓐ Ⓑ Ⓒ Ⓓ Ⓔ
PT41-S3-Q11	Ⓐ Ⓑ Ⓒ Ⓓ Ⓔ		PT46-S2-Q14	Ⓐ Ⓑ Ⓒ Ⓓ Ⓔ
PT41-S3-Q13	Ⓐ Ⓑ Ⓒ Ⓓ Ⓔ		PT46-S2-Q24	Ⓐ Ⓑ Ⓒ Ⓓ Ⓔ
PT41-S3-Q20	Ⓐ Ⓑ Ⓒ Ⓓ Ⓔ		PT46-S3-Q2	Ⓐ Ⓑ Ⓒ Ⓓ Ⓔ
PT41-S3-Q23	Ⓐ Ⓑ Ⓒ Ⓓ Ⓔ		PT46-S3-Q4	Ⓐ Ⓑ Ⓒ Ⓓ Ⓔ
PT42-S2-Q3	Ⓐ Ⓑ Ⓒ Ⓓ Ⓔ		PT46-S3-Q7	Ⓐ Ⓑ Ⓒ Ⓓ Ⓔ
PT42-S2-Q12	Ⓐ Ⓑ Ⓒ Ⓓ Ⓔ		PT46-S3-Q13	Ⓐ Ⓑ Ⓒ Ⓓ Ⓔ
PT42-S2-Q15	Ⓐ Ⓑ Ⓒ Ⓓ Ⓔ		PT46-S3-Q23	Ⓐ Ⓑ Ⓒ Ⓓ Ⓔ
PT42-S2-Q17	Ⓐ Ⓑ Ⓒ Ⓓ Ⓔ		PT47-S1-Q1	Ⓐ Ⓑ Ⓒ Ⓓ Ⓔ
PT42-S2-Q26	Ⓐ Ⓑ Ⓒ Ⓓ Ⓔ		PT47-S1-Q8	Ⓐ Ⓑ Ⓒ Ⓓ Ⓔ
PT42-S4-Q4	Ⓐ Ⓑ Ⓒ Ⓓ Ⓔ		PT47-S1-Q23	Ⓐ Ⓑ Ⓒ Ⓓ Ⓔ
PT42-S4-Q12	Ⓐ Ⓑ Ⓒ Ⓓ Ⓔ		PT47-S3-Q8	Ⓐ Ⓑ Ⓒ Ⓓ Ⓔ
PT42-S4-Q14	Ⓐ Ⓑ Ⓒ Ⓓ Ⓔ		PT47-S3-Q16	Ⓐ Ⓑ Ⓒ Ⓓ Ⓔ
PT42-S4-Q20	Ⓐ Ⓑ Ⓒ Ⓓ Ⓔ		PT47-S3-Q19	Ⓐ Ⓑ Ⓒ Ⓓ Ⓔ
PT43-S2-Q5	Ⓐ Ⓑ Ⓒ Ⓓ Ⓔ		PT47-S3-Q23	Ⓐ Ⓑ Ⓒ Ⓓ Ⓔ
PT43-S2-Q9	Ⓐ Ⓑ Ⓒ Ⓓ Ⓔ		PT48-S1-Q2	Ⓐ Ⓑ Ⓒ Ⓓ Ⓔ
PT43-S2-Q12	Ⓐ Ⓑ Ⓒ Ⓓ Ⓔ		PT48-S1-Q13	Ⓐ Ⓑ Ⓒ Ⓓ Ⓔ
PT43-S2-Q20	Ⓐ Ⓑ Ⓒ Ⓓ Ⓔ		PT48-S1-Q17	Ⓐ Ⓑ Ⓒ Ⓓ Ⓔ
PT43-S3-Q4	Ⓐ Ⓑ Ⓒ Ⓓ Ⓔ		PT48-S1-Q21	Ⓐ Ⓑ Ⓒ Ⓓ Ⓔ
PT43-S3-Q18	Ⓐ Ⓑ Ⓒ Ⓓ Ⓔ		PT48-S1-Q24	Ⓐ Ⓑ Ⓒ Ⓓ Ⓔ
PT43-S3-Q20	Ⓐ Ⓑ Ⓒ Ⓓ Ⓔ		PT48-S4-Q11	Ⓐ Ⓑ Ⓒ Ⓓ Ⓔ
PT44-S2-Q1	Ⓐ Ⓑ Ⓒ Ⓓ Ⓔ		PT48-S4-Q13	Ⓐ Ⓑ Ⓒ Ⓓ Ⓔ
PT44-S2-Q21	Ⓐ Ⓑ Ⓒ Ⓓ Ⓔ		PT48-S4-Q15	Ⓐ Ⓑ Ⓒ Ⓓ Ⓔ
PT44-S2-Q25	Ⓐ Ⓑ Ⓒ Ⓓ Ⓔ		PT48-S4-Q17	Ⓐ Ⓑ Ⓒ Ⓓ Ⓔ
PT44-S4-Q9	Ⓐ Ⓑ Ⓒ Ⓓ Ⓔ		PT48-S4-Q25	Ⓐ Ⓑ Ⓒ Ⓓ Ⓔ
PT44-S4-Q11	Ⓐ Ⓑ Ⓒ Ⓓ Ⓔ		PT49-S2-Q5	Ⓐ Ⓑ Ⓒ Ⓓ Ⓔ
PT44-S4-Q20	Ⓐ Ⓑ Ⓒ Ⓓ Ⓔ		PT49-S2-Q13	Ⓐ Ⓑ Ⓒ Ⓓ Ⓔ

	PT49-S2-Q18	Ⓐ Ⓑ Ⓒ Ⓓ Ⓔ	V4, Pg. 56	PT53-S3-Q2	Ⓐ Ⓑ Ⓒ Ⓓ Ⓔ
	PT49-S2-Q23	Ⓐ Ⓑ Ⓒ Ⓓ Ⓔ	V4, Pg. 58	PT53-S3-Q6	Ⓐ Ⓑ Ⓒ Ⓓ Ⓔ
	PT49-S4-Q1	Ⓐ Ⓑ Ⓒ Ⓓ Ⓔ	V4, Pg. 60	PT53-S3-Q17	Ⓐ Ⓑ Ⓒ Ⓓ Ⓔ
	PT49-S4-Q6	Ⓐ Ⓑ Ⓒ Ⓓ Ⓔ	V4, Pg. 88	PT54-S2-Q1	Ⓐ Ⓑ Ⓒ Ⓓ Ⓔ
	PT49-S4-Q12	Ⓐ Ⓑ Ⓒ Ⓓ Ⓔ	V4, Pg. 89	PT54-S2-Q5	Ⓐ Ⓑ Ⓒ Ⓓ Ⓔ
	PT49-S4-Q23	Ⓐ Ⓑ Ⓒ Ⓓ Ⓔ	V4, Pg. 91	PT54-S2-Q15	Ⓐ Ⓑ Ⓒ Ⓓ Ⓔ
	PT50-S2-Q3	Ⓐ Ⓑ Ⓒ Ⓓ Ⓔ	V4, Pg. 93	PT54-S2-Q19	Ⓐ Ⓑ Ⓒ Ⓓ Ⓔ
	PT50-S2-Q6	Ⓐ Ⓑ Ⓒ Ⓓ Ⓔ	V4, Pg. 94	PT54-S2-Q22	Ⓐ Ⓑ Ⓒ Ⓓ Ⓔ
	PT50-S2-Q10	Ⓐ Ⓑ Ⓒ Ⓓ Ⓔ	V4, Pg. 101	PT54-S4-Q4	Ⓐ Ⓑ Ⓒ Ⓓ Ⓔ
	PT50-S4-Q2	Ⓐ Ⓑ Ⓒ Ⓓ Ⓔ	V4, Pg. 104	PT54-S4-Q14	Ⓐ Ⓑ Ⓒ Ⓓ Ⓔ
	PT50-S4-Q4	Ⓐ Ⓑ Ⓒ Ⓓ Ⓔ	V4, Pg. 104	PT54-S4-Q16	Ⓐ Ⓑ Ⓒ Ⓓ Ⓔ
	PT50-S4-Q7	Ⓐ Ⓑ Ⓒ Ⓓ Ⓔ	V4, Pg. 105	PT54-S4-Q19	Ⓐ Ⓑ Ⓒ Ⓓ Ⓔ
	PT50-S4-Q17	Ⓐ Ⓑ Ⓒ Ⓓ Ⓔ	V4, Pg. 119	PT55-S1-Q14	Ⓐ Ⓑ Ⓒ Ⓓ Ⓔ
	PT50-S4-Q19	Ⓐ Ⓑ Ⓒ Ⓓ Ⓔ	V4, Pg. 121	PT55-S1-Q20	Ⓐ Ⓑ Ⓒ Ⓓ Ⓔ
	PT50-S4-Q22	Ⓐ Ⓑ Ⓒ Ⓓ Ⓔ	V4, Pg. 123	PT55-S1-Q24	Ⓐ Ⓑ Ⓒ Ⓓ Ⓔ
	PT51-S1-Q4	Ⓐ Ⓑ Ⓒ Ⓓ Ⓔ	V4, Pg. 132	PT55-S3-Q2	Ⓐ Ⓑ Ⓒ Ⓓ Ⓔ
	PT51-S1-Q6	Ⓐ Ⓑ Ⓒ Ⓓ Ⓔ	V4, Pg. 134	PT55-S3-Q11	Ⓐ Ⓑ Ⓒ Ⓓ Ⓔ
	PT51-S1-Q10	Ⓐ Ⓑ Ⓒ Ⓓ Ⓔ	V4, Pg. 137	PT55-S3-Q18	Ⓐ Ⓑ Ⓒ Ⓓ Ⓔ
	PT51-S1-Q12	Ⓐ Ⓑ Ⓒ Ⓓ Ⓔ	V4, Pg. 139	PT55-S3-Q25	Ⓐ Ⓑ Ⓒ Ⓓ Ⓔ
	PT51-S1-Q15	Ⓐ Ⓑ Ⓒ Ⓓ Ⓔ	V4, Pg. 156	PT56-S2-Q1	Ⓐ Ⓑ Ⓒ Ⓓ Ⓔ
	PT51-S1-Q18	Ⓐ Ⓑ Ⓒ Ⓓ Ⓔ	V4, Pg. 159	PT56-S2-Q12	Ⓐ Ⓑ Ⓒ Ⓓ Ⓔ
	PT51-S3-Q4	Ⓐ Ⓑ Ⓒ Ⓓ Ⓔ	V4, Pg. 160	PT56-S2-Q15	Ⓐ Ⓑ Ⓒ Ⓓ Ⓔ
	PT51-S3-Q6	Ⓐ Ⓑ Ⓒ Ⓓ Ⓔ	V4, Pg. 164	PT56-S3-Q1	Ⓐ Ⓑ Ⓒ Ⓓ Ⓔ
	PT51-S3-Q9	Ⓐ Ⓑ Ⓒ Ⓓ Ⓔ	V4, Pg. 165	PT56-S3-Q4	Ⓐ Ⓑ Ⓒ Ⓓ Ⓔ
	PT51-S3-Q17	Ⓐ Ⓑ Ⓒ Ⓓ Ⓔ	V4, Pg. 166	PT56-S3-Q10	Ⓐ Ⓑ Ⓒ Ⓓ Ⓔ
V4, Pg. 8	PT52-S1-Q2	Ⓐ Ⓑ Ⓒ Ⓓ Ⓔ	V4, Pg. 168	PT56-S3-Q17	Ⓐ Ⓑ Ⓒ Ⓓ Ⓔ
V4, Pg. 9	PT52-S1-Q6	Ⓐ Ⓑ Ⓒ Ⓓ Ⓔ	V4, Pg. 170	PT56-S3-Q21	Ⓐ Ⓑ Ⓒ Ⓓ Ⓔ
V4, Pg. 15	PT52-S1-Q23	Ⓐ Ⓑ Ⓒ Ⓓ Ⓔ	V4, Pg. 193	PT57-S2-Q4	Ⓐ Ⓑ Ⓒ Ⓓ Ⓔ
V4, Pg. 21	PT52-S3-Q4	Ⓐ Ⓑ Ⓒ Ⓓ Ⓔ	V4, Pg. 194	PT57-S2-Q6	Ⓐ Ⓑ Ⓒ Ⓓ Ⓔ
V4, Pg. 22	PT52-S3-Q8	Ⓐ Ⓑ Ⓒ Ⓓ Ⓔ	V4, Pg. 196	PT57-S2-Q15	Ⓐ Ⓑ Ⓒ Ⓓ Ⓔ
V4, Pg. 23	PT52-S3-Q12	Ⓐ Ⓑ Ⓒ Ⓓ Ⓔ	V4, Pg. 199	PT57-S2-Q26	Ⓐ Ⓑ Ⓒ Ⓓ Ⓔ
V4, Pg. 24	PT52-S3-Q16	Ⓐ Ⓑ Ⓒ Ⓓ Ⓔ	V4, Pg. 200	PT57-S3-Q2	Ⓐ Ⓑ Ⓒ Ⓓ Ⓔ
V4, Pg. 26	PT52-S3-Q21	Ⓐ Ⓑ Ⓒ Ⓓ Ⓔ	V4, Pg. 202	PT57-S3-Q8	Ⓐ Ⓑ Ⓒ Ⓓ Ⓔ
V4, Pg. 46	PT53-S1-Q12	Ⓐ Ⓑ Ⓒ Ⓓ Ⓔ	V4, Pg. 202	PT57-S3-Q10	Ⓐ Ⓑ Ⓒ Ⓓ Ⓔ
V4, Pg. 49	PT53-S1-Q18	Ⓐ Ⓑ Ⓒ Ⓓ Ⓔ	V4, Pg. 205	PT57-S3-Q18	Ⓐ Ⓑ Ⓒ Ⓓ Ⓔ
V4, Pg. 50	PT53-S1-Q22	Ⓐ Ⓑ Ⓒ Ⓓ Ⓔ	V4, Pg. 207	PT57-S3-Q22	Ⓐ Ⓑ Ⓒ Ⓓ Ⓔ
V4, Pg. 51	PT53-S1-Q25	Ⓐ Ⓑ Ⓒ Ⓓ Ⓔ	V4, Pg. 226	PT58-S1-Q9	Ⓐ Ⓑ Ⓒ Ⓓ Ⓔ

V4, Pg. 227	PT58-S1-Q11	Ⓐ Ⓑ Ⓒ Ⓓ Ⓔ	V5, Pg. 51	PT63-S1-Q25	Ⓐ Ⓑ Ⓒ Ⓓ Ⓔ
V4, Pg. 229	PT58-S1-Q18	Ⓐ Ⓑ Ⓒ Ⓓ Ⓔ	V5, Pg. 56	PT63-S3-Q2	Ⓐ Ⓑ Ⓒ Ⓓ Ⓔ
V4, Pg. 245	PT58-S4-Q5	Ⓐ Ⓑ Ⓒ Ⓓ Ⓔ	V5, Pg. 59	PT63-S3-Q14	Ⓐ Ⓑ Ⓒ Ⓓ Ⓔ
V4, Pg. 246	PT58-S4-Q8	Ⓐ Ⓑ Ⓒ Ⓓ Ⓔ	V5, Pg. 60	PT63-S3-Q18	Ⓐ Ⓑ Ⓒ Ⓓ Ⓔ
V4, Pg. 247	PT58-S4-Q14	Ⓐ Ⓑ Ⓒ Ⓓ Ⓔ	V5, Pg. 81	PT64-S1-Q5	Ⓐ Ⓑ Ⓒ Ⓓ Ⓔ
V4, Pg. 248	PT58-S4-Q18	Ⓐ Ⓑ Ⓒ Ⓓ Ⓔ	V5, Pg. 81	PT64-S1-Q7	Ⓐ Ⓑ Ⓒ Ⓓ Ⓔ
V4, Pg. 265	PT59-S2-Q4	Ⓐ Ⓑ Ⓒ Ⓓ Ⓔ	V5, Pg. 84	PT64-S1-Q16	Ⓐ Ⓑ Ⓒ Ⓓ Ⓔ
V4, Pg. 265	PT59-S2-Q6	Ⓐ Ⓑ Ⓒ Ⓓ Ⓔ	V5, Pg. 85	PT64-S1-Q19	Ⓐ Ⓑ Ⓒ Ⓓ Ⓔ
V4, Pg. 266	PT59-S2-Q8	Ⓐ Ⓑ Ⓒ Ⓓ Ⓔ	V5, Pg. 93	PT64-S3-Q4	Ⓐ Ⓑ Ⓒ Ⓓ Ⓔ
V4, Pg. 268	PT59-S2-Q15	Ⓐ Ⓑ Ⓒ Ⓓ Ⓔ	V5, Pg. 93	PT64-S3-Q6	Ⓐ Ⓑ Ⓒ Ⓓ Ⓔ
V4, Pg. 269	PT59-S2-Q20	Ⓐ Ⓑ Ⓒ Ⓓ Ⓔ	V5, Pg. 94	PT64-S3-Q11	Ⓐ Ⓑ Ⓒ Ⓓ Ⓔ
V4, Pg. 273	PT59-S3-Q5	Ⓐ Ⓑ Ⓒ Ⓓ Ⓔ	V5, Pg. 95	PT64-S3-Q14	Ⓐ Ⓑ Ⓒ Ⓓ Ⓔ
V4, Pg. 274	PT59-S3-Q8	Ⓐ Ⓑ Ⓒ Ⓓ Ⓔ	V5, Pg. 118	PT65-S1-Q8	Ⓐ Ⓑ Ⓒ Ⓓ Ⓔ
V4, Pg. 277	PT59-S3-Q20	Ⓐ Ⓑ Ⓒ Ⓓ Ⓔ	V5, Pg. 121	PT65-S1-Q15	Ⓐ Ⓑ Ⓒ Ⓓ Ⓔ
V4, Pg. 278	PT59-S3-Q22	Ⓐ Ⓑ Ⓒ Ⓓ Ⓔ	V5, Pg. 121	PT65-S1-Q17	Ⓐ Ⓑ Ⓒ Ⓓ Ⓔ
V4, Pg. 279	PT59-S3-Q24	Ⓐ Ⓑ Ⓒ Ⓓ Ⓔ	V5, Pg. 122	PT65-S1-Q20	Ⓐ Ⓑ Ⓒ Ⓓ Ⓔ
V4, Pg. 296	PT60-S1-Q1	Ⓐ Ⓑ Ⓒ Ⓓ Ⓔ	V5, Pg. 138	PT65-S4-Q8	Ⓐ Ⓑ Ⓒ Ⓓ Ⓔ
V4, Pg. 298	PT60-S1-Q10	Ⓐ Ⓑ Ⓒ Ⓓ Ⓔ	V5, Pg. 139	PT65-S4-Q11	Ⓐ Ⓑ Ⓒ Ⓓ Ⓔ
V4, Pg. 299	PT60-S1-Q12	Ⓐ Ⓑ Ⓒ Ⓓ Ⓔ	V5, Pg. 143	PT65-S4-Q26	Ⓐ Ⓑ Ⓒ Ⓓ Ⓔ
V4, Pg. 300	PT60-S1-Q15	Ⓐ Ⓑ Ⓒ Ⓓ Ⓔ	V5, Pg. 160	PT66-S2-Q1	Ⓐ Ⓑ Ⓒ Ⓓ Ⓔ
V4, Pg. 310	PT60-S3-Q8	Ⓐ Ⓑ Ⓒ Ⓓ Ⓔ	V5, Pg. 162	PT66-S2-Q8	Ⓐ Ⓑ Ⓒ Ⓓ Ⓔ
V4, Pg. 312	PT60-S3-Q16	Ⓐ Ⓑ Ⓒ Ⓓ Ⓔ	V5, Pg. 163	PT66-S2-Q11	Ⓐ Ⓑ Ⓒ Ⓓ Ⓔ
V4, Pg. 313	PT60-S3-Q19	Ⓐ Ⓑ Ⓒ Ⓓ Ⓔ	V5, Pg. 163	PT66-S2-Q13	Ⓐ Ⓑ Ⓒ Ⓓ Ⓔ
V4, Pg. 340	PT61-S2-Q1	Ⓐ Ⓑ Ⓒ Ⓓ Ⓔ	V5, Pg. 164	PT66-S2-Q15	Ⓐ Ⓑ Ⓒ Ⓓ Ⓔ
V4, Pg. 342	PT61-S2-Q8	Ⓐ Ⓑ Ⓒ Ⓓ Ⓔ	V5, Pg. 166	PT66-S2-Q21	Ⓐ Ⓑ Ⓒ Ⓓ Ⓔ
V4, Pg. 344	PT61-S2-Q18	Ⓐ Ⓑ Ⓒ Ⓓ Ⓔ	V5, Pg. 176	PT66-S4-Q1	Ⓐ Ⓑ Ⓒ Ⓓ Ⓔ
V4, Pg. 355	PT61-S4-Q11	Ⓐ Ⓑ Ⓒ Ⓓ Ⓔ	V5, Pg. 182	PT66-S4-Q22	Ⓐ Ⓑ Ⓒ Ⓓ Ⓔ
V4, Pg. 356	PT61-S4-Q15	Ⓐ Ⓑ Ⓒ Ⓓ Ⓔ	V5, Pg. 183	PT66-S4-Q25	Ⓐ Ⓑ Ⓒ Ⓓ Ⓔ
V4, Pg. 358	PT61-S4-Q24	Ⓐ Ⓑ Ⓒ Ⓓ Ⓔ	V5, Pg. 202	PT67-S2-Q9	Ⓐ Ⓑ Ⓒ Ⓓ Ⓔ
V5, Pg. 17	PT62-S2-Q5	Ⓐ Ⓑ Ⓒ Ⓓ Ⓔ	V5, Pg. 203	PT67-S2-Q13	Ⓐ Ⓑ Ⓒ Ⓓ Ⓔ
V5, Pg. 18	PT62-S2-Q8	Ⓐ Ⓑ Ⓒ Ⓓ Ⓔ	V5, Pg. 206	PT67-S2-Q21	Ⓐ Ⓑ Ⓒ Ⓓ Ⓔ
V5, Pg. 19	PT62-S2-Q11	Ⓐ Ⓑ Ⓒ Ⓓ Ⓔ	V5, Pg. 218	PT67-S4-Q9	Ⓐ Ⓑ Ⓒ Ⓓ Ⓔ
V5, Pg. 30	PT62-S4-Q10	Ⓐ Ⓑ Ⓒ Ⓓ Ⓔ	V5, Pg. 220	PT67-S4-Q14	Ⓐ Ⓑ Ⓒ Ⓓ Ⓔ
V5, Pg. 31	PT62-S4-Q13	Ⓐ Ⓑ Ⓒ Ⓓ Ⓔ	V5, Pg. 222	PT67-S4-Q21	Ⓐ Ⓑ Ⓒ Ⓓ Ⓔ
V5, Pg. 33	PT62-S4-Q19	Ⓐ Ⓑ Ⓒ Ⓓ Ⓔ	V5, Pg. 241	PT68-S2-Q7	Ⓐ Ⓑ Ⓒ Ⓓ Ⓔ
V5, Pg. 44	PT63-S1-Q3	Ⓐ Ⓑ Ⓒ Ⓓ Ⓔ	V5, Pg. 243	PT68-S2-Q12	Ⓐ Ⓑ Ⓒ Ⓓ Ⓔ
V5, Pg. 50	PT63-S1-Q23	Ⓐ Ⓑ Ⓒ Ⓓ Ⓔ	V5, Pg. 245	PT68-S2-Q20	Ⓐ Ⓑ Ⓒ Ⓓ Ⓔ

V5, Pg. 246	PT68-S2-Q24	Ⓐ Ⓑ Ⓒ Ⓓ Ⓔ	PT73, Pg. 18	PT73-S2-Q3	Ⓐ Ⓑ Ⓒ Ⓓ Ⓔ
V5, Pg. 249	PT68-S3-Q3	Ⓐ Ⓑ Ⓒ Ⓓ Ⓔ	PT73, Pg. 19	PT73-S2-Q5	Ⓐ Ⓑ Ⓒ Ⓓ Ⓔ
V5, Pg. 249	PT68-S3-Q5	Ⓐ Ⓑ Ⓒ Ⓓ Ⓔ	PT73, Pg. 21	PT73-S2-Q13	Ⓐ Ⓑ Ⓒ Ⓓ Ⓔ
V5, Pg. 252	PT68-S3-Q16	Ⓐ Ⓑ Ⓒ Ⓓ Ⓔ	PT73, Pg. 22	PT73-S2-Q15	Ⓐ Ⓑ Ⓒ Ⓓ Ⓔ
V5, Pg. 254	PT68-S3-Q21	Ⓐ Ⓑ Ⓒ Ⓓ Ⓔ	PT73, Pg. 23	PT73-S2-Q18	Ⓐ Ⓑ Ⓒ Ⓓ Ⓔ
V5, Pg. 273	PT69-S1-Q3	Ⓐ Ⓑ Ⓒ Ⓓ Ⓔ	PT73, Pg. 35	PT73-S4-Q3	Ⓐ Ⓑ Ⓒ Ⓓ Ⓔ
V5, Pg. 278	PT69-S1-Q20	Ⓐ Ⓑ Ⓒ Ⓓ Ⓔ	PT73, Pg. 36	PT73-S4-Q10	Ⓐ Ⓑ Ⓒ Ⓓ Ⓔ
V5, Pg. 279	PT69-S1-Q24	Ⓐ Ⓑ Ⓒ Ⓓ Ⓔ	PT73, Pg. 41	PT73-S4-Q25	Ⓐ Ⓑ Ⓒ Ⓓ Ⓔ
V5, Pg. 296	PT69-S4-Q3	Ⓐ Ⓑ Ⓒ Ⓓ Ⓔ	PT74, Pg. 11	PT74-S1-Q5	Ⓐ Ⓑ Ⓒ Ⓓ Ⓔ
V5, Pg. 299	PT69-S4-Q11	Ⓐ Ⓑ Ⓒ Ⓓ Ⓔ	PT74, Pg. 14	PT74-S1-Q16	Ⓐ Ⓑ Ⓒ Ⓓ Ⓔ
V5, Pg. 300	PT69-S4-Q16	Ⓐ Ⓑ Ⓒ Ⓓ Ⓔ	PT74, Pg. 15	PT74-S1-Q18	Ⓐ Ⓑ Ⓒ Ⓓ Ⓔ
V5, Pg. 301	PT69-S4-Q18	Ⓐ Ⓑ Ⓒ Ⓓ Ⓔ	PT74, Pg. 36	PT74-S4-Q8	Ⓐ Ⓑ Ⓒ Ⓓ Ⓔ
V5, Pg. 302	PT69-S4-Q22	Ⓐ Ⓑ Ⓒ Ⓓ Ⓔ	PT74, Pg. 37	PT74-S4-Q15	Ⓐ Ⓑ Ⓒ Ⓓ Ⓔ
V5, Pg. 312	PT70-S1-Q2	Ⓐ Ⓑ Ⓒ Ⓓ Ⓔ	PT74, Pg. 38	PT74-S4-Q18	Ⓐ Ⓑ Ⓒ Ⓓ Ⓔ
V5, Pg. 314	PT70-S1-Q9	Ⓐ Ⓑ Ⓒ Ⓓ Ⓔ	PT74, Pg. 39	PT74-S4-Q20	Ⓐ Ⓑ Ⓒ Ⓓ Ⓔ
V5, Pg. 316	PT70-S1-Q15	Ⓐ Ⓑ Ⓒ Ⓓ Ⓔ	PT74, Pg. 39	PT74-S4-Q22	Ⓐ Ⓑ Ⓒ Ⓓ Ⓔ
V5, Pg. 317	PT70-S1-Q20	Ⓐ Ⓑ Ⓒ Ⓓ Ⓔ	PT75, Pg. 12	PT75-S1-Q7	Ⓐ Ⓑ Ⓒ Ⓓ Ⓔ
V5, Pg. 336	PT70-S4-Q3	Ⓐ Ⓑ Ⓒ Ⓓ Ⓔ	PT75, Pg. 13	PT75-S1-Q12	Ⓐ Ⓑ Ⓒ Ⓓ Ⓔ
V5, Pg. 338	PT70-S4-Q9	Ⓐ Ⓑ Ⓒ Ⓓ Ⓔ	PT75, Pg. 14	PT75-S1-Q18	Ⓐ Ⓑ Ⓒ Ⓓ Ⓔ
V5, Pg. 338	PT70-S4-Q11	Ⓐ Ⓑ Ⓒ Ⓓ Ⓔ	PT75, Pg. 17	PT75-S1-Q24	Ⓐ Ⓑ Ⓒ Ⓓ Ⓔ
V5, Pg. 352	PT71-S1-Q3	Ⓐ Ⓑ Ⓒ Ⓓ Ⓔ	PT75, Pg. 27	PT75-S3-Q7	Ⓐ Ⓑ Ⓒ Ⓓ Ⓔ
V5, Pg. 357	PT71-S1-Q18	Ⓐ Ⓑ Ⓒ Ⓓ Ⓔ	PT75, Pg. 30	PT75-S3-Q16	Ⓐ Ⓑ Ⓒ Ⓓ Ⓔ
V5, Pg. 358	PT71-S1-Q21	Ⓐ Ⓑ Ⓒ Ⓓ Ⓔ	PT75, Pg. 31	PT75-S3-Q18	Ⓐ Ⓑ Ⓒ Ⓓ Ⓔ
V5, Pg. 359	PT71-S1-Q24	Ⓐ Ⓑ Ⓒ Ⓓ Ⓔ	PT76, Pg. 18	PT76-S2-Q1	Ⓐ Ⓑ Ⓒ Ⓓ Ⓔ
V5, Pg. 368	PT71-S3-Q1	Ⓐ Ⓑ Ⓒ Ⓓ Ⓔ	PT76, Pg. 19	PT76-S2-Q4	Ⓐ Ⓑ Ⓒ Ⓓ Ⓔ
V5, Pg. 369	PT71-S3-Q7	Ⓐ Ⓑ Ⓒ Ⓓ Ⓔ	PT76, Pg. 22	PT76-S2-Q16	Ⓐ Ⓑ Ⓒ Ⓓ Ⓔ
V5, Pg. 373	PT71-S3-Q18	Ⓐ Ⓑ Ⓒ Ⓓ Ⓔ	PT76, Pg. 23	PT76-S2-Q19	Ⓐ Ⓑ Ⓒ Ⓓ Ⓔ
V5, Pg. 373	PT71-S3-Q20	Ⓐ Ⓑ Ⓒ Ⓓ Ⓔ	PT76, Pg. 35	PT76-S4-Q5	Ⓐ Ⓑ Ⓒ Ⓓ Ⓔ
PT72, Pg. 19	PT72-S2-Q5	Ⓐ Ⓑ Ⓒ Ⓓ Ⓔ	PT76, Pg. 37	PT76-S4-Q13	Ⓐ Ⓑ Ⓒ Ⓓ Ⓔ
PT72, Pg. 21	PT72-S2-Q14	Ⓐ Ⓑ Ⓒ Ⓓ Ⓔ	PT76, Pg. 37	PT76-S4-Q15	Ⓐ Ⓑ Ⓒ Ⓓ Ⓔ
PT72, Pg. 22	PT72-S2-Q16	Ⓐ Ⓑ Ⓒ Ⓓ Ⓔ	PT77, Pg. 22	PT77-S2-Q14	Ⓐ Ⓑ Ⓒ Ⓓ Ⓔ
PT72, Pg. 22	PT72-S2-Q18	Ⓐ Ⓑ Ⓒ Ⓓ Ⓔ	PT77, Pg. 23	PT77-S2-Q18	Ⓐ Ⓑ Ⓒ Ⓓ Ⓔ
PT72, Pg. 23	PT72-S2-Q20	Ⓐ Ⓑ Ⓒ Ⓓ Ⓔ	PT77, Pg. 24	PT77-S2-Q22	Ⓐ Ⓑ Ⓒ Ⓓ Ⓔ
PT72, Pg. 28	PT72-S3-Q7	Ⓐ Ⓑ Ⓒ Ⓓ Ⓔ	PT77, Pg. 35	PT77-S4-Q6	Ⓐ Ⓑ Ⓒ Ⓓ Ⓔ
PT72, Pg. 29	PT72-S3-Q11	Ⓐ Ⓑ Ⓒ Ⓓ Ⓔ	PT77, Pg. 36	PT77-S4-Q9	Ⓐ Ⓑ Ⓒ Ⓓ Ⓔ
PT72, Pg. 30	PT72-S3-Q14	Ⓐ Ⓑ Ⓒ Ⓓ Ⓔ	PT77, Pg. 37	PT77-S4-Q12	Ⓐ Ⓑ Ⓒ Ⓓ Ⓔ
PT72, Pg. 32	PT72-S3-Q22	Ⓐ Ⓑ Ⓒ Ⓓ Ⓔ			

Parallel (Reasoning)

J07, Pg. 9	J07-S2-Q12	Ⓐ Ⓑ Ⓒ Ⓓ Ⓔ	V1, Pg. 192	PT13-S2-Q8	Ⓐ Ⓑ Ⓒ Ⓓ Ⓔ
SP1, Pg. 72	PTA-S1-Q14	Ⓐ Ⓑ Ⓒ Ⓓ Ⓔ	V1, Pg. 213	PT13-S4-Q24	Ⓐ Ⓑ Ⓒ Ⓓ Ⓔ
SP1, Pg. 95	PTA-S4-Q23	Ⓐ Ⓑ Ⓒ Ⓓ Ⓔ	V1, Pg. 228	PT14-S2-Q15	Ⓐ Ⓑ Ⓒ Ⓓ Ⓔ
SP1, Pg. 189	PTB-S1-Q12	Ⓐ Ⓑ Ⓒ Ⓓ Ⓔ	V1, Pg. 242	PT14-S4-Q8	Ⓐ Ⓑ Ⓒ Ⓓ Ⓔ
SP1, Pg. 304	PTC-S2-Q16	Ⓐ Ⓑ Ⓒ Ⓓ Ⓔ	V1, Pg. 267	PT15-S2-Q18	Ⓐ Ⓑ Ⓒ Ⓓ Ⓔ
SP1, Pg. 314	PTC-S3-Q24	Ⓐ Ⓑ Ⓒ Ⓓ Ⓔ	V1, Pg. 273	PT15-S3-Q13	Ⓐ Ⓑ Ⓒ Ⓓ Ⓔ
SP2, Pg. 360	PTC2-S2-Q23	Ⓐ Ⓑ Ⓒ Ⓓ Ⓔ	V1, Pg. 297	PT16-S2-Q19	Ⓐ Ⓑ Ⓒ Ⓓ Ⓔ
SP2, Pg. 362	PTC2-S3-Q3	Ⓐ Ⓑ Ⓒ Ⓓ Ⓔ	V1, Pg. 306	PT16-S3-Q22	Ⓐ Ⓑ Ⓒ Ⓓ Ⓔ
	PT1-S3-Q2	Ⓐ Ⓑ Ⓒ Ⓓ Ⓔ		PT17-S2-Q24	Ⓐ Ⓑ Ⓒ Ⓓ Ⓔ
	PT1-S3-Q6	Ⓐ Ⓑ Ⓒ Ⓓ Ⓔ		PT17-S3-Q13	Ⓐ Ⓑ Ⓒ Ⓓ Ⓔ
	PT1-S4-Q24	Ⓐ Ⓑ Ⓒ Ⓓ Ⓔ	V1, Pg. 330	PT18-S2-Q13	Ⓐ Ⓑ Ⓒ Ⓓ Ⓔ
	PT2-S2-Q1	Ⓐ Ⓑ Ⓒ Ⓓ Ⓔ	V1, Pg. 348	PT18-S4-Q20	Ⓐ Ⓑ Ⓒ Ⓓ Ⓔ
	PT2-S2-Q15	Ⓐ Ⓑ Ⓒ Ⓓ Ⓔ	V2, Pg. 26	PT19-S2-Q20	Ⓐ Ⓑ Ⓒ Ⓓ Ⓔ
	PT2-S4-Q20	Ⓐ Ⓑ Ⓒ Ⓓ Ⓔ	V2, Pg. 43	PT19-S4-Q24	Ⓐ Ⓑ Ⓒ Ⓓ Ⓔ
	PT3-S2-Q1	Ⓐ Ⓑ Ⓒ Ⓓ Ⓔ	V2, Pg. 55	PT20-S1-Q19	Ⓐ Ⓑ Ⓒ Ⓓ Ⓔ
	PT3-S2-Q13	Ⓐ Ⓑ Ⓒ Ⓓ Ⓔ	V2, Pg. 73	PT20-S4-Q15	Ⓐ Ⓑ Ⓒ Ⓓ Ⓔ
	PT3-S4-Q3	Ⓐ Ⓑ Ⓒ Ⓓ Ⓔ	V2, Pg. 102	PT21-S3-Q22	Ⓐ Ⓑ Ⓒ Ⓓ Ⓔ
	PT4-S1-Q20	Ⓐ Ⓑ Ⓒ Ⓓ Ⓔ	V2, Pg. 130	PT22-S2-Q16	Ⓐ Ⓑ Ⓒ Ⓓ Ⓔ
	PT4-S4-Q15	Ⓐ Ⓑ Ⓒ Ⓓ Ⓔ	V2, Pg. 143	PT22-S4-Q20	Ⓐ Ⓑ Ⓒ Ⓓ Ⓔ
	PT4-S4-Q20	Ⓐ Ⓑ Ⓒ Ⓓ Ⓔ	V2, Pg. 163	PT23-S2-Q25	Ⓐ Ⓑ Ⓒ Ⓓ Ⓔ
	PT5-S1-Q20	Ⓐ Ⓑ Ⓒ Ⓓ Ⓔ	V2, Pg. 168	PT23-S3-Q18	Ⓐ Ⓑ Ⓒ Ⓓ Ⓔ
	PT5-S3-Q25	Ⓐ Ⓑ Ⓒ Ⓓ Ⓔ	V2, Pg. 197	PT24-S2-Q13	Ⓐ Ⓑ Ⓒ Ⓓ Ⓔ
	PT6-S2-Q25	Ⓐ Ⓑ Ⓒ Ⓓ Ⓔ	V2, Pg. 207	PT24-S3-Q21	Ⓐ Ⓑ Ⓒ Ⓓ Ⓔ
	PT6-S3-Q14	Ⓐ Ⓑ Ⓒ Ⓓ Ⓔ	V2, Pg. 235	PT25-S2-Q22	Ⓐ Ⓑ Ⓒ Ⓓ Ⓔ
V1, Pg. 19	PT7-S1-Q13	Ⓐ Ⓑ Ⓒ Ⓓ Ⓔ	V2, Pg. 245	PT25-S4-Q20	Ⓐ Ⓑ Ⓒ Ⓓ Ⓔ
V1, Pg. 43	PT7-S4-Q25	Ⓐ Ⓑ Ⓒ Ⓓ Ⓔ	V2, Pg. 262	PT26-S2-Q16	Ⓐ Ⓑ Ⓒ Ⓓ Ⓔ
	PT8-S1-Q16	Ⓐ Ⓑ Ⓒ Ⓓ Ⓔ	V2, Pg. 295	PT27-S1-Q26	Ⓐ Ⓑ Ⓒ Ⓓ Ⓔ
	PT8-S4-Q12	Ⓐ Ⓑ Ⓒ Ⓓ Ⓔ	V2, Pg. 325	PT28-S1-Q13	Ⓐ Ⓑ Ⓒ Ⓓ Ⓔ
V1, Pg. 65	PT9-S2-Q24	Ⓐ Ⓑ Ⓒ Ⓓ Ⓔ	V2, Pg. 341	PT28-S3-Q26	Ⓐ Ⓑ Ⓒ Ⓓ Ⓔ
V1, Pg. 73	PT9-S4-Q15	Ⓐ Ⓑ Ⓒ Ⓓ Ⓔ	V3, Pg. 19	PT29-S1-Q13	Ⓐ Ⓑ Ⓒ Ⓓ Ⓔ
V1, Pg. 91	PT10-S1-Q25	Ⓐ Ⓑ Ⓒ Ⓓ Ⓔ	V3, Pg. 58	PT30-S2-Q14	Ⓐ Ⓑ Ⓒ Ⓓ Ⓔ
V1, Pg. 107	PT10-S4-Q12	Ⓐ Ⓑ Ⓒ Ⓓ Ⓔ	V3, Pg. 72	PT30-S4-Q9	Ⓐ Ⓑ Ⓒ Ⓓ Ⓔ
V1, Pg. 129	PT11-S2-Q25	Ⓐ Ⓑ Ⓒ Ⓓ Ⓔ	V3, Pg. 95	PT31-S2-Q23	Ⓐ Ⓑ Ⓒ Ⓓ Ⓔ
V1, Pg. 145	PT11-S4-Q22	Ⓐ Ⓑ Ⓒ Ⓓ Ⓔ	V3, Pg. 100	PT31-S3-Q18	Ⓐ Ⓑ Ⓒ Ⓓ Ⓔ
V1, Pg. 158	PT12-S1-Q23	Ⓐ Ⓑ Ⓒ Ⓓ Ⓔ	V3, Pg. 123	PT32-S1-Q16	Ⓐ Ⓑ Ⓒ Ⓓ Ⓔ
V1, Pg. 174	PT12-S4-Q9	Ⓐ Ⓑ Ⓒ Ⓓ Ⓔ	V3, Pg. 158	PT33-S1-Q23	Ⓐ Ⓑ Ⓒ Ⓓ Ⓔ

V3, Pg. 174	PT33-S3-Q22	ⓐ ⓑ ⓒ ⓓ ⓔ	V4, Pg. 197	PT57-S2-Q19	ⓐ ⓑ ⓒ ⓓ ⓔ
V3, Pg. 195	PT34-S2-Q6	ⓐ ⓑ ⓒ ⓓ ⓔ	V4, Pg. 206	PT57-S3-Q20	ⓐ ⓑ ⓒ ⓓ ⓔ
V3, Pg. 209	PT34-S3-Q25	ⓐ ⓑ ⓒ ⓓ ⓔ	V4, Pg. 268	PT59-S2-Q16	ⓐ ⓑ ⓒ ⓓ ⓔ
V3, Pg. 246	PT35-S4-Q23	ⓐ ⓑ ⓒ ⓓ ⓔ	V4, Pg. 300	PT60-S1-Q17	ⓐ ⓑ ⓒ ⓓ ⓔ
V3, Pg. 303	PT37-S2-Q26	ⓐ ⓑ ⓒ ⓓ ⓔ	V4, Pg. 309	PT60-S3-Q6	ⓐ ⓑ ⓒ ⓓ ⓔ
V3, Pg. 312	PT37-S4-Q14	ⓐ ⓑ ⓒ ⓓ ⓔ	V4, Pg. 354	PT61-S4-Q9	ⓐ ⓑ ⓒ ⓓ ⓔ
V3, Pg. 328	PT38-S1-Q22	ⓐ ⓑ ⓒ ⓓ ⓔ	V5, Pg. 35	PT62-S4-Q25	ⓐ ⓑ ⓒ ⓓ ⓔ
	PT39-S2-Q8	ⓐ ⓑ ⓒ ⓓ ⓔ	V5, Pg. 50	PT63-S1-Q21	ⓐ ⓑ ⓒ ⓓ ⓔ
	PT40-S1-Q23	ⓐ ⓑ ⓒ ⓓ ⓔ	V5, Pg. 61	PT63-S3-Q20	ⓐ ⓑ ⓒ ⓓ ⓔ
	PT40-S3-Q25	ⓐ ⓑ ⓒ ⓓ ⓔ	V5, Pg. 86	PT64-S1-Q21	ⓐ ⓑ ⓒ ⓓ ⓔ
	PT41-S1-Q15	ⓐ ⓑ ⓒ ⓓ ⓔ	V5, Pg. 99	PT64-S3-Q25	ⓐ ⓑ ⓒ ⓓ ⓔ
	PT41-S3-Q24	ⓐ ⓑ ⓒ ⓓ ⓔ	V5, Pg. 140	PT65-S4-Q17	ⓐ ⓑ ⓒ ⓓ ⓔ
	PT42-S2-Q22	ⓐ ⓑ ⓒ ⓓ ⓔ	V5, Pg. 164	PT66-S2-Q16	ⓐ ⓑ ⓒ ⓓ ⓔ
	PT43-S2-Q11	ⓐ ⓑ ⓒ ⓓ ⓔ	V5, Pg. 179	PT66-S4-Q13	ⓐ ⓑ ⓒ ⓓ ⓔ
	PT43-S3-Q25	ⓐ ⓑ ⓒ ⓓ ⓔ	V5, Pg. 205	PT67-S2-Q19	ⓐ ⓑ ⓒ ⓓ ⓔ
	PT44-S4-Q21	ⓐ ⓑ ⓒ ⓓ ⓔ	V5, Pg. 222	PT67-S4-Q19	ⓐ ⓑ ⓒ ⓓ ⓔ
	PT45-S1-Q25	ⓐ ⓑ ⓒ ⓓ ⓔ	V5, Pg. 242	PT68-S2-Q9	ⓐ ⓑ ⓒ ⓓ ⓔ
	PT46-S2-Q18	ⓐ ⓑ ⓒ ⓓ ⓔ	V5, Pg. 254	PT68-S3-Q22	ⓐ ⓑ ⓒ ⓓ ⓔ
	PT47-S1-Q15	ⓐ ⓑ ⓒ ⓓ ⓔ	V5, Pg. 299	PT69-S4-Q10	ⓐ ⓑ ⓒ ⓓ ⓔ
	PT48-S1-Q12	ⓐ ⓑ ⓒ ⓓ ⓔ	V5, Pg. 317	PT70-S1-Q19	ⓐ ⓑ ⓒ ⓓ ⓔ
	PT48-S4-Q22	ⓐ ⓑ ⓒ ⓓ ⓔ	V5, Pg. 340	PT70-S4-Q17	ⓐ ⓑ ⓒ ⓓ ⓔ
	PT49-S2-Q24	ⓐ ⓑ ⓒ ⓓ ⓔ	V5, Pg. 356	PT71-S1-Q14	ⓐ ⓑ ⓒ ⓓ ⓔ
	PT49-S4-Q17	ⓐ ⓑ ⓒ ⓓ ⓔ	V5, Pg. 375	PT71-S3-Q24	ⓐ ⓑ ⓒ ⓓ ⓔ
	PT50-S4-Q14	ⓐ ⓑ ⓒ ⓓ ⓔ	PT72, Pg. 25	PT72-S2-Q26	ⓐ ⓑ ⓒ ⓓ ⓔ
	PT51-S1-Q5	ⓐ ⓑ ⓒ ⓓ ⓔ	PT72, Pg. 33	PT72-S3-Q23	ⓐ ⓑ ⓒ ⓓ ⓔ
	PT51-S3-Q24	ⓐ ⓑ ⓒ ⓓ ⓔ	PT73, Pg. 23	PT73-S2-Q17	ⓐ ⓑ ⓒ ⓓ ⓔ
V4, Pg. 9	PT52-S1-Q3	ⓐ ⓑ ⓒ ⓓ ⓔ	PT73, Pg. 40	PT73-S4-Q21	ⓐ ⓑ ⓒ ⓓ ⓔ
V4, Pg. 49	PT53-S1-Q19	ⓐ ⓑ ⓒ ⓓ ⓔ	PT74, Pg. 15	PT74-S1-Q19	ⓐ ⓑ ⓒ ⓓ ⓔ
V4, Pg. 62	PT53-S3-Q23	ⓐ ⓑ ⓒ ⓓ ⓔ	PT74, Pg. 39	PT74-S4-Q19	ⓐ ⓑ ⓒ ⓓ ⓔ
V4, Pg. 94	PT54-S2-Q23	ⓐ ⓑ ⓒ ⓓ ⓔ	PT75, Pg. 17	PT75-S1-Q25	ⓐ ⓑ ⓒ ⓓ ⓔ
V4, Pg. 107	PT54-S4-Q25	ⓐ ⓑ ⓒ ⓓ ⓔ	PT75, Pg. 28	PT75-S3-Q9	ⓐ ⓑ ⓒ ⓓ ⓔ
V4, Pg. 136	PT55-S3-Q15	ⓐ ⓑ ⓒ ⓓ ⓔ	PT76, Pg. 40	PT76-S4-Q22	ⓐ ⓑ ⓒ ⓓ ⓔ
V4, Pg. 171	PT56-S3-Q24	ⓐ ⓑ ⓒ ⓓ ⓔ	PT77, Pg. 40	PT77-S4-Q23	ⓐ ⓑ ⓒ ⓓ ⓔ

Parallel (Flaw)

J07, Pg. 6	J07-S2-Q2	ⓐ ⓑ ⓒ ⓓ ⓔ	SP1, Pg. 74	PTA-S1-Q22	ⓐ ⓑ ⓒ ⓓ ⓔ
J07, Pg. 20	J07-S3-Q20	ⓐ ⓑ ⓒ ⓓ ⓔ	SP1, Pg. 92	PTA-S4-Q14	ⓐ ⓑ ⓒ ⓓ ⓔ

SP1, Pg. 192	PTB-S1-Q22	Ⓐ Ⓑ Ⓒ Ⓓ Ⓔ	V1, Pg. 343	PT18-S4-Q3	Ⓐ Ⓑ Ⓒ Ⓓ Ⓔ
SP1, Pg. 212	PTB-S4-Q23	Ⓐ Ⓑ Ⓒ Ⓓ Ⓔ	V2, Pg. 26	PT19-S2-Q22	Ⓐ Ⓑ Ⓒ Ⓓ Ⓔ
SP1, Pg. 306	PTC-S2-Q21	Ⓐ Ⓑ Ⓒ Ⓓ Ⓔ	V2, Pg. 41	PT19-S4-Q21	Ⓐ Ⓑ Ⓒ Ⓓ Ⓔ
SP1, Pg. 311	PTC-S3-Q14	Ⓐ Ⓑ Ⓒ Ⓓ Ⓔ	V2, Pg. 54	PT20-S1-Q17	Ⓐ Ⓑ Ⓒ Ⓓ Ⓔ
SP2, Pg. 358	PTC2-S2-Q18	Ⓐ Ⓑ Ⓒ Ⓓ Ⓔ	V2, Pg. 75	PT20-S4-Q20	Ⓐ Ⓑ Ⓒ Ⓓ Ⓔ
SP2, Pg. 368	PTC2-S3-Q23	Ⓐ Ⓑ Ⓒ Ⓓ Ⓔ	V2, Pg. 92	PT21-S2-Q15	Ⓐ Ⓑ Ⓒ Ⓓ Ⓔ
	PT1-S4-Q10	Ⓐ Ⓑ Ⓒ Ⓓ Ⓔ	V2, Pg. 94	PT21-S2-Q21	Ⓐ Ⓑ Ⓒ Ⓓ Ⓔ
	PT2-S2-Q20	Ⓐ Ⓑ Ⓒ Ⓓ Ⓔ	V2, Pg. 103	PT21-S3-Q25	Ⓐ Ⓑ Ⓒ Ⓓ Ⓔ
	PT2-S4-Q22	Ⓐ Ⓑ Ⓒ Ⓓ Ⓔ	V2, Pg. 132	PT22-S2-Q23	Ⓐ Ⓑ Ⓒ Ⓓ Ⓔ
	PT4-S1-Q24	Ⓐ Ⓑ Ⓒ Ⓓ Ⓔ	V2, Pg. 139	PT22-S4-Q6	Ⓐ Ⓑ Ⓒ Ⓓ Ⓔ
	PT5-S1-Q22	Ⓐ Ⓑ Ⓒ Ⓓ Ⓔ	V2, Pg. 162	PT23-S2-Q23	Ⓐ Ⓑ Ⓒ Ⓓ Ⓔ
	PT5-S3-Q15	Ⓐ Ⓑ Ⓒ Ⓓ Ⓔ	V2, Pg. 170	PT23-S3-Q23	Ⓐ Ⓑ Ⓒ Ⓓ Ⓔ
	PT6-S2-Q5	Ⓐ Ⓑ Ⓒ Ⓓ Ⓔ	V2, Pg. 195	PT24-S2-Q5	Ⓐ Ⓑ Ⓒ Ⓓ Ⓔ
	PT6-S3-Q10	Ⓐ Ⓑ Ⓒ Ⓓ Ⓔ	V2, Pg. 206	PT24-S3-Q16	Ⓐ Ⓑ Ⓒ Ⓓ Ⓔ
V1, Pg. 21	PT7-S1-Q20	Ⓐ Ⓑ Ⓒ Ⓓ Ⓔ	V2, Pg. 228	PT25-S2-Q2	Ⓐ Ⓑ Ⓒ Ⓓ Ⓔ
V1, Pg. 40	PT7-S4-Q14	Ⓐ Ⓑ Ⓒ Ⓓ Ⓔ	V2, Pg. 243	PT25-S4-Q12	Ⓐ Ⓑ Ⓒ Ⓓ Ⓔ
	PT8-S1-Q25	Ⓐ Ⓑ Ⓒ Ⓓ Ⓔ	V2, Pg. 263	PT26-S2-Q20	Ⓐ Ⓑ Ⓒ Ⓓ Ⓔ
	PT8-S4-Q3	Ⓐ Ⓑ Ⓒ Ⓓ Ⓔ	V2, Pg. 269	PT26-S3-Q13	Ⓐ Ⓑ Ⓒ Ⓓ Ⓔ
V1, Pg. 58	PT9-S2-Q1	Ⓐ Ⓑ Ⓒ Ⓓ Ⓔ	V2, Pg. 291	PT27-S1-Q11	Ⓐ Ⓑ Ⓒ Ⓓ Ⓔ
V1, Pg. 77	PT9-S4-Q24	Ⓐ Ⓑ Ⓒ Ⓓ Ⓔ	V2, Pg. 311	PT27-S4-Q13	Ⓐ Ⓑ Ⓒ Ⓓ Ⓔ
V1, Pg. 89	PT10-S1-Q20	Ⓐ Ⓑ Ⓒ Ⓓ Ⓔ	V2, Pg. 322	PT28-S1-Q3	Ⓐ Ⓑ Ⓒ Ⓓ Ⓔ
V1, Pg. 105	PT10-S4-Q5	Ⓐ Ⓑ Ⓒ Ⓓ Ⓔ	V2, Pg. 339	PT28-S3-Q21	Ⓐ Ⓑ Ⓒ Ⓓ Ⓔ
V1, Pg. 126	PT11-S2-Q17	Ⓐ Ⓑ Ⓒ Ⓓ Ⓔ	V3, Pg. 22	PT29-S1-Q23	Ⓐ Ⓑ Ⓒ Ⓓ Ⓔ
V1, Pg. 144	PT11-S4-Q20	Ⓐ Ⓑ Ⓒ Ⓓ Ⓔ	V3, Pg. 42	PT29-S4-Q21	Ⓐ Ⓑ Ⓒ Ⓓ Ⓔ
V1, Pg. 156	PT12-S1-Q17	Ⓐ Ⓑ Ⓒ Ⓓ Ⓔ	V3, Pg. 55	PT30-S2-Q6	Ⓐ Ⓑ Ⓒ Ⓓ Ⓔ
V1, Pg. 179	PT12-S4-Q23	Ⓐ Ⓑ Ⓒ Ⓓ Ⓔ	V3, Pg. 77	PT30-S4-Q25	Ⓐ Ⓑ Ⓒ Ⓓ Ⓔ
V1, Pg. 196	PT13-S2-Q23	Ⓐ Ⓑ Ⓒ Ⓓ Ⓔ	V3, Pg. 94	PT31-S2-Q21	Ⓐ Ⓑ Ⓒ Ⓓ Ⓔ
V1, Pg. 210	PT13-S4-Q15	Ⓐ Ⓑ Ⓒ Ⓓ Ⓔ	V3, Pg. 102	PT31-S3-Q23	Ⓐ Ⓑ Ⓒ Ⓓ Ⓔ
V1, Pg. 231	PT14-S2-Q25	Ⓐ Ⓑ Ⓒ Ⓓ Ⓔ	V3, Pg. 125	PT32-S1-Q22	Ⓐ Ⓑ Ⓒ Ⓓ Ⓔ
V1, Pg. 244	PT14-S4-Q14	Ⓐ Ⓑ Ⓒ Ⓓ Ⓔ	V3, Pg. 144	PT32-S4-Q21	Ⓐ Ⓑ Ⓒ Ⓓ Ⓔ
V1, Pg. 263	PT15-S2-Q4	Ⓐ Ⓑ Ⓒ Ⓓ Ⓔ	V3, Pg. 156	PT33-S1-Q15	Ⓐ Ⓑ Ⓒ Ⓓ Ⓔ
V1, Pg. 276	PT15-S3-Q22	Ⓐ Ⓑ Ⓒ Ⓓ Ⓔ	V3, Pg. 173	PT33-S3-Q18	Ⓐ Ⓑ Ⓒ Ⓓ Ⓔ
V1, Pg. 294	PT16-S2-Q7	Ⓐ Ⓑ Ⓒ Ⓓ Ⓔ	V3, Pg. 201	PT34-S2-Q24	Ⓐ Ⓑ Ⓒ Ⓓ Ⓔ
V1, Pg. 303	PT16-S3-Q15	Ⓐ Ⓑ Ⓒ Ⓓ Ⓔ	V3, Pg. 208	PT34-S3-Q23	Ⓐ Ⓑ Ⓒ Ⓓ Ⓔ
	PT17-S2-Q16	Ⓐ Ⓑ Ⓒ Ⓓ Ⓔ	V3, Pg. 227	PT35-S1-Q24	Ⓐ Ⓑ Ⓒ Ⓓ Ⓔ
	PT17-S3-Q19	Ⓐ Ⓑ Ⓒ Ⓓ Ⓔ	V3, Pg. 241	PT35-S4-Q6	Ⓐ Ⓑ Ⓒ Ⓓ Ⓔ
V1, Pg. 331	PT18-S2-Q17	Ⓐ Ⓑ Ⓒ Ⓓ Ⓔ	V3, Pg. 260	PT36-S1-Q21	Ⓐ Ⓑ Ⓒ Ⓓ Ⓔ

V3, Pg. 275	PT36-S3-Q19	Ⓐ Ⓑ Ⓒ Ⓓ Ⓔ	V4, Pg. 116	PT55-S1-Q1	Ⓐ Ⓑ Ⓒ Ⓓ Ⓔ
V3, Pg. 301	PT37-S2-Q21	Ⓐ Ⓑ Ⓒ Ⓓ Ⓔ	V4, Pg. 139	PT55-S3-Q23	Ⓐ Ⓑ Ⓒ Ⓓ Ⓔ
V3, Pg. 309	PT37-S4-Q4	Ⓐ Ⓑ Ⓒ Ⓓ Ⓔ	V4, Pg. 157	PT56-S2-Q7	Ⓐ Ⓑ Ⓒ Ⓓ Ⓔ
V3, Pg. 326	PT38-S1-Q16	Ⓐ Ⓑ Ⓒ Ⓓ Ⓔ	V4, Pg. 167	PT56-S3-Q14	Ⓐ Ⓑ Ⓒ Ⓓ Ⓔ
V3, Pg. 346	PT38-S4-Q17	Ⓐ Ⓑ Ⓒ Ⓓ Ⓔ	V4, Pg. 194	PT57-S2-Q8	Ⓐ Ⓑ Ⓒ Ⓓ Ⓔ
	PT39-S2-Q18	Ⓐ Ⓑ Ⓒ Ⓓ Ⓔ	V4, Pg. 204	PT57-S3-Q15	Ⓐ Ⓑ Ⓒ Ⓓ Ⓔ
	PT39-S4-Q26	Ⓐ Ⓑ Ⓒ Ⓓ Ⓔ	V4, Pg. 226	PT58-S1-Q7	Ⓐ Ⓑ Ⓒ Ⓓ Ⓔ
	PT40-S1-Q20	Ⓐ Ⓑ Ⓒ Ⓓ Ⓔ	V4, Pg. 250	PT58-S4-Q22	Ⓐ Ⓑ Ⓒ Ⓓ Ⓔ
	PT40-S3-Q17	Ⓐ Ⓑ Ⓒ Ⓓ Ⓔ	V4, Pg. 266	PT59-S2-Q9	Ⓐ Ⓑ Ⓒ Ⓓ Ⓔ
	PT41-S1-Q23	Ⓐ Ⓑ Ⓒ Ⓓ Ⓔ	V4, Pg. 276	PT59-S3-Q15	Ⓐ Ⓑ Ⓒ Ⓓ Ⓔ
	PT41-S3-Q8	Ⓐ Ⓑ Ⓒ Ⓓ Ⓔ	V4, Pg. 302	PT60-S1-Q21	Ⓐ Ⓑ Ⓒ Ⓓ Ⓔ
	PT42-S2-Q24	Ⓐ Ⓑ Ⓒ Ⓓ Ⓔ	V4, Pg. 314	PT60-S3-Q23	Ⓐ Ⓑ Ⓒ Ⓓ Ⓔ
	PT42-S4-Q22	Ⓐ Ⓑ Ⓒ Ⓓ Ⓔ	V4, Pg. 346	PT61-S2-Q23	Ⓐ Ⓑ Ⓒ Ⓓ Ⓔ
	PT43-S2-Q24	Ⓐ Ⓑ Ⓒ Ⓓ Ⓔ	V4, Pg. 359	PT61-S4-Q26	Ⓐ Ⓑ Ⓒ Ⓓ Ⓔ
	PT43-S3-Q22	Ⓐ Ⓑ Ⓒ Ⓓ Ⓔ	V5, Pg. 17	PT62-S2-Q7	Ⓐ Ⓑ Ⓒ Ⓓ Ⓔ
	PT44-S2-Q22	Ⓐ Ⓑ Ⓒ Ⓓ Ⓔ	V5, Pg. 30	PT62-S4-Q9	Ⓐ Ⓑ Ⓒ Ⓓ Ⓔ
	PT44-S4-Q19	Ⓐ Ⓑ Ⓒ Ⓓ Ⓔ	V5, Pg. 51	PT63-S1-Q24	Ⓐ Ⓑ Ⓒ Ⓓ Ⓔ
	PT45-S1-Q11	Ⓐ Ⓑ Ⓒ Ⓓ Ⓔ	V5, Pg. 63	PT63-S3-Q25	Ⓐ Ⓑ Ⓒ Ⓓ Ⓔ
	PT45-S4-Q20	Ⓐ Ⓑ Ⓒ Ⓓ Ⓔ	V5, Pg. 82	PT64-S1-Q9	Ⓐ Ⓑ Ⓒ Ⓓ Ⓔ
	PT46-S2-Q20	Ⓐ Ⓑ Ⓒ Ⓓ Ⓔ	V5, Pg. 98	PT64-S3-Q23	Ⓐ Ⓑ Ⓒ Ⓓ Ⓔ
	PT46-S3-Q19	Ⓐ Ⓑ Ⓒ Ⓓ Ⓔ	V5, Pg. 119	PT65-S1-Q11	Ⓐ Ⓑ Ⓒ Ⓓ Ⓔ
	PT47-S1-Q21	Ⓐ Ⓑ Ⓒ Ⓓ Ⓔ	V5, Pg. 142	PT65-S4-Q24	Ⓐ Ⓑ Ⓒ Ⓓ Ⓔ
	PT47-S3-Q25	Ⓐ Ⓑ Ⓒ Ⓓ Ⓔ	V5, Pg. 167	PT66-S2-Q24	Ⓐ Ⓑ Ⓒ Ⓓ Ⓔ
	PT48-S1-Q23	Ⓐ Ⓑ Ⓒ Ⓓ Ⓔ	V5, Pg. 182	PT66-S4-Q24	Ⓐ Ⓑ Ⓒ Ⓓ Ⓔ
	PT48-S4-Q4	Ⓐ Ⓑ Ⓒ Ⓓ Ⓔ	V5, Pg. 207	PT67-S2-Q23	Ⓐ Ⓑ Ⓒ Ⓓ Ⓔ
	PT49-S2-Q26	Ⓐ Ⓑ Ⓒ Ⓓ Ⓔ	V5, Pg. 223	PT67-S4-Q25	Ⓐ Ⓑ Ⓒ Ⓓ Ⓔ
	PT49-S4-Q24	Ⓐ Ⓑ Ⓒ Ⓓ Ⓔ	V5, Pg. 247	PT68-S2-Q25	Ⓐ Ⓑ Ⓒ Ⓓ Ⓔ
	PT50-S2-Q17	Ⓐ Ⓑ Ⓒ Ⓓ Ⓔ	V5, Pg. 255	PT68-S3-Q24	Ⓐ Ⓑ Ⓒ Ⓓ Ⓔ
	PT50-S4-Q24	Ⓐ Ⓑ Ⓒ Ⓓ Ⓔ	V5, Pg. 276	PT69-S1-Q14	Ⓐ Ⓑ Ⓒ Ⓓ Ⓔ
	PT51-S1-Q20	Ⓐ Ⓑ Ⓒ Ⓓ Ⓔ	V5, Pg. 300	PT69-S4-Q14	Ⓐ Ⓑ Ⓒ Ⓓ Ⓔ
	PT51-S3-Q22	Ⓐ Ⓑ Ⓒ Ⓓ Ⓔ	V5, Pg. 314	PT70-S1-Q10	Ⓐ Ⓑ Ⓒ Ⓓ Ⓔ
V4, Pg. 12	PT52-S1-Q16	Ⓐ Ⓑ Ⓒ Ⓓ Ⓔ	V5, Pg. 342	PT70-S4-Q23	Ⓐ Ⓑ Ⓒ Ⓓ Ⓔ
V4, Pg. 27	PT52-S3-Q24	Ⓐ Ⓑ Ⓒ Ⓓ Ⓔ	V5, Pg. 358	PT71-S1-Q23	Ⓐ Ⓑ Ⓒ Ⓓ Ⓔ
V4, Pg. 50	PT53-S1-Q21	Ⓐ Ⓑ Ⓒ Ⓓ Ⓔ	V5, Pg. 372	PT71-S3-Q15	Ⓐ Ⓑ Ⓒ Ⓓ Ⓔ
V4, Pg. 59	PT53-S3-Q13	Ⓐ Ⓑ Ⓒ Ⓓ Ⓔ	PT72, Pg. 24	PT72-S2-Q22	Ⓐ Ⓑ Ⓒ Ⓓ Ⓔ
V4, Pg. 94	PT54-S2-Q21	Ⓐ Ⓑ Ⓒ Ⓓ Ⓔ	PT72, Pg. 33	PT72-S3-Q25	Ⓐ Ⓑ Ⓒ Ⓓ Ⓔ
V4, Pg. 102	PT54-S4-Q8	Ⓐ Ⓑ Ⓒ Ⓓ Ⓔ	PT73, Pg. 20	PT73-S2-Q7	Ⓐ Ⓑ Ⓒ Ⓓ Ⓔ

PT73, Pg. 39	PT73-S4-Q18	Ⓐ Ⓑ Ⓒ Ⓓ Ⓔ	PT75, Pg. 29	PT75-S3-Q14	Ⓐ Ⓑ Ⓒ Ⓓ Ⓔ
PT74, Pg. 17	PT74-S1-Q25	Ⓐ Ⓑ Ⓒ Ⓓ Ⓔ	PT76, Pg. 24	PT76-S2-Q21	Ⓐ Ⓑ Ⓒ Ⓓ Ⓔ
PT74, Pg. 41	PT74-S4-Q25	Ⓐ Ⓑ Ⓒ Ⓓ Ⓔ	PT76, Pg. 35	PT76-S4-Q6	Ⓐ Ⓑ Ⓒ Ⓓ Ⓔ
PT75, Pg. 16	PT75-S1-Q22	Ⓐ Ⓑ Ⓒ Ⓓ Ⓔ	PT77, Pg. 19	PT77-S2-Q5	Ⓐ Ⓑ Ⓒ Ⓓ Ⓔ
PT75, Pg. 28	PT75-S3-Q10	Ⓐ Ⓑ Ⓒ Ⓓ Ⓔ	PT77, Pg. 41	PT77-S4-Q25	Ⓐ Ⓑ Ⓒ Ⓓ Ⓔ

Paradox

J07, Pg. 13	J07-S2-Q25	Ⓐ Ⓑ Ⓒ Ⓓ Ⓔ		PT6-S2-Q8	Ⓐ Ⓑ Ⓒ Ⓓ Ⓔ
J07, Pg. 14	J07-S3-Q2	Ⓐ Ⓑ Ⓒ Ⓓ Ⓔ		PT6-S2-Q12	Ⓐ Ⓑ Ⓒ Ⓓ Ⓔ
SP1, Pg. 71	PTA-S1-Q12	Ⓐ Ⓑ Ⓒ Ⓓ Ⓔ		PT6-S2-Q16	Ⓐ Ⓑ Ⓒ Ⓓ Ⓔ
SP1, Pg. 74	PTA-S1-Q20	Ⓐ Ⓑ Ⓒ Ⓓ Ⓔ		PT6-S3-Q6	Ⓐ Ⓑ Ⓒ Ⓓ Ⓔ
SP1, Pg. 75	PTA-S1-Q25	Ⓐ Ⓑ Ⓒ Ⓓ Ⓔ	V1, Pg. 19	PT7-S1-Q11	Ⓐ Ⓑ Ⓒ Ⓓ Ⓔ
SP1, Pg. 88	PTA-S4-Q1	Ⓐ Ⓑ Ⓒ Ⓓ Ⓔ	V1, Pg. 23	PT7-S1-Q25	Ⓐ Ⓑ Ⓒ Ⓓ Ⓔ
SP1, Pg. 91	PTA-S4-Q12	Ⓐ Ⓑ Ⓒ Ⓓ Ⓔ	V1, Pg. 41	PT7-S4-Q17	Ⓐ Ⓑ Ⓒ Ⓓ Ⓔ
SP1, Pg. 193	PTB-S1-Q25	Ⓐ Ⓑ Ⓒ Ⓓ Ⓔ		PT8-S1-Q1	Ⓐ Ⓑ Ⓒ Ⓓ Ⓔ
SP1, Pg. 206	PTB-S4-Q2	Ⓐ Ⓑ Ⓒ Ⓓ Ⓔ		PT8-S4-Q2	Ⓐ Ⓑ Ⓒ Ⓓ Ⓔ
SP1, Pg. 301	PTC-S2-Q4	Ⓐ Ⓑ Ⓒ Ⓓ Ⓔ		PT8-S4-Q4	Ⓐ Ⓑ Ⓒ Ⓓ Ⓔ
SP1, Pg. 309	PTC-S3-Q3	Ⓐ Ⓑ Ⓒ Ⓓ Ⓔ		PT8-S4-Q19	Ⓐ Ⓑ Ⓒ Ⓓ Ⓔ
SP1, Pg. 309	PTC-S3-Q6	Ⓐ Ⓑ Ⓒ Ⓓ Ⓔ	V1, Pg. 59	PT9-S2-Q6	Ⓐ Ⓑ Ⓒ Ⓓ Ⓔ
SP1, Pg. 312	PTC-S3-Q17	Ⓐ Ⓑ Ⓒ Ⓓ Ⓔ	V1, Pg. 60	PT9-S2-Q8	Ⓐ Ⓑ Ⓒ Ⓓ Ⓔ
SP2, Pg. 355	PTC2-S2-Q4	Ⓐ Ⓑ Ⓒ Ⓓ Ⓔ	V1, Pg. 70	PT9-S4-Q3	Ⓐ Ⓑ Ⓒ Ⓓ Ⓔ
SP2, Pg. 359	PTC2-S2-Q19	Ⓐ Ⓑ Ⓒ Ⓓ Ⓔ	V1, Pg. 84	PT10-S1-Q2	Ⓐ Ⓑ Ⓒ Ⓓ Ⓔ
SP2, Pg. 365	PTC2-S3-Q15	Ⓐ Ⓑ Ⓒ Ⓓ Ⓔ	V1, Pg. 87	PT10-S1-Q14	Ⓐ Ⓑ Ⓒ Ⓓ Ⓔ
	PT1-S3-Q1	Ⓐ Ⓑ Ⓒ Ⓓ Ⓔ	V1, Pg. 109	PT10-S4-Q17	Ⓐ Ⓑ Ⓒ Ⓓ Ⓔ
	PT1-S3-Q18	Ⓐ Ⓑ Ⓒ Ⓓ Ⓔ	V1, Pg. 111	PT10-S4-Q23	Ⓐ Ⓑ Ⓒ Ⓓ Ⓔ
	PT1-S4-Q17	Ⓐ Ⓑ Ⓒ Ⓓ Ⓔ	V1, Pg. 128	PT11-S2-Q23	Ⓐ Ⓑ Ⓒ Ⓓ Ⓔ
	PT2-S2-Q4	Ⓐ Ⓑ Ⓒ Ⓓ Ⓔ	V1, Pg. 138	PT11-S4-Q1	Ⓐ Ⓑ Ⓒ Ⓓ Ⓔ
	PT2-S4-Q12	Ⓐ Ⓑ Ⓒ Ⓓ Ⓔ	V1, Pg. 153	PT12-S1-Q4	Ⓐ Ⓑ Ⓒ Ⓓ Ⓔ
	PT3-S2-Q8	Ⓐ Ⓑ Ⓒ Ⓓ Ⓔ	V1, Pg. 154	PT12-S1-Q7	Ⓐ Ⓑ Ⓒ Ⓓ Ⓔ
	PT3-S4-Q8	Ⓐ Ⓑ Ⓒ Ⓓ Ⓔ	V1, Pg. 155	PT12-S1-Q12	Ⓐ Ⓑ Ⓒ Ⓓ Ⓔ
	PT4-S1-Q14	Ⓐ Ⓑ Ⓒ Ⓓ Ⓔ	V1, Pg. 175	PT12-S4-Q12	Ⓐ Ⓑ Ⓒ Ⓓ Ⓔ
	PT4-S4-Q2	Ⓐ Ⓑ Ⓒ Ⓓ Ⓔ	V1, Pg. 178	PT12-S4-Q22	Ⓐ Ⓑ Ⓒ Ⓓ Ⓔ
	PT4-S4-Q25	Ⓐ Ⓑ Ⓒ Ⓓ Ⓔ	V1, Pg. 190	PT13-S2-Q3	Ⓐ Ⓑ Ⓒ Ⓓ Ⓔ
	PT5-S1-Q14	Ⓐ Ⓑ Ⓒ Ⓓ Ⓔ	V1, Pg. 194	PT13-S2-Q15	Ⓐ Ⓑ Ⓒ Ⓓ Ⓔ
	PT5-S1-Q19	Ⓐ Ⓑ Ⓒ Ⓓ Ⓔ	V1, Pg. 195	PT13-S2-Q19	Ⓐ Ⓑ Ⓒ Ⓓ Ⓔ
	PT5-S3-Q13	Ⓐ Ⓑ Ⓒ Ⓓ Ⓔ	V1, Pg. 206	PT13-S4-Q2	Ⓐ Ⓑ Ⓒ Ⓓ Ⓔ
	PT5-S3-Q20	Ⓐ Ⓑ Ⓒ Ⓓ Ⓔ	V1, Pg. 208	PT13-S4-Q10	Ⓐ Ⓑ Ⓒ Ⓓ Ⓔ

V1, Pg. 209	PT13-S4-Q13	Ⓐ Ⓑ Ⓒ Ⓓ Ⓔ	V2, Pg. 233	PT25-S2-Q17	Ⓐ Ⓑ Ⓒ Ⓓ Ⓔ
V1, Pg. 224	PT14-S2-Q1	Ⓐ Ⓑ Ⓒ Ⓓ Ⓔ	V2, Pg. 244	PT25-S4-Q13	Ⓐ Ⓑ Ⓒ Ⓓ Ⓔ
V1, Pg. 225	PT14-S2-Q3	Ⓐ Ⓑ Ⓒ Ⓓ Ⓔ	V2, Pg. 261	PT26-S2-Q14	Ⓐ Ⓑ Ⓒ Ⓓ Ⓔ
V1, Pg. 225	PT14-S2-Q5	Ⓐ Ⓑ Ⓒ Ⓓ Ⓔ	V2, Pg. 263	PT26-S2-Q18	Ⓐ Ⓑ Ⓒ Ⓓ Ⓔ
V1, Pg. 240	PT14-S4-Q1	Ⓐ Ⓑ Ⓒ Ⓓ Ⓔ	V2, Pg. 266	PT26-S3-Q1	Ⓐ Ⓑ Ⓒ Ⓓ Ⓔ
V1, Pg. 241	PT14-S4-Q3	Ⓐ Ⓑ Ⓒ Ⓓ Ⓔ	V2, Pg. 271	PT26-S3-Q18	Ⓐ Ⓑ Ⓒ Ⓓ Ⓔ
V1, Pg. 263	PT15-S2-Q5	Ⓐ Ⓑ Ⓒ Ⓓ Ⓔ	V2, Pg. 290	PT27-S1-Q7	Ⓐ Ⓑ Ⓒ Ⓓ Ⓔ
V1, Pg. 265	PT15-S2-Q10	Ⓐ Ⓑ Ⓒ Ⓓ Ⓔ	V2, Pg. 310	PT27-S4-Q8	Ⓐ Ⓑ Ⓒ Ⓓ Ⓔ
V1, Pg. 275	PT15-S3-Q20	Ⓐ Ⓑ Ⓒ Ⓓ Ⓔ	V2, Pg. 324	PT28-S1-Q8	Ⓐ Ⓑ Ⓒ Ⓓ Ⓔ
V1, Pg. 292	PT16-S2-Q1	Ⓐ Ⓑ Ⓒ Ⓓ Ⓔ	V2, Pg. 326	PT28-S1-Q17	Ⓐ Ⓑ Ⓒ Ⓓ Ⓔ
V1, Pg. 293	PT16-S2-Q4	Ⓐ Ⓑ Ⓒ Ⓓ Ⓔ	V2, Pg. 334	PT28-S3-Q3	Ⓐ Ⓑ Ⓒ Ⓓ Ⓔ
V1, Pg. 296	PT16-S2-Q15	Ⓐ Ⓑ Ⓒ Ⓓ Ⓔ	V3, Pg. 16	PT29-S1-Q4	Ⓐ Ⓑ Ⓒ Ⓓ Ⓔ
V1, Pg. 302	PT16-S3-Q10	Ⓐ Ⓑ Ⓒ Ⓓ Ⓔ	V3, Pg. 18	PT29-S1-Q10	Ⓐ Ⓑ Ⓒ Ⓓ Ⓔ
V1, Pg. 304	PT16-S3-Q17	Ⓐ Ⓑ Ⓒ Ⓓ Ⓔ	V3, Pg. 23	PT29-S1-Q25	Ⓐ Ⓑ Ⓒ Ⓓ Ⓔ
	PT17-S2-Q14	Ⓐ Ⓑ Ⓒ Ⓓ Ⓔ	V3, Pg. 41	PT29-S4-Q19	Ⓐ Ⓑ Ⓒ Ⓓ Ⓔ
	PT17-S3-Q2	Ⓐ Ⓑ Ⓒ Ⓓ Ⓔ	V3, Pg. 57	PT30-S2-Q12	Ⓐ Ⓑ Ⓒ Ⓓ Ⓔ
V1, Pg. 329	PT18-S2-Q11	Ⓐ Ⓑ Ⓒ Ⓓ Ⓔ	V3, Pg. 71	PT30-S4-Q5	Ⓐ Ⓑ Ⓒ Ⓓ Ⓔ
V1, Pg. 332	PT18-S2-Q19	Ⓐ Ⓑ Ⓒ Ⓓ Ⓔ	V3, Pg. 91	PT31-S2-Q11	Ⓐ Ⓑ Ⓒ Ⓓ Ⓔ
V1, Pg. 333	PT18-S2-Q22	Ⓐ Ⓑ Ⓒ Ⓓ Ⓔ	V3, Pg. 92	PT31-S2-Q13	Ⓐ Ⓑ Ⓒ Ⓓ Ⓔ
V1, Pg. 345	PT18-S4-Q13	Ⓐ Ⓑ Ⓒ Ⓓ Ⓔ	V3, Pg. 96	PT31-S3-Q2	Ⓐ Ⓑ Ⓒ Ⓓ Ⓔ
V1, Pg. 346	PT18-S4-Q15	Ⓐ Ⓑ Ⓒ Ⓓ Ⓔ	V3, Pg. 97	PT31-S3-Q7	Ⓐ Ⓑ Ⓒ Ⓓ Ⓔ
V2, Pg. 21	PT19-S2-Q5	Ⓐ Ⓑ Ⓒ Ⓓ Ⓔ	V3, Pg. 118	PT32-S1-Q2	Ⓐ Ⓑ Ⓒ Ⓓ Ⓔ
V2, Pg. 41	PT19-S4-Q20	Ⓐ Ⓑ Ⓒ Ⓓ Ⓔ	V3, Pg. 139	PT32-S4-Q5	Ⓐ Ⓑ Ⓒ Ⓓ Ⓔ
V2, Pg. 42	PT19-S4-Q23	Ⓐ Ⓑ Ⓒ Ⓓ Ⓔ	V3, Pg. 142	PT32-S4-Q17	Ⓐ Ⓑ Ⓒ Ⓓ Ⓔ
V2, Pg. 55	PT20-S1-Q18	Ⓐ Ⓑ Ⓒ Ⓓ Ⓔ	V3, Pg. 154	PT33-S1-Q8	Ⓐ Ⓑ Ⓒ Ⓓ Ⓔ
V2, Pg. 77	PT20-S4-Q26	Ⓐ Ⓑ Ⓒ Ⓓ Ⓔ	V3, Pg. 156	PT33-S1-Q14	Ⓐ Ⓑ Ⓒ Ⓓ Ⓔ
V2, Pg. 88	PT21-S2-Q2	Ⓐ Ⓑ Ⓒ Ⓓ Ⓔ	V3, Pg. 168	PT33-S3-Q1	Ⓐ Ⓑ Ⓒ Ⓓ Ⓔ
V2, Pg. 89	PT21-S2-Q4	Ⓐ Ⓑ Ⓒ Ⓓ Ⓔ	V3, Pg. 169	PT33-S3-Q3	Ⓐ Ⓑ Ⓒ Ⓓ Ⓔ
V2, Pg. 96	PT21-S3-Q3	Ⓐ Ⓑ Ⓒ Ⓓ Ⓔ	V3, Pg. 195	PT34-S2-Q5	Ⓐ Ⓑ Ⓒ Ⓓ Ⓔ
V2, Pg. 97	PT21-S3-Q7	Ⓐ Ⓑ Ⓒ Ⓓ Ⓔ	V3, Pg. 196	PT34-S2-Q7	Ⓐ Ⓑ Ⓒ Ⓓ Ⓔ
V2, Pg. 131	PT22-S2-Q21	Ⓐ Ⓑ Ⓒ Ⓓ Ⓔ	V3, Pg. 202	PT34-S3-Q2	Ⓐ Ⓑ Ⓒ Ⓓ Ⓔ
V2, Pg. 142	PT22-S4-Q17	Ⓐ Ⓑ Ⓒ Ⓓ Ⓔ	V3, Pg. 222	PT35-S1-Q10	Ⓐ Ⓑ Ⓒ Ⓓ Ⓔ
V2, Pg. 161	PT23-S2-Q22	Ⓐ Ⓑ Ⓒ Ⓓ Ⓔ	V3, Pg. 226	PT35-S1-Q21	Ⓐ Ⓑ Ⓒ Ⓓ Ⓔ
V2, Pg. 164	PT23-S3-Q2	Ⓐ Ⓑ Ⓒ Ⓓ Ⓔ	V3, Pg. 227	PT35-S1-Q25	Ⓐ Ⓑ Ⓒ Ⓓ Ⓔ
V2, Pg. 199	PT24-S2-Q18	Ⓐ Ⓑ Ⓒ Ⓓ Ⓔ	V3, Pg. 241	PT35-S4-Q4	Ⓐ Ⓑ Ⓒ Ⓓ Ⓔ
V2, Pg. 205	PT24-S3-Q14	Ⓐ Ⓑ Ⓒ Ⓓ Ⓔ	V3, Pg. 243	PT35-S4-Q12	Ⓐ Ⓑ Ⓒ Ⓓ Ⓔ
V2, Pg. 232	PT25-S2-Q14	Ⓐ Ⓑ Ⓒ Ⓓ Ⓔ	V3, Pg. 257	PT36-S1-Q9	Ⓐ Ⓑ Ⓒ Ⓓ Ⓔ

V3, Pg. 258	PT36-S1-Q13	Ⓐ Ⓑ Ⓒ Ⓓ Ⓔ		PT46-S3-Q1	Ⓐ Ⓑ Ⓒ Ⓓ Ⓔ
V3, Pg. 260	PT36-S1-Q23	Ⓐ Ⓑ Ⓒ Ⓓ Ⓔ		PT47-S1-Q6	Ⓐ Ⓑ Ⓒ Ⓓ Ⓔ
V3, Pg. 270	PT36-S3-Q1	Ⓐ Ⓑ Ⓒ Ⓓ Ⓔ		PT47-S3-Q11	Ⓐ Ⓑ Ⓒ Ⓓ Ⓔ
V3, Pg. 298	PT37-S2-Q8	Ⓐ Ⓑ Ⓒ Ⓓ Ⓔ		PT47-S3-Q15	Ⓐ Ⓑ Ⓒ Ⓓ Ⓔ
V3, Pg. 300	PT37-S2-Q17	Ⓐ Ⓑ Ⓒ Ⓓ Ⓔ		PT48-S1-Q22	Ⓐ Ⓑ Ⓒ Ⓓ Ⓔ
V3, Pg. 309	PT37-S4-Q5	Ⓐ Ⓑ Ⓒ Ⓓ Ⓔ		PT48-S4-Q7	Ⓐ Ⓑ Ⓒ Ⓓ Ⓔ
V3, Pg. 324	PT38-S1-Q9	Ⓐ Ⓑ Ⓒ Ⓓ Ⓔ		PT48-S4-Q19	Ⓐ Ⓑ Ⓒ Ⓓ Ⓔ
V3, Pg. 344	PT38-S4-Q9	Ⓐ Ⓑ Ⓒ Ⓓ Ⓔ		PT48-S4-Q24	Ⓐ Ⓑ Ⓒ Ⓓ Ⓔ
	PT39-S2-Q3	Ⓐ Ⓑ Ⓒ Ⓓ Ⓔ		PT49-S2-Q2	Ⓐ Ⓑ Ⓒ Ⓓ Ⓔ
	PT39-S2-Q5	Ⓐ Ⓑ Ⓒ Ⓓ Ⓔ		PT49-S4-Q11	Ⓐ Ⓑ Ⓒ Ⓓ Ⓔ
	PT39-S4-Q5	Ⓐ Ⓑ Ⓒ Ⓓ Ⓔ		PT49-S4-Q25	Ⓐ Ⓑ Ⓒ Ⓓ Ⓔ
	PT39-S4-Q9	Ⓐ Ⓑ Ⓒ Ⓓ Ⓔ		PT50-S2-Q5	Ⓐ Ⓑ Ⓒ Ⓓ Ⓔ
	PT39-S4-Q12	Ⓐ Ⓑ Ⓒ Ⓓ Ⓔ		PT50-S2-Q8	Ⓐ Ⓑ Ⓒ Ⓓ Ⓔ
	PT40-S1-Q1	Ⓐ Ⓑ Ⓒ Ⓓ Ⓔ		PT50-S2-Q21	Ⓐ Ⓑ Ⓒ Ⓓ Ⓔ
	PT40-S3-Q1	Ⓐ Ⓑ Ⓒ Ⓓ Ⓔ		PT50-S4-Q16	Ⓐ Ⓑ Ⓒ Ⓓ Ⓔ
	PT40-S3-Q7	Ⓐ Ⓑ Ⓒ Ⓓ Ⓔ		PT51-S1-Q3	Ⓐ Ⓑ Ⓒ Ⓓ Ⓔ
	PT41-S1-Q2	Ⓐ Ⓑ Ⓒ Ⓓ Ⓔ		PT51-S1-Q22	Ⓐ Ⓑ Ⓒ Ⓓ Ⓔ
	PT41-S1-Q4	Ⓐ Ⓑ Ⓒ Ⓓ Ⓔ		PT51-S3-Q8	Ⓐ Ⓑ Ⓒ Ⓓ Ⓔ
	PT41-S1-Q8	Ⓐ Ⓑ Ⓒ Ⓓ Ⓔ		PT51-S3-Q10	Ⓐ Ⓑ Ⓒ Ⓓ Ⓔ
	PT41-S3-Q1	Ⓐ Ⓑ Ⓒ Ⓓ Ⓔ	V4, Pg. 11	PT52-S1-Q11	Ⓐ Ⓑ Ⓒ Ⓓ Ⓔ
	PT41-S3-Q5	Ⓐ Ⓑ Ⓒ Ⓓ Ⓔ	V4, Pg. 12	PT52-S1-Q14	Ⓐ Ⓑ Ⓒ Ⓓ Ⓔ
	PT41-S3-Q21	Ⓐ Ⓑ Ⓒ Ⓓ Ⓔ	V4, Pg. 25	PT52-S3-Q20	Ⓐ Ⓑ Ⓒ Ⓓ Ⓔ
	PT42-S2-Q5	Ⓐ Ⓑ Ⓒ Ⓓ Ⓔ	V4, Pg. 26	PT52-S3-Q22	Ⓐ Ⓑ Ⓒ Ⓓ Ⓔ
	PT42-S4-Q5	Ⓐ Ⓑ Ⓒ Ⓓ Ⓔ	V4, Pg. 51	PT53-S1-Q24	Ⓐ Ⓑ Ⓒ Ⓓ Ⓔ
	PT42-S4-Q11	Ⓐ Ⓑ Ⓒ Ⓓ Ⓔ	V4, Pg. 62	PT53-S3-Q22	Ⓐ Ⓑ Ⓒ Ⓓ Ⓔ
	PT42-S4-Q24	Ⓐ Ⓑ Ⓒ Ⓓ Ⓔ	V4, Pg. 88	PT54-S2-Q4	Ⓐ Ⓑ Ⓒ Ⓓ Ⓔ
	PT43-S2-Q3	Ⓐ Ⓑ Ⓒ Ⓓ Ⓔ	V4, Pg. 101	PT54-S4-Q6	Ⓐ Ⓑ Ⓒ Ⓓ Ⓔ
	PT43-S2-Q15	Ⓐ Ⓑ Ⓒ Ⓓ Ⓔ	V4, Pg. 104	PT54-S4-Q13	Ⓐ Ⓑ Ⓒ Ⓓ Ⓔ
	PT43-S2-Q25	Ⓐ Ⓑ Ⓒ Ⓓ Ⓔ	V4, Pg. 106	PT54-S4-Q21	Ⓐ Ⓑ Ⓒ Ⓓ Ⓔ
	PT43-S3-Q13	Ⓐ Ⓑ Ⓒ Ⓓ Ⓔ	V4, Pg. 119	PT55-S1-Q13	Ⓐ Ⓑ Ⓒ Ⓓ Ⓔ
	PT43-S3-Q15	Ⓐ Ⓑ Ⓒ Ⓓ Ⓔ	V4, Pg. 132	PT55-S3-Q1	Ⓐ Ⓑ Ⓒ Ⓓ Ⓔ
	PT44-S2-Q3	Ⓐ Ⓑ Ⓒ Ⓓ Ⓔ	V4, Pg. 159	PT56-S2-Q13	Ⓐ Ⓑ Ⓒ Ⓓ Ⓔ
	PT44-S2-Q10	Ⓐ Ⓑ Ⓒ Ⓓ Ⓔ	V4, Pg. 162	PT56-S2-Q22	Ⓐ Ⓑ Ⓒ Ⓓ Ⓔ
	PT44-S4-Q25	Ⓐ Ⓑ Ⓒ Ⓓ Ⓔ	V4, Pg. 165	PT56-S3-Q7	Ⓐ Ⓑ Ⓒ Ⓓ Ⓔ
	PT45-S4-Q5	Ⓐ Ⓑ Ⓒ Ⓓ Ⓔ	V4, Pg. 193	PT57-S2-Q3	Ⓐ Ⓑ Ⓒ Ⓓ Ⓔ
	PT45-S4-Q15	Ⓐ Ⓑ Ⓒ Ⓓ Ⓔ	V4, Pg. 200	PT57-S3-Q1	Ⓐ Ⓑ Ⓒ Ⓓ Ⓔ
	PT46-S2-Q6	Ⓐ Ⓑ Ⓒ Ⓓ Ⓔ	V4, Pg. 201	PT57-S3-Q4	Ⓐ Ⓑ Ⓒ Ⓓ Ⓔ

V4, Pg. 201	PT57-S3-Q7	Ⓐ Ⓑ Ⓒ Ⓓ Ⓔ	V5, Pg. 201	PT67-S2-Q4	Ⓐ Ⓑ Ⓒ Ⓓ Ⓔ
V4, Pg. 226	PT58-S1-Q8	Ⓐ Ⓑ Ⓒ Ⓓ Ⓔ	V5, Pg. 216	PT67-S4-Q3	Ⓐ Ⓑ Ⓒ Ⓓ Ⓔ
V4, Pg. 228	PT58-S1-Q17	Ⓐ Ⓑ Ⓒ Ⓓ Ⓔ	V5, Pg. 223	PT67-S4-Q23	Ⓐ Ⓑ Ⓒ Ⓓ Ⓔ
V4, Pg. 244	PT58-S4-Q1	Ⓐ Ⓑ Ⓒ Ⓓ Ⓔ	V5, Pg. 240	PT68-S2-Q3	Ⓐ Ⓑ Ⓒ Ⓓ Ⓔ
V4, Pg. 245	PT58-S4-Q7	Ⓐ Ⓑ Ⓒ Ⓓ Ⓔ	V5, Pg. 241	PT68-S2-Q6	Ⓐ Ⓑ Ⓒ Ⓓ Ⓔ
V4, Pg. 249	PT58-S4-Q20	Ⓐ Ⓑ Ⓒ Ⓓ Ⓔ	V5, Pg. 250	PT68-S3-Q6	Ⓐ Ⓑ Ⓒ Ⓓ Ⓔ
V4, Pg. 267	PT59-S2-Q11	Ⓐ Ⓑ Ⓒ Ⓓ Ⓔ	V5, Pg. 252	PT68-S3-Q14	Ⓐ Ⓑ Ⓒ Ⓓ Ⓔ
V4, Pg. 272	PT59-S3-Q1	Ⓐ Ⓑ Ⓒ Ⓓ Ⓔ	V5, Pg. 276	PT69-S1-Q15	Ⓐ Ⓑ Ⓒ Ⓓ Ⓔ
V4, Pg. 273	PT59-S3-Q4	Ⓐ Ⓑ Ⓒ Ⓓ Ⓔ	V5, Pg. 297	PT69-S4-Q5	Ⓐ Ⓑ Ⓒ Ⓓ Ⓔ
V4, Pg. 276	PT59-S3-Q17	Ⓐ Ⓑ Ⓒ Ⓓ Ⓔ	V5, Pg. 313	PT70-S1-Q5	Ⓐ Ⓑ Ⓒ Ⓓ Ⓔ
V4, Pg. 297	PT60-S1-Q5	Ⓐ Ⓑ Ⓒ Ⓓ Ⓔ	V5, Pg. 314	PT70-S1-Q10	Ⓐ Ⓑ Ⓒ Ⓓ Ⓔ
V4, Pg. 298	PT60-S1-Q9	Ⓐ Ⓑ Ⓒ Ⓓ Ⓔ	V5, Pg. 315	PT70-S1-Q12	Ⓐ Ⓑ Ⓒ Ⓓ Ⓔ
V4, Pg. 308	PT60-S3-Q1	Ⓐ Ⓑ Ⓒ Ⓓ Ⓔ	V5, Pg. 337	PT70-S4-Q7	Ⓐ Ⓑ Ⓒ Ⓓ Ⓔ
V4, Pg. 343	PT61-S2-Q12	Ⓐ Ⓑ Ⓒ Ⓓ Ⓔ	V5, Pg. 339	PT70-S4-Q13	Ⓐ Ⓑ Ⓒ Ⓓ Ⓔ
V4, Pg. 345	PT61-S2-Q19	Ⓐ Ⓑ Ⓒ Ⓓ Ⓔ	V5, Pg. 358	PT71-S1-Q20	Ⓐ Ⓑ Ⓒ Ⓓ Ⓔ
V4, Pg. 347	PT61-S2-Q25	Ⓐ Ⓑ Ⓒ Ⓓ Ⓔ	V5, Pg. 368	PT71-S3-Q3	Ⓐ Ⓑ Ⓒ Ⓓ Ⓔ
V4, Pg. 355	PT61-S4-Q12	Ⓐ Ⓑ Ⓒ Ⓓ Ⓔ	V5, Pg. 375	PT71-S3-Q26	Ⓐ Ⓑ Ⓒ Ⓓ Ⓔ
V4, Pg. 356	PT61-S4-Q14	Ⓐ Ⓑ Ⓒ Ⓓ Ⓔ	PT72, Pg. 20	PT72-S2-Q9	Ⓐ Ⓑ Ⓒ Ⓓ Ⓔ
V5, Pg. 21	PT62-S2-Q20	Ⓐ Ⓑ Ⓒ Ⓓ Ⓔ	PT72, Pg. 21	PT72-S2-Q11	Ⓐ Ⓑ Ⓒ Ⓓ Ⓔ
V5, Pg. 30	PT62-S4-Q7	Ⓐ Ⓑ Ⓒ Ⓓ Ⓔ	PT72, Pg. 26	PT72-S3-Q1	Ⓐ Ⓑ Ⓒ Ⓓ Ⓔ
V5, Pg. 32	PT62-S4-Q17	Ⓐ Ⓑ Ⓒ Ⓓ Ⓔ	PT72, Pg. 27	PT72-S3-Q5	Ⓐ Ⓑ Ⓒ Ⓓ Ⓔ
V5, Pg. 35	PT62-S4-Q26	Ⓐ Ⓑ Ⓒ Ⓓ Ⓔ	PT73, Pg. 18	PT73-S2-Q2	Ⓐ Ⓑ Ⓒ Ⓓ Ⓔ
V5, Pg. 45	PT63-S1-Q4	Ⓐ Ⓑ Ⓒ Ⓓ Ⓔ	PT73, Pg. 25	PT73-S2-Q24	Ⓐ Ⓑ Ⓒ Ⓓ Ⓔ
V5, Pg. 58	PT63-S3-Q8	Ⓐ Ⓑ Ⓒ Ⓓ Ⓔ	PT73, Pg. 38	PT73-S4-Q15	Ⓐ Ⓑ Ⓒ Ⓓ Ⓔ
V5, Pg. 59	PT63-S3-Q12	Ⓐ Ⓑ Ⓒ Ⓓ Ⓔ	PT73, Pg. 40	PT73-S4-Q22	Ⓐ Ⓑ Ⓒ Ⓓ Ⓔ
V5, Pg. 63	PT63-S3-Q26	Ⓐ Ⓑ Ⓒ Ⓓ Ⓔ	PT74, Pg. 12	PT74-S1-Q9	Ⓐ Ⓑ Ⓒ Ⓓ Ⓔ
V5, Pg. 81	PT64-S1-Q6	Ⓐ Ⓑ Ⓒ Ⓓ Ⓔ	PT74, Pg. 14	PT74-S1-Q15	Ⓐ Ⓑ Ⓒ Ⓓ Ⓔ
V5, Pg. 94	PT64-S3-Q8	Ⓐ Ⓑ Ⓒ Ⓓ Ⓔ	PT74, Pg. 36	PT74-S4-Q9	Ⓐ Ⓑ Ⓒ Ⓓ Ⓔ
V5, Pg. 95	PT64-S3-Q13	Ⓐ Ⓑ Ⓒ Ⓓ Ⓔ	PT75, Pg. 11	PT75-S1-Q6	Ⓐ Ⓑ Ⓒ Ⓓ Ⓔ
V5, Pg. 119	PT65-S1-Q12	Ⓐ Ⓑ Ⓒ Ⓓ Ⓔ	PT75, Pg. 15	PT75-S1-Q19	Ⓐ Ⓑ Ⓒ Ⓓ Ⓔ
V5, Pg. 136	PT65-S4-Q1	Ⓐ Ⓑ Ⓒ Ⓓ Ⓔ	PT75, Pg. 27	PT75-S3-Q5	Ⓐ Ⓑ Ⓒ Ⓓ Ⓔ
V5, Pg. 138	PT65-S4-Q10	Ⓐ Ⓑ Ⓒ Ⓓ Ⓔ	PT76, Pg. 20	PT76-S2-Q7	Ⓐ Ⓑ Ⓒ Ⓓ Ⓔ
V5, Pg. 166	PT66-S2-Q23	Ⓐ Ⓑ Ⓒ Ⓓ Ⓔ	PT76, Pg. 21	PT76-S2-Q11	Ⓐ Ⓑ Ⓒ Ⓓ Ⓔ
V5, Pg. 178	PT66-S4-Q10	Ⓐ Ⓑ Ⓒ Ⓓ Ⓔ	PT76, Pg. 23	PT76-S2-Q20	Ⓐ Ⓑ Ⓒ Ⓓ Ⓔ
V5, Pg. 180	PT66-S4-Q15	Ⓐ Ⓑ Ⓒ Ⓓ Ⓔ	PT76, Pg. 34	PT76-S4-Q3	Ⓐ Ⓑ Ⓒ Ⓓ Ⓔ
V5, Pg. 181	PT66-S4-Q18	Ⓐ Ⓑ Ⓒ Ⓓ Ⓔ	PT76, Pg. 41	PT76-S4-Q25	Ⓐ Ⓑ Ⓒ Ⓓ Ⓔ
V5, Pg. 200	PT67-S2-Q2	Ⓐ Ⓑ Ⓒ Ⓓ Ⓔ	PT77, Pg. 23	PT77-S2-Q19	Ⓐ Ⓑ Ⓒ Ⓓ Ⓔ

| PT77, Pg. 34 | PT77-S4-Q3 | Ⓐ Ⓑ Ⓒ Ⓓ Ⓔ | PT77, Pg. 39 | PT77-S4-Q21 | Ⓐ Ⓑ Ⓒ Ⓓ Ⓔ |

Principle (Identify)

J07, Pg. 13	J07-S2-Q24	Ⓐ Ⓑ Ⓒ Ⓓ Ⓔ	V1, Pg. 75	PT9-S4-Q21	Ⓐ Ⓑ Ⓒ Ⓓ Ⓔ
J07, Pg. 15	J07-S3-Q6	Ⓐ Ⓑ Ⓒ Ⓓ Ⓔ	V1, Pg. 90	PT10-S1-Q23	Ⓐ Ⓑ Ⓒ Ⓓ Ⓔ
J07, Pg. 18	J07-S3-Q14	Ⓐ Ⓑ Ⓒ Ⓓ Ⓔ	V1, Pg. 105	PT10-S4-Q6	Ⓐ Ⓑ Ⓒ Ⓓ Ⓔ
J07, Pg. 21	J07-S3-Q24	Ⓐ Ⓑ Ⓒ Ⓓ Ⓔ	V1, Pg. 108	PT10-S4-Q15	Ⓐ Ⓑ Ⓒ Ⓓ Ⓔ
SP1, Pg. 72	PTA-S1-Q15	Ⓐ Ⓑ Ⓒ Ⓓ Ⓔ	V1, Pg. 123	PT11-S2-Q6	Ⓐ Ⓑ Ⓒ Ⓓ Ⓔ
SP1, Pg. 92	PTA-S4-Q13	Ⓐ Ⓑ Ⓒ Ⓓ Ⓔ	V1, Pg. 124	PT11-S2-Q10	Ⓐ Ⓑ Ⓒ Ⓓ Ⓔ
SP1, Pg. 189	PTB-S1-Q14	Ⓐ Ⓑ Ⓒ Ⓓ Ⓔ	V1, Pg. 139	PT11-S4-Q6	Ⓐ Ⓑ Ⓒ Ⓓ Ⓔ
SP1, Pg. 192	PTB-S1-Q24	Ⓐ Ⓑ Ⓒ Ⓓ Ⓔ	V1, Pg. 153	PT12-S1-Q5	Ⓐ Ⓑ Ⓒ Ⓓ Ⓔ
SP1, Pg. 208	PTB-S4-Q7	Ⓐ Ⓑ Ⓒ Ⓓ Ⓔ	V1, Pg. 176	PT12-S4-Q13	Ⓐ Ⓑ Ⓒ Ⓓ Ⓔ
SP1, Pg. 209	PTB-S4-Q12	Ⓐ Ⓑ Ⓒ Ⓓ Ⓔ	V1, Pg. 177	PT12-S4-Q18	Ⓐ Ⓑ Ⓒ Ⓓ Ⓔ
SP1, Pg. 213	PTB-S4-Q24	Ⓐ Ⓑ Ⓒ Ⓓ Ⓔ	V1, Pg. 194	PT13-S2-Q16	Ⓐ Ⓑ Ⓒ Ⓓ Ⓔ
SP1, Pg. 302	PTC-S2-Q8	Ⓐ Ⓑ Ⓒ Ⓓ Ⓔ	V1, Pg. 212	PT13-S4-Q22	Ⓐ Ⓑ Ⓒ Ⓓ Ⓔ
SP1, Pg. 307	PTC-S2-Q24	Ⓐ Ⓑ Ⓒ Ⓓ Ⓔ	V1, Pg. 262	PT15-S2-Q1	Ⓐ Ⓑ Ⓒ Ⓓ Ⓔ
SP1, Pg. 313	PTC-S3-Q22	Ⓐ Ⓑ Ⓒ Ⓓ Ⓔ	V1, Pg. 266	PT15-S2-Q13	Ⓐ Ⓑ Ⓒ Ⓓ Ⓔ
SP2, Pg. 355	PTC2-S2-Q6	Ⓐ Ⓑ Ⓒ Ⓓ Ⓔ	V1, Pg. 271	PT15-S3-Q6	Ⓐ Ⓑ Ⓒ Ⓓ Ⓔ
SP2, Pg. 367	PTC2-S3-Q19	Ⓐ Ⓑ Ⓒ Ⓓ Ⓔ	V1, Pg. 295	PT16-S2-Q12	Ⓐ Ⓑ Ⓒ Ⓓ Ⓔ
	PT1-S3-Q3	Ⓐ Ⓑ Ⓒ Ⓓ Ⓔ	V1, Pg. 306	PT16-S3-Q23	Ⓐ Ⓑ Ⓒ Ⓓ Ⓔ
	PT1-S3-Q24	Ⓐ Ⓑ Ⓒ Ⓓ Ⓔ		PT17-S2-Q3	Ⓐ Ⓑ Ⓒ Ⓓ Ⓔ
	PT2-S4-Q1	Ⓐ Ⓑ Ⓒ Ⓓ Ⓔ		PT17-S3-Q8	Ⓐ Ⓑ Ⓒ Ⓓ Ⓔ
	PT3-S4-Q6	Ⓐ Ⓑ Ⓒ Ⓓ Ⓔ		PT17-S3-Q23	Ⓐ Ⓑ Ⓒ Ⓓ Ⓔ
	PT4-S1-Q11	Ⓐ Ⓑ Ⓒ Ⓓ Ⓔ	V1, Pg. 342	PT18-S4-Q1	Ⓐ Ⓑ Ⓒ Ⓓ Ⓔ
	PT4-S4-Q13	Ⓐ Ⓑ Ⓒ Ⓓ Ⓔ	V1, Pg. 346	PT18-S4-Q16	Ⓐ Ⓑ Ⓒ Ⓓ Ⓔ
	PT4-S4-Q22	Ⓐ Ⓑ Ⓒ Ⓓ Ⓔ	V2, Pg. 22	PT19-S2-Q10	Ⓐ Ⓑ Ⓒ Ⓓ Ⓔ
	PT5-S1-Q4	Ⓐ Ⓑ Ⓒ Ⓓ Ⓔ	V2, Pg. 51	PT20-S1-Q5	Ⓐ Ⓑ Ⓒ Ⓓ Ⓔ
	PT5-S1-Q18	Ⓐ Ⓑ Ⓒ Ⓓ Ⓔ	V2, Pg. 72	PT20-S4-Q12	Ⓐ Ⓑ Ⓒ Ⓓ Ⓔ
	PT5-S1-Q21	Ⓐ Ⓑ Ⓒ Ⓓ Ⓔ	V2, Pg. 77	PT20-S4-Q24	Ⓐ Ⓑ Ⓒ Ⓓ Ⓔ
	PT5-S3-Q21	Ⓐ Ⓑ Ⓒ Ⓓ Ⓔ	V2, Pg. 92	PT21-S2-Q16	Ⓐ Ⓑ Ⓒ Ⓓ Ⓔ
	PT6-S3-Q25	Ⓐ Ⓑ Ⓒ Ⓓ Ⓔ	V2, Pg. 99	PT21-S3-Q15	Ⓐ Ⓑ Ⓒ Ⓓ Ⓔ
V1, Pg. 37	PT7-S4-Q5	Ⓐ Ⓑ Ⓒ Ⓓ Ⓔ	V2, Pg. 100	PT21-S3-Q17	Ⓐ Ⓑ Ⓒ Ⓓ Ⓔ
	PT8-S1-Q20	Ⓐ Ⓑ Ⓒ Ⓓ Ⓔ	V2, Pg. 142	PT22-S4-Q15	Ⓐ Ⓑ Ⓒ Ⓓ Ⓔ
	PT8-S4-Q7	Ⓐ Ⓑ Ⓒ Ⓓ Ⓔ	V2, Pg. 159	PT23-S2-Q13	Ⓐ Ⓑ Ⓒ Ⓓ Ⓔ
	PT8-S4-Q16	Ⓐ Ⓑ Ⓒ Ⓓ Ⓔ	V2, Pg. 165	PT23-S3-Q5	Ⓐ Ⓑ Ⓒ Ⓓ Ⓔ
	PT8-S4-Q22	Ⓐ Ⓑ Ⓒ Ⓓ Ⓔ	V2, Pg. 196	PT24-S2-Q9	Ⓐ Ⓑ Ⓒ Ⓓ Ⓔ
V1, Pg. 72	PT9-S4-Q11	Ⓐ Ⓑ Ⓒ Ⓓ Ⓔ	V2, Pg. 200	PT24-S2-Q22	Ⓐ Ⓑ Ⓒ Ⓓ Ⓔ

V2, Pg. 201	PT24-S2-Q25	Ⓐ Ⓑ Ⓒ Ⓓ Ⓔ	V3, Pg. 276	PT36-S3-Q20	Ⓐ Ⓑ Ⓒ Ⓓ Ⓔ
V2, Pg. 207	PT24-S3-Q20	Ⓐ Ⓑ Ⓒ Ⓓ Ⓔ	V3, Pg. 300	PT37-S2-Q18	Ⓐ Ⓑ Ⓒ Ⓓ Ⓔ
V2, Pg. 209	PT24-S3-Q26	Ⓐ Ⓑ Ⓒ Ⓓ Ⓔ	V3, Pg. 302	PT37-S2-Q22	Ⓐ Ⓑ Ⓒ Ⓓ Ⓔ
V2, Pg. 231	PT25-S2-Q8	Ⓐ Ⓑ Ⓒ Ⓓ Ⓔ	V3, Pg. 302	PT37-S2-Q24	Ⓐ Ⓑ Ⓒ Ⓓ Ⓔ
V2, Pg. 232	PT25-S2-Q11	Ⓐ Ⓑ Ⓒ Ⓓ Ⓔ	V3, Pg. 314	PT37-S4-Q21	Ⓐ Ⓑ Ⓒ Ⓓ Ⓔ
V2, Pg. 235	PT25-S2-Q23	Ⓐ Ⓑ Ⓒ Ⓓ Ⓔ	V3, Pg. 322	PT38-S1-Q3	Ⓐ Ⓑ Ⓒ Ⓓ Ⓔ
V2, Pg. 235	PT25-S2-Q24	Ⓐ Ⓑ Ⓒ Ⓓ Ⓔ	V3, Pg. 343	PT38-S4-Q4	Ⓐ Ⓑ Ⓒ Ⓓ Ⓔ
V2, Pg. 235	PT25-S2-Q25	Ⓐ Ⓑ Ⓒ Ⓓ Ⓔ		PT39-S2-Q19	Ⓐ Ⓑ Ⓒ Ⓓ Ⓔ
V2, Pg. 241	PT25-S4-Q5	Ⓐ Ⓑ Ⓒ Ⓓ Ⓔ		PT39-S4-Q14	Ⓐ Ⓑ Ⓒ Ⓓ Ⓔ
V2, Pg. 244	PT25-S4-Q14	Ⓐ Ⓑ Ⓒ Ⓓ Ⓔ		PT40-S1-Q18	Ⓐ Ⓑ Ⓒ Ⓓ Ⓔ
V2, Pg. 258	PT26-S2-Q2	Ⓐ Ⓑ Ⓒ Ⓓ Ⓔ		PT40-S3-Q9	Ⓐ Ⓑ Ⓒ Ⓓ Ⓔ
V2, Pg. 264	PT26-S2-Q23	Ⓐ Ⓑ Ⓒ Ⓓ Ⓔ		PT41-S1-Q17	Ⓐ Ⓑ Ⓒ Ⓓ Ⓔ
V2, Pg. 295	PT27-S1-Q24	Ⓐ Ⓑ Ⓒ Ⓓ Ⓔ		PT41-S1-Q19	Ⓐ Ⓑ Ⓒ Ⓓ Ⓔ
V2, Pg. 323	PT28-S1-Q4	Ⓐ Ⓑ Ⓒ Ⓓ Ⓔ		PT41-S3-Q14	Ⓐ Ⓑ Ⓒ Ⓓ Ⓔ
V2, Pg. 338	PT28-S3-Q18	Ⓐ Ⓑ Ⓒ Ⓓ Ⓔ		PT42-S4-Q15	Ⓐ Ⓑ Ⓒ Ⓓ Ⓔ
V3, Pg. 21	PT29-S1-Q19	Ⓐ Ⓑ Ⓒ Ⓓ Ⓔ		PT43-S2-Q21	Ⓐ Ⓑ Ⓒ Ⓓ Ⓔ
V3, Pg. 22	PT29-S1-Q22	Ⓐ Ⓑ Ⓒ Ⓓ Ⓔ		PT43-S3-Q3	Ⓐ Ⓑ Ⓒ Ⓓ Ⓔ
V3, Pg. 38	PT29-S4-Q7	Ⓐ Ⓑ Ⓒ Ⓓ Ⓔ		PT43-S3-Q7	Ⓐ Ⓑ Ⓒ Ⓓ Ⓔ
V3, Pg. 40	PT29-S4-Q17	Ⓐ Ⓑ Ⓒ Ⓓ Ⓔ		PT43-S3-Q11	Ⓐ Ⓑ Ⓒ Ⓓ Ⓔ
V3, Pg. 55	PT30-S2-Q5	Ⓐ Ⓑ Ⓒ Ⓓ Ⓔ		PT43-S3-Q26	Ⓐ Ⓑ Ⓒ Ⓓ Ⓔ
V3, Pg. 59	PT30-S2-Q19	Ⓐ Ⓑ Ⓒ Ⓓ Ⓔ		PT44-S2-Q17	Ⓐ Ⓑ Ⓒ Ⓓ Ⓔ
V3, Pg. 76	PT30-S4-Q23	Ⓐ Ⓑ Ⓒ Ⓓ Ⓔ		PT44-S4-Q2	Ⓐ Ⓑ Ⓒ Ⓓ Ⓔ
V3, Pg. 94	PT31-S2-Q22	Ⓐ Ⓑ Ⓒ Ⓓ Ⓔ		PT44-S4-Q4	Ⓐ Ⓑ Ⓒ Ⓓ Ⓔ
V3, Pg. 95	PT31-S2-Q24	Ⓐ Ⓑ Ⓒ Ⓓ Ⓔ		PT44-S4-Q13	Ⓐ Ⓑ Ⓒ Ⓓ Ⓔ
V3, Pg. 97	PT31-S3-Q4	Ⓐ Ⓑ Ⓒ Ⓓ Ⓔ		PT45-S4-Q3	Ⓐ Ⓑ Ⓒ Ⓓ Ⓔ
V3, Pg. 103	PT31-S3-Q26	Ⓐ Ⓑ Ⓒ Ⓓ Ⓔ		PT46-S2-Q3	Ⓐ Ⓑ Ⓒ Ⓓ Ⓔ
V3, Pg. 119	PT32-S1-Q3	Ⓐ Ⓑ Ⓒ Ⓓ Ⓔ		PT46-S2-Q5	Ⓐ Ⓑ Ⓒ Ⓓ Ⓔ
V3, Pg. 140	PT32-S4-Q8	Ⓐ Ⓑ Ⓒ Ⓓ Ⓔ		PT46-S3-Q8	Ⓐ Ⓑ Ⓒ Ⓓ Ⓔ
V3, Pg. 157	PT33-S1-Q18	Ⓐ Ⓑ Ⓒ Ⓓ Ⓔ		PT46-S3-Q14	Ⓐ Ⓑ Ⓒ Ⓓ Ⓔ
V3, Pg. 158	PT33-S1-Q21	Ⓐ Ⓑ Ⓒ Ⓓ Ⓔ		PT47-S1-Q3	Ⓐ Ⓑ Ⓒ Ⓓ Ⓔ
V3, Pg. 169	PT33-S3-Q6	Ⓐ Ⓑ Ⓒ Ⓓ Ⓔ		PT47-S1-Q7	Ⓐ Ⓑ Ⓒ Ⓓ Ⓔ
V3, Pg. 199	PT34-S2-Q20	Ⓐ Ⓑ Ⓒ Ⓓ Ⓔ		PT47-S3-Q26	Ⓐ Ⓑ Ⓒ Ⓓ Ⓔ
V3, Pg. 202	PT34-S3-Q1	Ⓐ Ⓑ Ⓒ Ⓓ Ⓔ		PT48-S1-Q9	Ⓐ Ⓑ Ⓒ Ⓓ Ⓔ
V3, Pg. 206	PT34-S3-Q16	Ⓐ Ⓑ Ⓒ Ⓓ Ⓔ		PT48-S1-Q11	Ⓐ Ⓑ Ⓒ Ⓓ Ⓔ
V3, Pg. 220	PT35-S1-Q2	Ⓐ Ⓑ Ⓒ Ⓓ Ⓔ		PT48-S1-Q18	Ⓐ Ⓑ Ⓒ Ⓓ Ⓔ
V3, Pg. 243	PT35-S4-Q11	Ⓐ Ⓑ Ⓒ Ⓓ Ⓔ		PT48-S4-Q6	Ⓐ Ⓑ Ⓒ Ⓓ Ⓔ
V3, Pg. 258	PT36-S1-Q15	Ⓐ Ⓑ Ⓒ Ⓓ Ⓔ		PT49-S2-Q15	Ⓐ Ⓑ Ⓒ Ⓓ Ⓔ

	PT49-S4-Q9	Ⓐ Ⓑ Ⓒ Ⓓ Ⓔ	V4, Pg. 251	PT58-S4-Q25	Ⓐ Ⓑ Ⓒ Ⓓ Ⓔ
	PT49-S4-Q21	Ⓐ Ⓑ Ⓒ Ⓓ Ⓔ	V4, Pg. 267	PT59-S2-Q13	Ⓐ Ⓑ Ⓒ Ⓓ Ⓔ
	PT50-S2-Q12	Ⓐ Ⓑ Ⓒ Ⓓ Ⓔ	V4, Pg. 270	PT59-S2-Q23	Ⓐ Ⓑ Ⓒ Ⓓ Ⓔ
	PT50-S2-Q25	Ⓐ Ⓑ Ⓒ Ⓓ Ⓔ	V4, Pg. 277	PT59-S3-Q18	Ⓐ Ⓑ Ⓒ Ⓓ Ⓔ
	PT50-S4-Q3	Ⓐ Ⓑ Ⓒ Ⓓ Ⓔ	V4, Pg. 301	PT60-S1-Q18	Ⓐ Ⓑ Ⓒ Ⓓ Ⓔ
	PT50-S4-Q18	Ⓐ Ⓑ Ⓒ Ⓓ Ⓔ	V4, Pg. 302	PT60-S1-Q23	Ⓐ Ⓑ Ⓒ Ⓓ Ⓔ
	PT50-S4-Q20	Ⓐ Ⓑ Ⓒ Ⓓ Ⓔ	V4, Pg. 310	PT60-S3-Q9	Ⓐ Ⓑ Ⓒ Ⓓ Ⓔ
	PT51-S3-Q5	Ⓐ Ⓑ Ⓒ Ⓓ Ⓔ	V4, Pg. 315	PT60-S3-Q24	Ⓐ Ⓑ Ⓒ Ⓓ Ⓔ
	PT51-S3-Q7	Ⓐ Ⓑ Ⓒ Ⓓ Ⓔ	V4, Pg. 341	PT61-S2-Q5	Ⓐ Ⓑ Ⓒ Ⓓ Ⓔ
	PT51-S3-Q13	Ⓐ Ⓑ Ⓒ Ⓓ Ⓔ	V4, Pg. 345	PT61-S2-Q21	Ⓐ Ⓑ Ⓒ Ⓓ Ⓔ
V4, Pg. 10	PT52-S1-Q8	Ⓐ Ⓑ Ⓒ Ⓓ Ⓔ	V4, Pg. 352	PT61-S4-Q1	Ⓐ Ⓑ Ⓒ Ⓓ Ⓔ
V4, Pg. 13	PT52-S1-Q19	Ⓐ Ⓑ Ⓒ Ⓓ Ⓔ	V4, Pg. 358	PT61-S4-Q23	Ⓐ Ⓑ Ⓒ Ⓓ Ⓔ
V4, Pg. 20	PT52-S3-Q1	Ⓐ Ⓑ Ⓒ Ⓓ Ⓔ	V5, Pg. 16	PT62-S2-Q1	Ⓐ Ⓑ Ⓒ Ⓓ Ⓔ
V4, Pg. 23	PT52-S3-Q11	Ⓐ Ⓑ Ⓒ Ⓓ Ⓔ	V5, Pg. 22	PT62-S2-Q23	Ⓐ Ⓑ Ⓒ Ⓓ Ⓔ
V4, Pg. 25	PT52-S3-Q18	Ⓐ Ⓑ Ⓒ Ⓓ Ⓔ	V5, Pg. 23	PT62-S2-Q26	Ⓐ Ⓑ Ⓒ Ⓓ Ⓔ
V4, Pg. 45	PT53-S1-Q5	Ⓐ Ⓑ Ⓒ Ⓓ Ⓔ	V5, Pg. 28	PT62-S4-Q2	Ⓐ Ⓑ Ⓒ Ⓓ Ⓔ
V4, Pg. 59	PT53-S3-Q12	Ⓐ Ⓑ Ⓒ Ⓓ Ⓔ	V5, Pg. 32	PT62-S4-Q15	Ⓐ Ⓑ Ⓒ Ⓓ Ⓔ
V4, Pg. 61	PT53-S3-Q18	Ⓐ Ⓑ Ⓒ Ⓓ Ⓔ	V5, Pg. 56	PT63-S3-Q3	Ⓐ Ⓑ Ⓒ Ⓓ Ⓔ
V4, Pg. 89	PT54-S2-Q8	Ⓐ Ⓑ Ⓒ Ⓓ Ⓔ	V5, Pg. 62	PT63-S3-Q23	Ⓐ Ⓑ Ⓒ Ⓓ Ⓔ
V4, Pg. 92	PT54-S2-Q18	Ⓐ Ⓑ Ⓒ Ⓓ Ⓔ	V5, Pg. 83	PT64-S1-Q12	Ⓐ Ⓑ Ⓒ Ⓓ Ⓔ
V4, Pg. 102	PT54-S4-Q9	Ⓐ Ⓑ Ⓒ Ⓓ Ⓔ	V5, Pg. 123	PT65-S1-Q24	Ⓐ Ⓑ Ⓒ Ⓓ Ⓔ
V4, Pg. 117	PT55-S1-Q6	Ⓐ Ⓑ Ⓒ Ⓓ Ⓔ	V5, Pg. 137	PT65-S4-Q5	Ⓐ Ⓑ Ⓒ Ⓓ Ⓔ
V4, Pg. 118	PT55-S1-Q10	Ⓐ Ⓑ Ⓒ Ⓓ Ⓔ	V5, Pg. 140	PT65-S4-Q18	Ⓐ Ⓑ Ⓒ Ⓓ Ⓔ
V4, Pg. 121	PT55-S1-Q21	Ⓐ Ⓑ Ⓒ Ⓓ Ⓔ	V5, Pg. 142	PT65-S4-Q23	Ⓐ Ⓑ Ⓒ Ⓓ Ⓔ
V4, Pg. 133	PT55-S3-Q6	Ⓐ Ⓑ Ⓒ Ⓓ Ⓔ	V5, Pg. 162	PT66-S2-Q7	Ⓐ Ⓑ Ⓒ Ⓓ Ⓔ
V4, Pg. 137	PT55-S3-Q17	Ⓐ Ⓑ Ⓒ Ⓓ Ⓔ	V5, Pg. 162	PT66-S2-Q9	Ⓐ Ⓑ Ⓒ Ⓓ Ⓔ
V4, Pg. 160	PT56-S2-Q16	Ⓐ Ⓑ Ⓒ Ⓓ Ⓔ	V5, Pg. 163	PT66-S2-Q12	Ⓐ Ⓑ Ⓒ Ⓓ Ⓔ
V4, Pg. 161	PT56-S2-Q20	Ⓐ Ⓑ Ⓒ Ⓓ Ⓔ	V5, Pg. 176	PT66-S4-Q2	Ⓐ Ⓑ Ⓒ Ⓓ Ⓔ
V4, Pg. 164	PT56-S3-Q3	Ⓐ Ⓑ Ⓒ Ⓓ Ⓔ	V5, Pg. 178	PT66-S4-Q11	Ⓐ Ⓑ Ⓒ Ⓓ Ⓔ
V4, Pg. 167	PT56-S3-Q12	Ⓐ Ⓑ Ⓒ Ⓓ Ⓔ	V5, Pg. 202	PT67-S2-Q8	Ⓐ Ⓑ Ⓒ Ⓓ Ⓔ
V4, Pg. 192	PT57-S2-Q1	Ⓐ Ⓑ Ⓒ Ⓓ Ⓔ	V5, Pg. 204	PT67-S2-Q15	Ⓐ Ⓑ Ⓒ Ⓓ Ⓔ
V4, Pg. 195	PT57-S2-Q10	Ⓐ Ⓑ Ⓒ Ⓓ Ⓔ	V5, Pg. 205	PT67-S2-Q18	Ⓐ Ⓑ Ⓒ Ⓓ Ⓔ
V4, Pg. 204	PT57-S3-Q16	Ⓐ Ⓑ Ⓒ Ⓓ Ⓔ	V5, Pg. 217	PT67-S4-Q7	Ⓐ Ⓑ Ⓒ Ⓓ Ⓔ
V4, Pg. 205	PT57-S3-Q19	Ⓐ Ⓑ Ⓒ Ⓓ Ⓔ	V5, Pg. 244	PT68-S2-Q16	Ⓐ Ⓑ Ⓒ Ⓓ Ⓔ
V4, Pg. 225	PT58-S1-Q4	Ⓐ Ⓑ Ⓒ Ⓓ Ⓔ	V5, Pg. 248	PT68-S3-Q1	Ⓐ Ⓑ Ⓒ Ⓓ Ⓔ
V4, Pg. 230	PT58-S1-Q23	Ⓐ Ⓑ Ⓒ Ⓓ Ⓔ	V5, Pg. 251	PT68-S3-Q12	Ⓐ Ⓑ Ⓒ Ⓓ Ⓔ
V4, Pg. 248	PT58-S4-Q16	Ⓐ Ⓑ Ⓒ Ⓓ Ⓔ	V5, Pg. 273	PT69-S1-Q6	Ⓐ Ⓑ Ⓒ Ⓓ Ⓔ

V5, Pg. 301	PT69-S4-Q17	Ⓐ Ⓑ Ⓒ Ⓓ Ⓔ	PT74, Pg. 10	PT74-S1-Q3	Ⓐ Ⓑ Ⓒ Ⓓ Ⓔ
V5, Pg. 315	PT70-S1-Q14	Ⓐ Ⓑ Ⓒ Ⓓ Ⓔ	PT74, Pg. 11	PT74-S1-Q7	Ⓐ Ⓑ Ⓒ Ⓓ Ⓔ
V5, Pg. 318	PT70-S1-Q23	Ⓐ Ⓑ Ⓒ Ⓓ Ⓔ	PT74, Pg. 35	PT74-S4-Q5	Ⓐ Ⓑ Ⓒ Ⓓ Ⓔ
V5, Pg. 336	PT70-S4-Q1	Ⓐ Ⓑ Ⓒ Ⓓ Ⓔ	PT74, Pg. 37	PT74-S4-Q12	Ⓐ Ⓑ Ⓒ Ⓓ Ⓔ
V5, Pg. 339	PT70-S4-Q15	Ⓐ Ⓑ Ⓒ Ⓓ Ⓔ	PT74, Pg. 39	PT74-S4-Q21	Ⓐ Ⓑ Ⓒ Ⓓ Ⓔ
V5, Pg. 369	PT71-S3-Q6	Ⓐ Ⓑ Ⓒ Ⓓ Ⓔ	PT75, Pg. 10	PT75-S1-Q2	Ⓐ Ⓑ Ⓒ Ⓓ Ⓔ
V5, Pg. 370	PT71-S3-Q9	Ⓐ Ⓑ Ⓒ Ⓓ Ⓔ	PT75, Pg. 12	PT75-S1-Q10	Ⓐ Ⓑ Ⓒ Ⓓ Ⓔ
V5, Pg. 371	PT71-S3-Q13	Ⓐ Ⓑ Ⓒ Ⓓ Ⓔ	PT75, Pg. 26	PT75-S3-Q3	Ⓐ Ⓑ Ⓒ Ⓓ Ⓔ
PT72, Pg. 18	PT72-S2-Q1	Ⓐ Ⓑ Ⓒ Ⓓ Ⓔ	PT76, Pg. 19	PT76-S2-Q6	Ⓐ Ⓑ Ⓒ Ⓓ Ⓔ
PT72, Pg. 19	PT72-S2-Q6	Ⓐ Ⓑ Ⓒ Ⓓ Ⓔ	PT76, Pg. 24	PT76-S2-Q23	Ⓐ Ⓑ Ⓒ Ⓓ Ⓔ
PT72, Pg. 29	PT72-S3-Q13	Ⓐ Ⓑ Ⓒ Ⓓ Ⓔ	PT76, Pg. 34	PT76-S4-Q2	Ⓐ Ⓑ Ⓒ Ⓓ Ⓔ
PT72, Pg. 30	PT72-S3-Q17	Ⓐ Ⓑ Ⓒ Ⓓ Ⓔ	PT76, Pg. 36	PT76-S4-Q9	Ⓐ Ⓑ Ⓒ Ⓓ Ⓔ
PT72, Pg. 32	PT72-S3-Q21	Ⓐ Ⓑ Ⓒ Ⓓ Ⓔ	PT77, Pg. 20	PT77-S2-Q8	Ⓐ Ⓑ Ⓒ Ⓓ Ⓔ
PT73, Pg. 19	PT73-S2-Q6	Ⓐ Ⓑ Ⓒ Ⓓ Ⓔ	PT77, Pg. 22	PT77-S2-Q16	Ⓐ Ⓑ Ⓒ Ⓓ Ⓔ
PT73, Pg. 34	PT73-S4-Q2	Ⓐ Ⓑ Ⓒ Ⓓ Ⓔ	PT77, Pg. 34	PT77-S4-Q1	Ⓐ Ⓑ Ⓒ Ⓓ Ⓔ
PT73, Pg. 36	PT73-S4-Q7	Ⓐ Ⓑ Ⓒ Ⓓ Ⓔ			

Principle (Apply)

J07, Pg. 8	J07-S2-Q7	Ⓐ Ⓑ Ⓒ Ⓓ Ⓔ	V2, Pg. 272	PT26-S3-Q23	Ⓐ Ⓑ Ⓒ Ⓓ Ⓔ
J07, Pg. 14	J07-S3-Q1	Ⓐ Ⓑ Ⓒ Ⓓ Ⓔ	V2, Pg. 273	PT26-S3-Q25	Ⓐ Ⓑ Ⓒ Ⓓ Ⓔ
SP1, Pg. 209	PTB-S4-Q10	Ⓐ Ⓑ Ⓒ Ⓓ Ⓔ	V2, Pg. 308	PT27-S4-Q1	Ⓐ Ⓑ Ⓒ Ⓓ Ⓔ
SP1, Pg. 312	PTC-S3-Q16	Ⓐ Ⓑ Ⓒ Ⓓ Ⓔ	V2, Pg. 309	PT27-S4-Q3	Ⓐ Ⓑ Ⓒ Ⓓ Ⓔ
SP2, Pg. 357	PTC2-S2-Q12	Ⓐ Ⓑ Ⓒ Ⓓ Ⓔ	V2, Pg. 324	PT28-S1-Q10	Ⓐ Ⓑ Ⓒ Ⓓ Ⓔ
SP2, Pg. 357	PTC2-S2-Q14	Ⓐ Ⓑ Ⓒ Ⓓ Ⓔ	V2, Pg. 340	PT28-S3-Q23	Ⓐ Ⓑ Ⓒ Ⓓ Ⓔ
	PT3-S4-Q24	Ⓐ Ⓑ Ⓒ Ⓓ Ⓔ	V3, Pg. 38	PT29-S4-Q10	Ⓐ Ⓑ Ⓒ Ⓓ Ⓔ
	PT6-S2-Q24	Ⓐ Ⓑ Ⓒ Ⓓ Ⓔ	V3, Pg. 139	PT32-S4-Q3	Ⓐ Ⓑ Ⓒ Ⓓ Ⓔ
V1, Pg. 63	PT9-S2-Q18	Ⓐ Ⓑ Ⓒ Ⓓ Ⓔ	V3, Pg. 143	PT32-S4-Q18	Ⓐ Ⓑ Ⓒ Ⓓ Ⓔ
V1, Pg. 210	PT13-S4-Q16	Ⓐ Ⓑ Ⓒ Ⓓ Ⓔ	V3, Pg. 156	PT33-S1-Q16	Ⓐ Ⓑ Ⓒ Ⓓ Ⓔ
V1, Pg. 240	PT14-S4-Q2	Ⓐ Ⓑ Ⓒ Ⓓ Ⓔ	V3, Pg. 222	PT35-S1-Q7	Ⓐ Ⓑ Ⓒ Ⓓ Ⓔ
V1, Pg. 268	PT15-S2-Q21	Ⓐ Ⓑ Ⓒ Ⓓ Ⓔ	V3, Pg. 255	PT36-S1-Q5	Ⓐ Ⓑ Ⓒ Ⓓ Ⓔ
V1, Pg. 294	PT16-S2-Q8	Ⓐ Ⓑ Ⓒ Ⓓ Ⓔ	V3, Pg. 259	PT36-S1-Q17	Ⓐ Ⓑ Ⓒ Ⓓ Ⓔ
	PT17-S2-Q15	Ⓐ Ⓑ Ⓒ Ⓓ Ⓔ	V3, Pg. 274	PT36-S3-Q15	Ⓐ Ⓑ Ⓒ Ⓓ Ⓔ
V1, Pg. 347	PT18-S4-Q19	Ⓐ Ⓑ Ⓒ Ⓓ Ⓔ	V3, Pg. 323	PT38-S1-Q7	Ⓐ Ⓑ Ⓒ Ⓓ Ⓔ
V2, Pg. 130	PT22-S2-Q18	Ⓐ Ⓑ Ⓒ Ⓓ Ⓔ	V3, Pg. 343	PT38-S4-Q7	Ⓐ Ⓑ Ⓒ Ⓓ Ⓔ
V2, Pg. 140	PT22-S4-Q7	Ⓐ Ⓑ Ⓒ Ⓓ Ⓔ	V3, Pg. 348	PT38-S4-Q23	Ⓐ Ⓑ Ⓒ Ⓓ Ⓔ
V2, Pg. 170	PT23-S3-Q24	Ⓐ Ⓑ Ⓒ Ⓓ Ⓔ		PT39-S2-Q11	Ⓐ Ⓑ Ⓒ Ⓓ Ⓔ
V2, Pg. 208	PT24-S3-Q24	Ⓐ Ⓑ Ⓒ Ⓓ Ⓔ		PT39-S4-Q24	Ⓐ Ⓑ Ⓒ Ⓓ Ⓔ

	PT41-S1-Q14	Ⓐ Ⓑ Ⓒ Ⓓ Ⓔ	
	PT42-S2-Q9	Ⓐ Ⓑ Ⓒ Ⓓ Ⓔ	
	PT42-S2-Q21	Ⓐ Ⓑ Ⓒ Ⓓ Ⓔ	
	PT42-S4-Q8	Ⓐ Ⓑ Ⓒ Ⓓ Ⓔ	
	PT43-S3-Q5	Ⓐ Ⓑ Ⓒ Ⓓ Ⓔ	
	PT44-S2-Q12	Ⓐ Ⓑ Ⓒ Ⓓ Ⓔ	
	PT45-S1-Q9	Ⓐ Ⓑ Ⓒ Ⓓ Ⓔ	
	PT45-S4-Q2	Ⓐ Ⓑ Ⓒ Ⓓ Ⓔ	
	PT45-S4-Q21	Ⓐ Ⓑ Ⓒ Ⓓ Ⓔ	
	PT46-S2-Q15	Ⓐ Ⓑ Ⓒ Ⓓ Ⓔ	
	PT46-S2-Q21	Ⓐ Ⓑ Ⓒ Ⓓ Ⓔ	
	PT46-S3-Q12	Ⓐ Ⓑ Ⓒ Ⓓ Ⓔ	
	PT47-S1-Q5	Ⓐ Ⓑ Ⓒ Ⓓ Ⓔ	
	PT47-S1-Q24	Ⓐ Ⓑ Ⓒ Ⓓ Ⓔ	
	PT47-S3-Q18	Ⓐ Ⓑ Ⓒ Ⓓ Ⓔ	
	PT47-S3-Q22	Ⓐ Ⓑ Ⓒ Ⓓ Ⓔ	
	PT48-S1-Q4	Ⓐ Ⓑ Ⓒ Ⓓ Ⓔ	
	PT48-S4-Q16	Ⓐ Ⓑ Ⓒ Ⓓ Ⓔ	
	PT49-S2-Q3	Ⓐ Ⓑ Ⓒ Ⓓ Ⓔ	
	PT50-S2-Q1	Ⓐ Ⓑ Ⓒ Ⓓ Ⓔ	
	PT50-S2-Q23	Ⓐ Ⓑ Ⓒ Ⓓ Ⓔ	
	PT51-S1-Q9	Ⓐ Ⓑ Ⓒ Ⓓ Ⓔ	
	PT51-S1-Q17	Ⓐ Ⓑ Ⓒ Ⓓ Ⓔ	
V4, Pg. 14	PT52-S1-Q22	Ⓐ Ⓑ Ⓒ Ⓓ Ⓔ	
V4, Pg. 27	PT52-S3-Q25	Ⓐ Ⓑ Ⓒ Ⓓ Ⓔ	
V4, Pg. 48	PT53-S1-Q17	Ⓐ Ⓑ Ⓒ Ⓓ Ⓔ	
V4, Pg. 63	PT53-S3-Q25	Ⓐ Ⓑ Ⓒ Ⓓ Ⓔ	
V4, Pg. 105	PT54-S4-Q17	Ⓐ Ⓑ Ⓒ Ⓓ Ⓔ	
V4, Pg. 119	PT55-S1-Q11	Ⓐ Ⓑ Ⓒ Ⓓ Ⓔ	
V4, Pg. 120	PT55-S1-Q16	Ⓐ Ⓑ Ⓒ Ⓓ Ⓔ	
V4, Pg. 161	PT56-S2-Q18	Ⓐ Ⓑ Ⓒ Ⓓ Ⓔ	
V4, Pg. 170	PT56-S3-Q23	Ⓐ Ⓑ Ⓒ Ⓓ Ⓔ	
V4, Pg. 203	PT57-S3-Q14	Ⓐ Ⓑ Ⓒ Ⓓ Ⓔ	
V4, Pg. 224	PT58-S1-Q2	Ⓐ Ⓑ Ⓒ Ⓓ Ⓔ	
V4, Pg. 230	PT58-S1-Q21	Ⓐ Ⓑ Ⓒ Ⓓ Ⓔ	
V4, Pg. 245	PT58-S4-Q4	Ⓐ Ⓑ Ⓒ Ⓓ Ⓔ	
V4, Pg. 274	PT59-S3-Q6	Ⓐ Ⓑ Ⓒ Ⓓ Ⓔ	

V4, Pg. 313	PT60-S3-Q18	Ⓐ Ⓑ Ⓒ Ⓓ Ⓔ	
V4, Pg. 313	PT60-S3-Q20	Ⓐ Ⓑ Ⓒ Ⓓ Ⓔ	
V4, Pg. 340	PT61-S2-Q2	Ⓐ Ⓑ Ⓒ Ⓓ Ⓔ	
V4, Pg. 357	PT61-S4-Q19	Ⓐ Ⓑ Ⓒ Ⓓ Ⓔ	
V5, Pg. 19	PT62-S2-Q13	Ⓐ Ⓑ Ⓒ Ⓓ Ⓔ	
V5, Pg. 21	PT62-S2-Q18	Ⓐ Ⓑ Ⓒ Ⓓ Ⓔ	
V5, Pg. 49	PT63-S1-Q18	Ⓐ Ⓑ Ⓒ Ⓓ Ⓔ	
V5, Pg. 62	PT63-S3-Q22	Ⓐ Ⓑ Ⓒ Ⓓ Ⓔ	
V5, Pg. 87	PT64-S1-Q24	Ⓐ Ⓑ Ⓒ Ⓓ Ⓔ	
V5, Pg. 92	PT64-S3-Q2	Ⓐ Ⓑ Ⓒ Ⓓ Ⓔ	
V5, Pg. 96	PT64-S3-Q18	Ⓐ Ⓑ Ⓒ Ⓓ Ⓔ	
V5, Pg. 97	PT64-S3-Q20	Ⓐ Ⓑ Ⓒ Ⓓ Ⓔ	
V5, Pg. 117	PT65-S1-Q6	Ⓐ Ⓑ Ⓒ Ⓓ Ⓔ	
V5, Pg. 120	PT65-S1-Q14	Ⓐ Ⓑ Ⓒ Ⓓ Ⓔ	
V5, Pg. 179	PT66-S4-Q14	Ⓐ Ⓑ Ⓒ Ⓓ Ⓔ	
V5, Pg. 180	PT66-S4-Q16	Ⓐ Ⓑ Ⓒ Ⓓ Ⓔ	
V5, Pg. 207	PT67-S2-Q25	Ⓐ Ⓑ Ⓒ Ⓓ Ⓔ	
V5, Pg. 218	PT67-S4-Q8	Ⓐ Ⓑ Ⓒ Ⓓ Ⓔ	
V5, Pg. 241	PT68-S2-Q5	Ⓐ Ⓑ Ⓒ Ⓓ Ⓔ	
V5, Pg. 274	PT69-S1-Q8	Ⓐ Ⓑ Ⓒ Ⓓ Ⓔ	
V5, Pg. 277	PT69-S1-Q18	Ⓐ Ⓑ Ⓒ Ⓓ Ⓔ	
V5, Pg. 297	PT69-S4-Q6	Ⓐ Ⓑ Ⓒ Ⓓ Ⓔ	
V5, Pg. 313	PT70-S1-Q6	Ⓐ Ⓑ Ⓒ Ⓓ Ⓔ	
V5, Pg. 357	PT71-S1-Q19	Ⓐ Ⓑ Ⓒ Ⓓ Ⓔ	
V5, Pg. 359	PT71-S1-Q25	Ⓐ Ⓑ Ⓒ Ⓓ Ⓔ	
V5, Pg. 374	PT71-S3-Q22	Ⓐ Ⓑ Ⓒ Ⓓ Ⓔ	
PT72, Pg. 31	PT72-S3-Q19	Ⓐ Ⓑ Ⓒ Ⓓ Ⓔ	
PT73, Pg. 19	PT73-S2-Q4	Ⓐ Ⓑ Ⓒ Ⓓ Ⓔ	
PT73, Pg. 40	PT73-S4-Q23	Ⓐ Ⓑ Ⓒ Ⓓ Ⓔ	
PT74, Pg. 12	PT74-S1-Q10	Ⓐ Ⓑ Ⓒ Ⓓ Ⓔ	
PT74, Pg. 40	PT74-S4-Q23	Ⓐ Ⓑ Ⓒ Ⓓ Ⓔ	
PT75, Pg. 28	PT75-S3-Q12	Ⓐ Ⓑ Ⓒ Ⓓ Ⓔ	
PT76, Pg. 22	PT76-S2-Q14	Ⓐ Ⓑ Ⓒ Ⓓ Ⓔ	
PT76, Pg. 25	PT76-S2-Q26	Ⓐ Ⓑ Ⓒ Ⓓ Ⓔ	
PT76, Pg. 36	PT76-S4-Q11	Ⓐ Ⓑ Ⓒ Ⓓ Ⓔ	
PT77, Pg. 21	PT77-S2-Q12	Ⓐ Ⓑ Ⓒ Ⓓ Ⓔ	
PT77, Pg. 24	PT77-S2-Q21	Ⓐ Ⓑ Ⓒ Ⓓ Ⓔ	

| PT77, Pg. 38 | PT77-S4-Q17 | Ⓐ Ⓑ Ⓒ Ⓓ Ⓔ |

Except

J07, Pg. 11	J07-S2-Q19	Ⓐ Ⓑ Ⓒ Ⓓ Ⓔ	V1, Pg. 159	PT12-S1-Q25	Ⓐ Ⓑ Ⓒ Ⓓ Ⓔ
J07, Pg. 14	J07-S3-Q2	Ⓐ Ⓑ Ⓒ Ⓓ Ⓔ	V1, Pg. 197	PT13-S2-Q25	Ⓐ Ⓑ Ⓒ Ⓓ Ⓔ
SP1, Pg. 190	PTB-S1-Q16	Ⓐ Ⓑ Ⓒ Ⓓ Ⓔ	V1, Pg. 209	PT13-S4-Q14	Ⓐ Ⓑ Ⓒ Ⓓ Ⓔ
SP1, Pg. 191	PTB-S1-Q19	Ⓐ Ⓑ Ⓒ Ⓓ Ⓔ	V1, Pg. 212	PT13-S4-Q21	Ⓐ Ⓑ Ⓒ Ⓓ Ⓔ
SP1, Pg. 206	PTB-S4-Q2	Ⓐ Ⓑ Ⓒ Ⓓ Ⓔ	V1, Pg. 225	PT14-S2-Q5	Ⓐ Ⓑ Ⓒ Ⓓ Ⓔ
SP1, Pg. 211	PTB-S4-Q21	Ⓐ Ⓑ Ⓒ Ⓓ Ⓔ	V1, Pg. 231	PT14-S2-Q24	Ⓐ Ⓑ Ⓒ Ⓓ Ⓔ
SP1, Pg. 308	PTC-S3-Q1	Ⓐ Ⓑ Ⓒ Ⓓ Ⓔ	V1, Pg. 327	PT18-S2-Q5	Ⓐ Ⓑ Ⓒ Ⓓ Ⓔ
SP1, Pg. 309	PTC-S3-Q3	Ⓐ Ⓑ Ⓒ Ⓓ Ⓔ	V1, Pg. 333	PT18-S2-Q23	Ⓐ Ⓑ Ⓒ Ⓓ Ⓔ
SP1, Pg. 309	PTC-S3-Q6	Ⓐ Ⓑ Ⓒ Ⓓ Ⓔ	V1, Pg. 348	PT18-S4-Q23	Ⓐ Ⓑ Ⓒ Ⓓ Ⓔ
SP1, Pg. 312	PTC-S3-Q17	Ⓐ Ⓑ Ⓒ Ⓓ Ⓔ	V2, Pg. 51	PT20-S1-Q7	Ⓐ Ⓑ Ⓒ Ⓓ Ⓔ
SP1, Pg. 312	PTC-S3-Q18	Ⓐ Ⓑ Ⓒ Ⓓ Ⓔ	V2, Pg. 56	PT20-S1-Q20	Ⓐ Ⓑ Ⓒ Ⓓ Ⓔ
	PT1-S3-Q10	Ⓐ Ⓑ Ⓒ Ⓓ Ⓔ	V2, Pg. 71	PT20-S4-Q5	Ⓐ Ⓑ Ⓒ Ⓓ Ⓔ
	PT1-S4-Q4	Ⓐ Ⓑ Ⓒ Ⓓ Ⓔ	V2, Pg. 76	PT20-S4-Q23	Ⓐ Ⓑ Ⓒ Ⓓ Ⓔ
	PT1-S4-Q17	Ⓐ Ⓑ Ⓒ Ⓓ Ⓔ	V2, Pg. 77	PT20-S4-Q26	Ⓐ Ⓑ Ⓒ Ⓓ Ⓔ
	PT1-S4-Q20	Ⓐ Ⓑ Ⓒ Ⓓ Ⓔ	V2, Pg. 128	PT22-S2-Q8	Ⓐ Ⓑ Ⓒ Ⓓ Ⓔ
	PT2-S2-Q22	Ⓐ Ⓑ Ⓒ Ⓓ Ⓔ	V2, Pg. 131	PT22-S2-Q19	Ⓐ Ⓑ Ⓒ Ⓓ Ⓔ
	PT2-S4-Q3	Ⓐ Ⓑ Ⓒ Ⓓ Ⓔ	V2, Pg. 142	PT22-S4-Q15	Ⓐ Ⓑ Ⓒ Ⓓ Ⓔ
	PT2-S4-Q10	Ⓐ Ⓑ Ⓒ Ⓓ Ⓔ	V2, Pg. 163	PT23-S2-Q26	Ⓐ Ⓑ Ⓒ Ⓓ Ⓔ
	PT3-S2-Q20	Ⓐ Ⓑ Ⓒ Ⓓ Ⓔ	V2, Pg. 168	PT23-S3-Q15	Ⓐ Ⓑ Ⓒ Ⓓ Ⓔ
	PT3-S4-Q10	Ⓐ Ⓑ Ⓒ Ⓓ Ⓔ	V2, Pg. 194	PT24-S2-Q4	Ⓐ Ⓑ Ⓒ Ⓓ Ⓔ
	PT4-S1-Q24	Ⓐ Ⓑ Ⓒ Ⓓ Ⓔ	V2, Pg. 195	PT24-S2-Q7	Ⓐ Ⓑ Ⓒ Ⓓ Ⓔ
	PT4-S4-Q9	Ⓐ Ⓑ Ⓒ Ⓓ Ⓔ	V2, Pg. 200	PT24-S2-Q19	Ⓐ Ⓑ Ⓒ Ⓓ Ⓔ
	PT4-S4-Q24	Ⓐ Ⓑ Ⓒ Ⓓ Ⓔ	V2, Pg. 200	PT24-S2-Q20	Ⓐ Ⓑ Ⓒ Ⓓ Ⓔ
	PT4-S4-Q25	Ⓐ Ⓑ Ⓒ Ⓓ Ⓔ	V2, Pg. 205	PT24-S3-Q14	Ⓐ Ⓑ Ⓒ Ⓓ Ⓔ
	PT6-S2-Q7	Ⓐ Ⓑ Ⓒ Ⓓ Ⓔ	V2, Pg. 208	PT24-S3-Q22	Ⓐ Ⓑ Ⓒ Ⓓ Ⓔ
	PT6-S2-Q12	Ⓐ Ⓑ Ⓒ Ⓓ Ⓔ	V2, Pg. 233	PT25-S2-Q17	Ⓐ Ⓑ Ⓒ Ⓓ Ⓔ
	PT6-S3-Q3	Ⓐ Ⓑ Ⓒ Ⓓ Ⓔ	V2, Pg. 234	PT25-S2-Q19	Ⓐ Ⓑ Ⓒ Ⓓ Ⓔ
V1, Pg. 21	PT7-S1-Q19	Ⓐ Ⓑ Ⓒ Ⓓ Ⓔ	V2, Pg. 243	PT25-S4-Q11	Ⓐ Ⓑ Ⓒ Ⓓ Ⓔ
	PT8-S4-Q19	Ⓐ Ⓑ Ⓒ Ⓓ Ⓔ	V2, Pg. 244	PT25-S4-Q15	Ⓐ Ⓑ Ⓒ Ⓓ Ⓔ
V1, Pg. 62	PT9-S2-Q17	Ⓐ Ⓑ Ⓒ Ⓓ Ⓔ	V2, Pg. 244	PT25-S4-Q16	Ⓐ Ⓑ Ⓒ Ⓓ Ⓔ
V1, Pg. 71	PT9-S4-Q8	Ⓐ Ⓑ Ⓒ Ⓓ Ⓔ	V2, Pg. 262	PT26-S2-Q17	Ⓐ Ⓑ Ⓒ Ⓓ Ⓔ
V1, Pg. 86	PT10-S1-Q9	Ⓐ Ⓑ Ⓒ Ⓓ Ⓔ	V2, Pg. 263	PT26-S2-Q19	Ⓐ Ⓑ Ⓒ Ⓓ Ⓔ
V1, Pg. 88	PT10-S1-Q19	Ⓐ Ⓑ Ⓒ Ⓓ Ⓔ	V2, Pg. 264	PT26-S2-Q22	Ⓐ Ⓑ Ⓒ Ⓓ Ⓔ
V1, Pg. 111	PT10-S4-Q23	Ⓐ Ⓑ Ⓒ Ⓓ Ⓔ	V2, Pg. 272	PT26-S3-Q20	Ⓐ Ⓑ Ⓒ Ⓓ Ⓔ

V2, Pg. 295	PT27-S1-Q25	Ⓐ Ⓑ Ⓒ Ⓓ Ⓔ	V3, Pg. 298	PT37-S2-Q8	Ⓐ Ⓑ Ⓒ Ⓓ Ⓔ
V2, Pg. 312	PT27-S4-Q16	Ⓐ Ⓑ Ⓒ Ⓓ Ⓔ	V3, Pg. 300	PT37-S2-Q17	Ⓐ Ⓑ Ⓒ Ⓓ Ⓔ
V2, Pg. 322	PT28-S1-Q1	Ⓐ Ⓑ Ⓒ Ⓓ Ⓔ	V3, Pg. 301	PT37-S2-Q20	Ⓐ Ⓑ Ⓒ Ⓓ Ⓔ
V2, Pg. 324	PT28-S1-Q11	Ⓐ Ⓑ Ⓒ Ⓓ Ⓔ	V3, Pg. 311	PT37-S4-Q13	Ⓐ Ⓑ Ⓒ Ⓓ Ⓔ
V2, Pg. 328	PT28-S1-Q23	Ⓐ Ⓑ Ⓒ Ⓓ Ⓔ	V3, Pg. 343	PT38-S4-Q5	Ⓐ Ⓑ Ⓒ Ⓓ Ⓔ
V2, Pg. 329	PT28-S1-Q26	Ⓐ Ⓑ Ⓒ Ⓓ Ⓔ	V3, Pg. 343	PT38-S4-Q7	Ⓐ Ⓑ Ⓒ Ⓓ Ⓔ
V2, Pg. 334	PT28-S3-Q4	Ⓐ Ⓑ Ⓒ Ⓓ Ⓔ	V3, Pg. 344	PT38-S4-Q9	Ⓐ Ⓑ Ⓒ Ⓓ Ⓔ
V2, Pg. 336	PT28-S3-Q12	Ⓐ Ⓑ Ⓒ Ⓓ Ⓔ	V3, Pg. 349	PT38-S4-Q25	Ⓐ Ⓑ Ⓒ Ⓓ Ⓔ
V2, Pg. 339	PT28-S3-Q20	Ⓐ Ⓑ Ⓒ Ⓓ Ⓔ		PT39-S2-Q24	Ⓐ Ⓑ Ⓒ Ⓓ Ⓔ
V3, Pg. 16	PT29-S1-Q3	Ⓐ Ⓑ Ⓒ Ⓓ Ⓔ		PT39-S4-Q13	Ⓐ Ⓑ Ⓒ Ⓓ Ⓔ
V3, Pg. 19	PT29-S1-Q13	Ⓐ Ⓑ Ⓒ Ⓓ Ⓔ		PT39-S4-Q22	Ⓐ Ⓑ Ⓒ Ⓓ Ⓔ
V3, Pg. 23	PT29-S1-Q25	Ⓐ Ⓑ Ⓒ Ⓓ Ⓔ		PT40-S3-Q2	Ⓐ Ⓑ Ⓒ Ⓓ Ⓔ
V3, Pg. 41	PT29-S4-Q19	Ⓐ Ⓑ Ⓒ Ⓓ Ⓔ		PT40-S3-Q7	Ⓐ Ⓑ Ⓒ Ⓓ Ⓔ
V3, Pg. 41	PT29-S4-Q20	Ⓐ Ⓑ Ⓒ Ⓓ Ⓔ		PT40-S3-Q19	Ⓐ Ⓑ Ⓒ Ⓓ Ⓔ
V3, Pg. 57	PT30-S2-Q12	Ⓐ Ⓑ Ⓒ Ⓓ Ⓔ		PT40-S3-Q26	Ⓐ Ⓑ Ⓒ Ⓓ Ⓔ
V3, Pg. 59	PT30-S2-Q19	Ⓐ Ⓑ Ⓒ Ⓓ Ⓔ		PT41-S3-Q2	Ⓐ Ⓑ Ⓒ Ⓓ Ⓔ
V3, Pg. 71	PT30-S4-Q5	Ⓐ Ⓑ Ⓒ Ⓓ Ⓔ		PT41-S3-Q5	Ⓐ Ⓑ Ⓒ Ⓓ Ⓔ
V3, Pg. 71	PT30-S4-Q7	Ⓐ Ⓑ Ⓒ Ⓓ Ⓔ		PT41-S3-Q10	Ⓐ Ⓑ Ⓒ Ⓓ Ⓔ
V3, Pg. 90	PT31-S2-Q8	Ⓐ Ⓑ Ⓒ Ⓓ Ⓔ		PT41-S3-Q15	Ⓐ Ⓑ Ⓒ Ⓓ Ⓔ
V3, Pg. 92	PT31-S2-Q13	Ⓐ Ⓑ Ⓒ Ⓓ Ⓔ		PT41-S3-Q16	Ⓐ Ⓑ Ⓒ Ⓓ Ⓔ
V3, Pg. 99	PT31-S3-Q12	Ⓐ Ⓑ Ⓒ Ⓓ Ⓔ		PT41-S3-Q19	Ⓐ Ⓑ Ⓒ Ⓓ Ⓔ
V3, Pg. 123	PT32-S1-Q17	Ⓐ Ⓑ Ⓒ Ⓓ Ⓔ		PT42-S4-Q9	Ⓐ Ⓑ Ⓒ Ⓓ Ⓔ
V3, Pg. 124	PT32-S1-Q20	Ⓐ Ⓑ Ⓒ Ⓓ Ⓔ		PT43-S2-Q8	Ⓐ Ⓑ Ⓒ Ⓓ Ⓔ
V3, Pg. 142	PT32-S4-Q15	Ⓐ Ⓑ Ⓒ Ⓓ Ⓔ		PT43-S3-Q2	Ⓐ Ⓑ Ⓒ Ⓓ Ⓔ
V3, Pg. 154	PT33-S1-Q8	Ⓐ Ⓑ Ⓒ Ⓓ Ⓔ		PT43-S3-Q15	Ⓐ Ⓑ Ⓒ Ⓓ Ⓔ
V3, Pg. 156	PT33-S1-Q16	Ⓐ Ⓑ Ⓒ Ⓓ Ⓔ		PT43-S3-Q17	Ⓐ Ⓑ Ⓒ Ⓓ Ⓔ
V3, Pg. 157	PT33-S1-Q20	Ⓐ Ⓑ Ⓒ Ⓓ Ⓔ		PT44-S2-Q8	Ⓐ Ⓑ Ⓒ Ⓓ Ⓔ
V3, Pg. 158	PT33-S1-Q22	Ⓐ Ⓑ Ⓒ Ⓓ Ⓔ		PT44-S4-Q17	Ⓐ Ⓑ Ⓒ Ⓓ Ⓔ
V3, Pg. 169	PT33-S3-Q3	Ⓐ Ⓑ Ⓒ Ⓓ Ⓔ		PT44-S4-Q18	Ⓐ Ⓑ Ⓒ Ⓓ Ⓔ
V3, Pg. 202	PT34-S3-Q2	Ⓐ Ⓑ Ⓒ Ⓓ Ⓔ		PT45-S4-Q11	Ⓐ Ⓑ Ⓒ Ⓓ Ⓔ
V3, Pg. 207	PT34-S3-Q22	Ⓐ Ⓑ Ⓒ Ⓓ Ⓔ		PT45-S4-Q15	Ⓐ Ⓑ Ⓒ Ⓓ Ⓔ
V3, Pg. 222	PT35-S1-Q10	Ⓐ Ⓑ Ⓒ Ⓓ Ⓔ		PT47-S3-Q11	Ⓐ Ⓑ Ⓒ Ⓓ Ⓔ
V3, Pg. 224	PT35-S1-Q15	Ⓐ Ⓑ Ⓒ Ⓓ Ⓔ		PT47-S3-Q15	Ⓐ Ⓑ Ⓒ Ⓓ Ⓔ
V3, Pg. 240	PT35-S4-Q1	Ⓐ Ⓑ Ⓒ Ⓓ Ⓔ		PT48-S4-Q23	Ⓐ Ⓑ Ⓒ Ⓓ Ⓔ
V3, Pg. 244	PT35-S4-Q17	Ⓐ Ⓑ Ⓒ Ⓓ Ⓔ		PT49-S2-Q4	Ⓐ Ⓑ Ⓒ Ⓓ Ⓔ
V3, Pg. 246	PT35-S4-Q22	Ⓐ Ⓑ Ⓒ Ⓓ Ⓔ		PT49-S2-Q11	Ⓐ Ⓑ Ⓒ Ⓓ Ⓔ
V3, Pg. 260	PT36-S1-Q23	Ⓐ Ⓑ Ⓒ Ⓓ Ⓔ		PT49-S2-Q16	Ⓐ Ⓑ Ⓒ Ⓓ Ⓔ

	PT49-S2-Q21	Ⓐ Ⓑ Ⓒ Ⓓ Ⓔ
	PT49-S4-Q4	Ⓐ Ⓑ Ⓒ Ⓓ Ⓔ
	PT49-S4-Q25	Ⓐ Ⓑ Ⓒ Ⓓ Ⓔ
	PT50-S2-Q5	Ⓐ Ⓑ Ⓒ Ⓓ Ⓔ
	PT50-S2-Q24	Ⓐ Ⓑ Ⓒ Ⓓ Ⓔ
V4, Pg. 11	PT52-S1-Q11	Ⓐ Ⓑ Ⓒ Ⓓ Ⓔ
V4, Pg. 13	PT52-S1-Q18	Ⓐ Ⓑ Ⓒ Ⓓ Ⓔ
V4, Pg. 44	PT53-S1-Q1	Ⓐ Ⓑ Ⓒ Ⓓ Ⓔ
V4, Pg. 51	PT53-S1-Q24	Ⓐ Ⓑ Ⓒ Ⓓ Ⓔ
V4, Pg. 59	PT53-S3-Q13	Ⓐ Ⓑ Ⓒ Ⓓ Ⓔ
V4, Pg. 62	PT53-S3-Q22	Ⓐ Ⓑ Ⓒ Ⓓ Ⓔ
V4, Pg. 123	PT55-S1-Q25	Ⓐ Ⓑ Ⓒ Ⓓ Ⓔ
V4, Pg. 133	PT55-S3-Q6	Ⓐ Ⓑ Ⓒ Ⓓ Ⓔ
V4, Pg. 170	PT56-S3-Q22	Ⓐ Ⓑ Ⓒ Ⓓ Ⓔ
V4, Pg. 226	PT58-S1-Q8	Ⓐ Ⓑ Ⓒ Ⓓ Ⓔ
V4, Pg. 276	PT59-S3-Q17	Ⓐ Ⓑ Ⓒ Ⓓ Ⓔ
V4, Pg. 345	PT61-S2-Q19	Ⓐ Ⓑ Ⓒ Ⓓ Ⓔ
V4, Pg. 346	PT61-S2-Q22	Ⓐ Ⓑ Ⓒ Ⓓ Ⓔ
V4, Pg. 352	PT61-S4-Q3	Ⓐ Ⓑ Ⓒ Ⓓ Ⓔ
V5, Pg. 21	PT62-S2-Q18	Ⓐ Ⓑ Ⓒ Ⓓ Ⓔ
V5, Pg. 32	PT62-S4-Q17	Ⓐ Ⓑ Ⓒ Ⓓ Ⓔ
V5, Pg. 35	PT62-S4-Q26	Ⓐ Ⓑ Ⓒ Ⓓ Ⓔ
V5, Pg. 45	PT63-S1-Q7	Ⓐ Ⓑ Ⓒ Ⓓ Ⓔ
V5, Pg. 116	PT65-S1-Q3	Ⓐ Ⓑ Ⓒ Ⓓ Ⓔ
V5, Pg. 141	PT65-S4-Q19	Ⓐ Ⓑ Ⓒ Ⓓ Ⓔ
V5, Pg. 161	PT66-S2-Q3	Ⓐ Ⓑ Ⓒ Ⓓ Ⓔ
V5, Pg. 201	PT67-S2-Q4	Ⓐ Ⓑ Ⓒ Ⓓ Ⓔ
V5, Pg. 315	PT70-S1-Q11	Ⓐ Ⓑ Ⓒ Ⓓ Ⓔ
V5, Pg. 372	PT71-S3-Q16	Ⓐ Ⓑ Ⓒ Ⓓ Ⓔ
V5, Pg. 374	PT71-S3-Q21	Ⓐ Ⓑ Ⓒ Ⓓ Ⓔ
PT75, Pg. 32	PT75-S3-Q22	Ⓐ Ⓑ Ⓒ Ⓓ Ⓔ
PT77, Pg. 25	PT77-S2-Q25	Ⓐ Ⓑ Ⓒ Ⓓ Ⓔ
PT77, Pg. 39	PT77-S4-Q21	Ⓐ Ⓑ Ⓒ Ⓓ Ⓔ

Reading Comprehension Problem Sets

Humanities

J07, Pg. 22   J07-S4-P1

1 Ⓐ Ⓑ Ⓒ Ⓓ Ⓔ
2 Ⓐ Ⓑ Ⓒ Ⓓ Ⓔ
3 Ⓐ Ⓑ Ⓒ Ⓓ Ⓔ
4 Ⓐ Ⓑ Ⓒ Ⓓ Ⓔ
5 Ⓐ Ⓑ Ⓒ Ⓓ Ⓔ
6 Ⓐ Ⓑ Ⓒ Ⓓ Ⓔ
7 Ⓐ Ⓑ Ⓒ Ⓓ Ⓔ
8 Ⓐ Ⓑ Ⓒ Ⓓ Ⓔ

SP1, Pg. 78   PTA-S2-P2

9 Ⓐ Ⓑ Ⓒ Ⓓ Ⓔ
10 Ⓐ Ⓑ Ⓒ Ⓓ Ⓔ
11 Ⓐ Ⓑ Ⓒ Ⓓ Ⓔ
12 Ⓐ Ⓑ Ⓒ Ⓓ Ⓔ
13 Ⓐ Ⓑ Ⓒ Ⓓ Ⓔ

SP1, Pg. 204   PTB-S3-P4

22 Ⓐ Ⓑ Ⓒ Ⓓ Ⓔ
23 Ⓐ Ⓑ Ⓒ Ⓓ Ⓔ
24 Ⓐ Ⓑ Ⓒ Ⓓ Ⓔ
25 Ⓐ Ⓑ Ⓒ Ⓓ Ⓔ
26 Ⓐ Ⓑ Ⓒ Ⓓ Ⓔ

SP2, Pg. 372   PTC2-S4-P2

7 Ⓐ Ⓑ Ⓒ Ⓓ Ⓔ
8 Ⓐ Ⓑ Ⓒ Ⓓ Ⓔ
9 Ⓐ Ⓑ Ⓒ Ⓓ Ⓔ
10 Ⓐ Ⓑ Ⓒ Ⓓ Ⓔ
11 Ⓐ Ⓑ Ⓒ Ⓓ Ⓔ
12 Ⓐ Ⓑ Ⓒ Ⓓ Ⓔ

PT1-S1-P1

1 Ⓐ Ⓑ Ⓒ Ⓓ Ⓔ
2 Ⓐ Ⓑ Ⓒ Ⓓ Ⓔ
3 Ⓐ Ⓑ Ⓒ Ⓓ Ⓔ
4 Ⓐ Ⓑ Ⓒ Ⓓ Ⓔ
5 Ⓐ Ⓑ Ⓒ Ⓓ Ⓔ
6 Ⓐ Ⓑ Ⓒ Ⓓ Ⓔ
7 Ⓐ Ⓑ Ⓒ Ⓓ Ⓔ
8 Ⓐ Ⓑ Ⓒ Ⓓ Ⓔ

PT2-S1-P1

1 Ⓐ Ⓑ Ⓒ Ⓓ Ⓔ
2 Ⓐ Ⓑ Ⓒ Ⓓ Ⓔ
3 Ⓐ Ⓑ Ⓒ Ⓓ Ⓔ
4 Ⓐ Ⓑ Ⓒ Ⓓ Ⓔ
5 Ⓐ Ⓑ Ⓒ Ⓓ Ⓔ
6 Ⓐ Ⓑ Ⓒ Ⓓ Ⓔ

PT3-S3-P4

21 Ⓐ Ⓑ Ⓒ Ⓓ Ⓔ
22 Ⓐ Ⓑ Ⓒ Ⓓ Ⓔ
23 Ⓐ Ⓑ Ⓒ Ⓓ Ⓔ
24 Ⓐ Ⓑ Ⓒ Ⓓ Ⓔ
25 Ⓐ Ⓑ Ⓒ Ⓓ Ⓔ
26 Ⓐ Ⓑ Ⓒ Ⓓ Ⓔ
27 Ⓐ Ⓑ Ⓒ Ⓓ Ⓔ
28 Ⓐ Ⓑ Ⓒ Ⓓ Ⓔ

PT4-S2-P4

21 Ⓐ Ⓑ Ⓒ Ⓓ Ⓔ
22 Ⓐ Ⓑ Ⓒ Ⓓ Ⓔ
23 Ⓐ Ⓑ Ⓒ Ⓓ Ⓔ
24 Ⓐ Ⓑ Ⓒ Ⓓ Ⓔ
25 Ⓐ Ⓑ Ⓒ Ⓓ Ⓔ
26 Ⓐ Ⓑ Ⓒ Ⓓ Ⓔ
27 Ⓐ Ⓑ Ⓒ Ⓓ Ⓔ

PT5-S4-P4

22 Ⓐ Ⓑ Ⓒ Ⓓ Ⓔ
23 Ⓐ Ⓑ Ⓒ Ⓓ Ⓔ
24 Ⓐ Ⓑ Ⓒ Ⓓ Ⓔ
25 Ⓐ Ⓑ Ⓒ Ⓓ Ⓔ
26 Ⓐ Ⓑ Ⓒ Ⓓ Ⓔ
27 Ⓐ Ⓑ Ⓒ Ⓓ Ⓔ

PT6-S1-P3

13 Ⓐ Ⓑ Ⓒ Ⓓ Ⓔ
14 Ⓐ Ⓑ Ⓒ Ⓓ Ⓔ
15 Ⓐ Ⓑ Ⓒ Ⓓ Ⓔ
16 Ⓐ Ⓑ Ⓒ Ⓓ Ⓔ
17 Ⓐ Ⓑ Ⓒ Ⓓ Ⓔ
18 Ⓐ Ⓑ Ⓒ Ⓓ Ⓔ
19 Ⓐ Ⓑ Ⓒ Ⓓ Ⓔ
20 Ⓐ Ⓑ Ⓒ Ⓓ Ⓔ

V1, Pg. 30   PT7-S3-P2

8 Ⓐ Ⓑ Ⓒ Ⓓ Ⓔ
9 Ⓐ Ⓑ Ⓒ Ⓓ Ⓔ
10 Ⓐ Ⓑ Ⓒ Ⓓ Ⓔ
11 Ⓐ Ⓑ Ⓒ Ⓓ Ⓔ
12 Ⓐ Ⓑ Ⓒ Ⓓ Ⓔ
13 Ⓐ Ⓑ Ⓒ Ⓓ Ⓔ
14 Ⓐ Ⓑ Ⓒ Ⓓ Ⓔ

PT8-S3-P3

14 Ⓐ Ⓑ Ⓒ Ⓓ Ⓔ
15 Ⓐ Ⓑ Ⓒ Ⓓ Ⓔ
16 Ⓐ Ⓑ Ⓒ Ⓓ Ⓔ
17 Ⓐ Ⓑ Ⓒ Ⓓ Ⓔ
18 Ⓐ Ⓑ Ⓒ Ⓓ Ⓔ
19 Ⓐ Ⓑ Ⓒ Ⓓ Ⓔ
20 Ⓐ Ⓑ Ⓒ Ⓓ Ⓔ

V1, Pg. 50   PT9-S1-P1

1 Ⓐ Ⓑ Ⓒ Ⓓ Ⓔ
2 Ⓐ Ⓑ Ⓒ Ⓓ Ⓔ
3 Ⓐ Ⓑ Ⓒ Ⓓ Ⓔ
4 Ⓐ Ⓑ Ⓒ Ⓓ Ⓔ
5 Ⓐ Ⓑ Ⓒ Ⓓ Ⓔ
6 Ⓐ Ⓑ Ⓒ Ⓓ Ⓔ

V1, Pg. 98   PT10-S3-P2

9 Ⓐ Ⓑ Ⓒ Ⓓ Ⓔ
10 Ⓐ Ⓑ Ⓒ Ⓓ Ⓔ
11 Ⓐ Ⓑ Ⓒ Ⓓ Ⓔ
12 Ⓐ Ⓑ Ⓒ Ⓓ Ⓔ
13 Ⓐ Ⓑ Ⓒ Ⓓ Ⓔ
14 Ⓐ Ⓑ Ⓒ Ⓓ Ⓔ

V1, Pg. 130   PT11-S3-P1

1 Ⓐ Ⓑ Ⓒ Ⓓ Ⓔ
2 Ⓐ Ⓑ Ⓒ Ⓓ Ⓔ
3 Ⓐ Ⓑ Ⓒ Ⓓ Ⓔ
4 Ⓐ Ⓑ Ⓒ Ⓓ Ⓔ
5 Ⓐ Ⓑ Ⓒ Ⓓ Ⓔ
6 Ⓐ Ⓑ Ⓒ Ⓓ Ⓔ
7 Ⓐ Ⓑ Ⓒ Ⓓ Ⓔ

V1, Pg. 164   PT12-S3-P1

1 Ⓐ Ⓑ Ⓒ Ⓓ Ⓔ
2 Ⓐ Ⓑ Ⓒ Ⓓ Ⓔ
3 Ⓐ Ⓑ Ⓒ Ⓓ Ⓔ
4 Ⓐ Ⓑ Ⓒ Ⓓ Ⓔ
5 Ⓐ Ⓑ Ⓒ Ⓓ Ⓔ
6 Ⓐ Ⓑ Ⓒ Ⓓ Ⓔ
7 Ⓐ Ⓑ Ⓒ Ⓓ Ⓔ

V1, Pg. 202   PT13-S3-P3

14 Ⓐ Ⓑ Ⓒ Ⓓ Ⓔ
15 Ⓐ Ⓑ Ⓒ Ⓓ Ⓔ
16 Ⓐ Ⓑ Ⓒ Ⓓ Ⓔ
17 Ⓐ Ⓑ Ⓒ Ⓓ Ⓔ
18 Ⓐ Ⓑ Ⓒ Ⓓ Ⓔ
19 Ⓐ Ⓑ Ⓒ Ⓓ Ⓔ
20 Ⓐ Ⓑ Ⓒ Ⓓ Ⓔ

V1, Pg. 234   PT14-S3-P2

7   Ⓐ Ⓑ Ⓒ Ⓓ Ⓔ
8   Ⓐ Ⓑ Ⓒ Ⓓ Ⓔ
9   Ⓐ Ⓑ Ⓒ Ⓓ Ⓔ
10 Ⓐ Ⓑ Ⓒ Ⓓ Ⓔ
11 Ⓐ Ⓑ Ⓒ Ⓓ Ⓔ
12 Ⓐ Ⓑ Ⓒ Ⓓ Ⓔ
13 Ⓐ Ⓑ Ⓒ Ⓓ Ⓔ

V1, Pg. 256   PT15-S1-P2

8   Ⓐ Ⓑ Ⓒ Ⓓ Ⓔ
9   Ⓐ Ⓑ Ⓒ Ⓓ Ⓔ
10 Ⓐ Ⓑ Ⓒ Ⓓ Ⓔ
11 Ⓐ Ⓑ Ⓒ Ⓓ Ⓔ
12 Ⓐ Ⓑ Ⓒ Ⓓ Ⓔ
13 Ⓐ Ⓑ Ⓒ Ⓓ Ⓔ
14 Ⓐ Ⓑ Ⓒ Ⓓ Ⓔ
15 Ⓐ Ⓑ Ⓒ Ⓓ Ⓔ

V1, Pg. 308   PT16-S4-P1

1   Ⓐ Ⓑ Ⓒ Ⓓ Ⓔ
2   Ⓐ Ⓑ Ⓒ Ⓓ Ⓔ
3   Ⓐ Ⓑ Ⓒ Ⓓ Ⓔ
4   Ⓐ Ⓑ Ⓒ Ⓓ Ⓔ
5   Ⓐ Ⓑ Ⓒ Ⓓ Ⓔ
6   Ⓐ Ⓑ Ⓒ Ⓓ Ⓔ
7   Ⓐ Ⓑ Ⓒ Ⓓ Ⓔ
8   Ⓐ Ⓑ Ⓒ Ⓓ Ⓔ

PT17-S4-P1

1   Ⓐ Ⓑ Ⓒ Ⓓ Ⓔ
2   Ⓐ Ⓑ Ⓒ Ⓓ Ⓔ
3   Ⓐ Ⓑ Ⓒ Ⓓ Ⓔ
4   Ⓐ Ⓑ Ⓒ Ⓓ Ⓔ
5   Ⓐ Ⓑ Ⓒ Ⓓ Ⓔ
6   Ⓐ Ⓑ Ⓒ Ⓓ Ⓔ
7   Ⓐ Ⓑ Ⓒ Ⓓ Ⓔ
8   Ⓐ Ⓑ Ⓒ Ⓓ Ⓔ

V1, Pg. 340   PT18-S3-P4

22 Ⓐ Ⓑ Ⓒ Ⓓ Ⓔ
23 Ⓐ Ⓑ Ⓒ Ⓓ Ⓔ
24 Ⓐ Ⓑ Ⓒ Ⓓ Ⓔ
25 Ⓐ Ⓑ Ⓒ Ⓓ Ⓔ
26 Ⓐ Ⓑ Ⓒ Ⓓ Ⓔ
27 Ⓐ Ⓑ Ⓒ Ⓓ Ⓔ
28 Ⓐ Ⓑ Ⓒ Ⓓ Ⓔ

V2, Pg. 28   PT19-S3-P1

1   Ⓐ Ⓑ Ⓒ Ⓓ Ⓔ
2   Ⓐ Ⓑ Ⓒ Ⓓ Ⓔ
3   Ⓐ Ⓑ Ⓒ Ⓓ Ⓔ
4   Ⓐ Ⓑ Ⓒ Ⓓ Ⓔ
5   Ⓐ Ⓑ Ⓒ Ⓓ Ⓔ
6   Ⓐ Ⓑ Ⓒ Ⓓ Ⓔ
7   Ⓐ Ⓑ Ⓒ Ⓓ Ⓔ
8   Ⓐ Ⓑ Ⓒ Ⓓ Ⓔ

V2, Pg. 58   PT20-S2-P1

1   Ⓐ Ⓑ Ⓒ Ⓓ Ⓔ
2   Ⓐ Ⓑ Ⓒ Ⓓ Ⓔ
3   Ⓐ Ⓑ Ⓒ Ⓓ Ⓔ
4   Ⓐ Ⓑ Ⓒ Ⓓ Ⓔ
5   Ⓐ Ⓑ Ⓒ Ⓓ Ⓔ
6   Ⓐ Ⓑ Ⓒ Ⓓ Ⓔ

V2, Pg. 104   PT21-S4-P1

1   Ⓐ Ⓑ Ⓒ Ⓓ Ⓔ
2   Ⓐ Ⓑ Ⓒ Ⓓ Ⓔ
3   Ⓐ Ⓑ Ⓒ Ⓓ Ⓔ
4   Ⓐ Ⓑ Ⓒ Ⓓ Ⓔ
5   Ⓐ Ⓑ Ⓒ Ⓓ Ⓔ
6   Ⓐ Ⓑ Ⓒ Ⓓ Ⓔ
7   Ⓐ Ⓑ Ⓒ Ⓓ Ⓔ
8   Ⓐ Ⓑ Ⓒ Ⓓ Ⓔ

V2, Pg. 118   PT22-S1-P1

1   Ⓐ Ⓑ Ⓒ Ⓓ Ⓔ
2   Ⓐ Ⓑ Ⓒ Ⓓ Ⓔ
3   Ⓐ Ⓑ Ⓒ Ⓓ Ⓔ
4   Ⓐ Ⓑ Ⓒ Ⓓ Ⓔ
5   Ⓐ Ⓑ Ⓒ Ⓓ Ⓔ
6   Ⓐ Ⓑ Ⓒ Ⓓ Ⓔ
7   Ⓐ Ⓑ Ⓒ Ⓓ Ⓔ
8   Ⓐ Ⓑ Ⓒ Ⓓ Ⓔ

V2, Pg. 172   PT23-S4-P1

1   Ⓐ Ⓑ Ⓒ Ⓓ Ⓔ
2   Ⓐ Ⓑ Ⓒ Ⓓ Ⓔ
3   Ⓐ Ⓑ Ⓒ Ⓓ Ⓔ
4   Ⓐ Ⓑ Ⓒ Ⓓ Ⓔ
5   Ⓐ Ⓑ Ⓒ Ⓓ Ⓔ

V2, Pg. 192   PT24-S1-P4

21 Ⓐ Ⓑ Ⓒ Ⓓ Ⓔ
22 Ⓐ Ⓑ Ⓒ Ⓓ Ⓔ
23 Ⓐ Ⓑ Ⓒ Ⓓ Ⓔ
24 Ⓐ Ⓑ Ⓒ Ⓓ Ⓔ
25 Ⓐ Ⓑ Ⓒ Ⓓ Ⓔ
26 Ⓐ Ⓑ Ⓒ Ⓓ Ⓔ
27 Ⓐ Ⓑ Ⓒ Ⓓ Ⓔ

V2, Pg. 222   PT25-S1-P2

8   Ⓐ Ⓑ Ⓒ Ⓓ Ⓔ
9   Ⓐ Ⓑ Ⓒ Ⓓ Ⓔ
10 Ⓐ Ⓑ Ⓒ Ⓓ Ⓔ
11 Ⓐ Ⓑ Ⓒ Ⓓ Ⓔ
12 Ⓐ Ⓑ Ⓒ Ⓓ Ⓔ
13 Ⓐ Ⓑ Ⓒ Ⓓ Ⓔ

V2, Pg. 276   PT26-S4-P2

6   Ⓐ Ⓑ Ⓒ Ⓓ Ⓔ
7   Ⓐ Ⓑ Ⓒ Ⓓ Ⓔ
8   Ⓐ Ⓑ Ⓒ Ⓓ Ⓔ
9   Ⓐ Ⓑ Ⓒ Ⓓ Ⓔ
10 Ⓐ Ⓑ Ⓒ Ⓓ Ⓔ
11 Ⓐ Ⓑ Ⓒ Ⓓ Ⓔ
12 Ⓐ Ⓑ Ⓒ Ⓓ Ⓔ
13 Ⓐ Ⓑ Ⓒ Ⓓ Ⓔ

V2, Pg. 306   PT27-S3-P4

22 Ⓐ Ⓑ Ⓒ Ⓓ Ⓔ
23 Ⓐ Ⓑ Ⓒ Ⓓ Ⓔ
24 Ⓐ Ⓑ Ⓒ Ⓓ Ⓔ
25 Ⓐ Ⓑ Ⓒ Ⓓ Ⓔ
26 Ⓐ Ⓑ Ⓒ Ⓓ Ⓔ

V2, Pg. 348   PT28-S4-P4

22 Ⓐ Ⓑ Ⓒ Ⓓ Ⓔ
23 Ⓐ Ⓑ Ⓒ Ⓓ Ⓔ
24 Ⓐ Ⓑ Ⓒ Ⓓ Ⓔ
25 Ⓐ Ⓑ Ⓒ Ⓓ Ⓔ
26 Ⓐ Ⓑ Ⓒ Ⓓ Ⓔ

V3, Pg. 24   PT29-S2-P1

1   Ⓐ Ⓑ Ⓒ Ⓓ Ⓔ
2   Ⓐ Ⓑ Ⓒ Ⓓ Ⓔ
3   Ⓐ Ⓑ Ⓒ Ⓓ Ⓔ
4   Ⓐ Ⓑ Ⓒ Ⓓ Ⓔ
5   Ⓐ Ⓑ Ⓒ Ⓓ Ⓔ
6   Ⓐ Ⓑ Ⓒ Ⓓ Ⓔ
7   Ⓐ Ⓑ Ⓒ Ⓓ Ⓔ

V3, Pg. 64   PT30-S3-P2

7   Ⓐ Ⓑ Ⓒ Ⓓ Ⓔ
8   Ⓐ Ⓑ Ⓒ Ⓓ Ⓔ
9   Ⓐ Ⓑ Ⓒ Ⓓ Ⓔ
10 Ⓐ Ⓑ Ⓒ Ⓓ Ⓔ
11 Ⓐ Ⓑ Ⓒ Ⓓ Ⓔ
12 Ⓐ Ⓑ Ⓒ Ⓓ Ⓔ
13 Ⓐ Ⓑ Ⓒ Ⓓ Ⓔ
14 Ⓐ Ⓑ Ⓒ Ⓓ Ⓔ

V3, Pg. 110   PT31-S4-P4

21 Ⓐ Ⓑ Ⓒ Ⓓ Ⓔ
22 Ⓐ Ⓑ Ⓒ Ⓓ Ⓔ
23 Ⓐ Ⓑ Ⓒ Ⓓ Ⓔ
24 Ⓐ Ⓑ Ⓒ Ⓓ Ⓔ
25 Ⓐ Ⓑ Ⓒ Ⓓ Ⓔ
26 Ⓐ Ⓑ Ⓒ Ⓓ Ⓔ
27 Ⓐ Ⓑ Ⓒ Ⓓ Ⓔ
28 Ⓐ Ⓑ Ⓒ Ⓓ Ⓔ

V3, Pg. 130   PT32-S2-P3

14 Ⓐ Ⓑ Ⓒ Ⓓ Ⓔ
15 Ⓐ Ⓑ Ⓒ Ⓓ Ⓔ
16 Ⓐ Ⓑ Ⓒ Ⓓ Ⓔ
17 Ⓐ Ⓑ Ⓒ Ⓓ Ⓔ
18 Ⓐ Ⓑ Ⓒ Ⓓ Ⓔ
19 Ⓐ Ⓑ Ⓒ Ⓓ Ⓔ

V3, Pg. 162   PT33-S2-P2

8   Ⓐ Ⓑ Ⓒ Ⓓ Ⓔ
9   Ⓐ Ⓑ Ⓒ Ⓓ Ⓔ
10 Ⓐ Ⓑ Ⓒ Ⓓ Ⓔ
11 Ⓐ Ⓑ Ⓒ Ⓓ Ⓔ
12 Ⓐ Ⓑ Ⓒ Ⓓ Ⓔ
13 Ⓐ Ⓑ Ⓒ Ⓓ Ⓔ
14 Ⓐ Ⓑ Ⓒ Ⓓ Ⓔ

V3, Pg. 188   PT34-S1-P2

7   Ⓐ Ⓑ Ⓒ Ⓓ Ⓔ
8   Ⓐ Ⓑ Ⓒ Ⓓ Ⓔ
9   Ⓐ Ⓑ Ⓒ Ⓓ Ⓔ
10 Ⓐ Ⓑ Ⓒ Ⓓ Ⓔ
11 Ⓐ Ⓑ Ⓒ Ⓓ Ⓔ
12 Ⓐ Ⓑ Ⓒ Ⓓ Ⓔ

V3, Pg. 230   PT35-S2-P2

7   Ⓐ Ⓑ Ⓒ Ⓓ Ⓔ
8   Ⓐ Ⓑ Ⓒ Ⓓ Ⓔ
9   Ⓐ Ⓑ Ⓒ Ⓓ Ⓔ
10 Ⓐ Ⓑ Ⓒ Ⓓ Ⓔ
11 Ⓐ Ⓑ Ⓒ Ⓓ Ⓔ
12 Ⓐ Ⓑ Ⓒ Ⓓ Ⓔ
13 Ⓐ Ⓑ Ⓒ Ⓓ Ⓔ
14 Ⓐ Ⓑ Ⓒ Ⓓ Ⓔ

V3, Pg. 264   PT36-S2-P2

7   Ⓐ Ⓑ Ⓒ Ⓓ Ⓔ
8   Ⓐ Ⓑ Ⓒ Ⓓ Ⓔ
9   Ⓐ Ⓑ Ⓒ Ⓓ Ⓔ
10 Ⓐ Ⓑ Ⓒ Ⓓ Ⓔ
11 Ⓐ Ⓑ Ⓒ Ⓓ Ⓔ
12 Ⓐ Ⓑ Ⓒ Ⓓ Ⓔ
13 Ⓐ Ⓑ Ⓒ Ⓓ Ⓔ
14 Ⓐ Ⓑ Ⓒ Ⓓ Ⓔ

V3, Pg. 292   PT37-S1-P3

14 Ⓐ Ⓑ Ⓒ Ⓓ Ⓔ
15 Ⓐ Ⓑ Ⓒ Ⓓ Ⓔ
16 Ⓐ Ⓑ Ⓒ Ⓓ Ⓔ
17 Ⓐ Ⓑ Ⓒ Ⓓ Ⓔ
18 Ⓐ Ⓑ Ⓒ Ⓓ Ⓔ
19 Ⓐ Ⓑ Ⓒ Ⓓ Ⓔ
20 Ⓐ Ⓑ Ⓒ Ⓓ Ⓔ
21 Ⓐ Ⓑ Ⓒ Ⓓ Ⓔ

V3, Pg. 340   PT38-S3-P4

21 Ⓐ Ⓑ Ⓒ Ⓓ Ⓔ
22 Ⓐ Ⓑ Ⓒ Ⓓ Ⓔ
23 Ⓐ Ⓑ Ⓒ Ⓓ Ⓔ
24 Ⓐ Ⓑ Ⓒ Ⓓ Ⓔ
25 Ⓐ Ⓑ Ⓒ Ⓓ Ⓔ
26 Ⓐ Ⓑ Ⓒ Ⓓ Ⓔ
27 Ⓐ Ⓑ Ⓒ Ⓓ Ⓔ

PT39-S3-P1

1   Ⓐ Ⓑ Ⓒ Ⓓ Ⓔ
2   Ⓐ Ⓑ Ⓒ Ⓓ Ⓔ
3   Ⓐ Ⓑ Ⓒ Ⓓ Ⓔ
4   Ⓐ Ⓑ Ⓒ Ⓓ Ⓔ
5   Ⓐ Ⓑ Ⓒ Ⓓ Ⓔ
6   Ⓐ Ⓑ Ⓒ Ⓓ Ⓔ
7   Ⓐ Ⓑ Ⓒ Ⓓ Ⓔ
8   Ⓐ Ⓑ Ⓒ Ⓓ Ⓔ

PT40-S4-P2

6   Ⓐ Ⓑ Ⓒ Ⓓ Ⓔ
7   Ⓐ Ⓑ Ⓒ Ⓓ Ⓔ
8   Ⓐ Ⓑ Ⓒ Ⓓ Ⓔ
9   Ⓐ Ⓑ Ⓒ Ⓓ Ⓔ
10 Ⓐ Ⓑ Ⓒ Ⓓ Ⓔ
11 Ⓐ Ⓑ Ⓒ Ⓓ Ⓔ
12 Ⓐ Ⓑ Ⓒ Ⓓ Ⓔ

PT41-S4-P2

7   Ⓐ Ⓑ Ⓒ Ⓓ Ⓔ
8   Ⓐ Ⓑ Ⓒ Ⓓ Ⓔ
9   Ⓐ Ⓑ Ⓒ Ⓓ Ⓔ
10 Ⓐ Ⓑ Ⓒ Ⓓ Ⓔ
11 Ⓐ Ⓑ Ⓒ Ⓓ Ⓔ
12 Ⓐ Ⓑ Ⓒ Ⓓ Ⓔ
13 Ⓐ Ⓑ Ⓒ Ⓓ Ⓔ

PT42-S3-P2

8   Ⓐ Ⓑ Ⓒ Ⓓ Ⓔ
9   Ⓐ Ⓑ Ⓒ Ⓓ Ⓔ
10 Ⓐ Ⓑ Ⓒ Ⓓ Ⓔ
11 Ⓐ Ⓑ Ⓒ Ⓓ Ⓔ
12 Ⓐ Ⓑ Ⓒ Ⓓ Ⓔ
13 Ⓐ Ⓑ Ⓒ Ⓓ Ⓔ
14 Ⓐ Ⓑ Ⓒ Ⓓ Ⓔ
15 Ⓐ Ⓑ Ⓒ Ⓓ Ⓔ

PT43-S1-P3

14 Ⓐ Ⓑ Ⓒ Ⓓ Ⓔ
15 Ⓐ Ⓑ Ⓒ Ⓓ Ⓔ
16 Ⓐ Ⓑ Ⓒ Ⓓ Ⓔ
17 Ⓐ Ⓑ Ⓒ Ⓓ Ⓔ
18 Ⓐ Ⓑ Ⓒ Ⓓ Ⓔ
19 Ⓐ Ⓑ Ⓒ Ⓓ Ⓔ
20 Ⓐ Ⓑ Ⓒ Ⓓ Ⓔ
21 Ⓐ Ⓑ Ⓒ Ⓓ Ⓔ

PT44-S1-P4

21 Ⓐ Ⓑ Ⓒ Ⓓ Ⓔ
22 Ⓐ Ⓑ Ⓒ Ⓓ Ⓔ
23 Ⓐ Ⓑ Ⓒ Ⓓ Ⓔ
24 Ⓐ Ⓑ Ⓒ Ⓓ Ⓔ
25 Ⓐ Ⓑ Ⓒ Ⓓ Ⓔ
26 Ⓐ Ⓑ Ⓒ Ⓓ Ⓔ
27 Ⓐ Ⓑ Ⓒ Ⓓ Ⓔ

PT45-S2-P2

7   Ⓐ Ⓑ Ⓒ Ⓓ Ⓔ
8   Ⓐ Ⓑ Ⓒ Ⓓ Ⓔ
9   Ⓐ Ⓑ Ⓒ Ⓓ Ⓔ
10 Ⓐ Ⓑ Ⓒ Ⓓ Ⓔ
11 Ⓐ Ⓑ Ⓒ Ⓓ Ⓔ
12 Ⓐ Ⓑ Ⓒ Ⓓ Ⓔ
13 Ⓐ Ⓑ Ⓒ Ⓓ Ⓔ
14 Ⓐ Ⓑ Ⓒ Ⓓ Ⓔ

PT46-S1-P2

8   Ⓐ Ⓑ Ⓒ Ⓓ Ⓔ
9   Ⓐ Ⓑ Ⓒ Ⓓ Ⓔ
10 Ⓐ Ⓑ Ⓒ Ⓓ Ⓔ
11 Ⓐ Ⓑ Ⓒ Ⓓ Ⓔ
12 Ⓐ Ⓑ Ⓒ Ⓓ Ⓔ
13 Ⓐ Ⓑ Ⓒ Ⓓ Ⓔ
14 Ⓐ Ⓑ Ⓒ Ⓓ Ⓔ
15 Ⓐ Ⓑ Ⓒ Ⓓ Ⓔ

PT47-S2-P2

6   Ⓐ Ⓑ Ⓒ Ⓓ Ⓔ
7   Ⓐ Ⓑ Ⓒ Ⓓ Ⓔ
8   Ⓐ Ⓑ Ⓒ Ⓓ Ⓔ
9   Ⓐ Ⓑ Ⓒ Ⓓ Ⓔ
10 Ⓐ Ⓑ Ⓒ Ⓓ Ⓔ
11 Ⓐ Ⓑ Ⓒ Ⓓ Ⓔ

PT48-S3-P2

6   Ⓐ Ⓑ Ⓒ Ⓓ Ⓔ
7   Ⓐ Ⓑ Ⓒ Ⓓ Ⓔ
8   Ⓐ Ⓑ Ⓒ Ⓓ Ⓔ
9   Ⓐ Ⓑ Ⓒ Ⓓ Ⓔ
10 Ⓐ Ⓑ Ⓒ Ⓓ Ⓔ
11 Ⓐ Ⓑ Ⓒ Ⓓ Ⓔ
12 Ⓐ Ⓑ Ⓒ Ⓓ Ⓔ

PT49-S3-P2

7   Ⓐ Ⓑ Ⓒ Ⓓ Ⓔ
8   Ⓐ Ⓑ Ⓒ Ⓓ Ⓔ
9   Ⓐ Ⓑ Ⓒ Ⓓ Ⓔ
10 Ⓐ Ⓑ Ⓒ Ⓓ Ⓔ
11 Ⓐ Ⓑ Ⓒ Ⓓ Ⓔ
12 Ⓐ Ⓑ Ⓒ Ⓓ Ⓔ
13 Ⓐ Ⓑ Ⓒ Ⓓ Ⓔ

PT50-S1-P1

1 Ⓐ Ⓑ Ⓒ Ⓓ Ⓔ
2 Ⓐ Ⓑ Ⓒ Ⓓ Ⓔ
3 Ⓐ Ⓑ Ⓒ Ⓓ Ⓔ
4 Ⓐ Ⓑ Ⓒ Ⓓ Ⓔ
5 Ⓐ Ⓑ Ⓒ Ⓓ Ⓔ

PT51-S2-P1

1 Ⓐ Ⓑ Ⓒ Ⓓ Ⓔ
2 Ⓐ Ⓑ Ⓒ Ⓓ Ⓔ
3 Ⓐ Ⓑ Ⓒ Ⓓ Ⓔ
4 Ⓐ Ⓑ Ⓒ Ⓓ Ⓔ
5 Ⓐ Ⓑ Ⓒ Ⓓ Ⓔ
6 Ⓐ Ⓑ Ⓒ Ⓓ Ⓔ
7 Ⓐ Ⓑ Ⓒ Ⓓ Ⓔ

V4, Pg. 28   PT52-S4-P1

1 Ⓐ Ⓑ Ⓒ Ⓓ Ⓔ
2 Ⓐ Ⓑ Ⓒ Ⓓ Ⓔ
3 Ⓐ Ⓑ Ⓒ Ⓓ Ⓔ
4 Ⓐ Ⓑ Ⓒ Ⓓ Ⓔ
5 Ⓐ Ⓑ Ⓒ Ⓓ Ⓔ
6 Ⓐ Ⓑ Ⓒ Ⓓ Ⓔ

V4, Pg. 64   PT53-S4-P1

1 Ⓐ Ⓑ Ⓒ Ⓓ Ⓔ
2 Ⓐ Ⓑ Ⓒ Ⓓ Ⓔ
3 Ⓐ Ⓑ Ⓒ Ⓓ Ⓔ
4 Ⓐ Ⓑ Ⓒ Ⓓ Ⓔ
5 Ⓐ Ⓑ Ⓒ Ⓓ Ⓔ
6 Ⓐ Ⓑ Ⓒ Ⓓ Ⓔ

V4, Pg. 84   PT54-S1-P3

13 Ⓐ Ⓑ Ⓒ Ⓓ Ⓔ
14 Ⓐ Ⓑ Ⓒ Ⓓ Ⓔ
15 Ⓐ Ⓑ Ⓒ Ⓓ Ⓔ
16 Ⓐ Ⓑ Ⓒ Ⓓ Ⓔ
17 Ⓐ Ⓑ Ⓒ Ⓓ Ⓔ
18 Ⓐ Ⓑ Ⓒ Ⓓ Ⓔ
19 Ⓐ Ⓑ Ⓒ Ⓓ Ⓔ

V4, Pg. 128   PT55-S2-P3

14 Ⓐ Ⓑ Ⓒ Ⓓ Ⓔ
15 Ⓐ Ⓑ Ⓒ Ⓓ Ⓔ
16 Ⓐ Ⓑ Ⓒ Ⓓ Ⓔ
17 Ⓐ Ⓑ Ⓒ Ⓓ Ⓔ
18 Ⓐ Ⓑ Ⓒ Ⓓ Ⓔ
19 Ⓐ Ⓑ Ⓒ Ⓓ Ⓔ
20 Ⓐ Ⓑ Ⓒ Ⓓ Ⓔ
21 Ⓐ Ⓑ Ⓒ Ⓓ Ⓔ

V4, Pg. 172   PT56-S4-P1

1 Ⓐ Ⓑ Ⓒ Ⓓ Ⓔ
2 Ⓐ Ⓑ Ⓒ Ⓓ Ⓔ
3 Ⓐ Ⓑ Ⓒ Ⓓ Ⓔ
4 Ⓐ Ⓑ Ⓒ Ⓓ Ⓔ
5 Ⓐ Ⓑ Ⓒ Ⓓ Ⓔ
6 Ⓐ Ⓑ Ⓒ Ⓓ Ⓔ
7 Ⓐ Ⓑ Ⓒ Ⓓ Ⓔ

V4, Pg. 212   PT57-S4-P3

13 Ⓐ Ⓑ Ⓒ Ⓓ Ⓔ
14 Ⓐ Ⓑ Ⓒ Ⓓ Ⓔ
15 Ⓐ Ⓑ Ⓒ Ⓓ Ⓔ
16 Ⓐ Ⓑ Ⓒ Ⓓ Ⓔ
17 Ⓐ Ⓑ Ⓒ Ⓓ Ⓔ
18 Ⓐ Ⓑ Ⓒ Ⓓ Ⓔ
19 Ⓐ Ⓑ Ⓒ Ⓓ Ⓔ

V4, Pg. 238   PT58-S2-P4

21 Ⓐ Ⓑ Ⓒ Ⓓ Ⓔ
22 Ⓐ Ⓑ Ⓒ Ⓓ Ⓔ
23 Ⓐ Ⓑ Ⓒ Ⓓ Ⓔ
24 Ⓐ Ⓑ Ⓒ Ⓓ Ⓔ
25 Ⓐ Ⓑ Ⓒ Ⓓ Ⓔ
26 Ⓐ Ⓑ Ⓒ Ⓓ Ⓔ
27 Ⓐ Ⓑ Ⓒ Ⓓ Ⓔ

V4, Pg. 284   PT59-S4-P3

16 Ⓐ Ⓑ Ⓒ Ⓓ Ⓔ
17 Ⓐ Ⓑ Ⓒ Ⓓ Ⓔ
18 Ⓐ Ⓑ Ⓒ Ⓓ Ⓔ
19 Ⓐ Ⓑ Ⓒ Ⓓ Ⓔ
20 Ⓐ Ⓑ Ⓒ Ⓓ Ⓔ
21 Ⓐ Ⓑ Ⓒ Ⓓ Ⓔ
22 Ⓐ Ⓑ Ⓒ Ⓓ Ⓔ

V4, Pg. 320   PT60-S4-P3

13 Ⓐ Ⓑ Ⓒ Ⓓ Ⓔ
14 Ⓐ Ⓑ Ⓒ Ⓓ Ⓔ
15 Ⓐ Ⓑ Ⓒ Ⓓ Ⓔ
16 Ⓐ Ⓑ Ⓒ Ⓓ Ⓔ
17 Ⓐ Ⓑ Ⓒ Ⓓ Ⓔ
18 Ⓐ Ⓑ Ⓒ Ⓓ Ⓔ
19 Ⓐ Ⓑ Ⓒ Ⓓ Ⓔ
20 Ⓐ Ⓑ Ⓒ Ⓓ Ⓔ

V4, Pg. 334   PT61-S1-P2

7 Ⓐ Ⓑ Ⓒ Ⓓ Ⓔ
8 Ⓐ Ⓑ Ⓒ Ⓓ Ⓔ
9 Ⓐ Ⓑ Ⓒ Ⓓ Ⓔ
10 Ⓐ Ⓑ Ⓒ Ⓓ Ⓔ
11 Ⓐ Ⓑ Ⓒ Ⓓ Ⓔ
12 Ⓐ Ⓑ Ⓒ Ⓓ Ⓔ
13 Ⓐ Ⓑ Ⓒ Ⓓ Ⓔ

V5, Pg. 14   PT62-S1-P4

22 Ⓐ Ⓑ Ⓒ Ⓓ Ⓔ
23 Ⓐ Ⓑ Ⓒ Ⓓ Ⓔ
24 Ⓐ Ⓑ Ⓒ Ⓓ Ⓔ
25 Ⓐ Ⓑ Ⓒ Ⓓ Ⓔ
26 Ⓐ Ⓑ Ⓒ Ⓓ Ⓔ
27 Ⓐ Ⓑ Ⓒ Ⓓ Ⓔ

V5, Pg. 66   PT63-S4-P2

8 Ⓐ Ⓑ Ⓒ Ⓓ Ⓔ
9 Ⓐ Ⓑ Ⓒ Ⓓ Ⓔ
10 Ⓐ Ⓑ Ⓒ Ⓓ Ⓔ
11 Ⓐ Ⓑ Ⓒ Ⓓ Ⓔ
12 Ⓐ Ⓑ Ⓒ Ⓓ Ⓔ
13 Ⓐ Ⓑ Ⓒ Ⓓ Ⓔ
14 Ⓐ Ⓑ Ⓒ Ⓓ Ⓔ
15 Ⓐ Ⓑ Ⓒ Ⓓ Ⓔ

V5, Pg. 106   PT64-S4-P4

20 Ⓐ Ⓑ Ⓒ Ⓓ Ⓔ
21 Ⓐ Ⓑ Ⓒ Ⓓ Ⓔ
22 Ⓐ Ⓑ Ⓒ Ⓓ Ⓔ
23 Ⓐ Ⓑ Ⓒ Ⓓ Ⓔ
24 Ⓐ Ⓑ Ⓒ Ⓓ Ⓔ
25 Ⓐ Ⓑ Ⓒ Ⓓ Ⓔ
26 Ⓐ Ⓑ Ⓒ Ⓓ Ⓔ
27 Ⓐ Ⓑ Ⓒ Ⓓ Ⓔ

V5, Pg. 128   PT65-S3-P1

1 Ⓐ Ⓑ Ⓒ Ⓓ Ⓔ
2 Ⓐ Ⓑ Ⓒ Ⓓ Ⓔ
3 Ⓐ Ⓑ Ⓒ Ⓓ Ⓔ
4 Ⓐ Ⓑ Ⓒ Ⓓ Ⓔ
5 Ⓐ Ⓑ Ⓒ Ⓓ Ⓔ
6 Ⓐ Ⓑ Ⓒ Ⓓ Ⓔ
7 Ⓐ Ⓑ Ⓒ Ⓓ Ⓔ

V5, Pg. 156   PT66-S1-P3

15 Ⓐ Ⓑ Ⓒ Ⓓ Ⓔ
16 Ⓐ Ⓑ Ⓒ Ⓓ Ⓔ
17 Ⓐ Ⓑ Ⓒ Ⓓ Ⓔ
18 Ⓐ Ⓑ Ⓒ Ⓓ Ⓔ
19 Ⓐ Ⓑ Ⓒ Ⓓ Ⓔ
20 Ⓐ Ⓑ Ⓒ Ⓓ Ⓔ
21 Ⓐ Ⓑ Ⓒ Ⓓ Ⓔ
22 Ⓐ Ⓑ Ⓒ Ⓓ Ⓔ

V5, Pg. 192   PT67-S1-P1

1 Ⓐ Ⓑ Ⓒ Ⓓ Ⓔ
2 Ⓐ Ⓑ Ⓒ Ⓓ Ⓔ
3 Ⓐ Ⓑ Ⓒ Ⓓ Ⓔ
4 Ⓐ Ⓑ Ⓒ Ⓓ Ⓔ
5 Ⓐ Ⓑ Ⓒ Ⓓ Ⓔ
6 Ⓐ Ⓑ Ⓒ Ⓓ Ⓔ
7 Ⓐ Ⓑ Ⓒ Ⓓ Ⓔ

V5, Pg. 194 PT67-S1-P2

8 Ⓐ Ⓑ Ⓒ Ⓓ Ⓔ
9 Ⓐ Ⓑ Ⓒ Ⓓ Ⓔ
10 Ⓐ Ⓑ Ⓒ Ⓓ Ⓔ
11 Ⓐ Ⓑ Ⓒ Ⓓ Ⓔ
12 Ⓐ Ⓑ Ⓒ Ⓓ Ⓔ
13 Ⓐ Ⓑ Ⓒ Ⓓ Ⓔ
14 Ⓐ Ⓑ Ⓒ Ⓓ Ⓔ

V5, Pg. 232 PT68-S1-P1

1 Ⓐ Ⓑ Ⓒ Ⓓ Ⓔ
2 Ⓐ Ⓑ Ⓒ Ⓓ Ⓔ
3 Ⓐ Ⓑ Ⓒ Ⓓ Ⓔ
4 Ⓐ Ⓑ Ⓒ Ⓓ Ⓔ
5 Ⓐ Ⓑ Ⓒ Ⓓ Ⓔ
6 Ⓐ Ⓑ Ⓒ Ⓓ Ⓔ
7 Ⓐ Ⓑ Ⓒ Ⓓ Ⓔ

V5, Pg. 290 PT69-S3-P2

8 Ⓐ Ⓑ Ⓒ Ⓓ Ⓔ
9 Ⓐ Ⓑ Ⓒ Ⓓ Ⓔ
10 Ⓐ Ⓑ Ⓒ Ⓓ Ⓔ
11 Ⓐ Ⓑ Ⓒ Ⓓ Ⓔ
12 Ⓐ Ⓑ Ⓒ Ⓓ Ⓔ
13 Ⓐ Ⓑ Ⓒ Ⓓ Ⓔ
14 Ⓐ Ⓑ Ⓒ Ⓓ Ⓔ

V5, Pg. 322 PT70-S2-P2

8 Ⓐ Ⓑ Ⓒ Ⓓ Ⓔ
9 Ⓐ Ⓑ Ⓒ Ⓓ Ⓔ
10 Ⓐ Ⓑ Ⓒ Ⓓ Ⓔ
11 Ⓐ Ⓑ Ⓒ Ⓓ Ⓔ
12 Ⓐ Ⓑ Ⓒ Ⓓ Ⓔ
13 Ⓐ Ⓑ Ⓒ Ⓓ Ⓔ
14 Ⓐ Ⓑ Ⓒ Ⓓ Ⓔ

V5, Pg. 376 PT71-S4-P1

1 Ⓐ Ⓑ Ⓒ Ⓓ Ⓔ
2 Ⓐ Ⓑ Ⓒ Ⓓ Ⓔ
3 Ⓐ Ⓑ Ⓒ Ⓓ Ⓔ
4 Ⓐ Ⓑ Ⓒ Ⓓ Ⓔ
5 Ⓐ Ⓑ Ⓒ Ⓓ Ⓔ
6 Ⓐ Ⓑ Ⓒ Ⓓ Ⓔ

PT72, Pg. 12 PT72-S1-P2

7 Ⓐ Ⓑ Ⓒ Ⓓ Ⓔ
8 Ⓐ Ⓑ Ⓒ Ⓓ Ⓔ
9 Ⓐ Ⓑ Ⓒ Ⓓ Ⓔ
10 Ⓐ Ⓑ Ⓒ Ⓓ Ⓔ
11 Ⓐ Ⓑ Ⓒ Ⓓ Ⓔ
12 Ⓐ Ⓑ Ⓒ Ⓓ Ⓔ
13 Ⓐ Ⓑ Ⓒ Ⓓ Ⓔ

PT73, Pg. 12 PT73-S1-P2

8 Ⓐ Ⓑ Ⓒ Ⓓ Ⓔ
9 Ⓐ Ⓑ Ⓒ Ⓓ Ⓔ
10 Ⓐ Ⓑ Ⓒ Ⓓ Ⓔ
11 Ⓐ Ⓑ Ⓒ Ⓓ Ⓔ
12 Ⓐ Ⓑ Ⓒ Ⓓ Ⓔ
13 Ⓐ Ⓑ Ⓒ Ⓓ Ⓔ
14 Ⓐ Ⓑ Ⓒ Ⓓ Ⓔ
15 Ⓐ Ⓑ Ⓒ Ⓓ Ⓔ

PT74, Pg. 26 PT74-S3-P1

1 Ⓐ Ⓑ Ⓒ Ⓓ Ⓔ
2 Ⓐ Ⓑ Ⓒ Ⓓ Ⓔ
3 Ⓐ Ⓑ Ⓒ Ⓓ Ⓔ
4 Ⓐ Ⓑ Ⓒ Ⓓ Ⓔ
5 Ⓐ Ⓑ Ⓒ Ⓓ Ⓔ
6 Ⓐ Ⓑ Ⓒ Ⓓ Ⓔ
7 Ⓐ Ⓑ Ⓒ Ⓓ Ⓔ
8 Ⓐ Ⓑ Ⓒ Ⓓ Ⓔ

PT76, Pg. 10 PT76-S1-P1

1 Ⓐ Ⓑ Ⓒ Ⓓ Ⓔ
2 Ⓐ Ⓑ Ⓒ Ⓓ Ⓔ
3 Ⓐ Ⓑ Ⓒ Ⓓ Ⓔ
4 Ⓐ Ⓑ Ⓒ Ⓓ Ⓔ
5 Ⓐ Ⓑ Ⓒ Ⓓ Ⓔ
6 Ⓐ Ⓑ Ⓒ Ⓓ Ⓔ

PT77, Pg. 10 PT77-S1-P1

1 Ⓐ Ⓑ Ⓒ Ⓓ Ⓔ
2 Ⓐ Ⓑ Ⓒ Ⓓ Ⓔ
3 Ⓐ Ⓑ Ⓒ Ⓓ Ⓔ
4 Ⓐ Ⓑ Ⓒ Ⓓ Ⓔ
5 Ⓐ Ⓑ Ⓒ Ⓓ Ⓔ
6 Ⓐ Ⓑ Ⓒ Ⓓ Ⓔ
7 Ⓐ Ⓑ Ⓒ Ⓓ Ⓔ

Law

J07, Pg. 26 J07-S4-P3

15 Ⓐ Ⓑ Ⓒ Ⓓ Ⓔ
16 Ⓐ Ⓑ Ⓒ Ⓓ Ⓔ
17 Ⓐ Ⓑ Ⓒ Ⓓ Ⓔ
18 Ⓐ Ⓑ Ⓒ Ⓓ Ⓔ
19 Ⓐ Ⓑ Ⓒ Ⓓ Ⓔ
20 Ⓐ Ⓑ Ⓒ Ⓓ Ⓔ
21 Ⓐ Ⓑ Ⓒ Ⓓ Ⓔ
22 Ⓐ Ⓑ Ⓒ Ⓓ Ⓔ

SP1, Pg. 76 PTA-S2-P1

1 Ⓐ Ⓑ Ⓒ Ⓓ Ⓔ
2 Ⓐ Ⓑ Ⓒ Ⓓ Ⓔ
3 Ⓐ Ⓑ Ⓒ Ⓓ Ⓔ
4 Ⓐ Ⓑ Ⓒ Ⓓ Ⓔ
5 Ⓐ Ⓑ Ⓒ Ⓓ Ⓔ
6 Ⓐ Ⓑ Ⓒ Ⓓ Ⓔ
7 Ⓐ Ⓑ Ⓒ Ⓓ Ⓔ
8 Ⓐ Ⓑ Ⓒ Ⓓ Ⓔ

SP1, Pg. 200 PTB-S3-P2

8 Ⓐ Ⓑ Ⓒ Ⓓ Ⓔ
9 Ⓐ Ⓑ Ⓒ Ⓓ Ⓔ
10 Ⓐ Ⓑ Ⓒ Ⓓ Ⓔ
11 Ⓐ Ⓑ Ⓒ Ⓓ Ⓔ
12 Ⓐ Ⓑ Ⓒ Ⓓ Ⓔ
13 Ⓐ Ⓑ Ⓒ Ⓓ Ⓔ
14 Ⓐ Ⓑ Ⓒ Ⓓ Ⓔ

SP1, Pg. 318 PTC-S4-P2

8 Ⓐ Ⓑ Ⓒ Ⓓ Ⓔ
9 Ⓐ Ⓑ Ⓒ Ⓓ Ⓔ
10 Ⓐ Ⓑ Ⓒ Ⓓ Ⓔ
11 Ⓐ Ⓑ Ⓒ Ⓓ Ⓔ
12 Ⓐ Ⓑ Ⓒ Ⓓ Ⓔ
13 Ⓐ Ⓑ Ⓒ Ⓓ Ⓔ
14 Ⓐ Ⓑ Ⓒ Ⓓ Ⓔ
15 Ⓐ Ⓑ Ⓒ Ⓓ Ⓔ

SP2, Pg. 376 PTC2-S4-P4

20 Ⓐ Ⓑ Ⓒ Ⓓ Ⓔ
21 Ⓐ Ⓑ Ⓒ Ⓓ Ⓔ
22 Ⓐ Ⓑ Ⓒ Ⓓ Ⓔ
23 Ⓐ Ⓑ Ⓒ Ⓓ Ⓔ
24 Ⓐ Ⓑ Ⓒ Ⓓ Ⓔ
25 Ⓐ Ⓑ Ⓒ Ⓓ Ⓔ
26 Ⓐ Ⓑ Ⓒ Ⓓ Ⓔ
27 Ⓐ Ⓑ Ⓒ Ⓓ Ⓔ

PT1-S1-P3

17 Ⓐ Ⓑ Ⓒ Ⓓ Ⓔ
18 Ⓐ Ⓑ Ⓒ Ⓓ Ⓔ
19 Ⓐ Ⓑ Ⓒ Ⓓ Ⓔ
20 Ⓐ Ⓑ Ⓒ Ⓓ Ⓔ
21 Ⓐ Ⓑ Ⓒ Ⓓ Ⓔ

PT2-S1-P4

22 Ⓐ Ⓑ Ⓒ Ⓓ Ⓔ
23 Ⓐ Ⓑ Ⓒ Ⓓ Ⓔ
24 Ⓐ Ⓑ Ⓒ Ⓓ Ⓔ
25 Ⓐ Ⓑ Ⓒ Ⓓ Ⓔ
26 Ⓐ Ⓑ Ⓒ Ⓓ Ⓔ
27 Ⓐ Ⓑ Ⓒ Ⓓ Ⓔ
28 Ⓐ Ⓑ Ⓒ Ⓓ Ⓔ

PT3-S3-P3

16 Ⓐ Ⓑ Ⓒ Ⓓ Ⓔ
17 Ⓐ Ⓑ Ⓒ Ⓓ Ⓔ
18 Ⓐ Ⓑ Ⓒ Ⓓ Ⓔ
19 Ⓐ Ⓑ Ⓒ Ⓓ Ⓔ
20 Ⓐ Ⓑ Ⓒ Ⓓ Ⓔ

PT4-S2-P1

1 Ⓐ Ⓑ Ⓒ Ⓓ Ⓔ
2 Ⓐ Ⓑ Ⓒ Ⓓ Ⓔ
3 Ⓐ Ⓑ Ⓒ Ⓓ Ⓔ
4 Ⓐ Ⓑ Ⓒ Ⓓ Ⓔ
5 Ⓐ Ⓑ Ⓒ Ⓓ Ⓔ
6 Ⓐ Ⓑ Ⓒ Ⓓ Ⓔ

PT5-S4-P1

1 Ⓐ Ⓑ Ⓒ Ⓓ Ⓔ
2 Ⓐ Ⓑ Ⓒ Ⓓ Ⓔ
3 Ⓐ Ⓑ Ⓒ Ⓓ Ⓔ
4 Ⓐ Ⓑ Ⓒ Ⓓ Ⓔ
5 Ⓐ Ⓑ Ⓒ Ⓓ Ⓔ
6 Ⓐ Ⓑ Ⓒ Ⓓ Ⓔ
7 Ⓐ Ⓑ Ⓒ Ⓓ Ⓔ
8 Ⓐ Ⓑ Ⓒ Ⓓ Ⓔ

PT6-S1-P1

1 Ⓐ Ⓑ Ⓒ Ⓓ Ⓔ
2 Ⓐ Ⓑ Ⓒ Ⓓ Ⓔ
3 Ⓐ Ⓑ Ⓒ Ⓓ Ⓔ
4 Ⓐ Ⓑ Ⓒ Ⓓ Ⓔ
5 Ⓐ Ⓑ Ⓒ Ⓓ Ⓔ
6 Ⓐ Ⓑ Ⓒ Ⓓ Ⓔ

V1, Pg. 34   PT7-S3-P4

21 Ⓐ Ⓑ Ⓒ Ⓓ Ⓔ
22 Ⓐ Ⓑ Ⓒ Ⓓ Ⓔ
23 Ⓐ Ⓑ Ⓒ Ⓓ Ⓔ
24 Ⓐ Ⓑ Ⓒ Ⓓ Ⓔ
25 Ⓐ Ⓑ Ⓒ Ⓓ Ⓔ
26 Ⓐ Ⓑ Ⓒ Ⓓ Ⓔ
27 Ⓐ Ⓑ Ⓒ Ⓓ Ⓔ

PT8-S3-P2

7 Ⓐ Ⓑ Ⓒ Ⓓ Ⓔ
8 Ⓐ Ⓑ Ⓒ Ⓓ Ⓔ
9 Ⓐ Ⓑ Ⓒ Ⓓ Ⓔ
10 Ⓐ Ⓑ Ⓒ Ⓓ Ⓔ
11 Ⓐ Ⓑ Ⓒ Ⓓ Ⓔ
12 Ⓐ Ⓑ Ⓒ Ⓓ Ⓔ
13 Ⓐ Ⓑ Ⓒ Ⓓ Ⓔ

V1, Pg. 56   PT9-S1-P4

21 Ⓐ Ⓑ Ⓒ Ⓓ Ⓔ
22 Ⓐ Ⓑ Ⓒ Ⓓ Ⓔ
23 Ⓐ Ⓑ Ⓒ Ⓓ Ⓔ
24 Ⓐ Ⓑ Ⓒ Ⓓ Ⓔ
25 Ⓐ Ⓑ Ⓒ Ⓓ Ⓔ
26 Ⓐ Ⓑ Ⓒ Ⓓ Ⓔ
27 Ⓐ Ⓑ Ⓒ Ⓓ Ⓔ

V1, Pg. 100   PT10-S3-P3

15 Ⓐ Ⓑ Ⓒ Ⓓ Ⓔ
16 Ⓐ Ⓑ Ⓒ Ⓓ Ⓔ
17 Ⓐ Ⓑ Ⓒ Ⓓ Ⓔ
18 Ⓐ Ⓑ Ⓒ Ⓓ Ⓔ
19 Ⓐ Ⓑ Ⓒ Ⓓ Ⓔ
20 Ⓐ Ⓑ Ⓒ Ⓓ Ⓔ
21 Ⓐ Ⓑ Ⓒ Ⓓ Ⓔ

V1, Pg. 168   PT12-S3-P3

14 Ⓐ Ⓑ Ⓒ Ⓓ Ⓔ
15 Ⓐ Ⓑ Ⓒ Ⓓ Ⓔ
16 Ⓐ Ⓑ Ⓒ Ⓓ Ⓔ
17 Ⓐ Ⓑ Ⓒ Ⓓ Ⓔ
18 Ⓐ Ⓑ Ⓒ Ⓓ Ⓔ
19 Ⓐ Ⓑ Ⓒ Ⓓ Ⓔ
20 Ⓐ Ⓑ Ⓒ Ⓓ Ⓔ

V1, Pg. 204   PT13-S3-P4

21 Ⓐ Ⓑ Ⓒ Ⓓ Ⓔ
22 Ⓐ Ⓑ Ⓒ Ⓓ Ⓔ
23 Ⓐ Ⓑ Ⓒ Ⓓ Ⓔ
24 Ⓐ Ⓑ Ⓒ Ⓓ Ⓔ
25 Ⓐ Ⓑ Ⓒ Ⓓ Ⓔ
26 Ⓐ Ⓑ Ⓒ Ⓓ Ⓔ
27 Ⓐ Ⓑ Ⓒ Ⓓ Ⓔ

V1, Pg. 236   PT14-S3-P3

14 Ⓐ Ⓑ Ⓒ Ⓓ Ⓔ
15 Ⓐ Ⓑ Ⓒ Ⓓ Ⓔ
16 Ⓐ Ⓑ Ⓒ Ⓓ Ⓔ
17 Ⓐ Ⓑ Ⓒ Ⓓ Ⓔ
18 Ⓐ Ⓑ Ⓒ Ⓓ Ⓔ
19 Ⓐ Ⓑ Ⓒ Ⓓ Ⓔ
20 Ⓐ Ⓑ Ⓒ Ⓓ Ⓔ

V1, Pg. 260   PT15-S1-P4

22 Ⓐ Ⓑ Ⓒ Ⓓ Ⓔ
23 Ⓐ Ⓑ Ⓒ Ⓓ Ⓔ
24 Ⓐ Ⓑ Ⓒ Ⓓ Ⓔ
25 Ⓐ Ⓑ Ⓒ Ⓓ Ⓔ
26 Ⓐ Ⓑ Ⓒ Ⓓ Ⓔ
27 Ⓐ Ⓑ Ⓒ Ⓓ Ⓔ

V1, Pg. 310   PT16-S4-P2

9 Ⓐ Ⓑ Ⓒ Ⓓ Ⓔ
10 Ⓐ Ⓑ Ⓒ Ⓓ Ⓔ
11 Ⓐ Ⓑ Ⓒ Ⓓ Ⓔ
12 Ⓐ Ⓑ Ⓒ Ⓓ Ⓔ
13 Ⓐ Ⓑ Ⓒ Ⓓ Ⓔ
14 Ⓐ Ⓑ Ⓒ Ⓓ Ⓔ
15 Ⓐ Ⓑ Ⓒ Ⓓ Ⓔ

PT17-S4-P2

9 Ⓐ Ⓑ Ⓒ Ⓓ Ⓔ
10 Ⓐ Ⓑ Ⓒ Ⓓ Ⓔ
11 Ⓐ Ⓑ Ⓒ Ⓓ Ⓔ
12 Ⓐ Ⓑ Ⓒ Ⓓ Ⓔ
13 Ⓐ Ⓑ Ⓒ Ⓓ Ⓔ
14 Ⓐ Ⓑ Ⓒ Ⓓ Ⓔ
15 Ⓐ Ⓑ Ⓒ Ⓓ Ⓔ

V1, Pg. 334   PT18-S3-P1

1 Ⓐ Ⓑ Ⓒ Ⓓ Ⓔ
2 Ⓐ Ⓑ Ⓒ Ⓓ Ⓔ
3 Ⓐ Ⓑ Ⓒ Ⓓ Ⓔ
4 Ⓐ Ⓑ Ⓒ Ⓓ Ⓔ
5 Ⓐ Ⓑ Ⓒ Ⓓ Ⓔ
6 Ⓐ Ⓑ Ⓒ Ⓓ Ⓔ
7 Ⓐ Ⓑ Ⓒ Ⓓ Ⓔ

V2, Pg. 30   PT19-S3-P2

9 Ⓐ Ⓑ Ⓒ Ⓓ Ⓔ
10 Ⓐ Ⓑ Ⓒ Ⓓ Ⓔ
11 Ⓐ Ⓑ Ⓒ Ⓓ Ⓔ
12 Ⓐ Ⓑ Ⓒ Ⓓ Ⓔ
13 Ⓐ Ⓑ Ⓒ Ⓓ Ⓔ
14 Ⓐ Ⓑ Ⓒ Ⓓ Ⓔ

V2, Pg. 60   PT20-S2-P2

7 Ⓐ Ⓑ Ⓒ Ⓓ Ⓔ
8 Ⓐ Ⓑ Ⓒ Ⓓ Ⓔ
9 Ⓐ Ⓑ Ⓒ Ⓓ Ⓔ
10 Ⓐ Ⓑ Ⓒ Ⓓ Ⓔ
11 Ⓐ Ⓑ Ⓒ Ⓓ Ⓔ
12 Ⓐ Ⓑ Ⓒ Ⓓ Ⓔ
13 Ⓐ Ⓑ Ⓒ Ⓓ Ⓔ
14 Ⓐ Ⓑ Ⓒ Ⓓ Ⓔ

V2, Pg. 106   PT21-S4-P2

9 Ⓐ Ⓑ Ⓒ Ⓓ Ⓔ
10 Ⓐ Ⓑ Ⓒ Ⓓ Ⓔ
11 Ⓐ Ⓑ Ⓒ Ⓓ Ⓔ
12 Ⓐ Ⓑ Ⓒ Ⓓ Ⓔ
13 Ⓐ Ⓑ Ⓒ Ⓓ Ⓔ
14 Ⓐ Ⓑ Ⓒ Ⓓ Ⓔ
15 Ⓐ Ⓑ Ⓒ Ⓓ Ⓔ
16 Ⓐ Ⓑ Ⓒ Ⓓ Ⓔ

V2, Pg. 120   PT22-S1-P2

9 Ⓐ Ⓑ Ⓒ Ⓓ Ⓔ
10 Ⓐ Ⓑ Ⓒ Ⓓ Ⓔ
11 Ⓐ Ⓑ Ⓒ Ⓓ Ⓔ
12 Ⓐ Ⓑ Ⓒ Ⓓ Ⓔ
13 Ⓐ Ⓑ Ⓒ Ⓓ Ⓔ
14 Ⓐ Ⓑ Ⓒ Ⓓ Ⓔ
15 Ⓐ Ⓑ Ⓒ Ⓓ Ⓔ
16 Ⓐ Ⓑ Ⓒ Ⓓ Ⓔ

V2, Pg. 174   PT23-S4-P2

6 Ⓐ Ⓑ Ⓒ Ⓓ Ⓔ
7 Ⓐ Ⓑ Ⓒ Ⓓ Ⓔ
8 Ⓐ Ⓑ Ⓒ Ⓓ Ⓔ
9 Ⓐ Ⓑ Ⓒ Ⓓ Ⓔ
10 Ⓐ Ⓑ Ⓒ Ⓓ Ⓔ
11 Ⓐ Ⓑ Ⓒ Ⓓ Ⓔ
12 Ⓐ Ⓑ Ⓒ Ⓓ Ⓔ
13 Ⓐ Ⓑ Ⓒ Ⓓ Ⓔ

V2, Pg. 190   PT24-S1-P3

14 Ⓐ Ⓑ Ⓒ Ⓓ Ⓔ
15 Ⓐ Ⓑ Ⓒ Ⓓ Ⓔ
16 Ⓐ Ⓑ Ⓒ Ⓓ Ⓔ
17 Ⓐ Ⓑ Ⓒ Ⓓ Ⓔ
18 Ⓐ Ⓑ Ⓒ Ⓓ Ⓔ
19 Ⓐ Ⓑ Ⓒ Ⓓ Ⓔ
20 Ⓐ Ⓑ Ⓒ Ⓓ Ⓔ

V2, Pg. 220   PT25-S1-P1

1 Ⓐ Ⓑ Ⓒ Ⓓ Ⓔ
2 Ⓐ Ⓑ Ⓒ Ⓓ Ⓔ
3 Ⓐ Ⓑ Ⓒ Ⓓ Ⓔ
4 Ⓐ Ⓑ Ⓒ Ⓓ Ⓔ
5 Ⓐ Ⓑ Ⓒ Ⓓ Ⓔ
6 Ⓐ Ⓑ Ⓒ Ⓓ Ⓔ
7 Ⓐ Ⓑ Ⓒ Ⓓ Ⓔ

V2, Pg. 280   PT26-S4-P4

22 Ⓐ Ⓑ Ⓒ Ⓓ Ⓔ
23 Ⓐ Ⓑ Ⓒ Ⓓ Ⓔ
24 Ⓐ Ⓑ Ⓒ Ⓓ Ⓔ
25 Ⓐ Ⓑ Ⓒ Ⓓ Ⓔ
26 Ⓐ Ⓑ Ⓒ Ⓓ Ⓔ
27 Ⓐ Ⓑ Ⓒ Ⓓ Ⓔ

V2, Pg. 300   PT27-S3-P1

1 Ⓐ Ⓑ Ⓒ Ⓓ Ⓔ
2 Ⓐ Ⓑ Ⓒ Ⓓ Ⓔ
3 Ⓐ Ⓑ Ⓒ Ⓓ Ⓔ
4 Ⓐ Ⓑ Ⓒ Ⓓ Ⓔ
5 Ⓐ Ⓑ Ⓒ Ⓓ Ⓔ
6 Ⓐ Ⓑ Ⓒ Ⓓ Ⓔ
7 Ⓐ Ⓑ Ⓒ Ⓓ Ⓔ

V2, Pg. 342   PT28-S4-P1

1 Ⓐ Ⓑ Ⓒ Ⓓ Ⓔ
2 Ⓐ Ⓑ Ⓒ Ⓓ Ⓔ
3 Ⓐ Ⓑ Ⓒ Ⓓ Ⓔ
4 Ⓐ Ⓑ Ⓒ Ⓓ Ⓔ
5 Ⓐ Ⓑ Ⓒ Ⓓ Ⓔ

V3, Pg. 30   PT29-S2-P4

22 Ⓐ Ⓑ Ⓒ Ⓓ Ⓔ
23 Ⓐ Ⓑ Ⓒ Ⓓ Ⓔ
24 Ⓐ Ⓑ Ⓒ Ⓓ Ⓔ
25 Ⓐ Ⓑ Ⓒ Ⓓ Ⓔ
26 Ⓐ Ⓑ Ⓒ Ⓓ Ⓔ
27 Ⓐ Ⓑ Ⓒ Ⓓ Ⓔ

V3, Pg. 66   PT30-S3-P3

15 Ⓐ Ⓑ Ⓒ Ⓓ Ⓔ
16 Ⓐ Ⓑ Ⓒ Ⓓ Ⓔ
17 Ⓐ Ⓑ Ⓒ Ⓓ Ⓔ
18 Ⓐ Ⓑ Ⓒ Ⓓ Ⓔ
19 Ⓐ Ⓑ Ⓒ Ⓓ Ⓔ
20 Ⓐ Ⓑ Ⓒ Ⓓ Ⓔ
21 Ⓐ Ⓑ Ⓒ Ⓓ Ⓔ

V3, Pg. 106   PT31-S4-P2

6 Ⓐ Ⓑ Ⓒ Ⓓ Ⓔ
7 Ⓐ Ⓑ Ⓒ Ⓓ Ⓔ
8 Ⓐ Ⓑ Ⓒ Ⓓ Ⓔ
9 Ⓐ Ⓑ Ⓒ Ⓓ Ⓔ
10 Ⓐ Ⓑ Ⓒ Ⓓ Ⓔ
11 Ⓐ Ⓑ Ⓒ Ⓓ Ⓔ
12 Ⓐ Ⓑ Ⓒ Ⓓ Ⓔ

V3, Pg. 126   PT32-S2-P1

1 Ⓐ Ⓑ Ⓒ Ⓓ Ⓔ
2 Ⓐ Ⓑ Ⓒ Ⓓ Ⓔ
3 Ⓐ Ⓑ Ⓒ Ⓓ Ⓔ
4 Ⓐ Ⓑ Ⓒ Ⓓ Ⓔ
5 Ⓐ Ⓑ Ⓒ Ⓓ Ⓔ
6 Ⓐ Ⓑ Ⓒ Ⓓ Ⓔ
7 Ⓐ Ⓑ Ⓒ Ⓓ Ⓔ

V3, Pg. 166   PT33-S2-P4

23 Ⓐ Ⓑ Ⓒ Ⓓ Ⓔ
24 Ⓐ Ⓑ Ⓒ Ⓓ Ⓔ
25 Ⓐ Ⓑ Ⓒ Ⓓ Ⓔ
26 Ⓐ Ⓑ Ⓒ Ⓓ Ⓔ
27 Ⓐ Ⓑ Ⓒ Ⓓ Ⓔ
28 Ⓐ Ⓑ Ⓒ Ⓓ Ⓔ

V3, Pg. 234   PT35-S2-P4

21 Ⓐ Ⓑ Ⓒ Ⓓ Ⓔ
22 Ⓐ Ⓑ Ⓒ Ⓓ Ⓔ
23 Ⓐ Ⓑ Ⓒ Ⓓ Ⓔ
24 Ⓐ Ⓑ Ⓒ Ⓓ Ⓔ
25 Ⓐ Ⓑ Ⓒ Ⓓ Ⓔ
26 Ⓐ Ⓑ Ⓒ Ⓓ Ⓔ

V3, Pg. 268   PT36-S2-P4

21 Ⓐ Ⓑ Ⓒ Ⓓ Ⓔ
22 Ⓐ Ⓑ Ⓒ Ⓓ Ⓔ
23 Ⓐ Ⓑ Ⓒ Ⓓ Ⓔ
24 Ⓐ Ⓑ Ⓒ Ⓓ Ⓔ
25 Ⓐ Ⓑ Ⓒ Ⓓ Ⓔ
26 Ⓐ Ⓑ Ⓒ Ⓓ Ⓔ

V3, Pg. 288   PT37-S1-P1

1 Ⓐ Ⓑ Ⓒ Ⓓ Ⓔ
2 Ⓐ Ⓑ Ⓒ Ⓓ Ⓔ
3 Ⓐ Ⓑ Ⓒ Ⓓ Ⓔ
4 Ⓐ Ⓑ Ⓒ Ⓓ Ⓔ
5 Ⓐ Ⓑ Ⓒ Ⓓ Ⓔ
6 Ⓐ Ⓑ Ⓒ Ⓓ Ⓔ
7 Ⓐ Ⓑ Ⓒ Ⓓ Ⓔ

V3, Pg. 336   PT38-S3-P2

9 Ⓐ Ⓑ Ⓒ Ⓓ Ⓔ
10 Ⓐ Ⓑ Ⓒ Ⓓ Ⓔ
11 Ⓐ Ⓑ Ⓒ Ⓓ Ⓔ
12 Ⓐ Ⓑ Ⓒ Ⓓ Ⓔ
13 Ⓐ Ⓑ Ⓒ Ⓓ Ⓔ
14 Ⓐ Ⓑ Ⓒ Ⓓ Ⓔ

PT39-S3-P4

24 Ⓐ Ⓑ Ⓒ Ⓓ Ⓔ
25 Ⓐ Ⓑ Ⓒ Ⓓ Ⓔ
26 Ⓐ Ⓑ Ⓒ Ⓓ Ⓔ
27 Ⓐ Ⓑ Ⓒ Ⓓ Ⓔ
28 Ⓐ Ⓑ Ⓒ Ⓓ Ⓔ

PT40-S4-P4

20 Ⓐ Ⓑ Ⓒ Ⓓ Ⓔ
21 Ⓐ Ⓑ Ⓒ Ⓓ Ⓔ
22 Ⓐ Ⓑ Ⓒ Ⓓ Ⓔ
23 Ⓐ Ⓑ Ⓒ Ⓓ Ⓔ
24 Ⓐ Ⓑ Ⓒ Ⓓ Ⓔ
25 Ⓐ Ⓑ Ⓒ Ⓓ Ⓔ
26 Ⓐ Ⓑ Ⓒ Ⓓ Ⓔ
27 Ⓐ Ⓑ Ⓒ Ⓓ Ⓔ

PT41-S4-P1

1 Ⓐ Ⓑ Ⓒ Ⓓ Ⓔ
2 Ⓐ Ⓑ Ⓒ Ⓓ Ⓔ
3 Ⓐ Ⓑ Ⓒ Ⓓ Ⓔ
4 Ⓐ Ⓑ Ⓒ Ⓓ Ⓔ
5 Ⓐ Ⓑ Ⓒ Ⓓ Ⓔ
6 Ⓐ Ⓑ Ⓒ Ⓓ Ⓔ

PT42-S3-P1

1 Ⓐ Ⓑ Ⓒ Ⓓ Ⓔ
2 Ⓐ Ⓑ Ⓒ Ⓓ Ⓔ
3 Ⓐ Ⓑ Ⓒ Ⓓ Ⓔ
4 Ⓐ Ⓑ Ⓒ Ⓓ Ⓔ
5 Ⓐ Ⓑ Ⓒ Ⓓ Ⓔ
6 Ⓐ Ⓑ Ⓒ Ⓓ Ⓔ
7 Ⓐ Ⓑ Ⓒ Ⓓ Ⓔ

PT43-S1-P4

22 Ⓐ Ⓑ Ⓒ Ⓓ Ⓔ
23 Ⓐ Ⓑ Ⓒ Ⓓ Ⓔ
24 Ⓐ Ⓑ Ⓒ Ⓓ Ⓔ
25 Ⓐ Ⓑ Ⓒ Ⓓ Ⓔ
26 Ⓐ Ⓑ Ⓒ Ⓓ Ⓔ
27 Ⓐ Ⓑ Ⓒ Ⓓ Ⓔ
28 Ⓐ Ⓑ Ⓒ Ⓓ Ⓔ

PT44-S1-P1

1 Ⓐ Ⓑ Ⓒ Ⓓ Ⓔ
2 Ⓐ Ⓑ Ⓒ Ⓓ Ⓔ
3 Ⓐ Ⓑ Ⓒ Ⓓ Ⓔ
4 Ⓐ Ⓑ Ⓒ Ⓓ Ⓔ
5 Ⓐ Ⓑ Ⓒ Ⓓ Ⓔ
6 Ⓐ Ⓑ Ⓒ Ⓓ Ⓔ
7 Ⓐ Ⓑ Ⓒ Ⓓ Ⓔ

PT45-S2-P4

20 Ⓐ Ⓑ Ⓒ Ⓓ Ⓔ
21 Ⓐ Ⓑ Ⓒ Ⓓ Ⓔ
22 Ⓐ Ⓑ Ⓒ Ⓓ Ⓔ
23 Ⓐ Ⓑ Ⓒ Ⓓ Ⓔ
24 Ⓐ Ⓑ Ⓒ Ⓓ Ⓔ
25 Ⓐ Ⓑ Ⓒ Ⓓ Ⓔ
26 Ⓐ Ⓑ Ⓒ Ⓓ Ⓔ
27 Ⓐ Ⓑ Ⓒ Ⓓ Ⓔ

PT46-S1-P4

22 Ⓐ Ⓑ Ⓒ Ⓓ Ⓔ
23 Ⓐ Ⓑ Ⓒ Ⓓ Ⓔ
24 Ⓐ Ⓑ Ⓒ Ⓓ Ⓔ
25 Ⓐ Ⓑ Ⓒ Ⓓ Ⓔ
26 Ⓐ Ⓑ Ⓒ Ⓓ Ⓔ
27 Ⓐ Ⓑ Ⓒ Ⓓ Ⓔ

PT47-S2-P3

12 Ⓐ Ⓑ Ⓒ Ⓓ Ⓔ
13 Ⓐ Ⓑ Ⓒ Ⓓ Ⓔ
14 Ⓐ Ⓑ Ⓒ Ⓓ Ⓔ
15 Ⓐ Ⓑ Ⓒ Ⓓ Ⓔ
16 Ⓐ Ⓑ Ⓒ Ⓓ Ⓔ
17 Ⓐ Ⓑ Ⓒ Ⓓ Ⓔ
18 Ⓐ Ⓑ Ⓒ Ⓓ Ⓔ

PT48-S3-P3

13 Ⓐ Ⓑ Ⓒ Ⓓ Ⓔ
14 Ⓐ Ⓑ Ⓒ Ⓓ Ⓔ
15 Ⓐ Ⓑ Ⓒ Ⓓ Ⓔ
16 Ⓐ Ⓑ Ⓒ Ⓓ Ⓔ
17 Ⓐ Ⓑ Ⓒ Ⓓ Ⓔ
18 Ⓐ Ⓑ Ⓒ Ⓓ Ⓔ
19 Ⓐ Ⓑ Ⓒ Ⓓ Ⓔ

PT49-S3-P1

1 Ⓐ Ⓑ Ⓒ Ⓓ Ⓔ
2 Ⓐ Ⓑ Ⓒ Ⓓ Ⓔ
3 Ⓐ Ⓑ Ⓒ Ⓓ Ⓔ
4 Ⓐ Ⓑ Ⓒ Ⓓ Ⓔ
5 Ⓐ Ⓑ Ⓒ Ⓓ Ⓔ
6 Ⓐ Ⓑ Ⓒ Ⓓ Ⓔ

PT50-S1-P2

6 Ⓐ Ⓑ Ⓒ Ⓓ Ⓔ
7 Ⓐ Ⓑ Ⓒ Ⓓ Ⓔ
8 Ⓐ Ⓑ Ⓒ Ⓓ Ⓔ
9 Ⓐ Ⓑ Ⓒ Ⓓ Ⓔ
10 Ⓐ Ⓑ Ⓒ Ⓓ Ⓔ
11 Ⓐ Ⓑ Ⓒ Ⓓ Ⓔ
12 Ⓐ Ⓑ Ⓒ Ⓓ Ⓔ
13 Ⓐ Ⓑ Ⓒ Ⓓ Ⓔ

PT51-S2-P4

21 Ⓐ Ⓑ Ⓒ Ⓓ Ⓔ
22 Ⓐ Ⓑ Ⓒ Ⓓ Ⓔ
23 Ⓐ Ⓑ Ⓒ Ⓓ Ⓔ
24 Ⓐ Ⓑ Ⓒ Ⓓ Ⓔ
25 Ⓐ Ⓑ Ⓒ Ⓓ Ⓔ
26 Ⓐ Ⓑ Ⓒ Ⓓ Ⓔ
27 Ⓐ Ⓑ Ⓒ Ⓓ Ⓔ
28 Ⓐ Ⓑ Ⓒ Ⓓ Ⓔ

V4, Pg. 34   PT52-S4-P4

20 Ⓐ Ⓑ Ⓒ Ⓓ Ⓔ
21 Ⓐ Ⓑ Ⓒ Ⓓ Ⓔ
22 Ⓐ Ⓑ Ⓒ Ⓓ Ⓔ
23 Ⓐ Ⓑ Ⓒ Ⓓ Ⓔ
24 Ⓐ Ⓑ Ⓒ Ⓓ Ⓔ
25 Ⓐ Ⓑ Ⓒ Ⓓ Ⓔ
26 Ⓐ Ⓑ Ⓒ Ⓓ Ⓔ
27 Ⓐ Ⓑ Ⓒ Ⓓ Ⓔ

V4, Pg. 66   PT53-S4-P2

7 Ⓐ Ⓑ Ⓒ Ⓓ Ⓔ
8 Ⓐ Ⓑ Ⓒ Ⓓ Ⓔ
9 Ⓐ Ⓑ Ⓒ Ⓓ Ⓔ
10 Ⓐ Ⓑ Ⓒ Ⓓ Ⓔ
11 Ⓐ Ⓑ Ⓒ Ⓓ Ⓔ
12 Ⓐ Ⓑ Ⓒ Ⓓ Ⓔ
13 Ⓐ Ⓑ Ⓒ Ⓓ Ⓔ
14 Ⓐ Ⓑ Ⓒ Ⓓ Ⓔ

V4, Pg. 80   PT54-S1-P1

1 Ⓐ Ⓑ Ⓒ Ⓓ Ⓔ
2 Ⓐ Ⓑ Ⓒ Ⓓ Ⓔ
3 Ⓐ Ⓑ Ⓒ Ⓓ Ⓔ
4 Ⓐ Ⓑ Ⓒ Ⓓ Ⓔ
5 Ⓐ Ⓑ Ⓒ Ⓓ Ⓔ

V4, Pg. 124   PT55-S2-P1

1 Ⓐ Ⓑ Ⓒ Ⓓ Ⓔ
2 Ⓐ Ⓑ Ⓒ Ⓓ Ⓔ
3 Ⓐ Ⓑ Ⓒ Ⓓ Ⓔ
4 Ⓐ Ⓑ Ⓒ Ⓓ Ⓔ
5 Ⓐ Ⓑ Ⓒ Ⓓ Ⓔ
6 Ⓐ Ⓑ Ⓒ Ⓓ Ⓔ

V4, Pg. 208   PT57-S4-P1

1 Ⓐ Ⓑ Ⓒ Ⓓ Ⓔ
2 Ⓐ Ⓑ Ⓒ Ⓓ Ⓔ
3 Ⓐ Ⓑ Ⓒ Ⓓ Ⓔ
4 Ⓐ Ⓑ Ⓒ Ⓓ Ⓔ
5 Ⓐ Ⓑ Ⓒ Ⓓ Ⓔ

V4, Pg. 236   PT58-S2-P3

14 Ⓐ Ⓑ Ⓒ Ⓓ Ⓔ
15 Ⓐ Ⓑ Ⓒ Ⓓ Ⓔ
16 Ⓐ Ⓑ Ⓒ Ⓓ Ⓔ
17 Ⓐ Ⓑ Ⓒ Ⓓ Ⓔ
18 Ⓐ Ⓑ Ⓒ Ⓓ Ⓔ
19 Ⓐ Ⓑ Ⓒ Ⓓ Ⓔ
20 Ⓐ Ⓑ Ⓒ Ⓓ Ⓔ

V4, Pg. 282   PT59-S4-P2

9 Ⓐ Ⓑ Ⓒ Ⓓ Ⓔ
10 Ⓐ Ⓑ Ⓒ Ⓓ Ⓔ
11 Ⓐ Ⓑ Ⓒ Ⓓ Ⓔ
12 Ⓐ Ⓑ Ⓒ Ⓓ Ⓔ
13 Ⓐ Ⓑ Ⓒ Ⓓ Ⓔ
14 Ⓐ Ⓑ Ⓒ Ⓓ Ⓔ
15 Ⓐ Ⓑ Ⓒ Ⓓ Ⓔ

V4, Pg. 322   PT60-S4-P4

21 Ⓐ Ⓑ Ⓒ Ⓓ Ⓔ
22 Ⓐ Ⓑ Ⓒ Ⓓ Ⓔ
23 Ⓐ Ⓑ Ⓒ Ⓓ Ⓔ
24 Ⓐ Ⓑ Ⓒ Ⓓ Ⓔ
25 Ⓐ Ⓑ Ⓒ Ⓓ Ⓔ
26 Ⓐ Ⓑ Ⓒ Ⓓ Ⓔ
27 Ⓐ Ⓑ Ⓒ Ⓓ Ⓔ

V4, Pg. 332   PT61-S1-P1

1 Ⓐ Ⓑ Ⓒ Ⓓ Ⓔ
2 Ⓐ Ⓑ Ⓒ Ⓓ Ⓔ
3 Ⓐ Ⓑ Ⓒ Ⓓ Ⓔ
4 Ⓐ Ⓑ Ⓒ Ⓓ Ⓔ
5 Ⓐ Ⓑ Ⓒ Ⓓ Ⓔ
6 Ⓐ Ⓑ Ⓒ Ⓓ Ⓔ

V5, Pg. 10   PT62-S1-P2

9   Ⓐ Ⓑ Ⓒ Ⓓ Ⓔ
10 Ⓐ Ⓑ Ⓒ Ⓓ Ⓔ
11 Ⓐ Ⓑ Ⓒ Ⓓ Ⓔ
12 Ⓐ Ⓑ Ⓒ Ⓓ Ⓔ
13 Ⓐ Ⓑ Ⓒ Ⓓ Ⓔ
14 Ⓐ Ⓑ Ⓒ Ⓓ Ⓔ

V5, Pg. 64   PT63-S4-P1

1 Ⓐ Ⓑ Ⓒ Ⓓ Ⓔ
2 Ⓐ Ⓑ Ⓒ Ⓓ Ⓔ
3 Ⓐ Ⓑ Ⓒ Ⓓ Ⓔ
4 Ⓐ Ⓑ Ⓒ Ⓓ Ⓔ
5 Ⓐ Ⓑ Ⓒ Ⓓ Ⓔ
6 Ⓐ Ⓑ Ⓒ Ⓓ Ⓔ
7 Ⓐ Ⓑ Ⓒ Ⓓ Ⓔ

V5, Pg. 100   PT64-S4-P1

1 Ⓐ Ⓑ Ⓒ Ⓓ Ⓔ
2 Ⓐ Ⓑ Ⓒ Ⓓ Ⓔ
3 Ⓐ Ⓑ Ⓒ Ⓓ Ⓔ
4 Ⓐ Ⓑ Ⓒ Ⓓ Ⓔ
5 Ⓐ Ⓑ Ⓒ Ⓓ Ⓔ
6 Ⓐ Ⓑ Ⓒ Ⓓ Ⓔ

V5, Pg. 132   PT65-S3-P3

14 Ⓐ Ⓑ Ⓒ Ⓓ Ⓔ
15 Ⓐ Ⓑ Ⓒ Ⓓ Ⓔ
16 Ⓐ Ⓑ Ⓒ Ⓓ Ⓔ
17 Ⓐ Ⓑ Ⓒ Ⓓ Ⓔ
18 Ⓐ Ⓑ Ⓒ Ⓓ Ⓔ
19 Ⓐ Ⓑ Ⓒ Ⓓ Ⓔ

V5, Pg. 154   PT66-S1-P2

8   Ⓐ Ⓑ Ⓒ Ⓓ Ⓔ
9   Ⓐ Ⓑ Ⓒ Ⓓ Ⓔ
10 Ⓐ Ⓑ Ⓒ Ⓓ Ⓔ
11 Ⓐ Ⓑ Ⓒ Ⓓ Ⓔ
12 Ⓐ Ⓑ Ⓒ Ⓓ Ⓔ
13 Ⓐ Ⓑ Ⓒ Ⓓ Ⓔ
14 Ⓐ Ⓑ Ⓒ Ⓓ Ⓔ

V5, Pg. 198   PT67-S1-P4

20 Ⓐ Ⓑ Ⓒ Ⓓ Ⓔ
21 Ⓐ Ⓑ Ⓒ Ⓓ Ⓔ
22 Ⓐ Ⓑ Ⓒ Ⓓ Ⓔ
23 Ⓐ Ⓑ Ⓒ Ⓓ Ⓔ
24 Ⓐ Ⓑ Ⓒ Ⓓ Ⓔ
25 Ⓐ Ⓑ Ⓒ Ⓓ Ⓔ
26 Ⓐ Ⓑ Ⓒ Ⓓ Ⓔ
27 Ⓐ Ⓑ Ⓒ Ⓓ Ⓔ

V5, Pg. 238   PT68-S1-P4

23 Ⓐ Ⓑ Ⓒ Ⓓ Ⓔ
24 Ⓐ Ⓑ Ⓒ Ⓓ Ⓔ
25 Ⓐ Ⓑ Ⓒ Ⓓ Ⓔ
26 Ⓐ Ⓑ Ⓒ Ⓓ Ⓔ
27 Ⓐ Ⓑ Ⓒ Ⓓ Ⓔ

V5, Pg. 292   PT69-S3-P3

15 Ⓐ Ⓑ Ⓒ Ⓓ Ⓔ
16 Ⓐ Ⓑ Ⓒ Ⓓ Ⓔ
17 Ⓐ Ⓑ Ⓒ Ⓓ Ⓔ
18 Ⓐ Ⓑ Ⓒ Ⓓ Ⓔ
19 Ⓐ Ⓑ Ⓒ Ⓓ Ⓔ
20 Ⓐ Ⓑ Ⓒ Ⓓ Ⓔ
21 Ⓐ Ⓑ Ⓒ Ⓓ Ⓔ

V5, Pg. 326   PT70-S2-P4

21 Ⓐ Ⓑ Ⓒ Ⓓ Ⓔ
22 Ⓐ Ⓑ Ⓒ Ⓓ Ⓔ
23 Ⓐ Ⓑ Ⓒ Ⓓ Ⓔ
24 Ⓐ Ⓑ Ⓒ Ⓓ Ⓔ
25 Ⓐ Ⓑ Ⓒ Ⓓ Ⓔ
26 Ⓐ Ⓑ Ⓒ Ⓓ Ⓔ
27 Ⓐ Ⓑ Ⓒ Ⓓ Ⓔ

PT72, Pg. 16 PT72-S1-P4

22 Ⓐ Ⓑ Ⓒ Ⓓ Ⓔ
23 Ⓐ Ⓑ Ⓒ Ⓓ Ⓔ
24 Ⓐ Ⓑ Ⓒ Ⓓ Ⓔ
25 Ⓐ Ⓑ Ⓒ Ⓓ Ⓔ
26 Ⓐ Ⓑ Ⓒ Ⓓ Ⓔ
27 Ⓐ Ⓑ Ⓒ Ⓓ Ⓔ

PT73, Pg. 16 PT73-S1-P4

22 Ⓐ Ⓑ Ⓒ Ⓓ Ⓔ
23 Ⓐ Ⓑ Ⓒ Ⓓ Ⓔ
24 Ⓐ Ⓑ Ⓒ Ⓓ Ⓔ
25 Ⓐ Ⓑ Ⓒ Ⓓ Ⓔ
26 Ⓐ Ⓑ Ⓒ Ⓓ Ⓔ
27 Ⓐ Ⓑ Ⓒ Ⓓ Ⓔ

PT74, Pg. 28 PT74-S3-P2

9   Ⓐ Ⓑ Ⓒ Ⓓ Ⓔ
10 Ⓐ Ⓑ Ⓒ Ⓓ Ⓔ
11 Ⓐ Ⓑ Ⓒ Ⓓ Ⓔ
12 Ⓐ Ⓑ Ⓒ Ⓓ Ⓔ
13 Ⓐ Ⓑ Ⓒ Ⓓ Ⓔ
14 Ⓐ Ⓑ Ⓒ Ⓓ Ⓔ
15 Ⓐ Ⓑ Ⓒ Ⓓ Ⓔ
16 Ⓐ Ⓑ Ⓒ Ⓓ Ⓔ

PT75, Pg. 20 PT75-S2-P2

8   Ⓐ Ⓑ Ⓒ Ⓓ Ⓔ
9   Ⓐ Ⓑ Ⓒ Ⓓ Ⓔ
10 Ⓐ Ⓑ Ⓒ Ⓓ Ⓔ
11 Ⓐ Ⓑ Ⓒ Ⓓ Ⓔ
12 Ⓐ Ⓑ Ⓒ Ⓓ Ⓔ
13 Ⓐ Ⓑ Ⓒ Ⓓ Ⓔ
14 Ⓐ Ⓑ Ⓒ Ⓓ Ⓔ

PT76, Pg. 12 PT76-S1-P2

7   Ⓐ Ⓑ Ⓒ Ⓓ Ⓔ
8   Ⓐ Ⓑ Ⓒ Ⓓ Ⓔ
9   Ⓐ Ⓑ Ⓒ Ⓓ Ⓔ
10 Ⓐ Ⓑ Ⓒ Ⓓ Ⓔ
11 Ⓐ Ⓑ Ⓒ Ⓓ Ⓔ
12 Ⓐ Ⓑ Ⓒ Ⓓ Ⓔ
13 Ⓐ Ⓑ Ⓒ Ⓓ Ⓔ

PT77, Pg. 12 PT77-S1-P2

8   Ⓐ Ⓑ Ⓒ Ⓓ Ⓔ
9   Ⓐ Ⓑ Ⓒ Ⓓ Ⓔ
10 Ⓐ Ⓑ Ⓒ Ⓓ Ⓔ
11 Ⓐ Ⓑ Ⓒ Ⓓ Ⓔ
12 Ⓐ Ⓑ Ⓒ Ⓓ Ⓔ
13 Ⓐ Ⓑ Ⓒ Ⓓ Ⓔ

Natural Sciences

J07, Pg. 28   J07-S4-P4

23 Ⓐ Ⓑ Ⓒ Ⓓ Ⓔ
24 Ⓐ Ⓑ Ⓒ Ⓓ Ⓔ
25 Ⓐ Ⓑ Ⓒ Ⓓ Ⓔ
26 Ⓐ Ⓑ Ⓒ Ⓓ Ⓔ
27 Ⓐ Ⓑ Ⓒ Ⓓ Ⓔ

SP1, Pg. 80   PTA-S2-P3

14 Ⓐ Ⓑ Ⓒ Ⓓ Ⓔ
15 Ⓐ Ⓑ Ⓒ Ⓓ Ⓔ
16 Ⓐ Ⓑ Ⓒ Ⓓ Ⓔ
17 Ⓐ Ⓑ Ⓒ Ⓓ Ⓔ
18 Ⓐ Ⓑ Ⓒ Ⓓ Ⓔ
19 Ⓐ Ⓑ Ⓒ Ⓓ Ⓔ
20 Ⓐ Ⓑ Ⓒ Ⓓ Ⓔ

SP1, Pg. 198 PTB-S3-P1

1 Ⓐ Ⓑ Ⓒ Ⓓ Ⓔ
2 Ⓐ Ⓑ Ⓒ Ⓓ Ⓔ
3 Ⓐ Ⓑ Ⓒ Ⓓ Ⓔ
4 Ⓐ Ⓑ Ⓒ Ⓓ Ⓔ
5 Ⓐ Ⓑ Ⓒ Ⓓ Ⓔ
6 Ⓐ Ⓑ Ⓒ Ⓓ Ⓔ
7 Ⓐ Ⓑ Ⓒ Ⓓ Ⓔ

SP1, Pg. 316 PTC-S4-P1

1 Ⓐ Ⓑ Ⓒ Ⓓ Ⓔ
2 Ⓐ Ⓑ Ⓒ Ⓓ Ⓔ
3 Ⓐ Ⓑ Ⓒ Ⓓ Ⓔ
4 Ⓐ Ⓑ Ⓒ Ⓓ Ⓔ
5 Ⓐ Ⓑ Ⓒ Ⓓ Ⓔ
6 Ⓐ Ⓑ Ⓒ Ⓓ Ⓔ
7 Ⓐ Ⓑ Ⓒ Ⓓ Ⓔ

SP1, Pg. 322 PTC-S4-P4

21 Ⓐ Ⓑ Ⓒ Ⓓ Ⓔ
22 Ⓐ Ⓑ Ⓒ Ⓓ Ⓔ
23 Ⓐ Ⓑ Ⓒ Ⓓ Ⓔ
24 Ⓐ Ⓑ Ⓒ Ⓓ Ⓔ
25 Ⓐ Ⓑ Ⓒ Ⓓ Ⓔ
26 Ⓐ Ⓑ Ⓒ Ⓓ Ⓔ
27 Ⓐ Ⓑ Ⓒ Ⓓ Ⓔ

SP2, Pg. 374 PTC2-S4-P3

13 Ⓐ Ⓑ Ⓒ Ⓓ Ⓔ
14 Ⓐ Ⓑ Ⓒ Ⓓ Ⓔ
15 Ⓐ Ⓑ Ⓒ Ⓓ Ⓔ
16 Ⓐ Ⓑ Ⓒ Ⓓ Ⓔ
17 Ⓐ Ⓑ Ⓒ Ⓓ Ⓔ
18 Ⓐ Ⓑ Ⓒ Ⓓ Ⓔ
19 Ⓐ Ⓑ Ⓒ Ⓓ Ⓔ

PT1-S1-P2

9 Ⓐ Ⓑ Ⓒ Ⓓ Ⓔ
10 Ⓐ Ⓑ Ⓒ Ⓓ Ⓔ
11 Ⓐ Ⓑ Ⓒ Ⓓ Ⓔ
12 Ⓐ Ⓑ Ⓒ Ⓓ Ⓔ
13 Ⓐ Ⓑ Ⓒ Ⓓ Ⓔ
14 Ⓐ Ⓑ Ⓒ Ⓓ Ⓔ
15 Ⓐ Ⓑ Ⓒ Ⓓ Ⓔ
16 Ⓐ Ⓑ Ⓒ Ⓓ Ⓔ

PT2-S1-P3

14 Ⓐ Ⓑ Ⓒ Ⓓ Ⓔ
15 Ⓐ Ⓑ Ⓒ Ⓓ Ⓔ
16 Ⓐ Ⓑ Ⓒ Ⓓ Ⓔ
17 Ⓐ Ⓑ Ⓒ Ⓓ Ⓔ
18 Ⓐ Ⓑ Ⓒ Ⓓ Ⓔ
19 Ⓐ Ⓑ Ⓒ Ⓓ Ⓔ
20 Ⓐ Ⓑ Ⓒ Ⓓ Ⓔ
21 Ⓐ Ⓑ Ⓒ Ⓓ Ⓔ

PT3-S3-P1

1 Ⓐ Ⓑ Ⓒ Ⓓ Ⓔ
2 Ⓐ Ⓑ Ⓒ Ⓓ Ⓔ
3 Ⓐ Ⓑ Ⓒ Ⓓ Ⓔ
4 Ⓐ Ⓑ Ⓒ Ⓓ Ⓔ
5 Ⓐ Ⓑ Ⓒ Ⓓ Ⓔ
6 Ⓐ Ⓑ Ⓒ Ⓓ Ⓔ
7 Ⓐ Ⓑ Ⓒ Ⓓ Ⓔ

PT4-S2-P2

7 Ⓐ Ⓑ Ⓒ Ⓓ Ⓔ
8 Ⓐ Ⓑ Ⓒ Ⓓ Ⓔ
9 Ⓐ Ⓑ Ⓒ Ⓓ Ⓔ
10 Ⓐ Ⓑ Ⓒ Ⓓ Ⓔ
11 Ⓐ Ⓑ Ⓒ Ⓓ Ⓔ
12 Ⓐ Ⓑ Ⓒ Ⓓ Ⓔ
13 Ⓐ Ⓑ Ⓒ Ⓓ Ⓔ

PT5-S4-P3

16 Ⓐ Ⓑ Ⓒ Ⓓ Ⓔ
17 Ⓐ Ⓑ Ⓒ Ⓓ Ⓔ
18 Ⓐ Ⓑ Ⓒ Ⓓ Ⓔ
19 Ⓐ Ⓑ Ⓒ Ⓓ Ⓔ
20 Ⓐ Ⓑ Ⓒ Ⓓ Ⓔ
21 Ⓐ Ⓑ Ⓒ Ⓓ Ⓔ

V1, Pg. 32   PT7-S3-P3

15 Ⓐ Ⓑ Ⓒ Ⓓ Ⓔ
16 Ⓐ Ⓑ Ⓒ Ⓓ Ⓔ
17 Ⓐ Ⓑ Ⓒ Ⓓ Ⓔ
18 Ⓐ Ⓑ Ⓒ Ⓓ Ⓔ
19 Ⓐ Ⓑ Ⓒ Ⓓ Ⓔ
20 Ⓐ Ⓑ Ⓒ Ⓓ Ⓔ

PT8-S3-P1

1 Ⓐ Ⓑ Ⓒ Ⓓ Ⓔ
2 Ⓐ Ⓑ Ⓒ Ⓓ Ⓔ
3 Ⓐ Ⓑ Ⓒ Ⓓ Ⓔ
4 Ⓐ Ⓑ Ⓒ Ⓓ Ⓔ
5 Ⓐ Ⓑ Ⓒ Ⓓ Ⓔ
6 Ⓐ Ⓑ Ⓒ Ⓓ Ⓔ

V1, Pg. 96   PT10-S3-P1

1 Ⓐ Ⓑ Ⓒ Ⓓ Ⓔ
2 Ⓐ Ⓑ Ⓒ Ⓓ Ⓔ
3 Ⓐ Ⓑ Ⓒ Ⓓ Ⓔ
4 Ⓐ Ⓑ Ⓒ Ⓓ Ⓔ
5 Ⓐ Ⓑ Ⓒ Ⓓ Ⓔ
6 Ⓐ Ⓑ Ⓒ Ⓓ Ⓔ
7 Ⓐ Ⓑ Ⓒ Ⓓ Ⓔ
8 Ⓐ Ⓑ Ⓒ Ⓓ Ⓔ

V1, Pg. 134   PT11-S3-P3

15 Ⓐ Ⓑ Ⓒ Ⓓ Ⓔ
16 Ⓐ Ⓑ Ⓒ Ⓓ Ⓔ
17 Ⓐ Ⓑ Ⓒ Ⓓ Ⓔ
18 Ⓐ Ⓑ Ⓒ Ⓓ Ⓔ
19 Ⓐ Ⓑ Ⓒ Ⓓ Ⓔ
20 Ⓐ Ⓑ Ⓒ Ⓓ Ⓔ
21 Ⓐ Ⓑ Ⓒ Ⓓ Ⓔ

V1, Pg. 170   PT12-S3-P4

21 Ⓐ Ⓑ Ⓒ Ⓓ Ⓔ
22 Ⓐ Ⓑ Ⓒ Ⓓ Ⓔ
23 Ⓐ Ⓑ Ⓒ Ⓓ Ⓔ
24 Ⓐ Ⓑ Ⓒ Ⓓ Ⓔ
25 Ⓐ Ⓑ Ⓒ Ⓓ Ⓔ
26 Ⓐ Ⓑ Ⓒ Ⓓ Ⓔ
27 Ⓐ Ⓑ Ⓒ Ⓓ Ⓔ

V1, Pg. 198   PT13-S3-P1

1 Ⓐ Ⓑ Ⓒ Ⓓ Ⓔ
2 Ⓐ Ⓑ Ⓒ Ⓓ Ⓔ
3 Ⓐ Ⓑ Ⓒ Ⓓ Ⓔ
4 Ⓐ Ⓑ Ⓒ Ⓓ Ⓔ
5 Ⓐ Ⓑ Ⓒ Ⓓ Ⓔ
6 Ⓐ Ⓑ Ⓒ Ⓓ Ⓔ
7 Ⓐ Ⓑ Ⓒ Ⓓ Ⓔ
8 Ⓐ Ⓑ Ⓒ Ⓓ Ⓔ

V1, Pg. 232   PT14-S3-P1

1 Ⓐ Ⓑ Ⓒ Ⓓ Ⓔ
2 Ⓐ Ⓑ Ⓒ Ⓓ Ⓔ
3 Ⓐ Ⓑ Ⓒ Ⓓ Ⓔ
4 Ⓐ Ⓑ Ⓒ Ⓓ Ⓔ
5 Ⓐ Ⓑ Ⓒ Ⓓ Ⓔ
6 Ⓐ Ⓑ Ⓒ Ⓓ Ⓔ

V1, Pg. 254   PT15-S1-P1

1 Ⓐ Ⓑ Ⓒ Ⓓ Ⓔ
2 Ⓐ Ⓑ Ⓒ Ⓓ Ⓔ
3 Ⓐ Ⓑ Ⓒ Ⓓ Ⓔ
4 Ⓐ Ⓑ Ⓒ Ⓓ Ⓔ
5 Ⓐ Ⓑ Ⓒ Ⓓ Ⓔ
6 Ⓐ Ⓑ Ⓒ Ⓓ Ⓔ
7 Ⓐ Ⓑ Ⓒ Ⓓ Ⓔ

V1, Pg. 312   PT16-S4-P3

16 Ⓐ Ⓑ Ⓒ Ⓓ Ⓔ
17 Ⓐ Ⓑ Ⓒ Ⓓ Ⓔ
18 Ⓐ Ⓑ Ⓒ Ⓓ Ⓔ
19 Ⓐ Ⓑ Ⓒ Ⓓ Ⓔ
20 Ⓐ Ⓑ Ⓒ Ⓓ Ⓔ
21 Ⓐ Ⓑ Ⓒ Ⓓ Ⓔ

PT17-S4-P4

22 Ⓐ Ⓑ Ⓒ Ⓓ Ⓔ
23 Ⓐ Ⓑ Ⓒ Ⓓ Ⓔ
24 Ⓐ Ⓑ Ⓒ Ⓓ Ⓔ
25 Ⓐ Ⓑ Ⓒ Ⓓ Ⓔ
26 Ⓐ Ⓑ Ⓒ Ⓓ Ⓔ
27 Ⓐ Ⓑ Ⓒ Ⓓ Ⓔ

V1, Pg. 336   PT18-S3-P2

8   Ⓐ Ⓑ Ⓒ Ⓓ Ⓔ
9   Ⓐ Ⓑ Ⓒ Ⓓ Ⓔ
10 Ⓐ Ⓑ Ⓒ Ⓓ Ⓔ
11 Ⓐ Ⓑ Ⓒ Ⓓ Ⓔ
12 Ⓐ Ⓑ Ⓒ Ⓓ Ⓔ
13 Ⓐ Ⓑ Ⓒ Ⓓ Ⓔ
14 Ⓐ Ⓑ Ⓒ Ⓓ Ⓔ
15 Ⓐ Ⓑ Ⓒ Ⓓ Ⓔ

V2, Pg. 32   PT19-S3-P3

15 Ⓐ Ⓑ Ⓒ Ⓓ Ⓔ
16 Ⓐ Ⓑ Ⓒ Ⓓ Ⓔ
17 Ⓐ Ⓑ Ⓒ Ⓓ Ⓔ
18 Ⓐ Ⓑ Ⓒ Ⓓ Ⓔ
19 Ⓐ Ⓑ Ⓒ Ⓓ Ⓔ
20 Ⓐ Ⓑ Ⓒ Ⓓ Ⓔ

V2, Pg. 62   PT20-S2-P3

15 Ⓐ Ⓑ Ⓒ Ⓓ Ⓔ
16 Ⓐ Ⓑ Ⓒ Ⓓ Ⓔ
17 Ⓐ Ⓑ Ⓒ Ⓓ Ⓔ
18 Ⓐ Ⓑ Ⓒ Ⓓ Ⓔ
19 Ⓐ Ⓑ Ⓒ Ⓓ Ⓔ
20 Ⓐ Ⓑ Ⓒ Ⓓ Ⓔ
21 Ⓐ Ⓑ Ⓒ Ⓓ Ⓔ

V2, Pg. 108   PT21-S4-P3

17 Ⓐ Ⓑ Ⓒ Ⓓ Ⓔ
18 Ⓐ Ⓑ Ⓒ Ⓓ Ⓔ
19 Ⓐ Ⓑ Ⓒ Ⓓ Ⓔ
20 Ⓐ Ⓑ Ⓒ Ⓓ Ⓔ
21 Ⓐ Ⓑ Ⓒ Ⓓ Ⓔ

V2, Pg. 124   PT22-S1-P4

22 Ⓐ Ⓑ Ⓒ Ⓓ Ⓔ
23 Ⓐ Ⓑ Ⓒ Ⓓ Ⓔ
24 Ⓐ Ⓑ Ⓒ Ⓓ Ⓔ
25 Ⓐ Ⓑ Ⓒ Ⓓ Ⓔ
26 Ⓐ Ⓑ Ⓒ Ⓓ Ⓔ

V2, Pg. 176   PT23-S4-P3

14 Ⓐ Ⓑ Ⓒ Ⓓ Ⓔ
15 Ⓐ Ⓑ Ⓒ Ⓓ Ⓔ
16 Ⓐ Ⓑ Ⓒ Ⓓ Ⓔ
17 Ⓐ Ⓑ Ⓒ Ⓓ Ⓔ
18 Ⓐ Ⓑ Ⓒ Ⓓ Ⓔ

V2, Pg. 186   PT24-S1-P1

1 Ⓐ Ⓑ Ⓒ Ⓓ Ⓔ
2 Ⓐ Ⓑ Ⓒ Ⓓ Ⓔ
3 Ⓐ Ⓑ Ⓒ Ⓓ Ⓔ
4 Ⓐ Ⓑ Ⓒ Ⓓ Ⓔ
5 Ⓐ Ⓑ Ⓒ Ⓓ Ⓔ
6 Ⓐ Ⓑ Ⓒ Ⓓ Ⓔ

V2, Pg. 226   PT25-S1-P4

22 Ⓐ Ⓑ Ⓒ Ⓓ Ⓔ
23 Ⓐ Ⓑ Ⓒ Ⓓ Ⓔ
24 Ⓐ Ⓑ Ⓒ Ⓓ Ⓔ
25 Ⓐ Ⓑ Ⓒ Ⓓ Ⓔ
26 Ⓐ Ⓑ Ⓒ Ⓓ Ⓔ

V2, Pg. 278   PT26-S4-P3

14 Ⓐ Ⓑ Ⓒ Ⓓ Ⓔ
15 Ⓐ Ⓑ Ⓒ Ⓓ Ⓔ
16 Ⓐ Ⓑ Ⓒ Ⓓ Ⓔ
17 Ⓐ Ⓑ Ⓒ Ⓓ Ⓔ
18 Ⓐ Ⓑ Ⓒ Ⓓ Ⓔ
19 Ⓐ Ⓑ Ⓒ Ⓓ Ⓔ
20 Ⓐ Ⓑ Ⓒ Ⓓ Ⓔ
21 Ⓐ Ⓑ Ⓒ Ⓓ Ⓔ

V2, Pg. 304   PT27-S3-P3

15 Ⓐ Ⓑ Ⓒ Ⓓ Ⓔ
16 Ⓐ Ⓑ Ⓒ Ⓓ Ⓔ
17 Ⓐ Ⓑ Ⓒ Ⓓ Ⓔ
18 Ⓐ Ⓑ Ⓒ Ⓓ Ⓔ
19 Ⓐ Ⓑ Ⓒ Ⓓ Ⓔ
20 Ⓐ Ⓑ Ⓒ Ⓓ Ⓔ
21 Ⓐ Ⓑ Ⓒ Ⓓ Ⓔ

V2, Pg. 344   PT28-S4-P2

6   Ⓐ Ⓑ Ⓒ Ⓓ Ⓔ
7   Ⓐ Ⓑ Ⓒ Ⓓ Ⓔ
8   Ⓐ Ⓑ Ⓒ Ⓓ Ⓔ
9   Ⓐ Ⓑ Ⓒ Ⓓ Ⓔ
10 Ⓐ Ⓑ Ⓒ Ⓓ Ⓔ
11 Ⓐ Ⓑ Ⓒ Ⓓ Ⓔ
12 Ⓐ Ⓑ Ⓒ Ⓓ Ⓔ
13 Ⓐ Ⓑ Ⓒ Ⓓ Ⓔ

V3, Pg. 28   PT29-S2-P3

16 Ⓐ Ⓑ Ⓒ Ⓓ Ⓔ
17 Ⓐ Ⓑ Ⓒ Ⓓ Ⓔ
18 Ⓐ Ⓑ Ⓒ Ⓓ Ⓔ
19 Ⓐ Ⓑ Ⓒ Ⓓ Ⓔ
20 Ⓐ Ⓑ Ⓒ Ⓓ Ⓔ
21 Ⓐ Ⓑ Ⓒ Ⓓ Ⓔ

V3, Pg. 62   PT30-S3-P1

1 Ⓐ Ⓑ Ⓒ Ⓓ Ⓔ
2 Ⓐ Ⓑ Ⓒ Ⓓ Ⓔ
3 Ⓐ Ⓑ Ⓒ Ⓓ Ⓔ
4 Ⓐ Ⓑ Ⓒ Ⓓ Ⓔ
5 Ⓐ Ⓑ Ⓒ Ⓓ Ⓔ
6 Ⓐ Ⓑ Ⓒ Ⓓ Ⓔ

V3, Pg. 108   PT31-S4-P3

13 Ⓐ Ⓑ Ⓒ Ⓓ Ⓔ
14 Ⓐ Ⓑ Ⓒ Ⓓ Ⓔ
15 Ⓐ Ⓑ Ⓒ Ⓓ Ⓔ
16 Ⓐ Ⓑ Ⓒ Ⓓ Ⓔ
17 Ⓐ Ⓑ Ⓒ Ⓓ Ⓔ
18 Ⓐ Ⓑ Ⓒ Ⓓ Ⓔ
19 Ⓐ Ⓑ Ⓒ Ⓓ Ⓔ
20 Ⓐ Ⓑ Ⓒ Ⓓ Ⓔ

V3, Pg. 132   PT32-S2-P4

20 Ⓐ Ⓑ Ⓒ Ⓓ Ⓔ
21 Ⓐ Ⓑ Ⓒ Ⓓ Ⓔ
22 Ⓐ Ⓑ Ⓒ Ⓓ Ⓔ
23 Ⓐ Ⓑ Ⓒ Ⓓ Ⓔ
24 Ⓐ Ⓑ Ⓒ Ⓓ Ⓔ
25 Ⓐ Ⓑ Ⓒ Ⓓ Ⓔ
26 Ⓐ Ⓑ Ⓒ Ⓓ Ⓔ
27 Ⓐ Ⓑ Ⓒ Ⓓ Ⓔ

V3, Pg. 164   PT33-S2-P3

15 Ⓐ Ⓑ Ⓒ Ⓓ Ⓔ
16 Ⓐ Ⓑ Ⓒ Ⓓ Ⓔ
17 Ⓐ Ⓑ Ⓒ Ⓓ Ⓔ
18 Ⓐ Ⓑ Ⓒ Ⓓ Ⓔ
19 Ⓐ Ⓑ Ⓒ Ⓓ Ⓔ
20 Ⓐ Ⓑ Ⓒ Ⓓ Ⓔ
21 Ⓐ Ⓑ Ⓒ Ⓓ Ⓔ
22 Ⓐ Ⓑ Ⓒ Ⓓ Ⓔ

V3, Pg. 190 PT34-S1-P3

13 Ⓐ Ⓑ Ⓒ Ⓓ Ⓔ
14 Ⓐ Ⓑ Ⓒ Ⓓ Ⓔ
15 Ⓐ Ⓑ Ⓒ Ⓓ Ⓔ
16 Ⓐ Ⓑ Ⓒ Ⓓ Ⓔ
17 Ⓐ Ⓑ Ⓒ Ⓓ Ⓔ
18 Ⓐ Ⓑ Ⓒ Ⓓ Ⓔ

V3, Pg. 232 PT35-S2-P3

15 Ⓐ Ⓑ Ⓒ Ⓓ Ⓔ
16 Ⓐ Ⓑ Ⓒ Ⓓ Ⓔ
17 Ⓐ Ⓑ Ⓒ Ⓓ Ⓔ
18 Ⓐ Ⓑ Ⓒ Ⓓ Ⓔ
19 Ⓐ Ⓑ Ⓒ Ⓓ Ⓔ
20 Ⓐ Ⓑ Ⓒ Ⓓ Ⓔ

V3, Pg. 266 PT36-S2-P3

15 Ⓐ Ⓑ Ⓒ Ⓓ Ⓔ
16 Ⓐ Ⓑ Ⓒ Ⓓ Ⓔ
17 Ⓐ Ⓑ Ⓒ Ⓓ Ⓔ
18 Ⓐ Ⓑ Ⓒ Ⓓ Ⓔ
19 Ⓐ Ⓑ Ⓒ Ⓓ Ⓔ
20 Ⓐ Ⓑ Ⓒ Ⓓ Ⓔ

V3, Pg. 290 PT37-S1-P2

8   Ⓐ Ⓑ Ⓒ Ⓓ Ⓔ
9   Ⓐ Ⓑ Ⓒ Ⓓ Ⓔ
10 Ⓐ Ⓑ Ⓒ Ⓓ Ⓔ
11 Ⓐ Ⓑ Ⓒ Ⓓ Ⓔ
12 Ⓐ Ⓑ Ⓒ Ⓓ Ⓔ
13 Ⓐ Ⓑ Ⓒ Ⓓ Ⓔ

V3, Pg. 334 PT38-S3-P1

1   Ⓐ Ⓑ Ⓒ Ⓓ Ⓔ
2   Ⓐ Ⓑ Ⓒ Ⓓ Ⓔ
3   Ⓐ Ⓑ Ⓒ Ⓓ Ⓔ
4   Ⓐ Ⓑ Ⓒ Ⓓ Ⓔ
5   Ⓐ Ⓑ Ⓒ Ⓓ Ⓔ
6   Ⓐ Ⓑ Ⓒ Ⓓ Ⓔ
7   Ⓐ Ⓑ Ⓒ Ⓓ Ⓔ
8   Ⓐ Ⓑ Ⓒ Ⓓ Ⓔ

PT39-S3-P3

17 Ⓐ Ⓑ Ⓒ Ⓓ Ⓔ
18 Ⓐ Ⓑ Ⓒ Ⓓ Ⓔ
19 Ⓐ Ⓑ Ⓒ Ⓓ Ⓔ
20 Ⓐ Ⓑ Ⓒ Ⓓ Ⓔ
21 Ⓐ Ⓑ Ⓒ Ⓓ Ⓔ
22 Ⓐ Ⓑ Ⓒ Ⓓ Ⓔ
23 Ⓐ Ⓑ Ⓒ Ⓓ Ⓔ

PT40-S4-P3

13 Ⓐ Ⓑ Ⓒ Ⓓ Ⓔ
14 Ⓐ Ⓑ Ⓒ Ⓓ Ⓔ
15 Ⓐ Ⓑ Ⓒ Ⓓ Ⓔ
16 Ⓐ Ⓑ Ⓒ Ⓓ Ⓔ
17 Ⓐ Ⓑ Ⓒ Ⓓ Ⓔ
18 Ⓐ Ⓑ Ⓒ Ⓓ Ⓔ
19 Ⓐ Ⓑ Ⓒ Ⓓ Ⓔ

PT42-S3-P4

21 Ⓐ Ⓑ Ⓒ Ⓓ Ⓔ
22 Ⓐ Ⓑ Ⓒ Ⓓ Ⓔ
23 Ⓐ Ⓑ Ⓒ Ⓓ Ⓔ
24 Ⓐ Ⓑ Ⓒ Ⓓ Ⓔ
25 Ⓐ Ⓑ Ⓒ Ⓓ Ⓔ
26 Ⓐ Ⓑ Ⓒ Ⓓ Ⓔ

PT44-S1-P3

15 Ⓐ Ⓑ Ⓒ Ⓓ Ⓔ
16 Ⓐ Ⓑ Ⓒ Ⓓ Ⓔ
17 Ⓐ Ⓑ Ⓒ Ⓓ Ⓔ
18 Ⓐ Ⓑ Ⓒ Ⓓ Ⓔ
19 Ⓐ Ⓑ Ⓒ Ⓓ Ⓔ
20 Ⓐ Ⓑ Ⓒ Ⓓ Ⓔ

PT45-S2-P3

15 Ⓐ Ⓑ Ⓒ Ⓓ Ⓔ
16 Ⓐ Ⓑ Ⓒ Ⓓ Ⓔ
17 Ⓐ Ⓑ Ⓒ Ⓓ Ⓔ
18 Ⓐ Ⓑ Ⓒ Ⓓ Ⓔ
19 Ⓐ Ⓑ Ⓒ Ⓓ Ⓔ

PT46-S1-P3

16 Ⓐ Ⓑ Ⓒ Ⓓ Ⓔ
17 Ⓐ Ⓑ Ⓒ Ⓓ Ⓔ
18 Ⓐ Ⓑ Ⓒ Ⓓ Ⓔ
19 Ⓐ Ⓑ Ⓒ Ⓓ Ⓔ
20 Ⓐ Ⓑ Ⓒ Ⓓ Ⓔ
21 Ⓐ Ⓑ Ⓒ Ⓓ Ⓔ

PT47-S2-P4

19 Ⓐ Ⓑ Ⓒ Ⓓ Ⓔ
20 Ⓐ Ⓑ Ⓒ Ⓓ Ⓔ
21 Ⓐ Ⓑ Ⓒ Ⓓ Ⓔ
22 Ⓐ Ⓑ Ⓒ Ⓓ Ⓔ
23 Ⓐ Ⓑ Ⓒ Ⓓ Ⓔ
24 Ⓐ Ⓑ Ⓒ Ⓓ Ⓔ
25 Ⓐ Ⓑ Ⓒ Ⓓ Ⓔ
26 Ⓐ Ⓑ Ⓒ Ⓓ Ⓔ

PT48-S3-P4

20 Ⓐ Ⓑ Ⓒ Ⓓ Ⓔ
21 Ⓐ Ⓑ Ⓒ Ⓓ Ⓔ
22 Ⓐ Ⓑ Ⓒ Ⓓ Ⓔ
23 Ⓐ Ⓑ Ⓒ Ⓓ Ⓔ
24 Ⓐ Ⓑ Ⓒ Ⓓ Ⓔ
25 Ⓐ Ⓑ Ⓒ Ⓓ Ⓔ
26 Ⓐ Ⓑ Ⓒ Ⓓ Ⓔ
27 Ⓐ Ⓑ Ⓒ Ⓓ Ⓔ

PT49-S3-P4

21 Ⓐ Ⓑ Ⓒ Ⓓ Ⓔ
22 Ⓐ Ⓑ Ⓒ Ⓓ Ⓔ
23 Ⓐ Ⓑ Ⓒ Ⓓ Ⓔ
24 Ⓐ Ⓑ Ⓒ Ⓓ Ⓔ
25 Ⓐ Ⓑ Ⓒ Ⓓ Ⓔ
26 Ⓐ Ⓑ Ⓒ Ⓓ Ⓔ
27 Ⓐ Ⓑ Ⓒ Ⓓ Ⓔ

PT50-S1-P4

22 Ⓐ Ⓑ Ⓒ Ⓓ Ⓔ
23 Ⓐ Ⓑ Ⓒ Ⓓ Ⓔ
24 Ⓐ Ⓑ Ⓒ Ⓓ Ⓔ
25 Ⓐ Ⓑ Ⓒ Ⓓ Ⓔ
26 Ⓐ Ⓑ Ⓒ Ⓓ Ⓔ
27 Ⓐ Ⓑ Ⓒ Ⓓ Ⓔ
28 Ⓐ Ⓑ Ⓒ Ⓓ Ⓔ

PT51-S2-P2

8   Ⓐ Ⓑ Ⓒ Ⓓ Ⓔ
9   Ⓐ Ⓑ Ⓒ Ⓓ Ⓔ
10 Ⓐ Ⓑ Ⓒ Ⓓ Ⓔ
11 Ⓐ Ⓑ Ⓒ Ⓓ Ⓔ
12 Ⓐ Ⓑ Ⓒ Ⓓ Ⓔ
13 Ⓐ Ⓑ Ⓒ Ⓓ Ⓔ

V4, Pg. 32 PT52-S4-P3

13 Ⓐ Ⓑ Ⓒ Ⓓ Ⓔ
14 Ⓐ Ⓑ Ⓒ Ⓓ Ⓔ
15 Ⓐ Ⓑ Ⓒ Ⓓ Ⓔ
16 Ⓐ Ⓑ Ⓒ Ⓓ Ⓔ
17 Ⓐ Ⓑ Ⓒ Ⓓ Ⓔ
18 Ⓐ Ⓑ Ⓒ Ⓓ Ⓔ
19 Ⓐ Ⓑ Ⓒ Ⓓ Ⓔ

V4, Pg. 70 PT53-S4-P4

20 Ⓐ Ⓑ Ⓒ Ⓓ Ⓔ
21 Ⓐ Ⓑ Ⓒ Ⓓ Ⓔ
22 Ⓐ Ⓑ Ⓒ Ⓓ Ⓔ
23 Ⓐ Ⓑ Ⓒ Ⓓ Ⓔ
24 Ⓐ Ⓑ Ⓒ Ⓓ Ⓔ
25 Ⓐ Ⓑ Ⓒ Ⓓ Ⓔ
26 Ⓐ Ⓑ Ⓒ Ⓓ Ⓔ
27 Ⓐ Ⓑ Ⓒ Ⓓ Ⓔ

V4, Pg. 82   PT54-S1-P2

6 (A) (B) (C) (D) (E)
7 (A) (B) (C) (D) (E)
8 (A) (B) (C) (D) (E)
9 (A) (B) (C) (D) (E)
10 (A) (B) (C) (D) (E)
11 (A) (B) (C) (D) (E)
12 (A) (B) (C) (D) (E)

V4, Pg. 126   PT55-S2-P2

7 (A) (B) (C) (D) (E)
8 (A) (B) (C) (D) (E)
9 (A) (B) (C) (D) (E)
10 (A) (B) (C) (D) (E)
11 (A) (B) (C) (D) (E)
12 (A) (B) (C) (D) (E)
13 (A) (B) (C) (D) (E)

V4, Pg. 174   PT56-S4-P2

8 (A) (B) (C) (D) (E)
9 (A) (B) (C) (D) (E)
10 (A) (B) (C) (D) (E)
11 (A) (B) (C) (D) (E)
12 (A) (B) (C) (D) (E)
13 (A) (B) (C) (D) (E)
14 (A) (B) (C) (D) (E)
15 (A) (B) (C) (D) (E)

V4, Pg. 214   PT57-S4-P4

20 (A) (B) (C) (D) (E)
21 (A) (B) (C) (D) (E)
22 (A) (B) (C) (D) (E)
23 (A) (B) (C) (D) (E)
24 (A) (B) (C) (D) (E)
25 (A) (B) (C) (D) (E)
26 (A) (B) (C) (D) (E)
27 (A) (B) (C) (D) (E)

V4, Pg. 234   PT58-S2-P2

8 (A) (B) (C) (D) (E)
9 (A) (B) (C) (D) (E)
10 (A) (B) (C) (D) (E)
11 (A) (B) (C) (D) (E)
12 (A) (B) (C) (D) (E)
13 (A) (B) (C) (D) (E)

V4, Pg. 280   PT59-S4-P1

1 (A) (B) (C) (D) (E)
2 (A) (B) (C) (D) (E)
3 (A) (B) (C) (D) (E)
4 (A) (B) (C) (D) (E)
5 (A) (B) (C) (D) (E)
6 (A) (B) (C) (D) (E)
7 (A) (B) (C) (D) (E)
8 (A) (B) (C) (D) (E)

V4, Pg. 318   PT60-S4-P2

8 (A) (B) (C) (D) (E)
9 (A) (B) (C) (D) (E)
10 (A) (B) (C) (D) (E)
11 (A) (B) (C) (D) (E)
12 (A) (B) (C) (D) (E)

V4, Pg. 336   PT61-S1-P3

14 (A) (B) (C) (D) (E)
15 (A) (B) (C) (D) (E)
16 (A) (B) (C) (D) (E)
17 (A) (B) (C) (D) (E)
18 (A) (B) (C) (D) (E)
19 (A) (B) (C) (D) (E)

V5, Pg. 8   PT62-S1-P1

1 (A) (B) (C) (D) (E)
2 (A) (B) (C) (D) (E)
3 (A) (B) (C) (D) (E)
4 (A) (B) (C) (D) (E)
5 (A) (B) (C) (D) (E)
6 (A) (B) (C) (D) (E)
7 (A) (B) (C) (D) (E)
8 (A) (B) (C) (D) (E)

V5, Pg. 12   PT62-S1-P3

15 (A) (B) (C) (D) (E)
16 (A) (B) (C) (D) (E)
17 (A) (B) (C) (D) (E)
18 (A) (B) (C) (D) (E)
19 (A) (B) (C) (D) (E)
20 (A) (B) (C) (D) (E)
21 (A) (B) (C) (D) (E)

V5, Pg. 68   PT63-S4-P3

16 (A) (B) (C) (D) (E)
17 (A) (B) (C) (D) (E)
18 (A) (B) (C) (D) (E)
19 (A) (B) (C) (D) (E)
20 (A) (B) (C) (D) (E)
21 (A) (B) (C) (D) (E)

V5, Pg. 104   PT64-S4-P3

13 (A) (B) (C) (D) (E)
14 (A) (B) (C) (D) (E)
15 (A) (B) (C) (D) (E)
16 (A) (B) (C) (D) (E)
17 (A) (B) (C) (D) (E)
18 (A) (B) (C) (D) (E)
19 (A) (B) (C) (D) (E)

V5, Pg. 134   PT65-S3-P4

20 (A) (B) (C) (D) (E)
21 (A) (B) (C) (D) (E)
22 (A) (B) (C) (D) (E)
23 (A) (B) (C) (D) (E)
24 (A) (B) (C) (D) (E)
25 (A) (B) (C) (D) (E)
26 (A) (B) (C) (D) (E)
27 (A) (B) (C) (D) (E)

V5, Pg. 158   PT66-S1-P4

23 (A) (B) (C) (D) (E)
24 (A) (B) (C) (D) (E)
25 (A) (B) (C) (D) (E)
26 (A) (B) (C) (D) (E)
27 (A) (B) (C) (D) (E)

V5, Pg. 196   PT67-S1-P3

15 (A) (B) (C) (D) (E)
16 (A) (B) (C) (D) (E)
17 (A) (B) (C) (D) (E)
18 (A) (B) (C) (D) (E)
19 (A) (B) (C) (D) (E)

V5, Pg. 234   PT68-S1-P2

8 (A) (B) (C) (D) (E)
9 (A) (B) (C) (D) (E)
10 (A) (B) (C) (D) (E)
11 (A) (B) (C) (D) (E)
12 (A) (B) (C) (D) (E)
13 (A) (B) (C) (D) (E)
14 (A) (B) (C) (D) (E)

V5, Pg. 294   PT69-S3-P4

22 (A) (B) (C) (D) (E)
23 (A) (B) (C) (D) (E)
24 (A) (B) (C) (D) (E)
25 (A) (B) (C) (D) (E)
26 (A) (B) (C) (D) (E)
27 (A) (B) (C) (D) (E)

V5, Pg. 320   PT70-S2-P1

1 (A) (B) (C) (D) (E)
2 (A) (B) (C) (D) (E)
3 (A) (B) (C) (D) (E)
4 (A) (B) (C) (D) (E)
5 (A) (B) (C) (D) (E)
6 (A) (B) (C) (D) (E)
7 (A) (B) (C) (D) (E)

V5, Pg. 380   PT71-S4-P3

14 (A) (B) (C) (D) (E)
15 (A) (B) (C) (D) (E)
16 (A) (B) (C) (D) (E)
17 (A) (B) (C) (D) (E)
18 (A) (B) (C) (D) (E)
19 (A) (B) (C) (D) (E)

V5, Pg. 382   PT71-S4-P4

20 Ⓐ Ⓑ Ⓒ Ⓓ Ⓔ
21 Ⓐ Ⓑ Ⓒ Ⓓ Ⓔ
22 Ⓐ Ⓑ Ⓒ Ⓓ Ⓔ
23 Ⓐ Ⓑ Ⓒ Ⓓ Ⓔ
24 Ⓐ Ⓑ Ⓒ Ⓓ Ⓔ
25 Ⓐ Ⓑ Ⓒ Ⓓ Ⓔ
26 Ⓐ Ⓑ Ⓒ Ⓓ Ⓔ
27 Ⓐ Ⓑ Ⓒ Ⓓ Ⓔ

PT72, Pg. 10 PT72-S1-P1

1 Ⓐ Ⓑ Ⓒ Ⓓ Ⓔ
2 Ⓐ Ⓑ Ⓒ Ⓓ Ⓔ
3 Ⓐ Ⓑ Ⓒ Ⓓ Ⓔ
4 Ⓐ Ⓑ Ⓒ Ⓓ Ⓔ
5 Ⓐ Ⓑ Ⓒ Ⓓ Ⓔ
6 Ⓐ Ⓑ Ⓒ Ⓓ Ⓔ

PT73, Pg. 10 PT73-S1-P1

1 Ⓐ Ⓑ Ⓒ Ⓓ Ⓔ
2 Ⓐ Ⓑ Ⓒ Ⓓ Ⓔ
3 Ⓐ Ⓑ Ⓒ Ⓓ Ⓔ
4 Ⓐ Ⓑ Ⓒ Ⓓ Ⓔ
5 Ⓐ Ⓑ Ⓒ Ⓓ Ⓔ
6 Ⓐ Ⓑ Ⓒ Ⓓ Ⓔ
7 Ⓐ Ⓑ Ⓒ Ⓓ Ⓔ

PT74, Pg. 30 PT74-S3-P3

17 Ⓐ Ⓑ Ⓒ Ⓓ Ⓔ
18 Ⓐ Ⓑ Ⓒ Ⓓ Ⓔ
19 Ⓐ Ⓑ Ⓒ Ⓓ Ⓔ
20 Ⓐ Ⓑ Ⓒ Ⓓ Ⓔ
21 Ⓐ Ⓑ Ⓒ Ⓓ Ⓔ

PT75, Pg. 24 PT75-S2-P4

21 Ⓐ Ⓑ Ⓒ Ⓓ Ⓔ
22 Ⓐ Ⓑ Ⓒ Ⓓ Ⓔ
23 Ⓐ Ⓑ Ⓒ Ⓓ Ⓔ
24 Ⓐ Ⓑ Ⓒ Ⓓ Ⓔ
25 Ⓐ Ⓑ Ⓒ Ⓓ Ⓔ
26 Ⓐ Ⓑ Ⓒ Ⓓ Ⓔ
27 Ⓐ Ⓑ Ⓒ Ⓓ Ⓔ

PT76, Pg. 16 PT76-S1-P4

20 Ⓐ Ⓑ Ⓒ Ⓓ Ⓔ
21 Ⓐ Ⓑ Ⓒ Ⓓ Ⓔ
22 Ⓐ Ⓑ Ⓒ Ⓓ Ⓔ
23 Ⓐ Ⓑ Ⓒ Ⓓ Ⓔ
24 Ⓐ Ⓑ Ⓒ Ⓓ Ⓔ
25 Ⓐ Ⓑ Ⓒ Ⓓ Ⓔ
26 Ⓐ Ⓑ Ⓒ Ⓓ Ⓔ
27 Ⓐ Ⓑ Ⓒ Ⓓ Ⓔ

PT77, Pg. 16 PT77-S1-P4

20 Ⓐ Ⓑ Ⓒ Ⓓ Ⓔ
21 Ⓐ Ⓑ Ⓒ Ⓓ Ⓔ
22 Ⓐ Ⓑ Ⓒ Ⓓ Ⓔ
23 Ⓐ Ⓑ Ⓒ Ⓓ Ⓔ
24 Ⓐ Ⓑ Ⓒ Ⓓ Ⓔ
25 Ⓐ Ⓑ Ⓒ Ⓓ Ⓔ
26 Ⓐ Ⓑ Ⓒ Ⓓ Ⓔ
27 Ⓐ Ⓑ Ⓒ Ⓓ Ⓔ

Social Sciences

J07, Pg. 24   J07-S4-P2

9 Ⓐ Ⓑ Ⓒ Ⓓ Ⓔ
10 Ⓐ Ⓑ Ⓒ Ⓓ Ⓔ
11 Ⓐ Ⓑ Ⓒ Ⓓ Ⓔ
12 Ⓐ Ⓑ Ⓒ Ⓓ Ⓔ
13 Ⓐ Ⓑ Ⓒ Ⓓ Ⓔ
14 Ⓐ Ⓑ Ⓒ Ⓓ Ⓔ

SP1, Pg. 82   PTA-S2-P4

21 Ⓐ Ⓑ Ⓒ Ⓓ Ⓔ
22 Ⓐ Ⓑ Ⓒ Ⓓ Ⓔ
23 Ⓐ Ⓑ Ⓒ Ⓓ Ⓔ
24 Ⓐ Ⓑ Ⓒ Ⓓ Ⓔ
25 Ⓐ Ⓑ Ⓒ Ⓓ Ⓔ
26 Ⓐ Ⓑ Ⓒ Ⓓ Ⓔ
27 Ⓐ Ⓑ Ⓒ Ⓓ Ⓔ

SP1, Pg. 202 PTB-S3-P3

15 Ⓐ Ⓑ Ⓒ Ⓓ Ⓔ
16 Ⓐ Ⓑ Ⓒ Ⓓ Ⓔ
17 Ⓐ Ⓑ Ⓒ Ⓓ Ⓔ
18 Ⓐ Ⓑ Ⓒ Ⓓ Ⓔ
19 Ⓐ Ⓑ Ⓒ Ⓓ Ⓔ
20 Ⓐ Ⓑ Ⓒ Ⓓ Ⓔ
21 Ⓐ Ⓑ Ⓒ Ⓓ Ⓔ

SP1, Pg. 320 PTC-S4-P3

16 Ⓐ Ⓑ Ⓒ Ⓓ Ⓔ
17 Ⓐ Ⓑ Ⓒ Ⓓ Ⓔ
18 Ⓐ Ⓑ Ⓒ Ⓓ Ⓔ
19 Ⓐ Ⓑ Ⓒ Ⓓ Ⓔ
20 Ⓐ Ⓑ Ⓒ Ⓓ Ⓔ

SP2, Pg. 370 PTC2-S4-P1

1 Ⓐ Ⓑ Ⓒ Ⓓ Ⓔ
2 Ⓐ Ⓑ Ⓒ Ⓓ Ⓔ
3 Ⓐ Ⓑ Ⓒ Ⓓ Ⓔ
4 Ⓐ Ⓑ Ⓒ Ⓓ Ⓔ
5 Ⓐ Ⓑ Ⓒ Ⓓ Ⓔ
6 Ⓐ Ⓑ Ⓒ Ⓓ Ⓔ

PT1-S1-P4

22 Ⓐ Ⓑ Ⓒ Ⓓ Ⓔ
23 Ⓐ Ⓑ Ⓒ Ⓓ Ⓔ
24 Ⓐ Ⓑ Ⓒ Ⓓ Ⓔ
25 Ⓐ Ⓑ Ⓒ Ⓓ Ⓔ
26 Ⓐ Ⓑ Ⓒ Ⓓ Ⓔ
27 Ⓐ Ⓑ Ⓒ Ⓓ Ⓔ
28 Ⓐ Ⓑ Ⓒ Ⓓ Ⓔ

PT2-S1-P2

7 Ⓐ Ⓑ Ⓒ Ⓓ Ⓔ
8 Ⓐ Ⓑ Ⓒ Ⓓ Ⓔ
9 Ⓐ Ⓑ Ⓒ Ⓓ Ⓔ
10 Ⓐ Ⓑ Ⓒ Ⓓ Ⓔ
11 Ⓐ Ⓑ Ⓒ Ⓓ Ⓔ
12 Ⓐ Ⓑ Ⓒ Ⓓ Ⓔ
13 Ⓐ Ⓑ Ⓒ Ⓓ Ⓔ

PT3-S3-P2

8 Ⓐ Ⓑ Ⓒ Ⓓ Ⓔ
9 Ⓐ Ⓑ Ⓒ Ⓓ Ⓔ
10 Ⓐ Ⓑ Ⓒ Ⓓ Ⓔ
11 Ⓐ Ⓑ Ⓒ Ⓓ Ⓔ
12 Ⓐ Ⓑ Ⓒ Ⓓ Ⓔ
13 Ⓐ Ⓑ Ⓒ Ⓓ Ⓔ
14 Ⓐ Ⓑ Ⓒ Ⓓ Ⓔ
15 Ⓐ Ⓑ Ⓒ Ⓓ Ⓔ

PT4-S2-P3

14 Ⓐ Ⓑ Ⓒ Ⓓ Ⓔ
15 Ⓐ Ⓑ Ⓒ Ⓓ Ⓔ
16 Ⓐ Ⓑ Ⓒ Ⓓ Ⓔ
17 Ⓐ Ⓑ Ⓒ Ⓓ Ⓔ
18 Ⓐ Ⓑ Ⓒ Ⓓ Ⓔ
19 Ⓐ Ⓑ Ⓒ Ⓓ Ⓔ
20 Ⓐ Ⓑ Ⓒ Ⓓ Ⓔ

PT5-S4-P2

9 Ⓐ Ⓑ Ⓒ Ⓓ Ⓔ
10 Ⓐ Ⓑ Ⓒ Ⓓ Ⓔ
11 Ⓐ Ⓑ Ⓒ Ⓓ Ⓔ
12 Ⓐ Ⓑ Ⓒ Ⓓ Ⓔ
13 Ⓐ Ⓑ Ⓒ Ⓓ Ⓔ
14 Ⓐ Ⓑ Ⓒ Ⓓ Ⓔ
15 Ⓐ Ⓑ Ⓒ Ⓓ Ⓔ

PT6-S1-P2

7 Ⓐ Ⓑ Ⓒ Ⓓ Ⓔ
8 Ⓐ Ⓑ Ⓒ Ⓓ Ⓔ
9 Ⓐ Ⓑ Ⓒ Ⓓ Ⓔ
10 Ⓐ Ⓑ Ⓒ Ⓓ Ⓔ
11 Ⓐ Ⓑ Ⓒ Ⓓ Ⓔ
12 Ⓐ Ⓑ Ⓒ Ⓓ Ⓔ

PT6-S1-P4

21 Ⓐ Ⓑ Ⓒ Ⓓ Ⓔ
22 Ⓐ Ⓑ Ⓒ Ⓓ Ⓔ
23 Ⓐ Ⓑ Ⓒ Ⓓ Ⓔ
24 Ⓐ Ⓑ Ⓒ Ⓓ Ⓔ
25 Ⓐ Ⓑ Ⓒ Ⓓ Ⓔ
26 Ⓐ Ⓑ Ⓒ Ⓓ Ⓔ
27 Ⓐ Ⓑ Ⓒ Ⓓ Ⓔ

V1, Pg. 28   PT7-S3-P1

1 Ⓐ Ⓑ Ⓒ Ⓓ Ⓔ
2 Ⓐ Ⓑ Ⓒ Ⓓ Ⓔ
3 Ⓐ Ⓑ Ⓒ Ⓓ Ⓔ
4 Ⓐ Ⓑ Ⓒ Ⓓ Ⓔ
5 Ⓐ Ⓑ Ⓒ Ⓓ Ⓔ
6 Ⓐ Ⓑ Ⓒ Ⓓ Ⓔ
7 Ⓐ Ⓑ Ⓒ Ⓓ Ⓔ

PT8-S3-P4

21 Ⓐ Ⓑ Ⓒ Ⓓ Ⓔ
22 Ⓐ Ⓑ Ⓒ Ⓓ Ⓔ
23 Ⓐ Ⓑ Ⓒ Ⓓ Ⓔ
24 Ⓐ Ⓑ Ⓒ Ⓓ Ⓔ
25 Ⓐ Ⓑ Ⓒ Ⓓ Ⓔ
26 Ⓐ Ⓑ Ⓒ Ⓓ Ⓔ
27 Ⓐ Ⓑ Ⓒ Ⓓ Ⓔ

V1, Pg. 52   PT9-S1-P2

7 Ⓐ Ⓑ Ⓒ Ⓓ Ⓔ
8 Ⓐ Ⓑ Ⓒ Ⓓ Ⓔ
9 Ⓐ Ⓑ Ⓒ Ⓓ Ⓔ
10 Ⓐ Ⓑ Ⓒ Ⓓ Ⓔ
11 Ⓐ Ⓑ Ⓒ Ⓓ Ⓔ
12 Ⓐ Ⓑ Ⓒ Ⓓ Ⓔ
13 Ⓐ Ⓑ Ⓒ Ⓓ Ⓔ

V1, Pg. 54   PT9-S1-P3

14 Ⓐ Ⓑ Ⓒ Ⓓ Ⓔ
15 Ⓐ Ⓑ Ⓒ Ⓓ Ⓔ
16 Ⓐ Ⓑ Ⓒ Ⓓ Ⓔ
17 Ⓐ Ⓑ Ⓒ Ⓓ Ⓔ
18 Ⓐ Ⓑ Ⓒ Ⓓ Ⓔ
19 Ⓐ Ⓑ Ⓒ Ⓓ Ⓔ
20 Ⓐ Ⓑ Ⓒ Ⓓ Ⓔ

V1, Pg. 102   PT10-S3-P4

22 Ⓐ Ⓑ Ⓒ Ⓓ Ⓔ
23 Ⓐ Ⓑ Ⓒ Ⓓ Ⓔ
24 Ⓐ Ⓑ Ⓒ Ⓓ Ⓔ
25 Ⓐ Ⓑ Ⓒ Ⓓ Ⓔ
26 Ⓐ Ⓑ Ⓒ Ⓓ Ⓔ
27 Ⓐ Ⓑ Ⓒ Ⓓ Ⓔ

V1, Pg. 132   PT11-S3-P2

8 Ⓐ Ⓑ Ⓒ Ⓓ Ⓔ
9 Ⓐ Ⓑ Ⓒ Ⓓ Ⓔ
10 Ⓐ Ⓑ Ⓒ Ⓓ Ⓔ
11 Ⓐ Ⓑ Ⓒ Ⓓ Ⓔ
12 Ⓐ Ⓑ Ⓒ Ⓓ Ⓔ
13 Ⓐ Ⓑ Ⓒ Ⓓ Ⓔ
14 Ⓐ Ⓑ Ⓒ Ⓓ Ⓔ

V1, Pg. 136   PT11-S3-P4

22 Ⓐ Ⓑ Ⓒ Ⓓ Ⓔ
23 Ⓐ Ⓑ Ⓒ Ⓓ Ⓔ
24 Ⓐ Ⓑ Ⓒ Ⓓ Ⓔ
25 Ⓐ Ⓑ Ⓒ Ⓓ Ⓔ
26 Ⓐ Ⓑ Ⓒ Ⓓ Ⓔ
27 Ⓐ Ⓑ Ⓒ Ⓓ Ⓔ

V1, Pg. 166   PT12-S3-P2

8 Ⓐ Ⓑ Ⓒ Ⓓ Ⓔ
9 Ⓐ Ⓑ Ⓒ Ⓓ Ⓔ
10 Ⓐ Ⓑ Ⓒ Ⓓ Ⓔ
11 Ⓐ Ⓑ Ⓒ Ⓓ Ⓔ
12 Ⓐ Ⓑ Ⓒ Ⓓ Ⓔ
13 Ⓐ Ⓑ Ⓒ Ⓓ Ⓔ

V1, Pg. 200   PT13-S3-P2

9 Ⓐ Ⓑ Ⓒ Ⓓ Ⓔ
10 Ⓐ Ⓑ Ⓒ Ⓓ Ⓔ
11 Ⓐ Ⓑ Ⓒ Ⓓ Ⓔ
12 Ⓐ Ⓑ Ⓒ Ⓓ Ⓔ
13 Ⓐ Ⓑ Ⓒ Ⓓ Ⓔ

V1, Pg. 238   PT14-S3-P4

21 Ⓐ Ⓑ Ⓒ Ⓓ Ⓔ
22 Ⓐ Ⓑ Ⓒ Ⓓ Ⓔ
23 Ⓐ Ⓑ Ⓒ Ⓓ Ⓔ
24 Ⓐ Ⓑ Ⓒ Ⓓ Ⓔ
25 Ⓐ Ⓑ Ⓒ Ⓓ Ⓔ
26 Ⓐ Ⓑ Ⓒ Ⓓ Ⓔ
27 Ⓐ Ⓑ Ⓒ Ⓓ Ⓔ

V1, Pg. 258   PT15-S1-P3

16 Ⓐ Ⓑ Ⓒ Ⓓ Ⓔ
17 Ⓐ Ⓑ Ⓒ Ⓓ Ⓔ
18 Ⓐ Ⓑ Ⓒ Ⓓ Ⓔ
19 Ⓐ Ⓑ Ⓒ Ⓓ Ⓔ
20 Ⓐ Ⓑ Ⓒ Ⓓ Ⓔ
21 Ⓐ Ⓑ Ⓒ Ⓓ Ⓔ

V1, Pg. 314   PT16-S4-P4

22 Ⓐ Ⓑ Ⓒ Ⓓ Ⓔ
23 Ⓐ Ⓑ Ⓒ Ⓓ Ⓔ
24 Ⓐ Ⓑ Ⓒ Ⓓ Ⓔ
25 Ⓐ Ⓑ Ⓒ Ⓓ Ⓔ
26 Ⓐ Ⓑ Ⓒ Ⓓ Ⓔ
27 Ⓐ Ⓑ Ⓒ Ⓓ Ⓔ

PT17-S4-P3

16 Ⓐ Ⓑ Ⓒ Ⓓ Ⓔ
17 Ⓐ Ⓑ Ⓒ Ⓓ Ⓔ
18 Ⓐ Ⓑ Ⓒ Ⓓ Ⓔ
19 Ⓐ Ⓑ Ⓒ Ⓓ Ⓔ
20 Ⓐ Ⓑ Ⓒ Ⓓ Ⓔ
21 Ⓐ Ⓑ Ⓒ Ⓓ Ⓔ

V1, Pg. 338   PT18-S3-P3

16 Ⓐ Ⓑ Ⓒ Ⓓ Ⓔ
17 Ⓐ Ⓑ Ⓒ Ⓓ Ⓔ
18 Ⓐ Ⓑ Ⓒ Ⓓ Ⓔ
19 Ⓐ Ⓑ Ⓒ Ⓓ Ⓔ
20 Ⓐ Ⓑ Ⓒ Ⓓ Ⓔ
21 Ⓐ Ⓑ Ⓒ Ⓓ Ⓔ

V2, Pg. 34   PT19-S3-P4

21 Ⓐ Ⓑ Ⓒ Ⓓ Ⓔ
22 Ⓐ Ⓑ Ⓒ Ⓓ Ⓔ
23 Ⓐ Ⓑ Ⓒ Ⓓ Ⓔ
24 Ⓐ Ⓑ Ⓒ Ⓓ Ⓔ
25 Ⓐ Ⓑ Ⓒ Ⓓ Ⓔ
26 Ⓐ Ⓑ Ⓒ Ⓓ Ⓔ
27 Ⓐ Ⓑ Ⓒ Ⓓ Ⓔ

V2, Pg. 64   PT20-S2-P4

22 Ⓐ Ⓑ Ⓒ Ⓓ Ⓔ
23 Ⓐ Ⓑ Ⓒ Ⓓ Ⓔ
24 Ⓐ Ⓑ Ⓒ Ⓓ Ⓔ
25 Ⓐ Ⓑ Ⓒ Ⓓ Ⓔ
26 Ⓐ Ⓑ Ⓒ Ⓓ Ⓔ

V2, Pg. 110   PT21-S4-P4

22 Ⓐ Ⓑ Ⓒ Ⓓ Ⓔ
23 Ⓐ Ⓑ Ⓒ Ⓓ Ⓔ
24 Ⓐ Ⓑ Ⓒ Ⓓ Ⓔ
25 Ⓐ Ⓑ Ⓒ Ⓓ Ⓔ
26 Ⓐ Ⓑ Ⓒ Ⓓ Ⓔ
27 Ⓐ Ⓑ Ⓒ Ⓓ Ⓔ

V2, Pg. 122 PT22-S1-P3

17 Ⓐ Ⓑ Ⓒ Ⓓ Ⓔ
18 Ⓐ Ⓑ Ⓒ Ⓓ Ⓔ
19 Ⓐ Ⓑ Ⓒ Ⓓ Ⓔ
20 Ⓐ Ⓑ Ⓒ Ⓓ Ⓔ
21 Ⓐ Ⓑ Ⓒ Ⓓ Ⓔ

V2, Pg. 178 PT23-S4-P4

19 Ⓐ Ⓑ Ⓒ Ⓓ Ⓔ
20 Ⓐ Ⓑ Ⓒ Ⓓ Ⓔ
21 Ⓐ Ⓑ Ⓒ Ⓓ Ⓔ
22 Ⓐ Ⓑ Ⓒ Ⓓ Ⓔ
23 Ⓐ Ⓑ Ⓒ Ⓓ Ⓔ
24 Ⓐ Ⓑ Ⓒ Ⓓ Ⓔ
25 Ⓐ Ⓑ Ⓒ Ⓓ Ⓔ
26 Ⓐ Ⓑ Ⓒ Ⓓ Ⓔ

V2, Pg. 188 PT24-S1-P2

7 Ⓐ Ⓑ Ⓒ Ⓓ Ⓔ
8 Ⓐ Ⓑ Ⓒ Ⓓ Ⓔ
9 Ⓐ Ⓑ Ⓒ Ⓓ Ⓔ
10 Ⓐ Ⓑ Ⓒ Ⓓ Ⓔ
11 Ⓐ Ⓑ Ⓒ Ⓓ Ⓔ
12 Ⓐ Ⓑ Ⓒ Ⓓ Ⓔ
13 Ⓐ Ⓑ Ⓒ Ⓓ Ⓔ

V2, Pg. 224 PT25-S1-P3

14 Ⓐ Ⓑ Ⓒ Ⓓ Ⓔ
15 Ⓐ Ⓑ Ⓒ Ⓓ Ⓔ
16 Ⓐ Ⓑ Ⓒ Ⓓ Ⓔ
17 Ⓐ Ⓑ Ⓒ Ⓓ Ⓔ
18 Ⓐ Ⓑ Ⓒ Ⓓ Ⓔ
19 Ⓐ Ⓑ Ⓒ Ⓓ Ⓔ
20 Ⓐ Ⓑ Ⓒ Ⓓ Ⓔ
21 Ⓐ Ⓑ Ⓒ Ⓓ Ⓔ

V2, Pg. 274 PT26-S4-P1

1 Ⓐ Ⓑ Ⓒ Ⓓ Ⓔ
2 Ⓐ Ⓑ Ⓒ Ⓓ Ⓔ
3 Ⓐ Ⓑ Ⓒ Ⓓ Ⓔ
4 Ⓐ Ⓑ Ⓒ Ⓓ Ⓔ
5 Ⓐ Ⓑ Ⓒ Ⓓ Ⓔ

V2, Pg. 302 PT27-S3-P2

8 Ⓐ Ⓑ Ⓒ Ⓓ Ⓔ
9 Ⓐ Ⓑ Ⓒ Ⓓ Ⓔ
10 Ⓐ Ⓑ Ⓒ Ⓓ Ⓔ
11 Ⓐ Ⓑ Ⓒ Ⓓ Ⓔ
12 Ⓐ Ⓑ Ⓒ Ⓓ Ⓔ
13 Ⓐ Ⓑ Ⓒ Ⓓ Ⓔ
14 Ⓐ Ⓑ Ⓒ Ⓓ Ⓔ

V2, Pg. 346 PT28-S4-P3

14 Ⓐ Ⓑ Ⓒ Ⓓ Ⓔ
15 Ⓐ Ⓑ Ⓒ Ⓓ Ⓔ
16 Ⓐ Ⓑ Ⓒ Ⓓ Ⓔ
17 Ⓐ Ⓑ Ⓒ Ⓓ Ⓔ
18 Ⓐ Ⓑ Ⓒ Ⓓ Ⓔ
19 Ⓐ Ⓑ Ⓒ Ⓓ Ⓔ
20 Ⓐ Ⓑ Ⓒ Ⓓ Ⓔ
21 Ⓐ Ⓑ Ⓒ Ⓓ Ⓔ

V3, Pg. 26 PT29-S2-P2

8 Ⓐ Ⓑ Ⓒ Ⓓ Ⓔ
9 Ⓐ Ⓑ Ⓒ Ⓓ Ⓔ
10 Ⓐ Ⓑ Ⓒ Ⓓ Ⓔ
11 Ⓐ Ⓑ Ⓒ Ⓓ Ⓔ
12 Ⓐ Ⓑ Ⓒ Ⓓ Ⓔ
13 Ⓐ Ⓑ Ⓒ Ⓓ Ⓔ
14 Ⓐ Ⓑ Ⓒ Ⓓ Ⓔ
15 Ⓐ Ⓑ Ⓒ Ⓓ Ⓔ

V3, Pg. 68 PT30-S3-P4

22 Ⓐ Ⓑ Ⓒ Ⓓ Ⓔ
23 Ⓐ Ⓑ Ⓒ Ⓓ Ⓔ
24 Ⓐ Ⓑ Ⓒ Ⓓ Ⓔ
25 Ⓐ Ⓑ Ⓒ Ⓓ Ⓔ
26 Ⓐ Ⓑ Ⓒ Ⓓ Ⓔ
27 Ⓐ Ⓑ Ⓒ Ⓓ Ⓔ

V3, Pg. 104 PT31-S4-P1

1 Ⓐ Ⓑ Ⓒ Ⓓ Ⓔ
2 Ⓐ Ⓑ Ⓒ Ⓓ Ⓔ
3 Ⓐ Ⓑ Ⓒ Ⓓ Ⓔ
4 Ⓐ Ⓑ Ⓒ Ⓓ Ⓔ
5 Ⓐ Ⓑ Ⓒ Ⓓ Ⓔ

V3, Pg. 128 PT32-S2-P2

8 Ⓐ Ⓑ Ⓒ Ⓓ Ⓔ
9 Ⓐ Ⓑ Ⓒ Ⓓ Ⓔ
10 Ⓐ Ⓑ Ⓒ Ⓓ Ⓔ
11 Ⓐ Ⓑ Ⓒ Ⓓ Ⓔ
12 Ⓐ Ⓑ Ⓒ Ⓓ Ⓔ
13 Ⓐ Ⓑ Ⓒ Ⓓ Ⓔ

V3, Pg. 160 PT33-S2-P1

1 Ⓐ Ⓑ Ⓒ Ⓓ Ⓔ
2 Ⓐ Ⓑ Ⓒ Ⓓ Ⓔ
3 Ⓐ Ⓑ Ⓒ Ⓓ Ⓔ
4 Ⓐ Ⓑ Ⓒ Ⓓ Ⓔ
5 Ⓐ Ⓑ Ⓒ Ⓓ Ⓔ
6 Ⓐ Ⓑ Ⓒ Ⓓ Ⓔ
7 Ⓐ Ⓑ Ⓒ Ⓓ Ⓔ

V3, Pg. 186 PT34-S1-P1

1 Ⓐ Ⓑ Ⓒ Ⓓ Ⓔ
2 Ⓐ Ⓑ Ⓒ Ⓓ Ⓔ
3 Ⓐ Ⓑ Ⓒ Ⓓ Ⓔ
4 Ⓐ Ⓑ Ⓒ Ⓓ Ⓔ
5 Ⓐ Ⓑ Ⓒ Ⓓ Ⓔ
6 Ⓐ Ⓑ Ⓒ Ⓓ Ⓔ

V3, Pg. 192 PT34-S1-P4

19 Ⓐ Ⓑ Ⓒ Ⓓ Ⓔ
20 Ⓐ Ⓑ Ⓒ Ⓓ Ⓔ
21 Ⓐ Ⓑ Ⓒ Ⓓ Ⓔ
22 Ⓐ Ⓑ Ⓒ Ⓓ Ⓔ
23 Ⓐ Ⓑ Ⓒ Ⓓ Ⓔ
24 Ⓐ Ⓑ Ⓒ Ⓓ Ⓔ
25 Ⓐ Ⓑ Ⓒ Ⓓ Ⓔ
26 Ⓐ Ⓑ Ⓒ Ⓓ Ⓔ

V3, Pg. 228 PT35-S2-P1

1 Ⓐ Ⓑ Ⓒ Ⓓ Ⓔ
2 Ⓐ Ⓑ Ⓒ Ⓓ Ⓔ
3 Ⓐ Ⓑ Ⓒ Ⓓ Ⓔ
4 Ⓐ Ⓑ Ⓒ Ⓓ Ⓔ
5 Ⓐ Ⓑ Ⓒ Ⓓ Ⓔ
6 Ⓐ Ⓑ Ⓒ Ⓓ Ⓔ

V3, Pg. 262 PT36-S2-P1

1 Ⓐ Ⓑ Ⓒ Ⓓ Ⓔ
2 Ⓐ Ⓑ Ⓒ Ⓓ Ⓔ
3 Ⓐ Ⓑ Ⓒ Ⓓ Ⓔ
4 Ⓐ Ⓑ Ⓒ Ⓓ Ⓔ
5 Ⓐ Ⓑ Ⓒ Ⓓ Ⓔ
6 Ⓐ Ⓑ Ⓒ Ⓓ Ⓔ

V3, Pg. 294 PT37-S1-P4

22 Ⓐ Ⓑ Ⓒ Ⓓ Ⓔ
23 Ⓐ Ⓑ Ⓒ Ⓓ Ⓔ
24 Ⓐ Ⓑ Ⓒ Ⓓ Ⓔ
25 Ⓐ Ⓑ Ⓒ Ⓓ Ⓔ
26 Ⓐ Ⓑ Ⓒ Ⓓ Ⓔ

V3, Pg. 338 PT38-S3-P3

15 Ⓐ Ⓑ Ⓒ Ⓓ Ⓔ
16 Ⓐ Ⓑ Ⓒ Ⓓ Ⓔ
17 Ⓐ Ⓑ Ⓒ Ⓓ Ⓔ
18 Ⓐ Ⓑ Ⓒ Ⓓ Ⓔ
19 Ⓐ Ⓑ Ⓒ Ⓓ Ⓔ
20 Ⓐ Ⓑ Ⓒ Ⓓ Ⓔ

PT39-S3-P2

9 Ⓐ Ⓑ Ⓒ Ⓓ Ⓔ
10 Ⓐ Ⓑ Ⓒ Ⓓ Ⓔ
11 Ⓐ Ⓑ Ⓒ Ⓓ Ⓔ
12 Ⓐ Ⓑ Ⓒ Ⓓ Ⓔ
13 Ⓐ Ⓑ Ⓒ Ⓓ Ⓔ
14 Ⓐ Ⓑ Ⓒ Ⓓ Ⓔ
15 Ⓐ Ⓑ Ⓒ Ⓓ Ⓔ
16 Ⓐ Ⓑ Ⓒ Ⓓ Ⓔ

PT40-S4-P1

1 Ⓐ Ⓑ Ⓒ Ⓓ Ⓔ
2 Ⓐ Ⓑ Ⓒ Ⓓ Ⓔ
3 Ⓐ Ⓑ Ⓒ Ⓓ Ⓔ
4 Ⓐ Ⓑ Ⓒ Ⓓ Ⓔ
5 Ⓐ Ⓑ Ⓒ Ⓓ Ⓔ

PT41-S4-P3

14 Ⓐ Ⓑ Ⓒ Ⓓ Ⓔ
15 Ⓐ Ⓑ Ⓒ Ⓓ Ⓔ
16 Ⓐ Ⓑ Ⓒ Ⓓ Ⓔ
17 Ⓐ Ⓑ Ⓒ Ⓓ Ⓔ
18 Ⓐ Ⓑ Ⓒ Ⓓ Ⓔ
19 Ⓐ Ⓑ Ⓒ Ⓓ Ⓔ
20 Ⓐ Ⓑ Ⓒ Ⓓ Ⓔ

PT41-S4-P4

21 Ⓐ Ⓑ Ⓒ Ⓓ Ⓔ
22 Ⓐ Ⓑ Ⓒ Ⓓ Ⓔ
23 Ⓐ Ⓑ Ⓒ Ⓓ Ⓔ
24 Ⓐ Ⓑ Ⓒ Ⓓ Ⓔ
25 Ⓐ Ⓑ Ⓒ Ⓓ Ⓔ
26 Ⓐ Ⓑ Ⓒ Ⓓ Ⓔ

PT42-S3-P3

16 Ⓐ Ⓑ Ⓒ Ⓓ Ⓔ
17 Ⓐ Ⓑ Ⓒ Ⓓ Ⓔ
18 Ⓐ Ⓑ Ⓒ Ⓓ Ⓔ
19 Ⓐ Ⓑ Ⓒ Ⓓ Ⓔ
20 Ⓐ Ⓑ Ⓒ Ⓓ Ⓔ

PT43-S1-P1

1 Ⓐ Ⓑ Ⓒ Ⓓ Ⓔ
2 Ⓐ Ⓑ Ⓒ Ⓓ Ⓔ
3 Ⓐ Ⓑ Ⓒ Ⓓ Ⓔ
4 Ⓐ Ⓑ Ⓒ Ⓓ Ⓔ
5 Ⓐ Ⓑ Ⓒ Ⓓ Ⓔ

PT43-S1-P2

6 Ⓐ Ⓑ Ⓒ Ⓓ Ⓔ
7 Ⓐ Ⓑ Ⓒ Ⓓ Ⓔ
8 Ⓐ Ⓑ Ⓒ Ⓓ Ⓔ
9 Ⓐ Ⓑ Ⓒ Ⓓ Ⓔ
10 Ⓐ Ⓑ Ⓒ Ⓓ Ⓔ
11 Ⓐ Ⓑ Ⓒ Ⓓ Ⓔ
12 Ⓐ Ⓑ Ⓒ Ⓓ Ⓔ
13 Ⓐ Ⓑ Ⓒ Ⓓ Ⓔ

PT44-S1-P2

8 Ⓐ Ⓑ Ⓒ Ⓓ Ⓔ
9 Ⓐ Ⓑ Ⓒ Ⓓ Ⓔ
10 Ⓐ Ⓑ Ⓒ Ⓓ Ⓔ
11 Ⓐ Ⓑ Ⓒ Ⓓ Ⓔ
12 Ⓐ Ⓑ Ⓒ Ⓓ Ⓔ
13 Ⓐ Ⓑ Ⓒ Ⓓ Ⓔ
14 Ⓐ Ⓑ Ⓒ Ⓓ Ⓔ

PT45-S2-P1

1 Ⓐ Ⓑ Ⓒ Ⓓ Ⓔ
2 Ⓐ Ⓑ Ⓒ Ⓓ Ⓔ
3 Ⓐ Ⓑ Ⓒ Ⓓ Ⓔ
4 Ⓐ Ⓑ Ⓒ Ⓓ Ⓔ
5 Ⓐ Ⓑ Ⓒ Ⓓ Ⓔ
6 Ⓐ Ⓑ Ⓒ Ⓓ Ⓔ

PT46-S1-P1

1 Ⓐ Ⓑ Ⓒ Ⓓ Ⓔ
2 Ⓐ Ⓑ Ⓒ Ⓓ Ⓔ
3 Ⓐ Ⓑ Ⓒ Ⓓ Ⓔ
4 Ⓐ Ⓑ Ⓒ Ⓓ Ⓔ
5 Ⓐ Ⓑ Ⓒ Ⓓ Ⓔ
6 Ⓐ Ⓑ Ⓒ Ⓓ Ⓔ
7 Ⓐ Ⓑ Ⓒ Ⓓ Ⓔ

PT47-S2-P1

1 Ⓐ Ⓑ Ⓒ Ⓓ Ⓔ
2 Ⓐ Ⓑ Ⓒ Ⓓ Ⓔ
3 Ⓐ Ⓑ Ⓒ Ⓓ Ⓔ
4 Ⓐ Ⓑ Ⓒ Ⓓ Ⓔ
5 Ⓐ Ⓑ Ⓒ Ⓓ Ⓔ

PT48-S3-P1

1 Ⓐ Ⓑ Ⓒ Ⓓ Ⓔ
2 Ⓐ Ⓑ Ⓒ Ⓓ Ⓔ
3 Ⓐ Ⓑ Ⓒ Ⓓ Ⓔ
4 Ⓐ Ⓑ Ⓒ Ⓓ Ⓔ
5 Ⓐ Ⓑ Ⓒ Ⓓ Ⓔ

PT49-S3-P3

14 Ⓐ Ⓑ Ⓒ Ⓓ Ⓔ
15 Ⓐ Ⓑ Ⓒ Ⓓ Ⓔ
16 Ⓐ Ⓑ Ⓒ Ⓓ Ⓔ
17 Ⓐ Ⓑ Ⓒ Ⓓ Ⓔ
18 Ⓐ Ⓑ Ⓒ Ⓓ Ⓔ
19 Ⓐ Ⓑ Ⓒ Ⓓ Ⓔ
20 Ⓐ Ⓑ Ⓒ Ⓓ Ⓔ

PT50-S1-P3

14 Ⓐ Ⓑ Ⓒ Ⓓ Ⓔ
15 Ⓐ Ⓑ Ⓒ Ⓓ Ⓔ
16 Ⓐ Ⓑ Ⓒ Ⓓ Ⓔ
17 Ⓐ Ⓑ Ⓒ Ⓓ Ⓔ
18 Ⓐ Ⓑ Ⓒ Ⓓ Ⓔ
19 Ⓐ Ⓑ Ⓒ Ⓓ Ⓔ
20 Ⓐ Ⓑ Ⓒ Ⓓ Ⓔ
21 Ⓐ Ⓑ Ⓒ Ⓓ Ⓔ

PT51-S2-P3

14 Ⓐ Ⓑ Ⓒ Ⓓ Ⓔ
15 Ⓐ Ⓑ Ⓒ Ⓓ Ⓔ
16 Ⓐ Ⓑ Ⓒ Ⓓ Ⓔ
17 Ⓐ Ⓑ Ⓒ Ⓓ Ⓔ
18 Ⓐ Ⓑ Ⓒ Ⓓ Ⓔ
19 Ⓐ Ⓑ Ⓒ Ⓓ Ⓔ
20 Ⓐ Ⓑ Ⓒ Ⓓ Ⓔ

V4, Pg. 30   PT52-S4-P2

7 Ⓐ Ⓑ Ⓒ Ⓓ Ⓔ
8 Ⓐ Ⓑ Ⓒ Ⓓ Ⓔ
9 Ⓐ Ⓑ Ⓒ Ⓓ Ⓔ
10 Ⓐ Ⓑ Ⓒ Ⓓ Ⓔ
11 Ⓐ Ⓑ Ⓒ Ⓓ Ⓔ
12 Ⓐ Ⓑ Ⓒ Ⓓ Ⓔ

V4, Pg. 68   PT53-S4-P3

15 Ⓐ Ⓑ Ⓒ Ⓓ Ⓔ
16 Ⓐ Ⓑ Ⓒ Ⓓ Ⓔ
17 Ⓐ Ⓑ Ⓒ Ⓓ Ⓔ
18 Ⓐ Ⓑ Ⓒ Ⓓ Ⓔ
19 Ⓐ Ⓑ Ⓒ Ⓓ Ⓔ

V4, Pg. 86   PT54-S1-P4

20 Ⓐ Ⓑ Ⓒ Ⓓ Ⓔ
21 Ⓐ Ⓑ Ⓒ Ⓓ Ⓔ
22 Ⓐ Ⓑ Ⓒ Ⓓ Ⓔ
23 Ⓐ Ⓑ Ⓒ Ⓓ Ⓔ
24 Ⓐ Ⓑ Ⓒ Ⓓ Ⓔ
25 Ⓐ Ⓑ Ⓒ Ⓓ Ⓔ
26 Ⓐ Ⓑ Ⓒ Ⓓ Ⓔ
27 Ⓐ Ⓑ Ⓒ Ⓓ Ⓔ

V4, Pg. 130   PT55-S2-P4

22 Ⓐ Ⓑ Ⓒ Ⓓ Ⓔ
23 Ⓐ Ⓑ Ⓒ Ⓓ Ⓔ
24 Ⓐ Ⓑ Ⓒ Ⓓ Ⓔ
25 Ⓐ Ⓑ Ⓒ Ⓓ Ⓔ
26 Ⓐ Ⓑ Ⓒ Ⓓ Ⓔ
27 Ⓐ Ⓑ Ⓒ Ⓓ Ⓔ

V4, Pg. 176 PT56-S4-P3

16 Ⓐ Ⓑ Ⓒ Ⓓ Ⓔ
17 Ⓐ Ⓑ Ⓒ Ⓓ Ⓔ
18 Ⓐ Ⓑ Ⓒ Ⓓ Ⓔ
19 Ⓐ Ⓑ Ⓒ Ⓓ Ⓔ
20 Ⓐ Ⓑ Ⓒ Ⓓ Ⓔ
21 Ⓐ Ⓑ Ⓒ Ⓓ Ⓔ

V4, Pg. 178 PT56-S4-P4

22 Ⓐ Ⓑ Ⓒ Ⓓ Ⓔ
23 Ⓐ Ⓑ Ⓒ Ⓓ Ⓔ
24 Ⓐ Ⓑ Ⓒ Ⓓ Ⓔ
25 Ⓐ Ⓑ Ⓒ Ⓓ Ⓔ
26 Ⓐ Ⓑ Ⓒ Ⓓ Ⓔ
27 Ⓐ Ⓑ Ⓒ Ⓓ Ⓔ

V4, Pg. 210 PT57-S4-P2

6   Ⓐ Ⓑ Ⓒ Ⓓ Ⓔ
7   Ⓐ Ⓑ Ⓒ Ⓓ Ⓔ
8   Ⓐ Ⓑ Ⓒ Ⓓ Ⓔ
9   Ⓐ Ⓑ Ⓒ Ⓓ Ⓔ
10 Ⓐ Ⓑ Ⓒ Ⓓ Ⓔ
11 Ⓐ Ⓑ Ⓒ Ⓓ Ⓔ
12 Ⓐ Ⓑ Ⓒ Ⓓ Ⓔ

V4, Pg. 232 PT58-S2-P1

1   Ⓐ Ⓑ Ⓒ Ⓓ Ⓔ
2   Ⓐ Ⓑ Ⓒ Ⓓ Ⓔ
3   Ⓐ Ⓑ Ⓒ Ⓓ Ⓔ
4   Ⓐ Ⓑ Ⓒ Ⓓ Ⓔ
5   Ⓐ Ⓑ Ⓒ Ⓓ Ⓔ
6   Ⓐ Ⓑ Ⓒ Ⓓ Ⓔ
7   Ⓐ Ⓑ Ⓒ Ⓓ Ⓔ

V4, Pg. 286 PT59-S4-P4

23 Ⓐ Ⓑ Ⓒ Ⓓ Ⓔ
24 Ⓐ Ⓑ Ⓒ Ⓓ Ⓔ
25 Ⓐ Ⓑ Ⓒ Ⓓ Ⓔ
26 Ⓐ Ⓑ Ⓒ Ⓓ Ⓔ
27 Ⓐ Ⓑ Ⓒ Ⓓ Ⓔ

V4, Pg. 316 PT60-S4-P1

1   Ⓐ Ⓑ Ⓒ Ⓓ Ⓔ
2   Ⓐ Ⓑ Ⓒ Ⓓ Ⓔ
3   Ⓐ Ⓑ Ⓒ Ⓓ Ⓔ
4   Ⓐ Ⓑ Ⓒ Ⓓ Ⓔ
5   Ⓐ Ⓑ Ⓒ Ⓓ Ⓔ
6   Ⓐ Ⓑ Ⓒ Ⓓ Ⓔ
7   Ⓐ Ⓑ Ⓒ Ⓓ Ⓔ

V4, Pg. 338 PT61-S1-P4

20 Ⓐ Ⓑ Ⓒ Ⓓ Ⓔ
21 Ⓐ Ⓑ Ⓒ Ⓓ Ⓔ
22 Ⓐ Ⓑ Ⓒ Ⓓ Ⓔ
23 Ⓐ Ⓑ Ⓒ Ⓓ Ⓔ
24 Ⓐ Ⓑ Ⓒ Ⓓ Ⓔ
25 Ⓐ Ⓑ Ⓒ Ⓓ Ⓔ
26 Ⓐ Ⓑ Ⓒ Ⓓ Ⓔ
27 Ⓐ Ⓑ Ⓒ Ⓓ Ⓔ

V5, Pg. 70   PT63-S4-P4

22 Ⓐ Ⓑ Ⓒ Ⓓ Ⓔ
23 Ⓐ Ⓑ Ⓒ Ⓓ Ⓔ
24 Ⓐ Ⓑ Ⓒ Ⓓ Ⓔ
25 Ⓐ Ⓑ Ⓒ Ⓓ Ⓔ
26 Ⓐ Ⓑ Ⓒ Ⓓ Ⓔ
27 Ⓐ Ⓑ Ⓒ Ⓓ Ⓔ

V5, Pg. 102 PT64-S4-P2

7   Ⓐ Ⓑ Ⓒ Ⓓ Ⓔ
8   Ⓐ Ⓑ Ⓒ Ⓓ Ⓔ
9   Ⓐ Ⓑ Ⓒ Ⓓ Ⓔ
10 Ⓐ Ⓑ Ⓒ Ⓓ Ⓔ
11 Ⓐ Ⓑ Ⓒ Ⓓ Ⓔ
12 Ⓐ Ⓑ Ⓒ Ⓓ Ⓔ

V5, Pg. 130 PT65-S3-P2

8   Ⓐ Ⓑ Ⓒ Ⓓ Ⓔ
9   Ⓐ Ⓑ Ⓒ Ⓓ Ⓔ
10 Ⓐ Ⓑ Ⓒ Ⓓ Ⓔ
11 Ⓐ Ⓑ Ⓒ Ⓓ Ⓔ
12 Ⓐ Ⓑ Ⓒ Ⓓ Ⓔ
13 Ⓐ Ⓑ Ⓒ Ⓓ Ⓔ

V5, Pg. 152 PT66-S1-P1

1   Ⓐ Ⓑ Ⓒ Ⓓ Ⓔ
2   Ⓐ Ⓑ Ⓒ Ⓓ Ⓔ
3   Ⓐ Ⓑ Ⓒ Ⓓ Ⓔ
4   Ⓐ Ⓑ Ⓒ Ⓓ Ⓔ
5   Ⓐ Ⓑ Ⓒ Ⓓ Ⓔ
6   Ⓐ Ⓑ Ⓒ Ⓓ Ⓔ
7   Ⓐ Ⓑ Ⓒ Ⓓ Ⓔ

V5, Pg. 236 PT68-S1-P3

15 Ⓐ Ⓑ Ⓒ Ⓓ Ⓔ
16 Ⓐ Ⓑ Ⓒ Ⓓ Ⓔ
17 Ⓐ Ⓑ Ⓒ Ⓓ Ⓔ
18 Ⓐ Ⓑ Ⓒ Ⓓ Ⓔ
19 Ⓐ Ⓑ Ⓒ Ⓓ Ⓔ
20 Ⓐ Ⓑ Ⓒ Ⓓ Ⓔ
21 Ⓐ Ⓑ Ⓒ Ⓓ Ⓔ
22 Ⓐ Ⓑ Ⓒ Ⓓ Ⓔ

V5, Pg. 288 PT69-S3-P1

1   Ⓐ Ⓑ Ⓒ Ⓓ Ⓔ
2   Ⓐ Ⓑ Ⓒ Ⓓ Ⓔ
3   Ⓐ Ⓑ Ⓒ Ⓓ Ⓔ
4   Ⓐ Ⓑ Ⓒ Ⓓ Ⓔ
5   Ⓐ Ⓑ Ⓒ Ⓓ Ⓔ
6   Ⓐ Ⓑ Ⓒ Ⓓ Ⓔ
7   Ⓐ Ⓑ Ⓒ Ⓓ Ⓔ

V5, Pg. 324 PT70-S2-P3

15 Ⓐ Ⓑ Ⓒ Ⓓ Ⓔ
16 Ⓐ Ⓑ Ⓒ Ⓓ Ⓔ
17 Ⓐ Ⓑ Ⓒ Ⓓ Ⓔ
18 Ⓐ Ⓑ Ⓒ Ⓓ Ⓔ
19 Ⓐ Ⓑ Ⓒ Ⓓ Ⓔ
20 Ⓐ Ⓑ Ⓒ Ⓓ Ⓔ

V5, Pg. 378 PT71-S4-P2

7   Ⓐ Ⓑ Ⓒ Ⓓ Ⓔ
8   Ⓐ Ⓑ Ⓒ Ⓓ Ⓔ
9   Ⓐ Ⓑ Ⓒ Ⓓ Ⓔ
10 Ⓐ Ⓑ Ⓒ Ⓓ Ⓔ
11 Ⓐ Ⓑ Ⓒ Ⓓ Ⓔ
12 Ⓐ Ⓑ Ⓒ Ⓓ Ⓔ
13 Ⓐ Ⓑ Ⓒ Ⓓ Ⓔ

PT72, Pg. 14 PT72-S1-P3

14 Ⓐ Ⓑ Ⓒ Ⓓ Ⓔ
15 Ⓐ Ⓑ Ⓒ Ⓓ Ⓔ
16 Ⓐ Ⓑ Ⓒ Ⓓ Ⓔ
17 Ⓐ Ⓑ Ⓒ Ⓓ Ⓔ
18 Ⓐ Ⓑ Ⓒ Ⓓ Ⓔ
19 Ⓐ Ⓑ Ⓒ Ⓓ Ⓔ
20 Ⓐ Ⓑ Ⓒ Ⓓ Ⓔ
21 Ⓐ Ⓑ Ⓒ Ⓓ Ⓔ

PT73, Pg. 14 PT73-S1-P3

16 Ⓐ Ⓑ Ⓒ Ⓓ Ⓔ
17 Ⓐ Ⓑ Ⓒ Ⓓ Ⓔ
18 Ⓐ Ⓑ Ⓒ Ⓓ Ⓔ
19 Ⓐ Ⓑ Ⓒ Ⓓ Ⓔ
20 Ⓐ Ⓑ Ⓒ Ⓓ Ⓔ
21 Ⓐ Ⓑ Ⓒ Ⓓ Ⓔ

PT74, Pg. 32 PT74-S3-P4

22 Ⓐ Ⓑ Ⓒ Ⓓ Ⓔ
23 Ⓐ Ⓑ Ⓒ Ⓓ Ⓔ
24 Ⓐ Ⓑ Ⓒ Ⓓ Ⓔ
25 Ⓐ Ⓑ Ⓒ Ⓓ Ⓔ
26 Ⓐ Ⓑ Ⓒ Ⓓ Ⓔ
27 Ⓐ Ⓑ Ⓒ Ⓓ Ⓔ

PT75, Pg. 18 PT75-S2-P1

1 Ⓐ Ⓑ Ⓒ Ⓓ Ⓔ
2 Ⓐ Ⓑ Ⓒ Ⓓ Ⓔ
3 Ⓐ Ⓑ Ⓒ Ⓓ Ⓔ
4 Ⓐ Ⓑ Ⓒ Ⓓ Ⓔ
5 Ⓐ Ⓑ Ⓒ Ⓓ Ⓔ
6 Ⓐ Ⓑ Ⓒ Ⓓ Ⓔ
7 Ⓐ Ⓑ Ⓒ Ⓓ Ⓔ

PT75, Pg. 22 PT75-S2-P3

15 Ⓐ Ⓑ Ⓒ Ⓓ Ⓔ
16 Ⓐ Ⓑ Ⓒ Ⓓ Ⓔ
17 Ⓐ Ⓑ Ⓒ Ⓓ Ⓔ
18 Ⓐ Ⓑ Ⓒ Ⓓ Ⓔ
19 Ⓐ Ⓑ Ⓒ Ⓓ Ⓔ
20 Ⓐ Ⓑ Ⓒ Ⓓ Ⓔ

PT76, Pg. 14 PT76-S1-P3

14 Ⓐ Ⓑ Ⓒ Ⓓ Ⓔ
15 Ⓐ Ⓑ Ⓒ Ⓓ Ⓔ
16 Ⓐ Ⓑ Ⓒ Ⓓ Ⓔ
17 Ⓐ Ⓑ Ⓒ Ⓓ Ⓔ
18 Ⓐ Ⓑ Ⓒ Ⓓ Ⓔ
19 Ⓐ Ⓑ Ⓒ Ⓓ Ⓔ

PT77, Pg. 14 PT77-S1-P3

14 Ⓐ Ⓑ Ⓒ Ⓓ Ⓔ
15 Ⓐ Ⓑ Ⓒ Ⓓ Ⓔ
16 Ⓐ Ⓑ Ⓒ Ⓓ Ⓔ
17 Ⓐ Ⓑ Ⓒ Ⓓ Ⓔ
18 Ⓐ Ⓑ Ⓒ Ⓓ Ⓔ
19 Ⓐ Ⓑ Ⓒ Ⓓ Ⓔ

Comparative Passages

J07, Pg. 24   J07-S4-P2

9   Ⓐ Ⓑ Ⓒ Ⓓ Ⓔ
10 Ⓐ Ⓑ Ⓒ Ⓓ Ⓔ
11 Ⓐ Ⓑ Ⓒ Ⓓ Ⓔ
12 Ⓐ Ⓑ Ⓒ Ⓓ Ⓔ
13 Ⓐ Ⓑ Ⓒ Ⓓ Ⓔ
14 Ⓐ Ⓑ Ⓒ Ⓓ Ⓔ

SP2, Pg. 376 PTC2-S4-P4

20 Ⓐ Ⓑ Ⓒ Ⓓ Ⓔ
21 Ⓐ Ⓑ Ⓒ Ⓓ Ⓔ
22 Ⓐ Ⓑ Ⓒ Ⓓ Ⓔ
23 Ⓐ Ⓑ Ⓒ Ⓓ Ⓔ
24 Ⓐ Ⓑ Ⓒ Ⓓ Ⓔ
25 Ⓐ Ⓑ Ⓒ Ⓓ Ⓔ
26 Ⓐ Ⓑ Ⓒ Ⓓ Ⓔ
27 Ⓐ Ⓑ Ⓒ Ⓓ Ⓔ

V4, Pg. 30   PT52-S4-P2

7   Ⓐ Ⓑ Ⓒ Ⓓ Ⓔ
8   Ⓐ Ⓑ Ⓒ Ⓓ Ⓔ
9   Ⓐ Ⓑ Ⓒ Ⓓ Ⓔ
10 Ⓐ Ⓑ Ⓒ Ⓓ Ⓔ
11 Ⓐ Ⓑ Ⓒ Ⓓ Ⓔ
12 Ⓐ Ⓑ Ⓒ Ⓓ Ⓔ

V4, Pg. 68   PT53-S4-P3

15 Ⓐ Ⓑ Ⓒ Ⓓ Ⓔ
16 Ⓐ Ⓑ Ⓒ Ⓓ Ⓔ
17 Ⓐ Ⓑ Ⓒ Ⓓ Ⓔ
18 Ⓐ Ⓑ Ⓒ Ⓓ Ⓔ
19 Ⓐ Ⓑ Ⓒ Ⓓ Ⓔ

V4, Pg. 82   PT54-S1-P2

6   Ⓐ Ⓑ Ⓒ Ⓓ Ⓔ
7   Ⓐ Ⓑ Ⓒ Ⓓ Ⓔ
8   Ⓐ Ⓑ Ⓒ Ⓓ Ⓔ
9   Ⓐ Ⓑ Ⓒ Ⓓ Ⓔ
10 Ⓐ Ⓑ Ⓒ Ⓓ Ⓔ
11 Ⓐ Ⓑ Ⓒ Ⓓ Ⓔ
12 Ⓐ Ⓑ Ⓒ Ⓓ Ⓔ

V4, Pg. 126   PT55-S2-P2

7   Ⓐ Ⓑ Ⓒ Ⓓ Ⓔ
8   Ⓐ Ⓑ Ⓒ Ⓓ Ⓔ
9   Ⓐ Ⓑ Ⓒ Ⓓ Ⓔ
10 Ⓐ Ⓑ Ⓒ Ⓓ Ⓔ
11 Ⓐ Ⓑ Ⓒ Ⓓ Ⓔ
12 Ⓐ Ⓑ Ⓒ Ⓓ Ⓔ
13 Ⓐ Ⓑ Ⓒ Ⓓ Ⓔ

V4, Pg. 176   PT56-S4-P3

16 Ⓐ Ⓑ Ⓒ Ⓓ Ⓔ
17 Ⓐ Ⓑ Ⓒ Ⓓ Ⓔ
18 Ⓐ Ⓑ Ⓒ Ⓓ Ⓔ
19 Ⓐ Ⓑ Ⓒ Ⓓ Ⓔ
20 Ⓐ Ⓑ Ⓒ Ⓓ Ⓔ
21 Ⓐ Ⓑ Ⓒ Ⓓ Ⓔ

V4, Pg. 212   PT57-S4-P3

13 Ⓐ Ⓑ Ⓒ Ⓓ Ⓔ
14 Ⓐ Ⓑ Ⓒ Ⓓ Ⓔ
15 Ⓐ Ⓑ Ⓒ Ⓓ Ⓔ
16 Ⓐ Ⓑ Ⓒ Ⓓ Ⓔ
17 Ⓐ Ⓑ Ⓒ Ⓓ Ⓔ
18 Ⓐ Ⓑ Ⓒ Ⓓ Ⓔ
19 Ⓐ Ⓑ Ⓒ Ⓓ Ⓔ

V4, Pg. 238   PT58-S2-P4

21 Ⓐ Ⓑ Ⓒ Ⓓ Ⓔ
22 Ⓐ Ⓑ Ⓒ Ⓓ Ⓔ
23 Ⓐ Ⓑ Ⓒ Ⓓ Ⓔ
24 Ⓐ Ⓑ Ⓒ Ⓓ Ⓔ
25 Ⓐ Ⓑ Ⓒ Ⓓ Ⓔ
26 Ⓐ Ⓑ Ⓒ Ⓓ Ⓔ
27 Ⓐ Ⓑ Ⓒ Ⓓ Ⓔ

V4, Pg. 280   PT59-S4-P1

1   Ⓐ Ⓑ Ⓒ Ⓓ Ⓔ
2   Ⓐ Ⓑ Ⓒ Ⓓ Ⓔ
3   Ⓐ Ⓑ Ⓒ Ⓓ Ⓔ
4   Ⓐ Ⓑ Ⓒ Ⓓ Ⓔ
5   Ⓐ Ⓑ Ⓒ Ⓓ Ⓔ
6   Ⓐ Ⓑ Ⓒ Ⓓ Ⓔ
7   Ⓐ Ⓑ Ⓒ Ⓓ Ⓔ
8   Ⓐ Ⓑ Ⓒ Ⓓ Ⓔ

V4, Pg. 318   PT60-S4-P2

8   Ⓐ Ⓑ Ⓒ Ⓓ Ⓔ
9   Ⓐ Ⓑ Ⓒ Ⓓ Ⓔ
10 Ⓐ Ⓑ Ⓒ Ⓓ Ⓔ
11 Ⓐ Ⓑ Ⓒ Ⓓ Ⓔ
12 Ⓐ Ⓑ Ⓒ Ⓓ Ⓔ

V4, Pg. 336   PT61-S1-P3

14 Ⓐ Ⓑ Ⓒ Ⓓ Ⓔ
15 Ⓐ Ⓑ Ⓒ Ⓓ Ⓔ
16 Ⓐ Ⓑ Ⓒ Ⓓ Ⓔ
17 Ⓐ Ⓑ Ⓒ Ⓓ Ⓔ
18 Ⓐ Ⓑ Ⓒ Ⓓ Ⓔ
19 Ⓐ Ⓑ Ⓒ Ⓓ Ⓔ

V5, Pg. 12   PT62-S1-P3

15 Ⓐ Ⓑ Ⓒ Ⓓ Ⓔ
16 Ⓐ Ⓑ Ⓒ Ⓓ Ⓔ
17 Ⓐ Ⓑ Ⓒ Ⓓ Ⓔ
18 Ⓐ Ⓑ Ⓒ Ⓓ Ⓔ
19 Ⓐ Ⓑ Ⓒ Ⓓ Ⓔ
20 Ⓐ Ⓑ Ⓒ Ⓓ Ⓔ
21 Ⓐ Ⓑ Ⓒ Ⓓ Ⓔ

V5, Pg. 70   PT63-S4-P4

22 Ⓐ Ⓑ Ⓒ Ⓓ Ⓔ
23 Ⓐ Ⓑ Ⓒ Ⓓ Ⓔ
24 Ⓐ Ⓑ Ⓒ Ⓓ Ⓔ
25 Ⓐ Ⓑ Ⓒ Ⓓ Ⓔ
26 Ⓐ Ⓑ Ⓒ Ⓓ Ⓔ
27 Ⓐ Ⓑ Ⓒ Ⓓ Ⓔ

V5, Pg. 104   PT64-S4-P3

13 Ⓐ Ⓑ Ⓒ Ⓓ Ⓔ
14 Ⓐ Ⓑ Ⓒ Ⓓ Ⓔ
15 Ⓐ Ⓑ Ⓒ Ⓓ Ⓔ
16 Ⓐ Ⓑ Ⓒ Ⓓ Ⓔ
17 Ⓐ Ⓑ Ⓒ Ⓓ Ⓔ
18 Ⓐ Ⓑ Ⓒ Ⓓ Ⓔ
19 Ⓐ Ⓑ Ⓒ Ⓓ Ⓔ

V5, Pg. 132   PT65-S3-P3

14 Ⓐ Ⓑ Ⓒ Ⓓ Ⓔ
15 Ⓐ Ⓑ Ⓒ Ⓓ Ⓔ
16 Ⓐ Ⓑ Ⓒ Ⓓ Ⓔ
17 Ⓐ Ⓑ Ⓒ Ⓓ Ⓔ
18 Ⓐ Ⓑ Ⓒ Ⓓ Ⓔ
19 Ⓐ Ⓑ Ⓒ Ⓓ Ⓔ

V5, Pg. 154   PT66-S1-P2

8   Ⓐ Ⓑ Ⓒ Ⓓ Ⓔ
9   Ⓐ Ⓑ Ⓒ Ⓓ Ⓔ
10 Ⓐ Ⓑ Ⓒ Ⓓ Ⓔ
11 Ⓐ Ⓑ Ⓒ Ⓓ Ⓔ
12 Ⓐ Ⓑ Ⓒ Ⓓ Ⓔ
13 Ⓐ Ⓑ Ⓒ Ⓓ Ⓔ
14 Ⓐ Ⓑ Ⓒ Ⓓ Ⓔ

V5, Pg. 196   PT67-S1-P3

15 Ⓐ Ⓑ Ⓒ Ⓓ Ⓔ
16 Ⓐ Ⓑ Ⓒ Ⓓ Ⓔ
17 Ⓐ Ⓑ Ⓒ Ⓓ Ⓔ
18 Ⓐ Ⓑ Ⓒ Ⓓ Ⓔ
19 Ⓐ Ⓑ Ⓒ Ⓓ Ⓔ

V5, Pg. 238   PT68-S1-P4

23 Ⓐ Ⓑ Ⓒ Ⓓ Ⓔ
24 Ⓐ Ⓑ Ⓒ Ⓓ Ⓔ
25 Ⓐ Ⓑ Ⓒ Ⓓ Ⓔ
26 Ⓐ Ⓑ Ⓒ Ⓓ Ⓔ
27 Ⓐ Ⓑ Ⓒ Ⓓ Ⓔ

V5, Pg. 292   PT69-S3-P3

15 Ⓐ Ⓑ Ⓒ Ⓓ Ⓔ
16 Ⓐ Ⓑ Ⓒ Ⓓ Ⓔ
17 Ⓐ Ⓑ Ⓒ Ⓓ Ⓔ
18 Ⓐ Ⓑ Ⓒ Ⓓ Ⓔ
19 Ⓐ Ⓑ Ⓒ Ⓓ Ⓔ
20 Ⓐ Ⓑ Ⓒ Ⓓ Ⓔ
21 Ⓐ Ⓑ Ⓒ Ⓓ Ⓔ

V5, Pg. 324   PT70-S2-P3

15 Ⓐ Ⓑ Ⓒ Ⓓ Ⓔ
16 Ⓐ Ⓑ Ⓒ Ⓓ Ⓔ
17 Ⓐ Ⓑ Ⓒ Ⓓ Ⓔ
18 Ⓐ Ⓑ Ⓒ Ⓓ Ⓔ
19 Ⓐ Ⓑ Ⓒ Ⓓ Ⓔ
20 Ⓐ Ⓑ Ⓒ Ⓓ Ⓔ

V5, Pg. 378   PT71-S4-P2

7   Ⓐ Ⓑ Ⓒ Ⓓ Ⓔ
8   Ⓐ Ⓑ Ⓒ Ⓓ Ⓔ
9   Ⓐ Ⓑ Ⓒ Ⓓ Ⓔ
10 Ⓐ Ⓑ Ⓒ Ⓓ Ⓔ
11 Ⓐ Ⓑ Ⓒ Ⓓ Ⓔ
12 Ⓐ Ⓑ Ⓒ Ⓓ Ⓔ
13 Ⓐ Ⓑ Ⓒ Ⓓ Ⓔ

PT72, Pg. 16 PT72-S1-P4

22 Ⓐ Ⓑ Ⓒ Ⓓ Ⓔ
23 Ⓐ Ⓑ Ⓒ Ⓓ Ⓔ
24 Ⓐ Ⓑ Ⓒ Ⓓ Ⓔ
25 Ⓐ Ⓑ Ⓒ Ⓓ Ⓔ
26 Ⓐ Ⓑ Ⓒ Ⓓ Ⓔ
27 Ⓐ Ⓑ Ⓒ Ⓓ Ⓔ

PT73, Pg. 16 PT73-S1-P4

22 Ⓐ Ⓑ Ⓒ Ⓓ Ⓔ
23 Ⓐ Ⓑ Ⓒ Ⓓ Ⓔ
24 Ⓐ Ⓑ Ⓒ Ⓓ Ⓔ
25 Ⓐ Ⓑ Ⓒ Ⓓ Ⓔ
26 Ⓐ Ⓑ Ⓒ Ⓓ Ⓔ
27 Ⓐ Ⓑ Ⓒ Ⓓ Ⓔ

PT74, Pg. 30 PT74-S3-P3

17 Ⓐ Ⓑ Ⓒ Ⓓ Ⓔ
18 Ⓐ Ⓑ Ⓒ Ⓓ Ⓔ
19 Ⓐ Ⓑ Ⓒ Ⓓ Ⓔ
20 Ⓐ Ⓑ Ⓒ Ⓓ Ⓔ
21 Ⓐ Ⓑ Ⓒ Ⓓ Ⓔ

PT75, Pg. 22 PT75-S2-P3

15 Ⓐ Ⓑ Ⓒ Ⓓ Ⓔ
16 Ⓐ Ⓑ Ⓒ Ⓓ Ⓔ
17 Ⓐ Ⓑ Ⓒ Ⓓ Ⓔ
18 Ⓐ Ⓑ Ⓒ Ⓓ Ⓔ
19 Ⓐ Ⓑ Ⓒ Ⓓ Ⓔ
20 Ⓐ Ⓑ Ⓒ Ⓓ Ⓔ

PT76, Pg. 16 PT76-S1-P4

20 Ⓐ Ⓑ Ⓒ Ⓓ Ⓔ
21 Ⓐ Ⓑ Ⓒ Ⓓ Ⓔ
22 Ⓐ Ⓑ Ⓒ Ⓓ Ⓔ
23 Ⓐ Ⓑ Ⓒ Ⓓ Ⓔ
24 Ⓐ Ⓑ Ⓒ Ⓓ Ⓔ
25 Ⓐ Ⓑ Ⓒ Ⓓ Ⓔ
26 Ⓐ Ⓑ Ⓒ Ⓓ Ⓔ
27 Ⓐ Ⓑ Ⓒ Ⓓ Ⓔ

PT77, Pg. 14 PT77-S1-P3

14 Ⓐ Ⓑ Ⓒ Ⓓ Ⓔ
15 Ⓐ Ⓑ Ⓒ Ⓓ Ⓔ
16 Ⓐ Ⓑ Ⓒ Ⓓ Ⓔ
17 Ⓐ Ⓑ Ⓒ Ⓓ Ⓔ
18 Ⓐ Ⓑ Ⓒ Ⓓ Ⓔ
19 Ⓐ Ⓑ Ⓒ Ⓓ Ⓔ

Logic Games Answers

Relative Ordering

PTB-S2-G1
1. B
2. C
3. D
4. E
5. B
6. A

PTC-S1-G2
6. C
7. E
8. E
9. B
10. C
11. E
12. B

PT1-S2-G3
14. C
15. E
16. D
17. B
18. D

PT2-S3-G1
1. D
2. A
3. A
4. E
5. D

PT4-S3-G1
1. D
2. C
3. D
4. D
5. C
6. D

PT6-S4-G2
7. C
8. E
9. C
10. A
11. B
12. B

PT10-S2-G1
1. B
2. C
3. C
4. C
5. E

PT33-S4-G1
1. C
2. A
3. E
4. D
5. B

PT38-S2-G1
1. E
2. D
3. C
4. D
5. D
6. E
7. E

PT42-S1-G2
6. A
7. A
8. C
9. D
10. C
11. C
12. C

PT43-S4-G2
6. C
7. E
8. E
9. A
10. D
11. A
12. C

PT48-S2-G2
7. C
8. B
9. C
10. E
11. D
12. E

PT51-S4-G2
6. B
7. C
8. A
9. D
10. D

PT51-S4-G4
16. D
17. C
18. D
19. A
20. B
21. C
22. C

PT52-S2-G1
1. E
2. C
3. B
4. B
5. E
6. B
7. B

PT52-S2-G4
18. C
19. A
20. E
21. C
22. C
23. E

PT53-S2-G2
6. C
7. A
8. A
9. D
10. C
11. B

PT55-S4-G3
13. D
14. B
15. C
16. C
17. C
18. E

PT60-S2-G2
7. E
8. C
9. D
10. A
11. C
12. C

PT61-S3-G2
6. A
7. C
8. A
9. C
10. B
11. D

PT63-S2-G3
11. B
12. E
13. C
14. E
15. A
16. B
17. B

PT65-S2-G1
1. D
2. A
3. C
4. E
5. B

PT67-S3-G2
6. B
7. B
8. E
9. A
10. E
11. C
12. E

PT71-S2-G1
1. E
2. A
3. E
4. D
5. A

PT73-S3-G1
1. B
2. C
3. B
4. E
5. E
6. D
7. A

PT74-S2-G1
1. C
2. D
3. E
4. A
5. E

PT75-S4-G3
12. A
13. E
14. B
15. A
16. C
17. D
18. C

Simple Ordering

J07-S1-G1
1. A
2. C
3. C
4. E
5. E

J07-S1-G3
11. A
12. A
13. D
14. E
15. A
16. A
17. D

PTSP-S1-G1
1. D
2. A
3. A
4. B
5. E

PTA-S3-G1
1. D
2. B
3. E
4. D
5. D

PTC2-S1-G2
6. E
7. E
8. A
9. D
10. C

PT3-S1-G2
8. C
9. A
10. C
11. A
12. A
13. D

PT7-S2-G1
1. C
2. A
3. C
4. C
5. E
6. C
7. D

PT11-S1-G2
7. B
8. D
9. B
10. B
11. D

PT12-S2-G1
1. E
2. B
3. C
4. B
5. C
6. D

PT13-S1-G2
7. E
8. E
9. C
10. C
11. C

PT15-S4-G1
1. D
2. B
3. C
4. A
5. D
6. A

PT15-S4-G3
14. D
15. E
16. C
17. A
18. B
19. E

PT17-S1-G1
1. E
2. E
3. B
4. B
5. D

PT18-S1-G2
7. D
8. A
9. B
10. D
11. B
12. E
13. C

PT19-S1-G1
1. B
2. E
3. C
4. E
5. D
6. D
7. C

PT23-S1-G1
1. B
2. D
3. B
4. C
5. D

PT24-S4-G2
6. A
7. B
8. C
9. E
10. A

PT26-S1-G2
8. C
9. E
10. A
11. C
12. A

PT27-S2-G1
1. E
2. E
3. C
4. C
5. D
6. B

PT27-S2-G4
20. A
21. B
22. E
23. A
24. D

PT28-S2-G1
1. B
2. E
3. E
4. B
5. C

PT29-S3-G3
14. A
15. E
16. C
17. C
18. A
19. D

PT30-S1-G2
6. D
7. A
8. A
9. D
10. C

PT30-S1-G4
17. B
18. C
19. C
20. D
21. A
22. A
23. D

PT31-S1-G3
14. C
15. B
16. A
17. E
18. A

PT32-S3-G3
12. A
13. E
14. A
15. E
16. C
17. C
18. D

PT34-S4-G1
1. C
2. E
3. B
4. D
5. A
6. E
7. B

PT34-S4-G2
8. E
9. A
10. C
11. D
12. B

PT34-S4-G3
13. C
14. A
15. E
16. B
17. E
18. C

PT40-S2-G1
1. D
2. C
3. A
4. C
5. D

PT40-S2-G2
6. D
7. C
8. A
9. E
10. B

PT41-S2-G1
1. A
2. B
3. E
4. E
5. B
6. D
7. D

PT43-S4-G1
1. D
2. E
3. A
4. E
5. B

PT44-S3-G1
1. C
2. D
3. E
4. E
5. D
6. A

PT45-S3-G1
1. E
2. B
3. C
4. D
5. B
6. E

PT46-S4-G1
1. A
2. A
3. D
4. A
5. E
6. A

PT47-S4-G1
1. E
2. A
3. C
4. A
5. D

PT49-S1-G1
1. E
2. D
3. A
4. B
5. D
6. E
7. D

PT49-S1-G4
18. B
19. E
20. B
21. D
22. C

PT50-S3-G1
1. D
2. B
3. C
4. E
5. B

PT54-S3-G3
13. A
14. B
15. E
16. B
17. B

PT54-S3-G4
18. B
19. A
20. B
21. D
22. C
23. A

PT55-S4-G2
7. D
8. C
9. A
10. E
11. D
12. B

PT56-S1-G1
1. E
2. B
3. C
4. C
5. A
6. E

PT57-S1-G1
1. D
2. B
3. C
4. D
5. C

PT59-S1-G2
6. C
7. E
8. D
9. B
10. D

PT59-S1-G4
17. A
18. E
19. D
20. E
21. E
22. B
23. B

PT60-S2-G3
13. E
14. D
15. E
16. A
17. B

PT61-S3-G3
12. D
13. D
14. B
15. A
16. E
17. B

PT61-S3-G4
18. D
19. C
20. D
21. B
22. B
23. A

PT62-S3-G1
1. D
2. D
3. E
4. E
5. B
6. A

PT62-S3-G4
19. B
20. E
21. A
22. A
23. D

PT63-S2-G2
6. B
7. D
8. C
9. D
10. A

PT63-S2-G4
18. B
19. C
20. E
21. A
22. C
23. D

PT64-S2-G1
1. E
2. B
3. C
4. D
5. A
6. E

PT65-S2-G4
17. B
18. B
19. D
20. E
21. C
22. B
23. C

PT66-S3-G2
6. E
7. A
8. C
9. D
10. B
11. D

PT68-S4-G1
1. C
2. A
3. B
4. C
5. E

PT69-S2-G1
1. E
2. A
3. E
4. C
5. D

PT70-S3-G1
1. B
2. C
3. B
4. E
5. D
6. D
7. A

PT71-S2-G4
17. C
18. A
19. C
20. E
21. A
22. E
23. B

PT72-S4-G2
7. E
8. C
9. D
10. A
11. E
12. B

PT75-S4-G4
19. D
20. A
21. E
22. D
23. D

PT76-S3-G1
1. D
2. C
3. D
4. B
5. A
6. B

PT77-S3-G1
1. A
2. B
3. D
4. C
5. C

PT77-S3-G2
6. E
7. D
8. C
9. A
10. B
11. B
12. A

Complex Ordering

PTSP-S1-G4
18. D
19. E
20. C
21. B
22. D

PTA-S3-G3
11. B
12. C
13. A
14. A
15. E
16. E
17. D

PT2-S3-G4
18. E
19. B
20. E
21. A
22. E
23. B
24. D

PT5-S2-G4
18. B
19. C
20. C
21. D
22. A
23. E
24. E

PT7-S2-G4
19. E
20. D
21. B
22. D
23. B
24. A

PT8-S2-G3
13. C
14. C
15. E
16. B
17. D

PT14-S1-G2
7. E
8. A
9. B
10. C
11. E
12. A

PT20-S3-G4
19. E
20. C
21. D
22. D
23. B
24. C

PT22-S3-G2
8. B
9. B
10. D
11. B
12. B
13. A
14. A

PT23-S1-G4
19. D
20. D
21. B
22. E
23. C
24. A

PT24-S4-G3
11. B
12. A
13. D
14. B
15. E
16. A
17. D

PT25-S3-G4
19. E
20. D
21. A
22. A
23. A
24. D

PT26-S1-G1
1. C
2. B
3. A
4. D
5. E
6. A
7. D

PT30-S1-G3
11. B
12. A
13. B
14. E
15. B
16. A

PT31-S1-G1
1. E
2. B
3. D
4. C
5. A
6. C

PT32-S3-G4
19. E
20. B
21. D
22. B
23. A
24. D

PT36-S4-G2
7. E
8. A
9. C
10. C
11. A
12. A
13. B

PT36-S4-G4
19. A
20. C
21. D
22. C
23. D

PT37-S3-G2
6. A
7. B
8. C
9. A
10. B
11. E

PT37-S3-G4
19. A
20. A
21. D
22. B
23. B
24. C

PT38-S2-G2
8. C
9. A
10. B
11. A
12. D
13. E

PT38-S2-G4
20. D
21. A
22. A
23. B
24. D

PT39-S1-G1
1. D
2. C
3. A
4. C
5. C

PT39-S1-G3
12. E
13. D
14. C
15. B
16. D
17. D
18. D

PT41-S2-G2	PT46-S4-G3	PT53-S2-G3	PT58-S3-G3	PT66-S3-G4	PT70-S3-G4
8. B	12. A	12. B	13. D	19. C	19. E
9. E	13. C	13. E	14. D	20. A	20. B
10. C	14. E	14. A	15. B	21. C	21. A
11. E	15. D	15. E	16. B	22. B	22. A
12. A	16. B	16. A	17. C	23. C	23. D
		17. D			

PT44-S3-G3	PT51-S4-G3		PT65-S2-G2	PT68-S4-G4	PT71-S2-G3
13. E	11. D	PT55-S4-G4	6. C	17. C	12. A
14. C	12. E	19. E	7. D	18. A	13. A
15. A	13. D	20. D	8. E	19. E	14. C
16. E	14. D	21. D	9. B	20. B	15. B
17. D	15. E	22. C	10. B	21. E	16. D
		23. D	11. C	22. D	
				23. C	PT74-S2-G2

PT44-S3-G4					
18. A					6. E
19. E					7. B
20. E					8. E
21. D					9. A
22. C					10. A

In/Out Grouping

PTSP-S1-G2	PT10-S2-G4	PT24-S4-G4	PT33-S4-G3	PT41-S2-G3	PT49-S1-G3
6. B	19. B	18. E	13. D	13. E	13. A
7. D	20. C	19. E	14. E	14. C	14. C
8. E	21. E	20. E	15. E	15. C	15. A
9. C	22. B	21. E	16. D	16. D	16. D
10. A	23. D	22. D	17. D	17. B	17. E
11. B	24. A	23. C	18. B		

PTB-S2-G2	PT11-S1-G3	PT25-S3-G3	PT34-S4-G4	PT42-S1-G1	PT50-S3-G2
7. D	12. D	13. C	19. B	1. C	6. E
8. A	13. C	14. A	20. A	2. E	7. D
9. D	14. E	15. D	21. C	3. E	8. B
10. A	15. B	16. C	22. A	4. D	9. A
11. C	16. A	17. B	23. E	5. A	10. E
12. E	17. C	18. C	24. B		11. B
	18. A			PT45-S3-G3	

PT5-S2-G3	19. C	PT31-S1-G2	PT36-S4-G1	13. B	PT54-S3-G1
12. B		7. E	1. B	14. E	1. C
13. B	PT20-S3-G2	8. E	2. D	15. D	2. D
14. C	6. A	9. A	3. E	16. B	3. E
15. C	7. E	10. D	4. C	17. A	4. C
16. D	8. B	11. A	5. E		5. C
17. B	9. A	12. A	6. C	PT47-S4-G2	
	10. A	13. C		6. B	PT58-S3-G2
PT9-S3-G2	11. C		PT39-S1-G4	7. A	7. C
8. D	12. E	PT33-S4-G2	19. C	8. B	8. B
9. B		6. D	20. A	9. C	9. C
10. B	PT23-S1-G2	7. E	21. A	10. C	10. B
11. B	6. C	8. D	22. C	11. C	11. A
12. C	7. E	9. C	23. B		12. B
13. E	8. E	10. A		PT48-S2-G1	
	9. E	11. A	PT40-S2-G4	1. C	PT58-S3-G4
	10. B	12. B	18. D	2. E	18. C
	11. B		19. C	3. E	19. D
			20. C	4. A	20. B
			21. B	5. A	21. E
			22. A	6. A	22. B
			23. B		23. B

PT59-S1-G3	PT65-S2-G3	PT70-S3-G2	PT76-S3-G4
11. D	12. B	8. B	19. E
12. E	13. D	9. D	20. C
13. C	14. E	10. E	21. B
14. A	15. D	11. D	22. A
15. D	16. A	12. D	23. B
16. A			

Grouping (Distribution)

PTC-S1-G1
1. D
2. B
3. B
4. A
5. E

PT6-S4-G1
1. A
2. D
3. C
4. D
5. E
6. D

PT7-S2-G3
13. B
14. C
15. E
16. A
17. E
18. B

PT10-S2-G2
6. A
7. E
8. E
9. E
10. B
11. C
12. B

PT11-S1-G1
1. A
2. E
3. B
4. D
5. C
6. B

PT12-S2-G2
7. E
8. A
9. E
10. D
11. B

PT13-S1-G1
1. D
2. B
3. C
4. E
5. B
6. D

PT14-S1-G3
13. D
14. D
15. D
16. D
17. B
18. E

PT16-S1-G1
1. D
2. E
3. A
4. E
5. C
6. D

PT18-S1-G1
1. C
2. D
3. D
4. A
5. C
6. E

PT19-S1-G3
13. C
14. E
15. C
16. A
17. B
18. A
19. B

PT19-S1-G4
20. E
21. A
22. C
23. D
24. A

PT22-S3-G1
1. D
2. C
3. E
4. B
5. E
6. B
7. B

PT23-S1-G3
12. C
13. A
14. D
15. C
16. B
17. A
18. B

PT24-S4-G1
1. D
2. A
3. A
4. B
5. C

PT26-S1-G3
13. D
14. D
15. B
16. B
17. E
18. C

PT27-S2-G3
13. D
14. A
15. C
16. A
17. E
18. B
19. E

PT29-S3-G1
1. D
2. C
3. A
4. B
5. B
6. C

PT37-S3-G3
12. B
13. A
14. D
15. E
16. E
17. C
18. E

PT38-S2-G3
14. E
15. D
16. C
17. B
18. B
19. C

PT44-S3-G2
7. E
8. B
9. A
10. E
11. D
12. A

PT49-S1-G2
8. B
9. B
10. E
11. B
12. E

PT52-S2-G2
8. B
9. E
10. A
11. D
12. C

PT53-S2-G1
1. B
2. A
3. B
4. B
5. C

PT63-S2-G1
1. E
2. B
3. A
4. C
5. E

PT66-S3-G3
12. B
13. E
14. A
15. A
16. D
17. *
18. A

PT68-S4-G2
6. D
7. E
8. C
9. B
10. D

PT69-S2-G4
18. D
19. E
20. A
21. C
22. D
23. B

PT71-S2-G2
6. A
7. B
8. C
9. B
10. C
11. E

PT72-S4-G3
13. B
14. A
15. E
16. A
17. C
18. C

PT73-S3-G3
14. A
15. D
16. D
17. B
18. E

PT74-S2-G4
17. E
18. D
19. B
20. B
21. A
22. B
23. C

PT75-S4-G2
7. D
8. B
9. C
10. A
11. A

Determined Assignment

PTSP-S1-G3	**PT5-S2-G1**	**PT19-S1-G2**	**PT28-S2-G4**	**PT43-S4-G3**	**PT55-S4-G1**
12. A	1. C	8. B	19. D	13. B	1. D
13. B	2. D	9. C	20. E	14. B	2. C
14. A	3. E	10. A	21. A	15. D	3. A
15. B	4. E	11. A	22. C	16. B	4. B
16. D	5. C	12. C	23. E	17. B	5. E
17. E	6. E				6. C

PTA-S3-G2	**PT7-S2-G2**	**PT20-S3-G1**	**PT29-S3-G4**	**PT46-S4-G2**	**PT56-S1-G4**
6. E	8. B	1. A	20. E	7. B	17. A
7. D	9. C	2. A	21. A	8. C	18. A
8. C	10. E	3. D	22. B	9. B	19. C
9. D	11. E	4. A	23. D	10. C	20. D
10. E	12. E	5. B	24. E	11. B	21. E
					22. E
PTC2-S1-G1	**PT8-S2-G1**	**PT21-S1-G1**	**PT35-S3-G3**	**PT48-S2-G4**	23. B
1. A	1. D	1. C	13. A	18. A	
2. E	2. B	2. B	14. B	19. A	**PT57-S1-G2**
3. D	3. D	3. B	15. C	20. A	6. B
4. B	4. D	4. C	16. E	21. D	7. B
5. A	5. A	5. A	17. E	22. B	8. E
		6. C			9. D
PTC2-S1-G4	**PT9-S3-G3**		**PT35-S3-G4**	**PT50-S3-G3**	10. C
18. D	14. D	**PT21-S1-G3**	18. C	12. B	11. B
19. A	15. B	12. D	19. A	13. B	
20. B	16. B	13. D	20. E	14. C	**PT58-S3-G1**
21. E	17. C	14. B	21. D	15. A	1. E
22. D	18. D	15. E	22. A	16. E	2. C
23. B		16. E	23. E	17. E	3. E
	PT14-S1-G1	17. A			4. A
PT2-S3-G2	1. B		**PT36-S4-G3**	**PT50-S3-G4**	5. E
6. D	2. A	**PT25-S3-G2**	14. E	18. B	6. C
7. E	3. E	6. C	15. A	19. D	
8. A	4. B	7. A	16. D	20. E	**PT59-S1-G1**
9. E	5. D	8. B	17. B	21. D	1. C
10. C	6. C	9. E	18. C	22. A	2. A
11. B		10. B			3. C
12. C	**PT16-S1-G2**	11. E	**PT37-S3-G1**	**PT52-S2-G3**	4. D
	7. E	12. E	1. D	13. B	5. C
PT3-S1-G4	8. B		2. B	14. E	
20. B	9. C	**PT27-S2-G2**	3. D	15. C	**PT60-S2-G1**
21. C	10. E	7. B	4. D	16. B	1. B
22. D	11. C	8. E	5. D	17. D	2. D
23. B	12. B	9. C			3. A
24. C		10. D	**PT39-S1-G2**	**PT53-S2-G4**	4. A
	PT17-S1-G4	11. A	6. D	18. E	5. E
PT4-S3-G3	18. A	12. C	7. E	19. A	6. C
12. B	19. D		8. C	20. B	
13. C	20. E	**PT28-S2-G3**	9. B	21. C	**PT60-S2-G4**
14. E	21. C	13. D	10. A	22. E	18. A
15. A	22. C	14. C	11. A	23. B	19. B
16. D	23. B	15. B			20. B
17. B	24. B	16. B	**PT42-S1-G3**	**PT54-S3-G2**	21. D
		17. D	13. A	6. A	22. E
		18. D	14. A	7. A	23. C
			15. C	8. D	
			16. D	9. E	
			17. A	10. D	
			18. E	11. E	
				12. B	

PT61-S3-G1	PT64-S2-G4	PT67-S3-G3	PT69-S2-G3	PT72-S4-G1	PT75-S4-G1
1. A	19. B	13. D	12. A	1. B	1. C
2. E	20. A	14. A	13. D	2. E	2. B
3. A	21. A	15. B	14. C	3. B	3. A
4. C	22. D	16. A	15. A	4. D	4. E
5. D	23. C	17. E	16. D	5. A	5. D
			17. B	6. E	6. B

PT62-S3-G3	PT66-S3-G1	PT69-S2-G2		PT73-S3-G2	PT76-S3-G3
14. C	1. E	6. B	PT70-S3-G3	8. A	14. A
15. A	2. E	7. E	13. A	9. B	15. C
16. A	3. B	8. C	14. C	10. A	16. B
17. D	4. A	9. B	15. B	11. C	17. E
18. E	5. C	10. C	16. E	12. C	18. B
		11. A	17. E	13. E	
			18. A		

PT64-S2-G3	PT67-S3-G1
13. C	1. C
14. E	2. D
15. D	3. A
16. C	4. A
17. B	5. C
18. D	

Undetermined Assignment

J07-S1-G2	PTC-S1-G3	PT1-S2-G4	PT5-S2-G2	PT13-S1-G3	PT17-S1-G2
6. C	13. D	19. E	7. A	12. B	6. D
7. A	14. D	20. A	8. B	13. A	7. C
8. D	15. D	21. A	9. B	14. E	8. B
9. E	16. B	22. B	10. B	15. D	9. E
10. D	17. E	23. E	11. D	16. B	10. E
	18. A	24. C		17. E	11. E
J07-S1-G4	19. A		PT8-S2-G4		12. B
18. B		PT3-S1-G1	18. D	PT14-S1-G4	
19. D	PTC-S1-G4	1. D	19. B	19. B	PT17-S1-G3
20. C	20. A	2. B	20. E	20. A	13. E
21. D	21. B	3. A	21. D	21. C	14. D
22. B	22. B	4. E	22. B	22. B	15. D
23. A	23. E	5. C	23. E	23. B	16. B
	24. A	6. A	24. C	24. C	17. B
PTA-S3-G4		7. D			
18. D	PTC2-S1-G3		PT9-S3-G1	PT15-S4-G4	PT21-S1-G4
19. A	11. B	PT3-S1-G3	1. C	20. C	18. B
20. E	12. D	14. A	2. D	21. C	19. C
21. B	13. A	15. D	3. B	22. B	20. B
22. C	14. C	16. D	4. A	23. A	21. A
23. A	15. A	17. E	5. C	24. A	22. E
24. C	16. E	18. D	6. D		23. D
	17. E	19. A	7. A	PT16-S1-G3	24. E
PTB-S2-G4				13. D	
19. E	PT1-S2-G2	PT4-S3-G2	PT12-S2-G3	14. B	PT22-S3-G3
20. C	8. B	7. E	12. D	15. A	15. E
21. B	9. D	8. C	13. B	16. A	16. D
22. B	10. A	9. A	14. B	17. E	17. C
23. A	11. B	10. E	15. A	18. A	18. E
24. B	12. D	11. E	16. C		19. A
	13. C		17. C		

PT22-S3-G4	PT31-S1-G4	PT42-S1-G4	PT47-S4-G4	PT57-S1-G4	PT73-S3-G4
20. E	19. B	19. A	18. C	18. C	19. A
21. E	20. D	20. B	19. E	19. D	20. B
22. E	21. A	21. E	20. B	20. E	21. E
23. E	22. E	22. D	21. A	21. B	22. A
24. D	23. D	23. D	22. B	22. D	23. C
				23. E	

PT25-S3-G1	PT32-S3-G1	PT43-S4-G4	PT48-S2-G3		PT74-S2-G3
1. B	1. C	18. D	13. C	PT62-S3-G2	11. A
2. B	2. D	19. C	14. A	7. B	12. C
3. D	3. B	20. E	15. D	8. C	13. E
4. E	4. A	21. A	16. C	9. B	14. D
5. D	5. D	22. C	17. C	10. B	15. B
	6. B			11. A	16. A
PT26-S1-G4				12. C	
19. B	PT32-S3-G2	PT45-S3-G2	PT51-S4-G1	13. E	PT76-S3-G2
20. D	7. C	7. A	1. D		7. B
21. A	8. A	8. A	2. A	PT64-S2-G2	8. C
22. A	9. C	9. A	3. E	7. B	9. D
23. A	10. D	10. A	4. C	8. A	10. A
24. E	11. A	11. C	5. E	9. E	11. C
		12. E		10. A	12. E
PT28-S2-G2	PT33-S4-G4		PT56-S1-G2	11. C	13. C
6. D	19. B	PT45-S3-G4	7. A	12. D	
7. B	20. D	18. A	8. D		PT77-S3-G4
8. C	21. B	19. A	9. B		18. E
9. B	22. E	20. E	10. B	PT67-S3-G4	19. C
10. A	23. D	21. C	11. E	18. E	20. B
11. B		22. C		19. D	21. B
12. D	PT35-S3-G1		PT56-S1-G3	20. D	22. C
	1. D	PT46-S4-G4	12. D	21. B	23. C
PT29-S3-G2	2. A	17. C	13. C	22. A	
7. D	3. D	18. C	14. A	23. A	
8. E	4. B	19. B	15. A		
9. E	5. A	20. D	16. E		
10. E		21. E		PT68-S4-G3	
11. B	PT35-S3-G2	22. D	PT57-S1-G3	11. B	
12. B	6. C		12. B	12. E	
13. C	7. A	PT47-S4-G3	13. D	13. A	
	8. E	12. E	14. A	14. C	
	9. D	13. D	15. E	15. E	
	10. C	14. B	16. A	16. C	
	11. D	15. C	17. B		
	12. D	16. C			
		17. B			

Miscellaneous

PTB-S2-G3	PT1-S2-G1	PT2-S3-G3	PT4-S3-G4	PT6-S4-G3	PT6-S4-G4
13. E	1. B	13. A	18. E	13. E	20. D
14. B	2. A	14. D	19. C	14. A	21. C
15. E	3. B	15. D	20. D	15. D	22. B
16. A	4. E	16. B	21. A	16. A	23. B
17. C	5. E	17. C	22. A	17. D	24. A
18. E	6. C		23. C	18. B	
	7. E		24. B	19. C	

PT8-S2-G2	PT11-S1-G4	PT15-S4-G2	PT18-S1-G4	PT30-S1-G1	PT72-S4-G4
6. C	20. E	7. D	20. E	1. D	19. A
7. B	21. E	8. A	21. D	2. A	20. E
8. B	22. A	9. E	22. B	3. C	21. C
9. D	23. B	10. E	23. E	4. D	22. E
10. A	24. A	11. D	24. B	5. B	23. E
11. B		12. E			
12. E	PT12-S2-G4	13. A	PT20-S3-G3	PT40-S2-G3	PT77-S3-G3
	18. D		13. C	11. A	13. B
PT9-S3-G4	19. C	PT16-S1-G4	14. D	12. B	14. C
19. E	20. B	19. D	15. C	13. A	15. A
20. A	21. A	20. E	16. E	14. A	16. E
21. D	22. E	21. A	17. E	15. D	17. E
22. D	23. E	22. C	18. D	16. B	
23. B	24. D	23. A		17. C	
24. A		24. C	PT21-S1-G2		
	PT13-S1-G4		7. D	PT41-S2-G4	
PT10-S2-G3	18. E	PT18-S1-G3	8. A	18. C	
13. B	19. C	14. C	9. A	19. D	
14. D	20. A	15. C	10. B	20. A	
15. C	21. A	16. A	11. A	21. C	
16. D	22. D	17. C		22. A	
17. E	23. C	18. E		23. B	
18. C	24. E	19. A		24. C	

Limited Allocations

J07-S1-G3	PT9-S3-G1	PT30-S1-G2	PT42-S1-G4	PT45-S3-G4	PT49-S1-G2
11. A	1. C	6. D	19. A	18. A	8. B
12. A	2. D	7. A	20. B	19. A	9. B
13. D	3. B	8. A	21. E	20. E	10. E
14. E	4. A	9. D	22. D	21. C	11. B
15. A	5. C	10. C	23. D	22. C	12. E
16. A	6. D				
17. D	7. A	PT33-S4-G3	PT43-S4-G4	PT46-S4-G4	PT50-S3-G2
		13. D	18. D	17. C	6. E
PT2-S3-G3	PT11-S1-G2	14. E	19. C	18. C	7. D
13. A	7. B	15. E	20. E	19. B	8. B
14. D	8. D	16. D	21. A	20. D	9. A
15. D	9. B	17. D	22. C	21. E	10. E
16. B	10. B	18. B		22. D	11. B
17. C	11. D		PT44-S3-G1		
		PT35-S3-G2	1. C	PT47-S4-G3	PT54-S3-G2
PT6-S4-G1	PT15-S4-G3	6. C	2. D	12. E	6. A
1. A	14. D	7. A	3. E	13. D	7. A
2. D	15. E	8. E	4. E	14. B	8. D
3. C	16. C	9. D	5. D	15. C	9. E
4. D	17. A	10. C	6. A	16. C	10. D
5. E	18. B	11. D		17. B	11. E
6. D	19. E	12. D	PT44-S3-G4		12. B
			18. A	PT48-S2-G3	
PT7-S2-G3	PT29-S3-G4	PT41-S2-G3	19. E	13. C	PT56-S1-G2
13. B	20. E	13. E	20. E	14. A	7. A
14. C	21. A	14. C	21. D	15. D	8. D
15. E	22. B	15. C	22. C	16. C	9. B
16. A	23. D	16. D		17. C	10. B
17. E	24. E	17. B			11. E
18. B					

PT56-S1-G4	PT57-S1-G2	PT63-S2-G4	PT69-S2-G4	PT74-S2-G3
17. A	6. B	18. B	18. D	11. A
18. A	7. B	19. C	19. E	12. C
19. C	8. E	20. E	20. A	13. E
20. D	9. D	21. A	21. C	14. D
21. E	10. C	22. C	22. D	15. B
22. E	11. B	23. D	23. B	16. A
23. B				

	PT63-S2-G1	PT69-S2-G2	PT71-S2-G2	PT77-S3-G4
	1. E	6. B	6. A	18. E
	2. B	7. E	7. B	19. C
	3. A	8. C	8. C	20. B
	4. C	9. B	9. B	21. B
	5. E	10. C	10. C	22. C
		11. A	11. E	23. C

Limited Scenarios

PTC-S1-G2	PT7-S2-G4	PT16-S1-G2	PT21-S1-G3	PT26-S1-G3	PT29-S3-G2
6. C	19. E	7. E	12. D	13. D	7. D
7. E	20. D	8. B	13. D	14. D	8. E
8. E	21. B	9. C	14. B	15. B	9. E
9. B	22. D	10. E	15. E	16. B	10. E
10. C	23. B	11. C	16. E	17. E	11. B
11. E	24. A	12. B	17. A	18. C	12. B
12. B					13. C

PTC2-S1-G1	PT10-S2-G2	PT18-S1-G1	PT22-S3-G2	PT27-S2-G2	PT30-S1-G3
1. A	6. A	1. C	8. B	7. B	11. B
2. E	7. E	2. D	9. B	8. E	12. A
3. D	8. E	3. D	10. D	9. C	13. B
4. B	9. E	4. A	11. B	10. D	14. E
5. A	10. B	5. C	12. B	11. A	15. B
	11. C	6. E	13. A	12. C	16. A
	12. B		14. A		

PTC2-S1-G2		PT18-S1-G2		PT27-S2-G3	PT31-S1-G3
6. E	PT12-S2-G1	7. D	PT24-S4-G3	13. D	14. C
7. E	1. E	8. A	11. B	14. A	15. B
8. A	2. B	9. B	12. A	15. C	16. A
9. D	3. C	10. D	13. D	16. A	17. E
10. C	4. B	11. B	14. B	17. E	18. A
	5. C	12. E	15. E	18. B	
PTC2-S1-G3	6. D	13. C	16. A	19. E	
11. B			17. D		PT32-S3-G4
12. D	PT14-S1-G1	PT19-S1-G2		PT28-S2-G1	19. E
13. A	1. B	8. B		1. B	20. B
14. C	2. A	9. C	PT25-S3-G2	2. E	21. D
15. A	3. E	10. A	6. C	3. E	22. B
16. E	4. B	11. A	7. A	4. B	23. A
17. E	5. D	12. C	8. B	5. C	24. D
	6. C		9. E		
PT1-S2-G2		PT21-S1-G1	10. B	PT29-S3-G1	PT34-S4-G1
8. B		1. C	11. E	1. D	1. C
9. D	PT14-S1-G2	2. B	12. E	2. C	2. E
10. A	7. E	3. B		3. A	3. B
11. B	8. A	4. C		4. B	4. D
12. D	9. B	5. A	PT25-S3-G3	5. B	5. A
13. C	10. C	6. C	13. C	6. C	6. E
	11. E		14. A		7. B
	12. A		15. D		
			16. C		
			17. B		
			18. C		

PT34-S4-G3
13. C
14. A
15. E
16. B
17. E
18. C

PT35-S3-G3
13. A
14. B
15. C
16. E
17. E

PT36-S4-G2
7. E
8. A
9. C
10. C
11. A
12. A
13. B

PT36-S4-G4
19. A
20. C
21. D
22. C
23. D

PT37-S3-G3
12. B
13. A
14. D
15. E
16. E
17. C
18. E

PT37-S3-G4
19. A
20. A
21. D
22. B
23. B
24. C

PT38-S2-G3
14. E
15. D
16. C
17. B
18. B
19. C

PT38-S2-G4
20. D
21. A
22. A
23. B
24. D

PT39-S1-G3
12. E
13. D
14. C
15. B
16. D
17. D
18. D

PT41-S2-G1
1. A
2. B
3. E
4. E
5. B
6. D
7. D

PT41-S2-G2
8. B
9. E
10. C
11. E
12. A

PT42-S1-G3
13. A
14. A
15. C
16. D
17. A
18. E

PT43-S4-G1
1. D
2. E
3. A
4. E
5. B

PT44-S3-G2
7. E
8. B
9. A
10. E
11. D
12. A

PT45-S3-G2
7. A
8. A
9. A
10. A
11. C
12. E

PT46-S4-G3
12. A
13. C
14. E
15. D
16. B

PT48-S2-G4
18. A
19. A
20. A
21. D
22. B

PT49-S1-G4
18. B
19. E
20. B
21. D
22. C

PT51-S4-G1
1. D
2. A
3. E
4. C
5. E

PT51-S4-G2
6. B
7. C
8. A
9. D
10. D

PT52-S2-G4
18. C
19. A
20. E
21. C
22. C
23. E

PT53-S2-G1
1. B
2. A
3. B
4. B
5. C

PT53-S2-G4
18. E
19. A
20. B
21. C
22. E
23. B

PT54-S3-G4
18. B
19. A
20. B
21. D
22. C
23. A

PT55-S4-G2
7. D
8. C
9. A
10. E
11. D
12. B

PT56-S1-G1
1. E
2. B
3. C
4. C
5. A
6. E

PT57-S1-G4
18. C
19. D
20. E
21. B
22. D
23. E

PT59-S1-G1
1. C
2. A
3. C
4. D
5. C

PT59-S1-G4
17. A
18. E
19. D
20. E
21. E
22. B
23. B

PT60-S2-G4
18. A
19. B
20. B
21. D
22. E
23. C

PT61-S3-G1
1. A
2. E
3. A
4. C
5. D

PT61-S3-G2
6. A
7. C
8. A
9. C
10. B
11. D

PT61-S3-G3
12. D
13. D
14. B
15. A
16. E
17. B

PT62-S3-G1
1. D
2. D
3. E
4. E
5. B
6. A

PT62-S3-G2
7. B
8. C
9. B
10. B
11. A
12. C
13. E

PT62-S3-G3
14. C
15. A
16. A
17. D
18. E

PT63-S2-G3
11. A
12. E
13. C
14. E
15. A
16. B
17. B

PT64-S2-G1
1. E
2. B
3. C
4. D
5. A
6. E

PT64-S2-G2
7. B
8. A
9. E
10. A
11. C
12. D

PT64-S2-G3
13. C
14. E
15. D
16. C
17. B
18. D

PT64-S2-G4
19. B
20. A
21. A
22. D
23. C

PT65-S2-G2
6. C
7. D
8. E
9. B
10. B
11. C

PT65-S2-G4
17. B
18. B
19. D
20. E
21. C
22. B
23. C

PT66-S3-G1
1. E
2. E
3. B
4. A
5. C

PT66-S3-G2
6. E
7. A
8. C
9. D
10. B
11. D

PT66-S3-G3
12. B
13. E
14. A
15. A
16. D
17. *
18. A

PT66-S3-G4
19. C
20. A
21. C
22. B
23. C

PT67-S3-G2
6. B
7. B
8. E
9. A
10. E
11. C
12. E

PT67-S3-G3
13. D
14. A
15. B
16. A
17. E

PT69-S2-G3
12. A
13. D
14. C
15. A
16. D
17. B

PT72-S4-G2
7. E
8. C
9. D
10. A
11. E
12. B

PT72-S4-G4
19. A
20. E
21. C
22. E
23. E

PT73-S3-G1
1. B
2. C
3. B
4. E
5. E
6. D
7. A

PT73-S3-G3
14. A
15. D
16. D
17. B
18. E

PT74-S2-G1
1. C
2. D
3. E
4. A
5. E

PT74-S2-G2
6. E
7. B
8. E
9. A
10. A

PT75-S4-G2
7. D
8. B
9. C
10. A
11. A

PT76-S3-G1
1. D
2. C
3. D
4. B
5. A
6. B

PT76-S3-G2
7. B
8. C
9. D
10. A
11. C
12. E
13. C

PT76-S3-G3
14. A
15. C
16. B
17. E
18. B

Limited Solutions

J07-S1-G1
1. A
2. C
3. C
4. E
5. E

PT4-S3-G2
7. E
8. C
9. A
10. E
11. E

PT4-S3-G4
18. E
19. C
20. D
21. A
22. A
23. C
24. B

PT8-S2-G2
6. C
7. B
8. B
9. D
10. A
11. B
12. E

PT9-S3-G3
14. D
15. B
16. B
17. C
18. D

PT11-S1-G4
20. E
21. E
22. A
23. B
24. A

PT12-S2-G4
18. D
19. C
20. B
21. A
22. E
23. E
24. D

PT17-S1-G4
18. A
19. D
20. E
21. C
22. C
23. B
24. B

PT24-S4-G1
1. D
2. A
3. A
4. B
5. C

PT24-S4-G4
18. E
19. E
20. E
21. E
22. D
23. C

PT26-S1-G4
19. B
20. D
21. A
22. A
23. A
24. E

PT27-S2-G4
20. A
21. B
22. E
23. A
24. D

PT28-S2-G4
19. D
20. E
21. A
22. C
23. E

PT34-S4-G2
8. E
9. A
10. C
11. D
12. B

PT35-S3-G4
18. C
19. A
20. E
21. D
22. A
23. E

PT56-S1-G3
12. D
13. C
14. A
15. A
16. E

PT60-S2-G3
13. E
14. D
15. E
16. A
17. B

PT77-S3-G1
1. A
2. B
3. D
4. C
5. C

Must Be True

J07-S3-Q22 C	PT4-S1-Q12 ...... E	PT10-S4-Q22 .... E	PT18-S2-Q3 ...... A
PTA-S1-Q19 ...... E	PT4-S1-Q15 ...... D	PT11-S2-Q7 ...... D	PT18-S4-Q6 ...... D
PTA-S4-Q22 C	PT4-S4-Q5 .... D	PT11-S2-Q12 .... E	PT18-S4-Q10 .... A
PTA-S4-Q24 ...... D	PT4-S4-Q7 .... D	PT11-S2-Q16 C	PT19-S2-Q17 C
PTB-S1-Q6 C	PT4-S4-Q9 .... B	PT11-S4-Q16 .... A	PT20-S1-Q7 ...... E
PTB-S4-Q17 ...... D	PT4-S4-Q17 ...... B	PT12-S1-Q8 C	PT20-S1-Q24 .... B
PTC2-S3-Q13 .... B	PT4-S4-Q21 ...... E	PT12-S1-Q21 C	PT20-S4-Q6 C
PT1-S3-Q4 .... D	PT5-S1-Q25 ...... E	PT12-S1-Q25 .... B	PT20-S4-Q19 .... D
PT1-S3-Q7 .... A	PT5-S3-Q12 C	PT13-S2-Q10 .... A	PT21-S2-Q8 ...... E
PT1-S3-Q14 ...... E	PT5-S3-Q22 ...... E	PT13-S2-Q25 .... A	PT21-S2-Q10 ... A
PT1-S3-Q16 C	PT5-S3-Q23 ...... D	PT13-S4-Q5 ...... E	PT21-S2-Q18 .... A
PT1-S4-Q2 .... A	PT6-S2-Q3 .... D	PT13-S4-Q7 ...... E	PT21-S3-Q1 ...... E
PT1-S4-Q6 .... D	PT6-S2-Q6 C	PT13-S4-Q14 .... E	PT21-S3-Q24 .... E
PT1-S4-Q9 .... E	PT6-S2-Q10 ...... E	PT13-S4-Q18 .... B	PT22-S4-Q4 ...... A
PT1-S4-Q11 ...... B	PT6-S2-Q11 ...... B	PT13-S4-Q21 .... D	PT22-S4-Q25 .... A
PT1-S4-Q14 ...... E	PT6-S2-Q13 ...... E	PT14-S2-Q11 .... D	PT23-S2-Q10 C
PT1-S4-Q21 ...... D	PT6-S2-Q23 ...... E	PT14-S2-Q16 .... D	PT23-S2-Q12 .... B
PT2-S2-Q9 .... B	PT6-S3-Q1 .... A	PT14-S4-Q17 .... E	PT23-S2-Q20 .... B
PT2-S2-Q11 ...... B	PT6-S3-Q11 ...... A	PT15-S2-Q12 C	PT24-S2-Q11 .... E
PT2-S2-Q13 C	PT7-S1-Q3 .... E	PT15-S3-Q5 ...... B	PT24-S3-Q8 C
PT2-S2-Q16 ...... E	PT7-S1-Q12 ...... A	PT15-S3-Q7 ...... B	PT24-S3-Q11 .... B
PT2-S2-Q21 ...... D	PT7-S4-Q7 .... A	PT15-S3-Q26 .... E	PT24-S3-Q15 .... E
PT2-S2-Q24 ...... E	PT7-S4-Q15 ...... E	PT16-S2-Q3 ...... D	PT25-S2-Q21 .... E
PT2-S4-Q18 ...... D	PT8-S1-Q9 .... D	PT16-S2-Q9 C	PT25-S4-Q2 ...... B
PT2-S4-Q21 ...... E	PT8-S1-Q19 ...... E	PT16-S2-Q20 .... E	PT26-S2-Q6 ...... D
PT2-S4-Q23 C	PT8-S1-Q24 ...... B	PT16-S3-Q8 ...... B	PT26-S2-Q19 .... B
PT3-S2-Q4 .... B	PT8-S4-Q5 C	PT16-S3-Q16 C	PT26-S3-Q22 .... D
PT3-S2-Q7 .... A	PT9-S2-Q13 ...... D	PT16-S3-Q21 .... D	PT27-S1-Q9 ...... A
PT3-S2-Q10 ...... E	PT9-S2-Q16 ...... A	PT17-S2-Q1 ...... B	PT27-S1-Q19 .... E
PT3-S2-Q22 ...... A	PT9-S4-Q4 C	PT17-S2-Q9 ...... A	PT27-S1-Q22 .... D
PT3-S4-Q10 ...... E	PT9-S4-Q13 ...... A	PT17-S2-Q20 .... B	PT27-S4-Q5 C
PT3-S4-Q13 C	PT9-S4-Q16 ...... E	PT17-S3-Q1 ...... B	PT27-S4-Q14 C
PT3-S4-Q22 ...... B	PT9-S4-Q23 ...... E	PT17-S3-Q11 .... B	PT27-S4-Q17 .... A
PT4-S1-Q7 .... D	PT10-S1-Q18 .... E	PT17-S3-Q24 .... E	PT27-S4-Q22 .... E

PT28-S1-Q14 .... B	PT40-S1-Q22 C	PT51-S3-Q19 .... D	PT63-S3-Q5 ...... D
PT28-S3-Q1 ...... D	PT40-S1-Q24 C	PT52-S1-Q5 ...... B	PT64-S1-Q2 C
PT28-S3-Q8 ...... B	PT40-S3-Q11 .... E	PT53-S1-Q7 ...... A	PT64-S1-Q18 .... B
PT29-S1-Q6 ...... E	PT41-S1-Q21 .... B	PT53-S1-Q16 .... E	PT64-S1-Q20 .... D
PT29-S1-Q18 .... E	PT41-S3-Q25 .... B	PT53-S3-Q19 .... A	PT65-S1-Q25 .... D
PT29-S1-Q21 .... B	PT42-S2-Q16 .... E	PT54-S2-Q16 .... D	PT65-S4-Q6 ...... E
PT29-S4-Q23 .... E	PT42-S4-Q17 C	PT54-S2-Q25 .... D	PT66-S2-Q14 C
PT30-S2-Q18 .... A	PT42-S4-Q26 .... E	PT54-S4-Q23 .... B	PT66-S4-Q21 .... D
PT30-S2-Q20 .... E	PT43-S2-Q7 C	PT55-S1-Q15 .... D	PT67-S4-Q17 .... B
PT30-S2-Q23 .... D	PT43-S2-Q17 .... E	PT55-S1-Q25 C	PT68-S2-Q1 C
PT30-S4-Q4 ...... A	PT43-S2-Q22 .... A	PT56-S2-Q5 ...... E	PT68-S2-Q18 C
PT31-S2-Q17 .... A	PT43-S3-Q9 ...... A	PT56-S2-Q19 .... A	PT68-S3-Q4 ...... E
PT31-S3-Q10 .... D	PT43-S3-Q21 .... B	PT56-S2-Q23 .... E	PT69-S1-Q21 C
PT32-S1-Q7 C	PT43-S3-Q24 .... B	PT57-S2-Q25 C	PT69-S4-Q20 .... E
PT32-S1-Q11 .... B	PT44-S4-Q15 .... E	PT58-S1-Q15 .... D	PT70-S1-Q8 ...... B
PT32-S4-Q24 .... B	PT45-S1-Q8 ...... A	PT58-S1-Q20 .... E	PT70-S1-Q22 C
PT33-S1-Q11 .... E	PT45-S1-Q22 .... E	PT58-S4-Q9 ...... A	PT70-S1-Q24 C
PT33-S3-Q8 ...... A	PT46-S2-Q2 ...... E	PT59-S2-Q19 C	PT70-S4-Q14 .... B
PT34-S2-Q23 .... E	PT46-S2-Q7 ...... B	PT59-S3-Q19 .... E	PT70-S4-Q21 .... E
PT34-S3-Q13 .... D	PT46-S3-Q11 .... B	PT60-S1-Q3 ...... B	PT71-S1-Q17 .... B
PT36-S1-Q11 .... D	PT46-S3-Q25 .... E	PT60-S3-Q12 .... E	PT71-S3-Q10 .... A
PT36-S1-Q14 .... E	PT47-S1-Q18 .... D	PT60-S3-Q17 .... D	PT72-S2-Q24 .... A
PT37-S2-Q2 ...... E	PT48-S1-Q14 .... D	PT61-S2-Q3 C	PT72-S3-Q24 .... A
PT37-S2-Q7 ...... B	PT48-S1-Q26 .... A	PT61-S2-Q10 .... A	PT73-S2-Q21 .... E
PT37-S2-Q12 .... A	PT48-S4-Q14 .... D	PT61-S2-Q17 .... A	PT74-S1-Q24 .... B
PT38-S4-Q1 ...... B	PT49-S4-Q3 ...... D	PT62-S2-Q6 ...... A	PT74-S4-Q13 .... D
PT39-S2-Q7 C	PT49-S4-Q10 .... D	PT62-S2-Q19 .... D	PT76-S2-Q13 .... D
PT39-S2-Q12 .... A	PT50-S2-Q9 ...... B	PT62-S4-Q6 ...... A	PT76-S4-Q19 .... A
PT39-S4-Q6 ...... A	PT50-S4-Q10 .... E	PT63-S1-Q6 ...... A	PT77-S2-Q23 .... D
PT39-S4-Q10 .... B	PT51-S1-Q11 .... B	PT63-S1-Q9 ...... D	PT77-S4-Q13 .... D
PT40-S1-Q3 ...... B	PT51-S3-Q14 C	PT63-S1-Q20 .... B	PT77-S4-Q18 .... D

Most Strongly Supported

J07-S2-Q18 .... B	PTA-S1-Q8 .... A	PTB-S1-Q20 ...... A	PTC-S2-Q7 .... E
J07-S2-Q22 .... D	PTA-S4-Q6 C	PTB-S4-Q1 .... A	PTC-S2-Q17 ...... E
PTA-S1-Q1 C	PTA-S4-Q16 ...... B	PTB-S4-Q3 .... E	PTC-S3-Q23 ...... B
PTA-S1-Q3 .... D	PTB-S1-Q17 ...... A	PTB-S4-Q15 ...... A	PTC2-S2-Q2 C

PTC2-S2-Q21.... E	PT13-S2-Q6 ...... E	PT24-S3-Q7 ...... E	PT35-S1-Q19 C
PTC2-S3-Q21.... E	PT13-S2-Q18 .... A	PT25-S2-Q13 .... B	PT35-S4-Q1 ...... B
PT1-S3-Q11 ...... B	PT14-S2-Q23 .... E	PT25-S2-Q19 .... B	PT35-S4-Q3 ...... B
PT1-S3-Q20 ...... E	PT14-S4-Q5 ...... B	PT26-S2-Q9 ...... B	PT35-S4-Q21 C
PT1-S4-Q18 ...... E	PT14-S4-Q12 .... E	PT26-S3-Q15 C	PT35-S4-Q26 .... B
PT2-S4-Q2 C	PT14-S4-Q21 .... B	PT26-S3-Q20 .... B	PT36-S1-Q4 C
PT2-S4-Q8 C	PT15-S2-Q9 ...... E	PT27-S1-Q3 ...... D	PT36-S1-Q16 C
PT3-S4-Q1 .... D	PT15-S2-Q15 C	PT27-S1-Q12 .... E	PT36-S3-Q17 .... D
PT3-S4-Q4 .... D	PT16-S2-Q11 .... D	PT27-S1-Q20 C	PT37-S4-Q3 ...... D
PT3-S4-Q9 .... A	PT16-S3-Q5 ...... D	PT27-S4-Q23 .... E	PT37-S4-Q6 ...... E
PT3-S4-Q16 ...... A	PT18-S2-Q20 .... A	PT28-S1-Q16 .... B	PT38-S1-Q13 .... B
PT4-S1-Q17 C	PT18-S4-Q24 .... D	PT28-S1-Q22 .... B	PT38-S1-Q15 C
PT4-S1-Q19 ...... D	PT19-S2-Q3 ...... D	PT28-S3-Q4 ...... A	PT38-S1-Q20 C
PT4-S1-Q22 ...... B	PT19-S2-Q24 .... A	PT29-S1-Q8 ...... D	PT38-S1-Q21 .... D
PT5-S1-Q1 .... E	PT19-S4-Q12 C	PT29-S4-Q3 ...... A	PT38-S4-Q24 .... E
PT6-S3-Q5 .... D	PT19-S4-Q19 C	PT29-S4-Q12 .... A	PT39-S4-Q16 C
PT7-S1-Q8 .... A	PT20-S1-Q1 ...... B	PT30-S2-Q16 .... B	PT40-S3-Q3 C
PT7-S1-Q9 .... D	PT20-S1-Q6 ...... D	PT30-S4-Q10 .... E	PT41-S1-Q9 ...... B
PT7-S1-Q16 ...... B	PT20-S1-Q23 .... E	PT30-S4-Q22 .... D	PT41-S1-Q11 C
PT7-S1-Q21 ...... B	PT20-S4-Q10 C	PT31-S2-Q7 ...... D	PT41-S3-Q3 ...... A
PT7-S4-Q10 ...... D	PT21-S2-Q13 .... D	PT31-S2-Q20 .... B	PT41-S3-Q6 ...... A
PT7-S4-Q19 ...... B	PT21-S3-Q12 .... B	PT31-S3-Q3 C	PT42-S2-Q7 ...... D
PT8-S1-Q14 ...... B	PT21-S3-Q16 C	PT31-S3-Q6 ...... D	PT42-S2-Q11 .... E
PT8-S1-Q22 ...... A	PT21-S3-Q18 .... D	PT31-S3-Q22 .... E	PT42-S4-Q7 ...... E
PT9-S4-Q7 .... D	PT22-S2-Q5 ...... A	PT32-S1-Q9 ...... D	PT43-S2-Q4 ...... B
PT10-S1-Q22 C	PT22-S2-Q15 .... D	PT32-S1-Q18 .... E	PT44-S2-Q2 ...... E
PT10-S1-Q24 .... E	PT22-S2-Q17 .... D	PT32-S1-Q24 C	PT44-S2-Q11 .... B
PT10-S4-Q3 C	PT22-S2-Q22 .... D	PT32-S4-Q10 C	PT44-S2-Q14 .... D
PT10-S4-Q10 .... A	PT22-S4-Q12 .... B	PT32-S4-Q14 .... E	PT44-S4-Q3 ...... D
PT10-S4-Q16 .... D	PT22-S4-Q14 .... A	PT33-S1-Q7 ...... B	PT44-S4-Q12 .... D
PT10-S4-Q20 .... E	PT23-S2-Q7 ...... A	PT33-S1-Q9 ...... A	PT45-S4-Q16 .... E
PT11-S4-Q4 ...... D	PT23-S2-Q24 .... D	PT33-S3-Q10 .... E	PT45-S4-Q18 .... A
PT11-S4-Q14 .... A	PT23-S3-Q4 ...... A	PT33-S3-Q13 .... E	PT46-S2-Q12 .... E
PT12-S4-Q1 ...... D	PT23-S3-Q6 C	PT34-S2-Q4 C	PT46-S3-Q9 ...... A
PT12-S4-Q3 ...... E	PT23-S3-Q12 .... B	PT34-S2-Q19 .... D	PT47-S1-Q16 .... B
PT12-S4-Q16 .... E	PT23-S3-Q20 .... E	PT34-S3-Q19 .... B	PT47-S3-Q1 ...... E
PT13-S2-Q4 ...... A	PT24-S2-Q2 ...... D	PT35-S1-Q12 .... B	PT47-S3-Q3 ...... D

PT47-S3-Q10 C
PT48-S4-Q3 ...... D
PT49-S2-Q9 ...... B
PT49-S2-Q20 .... B
PT49-S4-Q14 .... E
PT49-S4-Q19 .... A
PT50-S2-Q18 C
PT50-S4-Q1 ...... E
PT50-S4-Q15 .... D
PT51-S1-Q21 .... D
PT51-S3-Q12 .... A
PT51-S3-Q21 ..... E
PT52-S1-Q7 ...... A
PT52-S1-Q15 .... B
PT52-S1-Q24 .... E
PT52-S3-Q14 C
PT52-S3-Q23 ..... A
PT53-S3-Q21 C
PT54-S2-Q12 .... D
PT54-S2-Q20 .... E
PT54-S4-Q5 ...... E
PT54-S4-Q12 .... D
PT55-S1-Q5 ...... B
PT55-S1-Q8 ...... D

PT55-S3-Q5 ...... A
PT55-S3-Q12 .... D
PT55-S3-Q16 C
PT56-S3-Q2 ...... E
PT56-S3-Q11 .... E
PT56-S3-Q15 .... D
PT57-S3-Q13 .... D
PT57-S3-Q23 C
PT57-S3-Q25 .... E
PT58-S1-Q10 .... B
PT58-S4-Q6 ...... D
PT58-S4-Q13 C
PT58-S4-Q15 .... B
PT59-S3-Q3 C
PT59-S3-Q7 ...... A
PT59-S3-Q21 .... E
PT60-S1-Q24 C
PT60-S3-Q10 C
PT61-S4-Q3 ...... A
PT61-S4-Q5 C
PT61-S4-Q7 ...... E
PT61-S4-Q10 .... A
PT62-S2-Q21 .... E
PT62-S4-Q8 C

PT62-S4-Q11 .... B
PT63-S1-Q12 .... B
PT63-S3-Q7 ...... B
PT63-S3-Q13 .... B
PT64-S3-Q22 C
PT65-S4-Q9 ...... E
PT66-S2-Q22 .... D
PT67-S2-Q7 ...... E
PT67-S2-Q11 C
PT67-S4-Q5 ...... A
PT67-S4-Q15 .... E
PT68-S2-Q8 C
PT68-S2-Q10 C
PT68-S3-Q2 ...... D
PT68-S3-Q10 C
PT68-S3-Q13 .... E
PT69-S1-Q10 .... D
PT69-S1-Q12 .... E
PT69-S4-Q2 ...... D
PT69-S4-Q9 ...... B
PT70-S4-Q2 C
PT70-S4-Q18 .... E
PT71-S1-Q8 ...... D
PT71-S1-Q15 .... B

PT71-S3-Q17 C
PT71-S3-Q23 .... E
PT72-S2-Q17 .... B
PT72-S3-Q20 .... B
PT73-S2-Q23 C
PT73-S4-Q8 ...... D
PT73-S4-Q12 .... A
PT73-S4-Q14 C
PT73-S4-Q16 .... E
PT74-S1-Q11 .... D
PT74-S1-Q22 .... E
PT74-S4-Q1 ...... B
PT74-S4-Q11 .... A
PT75-S1-Q13 C
PT75-S1-Q17 .... D
PT75-S1-Q20 .... E
PT75-S3-Q4 ...... D
PT75-S3-Q24 .... B
PT76-S2-Q17 .... D
PT76-S4-Q17 .... A
PT77-S4-Q15 C

Complete the Passage

J07-S2-Q3 .... D
J07-S2-Q8 .... A
J07-S3-Q10 .... E
J07-S3-Q16 .... B
PTC2-S2-Q5 C
PT3-S2-Q24 ...... A
PT5-S1-Q9 .... A
PT7-S1-Q5 .... B
PT7-S4-Q18 ...... A
PT10-S4-Q24 C
PT13-S2-Q9 ...... D

PT15-S3-Q21 .... D
PT18-S2-Q18 .... A
PT18-S4-Q4 C
PT19-S2-Q19 .... E
PT20-S4-Q13 .... A
PT25-S2-Q3 ...... A
PT26-S3-Q7 ...... E
PT34-S3-Q12 C
PT37-S2-Q9 ...... E
PT37-S4-Q1 C
PT37-S4-Q8 ...... B

PT38-S1-Q19 C
PT38-S4-Q10 .... D
PT39-S2-Q6 ...... D
PT40-S1-Q7 ...... B
PT44-S4-Q8 ...... B
PT44-S4-Q23 .... B
PT47-S1-Q13 C
PT47-S3-Q12 .... A
PT48-S1-Q6 ...... A
PT52-S1-Q13 .... E
PT53-S3-Q7 ...... A

PT54-S2-Q7 C
PT55-S3-Q3 ...... B
PT57-S2-Q2 ...... A
PT57-S2-Q18 .... D
PT59-S2-Q12 C
PT59-S2-Q24 .... B
PT60-S3-Q14 .... D
PT61-S2-Q15 .... B
PT62-S4-Q24 C
PT63-S1-Q1 C
PT64-S3-Q1 ...... B

PT64-S3-Q3 C	PT67-S4-Q20 .... E	PT72-S3-Q16 .... D	PT76-S2-Q15 .... A
PT65-S1-Q4 C	PT68-S3-Q19 .... E	PT73-S2-Q25 C	PT77-S2-Q13 .... B
PT65-S1-Q7 ...... D	PT69-S1-Q16 .... D	PT74-S1-Q1 C	PT77-S4-Q5 ...... A
PT65-S4-Q15 .... E	PT70-S1-Q1 ...... A	PT74-S4-Q7 ..... A	
PT67-S2-Q5 ...... E	PT71-S1-Q4 ...... D	PT75-S3-Q1 C	
PT67-S2-Q24 .... D	PT71-S3-Q5 C	PT76-S2-Q2 ...... B	

Cannot Be True

PTA-S1-Q23 ...... E	PT14-S2-Q2 C	PT30-S4-Q7 ..... B	PT44-S4-Q18 .... B
PTB-S4-Q21 C	PT17-S3-Q15 .... B	PT31-S2-Q8 ...... B	PT48-S4-Q18 .... E
PTC-S3-Q18 ...... D	PT18-S2-Q23 .... E	PT31-S2-Q15 .... A	PT49-S2-Q16 .... D
PT2-S2-Q17 ...... B	PT19-S4-Q13 .... E	PT34-S3-Q22 .... E	PT49-S2-Q21 .... B
PT3-S4-Q14 ...... D	PT25-S4-Q15 .... E	PT35-S4-Q22 .... A	PT49-S4-Q5 C
PT4-S4-Q24 ...... D	PT25-S4-Q16 .... D	PT38-S4-Q25 .... D	PT52-S1-Q18 .... B
PT5-S1-Q15 ...... A	PT25-S4-Q26 .... E	PT39-S2-Q24 .... B	PT56-S3-Q22 .... B
PT6-S3-Q19 ...... D	PT26-S3-Q12 .... D	PT41-S1-Q7 ...... A	PT57-S2-Q23 .... B
PT7-S1-Q19 C	PT28-S1-Q11 .... A	PT41-S3-Q2 ...... E	PT62-S2-Q24 .... E
PT7-S4-Q12 ...... A	PT28-S1-Q20 .... A	PT41-S3-Q10 .... A	PT77-S2-Q25 .... D
PT8-S1-Q8 .... B	PT28-S3-Q12 C	PT42-S4-Q25 .... A	PT77-S4-Q10 .... D
PT9-S2-Q17 ...... B	PT29-S4-Q22 C	PT43-S3-Q17 .... E	

Main Conclusion

J07-S2-Q1 .... B	PT3-S2-Q18 C	PT14-S2-Q14 C	PT23-S2-Q2 ...... B
J07-S2-Q10 .... B	PT5-S3-Q3 .... E	PT14-S2-Q19 .... E	PT23-S3-Q21 .... D
J07-S3-Q12 .... D	PT6-S2-Q1 C	PT15-S2-Q8 ...... A	PT23-S3-Q25 C
PTA-S1-Q9 .... B	PT6-S2-Q18 ...... E	PT15-S2-Q11 .... E	PT24-S2-Q12 C
PTA-S4-Q2 .... A	PT6-S3-Q12 C	PT15-S3-Q1 ...... B	PT24-S2-Q15 .... A
PTB-S1-Q1 .... E	PT7-S4-Q2 .... E	PT15-S3-Q4 ...... A	PT25-S2-Q1 ...... A
PTB-S4-Q6 C	PT9-S2-Q3 .... B	PT16-S3-Q19 .... A	PT25-S2-Q7 C
PTB-S4-Q25 ...... A	PT9-S4-Q18 C	PT17-S2-Q6 ...... D	PT25-S4-Q1 ...... A
PTC-S3-Q8 .... A	PT10-S1-Q11 C	PT17-S2-Q19 .... E	PT26-S2-Q8 ...... A
PTC2-S2-Q13 .... E	PT11-S2-Q4 ...... B	PT18-S2-Q10 .... E	PT28-S1-Q18 .... E
PTC2-S3-Q2 ...... E	PT11-S2-Q20 .... A	PT18-S4-Q2 ...... B	PT28-S3-Q14 .... A
PTC2-S3-Q16 .... D	PT11-S4-Q8 C	PT21-S2-Q1 ...... B	PT29-S1-Q11 C
PT1-S3-Q13 C	PT12-S1-Q1 ...... D	PT21-S2-Q14 C	PT29-S4-Q6 ...... E
PT1-S4-Q19 ...... A	PT12-S1-Q9 ...... E	PT21-S3-Q2 ...... A	PT30-S4-Q2 ...... B
PT2-S2-Q6 .... B	PT12-S4-Q10 .... A	PT21-S3-Q10 .... D	PT31-S2-Q4 ...... E
PT2-S4-Q19 ...... D	PT13-S4-Q3 ...... D	PT22-S2-Q2 ...... B	PT31-S3-Q14 C

PT32-S1-Q13 C	PT45-S4-Q1 ...... D	PT56-S3-Q5 ...... D	PT67-S4-Q1 ...... B
PT32-S4-Q12 .... A	PT45-S4-Q9 C	PT56-S3-Q19 .... E	PT68-S2-Q17 .... A
PT33-S1-Q5 ...... E	PT46-S3-Q5 C	PT57-S3-Q3 ...... A	PT68-S2-Q19 .... B
PT34-S2-Q15 C	PT46-S3-Q21 .... A	PT58-S1-Q13 .... B	PT68-S3-Q8 ...... B
PT34-S2-Q18 .... B	PT47-S3-Q6 ...... A	PT58-S4-Q3 ...... A	PT68-S3-Q11 .... D
PT35-S1-Q3 ...... A	PT48-S1-Q5 ...... A	PT59-S2-Q10 .... D	PT69-S1-Q9 ...... A
PT35-S1-Q16 C	PT48-S1-Q8 C	PT59-S3-Q9 ...... D	PT69-S4-Q1 ...... E
PT35-S4-Q9 ...... D	PT48-S4-Q1 C	PT60-S1-Q8 ...... E	PT69-S4-Q24 .... D
PT36-S1-Q6 ...... D	PT48-S4-Q12 .... B	PT60-S3-Q15 .... D	PT70-S1-Q18 .... A
PT36-S3-Q3 C	PT49-S4-Q7 C	PT61-S2-Q9 ...... E	PT70-S4-Q16 C
PT36-S3-Q9 C	PT50-S2-Q4 ...... E	PT61-S4-Q6 C	PT71-S1-Q5 ...... E
PT36-S3-Q23 C	PT50-S2-Q20 C	PT61-S4-Q16 C	PT71-S1-Q7 ...... E
PT38-S1-Q2 C	PT50-S4-Q25 .... E	PT62-S2-Q10 .... B	PT71-S3-Q12 .... A
PT38-S4-Q3 ...... E	PT51-S1-Q1 ...... D	PT62-S4-Q1 C	PT72-S2-Q4 ...... A
PT38-S4-Q11 .... E	PT51-S1-Q13 .... B	PT62-S4-Q12 .... D	PT72-S3-Q3 ...... D
PT39-S2-Q1 C	PT51-S3-Q16 .... D	PT63-S1-Q8 ...... E	PT72-S3-Q9 ...... E
PT40-S1-Q9 C	PT52-S1-Q1 C	PT63-S1-Q13 .... D	PT73-S2-Q11 .... B
PT40-S3-Q4 ...... A	PT52-S3-Q2 ...... D	PT63-S3-Q10 .... A	PT73-S4-Q5 ...... A
PT41-S1-Q5 ...... B	PT53-S1-Q4 ...... A	PT64-S1-Q1 C	PT73-S4-Q11 .... B
PT41-S3-Q18 C	PT53-S3-Q3 ...... E	PT65-S1-Q2 ...... A	PT74-S1-Q13 .... A
PT42-S4-Q10 .... D	PT53-S3-Q5 ...... E	PT65-S1-Q9 C	PT74-S4-Q2 C
PT43-S3-Q14 C	PT54-S2-Q11 .... B	PT65-S4-Q14 .... E	PT75-S1-Q8 C
PT43-S3-Q23 .... B	PT54-S4-Q11 C	PT66-S2-Q18 .... A	PT75-S3-Q8 C
PT44-S2-Q16 .... E	PT55-S1-Q18 .... E	PT66-S4-Q5 ...... B	PT77-S2-Q11 .... B
PT45-S1-Q1 ...... A	PT55-S3-Q13 .... D	PT66-S4-Q9 ...... A	PT77-S4-Q8 ...... A
PT45-S1-Q17 .... B	PT55-S3-Q20 .... B	PT66-S4-Q26 .... B	

Point

J07-S2-Q16 .... D	PTC-S3-Q20 ...... E	PT5-S3-Q18 ...... A	PT16-S2-Q13 .... D
J07-S3-Q3 .... E	PTC-S3-Q26 ...... D	PT8-S1-Q17 ...... B	PT16-S3-Q4 C
J07-S3-Q7 .... B	PTC2-S2-Q16 C	PT8-S4-Q6 C	PT17-S3-Q5 ...... E
PTA-S1-Q6 .... B	PTC2-S2-Q24 .... D	PT8-S4-Q15 ...... A	PT19-S2-Q16 C
PTA-S4-Q18 ...... D	PTC2-S3-Q4 ...... D	PT8-S4-Q23 ...... E	PT19-S4-Q16 C
PTB-S1-Q15 ...... E	PT1-S3-Q25 ...... A	PT10-S4-Q7 ...... A	PT20-S1-Q13 .... D
PTC-S2-Q1 .... D	PT2-S4-Q13 ...... B	PT11-S4-Q2 C	PT20-S4-Q21 ... D
PTC-S2-Q11 ...... A	PT4-S4-Q14 ...... E	PT13-S2-Q11 .... D	PT22-S4-Q3 C
PTC-S2-Q13 C	PT5-S1-Q7 .... A	PT14-S4-Q11 .... E	PT22-S4-Q10 ... E

PT24-S2-Q14 .... A	PT37-S2-Q11 .... D	PT47-S1-Q4 ...... B	PT65-S1-Q23 .... E
PT24-S3-Q1 ...... B	PT37-S2-Q23 .... B	PT47-S1-Q25 .... E	PT65-S4-Q4 ...... B
PT25-S4-Q22 C	PT37-S4-Q7 C	PT47-S3-Q5 ...... D	PT65-S4-Q25 C
PT26-S2-Q3 ...... A	PT38-S1-Q5 ...... E	PT47-S3-Q9 ...... D	PT66-S2-Q20 .... D
PT26-S2-Q24 .... E	PT38-S4-Q26 .... A	PT49-S2-Q1 ...... D	PT66-S4-Q19 .... D
PT27-S1-Q1 ...... B	PT39-S2-Q13 .... E	PT49-S2-Q10 .... E	PT66-S4-Q23 .... B
PT27-S4-Q11 .... D	PT39-S2-Q23 .... D	PT50-S2-Q11 .... E	PT67-S2-Q10 .... D
PT28-S1-Q6 ...... D	PT39-S4-Q2 ...... A	PT50-S4-Q8 ...... B	PT67-S2-Q16 C
PT29-S1-Q1 ...... A	PT39-S4-Q7 ...... A	PT51-S1-Q23 .... A	PT68-S2-Q21 .... E
PT29-S1-Q9 ...... D	PT40-S3-Q16 .... E	PT52-S3-Q10 .... E	PT68-S3-Q25 C
PT29-S4-Q13 .... B	PT42-S2-Q8 ...... A	PT53-S1-Q2 ...... B	PT69-S1-Q2 ...... A
PT29-S4-Q16 .... D	PT42-S2-Q13 C	PT56-S2-Q2 ...... A	PT69-S4-Q25 .... B
PT30-S2-Q10 .... D	PT43-S2-Q1 C	PT56-S2-Q17 .... E	PT70-S1-Q4 ...... A
PT30-S4-Q21 .... E	PT43-S2-Q13 .... D	PT56-S2-Q21 .... B	PT70-S4-Q5 ...... B
PT31-S2-Q1 ...... D	PT43-S2-Q19 .... D	PT57-S2-Q11 C	PT71-S1-Q10 C
PT31-S3-Q19 .... E	PT43-S3-Q6 ...... E	PT59-S2-Q2 ...... D	PT71-S3-Q2 ...... D
PT32-S4-Q20 .... B	PT44-S2-Q6 ...... B	PT60-S3-Q25 C	PT72-S2-Q19 C
PT33-S1-Q3 ...... A	PT44-S4-Q10 .... E	PT61-S2-Q7 ...... D	PT76-S2-Q3 C
PT33-S3-Q19 .... B	PT45-S1-Q6 ...... D	PT61-S4-Q18 .... A	PT76-S4-Q4 ...... B
PT34-S3-Q7 ...... E	PT45-S1-Q10 .... A	PT63-S1-Q14 .... D	PT76-S4-Q10 .... E
PT34-S3-Q15 .... D	PT45-S4-Q8 ...... D	PT63-S3-Q4 ...... A	PT77-S4-Q2 C
PT35-S1-Q26 .... B	PT46-S2-Q1 ...... D	PT64-S3-Q5 ...... D	
PT36-S3-Q4 ...... B	PT46-S2-Q9 ...... B	PT64-S3-Q7 ...... B	

Necessary Assumption

J07-S3-Q9 .... D	PTB-S4-Q4 .... B	PTC2-S3-Q25.... E	PT2-S4-Q9 .... D
J07-S3-Q11 .... E	PTB-S4-Q14 ...... D	PT1-S3-Q10 C	PT2-S4-Q15 ...... A
J07-S3-Q17 .... B	PTC-S2-Q5 .... B	PT1-S3-Q17 ...... D	PT3-S2-Q3 .... D
PTA-S1-Q5 .... E	PTC-S2-Q15 ...... D	PT1-S3-Q19 C	PT3-S2-Q15 ...... D
PTA-S1-Q11 ...... A	PTC-S2-Q20 ...... B	PT1-S3-Q21 C	PT3-S2-Q21 ...... B
PTA-S4-Q8 .... E	PTC-S2-Q23 C	PT1-S4-Q3 C	PT3-S4-Q12 ...... E
PTA-S4-Q17 ...... B	PTC-S3-Q1 .... E	PT1-S4-Q7 .... D	PT3-S4-Q19 ...... D
PTA-S4-Q19 ...... D	PTC-S3-Q11 ...... B	PT1-S4-Q13 ...... B	PT4-S1-Q5 C
PTB-S1-Q8 .... A	PTC2-S2-Q10.... C	PT1-S4-Q22 ...... B	PT4-S1-Q10 ...... E
PTB-S1-Q18 ...... D	PTC2-S3-Q17.... C	PT2-S2-Q3 .... E	PT4-S4-Q3 C
PTB-S1-Q21 ...... A	PTC2-S3-Q20.... C	PT2-S2-Q19 ...... D	PT4-S4-Q10 ...... D
PTB-S1-Q23 C	PTC2-S3-Q22.... E	PT2-S2-Q23 ...... E	PT4-S4-Q23 ...... B

PT5-S1-Q3 .... B	PT10-S4-Q4 ...... D	PT17-S2-Q10 .... A	PT22-S2-Q19 .... A
PT5-S3-Q5 .... B	PT10-S4-Q8 C	PT17-S2-Q12 C	PT22-S4-Q11 C
PT5-S3-Q7 .... E	PT10-S4-Q18 .... E	PT17-S2-Q21 C	PT22-S4-Q16 .... E
PT5-S3-Q10 ...... A	PT11-S2-Q5 ...... E	PT17-S2-Q23 C	PT22-S4-Q22 .... D
PT5-S3-Q14 ...... B	PT11-S2-Q13 .... A	PT17-S3-Q3 ...... D	PT23-S2-Q6 ...... D
PT5-S3-Q17 ...... A	PT11-S2-Q18 .... D	PT17-S3-Q21 .... A	PT23-S2-Q9 ...... E
PT6-S2-Q2 .... A	PT11-S2-Q24 .... A	PT17-S3-Q25 .... E	PT23-S2-Q17 .... D
PT6-S2-Q9 C	PT11-S4-Q7 C	PT18-S2-Q9 ...... E	PT23-S3-Q3 ...... A
PT6-S2-Q15 C	PT11-S4-Q13 .... A	PT18-S2-Q15 .... A	PT23-S3-Q9 ...... E
PT6-S3-Q3 .... D	PT11-S4-Q15 .... E	PT18-S4-Q8 ...... B	PT23-S3-Q11 .... B
PT6-S3-Q7 .... A	PT12-S1-Q2 C	PT18-S4-Q18 .... D	PT24-S2-Q17 .... B
PT6-S3-Q9 .... A	PT12-S1-Q10 .... B	PT18-S4-Q22 .... E	PT24-S3-Q5 ...... D
PT6-S3-Q15 ...... B	PT12-S1-Q13 .... D	PT19-S2-Q2 C	PT24-S3-Q13 .... B
PT7-S1-Q2 C	PT12-S4-Q2 ...... E	PT19-S2-Q9 ...... B	PT24-S3-Q18 .... A
PT7-S1-Q14 ...... E	PT12-S4-Q6 ...... B	PT19-S2-Q13 .... A	PT25-S2-Q6 C
PT7-S1-Q24 ...... A	PT12-S4-Q8 C	PT19-S2-Q15 .... B	PT25-S2-Q12 .... A
PT7-S4-Q6 C	PT13-S2-Q12 .... D	PT19-S4-Q4 ...... B	PT25-S2-Q16 .... E
PT7-S4-Q13 ...... D	PT13-S2-Q14 .... D	PT19-S4-Q8 ...... E	PT25-S4-Q9 ...... B
PT7-S4-Q24 ...... D	PT13-S4-Q4 ...... E	PT19-S4-Q14 .... B	PT25-S4-Q25 .... E
PT8-S1-Q2 .... A	PT13-S4-Q8 ...... D	PT20-S1-Q3 ...... B	PT26-S2-Q7 C
PT8-S1-Q6 C	PT13-S4-Q11 C	PT20-S1-Q11 .... D	PT26-S2-Q10 C
PT8-S1-Q12 ...... E	PT14-S2-Q17 C	PT20-S1-Q16 .... A	PT26-S2-Q13 .... A
PT8-S4-Q10 C	PT14-S2-Q18 .... D	PT20-S1-Q20 C	PT26-S2-Q22 C
PT8-S4-Q13 ...... E	PT14-S2-Q20 .... B	PT20-S4-Q1 ...... D	PT26-S2-Q25 .... E
PT8-S4-Q18 ...... D	PT14-S4-Q13 C	PT20-S4-Q8 ...... A	PT26-S3-Q9 C
PT8-S4-Q21 ...... A	PT14-S4-Q19 .... A	PT20-S4-Q11 .... D	PT26-S3-Q11 .... A
PT9-S2-Q19 ...... D	PT15-S2-Q6 ...... B	PT20-S4-Q16 .... D	PT27-S1-Q13 C
PT9-S2-Q21 ...... D	PT15-S2-Q16 .... E	PT21-S2-Q3 ...... B	PT27-S1-Q21 .... B
PT9-S2-Q25 ...... A	PT15-S2-Q23 .... B	PT21-S2-Q6 ...... B	PT27-S4-Q4 ...... D
PT9-S4-Q6 C	PT15-S3-Q3 C	PT21-S2-Q11 C	PT27-S4-Q9 ...... E
PT9-S4-Q10 ...... B	PT15-S3-Q12 .... E	PT21-S2-Q19 C	PT27-S4-Q19 .... A
PT9-S4-Q19 ...... A	PT15-S3-Q24 C	PT21-S3-Q4 ...... A	PT27-S4-Q20 .... A
PT9-S4-Q25 ...... D	PT16-S2-Q6 ...... D	PT21-S3-Q6 C	PT28-S1-Q2 ...... B
PT10-S1-Q1 ...... B	PT16-S2-Q14 .... D	PT21-S3-Q8 C	PT28-S1-Q12 .... B
PT10-S1-Q3 ...... E	PT16-S3-Q3 ...... B	PT21-S3-Q13 .... A	PT28-S1-Q21 C
PT10-S1-Q7 ...... A	PT16-S3-Q12 .... A	PT22-S2-Q1 C	PT28-S3-Q16 .... B
PT10-S1-Q15 .... A	PT16-S3-Q14 .... E	PT22-S2-Q14 .... D	PT28-S3-Q19 .... A

PT28-S3-Q22 .... B	PT35-S1-Q14 .... D	PT43-S2-Q10 .... A	PT51-S1-Q7 C
PT29-S1-Q5 C	PT35-S1-Q18 .... B	PT43-S2-Q16 .... E	PT51-S3-Q2 ...... D
PT29-S1-Q15 .... A	PT35-S4-Q16 .... A	PT43-S3-Q1 ...... A	PT51-S3-Q15 .... A
PT29-S4-Q4 ...... B	PT36-S1-Q3 C	PT43-S3-Q12 C	PT51-S3-Q18 .... B
PT29-S4-Q5 ...... B	PT36-S1-Q20 .... E	PT43-S3-Q16 .... B	PT52-S1-Q10 .... A
PT29-S4-Q8 ...... D	PT36-S3-Q14 C	PT44-S2-Q5 ...... A	PT52-S1-Q25 .... E
PT30-S2-Q11 .... D	PT36-S3-Q16 .... D	PT44-S2-Q9 C	PT52-S3-Q7 ...... A
PT30-S2-Q15 .... A	PT36-S3-Q18 .... B	PT44-S2-Q18 .... D	PT52-S3-Q9 C
PT30-S2-Q22 .... E	PT36-S3-Q22 .... E	PT44-S2-Q23 .... B	PT52-S3-Q13 .... D
PT30-S4-Q19 C	PT37-S2-Q15 .... B	PT44-S4-Q7 ...... A	PT53-S1-Q9 ...... A
PT31-S2-Q2 ...... D	PT37-S2-Q19 C	PT44-S4-Q16 .... D	PT53-S1-Q13 .... A
PT31-S2-Q14 .... E	PT37-S4-Q15 .... B	PT45-S1-Q3 ...... B	PT53-S1-Q15 .... B
PT31-S3-Q11 .... E	PT37-S4-Q19 .... A	PT45-S4-Q6 ...... E	PT53-S1-Q23 .... D
PT31-S3-Q13 C	PT37-S4-Q23 C	PT45-S4-Q13 .... B	PT53-S3-Q8 ...... A
PT31-S3-Q17 .... E	PT38-S1-Q12 .... D	PT46-S2-Q10 .... A	PT53-S3-Q15 .... E
PT31-S3-Q21 C	PT38-S1-Q14 .... D	PT46-S2-Q13 .... D	PT53-S3-Q20 .... D
PT32-S1-Q1 ...... E	PT38-S1-Q24 .... A	PT46-S3-Q15 .... B	PT54-S2-Q2 ...... E
PT32-S1-Q21 .... D	PT38-S4-Q6 ...... B	PT46-S3-Q17 .... E	PT54-S2-Q6 C
PT32-S1-Q23 .... D	PT38-S4-Q20 .... B	PT46-S3-Q20 C	PT54-S2-Q9 ...... A
PT32-S1-Q25 .... E	PT38-S4-Q22 .... D	PT46-S3-Q26 .... B	PT54-S4-Q3 ...... A
PT32-S4-Q7 ...... B	PT39-S2-Q17 .... B	PT47-S1-Q14 .... E	PT54-S4-Q7 ...... D
PT32-S4-Q16 C	PT39-S4-Q4 ...... D	PT47-S1-Q17 .... D	PT54-S4-Q18 C
PT32-S4-Q19 .... E	PT39-S4-Q19 .... D	PT47-S1-Q20 .... D	PT54-S4-Q24 .... E
PT33-S1-Q10 .... D	PT39-S4-Q25 C	PT47-S3-Q13 .... A	PT55-S1-Q2 ...... A
PT33-S1-Q13 .... B	PT40-S1-Q5 ...... B	PT47-S3-Q17 .... D	PT55-S1-Q12 C
PT33-S1-Q19 .... D	PT40-S1-Q16 .... D	PT48-S1-Q15 .... A	PT55-S1-Q17 .... D
PT33-S3-Q11 C	PT40-S3-Q20 .... E	PT48-S1-Q20 .... E	PT55-S3-Q8 ...... E
PT33-S3-Q16 .... D	PT40-S3-Q22 .... A	PT48-S4-Q10 .... E	PT55-S3-Q19 C
PT33-S3-Q25 .... E	PT41-S1-Q6 ...... D	PT49-S2-Q17 .... A	PT55-S3-Q24 .... D
PT34-S2-Q13 .... B	PT41-S1-Q10 .... B	PT49-S2-Q22 .... E	PT56-S2-Q4 C
PT34-S2-Q16 .... B	PT41-S1-Q24 .... E	PT49-S4-Q13 .... B	PT56-S2-Q6 ...... E
PT34-S2-Q21 .... E	PT41-S3-Q7 ...... A	PT49-S4-Q16 .... A	PT56-S3-Q9 ...... A
PT34-S3-Q3 ...... B	PT41-S3-Q17 .... B	PT49-S4-Q20 .... D	PT56-S3-Q18 .... E
PT34-S3-Q5 ...... D	PT42-S2-Q14 .... B	PT50-S2-Q14 .... D	PT56-S3-Q25 .... E
PT34-S3-Q9 ...... A	PT42-S4-Q2 ...... D	PT50-S2-Q16 C	PT57-S2-Q24 .... E
PT34-S3-Q11 C	PT42-S4-Q13 .... A	PT50-S4-Q11 .... D	PT57-S3-Q12 .... E
PT34-S3-Q17 .... D	PT42-S4-Q19 .... D	PT50-S4-Q21 C	PT57-S3-Q17 .... D

PT58-S1-Q1 C

PT58-S1-Q14 .... D

PT58-S1-Q16 .... E

PT58-S1-Q19 .... D

PT58-S1-Q22 C

PT58-S4-Q11 .... E

PT58-S4-Q17 .... D

PT58-S4-Q21 .... D

PT59-S2-Q14 .... D

PT59-S3-Q12 .... A

PT59-S3-Q16 .... E

PT59-S3-Q25 .... B

PT60-S1-Q7 C

PT60-S1-Q14 .... D

PT60-S1-Q20 .... D

PT60-S3-Q11 .... D

PT60-S3-Q22 .... A

PT61-S2-Q16 C

PT61-S4-Q20 .... A

PT62-S2-Q12 .... E

PT62-S2-Q25 .... A

PT62-S4-Q23 .... D

PT63-S1-Q5 ...... B

PT63-S1-Q19 C

PT63-S3-Q6 ...... D

PT63-S3-Q11 .... B

PT63-S3-Q15 .... E

PT64-S1-Q15 .... B

PT64-S3-Q12 C

PT64-S3-Q19 .... D

PT65-S1-Q18 .... B

PT65-S1-Q21 .... D

PT65-S4-Q2 ...... E

PT65-S4-Q13 .... E

PT65-S4-Q20 .... D

PT66-S2-Q2 ...... D

PT66-S2-Q4 ...... B

PT66-S2-Q10 .... A

PT66-S4-Q3 ...... E

PT66-S4-Q7 ...... B

PT67-S2-Q6 ...... A

PT67-S2-Q14 .... A

PT67-S4-Q2 ...... A

PT67-S4-Q11 .... A

PT67-S4-Q16 .... D

PT67-S4-Q18 .... A

PT68-S2-Q15 .... D

PT68-S3-Q18 .... E

PT68-S3-Q23 .... B

PT69-S1-Q4 ...... D

PT69-S1-Q7 ...... B

PT69-S1-Q19 .... E

PT69-S4-Q8 C

PT70-S1-Q13 .... B

PT70-S1-Q21 .... D

PT70-S4-Q6 ...... A

PT70-S4-Q10 .... B

PT70-S4-Q20 .... A

PT70-S4-Q25 .... D

PT71-S1-Q16 .... B

PT71-S1-Q22 .... E

PT71-S3-Q19 .... D

PT72-S2-Q12 .... E

PT72-S2-Q15 .... D

PT72-S2-Q21 .... B

PT72-S3-Q4 ...... E

PT72-S3-Q18 C

PT73-S2-Q1 C

PT73-S2-Q8 ...... B

PT73-S2-Q20 .... E

PT73-S4-Q13 .... B

PT73-S4-Q19 .... B

PT73-S4-Q26 .... A

PT74-S1-Q8 ...... A

PT74-S4-Q4 ...... D

PT74-S4-Q6 ...... B

PT75-S1-Q1 ...... B

PT75-S1-Q3 ...... A

PT75-S3-Q2 ...... B

PT75-S3-Q17 .... B

PT75-S3-Q19 C

PT75-S3-Q23 .... A

PT75-S3-Q25 .... A

PT76-S2-Q5 C

PT76-S2-Q18 .... B

PT76-S2-Q24 .... D

PT76-S4-Q12 .... B

PT76-S4-Q16 .... B

PT76-S4-Q18 .... E

PT76-S4-Q20 C

PT76-S4-Q24 .... D

PT77-S2-Q3 ...... E

PT77-S2-Q6 ...... D

PT77-S2-Q24 .... A

PT77-S4-Q26 .... E

Sufficient Assumption

J07-S2-Q6 .... B

J07-S2-Q13 C

J07-S2-Q15 .... D

J07-S2-Q23 C

J07-S3-Q5 C

PTA-S1-Q24 ...... D

PTB-S1-Q9 C

PTB-S4-Q22 ...... D

PTC-S3-Q4 .... B

PTC2-S2-Q15 .... E

PTC2-S2-Q20 .... B

PTC2-S3-Q11 C

PT2-S4-Q17 ...... A

PT3-S2-Q12 ...... D

PT3-S4-Q17 ...... D

PT4-S1-Q2 .... A

PT5-S1-Q12 ...... D

PT5-S1-Q16 ...... B

PT7-S4-Q23 C

PT8-S1-Q5 C

PT8-S4-Q9 .... B

PT9-S2-Q23 ...... A

PT9-S4-Q12 C

PT11-S2-Q22 .... A

PT12-S1-Q22 C

PT12-S4-Q20 .... A

PT14-S2-Q13 .... B

PT14-S4-Q7 C

PT14-S4-Q23 C

PT15-S3-Q18 .... A

PT17-S3-Q14 .... E

PT18-S4-Q12 C

PT19-S2-Q18 .... E

PT19-S4-Q11 .... B

PT21-S2-Q20 .... D

PT22-S4-Q2 C

PT22-S4-Q5 C

PT22-S4-Q13 .... D

PT23-S2-Q5 C

PT23-S3-Q14 .... D

PT24-S2-Q21 .... A

PT24-S2-Q24 .... E

PT24-S3-Q10 .... D

PT24-S3-Q19 .... D

PT25-S4-Q18 .... D	PT42-S2-Q23 .... E	PT55-S1-Q4 ...... A	PT66-S2-Q6 ...... E
PT26-S3-Q21 C	PT43-S2-Q18 .... D	PT55-S3-Q10 .... D	PT66-S2-Q19 .... D
PT27-S1-Q16 .... D	PT44-S2-Q13 .... A	PT55-S3-Q21 .... A	PT66-S4-Q17 .... E
PT28-S1-Q24 .... A	PT44-S4-Q26 C	PT56-S2-Q10 .... D	PT66-S4-Q20 .... D
PT29-S1-Q20 .... B	PT45-S1-Q21 .... A	PT56-S3-Q16 .... A	PT67-S4-Q13 .... B
PT30-S4-Q1 ...... A	PT45-S1-Q23 C	PT57-S2-Q7 ...... A	PT68-S2-Q23 C
PT31-S2-Q10 .... D	PT45-S4-Q22 .... E	PT57-S2-Q12 .... D	PT68-S3-Q15 .... E
PT32-S1-Q5 ...... B	PT46-S2-Q4 ...... A	PT57-S3-Q24 C	PT69-S1-Q25 .... B
PT32-S4-Q4 ...... B	PT46-S2-Q23 .... D	PT58-S1-Q12 .... D	PT69-S4-Q13 C
PT33-S3-Q21 .... A	PT46-S3-Q24 .... A	PT58-S1-Q25 .... A	PT69-S4-Q21 .... A
PT33-S3-Q23 C	PT47-S1-Q9 ...... E	PT58-S4-Q19 .... B	PT70-S1-Q7 ...... E
PT34-S2-Q2 ...... E	PT47-S1-Q12 .... E	PT58-S4-Q24 .... B	PT70-S4-Q22 .... D
PT34-S2-Q10 .... D	PT47-S3-Q21 .... E	PT59-S2-Q17 .... E	PT71-S1-Q1 ...... E
PT35-S1-Q20 .... A	PT48-S1-Q25 C	PT59-S2-Q26 .... B	PT71-S3-Q11 .... A
PT35-S1-Q22 .... B	PT48-S4-Q8 ...... B	PT59-S3-Q10 .... E	PT71-S3-Q14 .... B
PT35-S4-Q14 .... B	PT48-S4-Q21 .... A	PT60-S1-Q22 .... A	PT72-S2-Q8 ...... D
PT35-S4-Q19 C	PT49-S2-Q7 ...... E	PT60-S3-Q3 ...... A	PT73-S2-Q10 .... A
PT36-S1-Q18 .... D	PT49-S2-Q19 .... D	PT61-S2-Q13 .... B	PT73-S2-Q12 .... A
PT36-S1-Q22 C	PT49-S2-Q25 C	PT61-S2-Q24 .... B	PT73-S4-Q24 .... E
PT36-S1-Q26 .... E	PT49-S4-Q18 .... D	PT61-S4-Q13 .... A	PT74-S1-Q12 .... E
PT36-S3-Q12 .... A	PT49-S4-Q22 C	PT61-S4-Q25 .... B	PT74-S1-Q20 .... E
PT37-S2-Q5 ...... B	PT50-S2-Q7 ...... B	PT62-S2-Q9 C	PT74-S4-Q16 .... E
PT37-S4-Q9 ...... B	PT50-S2-Q22 .... D	PT62-S2-Q15 .... B	PT75-S1-Q23 C
PT37-S4-Q20 .... A	PT50-S4-Q13 .... B	PT62-S2-Q17 .... A	PT75-S3-Q15 .... E
PT38-S1-Q1 ...... A	PT51-S1-Q16 .... B	PT62-S4-Q16 .... B	PT76-S2-Q10 .... B
PT38-S4-Q16 C	PT51-S1-Q19 .... B	PT62-S4-Q18 .... D	PT76-S2-Q22 .... A
PT39-S2-Q21 .... E	PT51-S3-Q20 C	PT63-S1-Q10 .... A	PT76-S4-Q1 C
PT39-S4-Q17 .... B	PT52-S1-Q17 .... E	PT63-S3-Q17 .... D	PT76-S4-Q14 .... B
PT40-S1-Q8 ...... A	PT52-S1-Q20 .... E	PT63-S3-Q24 .... A	PT77-S2-Q9 ...... B
PT40-S1-Q19 C	PT52-S3-Q15 .... D	PT64-S1-Q11 .... E	PT77-S2-Q15 C
PT40-S1-Q21 .... E	PT53-S1-Q20 C	PT64-S1-Q23 .... D	PT77-S4-Q20 .... B
PT40-S3-Q15 .... E	PT54-S2-Q13 .... B	PT64-S3-Q21 .... A	PT77-S4-Q24 .... D
PT41-S3-Q22 .... D	PT54-S2-Q26 .... D	PT64-S3-Q26 .... E	
PT42-S2-Q19 C	PT54-S4-Q22 .... B	PT65-S1-Q16 .... B	

Strengthen

J07-S2-Q19 .... A	J07-S3-Q13 .... B	J07-S3-Q19 .... A	PTA-S1-Q17 ...... E

PTA-S4-Q3........ B	PT9-S2-Q10 ...... B	PT23-S2-Q16 C	PT31-S3-Q9 ...... A
PTA-S4-Q5........ A	PT9-S4-Q17 ...... B	PT23-S2-Q18 .... B	PT32-S1-Q20 .... B
PTA-S4-Q7........ D	PT10-S1-Q9 ...... D	PT23-S3-Q10 .... B	PT32-S4-Q9 ...... D
PTB-S1-Q3........ C	PT10-S4-Q2 ...... B	PT23-S3-Q13 .... E	PT32-S4-Q11 C
PTB-S1-Q7........ B	PT10-S4-Q11 .... A	PT23-S3-Q15 .... B	PT33-S1-Q1 ...... E
PTB-S1-Q19...... D	PT11-S4-Q18 .... A	PT24-S2-Q4 C	PT33-S1-Q6 ...... D
PTB-S4-Q11...... B	PT12-S1-Q11 .... D	PT24-S3-Q23 .... B	PT33-S3-Q4 C
PTB-S4-Q16...... A	PT12-S1-Q15 .... B	PT25-S2-Q4 ...... A	PT33-S3-Q9 ...... D
PTC-S2-Q14...... B	PT12-S1-Q19 .... B	PT25-S2-Q10 .... E	PT33-S3-Q20 .... D
PTC-S2-Q19...... A	PT13-S2-Q5 ...... A	PT25-S4-Q6 ...... D	PT34-S2-Q14 C
PTC-S3-Q7........ A	PT13-S4-Q23 .... E	PT25-S4-Q7 ...... A	PT34-S3-Q21 C
PTC-S3-Q12...... B	PT14-S2-Q6 ...... D	PT26-S2-Q11 .... A	PT34-S3-Q24 .... E
PTC2-S2-Q1...... A	PT14-S2-Q7 ...... D	PT26-S3-Q3 ...... D	PT35-S1-Q15 .... E
PTC2-S2-Q11.... D	PT15-S2-Q3 ...... E	PT27-S1-Q5 C	PT35-S4-Q10 .... D
PTC2-S3-Q1...... C	PT15-S3-Q8 ...... A	PT27-S1-Q18 .... A	PT36-S3-Q7 ...... B
PT1-S3-Q15 ...... B	PT15-S3-Q10 .... B	PT27-S4-Q2 ...... B	PT36-S3-Q11 C
PT1-S3-Q23 C	PT15-S3-Q23 .... E	PT27-S4-Q16 .... D	PT36-S3-Q26 .... B
PT1-S4-Q4 C	PT16-S2-Q18 .... A	PT28-S1-Q1 ...... A	PT37-S2-Q1 C
PT1-S4-Q23 C	PT16-S2-Q21 .... A	PT28-S1-Q15 C	PT37-S2-Q6 ...... E
PT2-S2-Q10 C	PT16-S3-Q13 .... B	PT28-S1-Q26 .... E	PT37-S2-Q20 .... B
PT2-S2-Q22 ...... A	PT17-S2-Q7 C	PT28-S3-Q6 ...... B	PT37-S4-Q13 .... D
PT2-S4-Q7 .... D	PT17-S3-Q6 ...... E	PT28-S3-Q9 ...... A	PT37-S4-Q25 .... B
PT2-S4-Q10 ...... D	PT17-S3-Q12 .... D	PT28-S3-Q13 .... E	PT38-S1-Q4 C
PT2-S4-Q14 ...... E	PT17-S3-Q18 .... E	PT28-S3-Q24 .... D	PT38-S4-Q5 ...... B
PT2-S4-Q25 ...... A	PT18-S2-Q2 C	PT29-S1-Q3 C	PT39-S2-Q10 C
PT3-S2-Q9 .... D	PT18-S2-Q16 .... D	PT29-S4-Q1 ...... D	PT39-S2-Q15 .... A
PT3-S2-Q17 C	PT18-S2-Q21 .... A	PT29-S4-Q11 .... B	PT39-S4-Q13 .... D
PT3-S4-Q21 ...... B	PT19-S2-Q21 .... A	PT29-S4-Q20 .... A	PT39-S4-Q18 .... E
PT5-S1-Q23 ...... B	PT19-S4-Q7 ...... E	PT30-S2-Q3 ...... B	PT40-S1-Q6 ...... E
PT5-S3-Q6 .... A	PT19-S4-Q15 C	PT30-S2-Q4 C	PT40-S1-Q11 .... A
PT6-S2-Q21 ...... D	PT20-S1-Q9 C	PT30-S2-Q21 .... A	PT40-S1-Q13 .... D
PT7-S1-Q15 ...... A	PT20-S4-Q5 ...... D	PT30-S2-Q24 C	PT40-S3-Q2 C
PT7-S1-Q23 ...... D	PT21-S2-Q23 .... B	PT30-S4-Q12 C	PT40-S3-Q8 ...... D
PT7-S4-Q1 .... D	PT21-S3-Q9 ...... B	PT30-S4-Q15 C	PT40-S3-Q18 .... B
PT8-S1-Q10 ...... B	PT22-S2-Q9 C	PT30-S4-Q18 .... B	PT40-S3-Q24 C
PT8-S4-Q11 ...... A	PT22-S4-Q8 ...... D	PT30-S4-Q20 .... A	PT41-S1-Q12 .... E
PT9-S2-Q9 .... A	PT23-S2-Q14 .... A	PT31-S2-Q5 ...... E	PT41-S3-Q15 .... E

PT41-S3-Q19 .... E	PT50-S4-Q9 ...... A	PT61-S2-Q6 C	PT70-S1-Q3 ...... D
PT42-S2-Q10 C	PT50-S4-Q23 C	PT61-S2-Q22 C	PT70-S1-Q25 .... B
PT42-S2-Q18 .... A	PT51-S1-Q24 .... B	PT61-S4-Q4 ...... D	PT70-S4-Q4 C
PT42-S4-Q1 ...... D	PT51-S3-Q3 C	PT62-S2-Q2 ...... E	PT71-S1-Q6 ...... D
PT42-S4-Q9 ...... B	PT51-S3-Q25 C	PT62-S2-Q3 ...... B	PT71-S1-Q12 .... B
PT42-S4-Q23 .... E	PT52-S1-Q4 C	PT62-S2-Q4 ...... E	PT71-S3-Q4 ...... E
PT43-S2-Q8 C	PT52-S3-Q3 ...... B	PT62-S2-Q16 .... E	PT71-S3-Q8 C
PT43-S2-Q14 C	PT53-S1-Q1 C	PT62-S4-Q3 ...... A	PT71-S3-Q16 .... B
PT43-S3-Q2 ...... E	PT53-S1-Q6 ...... A	PT62-S4-Q20 .... E	PT71-S3-Q25 .... A
PT43-S3-Q10 .... B	PT53-S1-Q10 .... D	PT62-S4-Q22 .... E	PT72-S2-Q3 ...... B
PT44-S2-Q7 ...... D	PT53-S3-Q1 ...... A	PT63-S1-Q11 .... D	PT72-S2-Q7 ...... E
PT44-S2-Q15 .... D	PT53-S3-Q11 C	PT63-S1-Q15 C	PT72-S2-Q23 .... A
PT44-S4-Q14 .... B	PT54-S2-Q24 .... A	PT63-S1-Q16 .... D	PT72-S2-Q25 .... B
PT44-S4-Q17 .... D	PT54-S4-Q1 ...... E	PT63-S1-Q22 .... B	PT72-S3-Q6 C
PT45-S1-Q14 .... E	PT54-S4-Q20 .... A	PT63-S3-Q21 .... B	PT72-S3-Q8 ...... A
PT45-S1-Q19 .... A	PT55-S1-Q23 .... B	PT64-S1-Q17 .... A	PT72-S3-Q12 C
PT45-S1-Q26 .... E	PT55-S3-Q14 .... B	PT64-S1-Q22 .... B	PT73-S2-Q22 .... A
PT45-S4-Q7 C	PT56-S2-Q14 .... D	PT64-S3-Q9 ...... A	PT73-S4-Q20 .... D
PT45-S4-Q25 .... B	PT56-S2-Q24 .... A	PT64-S3-Q17 .... B	PT74-S1-Q2 C
PT46-S2-Q16 .... B	PT56-S3-Q8 ...... A	PT64-S3-Q24 .... B	PT74-S1-Q4 C
PT46-S2-Q19 .... B	PT56-S3-Q13 .... A	PT65-S1-Q1 ...... B	PT74-S1-Q17 .... A
PT46-S3-Q22 .... A	PT57-S2-Q5 ...... E	PT65-S1-Q13 .... E	PT74-S4-Q3 ...... E
PT47-S1-Q11 .... D	PT57-S2-Q22 .... A	PT65-S1-Q19 C	PT74-S4-Q26 .... B
PT47-S1-Q26 C	PT57-S3-Q9 ...... D	PT65-S4-Q22 .... A	PT75-S1-Q9 ...... A
PT47-S3-Q2 ...... A	PT58-S1-Q3 ...... E	PT66-S2-Q17 C	PT75-S1-Q15 C
PT48-S1-Q3 C	PT58-S4-Q23 .... B	PT66-S4-Q12 .... A	PT75-S1-Q21 .... B
PT48-S1-Q7 C	PT59-S2-Q1 ...... A	PT67-S2-Q3 ...... B	PT75-S3-Q6 ...... B
PT48-S1-Q10 .... D	PT59-S2-Q3 ...... A	PT67-S4-Q4 C	PT75-S3-Q21 .... E
PT48-S1-Q16 .... D	PT59-S2-Q5 ...... E	PT68-S2-Q13 .... B	PT76-S2-Q25 .... D
PT48-S4-Q2 ...... E	PT59-S2-Q22 .... A	PT68-S3-Q7 ...... E	PT76-S4-Q8 ...... E
PT49-S2-Q4 ...... B	PT59-S3-Q11 .... B	PT68-S3-Q17 .... D	PT77-S2-Q1 C
PT49-S2-Q11 C	PT60-S1-Q11 C	PT69-S1-Q1 ...... B	PT77-S2-Q2 ...... D
PT49-S4-Q4 ...... E	PT60-S3-Q2 ...... B	PT69-S1-Q13 ... B	PT77-S2-Q7 ...... E
PT50-S2-Q13 .... D	PT60-S3-Q21 .... E	PT69-S4-Q23 .... E	PT77-S4-Q4 ...... B

Weaken

J07-S2-Q5 .... B	J07-S2-Q9 .... E	J07-S2-Q14 .... E	J07-S3-Q15 C

J07-S3-Q21 .... B	PT4-S4-Q1 .... B	PT11-S2-Q19 .... A	PT18-S4-Q23 .... B
PTA-S1-Q16 ...... A	PT4-S4-Q6 .... A	PT11-S2-Q21 .... B	PT19-S2-Q4 ...... D
PTA-S4-Q10 ...... D	PT4-S4-Q8 .... B	PT11-S4-Q5 C	PT19-S2-Q12 .... D
PTB-S1-Q4 .... D	PT4-S4-Q11 ...... B	PT11-S4-Q11 .... B	PT19-S4-Q9 ...... B
PTB-S1-Q16 ...... D	PT5-S1-Q5 .... B	PT11-S4-Q21 .... E	PT19-S4-Q10 .... A
PTB-S4-Q5 .... B	PT5-S1-Q8 .... B	PT12-S1-Q16 .... B	PT19-S4-Q26 .... D
PTB-S4-Q9 C	PT5-S1-Q10 C	PT12-S4-Q4 ...... B	PT20-S1-Q2 ...... A
PTB-S4-Q18 ...... E	PT5-S1-Q17 ...... D	PT12-S4-Q11 .... A	PT20-S1-Q4 ...... B
PTC-S2-Q3 .... A	PT5-S3-Q2 .... B	PT12-S4-Q21 .... D	PT20-S1-Q12 .... D
PTC-S3-Q2 C	PT5-S3-Q8 C	PT13-S2-Q1 ...... D	PT20-S4-Q3 ...... B
PTC-S3-Q10 C	PT5-S3-Q24 ...... B	PT13-S2-Q13 .... A	PT20-S4-Q17 .... E
PTC-S3-Q21 ...... B	PT6-S2-Q7 .... E	PT13-S2-Q21 C	PT20-S4-Q23 .... D
PTC2-S2-Q7 ...... D	PT6-S2-Q19 ...... E	PT13-S4-Q12 .... B	PT20-S4-Q25 .... D
PTC2-S2-Q17 C	PT6-S3-Q2 .... B	PT13-S4-Q17 .... D	PT21-S2-Q7 ...... B
PTC2-S3-Q5 ...... B	PT6-S3-Q4 .... B	PT13-S4-Q19 .... D	PT21-S2-Q17 C
PTC2-S3-Q7 ...... B	PT6-S3-Q13 ...... E	PT14-S2-Q12 .... A	PT21-S3-Q21 .... B
PT1-S3-Q5 C	PT6-S3-Q17 ...... A	PT14-S2-Q21 .... A	PT21-S3-Q23 C
PT1-S3-Q9 .... A	PT7-S1-Q1 C	PT14-S2-Q24 .... D	PT22-S2-Q4 ...... D
PT1-S4-Q12 ...... A	PT7-S1-Q4 .... E	PT14-S4-Q4 C	PT22-S2-Q8 ...... A
PT1-S4-Q15 ...... E	PT7-S4-Q4 .... E	PT14-S4-Q6 ...... A	PT22-S4-Q19 .... B
PT2-S2-Q7 .... A	PT8-S1-Q7 C	PT14-S4-Q22 .... A	PT22-S4-Q24 .... E
PT2-S2-Q14 C	PT8-S1-Q11 ...... B	PT14-S4-Q25 .... B	PT22-S4-Q26 .... D
PT2-S2-Q18 ...... B	PT8-S1-Q13 ...... D	PT15-S2-Q7 ...... B	PT23-S2-Q8 ...... D
PT2-S4-Q5 .... B	PT8-S4-Q14 ...... A	PT15-S3-Q25 .... D	PT23-S2-Q26 .... D
PT2-S4-Q16 C	PT8-S4-Q24 C	PT16-S2-Q2 ...... A	PT23-S3-Q19 .... B
PT3-S2-Q14 ...... B	PT8-S4-Q25 ...... B	PT16-S2-Q5 C	PT24-S2-Q7 ...... A
PT3-S2-Q16 C	PT9-S2-Q4 .... B	PT16-S2-Q16 .... E	PT24-S2-Q19 .... E
PT3-S2-Q20 C	PT9-S2-Q7 .... D	PT16-S3-Q1 ...... D	PT24-S2-Q20 .... B
PT3-S2-Q23 C	PT9-S2-Q12 ...... A	PT16-S3-Q6 C	PT24-S3-Q6 ...... D
PT3-S4-Q2 C	PT9-S4-Q2 .... E	PT16-S3-Q18 .... D	PT24-S3-Q9 ...... E
PT3-S4-Q5 C	PT9-S4-Q22 ...... E	PT17-S2-Q8 ...... B	PT24-S3-Q22 C
PT3-S4-Q11 ...... E	PT10-S1-Q16 .... E	PT17-S2-Q13 .... A	PT25-S2-Q5 ...... B
PT4-S1-Q1 .... E	PT10-S1-Q19 .... D	PT17-S3-Q17 .... B	PT25-S2-Q15 .... D
PT4-S1-Q3 .... E	PT10-S4-Q1 ...... A	PT18-S2-Q6 ...... B	PT25-S4-Q3 ...... E
PT4-S1-Q4 .... D	PT10-S4-Q9 ...... D	PT18-S2-Q24 .... A	PT25-S4-Q10 .... B
PT4-S1-Q9 .... A	PT11-S2-Q1 ...... E	PT18-S4-Q7 C	PT25-S4-Q11 .... D
PT4-S1-Q13 ...... D	PT11-S2-Q11 .... B	PT18-S4-Q14 .... D	PT25-S4-Q24 .... D

PT26-S2-Q5 ...... A	PT33-S1-Q25 .... D	PT41-S3-Q16 C	PT48-S4-Q26 .... B
PT26-S2-Q12 .... D	PT33-S3-Q7 ...... A	PT41-S3-Q26 .... B	PT49-S2-Q6 C
PT26-S3-Q6 ...... E	PT33-S3-Q24 .... B	PT42-S2-Q1 ...... A	PT49-S2-Q8 ...... D
PT26-S3-Q14 .... A	PT34-S2-Q12 .... A	PT42-S2-Q4 ...... A	PT49-S2-Q14 .... B
PT26-S3-Q24 .... E	PT34-S2-Q17 .... A	PT42-S2-Q6 ...... B	PT49-S4-Q8 ...... A
PT27-S1-Q4 ...... A	PT34-S2-Q25 C	PT42-S2-Q20 .... B	PT50-S2-Q2 ...... B
PT27-S1-Q8 ...... B	PT34-S3-Q6 ...... B	PT42-S2-Q25 C	PT50-S2-Q24 .... A
PT27-S1-Q10 .... E	PT34-S3-Q18 .... E	PT42-S4-Q6 C	PT50-S4-Q5 ...... E
PT27-S4-Q15 C	PT34-S3-Q20 .... A	PT43-S2-Q6 ...... E	PT50-S4-Q12 .... A
PT27-S4-Q18 .... B	PT35-S1-Q4 C	PT43-S3-Q8 C	PT51-S1-Q8 C
PT28-S1-Q5 ...... D	PT35-S1-Q8 ...... E	PT43-S3-Q19 .... B	PT51-S1-Q25 .... A
PT28-S1-Q23 .... A	PT35-S1-Q13 .... D	PT44-S2-Q4 C	PT51-S3-Q1 ...... A
PT28-S3-Q11 C	PT35-S4-Q5 ...... D	PT44-S2-Q8 ...... E	PT52-S1-Q9 ...... D
PT28-S3-Q15 .... B	PT35-S4-Q17 .... E	PT44-S2-Q20 .... B	PT52-S1-Q12 .... E
PT28-S3-Q17 .... B	PT35-S4-Q20 .... A	PT44-S4-Q1 C	PT52-S1-Q21 C
PT28-S3-Q25 .... E	PT36-S1-Q2 ...... A	PT44-S4-Q5 ...... D	PT52-S3-Q6 C
PT29-S1-Q16 .... B	PT36-S1-Q8 ...... D	PT45-S1-Q2 C	PT52-S3-Q19 .... A
PT29-S1-Q24 C	PT36-S1-Q25 C	PT45-S1-Q12 C	PT53-S1-Q3 ...... B
PT29-S4-Q9 ...... D	PT36-S3-Q2 ...... A	PT45-S1-Q16 C	PT53-S1-Q8 ...... D
PT29-S4-Q24 .... B	PT36-S3-Q5 ...... E	PT45-S1-Q18 .... D	PT53-S3-Q4 ...... A
PT30-S2-Q1 ...... A	PT37-S2-Q4 ...... B	PT45-S4-Q4 ...... D	PT53-S3-Q9 ...... E
PT30-S2-Q8 ...... A	PT37-S2-Q14 .... D	PT46-S2-Q8 ...... E	PT53-S3-Q14 .... A
PT30-S2-Q9 C	PT37-S4-Q2 ...... A	PT46-S2-Q22 C	PT53-S3-Q16 .... B
PT30-S4-Q11 .... A	PT37-S4-Q11 .... D	PT46-S2-Q25 C	PT54-S2-Q3 ...... A
PT30-S4-Q17 C	PT37-S4-Q18 .... B	PT46-S3-Q6 ...... D	PT54-S2-Q14 C
PT30-S4-Q24 .... D	PT38-S1-Q10 .... A	PT47-S1-Q2 ...... B	PT54-S4-Q10 .... D
PT31-S2-Q6 C	PT38-S1-Q17 .... B	PT47-S1-Q19 .... A	PT55-S1-Q7 ...... A
PT31-S2-Q16 .... E	PT38-S4-Q13 .... A	PT47-S1-Q22 C	PT55-S1-Q9 ...... D
PT31-S2-Q19 .... B	PT38-S4-Q15 .... D	PT47-S3-Q4 ...... B	PT55-S1-Q22 .... E
PT31-S3-Q12 C	PT39-S2-Q9 ...... D	PT47-S3-Q7 ...... B	PT55-S3-Q4 ...... A
PT31-S3-Q24 .... D	PT39-S4-Q1 ...... E	PT47-S3-Q14 .... A	PT55-S3-Q9 ...... D
PT32-S1-Q12 .... B	PT39-S4-Q22 .... D	PT47-S3-Q24 .... E	PT55-S3-Q22 .... A
PT32-S1-Q17 .... D	PT40-S1-Q17 .... E	PT48-S1-Q1 ...... D	PT56-S2-Q3 ...... B
PT32-S4-Q2 C	PT40-S3-Q5 ...... B	PT48-S1-Q19 .... B	PT56-S2-Q8 ...... D
PT33-S1-Q4 ...... D	PT40-S3-Q26 .... B	PT48-S4-Q9 ...... A	PT56-S3-Q20 .... D
PT33-S1-Q17 C	PT41-S1-Q13 C	PT48-S4-Q20 .... D	PT57-S2-Q9 C
PT33-S1-Q20 C	PT41-S1-Q16 C	PT48-S4-Q23 .... D	PT57-S2-Q14 .... E

PT57-S2-Q17 .... E	PT61-S4-Q8 ...... E	PT66-S4-Q8 ...... D	PT72-S3-Q2 ...... B
PT57-S2-Q20 .... D	PT61-S4-Q21 C	PT67-S2-Q1 ...... A	PT72-S3-Q10 .... D
PT57-S3-Q6 ...... A	PT62-S2-Q22 .... D	PT67-S2-Q17 .... B	PT73-S2-Q9 C
PT57-S3-Q11 .... A	PT62-S4-Q5 ...... B	PT67-S4-Q6 ...... A	PT73-S2-Q19 .... B
PT58-S1-Q5 ...... A	PT62-S4-Q14 .... E	PT67-S4-Q10 .... B	PT73-S4-Q1 ...... D
PT58-S1-Q24 .... E	PT63-S1-Q2 ...... B	PT67-S4-Q24 C	PT73-S4-Q17 C
PT58-S4-Q2 C	PT63-S1-Q7 ...... B	PT68-S2-Q4 ...... B	PT74-S1-Q6 ...... A
PT58-S4-Q10 .... D	PT63-S3-Q9 C	PT68-S3-Q9 ...... A	PT74-S1-Q23 .... D
PT59-S2-Q21 C	PT63-S3-Q16 .... E	PT69-S1-Q17 C	PT74-S4-Q24 .... D
PT59-S2-Q25 .... B	PT64-S1-Q4 ...... A	PT69-S1-Q22 .... B	PT75-S1-Q5 C
PT59-S3-Q2 ...... A	PT64-S1-Q8 ...... B	PT69-S4-Q7 ...... E	PT75-S1-Q11 .... D
PT59-S3-Q13 .... D	PT64-S1-Q10 .... A	PT69-S4-Q15 .... D	PT75-S3-Q13 C
PT60-S1-Q6 ...... B	PT64-S1-Q13 .... D	PT69-S4-Q19 .... E	PT75-S3-Q22 .... A
PT60-S1-Q13 C	PT64-S3-Q15 .... B	PT70-S1-Q16 .... E	PT76-S2-Q9 ...... B
PT60-S1-Q16 C	PT65-S1-Q5 ...... D	PT70-S4-Q12 .... B	PT76-S2-Q12 .... B
PT60-S3-Q4 ...... B	PT65-S4-Q3 ...... D	PT70-S4-Q19 .... D	PT76-S4-Q21 C
PT60-S3-Q13 .... D	PT65-S4-Q19 .... B	PT71-S1-Q13 .... A	PT76-S4-Q23 .... D
PT61-S2-Q11 .... A	PT66-S2-Q5 C	PT71-S3-Q21 .... A	PT77-S2-Q4 ...... A
PT61-S2-Q14 .... D	PT66-S4-Q4 ...... B	PT72-S2-Q2 C	PT77-S4-Q11 .... D
PT61-S2-Q20 C	PT66-S4-Q6 C	PT72-S2-Q10 C	PT77-S4-Q19 .... A

Evaluate

PTC-S2-Q9 .... D	PT15-S2-Q22 .... E	PT38-S4-Q19 .... A	PT68-S2-Q2 ...... A
PT3-S4-Q23 ...... A	PT15-S3-Q16 C	PT45-S4-Q11 C	PT68-S2-Q14 .... E
PT7-S1-Q22 ...... E	PT19-S4-Q22 .... D	PT46-S3-Q3 ...... D	PT69-S1-Q5 C
PT7-S4-Q8 .... E	PT20-S4-Q7 ...... E	PT49-S4-Q2 ...... B	PT73-S4-Q6 ...... E
PT9-S4-Q8 C	PT21-S3-Q11 C	PT51-S1-Q2 ...... A	PT74-S1-Q21 .... B
PT10-S1-Q6 C	PT24-S2-Q16 .... A	PT61-S4-Q2 ...... B	PT74-S4-Q10 C
PT11-S2-Q2 ...... D	PT27-S4-Q6 ...... E	PT65-S1-Q3 ...... B	PT77-S2-Q10 C
PT13-S2-Q22 .... D	PT36-S1-Q24 .... B	PT65-S4-Q7 ...... A	

Method (Argument)

J07-S2-Q20 .... E	PTB-S4-Q20 ...... D	PT1-S4-Q20 ...... D	PT3-S2-Q11 ...... D
PTA-S1-Q7 .... D	PTC-S2-Q10 C	PT2-S2-Q8 .... E	PT3-S2-Q19 ...... B
PTA-S1-Q13 ...... D	PTC-S3-Q13 ...... B	PT2-S2-Q12 ...... A	PT4-S1-Q6 .... E
PTA-S1-Q18 ...... A	PTC-S3-Q25 C	PT2-S4-Q3 .... E	PT4-S1-Q18 ...... D
PTA-S4-Q4 .... D	PTC2-S3-Q8 ...... D	PT2-S4-Q24 ...... D	PT4-S1-Q21 ...... B
PTB-S1-Q13 ...... B	PT1-S4-Q5 .... B	PT3-S2-Q6 C	PT4-S4-Q16 C

PT4-S4-Q18 ...... B	PT15-S2-Q24 .... A	PT23-S2-Q1 C	PT37-S2-Q10 C
PT5-S1-Q6 .... E	PT15-S3-Q15 .... B	PT23-S2-Q3 ...... E	PT37-S2-Q13 C
PT5-S3-Q4 .... E	PT15-S3-Q17 .... A	PT23-S2-Q15 .... D	PT37-S4-Q10 .... E
PT5-S3-Q19 ...... E	PT16-S2-Q17 .... B	PT23-S3-Q8 ...... B	PT37-S4-Q24 .... B
PT6-S2-Q20 C	PT16-S2-Q23 .... D	PT24-S2-Q3 ...... B	PT39-S2-Q4 C
PT6-S3-Q21 ...... E	PT16-S3-Q7 ...... A	PT24-S3-Q3 ...... D	PT39-S4-Q3 ...... E
PT6-S3-Q23 ...... D	PT16-S3-Q20 .... D	PT24-S3-Q17 .... A	PT39-S4-Q8 ...... D
PT6-S3-Q26 C	PT16-S3-Q25 C	PT25-S4-Q19 .... A	PT40-S1-Q2 ...... B
PT7-S1-Q6 .... E	PT17-S2-Q4 ...... E	PT25-S4-Q21 C	PT40-S1-Q4 ...... D
PT7-S1-Q7 C	PT17-S2-Q18 .... D	PT26-S3-Q2 ...... B	PT40-S3-Q13 .... E
PT7-S4-Q16 ...... E	PT17-S2-Q25 .... D	PT26-S3-Q16 .... D	PT41-S1-Q3 C
PT7-S4-Q20 ...... A	PT17-S3-Q4 ...... D	PT27-S1-Q6 C	PT41-S3-Q9 C
PT7-S4-Q21 ...... A	PT17-S3-Q10 .... D	PT27-S1-Q15 .... A	PT41-S3-Q12 .... B
PT8-S1-Q4 C	PT18-S2-Q1 ...... D	PT27-S4-Q12 .... A	PT45-S1-Q4 C
PT8-S1-Q15 ...... A	PT18-S2-Q5 ...... D	PT27-S4-Q21 .... D	PT45-S1-Q7 ...... B
PT8-S1-Q18 ...... E	PT18-S2-Q7 ...... B	PT28-S1-Q7 ...... E	PT45-S4-Q12 .... A
PT8-S4-Q17 ...... A	PT18-S2-Q12 .... D	PT28-S3-Q7 C	PT46-S2-Q17 .... E
PT9-S2-Q11 ...... E	PT18-S4-Q21 .... E	PT28-S3-Q10 .... A	PT46-S3-Q10 C
PT9-S2-Q15 ...... B	PT19-S2-Q6 ...... B	PT29-S1-Q2 ...... A	PT47-S1-Q10 .... D
PT9-S4-Q9 .... B	PT19-S2-Q8 C	PT29-S1-Q12 .... D	PT47-S3-Q20 .... B
PT10-S1-Q4 ...... D	PT19-S2-Q11 .... B	PT30-S2-Q7 ...... D	PT49-S4-Q15 .... A
PT10-S1-Q12 .... B	PT19-S4-Q2 ...... A	PT30-S4-Q16 .... D	PT50-S4-Q6 C
PT10-S4-Q25 C	PT19-S4-Q18 C	PT31-S3-Q20 .... A	PT52-S3-Q5 ...... D
PT11-S2-Q3 C	PT19-S4-Q25 .... B	PT32-S1-Q8 ...... A	PT53-S3-Q24 .... A
PT11-S2-Q8 ...... B	PT20-S1-Q8 ...... B	PT32-S4-Q1 ...... B	PT54-S2-Q10 .... B
PT11-S2-Q14 .... E	PT20-S1-Q21 .... A	PT33-S1-Q2 ...... A	PT54-S4-Q2 ...... D
PT11-S4-Q10 .... D	PT20-S1-Q25 .... D	PT33-S3-Q12 .... A	PT55-S1-Q3 C
PT11-S4-Q12 .... D	PT20-S4-Q4 ...... A	PT34-S2-Q8 ...... A	PT56-S2-Q11 .... B
PT12-S1-Q6 ...... A	PT21-S2-Q9 ...... E	PT34-S3-Q8 ...... B	PT56-S3-Q6 ...... D
PT12-S4-Q14 .... D	PT21-S2-Q12 .... B	PT35-S1-Q5 ...... E	PT57-S3-Q5 ...... A
PT13-S2-Q2 C	PT21-S2-Q24 .... A	PT35-S1-Q11 .... E	PT58-S1-Q6 ...... A
PT13-S2-Q17 .... A	PT21-S3-Q14 .... D	PT35-S4-Q25 .... A	PT58-S1-Q26 .... A
PT13-S4-Q1 ...... A	PT21-S3-Q20 .... D	PT36-S1-Q1 ...... A	PT58-S4-Q12 .... A
PT13-S4-Q6 ...... B	PT22-S2-Q3 ...... D	PT36-S1-Q7 ...... B	PT59-S3-Q14 C
PT14-S2-Q8 ...... B	PT22-S2-Q11 .... E	PT36-S3-Q8 .... A	PT59-S3-Q23 .... B
PT14-S4-Q16 .... A	PT22-S2-Q13 C	PT36-S3-Q10 .... E	PT60-S1-Q2 ...... E
PT14-S4-Q24 C	PT22-S4-Q23 .... B	PT36-S3-Q24 C	PT60-S1-Q25 C

PT61-S2-Q4 ...... D	PT66-S2-Q25 .... E	PT70-S4-Q8 ...... E	PT74-S4-Q14 .... A
PT62-S2-Q14 .... B	PT67-S2-Q12 .... D	PT70-S4-Q26 .... D	PT74-S4-Q17 .... E
PT62-S4-Q21 .... A	PT67-S4-Q12 .... D	PT71-S1-Q2 ...... D	PT75-S1-Q4 ...... E
PT63-S1-Q17 C	PT68-S2-Q26 .... D	PT71-S1-Q9 ...... A	PT75-S3-Q11 .... E
PT63-S3-Q19 C	PT68-S3-Q20 .... D	PT73-S2-Q14 .... E	PT76-S2-Q8 ...... E
PT64-S1-Q3 ...... B	PT69-S1-Q23 .... A	PT73-S2-Q16 .... A	PT77-S2-Q17 .... B
PT65-S4-Q16 .... A	PT69-S4-Q4 ...... B	PT73-S4-Q4 C	

Method (Statement)

J07-S2-Q11 C	PT29-S4-Q2 ...... A	PT43-S2-Q2 ...... A	PT57-S2-Q21 .... E
PTA-S4-Q9 C	PT29-S4-Q15 .... D	PT43-S2-Q23 .... D	PT57-S3-Q21 .... B
PTA-S4-Q15 ...... E	PT30-S4-Q3 C	PT44-S2-Q19 .... B	PT59-S2-Q7 ...... E
PTA-S4-Q21 ...... A	PT30-S4-Q13 .... B	PT44-S2-Q24 .... E	PT59-S2-Q18 .... D
PTB-S1-Q2 C	PT31-S2-Q12 .... A	PT44-S4-Q6 C	PT60-S1-Q4 ...... D
PTB-S1-Q11 ...... E	PT31-S3-Q16 .... D	PT44-S4-Q24 C	PT60-S3-Q5 ...... D
PTC-S2-Q22 C	PT32-S1-Q15 C	PT45-S4-Q23 .... E	PT60-S3-Q7 C
PTC2-S2-Q8 ...... E	PT32-S4-Q23 .... D	PT46-S3-Q16 .... D	PT61-S4-Q17 .... D
PTC2-S3-Q10 .... B	PT33-S3-Q14 .... E	PT46-S3-Q18 C	PT61-S4-Q22 C
PT3-S4-Q20 C	PT34-S2-Q22 .... E	PT48-S4-Q5 ...... B	PT62-S4-Q4 C
PT7-S1-Q18 C	PT34-S3-Q14 .... B	PT49-S2-Q12 C	PT63-S3-Q1 ...... E
PT9-S2-Q20 ...... A	PT34-S3-Q26 .... E	PT50-S2-Q15 .... E	PT64-S1-Q14 .... A
PT9-S4-Q20 C	PT35-S1-Q1 ...... D	PT50-S2-Q19 .... A	PT64-S1-Q25 .... B
PT10-S4-Q13 .... B	PT35-S1-Q9 ...... E	PT51-S1-Q14 C	PT64-S3-Q10 .... D
PT11-S4-Q24 .... A	PT35-S4-Q2 ...... A	PT51-S3-Q11 .... E	PT64-S3-Q16 .... D
PT12-S1-Q3 ...... E	PT35-S4-Q15 .... E	PT51-S3-Q23 .... B	PT65-S1-Q10 .... B
PT14-S2-Q9 C	PT36-S3-Q6 ...... B	PT52-S3-Q17 .... B	PT65-S1-Q22 .... E
PT15-S2-Q14 .... B	PT38-S1-Q18 .... B	PT53-S1-Q11 .... D	PT65-S4-Q12 C
PT15-S3-Q11 C	PT38-S4-Q18 .... B	PT53-S1-Q14 .... D	PT65-S4-Q21 .... E
PT18-S4-Q5 C	PT39-S2-Q16 .... D	PT53-S3-Q10 .... B	PT67-S2-Q20 C
PT19-S4-Q17 .... B	PT39-S2-Q22 .... D	PT54-S2-Q17 .... D	PT67-S2-Q22 .... B
PT20-S4-Q9 ...... B	PT40-S1-Q25 .... B	PT54-S4-Q15 .... B	PT67-S4-Q22 .... E
PT23-S2-Q11 C	PT40-S3-Q6 ...... E	PT55-S1-Q19 C	PT68-S2-Q11 C
PT24-S2-Q10 .... E	PT42-S2-Q2 ...... D	PT55-S3-Q7 ...... E	PT68-S2-Q22 .... B
PT26-S3-Q4 C	PT42-S4-Q3 ...... A	PT56-S2-Q9 ...... B	PT69-S1-Q11 .... E
PT27-S1-Q14 .... B	PT42-S4-Q16 .... E	PT56-S2-Q25 .... B	PT69-S4-Q12 .... A
PT27-S1-Q17 .... B	PT42-S4-Q18 .... D	PT57-S2-Q13 C	PT70-S1-Q17 .... D
PT27-S4-Q24 C	PT42-S4-Q21 .... D	PT57-S2-Q16 .... B	PT70-S4-Q24 C

PT71-S1-Q11 .... E	PT74-S1-Q14 .... D	PT76-S4-Q7 C	PT77-S4-Q16 .... B
PT72-S2-Q13 C	PT75-S1-Q14 .... A	PT77-S2-Q20 .... B	PT77-S4-Q22 C
PT72-S3-Q15 .... B	PT75-S1-Q16 C	PT77-S4-Q7 ...... D	
PT73-S4-Q9 ...... D	PT75-S3-Q20 .... D	PT77-S4-Q14 .... E	

Flaw

J07-S2-Q4 .... A	PTC2-S2-Q22.... A	PT5-S1-Q2 .... A	PT9-S2-Q5 .... D
J07-S2-Q17 .... B	PTC2-S2-Q25.... D	PT5-S1-Q11 ...... D	PT9-S2-Q14 C
J07-S2-Q21 .... A	PTC2-S3-Q6...... A	PT5-S1-Q13 ...... E	PT9-S2-Q22 ...... D
J07-S3-Q4 .... E	PTC2-S3-Q9...... E	PT5-S1-Q24 C	PT9-S4-Q1 C
J07-S3-Q8 .... E	PTC2-S3-Q12.... D	PT5-S3-Q1 C	PT9-S4-Q5 .... E
J07-S3-Q18 .... B	PTC2-S3-Q14.... E	PT5-S3-Q9 C	PT9-S4-Q14 ...... A
J07-S3-Q23 .... D	PTC2-S3-Q18.... A	PT5-S3-Q11 C	PT10-S1-Q5 ...... B
J07-S3-Q25 .... A	PTC2-S3-Q24.... B	PT5-S3-Q16 ...... B	PT10-S1-Q8 ...... E
PTA-S1-Q2 .... D	PT1-S3-Q8 .... B	PT6-S2-Q4 .... E	PT10-S1-Q10 .... E
PTA-S1-Q4 .... E	PT1-S3-Q12 ...... D	PT6-S2-Q14 ...... D	PT10-S1-Q13 .... B
PTA-S1-Q10 C	PT1-S3-Q22 ...... E	PT6-S2-Q17 ...... B	PT10-S1-Q17 .... B
PTA-S1-Q21 C	PT1-S4-Q1 C	PT6-S2-Q22 ...... D	PT10-S1-Q21 .... B
PTA-S4-Q11 ...... B	PT1-S4-Q8 C	PT6-S3-Q8 .... D	PT10-S4-Q14 .... B
PTA-S4-Q20 ...... D	PT1-S4-Q16 ...... A	PT6-S3-Q16 ...... E	PT10-S4-Q19 .... A
PTA-S4-Q25 ...... A	PT2-S2-Q2 .... E	PT6-S3-Q18 ...... A	PT10-S4-Q21 .... E
PTB-S1-Q5 .... E	PT2-S2-Q5 C	PT6-S3-Q20 C	PT11-S2-Q9 ...... D
PTB-S1-Q10 ...... B	PT2-S4-Q4 .... A	PT6-S3-Q22 ...... A	PT11-S2-Q15 .... D
PTB-S1-Q26 ...... D	PT2-S4-Q6 .... B	PT6-S3-Q24 ...... B	PT11-S2-Q26 .... E
PTB-S4-Q8 .... B	PT2-S4-Q11 ...... B	PT7-S1-Q10 ...... B	PT11-S4-Q3 ...... E
PTB-S4-Q13 ...... B	PT3-S2-Q2 .... E	PT7-S1-Q17 ...... B	PT11-S4-Q9 ...... E
PTB-S4-Q19 ...... D	PT3-S2-Q5 .... E	PT7-S4-Q3 .... B	PT11-S4-Q17 .... B
PTC-S2-Q2 .... E	PT3-S2-Q25 ...... E	PT7-S4-Q9 C	PT11-S4-Q19 .... A
PTC-S2-Q6 .... A	PT3-S4-Q7 .... B	PT7-S4-Q11 ...... A	PT11-S4-Q23 .... B
PTC-S2-Q12 C	PT3-S4-Q15 ...... E	PT7-S4-Q22 ...... D	PT12-S1-Q14 .... D
PTC-S2-Q18 ...... B	PT3-S4-Q18 ...... E	PT8-S1-Q3 .... A	PT12-S1-Q18 .... A
PTC-S3-Q5 .... A	PT4-S1-Q8 .... D	PT8-S1-Q21 ...... D	PT12-S1-Q20 .... D
PTC-S3-Q9 .... D	PT4-S1-Q16 ...... A	PT8-S1-Q23 ...... E	PT12-S1-Q24 .... A
PTC-S3-Q15 C	PT4-S1-Q23 C	PT8-S4-Q1 C	PT12-S1-Q26 .... E
PTC-S3-Q19 ...... D	PT4-S4-Q4 .... A	PT8-S4-Q8 C	PT12-S4-Q5 ...... A
PTC2-S2-Q3 C	PT4-S4-Q12 C	PT8-S4-Q20 ...... B	PT12-S4-Q7 ...... D
PTC2-S2-Q9 C	PT4-S4-Q19 ...... E	PT9-S2-Q2 .... D	PT12-S4-Q15 .... B

PT12-S4-Q17 C	PT17-S2-Q22 .... D	PT22-S2-Q12 .... B	PT26-S3-Q10 .... D
PT12-S4-Q19 .... B	PT17-S3-Q7 C	PT22-S2-Q20 .... E	PT26-S3-Q17 .... D
PT12-S4-Q24 .... A	PT17-S3-Q9 ...... D	PT22-S2-Q24 C	PT26-S3-Q19 .... D
PT13-S2-Q7 ...... B	PT17-S3-Q16 .... A	PT22-S2-Q25 .... B	PT27-S1-Q2 ...... D
PT13-S2-Q20 .... A	PT17-S3-Q20 .... A	PT22-S4-Q1 ...... A	PT27-S1-Q23 C
PT13-S2-Q24 .... E	PT17-S3-Q22 .... E	PT22-S4-Q9 ...... A	PT27-S1-Q25 .... B
PT13-S2-Q26 .... B	PT18-S2-Q4 ...... D	PT22-S4-Q18 .... B	PT27-S4-Q7 ...... D
PT13-S4-Q9 C	PT18-S2-Q8 ...... E	PT22-S4-Q21 .... D	PT27-S4-Q10 .... B
PT13-S4-Q20 .... E	PT18-S2-Q14 .... D	PT23-S2-Q4 ...... D	PT27-S4-Q25 .... E
PT14-S2-Q4 ...... E	PT18-S4-Q9 C	PT23-S2-Q19 .... B	PT28-S1-Q9 C
PT14-S2-Q10 .... B	PT18-S4-Q11 .... D	PT23-S2-Q21 .... E	PT28-S1-Q19 .... A
PT14-S2-Q22 .... D	PT18-S4-Q17 .... A	PT23-S3-Q7 ...... E	PT28-S1-Q25 .... D
PT14-S4-Q9 ...... D	PT18-S4-Q25 .... E	PT23-S3-Q16 C	PT28-S3-Q2 ...... E
PT14-S4-Q10 .... A	PT19-S2-Q1 ...... A	PT23-S3-Q17 C	PT28-S3-Q5 C
PT14-S4-Q15 C	PT19-S2-Q7 ...... B	PT23-S3-Q22 .... E	PT28-S3-Q20 .... B
PT14-S4-Q18 .... D	PT19-S2-Q14 C	PT24-S2-Q1 ...... B	PT29-S1-Q7 ...... A
PT14-S4-Q20 .... E	PT19-S2-Q23 .... E	PT24-S2-Q6 C	PT29-S1-Q14 .... E
PT15-S2-Q2 ...... D	PT19-S4-Q1 ...... D	PT24-S2-Q8 ...... B	PT29-S1-Q17 .... A
PT15-S2-Q17 .... D	PT19-S4-Q3 ...... E	PT24-S2-Q23 .... A	PT29-S4-Q14 .... A
PT15-S2-Q19 .... A	PT19-S4-Q5 ...... A	PT24-S3-Q2 ...... E	PT29-S4-Q18 .... B
PT15-S2-Q20 .... A	PT19-S4-Q6 C	PT24-S3-Q4 ...... E	PT29-S4-Q25 .... E
PT15-S3-Q2 ...... E	PT20-S1-Q10 C	PT24-S3-Q12 .... D	PT30-S2-Q2 ...... E
PT15-S3-Q9 ...... B	PT20-S1-Q14 C	PT24-S3-Q25 .... D	PT30-S2-Q13 .... D
PT15-S3-Q14 C	PT20-S1-Q15 C	PT25-S2-Q9 ...... E	PT30-S2-Q17 .... B
PT15-S3-Q19 .... A	PT20-S1-Q22 .... E	PT25-S2-Q18 .... E	PT30-S2-Q25 .... D
PT16-S2-Q10 .... E	PT20-S4-Q2 C	PT25-S2-Q20 .... D	PT30-S2-Q26 .... B
PT16-S2-Q22 .... E	PT20-S4-Q14 C	PT25-S4-Q4 ...... B	PT30-S4-Q6 ...... B
PT16-S2-Q24 .... E	PT20-S4-Q18 .... A	PT25-S4-Q8 ...... A	PT30-S4-Q8 ...... E
PT16-S3-Q2 ...... B	PT20-S4-Q22 .... A	PT25-S4-Q17 .... B	PT30-S4-Q14 C
PT16-S3-Q9 ...... A	PT21-S2-Q5 C	PT25-S4-Q23 .... B	PT31-S2-Q3 C
PT16-S3-Q11 .... E	PT21-S2-Q22 .... E	PT26-S2-Q1 ...... B	PT31-S2-Q9 ...... A
PT16-S3-Q24 .... B	PT21-S2-Q25 .... E	PT26-S2-Q4 C	PT31-S2-Q18 C
PT16-S3-Q26 .... A	PT21-S3-Q5 C	PT26-S2-Q15 C	PT31-S3-Q1 ...... E
PT17-S2-Q2 ...... E	PT21-S3-Q19 .... B	PT26-S2-Q17 .... B	PT31-S3-Q5 ...... D
PT17-S2-Q5 ...... D	PT22-S2-Q6 ...... E	PT26-S2-Q21 .... E	PT31-S3-Q8 ...... B
PT17-S2-Q11 .... E	PT22-S2-Q7 ...... E	PT26-S3-Q5 C	PT31-S3-Q15 .... A
PT17-S2-Q17 .... B	PT22-S2-Q10 .... B	PT26-S3-Q8 ...... E	PT31-S3-Q25 .... B

PT32-S1-Q4 ...... A	PT37-S2-Q16 .... D	PT41-S3-Q4 C	PT46-S2-Q11 .... A
PT32-S1-Q6 ...... D	PT37-S2-Q25 .... D	PT41-S3-Q11 .... D	PT46-S2-Q14 .... E
PT32-S1-Q10 .... A	PT37-S4-Q12 .... A	PT41-S3-Q13 C	PT46-S2-Q24 .... D
PT32-S1-Q14 .... B	PT37-S4-Q16 C	PT41-S3-Q20 .... B	PT46-S3-Q2 C
PT32-S1-Q19 .... E	PT37-S4-Q17 .... E	PT41-S3-Q23 .... A	PT46-S3-Q4 ...... D
PT32-S4-Q6 C	PT37-S4-Q22 .... E	PT42-S2-Q3 ...... D	PT46-S3-Q7 ...... D
PT32-S4-Q13 .... D	PT38-S1-Q6 ...... E	PT42-S2-Q12 .... D	PT46-S3-Q13 .... E
PT32-S4-Q15 .... A	PT38-S1-Q8 ...... E	PT42-S2-Q15 .... D	PT46-S3-Q23 .... E
PT32-S4-Q25 .... D	PT38-S1-Q11 .... E	PT42-S2-Q17 .... A	PT47-S1-Q1 ...... D
PT33-S1-Q12 .... B	PT38-S1-Q23 .... A	PT42-S2-Q26 .... B	PT47-S1-Q8 ...... E
PT33-S1-Q22 .... B	PT38-S4-Q2 C	PT42-S4-Q4 C	PT47-S1-Q23 .... D
PT33-S1-Q24 C	PT38-S4-Q8 ...... D	PT42-S4-Q12 .... B	PT47-S3-Q8 ...... A
PT33-S3-Q2 ...... D	PT38-S4-Q14 .... D	PT42-S4-Q14 .... E	PT47-S3-Q16 .... B
PT33-S3-Q5 ...... D	PT38-S4-Q21 .... D	PT42-S4-Q20 .... A	PT47-S3-Q19 C
PT33-S3-Q15 .... A	PT39-S2-Q2 ...... E	PT43-S2-Q5 ...... D	PT47-S3-Q23 .... A
PT33-S3-Q17 C	PT39-S2-Q14 C	PT43-S2-Q9 ...... D	PT48-S1-Q2 ...... D
PT34-S2-Q1 ...... A	PT39-S2-Q20 .... B	PT43-S2-Q12 .... B	PT48-S1-Q13 C
PT34-S2-Q3 ...... E	PT39-S4-Q11 .... B	PT43-S2-Q20 .... D	PT48-S1-Q17 .... E
PT34-S2-Q9 ...... D	PT39-S4-Q15 C	PT43-S3-Q4 C	PT48-S1-Q21 .... B
PT34-S2-Q11 C	PT39-S4-Q20 .... D	PT43-S3-Q18 .... B	PT48-S1-Q24 .... E
PT34-S3-Q4 ...... E	PT39-S4-Q21 .... B	PT43-S3-Q20 .... E	PT48-S4-Q11 .... D
PT34-S3-Q10 .... A	PT39-S4-Q23 .... D	PT44-S2-Q1 ...... B	PT48-S4-Q13 .... A
PT35-S1-Q6 ...... B	PT40-S1-Q10 .... B	PT44-S2-Q21 .... E	PT48-S4-Q15 .... D
PT35-S1-Q17 .... E	PT40-S1-Q12 .... D	PT44-S2-Q25 .... E	PT48-S4-Q17 C
PT35-S1-Q23 .... A	PT40-S1-Q14 C	PT44-S4-Q9 ...... D	PT48-S4-Q25 .... B
PT35-S4-Q7 C	PT40-S1-Q15 .... D	PT44-S4-Q11 .... A	PT49-S2-Q5 ...... A
PT35-S4-Q8 ...... E	PT40-S3-Q10 .... B	PT44-S4-Q20 .... D	PT49-S2-Q13 .... E
PT35-S4-Q13 .... D	PT40-S3-Q12 .... E	PT44-S4-Q22 C	PT49-S2-Q18 .... E
PT35-S4-Q18 .... B	PT40-S3-Q14 .... A	PT45-S1-Q13 .... E	PT49-S2-Q23 .... B
PT35-S4-Q24 .... B	PT40-S3-Q19 .... D	PT45-S1-Q15 .... E	PT49-S4-Q1 C
PT36-S1-Q10 C	PT40-S3-Q21 .... B	PT45-S1-Q20 .... D	PT49-S4-Q6 ...... A
PT36-S1-Q12 .... E	PT40-S3-Q23 .... B	PT45-S1-Q24 .... B	PT49-S4-Q12 .... A
PT36-S1-Q19 C	PT41-S1-Q1 C	PT45-S4-Q10 .... B	PT49-S4-Q23 .... D
PT36-S3-Q13 .... A	PT41-S1-Q18 .... E	PT45-S4-Q14 .... D	PT50-S2-Q3 ...... A
PT36-S3-Q21 .... B	PT41-S1-Q20 .... B	PT45-S4-Q17 C	PT50-S2-Q6 C
PT36-S3-Q25 .... D	PT41-S1-Q22 .... D	PT45-S4-Q19 C	PT50-S2-Q10 .... B
PT37-S2-Q3 ...... B	PT41-S1-Q25 .... B	PT45-S4-Q24 .... D	PT50-S4-Q2 C

PT50-S4-Q4 ...... E	PT54-S4-Q16 .... A	PT59-S2-Q20 .... D	PT64-S3-Q11 .... E
PT50-S4-Q7 ...... B	PT54-S4-Q19 .... B	PT59-S3-Q5 C	PT64-S3-Q14 .... A
PT50-S4-Q17 .... A	PT55-S1-Q14 .... E	PT59-S3-Q8 ...... B	PT65-S1-Q8 ...... A
PT50-S4-Q19 .... A	PT55-S1-Q20 .... A	PT59-S3-Q20 .... D	PT65-S1-Q15 C
PT50-S4-Q22 .... E	PT55-S1-Q24 .... D	PT59-S3-Q22 .... D	PT65-S1-Q17 .... D
PT51-S1-Q4 ...... B	PT55-S3-Q2 C	PT59-S3-Q24 .... E	PT65-S1-Q20 .... D
PT51-S1-Q6 C	PT55-S3-Q11 .... B	PT60-S1-Q1 ...... D	PT65-S4-Q8 C
PT51-S1-Q10 .... E	PT55-S3-Q18 .... E	PT60-S1-Q10 .... D	PT65-S4-Q11 .... D
PT51-S1-Q12 .... D	PT55-S3-Q25 .... B	PT60-S1-Q12 .... A	PT65-S4-Q26 .... E
PT51-S1-Q15 C	PT56-S2-Q1 ...... E	PT60-S1-Q15 .... B	PT66-S2-Q1 ...... E
PT51-S1-Q18 .... E	PT56-S2-Q12 .... E	PT60-S3-Q8 C	PT66-S2-Q8 ...... B
PT51-S3-Q4 ...... B	PT56-S2-Q15 .... B	PT60-S3-Q16 .... E	PT66-S2-Q11 .... E
PT51-S3-Q6 ...... A	PT56-S3-Q1 C	PT60-S3-Q19 .... D	PT66-S2-Q13 .... A
PT51-S3-Q9 ...... D	PT56-S3-Q4 ...... A	PT61-S2-Q1 ...... D	PT66-S2-Q15 .... E
PT51-S3-Q17 .... D	PT56-S3-Q10 C	PT61-S2-Q8 ...... A	PT66-S2-Q21 .... A
PT52-S1-Q2 ...... D	PT56-S3-Q17 C	PT61-S2-Q18 .... A	PT66-S4-Q1 ...... A
PT52-S1-Q6 ...... E	PT56-S3-Q21 .... D	PT61-S4-Q11 .... A	PT66-S4-Q22 C
PT52-S1-Q23 .... D	PT57-S2-Q4 ...... D	PT61-S4-Q15 .... B	PT66-S4-Q25 .... E
PT52-S3-Q4 ...... B	PT57-S2-Q6 C	PT61-S4-Q24 .... E	PT67-S2-Q9 ...... B
PT52-S3-Q8 ...... A	PT57-S2-Q15 .... A	PT62-S2-Q5 C	PT67-S2-Q13 .... E
PT52-S3-Q12 .... E	PT57-S2-Q26 .... B	PT62-S2-Q8 ...... A	PT67-S2-Q21 .... D
PT52-S3-Q16 C	PT57-S3-Q2 C	PT62-S2-Q11 .... A	PT67-S4-Q9 C
PT52-S3-Q21 .... E	PT57-S3-Q8 C	PT62-S4-Q10 .... B	PT67-S4-Q14 .... B
PT53-S1-Q12 C	PT57-S3-Q10 C	PT62-S4-Q13 C	PT67-S4-Q21 C
PT53-S1-Q18 .... B	PT57-S3-Q18 .... B	PT62-S4-Q19 .... B	PT68-S2-Q7 ...... B
PT53-S1-Q22 .... E	PT57-S3-Q22 .... B	PT63-S1-Q3 C	PT68-S2-Q12 .... D
PT53-S1-Q25 .... B	PT58-S1-Q9 ...... E	PT63-S1-Q23 .... B	PT68-S2-Q20 .... D
PT53-S3-Q2 C	PT58-S1-Q11 .... A	PT63-S1-Q25 .... A	PT68-S2-Q24 .... E
PT53-S3-Q6 ...... D	PT58-S1-Q18 C	PT63-S3-Q2 ...... D	PT68-S3-Q3 ...... B
PT53-S3-Q17 .... A	PT58-S4-Q5 ...... A	PT63-S3-Q14 .... B	PT68-S3-Q5 ...... A
PT54-S2-Q1 ...... D	PT58-S4-Q8 ...... B	PT63-S3-Q18 .... A	PT68-S3-Q16 .... A
PT54-S2-Q5 ...... B	PT58-S4-Q14 .... D	PT64-S1-Q5 ...... A	PT68-S3-Q21 .... A
PT54-S2-Q15 .... E	PT58-S4-Q18 .... E	PT64-S1-Q7 C	PT69-S1-Q3 ...... D
PT54-S2-Q19 .... D	PT59-S2-Q4 ...... E	PT64-S1-Q16 .... A	PT69-S1-Q20 .... B
PT54-S2-Q22 .... E	PT59-S2-Q6 C	PT64-S1-Q19 C	PT69-S1-Q24 C
PT54-S4-Q4 ...... D	PT59-S2-Q8 ...... B	PT64-S3-Q4 ...... B	PT69-S4-Q3 ...... B
PT54-S4-Q14 .... D	PT59-S2-Q15 .... A	PT64-S3-Q6 ...... D	PT69-S4-Q11 .... E

PT69-S4-Q16 .... B	PT71-S3-Q18 .... D	PT73-S4-Q3 ...... E	PT75-S3-Q16 .... A
PT69-S4-Q18 .... A	PT71-S3-Q20 .... B	PT73-S4-Q10 .... E	PT75-S3-Q18 .... E
PT69-S4-Q22 .... E	PT72-S2-Q5 ...... E	PT73-S4-Q25 .... E	PT76-S2-Q1 ...... B
PT70-S1-Q2 ...... D	PT72-S2-Q14 C	PT74-S1-Q5 C	PT76-S2-Q4 C
PT70-S1-Q9 ...... A	PT72-S2-Q16 .... D	PT74-S1-Q16 .... D	PT76-S2-Q16 C
PT70-S1-Q15 .... A	PT72-S2-Q18 .... E	PT74-S1-Q18 .... A	PT76-S2-Q19 C
PT70-S1-Q20 .... E	PT72-S2-Q20 .... B	PT74-S4-Q8 ...... B	PT76-S4-Q5 C
PT70-S4-Q3 ...... A	PT72-S3-Q7 ...... A	PT74-S4-Q15 C	PT76-S4-Q13 .... D
PT70-S4-Q9 ...... E	PT72-S3-Q11 .... A	PT74-S4-Q18 .... E	PT76-S4-Q15 .... D
PT70-S4-Q11 C	PT72-S3-Q14 .... B	PT74-S4-Q20 .... D	PT77-S2-Q14 .... A
PT71-S1-Q3 ...... D	PT72-S3-Q22 .... E	PT74-S4-Q22 C	PT77-S2-Q18 .... D
PT71-S1-Q18 C	PT73-S2-Q3 ...... A	PT75-S1-Q7 ...... E	PT77-S2-Q22 .... A
PT71-S1-Q21 C	PT73-S2-Q5 ...... D	PT75-S1-Q12 .... D	PT77-S4-Q6 C
PT71-S1-Q24 .... E	PT73-S2-Q13 .... B	PT75-S1-Q18 .... B	PT77-S4-Q9 ...... D
PT71-S3-Q1 C	PT73-S2-Q15 .... B	PT75-S1-Q24 .... E	PT77-S4-Q12 .... A
PT71-S3-Q7 ...... A	PT73-S2-Q18 .... E	PT75-S3-Q7 ...... B	

Parallel (Reasoning)

J07-S2-Q12 .... A	PT4-S4-Q20 ...... D	PT14-S2-Q15 .... E	PT24-S2-Q13 .... D
PTA-S1-Q14 ...... A	PT5-S1-Q20 ...... B	PT14-S4-Q8 ...... E	PT24-S3-Q21 .... A
PTA-S4-Q23 ...... D	PT5-S3-Q25 ...... E	PT15-S2-Q18 .... B	PT25-S2-Q22 .... A
PTB-S1-Q12 C	PT6-S2-Q25 C	PT15-S3-Q13 .... A	PT25-S4-Q20 C
PTC-S2-Q16 ...... B	PT6-S3-Q14 ...... B	PT16-S2-Q19 .... A	PT26-S2-Q16 C
PTC-S3-Q24 ...... A	PT7-S1-Q13 C	PT16-S3-Q22 .... B	PT27-S1-Q26 .... D
PTC2-S2-Q23 C	PT7-S4-Q25 ...... E	PT17-S2-Q24 .... A	PT28-S1-Q13 C
PTC2-S3-Q3 ...... D	PT8-S1-Q16 ...... B	PT17-S3-Q13 .... D	PT28-S3-Q26 .... D
PT1-S3-Q2 .... B	PT8-S4-Q12 ...... D	PT18-S2-Q13 C	PT29-S1-Q13 .... E
PT1-S3-Q6 .... A	PT9-S2-Q24 ...... D	PT18-S4-Q20 .... A	PT30-S2-Q14 .... D
PT1-S4-Q24 ...... E	PT9-S4-Q15 ...... D	PT19-S2-Q20 .... B	PT30-S4-Q9 ...... B
PT2-S2-Q1 .... D	PT10-S1-Q25 .... E	PT19-S4-Q24 .... A	PT31-S2-Q23 .... B
PT2-S2-Q15 ...... B	PT10-S4-Q12 .... D	PT20-S1-Q19 .... D	PT31-S3-Q18 .... A
PT2-S4-Q20 ...... D	PT11-S2-Q25 .... E	PT20-S4-Q15 .... B	PT32-S1-Q16 .... A
PT3-S2-Q1 C	PT11-S4-Q22 .... B	PT21-S3-Q22 C	PT33-S1-Q23 .... B
PT3-S2-Q13 ...... A	PT12-S1-Q23 C	PT22-S2-Q16 .... E	PT33-S3-Q22 C
PT3-S4-Q3 C	PT12-S4-Q9 ...... D	PT22-S4-Q20 .... B	PT34-S2-Q6 ...... B
PT4-S1-Q20 ...... B	PT13-S2-Q8 ...... A	PT23-S2-Q25 .... B	PT34-S3-Q25 .... A
PT4-S4-Q15 ...... A	PT13-S4-Q24 C	PT23-S3-Q18 C	PT35-S4-Q23 .... D

PT37-S2-Q26 .... D	PT48-S4-Q22 .... D	PT60-S1-Q17 .... A	PT70-S1-Q19 C
PT37-S4-Q14 .... E	PT49-S2-Q24 .... A	PT60-S3-Q6 ...... D	PT70-S4-Q17 .... B
PT38-S1-Q22 C	PT49-S4-Q17 .... A	PT61-S4-Q9 ...... D	PT71-S1-Q14 C
PT39-S2-Q8 ...... B	PT50-S4-Q14 .... D	PT62-S4-Q25 C	PT71-S3-Q24 .... A
PT40-S1-Q23 .... A	PT51-S1-Q5 ...... D	PT63-S1-Q21 .... E	PT72-S2-Q26 .... D
PT40-S3-Q25 .... D	PT51-S3-Q24 C	PT63-S3-Q20 .... E	PT72-S3-Q23 C
PT41-S1-Q15 C	PT52-S1-Q3 ...... A	PT64-S1-Q21 .... E	PT73-S2-Q17 .... B
PT41-S3-Q24 .... E	PT53-S1-Q19 .... A	PT64-S3-Q25 .... D	PT73-S4-Q21 .... E
PT42-S2-Q22 .... B	PT53-S3-Q23 .... D	PT65-S4-Q17 C	PT74-S1-Q19 .... A
PT43-S2-Q11 .... E	PT54-S2-Q23 C	PT66-S2-Q16 .... A	PT74-S4-Q19 C
PT43-S3-Q25 .... A	PT54-S4-Q25 C	PT66-S4-Q13 .... D	PT75-S1-Q25 .... A
PT44-S4-Q21 .... E	PT55-S3-Q15 .... E	PT67-S2-Q19 .... B	PT75-S3-Q9 ...... E
PT45-S1-Q25 C	PT56-S3-Q24 .... D	PT67-S4-Q19 .... B	PT76-S4-Q22 .... A
PT46-S2-Q18 C	PT57-S2-Q19 C	PT68-S2-Q9 C	PT77-S4-Q23 .... B
PT47-S1-Q15 .... D	PT57-S3-Q20 .... E	PT68-S3-Q22 .... B	
PT48-S1-Q12 .... B	PT59-S2-Q16 .... E	PT69-S4-Q10 .... B	

Parallel (Flaw)

J07-S2-Q2 .... B	PT7-S4-Q14 ...... D	PT17-S2-Q16 .... B	PT26-S2-Q20 C
J07-S3-Q20 C	PT8-S1-Q25 ...... B	PT17-S3-Q19 .... E	PT26-S3-Q13 .... E
PTA-S1-Q22 ...... D	PT8-S4-Q3 .... D	PT18-S2-Q17 C	PT27-S1-Q11 .... B
PTA-S4-Q14 ...... A	PT9-S2-Q1 .... A	PT18-S4-Q3 ...... E	PT27-S4-Q13 .... D
PTB-S1-Q22 ...... B	PT9-S4-Q24 ...... D	PT19-S2-Q22 .... D	PT28-S1-Q3 ...... A
PTB-S4-Q23 ...... D	PT10-S1-Q20 .... D	PT19-S4-Q21 C	PT28-S3-Q21 .... D
PTC-S2-Q21 C	PT10-S4-Q5 ...... B	PT20-S1-Q17 .... D	PT29-S1-Q23 .... B
PTC-S3-Q14 ...... A	PT11-S2-Q17 .... E	PT20-S4-Q20 .... E	PT29-S4-Q21 C
PTC2-S2-Q18.... A	PT11-S4-Q20 .... D	PT21-S2-Q15 .... A	PT30-S2-Q6 ...... B
PTC2-S3-Q23.... B	PT12-S1-Q17 C	PT21-S2-Q21 .... A	PT30-S4-Q25 .... A
PT1-S4-Q10 C	PT12-S4-Q23 C	PT21-S3-Q25 .... E	PT31-S2-Q21 C
PT2-S2-Q20 C	PT13-S2-Q23 .... D	PT22-S2-Q23 .... E	PT31-S3-Q23 C
PT2-S4-Q22 ...... D	PT13-S4-Q15 .... B	PT22-S4-Q6 C	PT32-S1-Q22 .... D
PT4-S1-Q24 ...... E	PT14-S2-Q25 .... E	PT23-S2-Q23 .... E	PT32-S4-Q21 .... A
PT5-S1-Q22 C	PT14-S4-Q14 .... D	PT23-S3-Q23 .... B	PT33-S1-Q15 C
PT5-S3-Q15 C	PT15-S2-Q4 ...... D	PT24-S2-Q5 ...... D	PT33-S3-Q18 .... B
PT6-S2-Q5 .... B	PT15-S3-Q22 C	PT24-S3-Q16 .... A	PT34-S2-Q24 .... B
PT6-S3-Q10 ...... D	PT16-S2-Q7 C	PT25-S2-Q2 C	PT34-S3-Q23 .... D
PT7-S1-Q20 ...... B	PT16-S3-Q15 C	PT25-S4-Q12 .... D	PT35-S1-Q24 C

PT35-S4-Q6 ...... B	PT46-S3-Q19 .... E	PT57-S3-Q15 C	PT68-S3-Q24 C
PT36-S1-Q21 .... A	PT47-S1-Q21 .... B	PT58-S1-Q7 ...... B	PT69-S1-Q14 .... A
PT36-S3-Q19 .... B	PT47-S3-Q25 .... D	PT58-S4-Q22 C	PT69-S4-Q14 C
PT37-S2-Q21 .... A	PT48-S1-Q23 .... E	PT59-S2-Q9 C	PT70-S1-Q10 .... A
PT37-S4-Q4 ...... E	PT48-S4-Q4 ...... B	PT59-S3-Q15 C	PT70-S4-Q23 .... D
PT38-S1-Q16 .... D	PT49-S2-Q26 C	PT60-S1-Q21 .... B	PT71-S1-Q23 C
PT38-S4-Q17 .... B	PT49-S4-Q24 .... A	PT60-S3-Q23 C	PT71-S3-Q15 .... A
PT39-S2-Q18 .... A	PT50-S2-Q17 .... A	PT61-S2-Q23 .... D	PT72-S2-Q22 C
PT39-S4-Q26 .... D	PT50-S4-Q24 .... D	PT61-S4-Q26 .... B	PT72-S3-Q25 .... D
PT40-S1-Q20 .... D	PT51-S1-Q20 .... B	PT62-S2-Q7 C	PT73-S2-Q7 C
PT40-S3-Q17 .... A	PT51-S3-Q22 .... B	PT62-S4-Q9 C	PT73-S4-Q18 C
PT41-S1-Q23 .... A	PT52-S1-Q16 .... A	PT63-S1-Q24 .... E	PT74-S1-Q25 .... D
PT41-S3-Q8 ...... B	PT52-S3-Q24 C	PT63-S3-Q25 .... A	PT74-S4-Q25 .... A
PT42-S2-Q24 .... B	PT53-S1-Q21 .... A	PT64-S1-Q9 ...... B	PT75-S1-Q22 C
PT42-S4-Q22 .... A	PT53-S3-Q13 .... B	PT64-S3-Q23 .... E	PT75-S3-Q10 C
PT43-S2-Q24 C	PT54-S2-Q21 .... A	PT65-S1-Q11 .... A	PT75-S3-Q14 .... D
PT43-S3-Q22 .... D	PT54-S4-Q8 C	PT65-S4-Q24 .... A	PT76-S2-Q21 .... B
PT44-S2-Q22 .... E	PT55-S1-Q1 ...... B	PT66-S2-Q24 C	PT76-S4-Q6 ...... D
PT44-S4-Q19 .... B	PT55-S3-Q23 C	PT66-S4-Q24 .... D	PT77-S2-Q5 ...... A
PT45-S1-Q11 C	PT56-S2-Q7 C	PT67-S2-Q23 .... B	PT77-S4-Q25 .... B
PT45-S4-Q20 .... A	PT56-S3-Q14 .... B	PT67-S4-Q25 .... D	
PT46-S2-Q20 .... B	PT57-S2-Q8 ...... E	PT68-S2-Q25 .... B	

Paradox

J07-S2-Q25 C	PTC2-S2-Q4 ...... B	PT5-S1-Q14 ...... A	PT8-S4-Q4 .... A
J07-S3-Q2 .... A	PTC2-S2-Q19 .... E	PT5-S1-Q19 C	PT8-S4-Q19 ...... D
PTA-S1-Q12 ...... A	PTC2-S3-Q15 .... A	PT5-S3-Q13 ...... D	PT9-S2-Q6 C
PTA-S1-Q20 ...... A	PT1-S3-Q1 .... A	PT5-S3-Q20 ...... B	PT9-S2-Q8 .... D
PTA-S1-Q25 ...... E	PT1-S3-Q18 ...... E	PT6-S2-Q8 .... A	PT9-S4-Q3 C
PTA-S4-Q1 C	PT1-S4-Q17 ...... B	PT6-S2-Q12 ...... E	PT10-S1-Q2 ...... E
PTA-S4-Q12 C	PT2-S2-Q4 .... D	PT6-S2-Q16 ...... E	PT10-S1-Q14 .... E
PTB-S1-Q25 ...... E	PT2-S4-Q12 ...... A	PT6-S3-Q6 .... E	PT10-S4-Q17 .... E
PTB-S4-Q2 .... B	PT3-S2-Q8 .... B	PT7-S1-Q11 C	PT10-S4-Q23 .... D
PTC-S2-Q4 .... D	PT3-S4-Q8 .... E	PT7-S1-Q25 ...... D	PT11-S2-Q23 .... A
PTC-S3-Q3 .... E	PT4-S1-Q14 C	PT7-S4-Q17 ...... D	PT11-S4-Q1 ...... D
PTC-S3-Q6 C	PT4-S4-Q2 .... E	PT8-S1-Q1 .... D	PT12-S1-Q4 ...... B
PTC-S3-Q17 ...... E	PT4-S4-Q25 ...... E	PT8-S4-Q2 .... D	PT12-S1-Q7 ...... B

PT12-S1-Q12 .... D	PT21-S3-Q7 ...... D	PT34-S2-Q7 ...... A	PT43-S3-Q13 .... A
PT12-S4-Q12 .... A	PT22-S2-Q21 .... D	PT34-S3-Q2 ...... D	PT43-S3-Q15 .... D
PT12-S4-Q22 C	PT22-S4-Q17 .... D	PT35-S1-Q10 .... B	PT44-S2-Q3 C
PT13-S2-Q3 C	PT23-S2-Q22 .... D	PT35-S1-Q21 .... E	PT44-S2-Q10 .... B
PT13-S2-Q15 .... E	PT23-S3-Q2 C	PT35-S1-Q25 .... D	PT44-S4-Q25 .... D
PT13-S2-Q19 C	PT24-S2-Q18 .... E	PT35-S4-Q4 ...... D	PT45-S4-Q5 ...... A
PT13-S4-Q2 C	PT24-S3-Q14 C	PT35-S4-Q12 C	PT45-S4-Q15 .... A
PT13-S4-Q10 .... D	PT25-S2-Q14 .... A	PT36-S1-Q9 ...... B	PT46-S2-Q6 ...... B
PT13-S4-Q13 .... B	PT25-S2-Q17 .... D	PT36-S1-Q13 C	PT46-S3-Q1 ...... A
PT14-S2-Q1 C	PT25-S4-Q13 .... B	PT36-S1-Q23 .... E	PT47-S1-Q6 ...... B
PT14-S2-Q3 ...... B	PT26-S2-Q14 .... D	PT36-S3-Q1 ...... D	PT47-S3-Q11 C
PT14-S2-Q5 ...... D	PT26-S2-Q18 C	PT37-S2-Q8 ...... A	PT47-S3-Q15 C
PT14-S4-Q1 ...... E	PT26-S3-Q1 ...... B	PT37-S2-Q17 .... E	PT48-S1-Q22 .... E
PT14-S4-Q3 C	PT26-S3-Q18 .... A	PT37-S4-Q5 ...... D	PT48-S4-Q7 C
PT15-S2-Q5 ...... A	PT27-S1-Q7 C	PT38-S1-Q9 ...... E	PT48-S4-Q19 .... D
PT15-S2-Q10 C	PT27-S4-Q8 ...... B	PT38-S4-Q9 C	PT48-S4-Q24 C
PT15-S3-Q20 .... B	PT28-S1-Q8 C	PT39-S2-Q3 ...... A	PT49-S2-Q2 ...... E
PT16-S2-Q1 ...... B	PT28-S1-Q17 .... D	PT39-S2-Q5 ...... A	PT49-S4-Q11 .... A
PT16-S2-Q4 ...... E	PT28-S3-Q3 ...... E	PT39-S4-Q5 C	PT49-S4-Q25 .... B
PT16-S2-Q15 .... E	PT29-S1-Q4 ...... D	PT39-S4-Q9 ...... E	PT50-S2-Q5 ...... B
PT16-S3-Q10 .... A	PT29-S1-Q10 .... D	PT39-S4-Q12 C	PT50-S2-Q8 ...... A
PT16-S3-Q17 .... A	PT29-S1-Q25 .... B	PT40-S1-Q1 C	PT50-S2-Q21 .... E
PT17-S2-Q14 C	PT29-S4-Q19 .... B	PT40-S3-Q1 ...... B	PT50-S4-Q16 C
PT17-S3-Q2 ...... D	PT30-S2-Q12 .... E	PT40-S3-Q7 C	PT51-S1-Q3 ...... B
PT18-S2-Q11 .... B	PT30-S4-Q5 ...... A	PT41-S1-Q2 ...... B	PT51-S1-Q22 ... B
PT18-S2-Q19 .... B	PT31-S2-Q11 .... E	PT41-S1-Q4 ...... B	PT51-S3-Q8 ...... D
PT18-S2-Q22 .... B	PT31-S2-Q13 C	PT41-S1-Q8 ...... D	PT51-S3-Q10 .... E
PT18-S4-Q13 .... A	PT31-S3-Q2 ...... D	PT41-S3-Q1 ...... A	PT52-S1-Q11 C
PT18-S4-Q15 .... A	PT31-S3-Q7 ...... B	PT41-S3-Q5 ...... E	PT52-S1-Q14 C
PT19-S2-Q5 ...... D	PT32-S1-Q2 C	PT41-S3-Q21 .... D	PT52-S3-Q20 .... E
PT19-S4-Q20 C	PT32-S4-Q5 ...... A	PT42-S2-Q5 ...... B	PT52-S3-Q22 .... E
PT19-S4-Q23 .... D	PT32-S4-Q17 .... E	PT42-S4-Q5 ...... A	PT53-S1-Q24 .... D
PT20-S1-Q18 C	PT33-S1-Q8 ...... E	PT42-S4-Q11 .... B	PT53-S3-Q22 .... B
PT20-S4-Q26 .... B	PT33-S1-Q14 .... B	PT42-S4-Q24 C	PT54-S2-Q4 ...... E
PT21-S2-Q2 C	PT33-S3-Q1 ...... B	PT43-S2-Q3 ...... E	PT54-S4-Q6 C
PT21-S2-Q4 ...... D	PT33-S3-Q3 ...... B	PT43-S2-Q15 .... D	PT54-S4-Q13 .... A
PT21-S3-Q3 ...... E	PT34-S2-Q5 ...... B	PT43-S2-Q25 C	PT54-S4-Q21 C

PT55-S1-Q13 .... D	PT61-S2-Q12 .... A	PT66-S4-Q15 .... B	PT72-S3-Q1 C
PT55-S3-Q1 ...... B	PT61-S2-Q19 .... D	PT66-S4-Q18 .... E	PT72-S3-Q5 C
PT56-S2-Q13 .... A	PT61-S2-Q25 .... D	PT67-S2-Q2 ...... A	PT73-S2-Q2 ...... E
PT56-S2-Q22 C	PT61-S4-Q12 C	PT67-S2-Q4 ...... B	PT73-S2-Q24 .... D
PT56-S3-Q7 ...... E	PT61-S4-Q14 .... A	PT67-S4-Q3 C	PT73-S4-Q15 .... A
PT57-S2-Q3 ...... D	PT62-S2-Q20 C	PT67-S4-Q23 .... B	PT73-S4-Q22 .... D
PT57-S3-Q1 ...... A	PT62-S4-Q7 C	PT68-S2-Q3 ...... B	PT74-S1-Q9 ...... E
PT57-S3-Q4 ...... B	PT62-S4-Q17 .... D	PT68-S2-Q6 ...... D	PT74-S1-Q15 .... E
PT57-S3-Q7 C	PT62-S4-Q26 .... D	PT68-S3-Q6 ...... A	PT74-S4-Q9 ...... B
PT58-S1-Q8 ...... E	PT63-S1-Q4 ...... D	PT68-S3-Q14 .... B	PT75-S1-Q6 ...... D
PT58-S1-Q17 .... B	PT63-S3-Q8 ...... B	PT69-S1-Q15 C	PT75-S1-Q19 .... B
PT58-S4-Q1 ...... E	PT63-S3-Q12 .... A	PT69-S4-Q5 ...... E	PT75-S3-Q5 ...... A
PT58-S4-Q7 ...... A	PT63-S3-Q26 .... A	PT70-S1-Q5 ...... E	PT76-S2-Q7 C
PT58-S4-Q20 .... E	PT64-S1-Q6 ...... E	PT70-S1-Q12 .... E	PT76-S2-Q11 .... A
PT59-S2-Q11 .... B	PT64-S3-Q8 ...... D	PT70-S4-Q7 C	PT76-S2-Q20 .... E
PT59-S3-Q1 ...... A	PT64-S3-Q13 .... A	PT70-S4-Q13 .... E	PT76-S4-Q3 ...... D
PT59-S3-Q4 C	PT65-S1-Q12 C	PT71-S1-Q20 C	PT76-S4-Q25 C
PT59-S3-Q17 .... A	PT65-S4-Q1 C	PT71-S3-Q3 ...... B	PT77-S2-Q19 .... B
PT60-S1-Q5 C	PT65-S4-Q10 .... D	PT71-S3-Q26 .... E	PT77-S4-Q3 ...... E
PT60-S1-Q9 ...... D	PT66-S2-Q23 .... B	PT72-S2-Q9 ...... D	PT77-S4-Q21 .... B
PT60-S3-Q1 ...... A	PT66-S4-Q10 .... A	PT72-S2-Q11 C	

Principle (Identify)

J07-S2-Q24 .... A	PTC2-S2-Q6 ...... B	PT7-S4-Q5 .... A	PT12-S4-Q13 C
J07-S3-Q6 .... B	PTC2-S3-Q19 .... D	PT8-S1-Q20 ...... B	PT12-S4-Q18 .... E
J07-S3-Q14 C	PT1-S3-Q3 .... E	PT8-S4-Q7 .... E	PT13-S2-Q16 C
J07-S3-Q24 .... E	PT1-S3-Q24 ...... E	PT8-S4-Q16 C	PT13-S4-Q22 .... A
PTA-S1-Q15 ...... B	PT2-S4-Q1 C	PT8-S4-Q22 ...... D	PT15-S2-Q1 ...... A
PTA-S4-Q13 ...... E	PT3-S4-Q6 .... A	PT9-S4-Q11 ...... D	PT15-S2-Q13 .... E
PTB-S1-Q14 C	PT4-S1-Q11 C	PT9-S4-Q21 ...... E	PT15-S3-Q6 ...... E
PTB-S1-Q24 ...... D	PT4-S4-Q13 ...... D	PT10-S1-Q23 .... D	PT16-S2-Q12 .... B
PTB-S4-Q7 .... E	PT4-S4-Q22 ...... D	PT10-S4-Q6 ...... D	PT16-S3-Q23 .... D
PTB-S4-Q12 ...... A	PT5-S1-Q4 .... A	PT10-S4-Q15 .... B	PT17-S2-Q3 C
PTB-S4-Q24 C	PT5-S1-Q18 ...... B	PT11-S2-Q6 ...... E	PT17-S3-Q8 ...... A
PTC-S2-Q8 .... A	PT5-S1-Q21 ...... E	PT11-S2-Q10 .... D	PT17-S3-Q23 C
PTC-S2-Q24 ...... B	PT5-S3-Q21 C	PT11-S4-Q6 ...... B	PT18-S4-Q1 ...... B
PTC-S3-Q22 ...... D	PT6-S3-Q25 ...... E	PT12-S1-Q5 ...... D	PT18-S4-Q16 C

PT19-S2-Q10 .... B	PT31-S3-Q26 .... B	PT46-S2-Q3 ...... B	PT55-S3-Q17 .... A
PT20-S1-Q5 ...... E	PT32-S1-Q3 ...... D	PT46-S2-Q5 ...... A	PT56-S2-Q16 .... D
PT20-S4-Q12 .... B	PT32-S4-Q8 C	PT46-S3-Q8 ...... D	PT56-S2-Q20 .... E
PT20-S4-Q24 .... B	PT33-S1-Q18 .... A	PT46-S3-Q14 .... B	PT56-S3-Q3 ...... B
PT21-S2-Q16 .... E	PT33-S1-Q21 C	PT47-S1-Q3 C	PT56-S3-Q12 .... A
PT21-S3-Q15 .... E	PT33-S3-Q6 C	PT47-S1-Q7 ...... A	PT57-S2-Q1 ...... A
PT21-S3-Q17 .... D	PT34-S2-Q20 .... D	PT47-S3-Q26 .... D	PT57-S2-Q10 .... B
PT22-S4-Q15 C	PT34-S3-Q1 C	PT48-S1-Q9 ...... D	PT57-S3-Q16 C
PT23-S2-Q13 .... A	PT34-S3-Q16 .... E	PT48-S1-Q11 .... E	PT57-S3-Q19 .... D
PT23-S3-Q5 ...... A	PT35-S1-Q2 ...... D	PT48-S1-Q18 .... D	PT58-S1-Q4 ...... E
PT24-S2-Q9 C	PT35-S4-Q11 .... B	PT48-S4-Q6 ...... A	PT58-S1-Q23 C
PT24-S2-Q22 .... D	PT36-S1-Q15 .... D	PT49-S2-Q15 C	PT58-S4-Q16 .... B
PT24-S2-Q25 .... A	PT36-S3-Q20 .... B	PT49-S4-Q9 ...... E	PT58-S4-Q25 .... A
PT24-S3-Q20 .... B	PT37-S2-Q18 .... A	PT49-S4-Q21 C	PT59-S2-Q13 C
PT24-S3-Q26 .... B	PT37-S2-Q22 .... B	PT50-S2-Q12 .... A	PT59-S2-Q23 .... D
PT25-S2-Q8 ...... A	PT37-S2-Q24 .... E	PT50-S2-Q25 .... D	PT59-S3-Q18 .... D
PT25-S2-Q11 .... D	PT37-S4-Q21 .... B	PT50-S4-Q3 ...... B	PT60-S1-Q18 .... E
PT25-S2-Q23 C	PT38-S1-Q3 ...... E	PT50-S4-Q18 .... D	PT60-S1-Q23 .... E
PT25-S2-Q24 .... E	PT38-S4-Q4 ...... A	PT50-S4-Q20 .... E	PT60-S3-Q9 C
PT25-S2-Q25 .... D	PT39-S2-Q19 .... E	PT51-S3-Q5 ...... A	PT60-S3-Q24 .... B
PT25-S4-Q5 ...... A	PT39-S4-Q14 .... A	PT51-S3-Q7 ...... B	PT61-S2-Q5 ...... A
PT25-S4-Q14 .... D	PT40-S1-Q18 .... B	PT51-S3-Q13 .... B	PT61-S2-Q21 .... E
PT26-S2-Q2 ...... B	PT40-S3-Q9 C	PT52-S1-Q8 C	PT61-S4-Q1 ...... E
PT26-S2-Q23 C	PT41-S1-Q17 C	PT52-S1-Q19 .... E	PT61-S4-Q23 .... D
PT27-S1-Q24 .... D	PT41-S1-Q19 .... E	PT52-S3-Q1 ...... D	PT62-S2-Q1 ...... D
PT28-S1-Q4 C	PT41-S3-Q14 .... B	PT52-S3-Q11 .... B	PT62-S2-Q23 C
PT28-S3-Q18 C	PT42-S4-Q15 .... B	PT52-S3-Q18 .... D	PT62-S2-Q26 .... E
PT29-S1-Q19 .... A	PT43-S2-Q21 .... E	PT53-S1-Q5 ...... E	PT62-S4-Q2 ...... D
PT29-S1-Q22 .... D	PT43-S3-Q3 ...... B	PT53-S3-Q12 .... B	PT62-S4-Q15 .... D
PT29-S4-Q7 C	PT43-S3-Q7 ...... D	PT53-S3-Q18 .... E	PT63-S3-Q3 ...... E
PT29-S4-Q17 .... A	PT43-S3-Q11 .... D	PT54-S2-Q8 ...... A	PT63-S3-Q23 C
PT30-S2-Q5 ...... B	PT43-S3-Q26 .... E	PT54-S2-Q18 C	PT64-S1-Q12 .... D
PT30-S2-Q19 C	PT44-S2-Q17 C	PT54-S4-Q9 ...... A	PT65-S1-Q24 C
PT30-S4-Q23 C	PT44-S4-Q2 ...... B	PT55-S1-Q6 ...... A	PT65-S4-Q5 ...... B
PT31-S2-Q22 .... D	PT44-S4-Q4 ...... A	PT55-S1-Q10 .... B	PT65-S4-Q18 .... B
PT31-S2-Q24 .... E	PT44-S4-Q13 .... D	PT55-S1-Q21 .... B	PT65-S4-Q23 .... B
PT31-S3-Q4 ...... E	PT45-S4-Q3 ...... E	PT55-S3-Q6 ...... D	PT66-S2-Q7 ...... D

PT66-S2-Q9 ...... A	PT69-S1-Q6 ...... A	PT72-S3-Q13 C	PT75-S1-Q2 C
PT66-S2-Q12 .... B	PT69-S4-Q17 .... D	PT72-S3-Q17 .... D	PT75-S1-Q10 .... E
PT66-S4-Q2 C	PT70-S1-Q14 .... D	PT72-S3-Q21 .... E	PT75-S3-Q3 C
PT66-S4-Q11 .... B	PT70-S1-Q23 .... E	PT73-S2-Q6 ...... D	PT76-S2-Q6 ...... D
PT67-S2-Q8 ...... E	PT70-S4-Q1 ...... A	PT73-S4-Q2 ...... D	PT76-S2-Q23 .... E
PT67-S2-Q15 C	PT70-S4-Q15 C	PT73-S4-Q7 ...... E	PT76-S4-Q2 ...... B
PT67-S2-Q18 .... D	PT71-S3-Q6 ...... D	PT74-S1-Q3 ...... B	PT76-S4-Q9 C
PT67-S4-Q7 ...... E	PT71-S3-Q9 ...... D	PT74-S1-Q7 ...... E	PT77-S2-Q8 ...... A
PT68-S2-Q16 C	PT71-S3-Q13 .... E	PT74-S4-Q5 ...... D	PT77-S2-Q16 .... B
PT68-S3-Q1 C	PT72-S2-Q1 ...... D	PT74-S4-Q12 .... D	PT77-S4-Q1 ...... A
PT68-S3-Q12 .... B	PT72-S2-Q6 C	PT74-S4-Q21 .... A	

Principle (Apply)

J07-S2-Q7 .... D	PT28-S3-Q23 .... D	PT46-S2-Q21 .... A	PT58-S1-Q21 C
J07-S3-Q1 C	PT29-S4-Q10 C	PT46-S3-Q12 C	PT58-S4-Q4 C
PTB-S4-Q10 ...... D	PT32-S4-Q3 ...... A	PT47-S1-Q5 ...... A	PT59-S3-Q6 ...... B
PTC-S3-Q16 C	PT32-S4-Q18 .... E	PT47-S1-Q24 C	PT60-S3-Q18 C
PTC2-S2-Q12 .... D	PT33-S1-Q16 C	PT47-S3-Q18 C	PT60-S3-Q20 .... A
PTC2-S2-Q14 .... B	PT35-S1-Q7 C	PT47-S3-Q22 .... D	PT61-S2-Q2 ...... E
PT3-S4-Q24 ...... E	PT36-S1-Q5 ...... A	PT48-S1-Q4 ...... B	PT61-S4-Q19 .... E
PT6-S2-Q24 C	PT36-S1-Q17 .... E	PT48-S4-Q16 C	PT62-S2-Q13 .... D
PT9-S2-Q18 ...... E	PT36-S3-Q15 .... A	PT49-S2-Q3 C	PT62-S2-Q18 .... D
PT13-S4-Q16 C	PT38-S1-Q7 ...... D	PT50-S2-Q1 ...... B	PT63-S1-Q18 .... E
PT14-S4-Q2 ...... D	PT38-S4-Q7 ...... B	PT50-S2-Q23 .... E	PT63-S3-Q22 .... A
PT15-S2-Q21 .... E	PT38-S4-Q23 .... D	PT51-S1-Q9 ...... E	PT64-S1-Q24 .... E
PT16-S2-Q8 ...... E	PT39-S2-Q11 .... D	PT51-S1-Q17 C	PT64-S3-Q2 ...... E
PT17-S2-Q15 .... A	PT39-S4-Q24 .... E	PT52-S1-Q22 .... D	PT64-S3-Q18 .... B
PT18-S4-Q19 .... B	PT41-S1-Q14 .... D	PT52-S3-Q25 .... A	PT64-S3-Q20 C
PT22-S2-Q18 .... B	PT42-S2-Q9 ...... A	PT53-S1-Q17 .... B	PT65-S1-Q6 ...... A
PT22-S4-Q7 C	PT42-S2-Q21 C	PT53-S3-Q25 C	PT65-S1-Q14 .... B
PT23-S3-Q24 .... D	PT42-S4-Q8 ...... D	PT54-S4-Q17 .... E	PT66-S4-Q14 .... E
PT24-S3-Q24 .... D	PT43-S3-Q5 ...... E	PT55-S1-Q11 .... E	PT66-S4-Q16 C
PT26-S3-Q23 .... B	PT44-S2-Q12 .... A	PT55-S1-Q16 .... B	PT67-S2-Q25 C
PT26-S3-Q25 .... B	PT45-S1-Q9 ...... E	PT56-S2-Q18 C	PT67-S4-Q8 ...... D
PT27-S4-Q1 C	PT45-S4-Q2 ...... B	PT56-S3-Q23 .... E	PT68-S2-Q5 ...... A
PT27-S4-Q3 ...... A	PT45-S4-Q21 .... E	PT57-S3-Q14 .... D	PT69-S1-Q8 C
PT28-S1-Q10 .... D	PT46-S2-Q15 C	PT58-S1-Q2 ...... D	PT69-S1-Q18 .... E

PT69-S4-Q6 ...... D	PT72-S3-Q19 .... D	PT75-S3-Q12 .... B	PT77-S2-Q21 .... A
PT70-S1-Q6 C	PT73-S2-Q4 ...... D	PT76-S2-Q14 .... E	PT77-S4-Q17 .... B
PT71-S1-Q19 .... A	PT73-S4-Q23 .... E	PT76-S2-Q26 .... E	
PT71-S1-Q25 .... D	PT74-S1-Q10 .... E	PT76-S4-Q11 .... B	
PT71-S3-Q22 .... B	PT74-S4-Q23 .... E	PT77-S2-Q12 .... B	

Except

J07-S2-Q19 .... A	PT9-S4-Q8 C	PT25-S2-Q19 .... B	PT32-S1-Q20 .... B
J07-S3-Q2 .... A	PT10-S1-Q9 ...... D	PT25-S4-Q11 .... D	PT32-S4-Q15 .... A
PTB-S1-Q16 ...... D	PT10-S1-Q19 .... D	PT25-S4-Q15 .... E	PT33-S1-Q8 ...... E
PTB-S1-Q19 ...... D	PT10-S4-Q23 .... D	PT25-S4-Q16 .... D	PT33-S1-Q16 C
PTB-S4-Q2 .... B	PT12-S1-Q25 .... B	PT26-S2-Q17 .... B	PT33-S1-Q20 C
PTB-S4-Q21 C	PT13-S2-Q25 .... A	PT26-S2-Q19 .... B	PT33-S1-Q22 .... B
PTC-S3-Q1 .... E	PT13-S4-Q14 .... E	PT26-S2-Q22 C	PT33-S3-Q3 ...... B
PTC-S3-Q3 .... E	PT13-S4-Q21 .... D	PT26-S3-Q20 .... B	PT34-S3-Q2 ...... D
PTC-S3-Q6 C	PT14-S2-Q5 ...... D	PT27-S1-Q25 .... B	PT34-S3-Q22 .... E
PTC-S3-Q17 ...... E	PT14-S2-Q24 .... D	PT27-S4-Q16 .... D	PT35-S1-Q10 .... B
PTC-S3-Q18 ...... D	PT18-S2-Q5 ...... D	PT28-S1-Q1 ...... A	PT35-S1-Q15 .... E
PT1-S3-Q10 C	PT18-S2-Q23 .... E	PT28-S1-Q11 .... A	PT35-S4-Q1 ...... B
PT1-S4-Q4 C	PT18-S4-Q23 .... B	PT28-S1-Q23 .... A	PT35-S4-Q17 .... E
PT1-S4-Q17 ...... B	PT20-S1-Q7 ...... E	PT28-S1-Q26 .... E	PT35-S4-Q22 .... A
PT1-S4-Q20 ...... D	PT20-S1-Q20 C	PT28-S3-Q4 ...... A	PT36-S1-Q23 .... E
PT2-S2-Q22 ...... A	PT20-S4-Q5 ...... D	PT28-S3-Q12 C	PT37-S2-Q8 ...... A
PT2-S4-Q3 .... E	PT20-S4-Q23 .... D	PT28-S3-Q20 .... B	PT37-S2-Q17 .... E
PT2-S4-Q10 ...... D	PT20-S4-Q26 .... B	PT29-S1-Q3 C	PT37-S2-Q20 .... B
PT3-S2-Q20 C	PT22-S2-Q8 ...... A	PT29-S1-Q13 .... E	PT37-S4-Q13 .... D
PT3-S4-Q10 ...... E	PT22-S2-Q19 .... A	PT29-S1-Q25 .... B	PT38-S4-Q5 ...... B
PT4-S1-Q24 ...... E	PT22-S4-Q15 C	PT29-S4-Q19 .... B	PT38-S4-Q7 ...... B
PT4-S4-Q9 .... B	PT23-S2-Q26 .... D	PT29-S4-Q20 .... A	PT38-S4-Q9 C
PT4-S4-Q24 ...... D	PT23-S3-Q15 .... B	PT30-S2-Q12 .... E	PT38-S4-Q25 .... D
PT4-S4-Q25 ...... E	PT24-S2-Q4 C	PT30-S2-Q19 C	PT39-S2-Q24 .... B
PT6-S2-Q7 .... E	PT24-S2-Q7 ...... A	PT30-S4-Q5 ...... A	PT39-S4-Q13 .... D
PT6-S2-Q12 ...... E	PT24-S2-Q19 .... E	PT30-S4-Q7 ...... B	PT39-S4-Q22 .... D
PT6-S3-Q3 .... D	PT24-S2-Q20 .... B	PT31-S2-Q8 ...... B	PT40-S3-Q2 C
PT7-S1-Q19 C	PT24-S3-Q14 C	PT31-S2-Q13 C	PT40-S3-Q7 C
PT8-S4-Q19 ...... D	PT24-S3-Q22 C	PT31-S3-Q12 C	PT40-S3-Q19 ... D
PT9-S2-Q17 ...... B	PT25-S2-Q17 .... D	PT32-S1-Q17 .... D	PT40-S3-Q26 .... B

PT41-S3-Q2 ...... E

PT41-S3-Q5 ...... E

PT41-S3-Q10 .... A

PT41-S3-Q15 .... E

PT41-S3-Q16 C

PT41-S3-Q19 .... E

PT42-S4-Q9 ...... B

PT43-S2-Q8 C

PT43-S3-Q2 ...... E

PT43-S3-Q15 .... D

PT43-S3-Q17 .... E

PT44-S2-Q8 ...... E

PT44-S4-Q17 .... D

PT44-S4-Q18 .... B

PT45-S4-Q11 C

PT45-S4-Q15 .... A

PT47-S3-Q11 C

PT47-S3-Q15 C

PT48-S4-Q23 .... D

PT49-S2-Q4 ...... B

PT49-S2-Q11 C

PT49-S2-Q16 .... D

PT49-S2-Q21 .... B

PT49-S4-Q4 ...... E

PT49-S4-Q25 .... B

PT50-S2-Q5 ...... B

PT50-S2-Q24 .... A

PT52-S1-Q11 C

PT52-S1-Q18 .... B

PT53-S1-Q1 C

PT53-S1-Q24 .... D

PT53-S3-Q13 .... B

PT53-S3-Q22 .... B

PT55-S1-Q25 C

PT55-S3-Q6 ...... D

PT56-S3-Q22 .... B

PT58-S1-Q8 ...... E

PT59-S3-Q17 .... A

PT61-S2-Q19 .... D

PT61-S2-Q22 C

PT61-S4-Q3 ...... A

PT62-S2-Q18 .... D

PT62-S4-Q17 .... D

PT62-S4-Q26 .... D

PT63-S1-Q7 ...... B

PT65-S1-Q3 ...... B

PT65-S4-Q19 .... B

PT66-S2-Q3 ...... D

PT67-S2-Q4 ...... B

PT70-S1-Q11 .... B

PT71-S3-Q16 .... B

PT71-S3-Q21 .... A

PT75-S3-Q22 .... A

PT77-S2-Q25 .... D

PT77-S4-Q21 .... B

Reading Comprehension Answers

Humanities

J07-S4-P1
1. E
2. D
3. A
4. E
5. D
6. B
7. A
8. A

PTA-S2-P2
9. B
10. D
11. D
12. C
13. D

PTB-S3-P4
22. B
23. D
24. E
25. D
26. C

PTC2-S4-P2
7. A
8. C
9. D
10. E
11. C
12. B

PT1-S1-P1
1. C
2. E
3. D
4. D
5. A
6. E
7. D
8. B

PT2-S1-P1
1. C
2. B
3. D
4. B
5. A
6. D

PT3-S3-P4
21. E
22. A
23. C
24. D
25. D
26. C
27. B
28. B

PT4-S2-P4
21. B
22. C
23. C
24. A
25. D
26. D
27. E

PT5-S4-P4
22. C
23. E
24. B
25. E
26. C
27. C

PT6-S1-P3
13. D
14. A
15. D
16. B
17. B
18. D
19. D
20. C

PT7-S3-P2
8. D
9. A
10. B
11. C
12. C
13. E
14. D

PT8-S3-P3
14. D
15. E
16. B
17. D
18. A
19. C
20. B

PT9-S1-P1
1. B
2. A
3. D
4. E
5. C
6. E

PT10-S3-P2
9. B
10. C
11. B
12. E
13. A
14. C

PT11-S3-P1
1. D
2. E
3. B
4. E
5. D
6. C
7. C

PT12-S3-P1
1. D
2. E
3. B
4. C
5. B
6. E
7. E

PT13-S3-P3
14. E
15. D
16. E
17. B
18. C
19. A
20. D

PT14-S3-P2
7. A
8. E
9. C
10. B
11. C
12. B
13. D

PT15-S1-P2
8. E
9. E
10. C
11. B
12. A
13. A
14. D
15. B

PT16-S4-P1
1. B
2. D
3. C
4. C
5. C
6. E
7. B
8. A

PT17-S4-P1
1. E
2. B
3. C
4. E
5. C
6. B
7. C
8. B

PT18-S3-P4
22. B
23. E
24. D
25. C
26. B
27. B
28. E

PT19-S3-P1
1. A
2. E
3. B
4. E
5. A
6. D
7. D
8. C

PT20-S2-P1
1. B
2. E
3. A
4. E
5. D
6. B

PT21-S4-P1
1. B
2. E
3. D
4. A
5. B
6. B
7. E
8. B

PT22-S1-P1
1. C
2. B
3. A
4. B
5. C
6. E
7. C
8. D

PT23-S4-P1
1. D
2. D
3. E
4. D
5. A

PT24-S1-P4
21. C
22. D
23. C
24. E
25. C
26. E
27. D

PT25-S1-P2
8. C
9. B
10. A
11. C
12. D
13. A

PT26-S4-P2
6. E
7. B
8. B
9. D
10. D
11. C
12. A
13. E

PT27-S3-P4
22. B
23. C
24. C
25. A
26. E

PT28-S4-P4
22. A
23. C
24. D
25. B
26. D

PT29-S2-P1
1. B
2. D
3. D
4. B
5. A
6. E
7. E

PT30-S3-P2
7. C
8. C
9. D
10. C
11. E
12. D
13. B
14. C

PT31-S4-P4
21. D
22. B
23. B
24. B
25. A
26. A
27. D
28. E

PT32-S2-P3
14. D
15. A
16. E
17. C
18. A
19. B

PT33-S2-P2
8. A
9. D
10. E
11. A
12. C
13. B
14. C

PT34-S1-P2
7. E
8. E
9. C
10. A
11. B
12. E

PT35-S2-P2
7. B
8. C
9. A
10. B
11. D
12. A
13. D
14. A

PT36-S2-P2
7. E
8. B
9. D
10. D
11. C
12. C
13. E
14. D

PT37-S1-P3
14. A
15. A
16. E
17. E
18. C
19. C
20. D
21. B

PT38-S3-P4
21. A
22. D
23. E
24. D
25. E
26. C
27. E

PT39-S3-P1
1. B
2. D
3. C
4. D
5. C
6. A
7. E
8. E

PT40-S4-P2
6. B
7. A
8. C
9. D
10. B
11. D
12. C

PT41-S4-P2
7. B
8. E
9. C
10. A
11. B
12. A
13. E

PT42-S3-P2
8. B
9. E
10. A
11. E
12. D
13. B
14. A
15. B

PT43-S1-P3
14. E
15. E
16. B
17. A
18. D
19. B
20. B
21. A

PT44-S1-P4
21. A
22. A
23. C
24. E
25. D
26. B
27. A

PT45-S2-P2
7. B
8. E
9. D
10. A
11. E
12. B
13. C
14. E

PT46-S1-P2
8. A
9. *
10. E
11. A
12. B
13. E
14. C
15. C

PT47-S2-P2
6. E
7. C
8. B
9. D
10. A
11. E

PT48-S3-P2
6. D
7. E
8. C
9. A
10. C
11. E
12. D

PT49-S3-P2
7. A
8. E
9. E
10. E
11. D
12. B
13. C

PT50-S1-P1
1. C
2. D
3. C
4. B
5. D

PT51-S2-P1
1. B
2. B
3. E
4. A
5. C
6. A
7. D

PT52-S4-P1
1. E
2. E
3. A
4. D
5. C
6. A

PT53-S4-P1
1. A
2. C
3. D
4. C
5. D
6. D

PT54-S1-P3
13. C
14. D
15. C
16. E
17. E
18. A
19. A

PT55-S2-P3
14. A
15. D
16. C
17. B
18. D
19. D
20. B
21. A

PT56-S4-P1
1. B
2. D
3. A
4. D
5. E
6. A
7. C

PT57-S4-P3
13. E
14. C
15. C
16. A
17. E
18. E
19. B

PT58-S2-P4
21. E
22. C
23. B
24. A
25. C
26. B
27. D

PT59-S4-P3
16. C
17. D
18. D
19. C
20. E
21. B
22. A

PT60-S4-P3
13. C
14. E
15. A
16. D
17. D
18. C
19. C
20. B

PT61-S1-P2
7. C
8. A
9. E
10. C
11. B
12. E
13. B

PT62-S1-P4
22. D
23. C
24. B
25. E
26. E
27. C

PT63-S4-P2
8. B
9. A
10. C
11. A
12. C
13. C
14. B
15. D

PT64-S4-P4
20. E
21. B
22. A
23. C
24. C
25. C
26. A
27. D

PT65-S3-P1
1. B
2. D
3. E
4. A
5. B
6. A
7. D

PT66-S1-P3
15. E
16. B
17. B
18. D
19. C
20. A
21. D
22. E

PT67-S1-P1
1. B
2. A
3. A
4. C
5. E
6. D
7. D

PT67-S1-P2
8. E
9. C
10. C
11. D
12. E
13. A
14. B

PT68-S1-P1
1. E
2. C
3. E
4. B
5. A
6. C
7. E

PT69-S3-P2
8. A
9. B
10. E
11. C
12. D
13. B
14. A

PT70-S2-P2
8. E
9. C
10. C
11. D
12. E
13. D
14. D

PT71-S4-P1
1. A
2. E
3. D
4. B
5. E
6. D

PT72-S1-P2
7. B
8. B
9. C
10. A
11. C
12. D
13. B

PT73-S1-P2
8. B
9. A
10. D
11. C
12. E
13. E
14. B
15. B

PT74-S3-P1
1. D
2. E
3. A
4. A
5. B
6. B
7. B
8. D

PT76-S1-P1
1. C
2. B
3. D
4. A
5. D
6. A

PT77-S1-P1
1. C
2. A
3. C
4. D
5. B
6. E
7. C

Law

J07-S4-P3
15. A
16. A
17. E
18. C
19. B
20. E
21. D
22. D

PTA-S2-P1
1. B
2. D
3. B
4. A
5. E
6. C
7. D
8. C

PTB-S3-P2
8. E
9. A
10. B
11. C
12. B
13. E
14. A

PTC-S4-P2
8. E
9. D
10. B
11. D
12. B
13. D
14. B
15. E

PTC2-S4-P4
20. A
21. B
22. A
23. B
24. D
25. D
26. E
27. D

PT1-S1-P3
17. A
18. E
19. B
20. D
21. B

PT2-S1-P4
22. B
23. E
24. B
25. B
26. C
27. A
28. D

PT3-S3-P3
16. E
17. E
18. D
19. B
20. A

PT4-S2-P1
1. B
2. C
3. A
4. C
5. C
6. D

PT5-S4-P1
1. A
2. D
3. D
4. E
5. E
6. C
7. D
8. A

PT6-S1-P1
1. E
2. C
3. A
4. E
5. B
6. D

PT7-S3-P4
21. C
22. C
23. D
24. E
25. B
26. B
27. D

PT8-S3-P2
7. A
8. D
9. B
10. A
11. B
12. C
13. C

PT9-S1-P4
21. C
22. D
23. C
24. C
25. E
26. C
27. E

PT10-S3-P3
15. E
16. E
17. B
18. A
19. D
20. D
21. D

PT12-S3-P3
14. C
15. E
16. E
17. D
18. A
19. C
20. A

PT13-S3-P4
21. A
22. D
23. D
24. C
25. B
26. A
27. E

PT14-S3-P3
14. C
15. B
16. C
17. C
18. A
19. D
20. E

PT15-S1-P4
22. E
23. B
24. C
25. C
26. A
27. D

PT16-S4-P2
9. E
10. A
11. C
12. B
13. D
14. E
15. B

PT17-S4-P2
9. C
10. C
11. D
12. D
13. B
14. B
15. E

PT18-S3-P1
1. A
2. E
3. A
4. C
5. B
6. A
7. A

PT19-S3-P2
9. C
10. E
11. D
12. B
13. A
14. D

PT20-S2-P2
7. C
8. A
9. B
10. C
11. A
12. B
13. B
14. C

PT21-S4-P2
9. A
10. B
11. B
12. D
13. E
14. D
15. C
16. A

PT22-S1-P2
9. C
10. A
11. A
12. D
13. D
14. B
15. B
16. A

PT23-S4-P2
6. C
7. E
8. B
9. C
10. E
11. D
12. A
13. B

PT24-S1-P3
14. D
15. B
16. E
17. A
18. A
19. D
20. A

PT25-S1-P1
1. D
2. B
3. A
4. D
5. B
6. C
7. D

PT26-S4-P4
22. C
23. E
24. B
25. A
26. C
27. D

PT27-S3-P1
1. E
2. A
3. B
4. C
5. C
6. B
7. E

PT28-S4-P1
1. C
2. E
3. E
4. D
5. B

PT29-S2-P4
22. D
23. D
24. D
25. A
26. C
27. A

PT30-S3-P3
15. E
16. B
17. D
18. E
19. A
20. A
21. C

PT31-S4-P2
6. C
7. D
8. B
9. B
10. B
11. A
12. C

PT32-S2-P1
1. D
2. E
3. A
4. C
5. B
6. A
7. B

PT33-S2-P4
23. B
24. B
25. A
26. B
27. A
28. D

PT35-S2-P4
21. B
22. D
23. A
24. E
25. E
26. D

PT36-S2-P4
21. D
22. C
23. D
24. C
25. E
26. A

PT37-S1-P1
1. E
2. D
3. A
4. C
5. A
6. C
7. D

PT38-S3-P2
9. D
10. A
11. E
12. B
13. D
14. C

PT39-S3-P4
24. B
25. A
26. B
27. C
28. A

PT40-S4-P4
20. B
21. E
22. A
23. D
24. E
25. A
26. E
27. D

PT41-S4-P1
1. A
2. E
3. C
4. D
5. B
6. D

PT42-S3-P1
1. B
2. D
3. A
4. C
5. B
6. E
7. D

PT43-S1-P4
22. D
23. A
24. B
25. D
26. E
27. A
28. E

PT44-S1-P1
1. E
2. D
3. E
4. D
5. C
6. A
7. A

PT45-S2-P4
20. C
21. B
22. C
23. E
24. B
25. A
26. E
27. C

PT46-S1-P4
22. E
23. D
24. C
25. A
26. E
27. C

PT47-S2-P3
12. D
13. A
14. A
15. E
16. B
17. C
18. C

PT48-S3-P3
13. B
14. C
15. E
16. D
17. D
18. A
19. C

PT49-S3-P1
1. A
2. D
3. E
4. B
5. C
6. E

PT50-S1-P2
6. A
7. D
8. A
9. E
10. A
11. B
12. D
13. E

PT51-S2-P4
21. A
22. A
23. B
24. E
25. D
26. C
27. C
28. B

PT52-S4-P4
20. C
21. A
22. B
23. A
24. B
25. C
26. D
27. D

PT53-S4-P2
7. D
8. A
9. C
10. E
11. D
12. B
13. B
14. A

PT54-S1-P1
1. A
2. C
3. D
4. D
5. E

PT55-S2-P1
1. D
2. A
3. A
4. B
5. E
6. E

PT57-S4-P1
1. A
2. A
3. D
4. C
5. E

PT58-S2-P3
14. B
15. A
16. B
17. A
18. E
19. C
20. D

PT59-S4-P2
9. C
10. E
11. B
12. A
13. E
14. B
15. A

PT60-S4-P4
21. B
22. A
23. E
24. C
25. B
26. D
27. B

PT61-S1-P1
1. D
2. B
3. B
4. D
5. E
6. A

PT62-S1-P2
9. A
10. E
11. E
12. D
13. C
14. B

PT63-S4-P1
1. A
2. C
3. E
4. B
5. A
6. E
7. C

PT64-S4-P1
1. D
2. B
3. E
4. B
5. A
6. C

PT65-S3-P3
14. C
15. B
16. A
17. A
18. E
19. D

PT66-S1-P2
8. D
9. B
10. A
11. C
12. E
13. C
14. B

PT67-S1-P4
20. A
21. E
22. B
23. B
24. A
25. D
26. C
27. E

PT68-S1-P4
23. C
24. D
25. D
26. B
27. E

PT69-S3-P3
15. C
16. B
17. E
18. B
19. A
20. D
21. D

PT70-S2-P4
21. B
22. C
23. D
24. B
25. E
26. B
27. C

PT72-S1-P4
22. C
23. E
24. D
25. D
26. B
27. B

PT73-S1-P4
22. B
23. A
24. D
25. E
26. D
27. A

PT74-S3-P2
9. C
10. B
11. D
12. A
13. D
14. E
15. A
16. D

PT75-S2-P2
8. B
9. A
10. A
11. C
12. B
13. C
14. E

PT76-S1-P2
7. D
8. B
9. B
10. C
11. B
12. D
13. D

PT77-S1-P2
8. E
9. D
10. C
11. E
12. A
13. A

Natural Sciences

J07-S4-P4
23. A
24. B
25. D
26. E
27. C

PTA-S2-P3
14. E
15. A
16. E
17. C
18. C
19. D
20. A

PTB-S3-P1
1. D
2. B
3. D
4. E
5. A
6. C
7. C

PTC-S4-P1
1. E
2. A
3. D
4. B
5. B
6. A
7. D

PTC-S4-P4
21. C
22. C
23. D
24. B
25. B
26. C
27. D

PTC2-S4-P3
13. B
14. C
15. D
16. B
17. A
18. E
19. B

PT1-S1-P2
9. B
10. E
11. A
12. B
13. A
14. A
15. B
16. C

PT2-S1-P3
14. D
15. D
16. A
17. A
18. B
19. E
20. C
21. A

PT3-S3-P1
1. E
2. D
3. A
4. C
5. D
6. C
7. C

PT4-S2-P2
7. E
8. E
9. D
10. B
11. B
12. A
13. C

PT5-S4-P3
16. B
17. E
18. E
19. C
20. B
21. A

PT7-S3-P3
15. B
16. D
17. C
18. E
19. A
20. D

PT8-S3-P1
1. D
2. A
3. D
4. A
5. E
6. B

PT10-S3-P1
1. A
2. D
3. B
4. E
5. C
6. B
7. E
8. D

PT11-S3-P3
15. C
16. C
17. D
18. A
19. E
20. E
21. E

PT12-S3-P4
21. D
22. A
23. B
24. A
25. E
26. C
27. E

PT13-S3-P1
1. A
2. D
3. B
4. C
5. D
6. A
7. C
8. C

PT14-S3-P1
1. C
2. E
3. A
4. B
5. D
6. D

PT15-S1-P1
1. C
2. A
3. D
4. A
5. D
6. B
7. B

PT16-S4-P3
16. C
17. E
18. A
19. E
20. E
21. D

PT17-S4-P4
22. B
23. B
24. D
25. A
26. D
27. E

PT18-S3-P2
8. C
9. A
10. C
11. E
12. B
13. D
14. A
15. D

PT19-S3-P3
15. C
16. E
17. A
18. E
19. D
20. B

PT20-S2-P3
15. B
16. A
17. B
18. A
19. E
20. D
21. B

PT21-S4-P3
17. D
18. B
19. A
20. B
21. C

PT22-S1-P4
22. D
23. A
24. B
25. B
26. A

PT23-S4-P3
14. D
15. A
16. E
17. C
18. D

PT24-S1-P1
1. B
2. A
3. C
4. D
5. E
6. B

PT25-S1-P4
22. D
23. A
24. E
25. B
26. B

PT26-S4-P3
14. D
15. E
16. A
17. A
18. E
19. E
20. C
21. D

PT27-S3-P3
15. B
16. B
17. A
18. C
19. B
20. D
21. C

PT28-S4-P2
6. D
7. E
8. D
9. D
10. A
11. C
12. C
13. C

PT29-S2-P3
16. B
17. B
18. E
19. C
20. C
21. B

PT30-S3-P1
1. C
2. D
3. D
4. E
5. E
6. C

PT31-S4-P3
13. C
14. A
15. E
16. D
17. A
18. A
19. E
20. C

PT32-S2-P4
20. E
21. D
22. A
23. A
24. C
25. D
26. C
27. D

PT33-S2-P3
15. C
16. B
17. A
18. D
19. A
20. A
21. C
22. C

PT34-S1-P3
13. E
14. C
15. E
16. B
17. D
18. C

PT35-S2-P3
15. B
16. D
17. E
18. C
19. C
20. E

PT36-S2-P3
15. D
16. C
17. B
18. A
19. A
20. B

PT37-S1-P2
8. B
9. D
10. A
11. A
12. C
13. A

PT38-S3-P1
1. C
2. A
3. E
4. B
5. D
6. A
7. D
8. A

PT39-S3-P3
17. D
18. E
19. A
20. E
21. D
22. B
23. D

PT40-S4-P3
13. C
14. B
15. D
16. D
17. A
18. B
19. A

PT42-S3-P4
21. D
22. B
23. E
24. D
25. C
26. D

PT44-S1-P3
15. B
16. A
17. C
18. E
19. A
20. D

PT45-S2-P3
15. D
16. B
17. C
18. A
19. E

PT46-S1-P3
16. A
17. D
18. C
19. D
20. B
21. E

PT47-S2-P4
19. E
20. D
21. D
22. B
23. E
24. A
25. B
26. C

PT48-S3-P4
20. C
21. C
22. D
23. A
24. E
25. A
26. E
27. B

PT49-S3-P4
21. A
22. B
23. B
24. D
25. D
26. E
27. A

PT50-S1-P4
22. B
23. D
24. C
25. E
26. C
27. D
28. B

PT51-S2-P2
8. E
9. B
10. D
11. C
12. B
13. A

PT52-S4-P3
13. C
14. E
15. *
16. D
17. E
18. B
19. A

PT53-S4-P4
20. C
21. D
22. E
23. A
24. C
25. D
26. E
27. A

PT54-S1-P2
6. B
7. E
8. E
9. B
10. B
11. C
12. A

PT55-S2-P2
7. A
8. E
9. B
10. E
11. A
12. C
13. A

PT56-S4-P2
8. A
9. C
10. D
11. A
12. A
13. B
14. E
15. C

PT57-S4-P4
20. B
21. C
22. D
23. D
24. E
25. A
26. E
27. D

PT58-S2-P2
8. D
9. C
10. A
11. B
12. A
13. E

PT59-S4-P1
1. C
2. C
3. E
4. B
5. C
6. B
7. A
8. E

PT60-S4-P2
8. C
9. A
10. D
11. D
12. C

PT61-S1-P3
14. B
15. A
16. D
17. D
18. C
19. B

PT62-S1-P1
1. A
2. C
3. E
4. B
5. B
6. E
7. D
8. D

PT62-S1-P3
15. A
16. B
17. A
18. B
19. D
20. C
21. D

PT63-S4-P3
16. C
17. D
18. A
19. C
20. B
21. A

PT64-S4-P3
13. E
14. B
15. C
16. A
17. E
18. D
19. C

PT65-S3-P4
20. A
21. E
22. B
23. D
24. E
25. B
26. C
27. B

PT66-S1-P4
23. B
24. D
25. A
26. B
27. E

PT67-S1-P3
15. D
16. E
17. E
18. B
19. D

PT68-S1-P2
8. C
9. A
10. B
11. A
12. B
13. A
14. D

PT69-S3-P4
22. B
23. A
24. D
25. A
26. E
27. C

PT70-S2-P1
1. B
2. A
3. E
4. C
5. B
6. A
7. E

PT71-S4-P3
14. D
15. E
16. A
17. A
18. C
19. D

PT71-S4-P4
20. A
21. B
22. B
23. E
24. D
25. C
26. B
27. C

PT72-S1-P1
1. D
2. E
3. C
4. A
5. B
6. D

PT73-S1-P1
1. A
2. B
3. D
4. B
5. A
6. E
7. C

PT74-S3-P3
17. B
18. A
19. B
20. C
21. C

PT75-S2-P4
21. E
22. B
23. A
24. D
25. B
26. B
27. C

PT76-S1-P4
20. C
21. C
22. C
23. D
24. B
25. A
26. B
27. E

PT77-S1-P4
20. B
21. C
22. D
23. B
24. E
25. B
26. A
27. E

Social Sciences

J07-S4-P2
9. C
10. B
11. D
12. C
13. E
14. A

PTA-S2-P4
21. B
22. C
23. D
24. D
25. C
26. C
27. D

PTB-S3-P3
15. B
16. A
17. E
18. E
19. A
20. B
21. B

PTC-S4-P3
16. E
17. A
18. A
19. A
20. B

PTC2-S4-P1
1. D
2. B
3. E
4. E
5. D
6. A

PT1-S1-P4
22. E
23. D
24. C
25. D
26. E
27. B
28. C

PT2-S1-P2
7. E
8. B
9. B
10. E
11. C
12. D
13. A

PT3-S3-P2
8. C
9. E
10. C
11. D
12. A
13. D
14. A
15. D

PT4-S2-P3
14. D
15. C
16. B
17. D
18. A
19. E
20. B

PT5-S4-P2
9. C
10. C
11. C
12. B
13. E
14. B
15. D

PT6-S1-P2
7. E
8. D
9. A
10. A
11. D
12. D

PT6-S1-P4
21. C
22. A
23. C
24. E
25. E
26. A
27. E

PT7-S3-P1
1. E
2. D
3. C
4. B
5. D
6. A
7. A

PT8-S3-P4
21. C
22. D
23. A
24. E
25. B
26. D
27. E

PT9-S1-P2
7. C
8. A
9. A
10. C
11. B
12. A
13. B

PT9-S1-P3
14. B
15. D
16. C
17. A
18. D
19. B
20. B

PT10-S3-P4
22. B
23. D
24. E
25. B
26. A
27. E

PT11-S3-P2
8. A
9. E
10. B
11. A
12. B
13. E
14. D

PT11-S3-P4
22. B
23. B
24. E
25. B
26. D
27. D

PT12-S3-P2
8. E
9. C
10. D
11. E
12. A
13. A

PT13-S3-P2
9. E
10. B
11. A
12. D
13. D

PT14-S3-P4
21. A
22. B
23. C
24. C
25. A
26. D
27. D

PT15-S1-P3
16. C
17. C
18. D
19. B
20. D
21. A

PT16-S4-P4
22. C
23. D
24. C
25. A
26. A
27. B

PT17-S4-P3
16. B
17. A
18. A
19. B
20. C
21. E

PT18-S3-P3
16. B
17. D
18. E
19. C
20. D
21. B

PT19-S3-P4
21. B
22. A
23. D
24. C
25. B
26. A
27. C

PT20-S2-P4
22. D
23. E
24. E
25. B
26. E

PT21-S4-P4
22. C
23. B
24. B
25. A
26. A
27. B

PT22-S1-P3
17. A
18. B
19. B
20. A
21. C

PT23-S4-P4
19. C
20. E
21. C
22. D
23. B
24. C
25. A
26. B

PT24-S1-P2
7. D
8. C
9. B
10. A
11. C
12. B
13. C

PT25-S1-P3
14. C
15. A
16. A
17. E
18. E
19. C
20. B
21. C

PT26-S4-P1
1. E
2. A
3. A
4. E
5. B

PT27-S3-P2
8. E
9. B
10. E
11. D
12. A
13. D
14. D

PT28-S4-P3
14. D
15. A
16. E
17. B
18. C
19. C
20. D
21. B

PT29-S2-P2
8. D
9. A
10. A
11. C
12. C
13. B
14. A
15. B

PT30-S3-P4
22. A
23. B
24. D
25. C
26. B
27. C

PT31-S4-P1
1. D
2. D
3. D
4. C
5. D

PT32-S2-P2
8. E
9. B
10. C
11. B
12. D
13. A

PT33-S2-P1
1. C
2. A
3. E
4. B
5. E
6. A
7. B

PT34-S1-P1
1. E
2. C
3. D
4. B
5. D
6. E

PT34-S1-P4
19. D
20. C
21. D
22. D
23. A
24. E
25. C
26. A

PT35-S2-P1
1. C
2. D
3. D
4. A
5. C
6. A

PT36-S2-P1
1. D
2. C
3. E
4. E
5. C
6. B

PT37-S1-P4
22. A
23. C
24. B
25. D
26. C

PT38-S3-P3
15. D
16. E
17. B
18. A
19. E
20. C

PT39-S3-P2
9. D
10. A
11. C
12. E
13. D
14. E
15. D
16. B

PT40-S4-P1
1. E
2. D
3. A
4. C
5. D

PT41-S4-P3
14. D
15. A
16. B
17. C
18. B
19. D
20. A

PT41-S4-P4
21. D
22. D
23. A
24. D
25. E
26. A

PT42-S3-P3
16. E
17. A
18. D
19. B
20. C

PT43-S1-P1
1. D
2. E
3. C
4. B
5. E

PT43-S1-P2
6. E
7. A
8. D
9. C
10. D
11. E
12. B
13. A

PT44-S1-P2
8. C
9. C
10. E
11. E
12. D
13. B
14. B

PT45-S2-P1
1. D
2. B
3. D
4. C
5. A
6. E

PT46-S1-P1
1. B
2. C
3. D
4. A
5. E
6. D
7. D

PT47-S2-P1
1. D
2. B
3. E
4. D
5. A

PT48-S3-P1
1. A
2. D
3. E
4. B
5. C

PT49-S3-P3
14. A
15. E
16. A
17. B
18. D
19. D
20. C

PT50-S1-P3
14. E
15. C
16. A
17. D
18. C
19. D
20. A
21. D

PT51-S2-P3
14. C
15. B
16. C
17. D
18. E
19. B
20. A

PT52-S4-P2
7. D
8. B
9. A
10. C
11. B
12. D

PT53-S4-P3
15. A
16. C
17. D
18. C
19. D

PT54-S1-P4
20. A
21. C
22. C
23. B
24. E
25. E
26. A
27. B

PT55-S2-P4
22. D
23. D
24. B
25. B
26. C
27. D

PT56-S4-P3
16. E
17. C
18. D
19. E
20. A
21. B

PT56-S4-P4
22. C
23. E
24. A
25. B
26. E
27. C

PT57-S4-P2
6. E
7. C
8. D
9. B
10. D
11. C
12. B

PT58-S2-P1
1. B
2. E
3. E
4. D
5. C
6. E
7. A

PT59-S4-P4
23. B
24. D
25. D
26. C
27. D

PT60-S4-P1
1. D
2. C
3. D
4. B
5. D
6. E
7. A

PT61-S1-P4
20. D
21. E
22. A
23. E
24. E
25. B
26. A
27. B

PT63-S4-P4
22. B
23. C
24. B
25. B
26. D
27. E

PT64-S4-P2
7. B
8. A
9. E
10. B
11. D
12. D

PT65-S3-P2
8. A
9. C
10. A
11. B
12. D
13. E

PT66-S1-P1
1. E
2. D
3. A
4. B
5. A
6. C
7. B

PT68-S1-P3
15. E
16. E
17. B
18. C
19. D
20. B
21. C
22. E

PT69-S3-P1
1. A
2. B
3. C
4. A
5. D
6. D
7. B

PT70-S2-P3
15. B
16. C
17. A
18. D
19. D
20. E

PT71-S4-P2
7. B
8. B
9. C
10. D
11. A
12. A
13. D

PT72-S1-P3
14. B
15. D
16. C
17. D
18. D
19. A
20. C
21. A

PT73-S1-P3
16. C
17. B
18. E
19. A
20. E
21. A

PT74-S3-P4
22. E
23. A
24. B
25. B
26. D
27. E

PT75-S2-P1
1. C
2. A
3. B
4. C
5. A
6. D
7. E

PT75-S2-P3
15. C
16. A
17. D
18. C
19. E
20. B

PT76-S1-P3
14. B
15. E
16. C
17. C
18. B
19. E

PT77-S1-P3
14. B
15. C
16. A
17. D
18. B
19. E

Comparative Passages

J07-S4-P2
9. C
10. B
11. D
12. C
13. E
14. A

PTC2-S4-P4
20. A
21. B
22. A
23. B
24. D
25. D
26. E
27. D

PT52-S4-P2
7. D
8. B
9. A
10. C
11. B
12. D

PT53-S4-P3
15. A
16. C
17. D
18. C
19. D

PT54-S1-P2
6. B
7. E
8. E
9. B
10. B
11. C
12. A

PT55-S2-P2
7. A
8. E
9. B
10. E
11. A
12. C
13. A

PT56-S4-P3
16. E
17. C
18. D
19. E
20. A
21. B

PT57-S4-P3
13. E
14. C
15. C
16. A
17. E
18. E
19. B

PT58-S2-P4
21. E
22. C
23. B
24. A
25. C
26. B
27. D

PT59-S4-P1
1. C
2. C
3. E
4. B
5. C
6. B
7. A
8. E

PT60-S4-P2
8. C
9. A
10. D
11. D
12. C

PT61-S1-P3
14. B
15. A
16. D
17. D
18. C
19. B

PT62-S1-P3
15. A
16. B
17. A
18. B
19. D
20. C
21. D

PT63-S4-P4
22. B
23. C
24. B
25. B
26. D
27. E

PT64-S4-P3
13. E
14. B
15. C
16. A
17. E
18. D
19. C

PT65-S3-P3
14. C
15. B
16. A
17. A
18. E
19. D

PT66-S1-P2
8. D
9. B
10. A
11. C
12. E
13. C
14. B

PT67-S1-P3
15. D
16. E
17. E
18. B
19. D

PT68-S1-P4
23. C
24. D
25. D
26. B
27. E

PT69-S3-P3
15. C
16. B
17. E
18. B
19. A
20. D
21. D

PT70-S2-P3
15. B
16. C
17. A
18. D
19. D
20. E

PT71-S4-P2
7. B
8. B
9. C
10. D
11. A
12. A
13. D

PT72-S1-P4
22. C
23. E
24. D
25. D
26. B
27. B

PT73-S1-P4
22. B
23. A
24. D
25. E
26. D
27. A

PT74-S3-P3
17. B
18. A
19. B
20. C
21. C

PT75-S2-P3
15. C
16. A
17. D
18. C
19. E
20. B

PT76-S1-P4
20. C
21. C
22. C
23. D
24. B
25. A
26. B
27. E

PT77-S1-P3
14. B
15. C
16. A
17. D
18. B
19. E

June 2007 PrepTest

Section 1: Logic Games

1   Simple Ordering – Limited Solutions
2   Undetermined Assignment
3   Simple Ordering – Limited Allocations
4   Undetermined Assignment

Section 2: Logical Reasoning A

1   Main Conclusion
2   Parallel (Flaw)
3   Complete the Passage
4   Flaw
5   Weaken
6   Sufficient Assumption
7   Principle (Apply)
8   Complete the Passage
9   Weaken
10   Main Conclusion
11   Method (Statement)
12   Parallel (Reasoning)
13   Sufficient Assumption
14   Weaken
15   Sufficient Assumption
16   Point
17   Flaw
18   Most Strongly Supported
19   Strengthen – Except
20   Method (Argument)
21   Flaw
22   Most Strongly Supported
23   Sufficient Assumption
24   Principle (Identify)
25   Paradox

Section 3: Logical Reasoning B

1   Principle (Apply)
2   Paradox – Except
3   Point
4   Flaw
5   Sufficient Assumption
6   Principle (Identify)
7   Point
8   Flaw
9   Necessary Assumption
10   Complete the Passage
11   Necessary Assumption
12   Main Conclusion
13   Strengthen
14   Principle (Identify)
15   Weaken
16   Complete the Passage
17   Necessary Assumption
18   Flaw
19   Strengthen
20   Parallel (Flaw)
21   Weaken
22   Must Be True
23   Flaw
24   Principle (Identify)
25   Flaw

Section 4: Reading Comprehension

1   Humanities
2   Social Sciences – Comparative
3   Law
4   Natural Sciences

PrepTest A (February 1996)

Section 1: Logical Reasoning A

1   Most Strongly Supported
2   Flaw
3   Most Strongly Supported
4   Flaw
5   Necessary Assumption
6   Point
7   Method (Argument)
8   Most Strongly Supported
9   Main Conclusion
10   Flaw

11	Necessary Assumption		19	Must Be True
12	Paradox		20	Paradox
13	Method (Argument)		21	Flaw
14	Parallel (Reasoning)		22	Parallel (Flaw)
15	Principle (Identify)		23	Cannot Be True
16	Weaken		24	Sufficient Assumption
17	Strengthen		25	Paradox
18	Method (Argument)			

Section 2: Reading Comprehension

1	Law		3	Natural Sciences
2	Humanities		4	Social Sciences

Section 3: Logic Games

1	Simple Ordering		3	Complex Ordering
2	Determined Assignment		4	Undetermined Assignment

Section 4: Logical Reasoning B

1	Paradox		14	Parallel (Flaw)
2	Main Conclusion		15	Method (Statement)
3	Strengthen		16	Most Strongly Supported
4	Method (Argument)		17	Necessary Assumption
5	Strengthen		18	Point
6	Most Strongly Supported		19	Necessary Assumption
7	Strengthen		20	Flaw
8	Necessary Assumption		21	Method (Statement)
9	Method (Statement)		22	Must Be True
10	Weaken		23	Parallel (Reasoning)
11	Flaw		24	Must Be True
12	Paradox		25	Flaw
13	Principle (Identify)			

PrepTest B (February 1999)

Section 1: Logical Reasoning A

1	Main Conclusion		14	Principle (Identify)
2	Method (Statement)		15	Point
3	Strengthen		16	Weaken – Except
4	Weaken		17	Most Strongly Supported
5	Flaw		18	Necessary Assumption
6	Must Be True		19	Strengthen – Except
7	Strengthen		20	Most Strongly Supported
8	Necessary Assumption		21	Necessary Assumption
9	Sufficient Assumption		22	Parallel (Flaw)
10	Flaw		23	Necessary Assumption
11	Method (Statement)		24	Principle (Identify)
12	Parallel (Reasoning)		25	Paradox
13	Method (Argument)		26	Flaw

Section 2: Logic Games

1	Relative Ordering		2	In/Out Grouping

PrepTest C (February 2000)

Section 1: Logic Games

Section 2: Logical Reasoning A

Section 3: Logical Reasoning B

19	Flaw	23	Most Strongly Supported
20	Point	24	Parallel (Reasoning)
21	Weaken	25	Method (Argument)
22	Principle (Identify)	26	Point

Section 4: Reading Comprehension

1	Natural Sciences	3	Social Sciences
2	Law	4	Natural Sciences

PrepTest C2 (0 0)

Section 1: Logic Games

1	Determined Assignment – Limited Scenarios	3	Undetermined Assignment – Limited Scenarios
2	Simple Ordering – Limited Scenarios	4	Determined Assignment

Section 2: Logical Reasoning A

1	Strengthen	14	Principle (Apply)
2	Most Strongly Supported	15	Sufficient Assumption
3	Flaw	16	Point
4	Paradox	17	Weaken
5	Complete the Passage	18	Parallel (Flaw)
6	Principle (Identify)	19	Paradox
7	Weaken	20	Sufficient Assumption
8	Method (Statement)	21	Most Strongly Supported
9	Flaw	22	Flaw
10	Necessary Assumption	23	Parallel (Reasoning)
11	Strengthen	24	Point
12	Principle (Apply)	25	Flaw
13	Main Conclusion		

Section 3: Logical Reasoning B

1	Strengthen	14	Flaw
2	Main Conclusion	15	Paradox
3	Parallel (Reasoning)	16	Main Conclusion
4	Point	17	Necessary Assumption
5	Weaken	18	Flaw
6	Flaw	19	Principle (Identify)
7	Weaken	20	Necessary Assumption
8	Method (Argument)	21	Most Strongly Supported
9	Flaw	22	Necessary Assumption
10	Method (Statement)	23	Parallel (Flaw)
11	Sufficient Assumption	24	Flaw
12	Flaw	25	Necessary Assumption
13	Must Be True		

Section 4: Reading Comprehension

1	Social Sciences
2	Humanities
3	Natural Sciences
4	Law – Comparative

PrepTest 1 (June 1991)

Section 1: Reading Comprehension

1 Humanities
2 Natural Sciences
3 Law
4 Social Sciences

Section 2: Logic Games

1 Miscellaneous
2 Undetermined Assignment – Limited Scenarios
3 Relative Ordering
4 Undetermined Assignment

Section 3: Logical Reasoning A

1 Paradox
2 Parallel (Reasoning)
3 Principle (Identify)
4 Must Be True
5 Weaken
6 Parallel (Reasoning)
7 Must Be True
8 Flaw
9 Weaken
10 Necessary Assumption – Except
11 Most Strongly Supported
12 Flaw
13 Main Conclusion
14 Must Be True
15 Strengthen
16 Must Be True
17 Necessary Assumption
18 Paradox
19 Necessary Assumption
20 Most Strongly Supported
21 Necessary Assumption
22 Flaw
23 Strengthen
24 Principle (Identify)
25 Point

Section 4: Logical Reasoning B

1 Flaw
2 Must Be True
3 Necessary Assumption
4 Strengthen – Except
5 Method (Argument)
6 Must Be True
7 Necessary Assumption
8 Flaw
9 Must Be True
10 Parallel (Flaw)
11 Must Be True
12 Weaken
13 Necessary Assumption
14 Must Be True
15 Weaken
16 Flaw
17 Paradox – Except
18 Most Strongly Supported
19 Main Conclusion
20 Method (Argument) – Except
21 Must Be True
22 Necessary Assumption
23 Strengthen
24 Parallel (Reasoning)

PrepTest 2 (October 1991)

Section 1: Reading Comprehension

1 Humanities
2 Social Sciences
3 Natural Sciences
4 Law

Section 2: Logical Reasoning A

1 Parallel (Reasoning)
2 Flaw
3 Necessary Assumption
4 Paradox
5 Flaw
6 Main Conclusion

7	Weaken	16	Must Be True
8	Method (Argument)	17	Cannot Be True
9	Must Be True	18	Weaken
10	Strengthen	19	Necessary Assumption
11	Must Be True	20	Parallel (Flaw)
12	Method (Argument)	21	Must Be True
13	Must Be True	22	Strengthen – Except
14	Weaken	23	Necessary Assumption
15	Parallel (Reasoning)	24	Must Be True

Section 3: Logic Games

1	Relative Ordering	3	Miscellaneous – Limited Allocations
2	Determined Assignment	4	Complex Ordering

Section 4: Logical Reasoning B

1	Principle (Identify)	14	Strengthen
2	Most Strongly Supported	15	Necessary Assumption
3	Method (Argument) – Except	16	Weaken
4	Flaw	17	Sufficient Assumption
5	Weaken	18	Must Be True
6	Flaw	19	Main Conclusion
7	Strengthen	20	Parallel (Reasoning)
8	Most Strongly Supported	21	Must Be True
9	Necessary Assumption	22	Parallel (Flaw)
10	Strengthen – Except	23	Must Be True
11	Flaw	24	Method (Argument)
12	Paradox	25	Strengthen
13	Point		

PrepTest 3 (December 1991)

Section 1: Logic Games

1	Undetermined Assignment	3	Undetermined Assignment
2	Simple Ordering	4	Determined Assignment

Section 2: Logical Reasoning A

1	Parallel (Reasoning)	18	Main Conclusion
2	Flaw	19	Method (Argument)
3	Necessary Assumption	20	Weaken – Except
4	Must Be True	21	Necessary Assumption
5	Flaw	22	Must Be True
6	Method (Argument)	23	Weaken
7	Must Be True	24	Complete the Passage
8	Paradox	25	Flaw
9	Strengthen		
10	Must Be True		
11	Method (Argument)		
12	Sufficient Assumption		
13	Parallel (Reasoning)		
14	Weaken		
15	Necessary Assumption		
16	Weaken		
17	Strengthen		

Section 3: Reading Comprehension

1	Natural Sciences		3	Law
2	Social Sciences		4	Humanities

Section 4: Logical Reasoning B

1	Most Strongly Supported		13	Must Be True
2	Weaken		14	Cannot Be True
3	Parallel (Reasoning)		15	Flaw
4	Most Strongly Supported		16	Most Strongly Supported
5	Weaken		17	Sufficient Assumption
6	Principle (Identify)		18	Flaw
7	Flaw		19	Necessary Assumption
8	Paradox		20	Method (Statement)
9	Most Strongly Supported		21	Strengthen
10	Must Be True – Except		22	Must Be True
11	Weaken		23	Evaluate
12	Necessary Assumption		24	Principle (Apply)

PrepTest 4 (June 1992)

Section 1: Logical Reasoning A

1	Weaken		13	Weaken
2	Sufficient Assumption		14	Paradox
3	Weaken		15	Must Be True
4	Weaken		16	Flaw
5	Necessary Assumption		17	Most Strongly Supported
6	Method (Argument)		18	Method (Argument)
7	Must Be True		19	Most Strongly Supported
8	Flaw		20	Parallel (Reasoning)
9	Weaken		21	Method (Argument)
10	Necessary Assumption		22	Most Strongly Supported
11	Principle (Identify)		23	Flaw
12	Must Be True		24	Parallel (Flaw) – Except

Section 2: Reading Comprehension

1	Law		3	Social Sciences
2	Natural Sciences		4	Humanities

Section 3: Logic Games

1	Relative Ordering		3	Determined Assignment
2	Undetermined Assignment – Limited Solutions		4	Miscellaneous – Limited Solutions

Section 4: Logical Reasoning B

1	Weaken		7	Must Be True
2	Paradox		8	Weaken
3	Necessary Assumption		9	Must Be True – Except
4	Flaw		10	Necessary Assumption
5	Must Be True		11	Weaken
6	Weaken		12	Flaw

PrepTest 5 (October 1992)

Section 1: Logical Reasoning A

1   Most Strongly Supported
2   Flaw
3   Necessary Assumption
4   Principle (Identify)
5   Weaken
6   Method (Argument)
7   Point
8   Weaken
9   Complete the Passage
10 Weaken
11 Flaw
12 Sufficient Assumption
13 Flaw

14 Paradox
15 Cannot Be True
16 Sufficient Assumption
17 Weaken
18 Principle (Identify)
19 Paradox
20 Parallel (Reasoning)
21 Principle (Identify)
22 Parallel (Flaw)
23 Strengthen
24 Flaw
25 Must Be True

Section 2: Logic Games

1   Determined Assignment
2   Undetermined Assignment

3   In/Out Grouping
4   Complex Ordering

Section 3: Logical Reasoning B

1   Flaw
2   Weaken
3   Main Conclusion
4   Method (Argument)
5   Necessary Assumption
6   Strengthen
7   Necessary Assumption
8   Weaken
9   Flaw
10 Necessary Assumption
11 Flaw
12 Must Be True
13 Paradox

14 Necessary Assumption
15 Parallel (Flaw)
16 Flaw
17 Necessary Assumption
18 Point
19 Method (Argument)
20 Paradox
21 Principle (Identify)
22 Must Be True
23 Must Be True
24 Weaken
25 Parallel (Reasoning)

Section 4: Reading Comprehension

1   Law
2   Social Sciences
3   Natural Sciences
4   Humanities

PrepTest 6 (December 1992)

Section 1: Reading Comprehension

Section 2: Logical Reasoning A

Section 3: Logical Reasoning B

Section 4: Logic Games

PrepTest 7 (June 1993)

Section 1: Logical Reasoning A

17	Flaw
18	Method (Statement)
19	Cannot Be True – Except
20	Parallel (Flaw)
21	Most Strongly Supported

22	Evaluate
23	Strengthen
24	Necessary Assumption
25	Paradox

Section 2: Logic Games

1	Simple Ordering
2	Determined Assignment

3	Grouping (Distribution) – Limited Allocations
4	Complex Ordering – Limited Scenarios

Section 3: Reading Comprehension

1	Social Sciences
2	Humanities

3	Natural Sciences
4	Law

Section 4: Logical Reasoning B

1	Strengthen
2	Main Conclusion
3	Flaw
4	Weaken
5	Principle (Identify)
6	Necessary Assumption
7	Must Be True
8	Evaluate
9	Flaw
10	Most Strongly Supported
11	Flaw
12	Cannot Be True
13	Necessary Assumption

14	Parallel (Flaw)
15	Must Be True
16	Method (Argument)
17	Paradox
18	Complete the Passage
19	Most Strongly Supported
20	Method (Argument)
21	Method (Argument)
22	Flaw
23	Sufficient Assumption
24	Necessary Assumption
25	Parallel (Reasoning)

PrepTest 8 (October 1993)

Section 1: Logical Reasoning A

1	Paradox
2	Necessary Assumption
3	Flaw
4	Method (Argument)
5	Sufficient Assumption
6	Necessary Assumption
7	Weaken
8	Cannot Be True
9	Must Be True
10	Strengthen
11	Weaken
12	Necessary Assumption
13	Weaken

14	Most Strongly Supported
15	Method (Argument)
16	Parallel (Reasoning)
17	Point
18	Method (Argument)
19	Must Be True
20	Principle (Identify)
21	Flaw
22	Most Strongly Supported
23	Flaw
24	Must Be True
25	Parallel (Flaw)

Section 2: Logic Games

1	Determined Assignment
2	Miscellaneous – Limited Solutions
3	Complex Ordering
4	Undetermined Assignment

Section 3: Reading Comprehension

1	Natural Sciences		3	Humanities
2	Law		4	Social Sciences

Section 4: Logical Reasoning B

1	Flaw		14	Weaken
2	Paradox		15	Point
3	Parallel (Flaw)		16	Principle (Identify)
4	Paradox		17	Method (Argument)
5	Must Be True		18	Necessary Assumption
6	Point		19	Paradox – Except
7	Principle (Identify)		20	Flaw
8	Flaw		21	Necessary Assumption
9	Sufficient Assumption		22	Principle (Identify)
10	Necessary Assumption		23	Point
11	Strengthen		24	Weaken
12	Parallel (Reasoning)		25	Weaken
13	Necessary Assumption			

PrepTest 9 (December 1993)

Section 1: Reading Comprehension

1	Humanities		3	Social Sciences
2	Social Sciences		4	Law

Section 2: Logical Reasoning A

1	Parallel (Flaw)		14	Flaw
2	Flaw		15	Method (Argument)
3	Main Conclusion		16	Must Be True
4	Weaken		17	Cannot Be True – Except
5	Flaw		18	Principle (Apply)
6	Paradox		19	Necessary Assumption
7	Weaken		20	Method (Statement)
8	Paradox		21	Necessary Assumption
9	Strengthen		22	Flaw
10	Strengthen		23	Sufficient Assumption
11	Method (Argument)		24	Parallel (Reasoning)
12	Weaken		25	Necessary Assumption
13	Must Be True			

Section 3: Logic Games

1	Undetermined Assignment – Limited Allocations		3	Determined Assignment – Limited Solutions
2	In/Out Grouping		4	Miscellaneous

Section 4: Logical Reasoning B

1	Flaw		5	Flaw
2	Weaken		6	Necessary Assumption
3	Paradox		7	Most Strongly Supported
4	Must Be True		8	Evaluate – Except

9	Method (Argument)	18	Main Conclusion
10	Necessary Assumption	19	Necessary Assumption
11	Principle (Identify)	20	Method (Statement)
12	Sufficient Assumption	21	Principle (Identify)
13	Must Be True	22	Weaken
14	Flaw	23	Must Be True
15	Parallel (Reasoning)	24	Parallel (Flaw)
16	Must Be True	25	Necessary Assumption
17	Strengthen		

PrepTest 10 (June 1994)

Section 1: Logical Reasoning A

1	Necessary Assumption	14	Paradox
2	Paradox	15	Necessary Assumption
3	Necessary Assumption	16	Weaken
4	Method (Argument)	17	Flaw
5	Flaw	18	Must Be True
6	Evaluate	19	Weaken – Except
7	Necessary Assumption	20	Parallel (Flaw)
8	Flaw	21	Flaw
9	Strengthen – Except	22	Most Strongly Supported
10	Flaw	23	Principle (Identify)
11	Main Conclusion	24	Most Strongly Supported
12	Method (Argument)	25	Parallel (Reasoning)
13	Flaw		

Section 2: Logic Games

1	Relative Ordering	3	Miscellaneous
2	Grouping (Distribution) – Limited Scenarios	4	In/Out Grouping

Section 3: Reading Comprehension

1	Natural Sciences	3	Law
2	Humanities	4	Social Sciences

Section 4: Logical Reasoning B

1	Weaken	18	Necessary Assumption
2	Strengthen	19	Flaw
3	Most Strongly Supported	20	Most Strongly Supported
4	Necessary Assumption	21	Flaw
5	Parallel (Flaw)	22	Must Be True
6	Principle (Identify)	23	Paradox – Except
7	Point	24	Complete the Passage
8	Necessary Assumption	25	Method (Argument)
9	Weaken		
10	Most Strongly Supported		
11	Strengthen		
12	Parallel (Reasoning)		
13	Method (Statement)		
14	Flaw		
15	Principle (Identify)		
16	Most Strongly Supported		
17	Paradox		

PrepTest 11 (October 1994)

Section 1: Logic Games

1   Grouping (Distribution)
2   Simple Ordering – Limited Allocations

3   In/Out Grouping
4   Miscellaneous – Limited Solutions

Section 2: Logical Reasoning A

1   Weaken
2   Evaluate
3   Method (Argument)
4   Main Conclusion
5   Necessary Assumption
6   Principle (Identify)
7   Must Be True
8   Method (Argument)
9   Flaw
10   Principle (Identify)
11   Weaken
12   Must Be True
13   Necessary Assumption

14   Method (Argument)
15   Flaw
16   Must Be True
17   Parallel (Flaw)
18   Necessary Assumption
19   Weaken
20   Main Conclusion
21   Weaken
22   Sufficient Assumption
23   Paradox
24   Necessary Assumption
25   Parallel (Reasoning)
26   Flaw

Section 3: Reading Comprehension

1   Humanities
2   Social Sciences

3   Natural Sciences
4   Social Sciences

Section 4: Logical Reasoning B

1   Paradox
2   Point
3   Flaw
4   Most Strongly Supported
5   Weaken
6   Principle (Identify)
7   Necessary Assumption
8   Main Conclusion
9   Flaw
10   Method (Argument)
11   Weaken
12   Method (Argument)

13   Necessary Assumption
14   Most Strongly Supported
15   Necessary Assumption
16   Must Be True
17   Flaw
18   Strengthen
19   Flaw
20   Parallel (Flaw)
21   Weaken
22   Parallel (Reasoning)
23   Flaw
24   Method (Statement)

PrepTest 12 (December 1994)

Section 1: Logical Reasoning A

1   Main Conclusion
2   Necessary Assumption
3   Method (Statement)
4   Paradox
5   Principle (Identify)
6   Method (Argument)
7   Paradox
8   Must Be True
9   Main Conclusion

10   Necessary Assumption
11   Strengthen
12   Paradox
13   Necessary Assumption
14   Flaw
15   Strengthen
16   Weaken
17   Parallel (Flaw)
18   Flaw

19	Strengthen		23	Parallel (Reasoning)
20	Flaw		24	Flaw
21	Must Be True		25	Must Be True – Except
22	Sufficient Assumption		26	Flaw

Section 2: Logic Games

1	Simple Ordering – Limited Scenarios		3	Undetermined Assignment
2	Grouping (Distribution)		4	Miscellaneous – Limited Solutions

Section 3: Reading Comprehension

1	Humanities		3	Law
2	Social Sciences		4	Natural Sciences

Section 4: Logical Reasoning B

1	Most Strongly Supported		13	Principle (Identify)
2	Necessary Assumption		14	Method (Argument)
3	Most Strongly Supported		15	Flaw
4	Weaken		16	Most Strongly Supported
5	Flaw		17	Flaw
6	Necessary Assumption		18	Principle (Identify)
7	Flaw		19	Flaw
8	Necessary Assumption		20	Sufficient Assumption
9	Parallel (Reasoning)		21	Weaken
10	Main Conclusion		22	Paradox
11	Weaken		23	Parallel (Flaw)
12	Paradox		24	Flaw

PrepTest 13 (June 1994)

Section 1: Logic Games

1	Grouping (Distribution)		3	Undetermined Assignment
2	Simple Ordering		4	Miscellaneous

Section 2: Logical Reasoning A

1	Weaken		18	Most Strongly Supported
2	Method (Argument)		19	Paradox
3	Paradox		20	Flaw
4	Most Strongly Supported		21	Weaken
5	Strengthen		22	Evaluate
6	Most Strongly Supported		23	Parallel (Flaw)
7	Flaw		24	Flaw
8	Parallel (Reasoning)		25	Must Be True – Except
9	Complete the Passage		26	Flaw
10	Must Be True			
11	Point			
12	Necessary Assumption			
13	Weaken			
14	Necessary Assumption			
15	Paradox			
16	Principle (Identify)			
17	Method (Argument)			

Section 3: Reading Comprehension

Section 4: Logical Reasoning B

PrepTest 14 (October 1995)

Section 1: Logic Games

Section 2: Logical Reasoning A

Section 3: Reading Comprehension

Section 4: Logical Reasoning B

11	Point	19	Necessary Assumption
12	Most Strongly Supported	20	Flaw
13	Necessary Assumption	21	Most Strongly Supported
14	Parallel (Flaw)	22	Weaken
15	Flaw	23	Sufficient Assumption
16	Method (Argument)	24	Method (Argument)
17	Must Be True	25	Weaken
18	Flaw		

PrepTest 15 (December 1995)

Section 1: Reading Comprehension

1	Natural Sciences	3	Social Sciences
2	Humanities	4	Law

Section 2: Logical Reasoning A

1	Principle (Identify)	13	Principle (Identify)
2	Flaw	14	Method (Statement)
3	Strengthen	15	Most Strongly Supported
4	Parallel (Flaw)	16	Necessary Assumption
5	Paradox	17	Flaw
6	Necessary Assumption	18	Parallel (Reasoning)
7	Weaken	19	Flaw
8	Main Conclusion	20	Flaw
9	Most Strongly Supported	21	Principle (Apply)
10	Paradox	22	Evaluate
11	Main Conclusion	23	Necessary Assumption
12	Must Be True	24	Method (Argument)

Section 3: Logical Reasoning B

1	Main Conclusion	14	Flaw
2	Flaw	15	Method (Argument)
3	Necessary Assumption	16	Evaluate
4	Main Conclusion	17	Method (Argument)
5	Must Be True	18	Sufficient Assumption
6	Principle (Identify)	19	Flaw
7	Must Be True	20	Paradox
8	Strengthen	21	Complete the Passage
9	Flaw	22	Parallel (Flaw)
10	Strengthen	23	Strengthen
11	Method (Statement)	24	Necessary Assumption
12	Necessary Assumption	25	Weaken
13	Parallel (Reasoning)	26	Must Be True

Section 4: Logic Games

1	Simple Ordering
2	Miscellaneous
3	Simple Ordering – Limited Allocations
4	Undetermined Assignment

PrepTest 16 (June 1995)

Section 1: Logic Games

1   Grouping (Distribution)
2   Determined Assignment – Limited Scenarios
3   Undetermined Assignment
4   Miscellaneous

Section 2: Logical Reasoning A

1   Paradox
2   Weaken
3   Must Be True
4   Paradox
5   Weaken
6   Necessary Assumption
7   Parallel (Flaw)
8   Principle (Apply)
9   Must Be True
10 Flaw
11 Most Strongly Supported
12 Principle (Identify)
13 Point
14 Necessary Assumption
15 Paradox
16 Weaken
17 Method (Argument)
18 Strengthen
19 Parallel (Reasoning)
20 Must Be True
21 Strengthen
22 Flaw
23 Method (Argument)
24 Flaw

Section 3: Logical Reasoning B

1   Weaken
2   Flaw
3   Necessary Assumption
4   Point
5   Most Strongly Supported
6   Weaken
7   Method (Argument)
8   Must Be True
9   Flaw
10 Paradox
11 Flaw
12 Necessary Assumption
13 Strengthen
14 Necessary Assumption
15 Parallel (Flaw)
16 Must Be True
17 Paradox
18 Weaken
19 Main Conclusion
20 Method (Argument)
21 Must Be True
22 Parallel (Reasoning)
23 Principle (Identify)
24 Flaw
25 Method (Argument)
26 Flaw

Section 4: Reading Comprehension

1   Humanities
2   Law
3   Natural Sciences
4   Social Sciences

PrepTest 17 (October 1995)

Section 1: Logic Games

1   Simple Ordering
2   Undetermined Assignment
3   Undetermined Assignment
4   Determined Assignment – Limited Solutions

Section 2: Logical Reasoning A

1   Must Be True
2   Flaw
3   Principle (Identify)
4   Method (Argument)
5   Flaw
6   Main Conclusion

7	Strengthen	17	Flaw
8	Weaken	18	Method (Argument)
9	Must Be True	19	Main Conclusion
10	Necessary Assumption	20	Must Be True
11	Flaw	21	Necessary Assumption
12	Necessary Assumption	22	Flaw
13	Weaken	23	Necessary Assumption
14	Paradox	24	Parallel (Reasoning)
15	Principle (Apply)	25	Method (Argument)
16	Parallel (Flaw)		

Section 3: Logical Reasoning B

1	Must Be True	14	Sufficient Assumption
2	Paradox	15	Cannot Be True
3	Necessary Assumption	16	Flaw
4	Method (Argument)	17	Weaken
5	Point	18	Strengthen
6	Strengthen	19	Parallel (Flaw)
7	Flaw	20	Flaw
8	Principle (Identify)	21	Necessary Assumption
9	Flaw	22	Flaw
10	Method (Argument)	23	Principle (Identify)
11	Must Be True	24	Must Be True
12	Strengthen	25	Necessary Assumption
13	Parallel (Reasoning)		

Section 4: Reading Comprehension

1	Humanities	3	Social Sciences
2	Law	4	Natural Sciences

PrepTest 18 (December 1992)

Section 1: Logic Games

1	Grouping (Distribution) – Limited Scenarios	3	Miscellaneous
2	Simple Ordering – Limited Scenarios	4	Miscellaneous

Section 2: Logical Reasoning A

1	Method (Argument)	17	Parallel (Flaw)
2	Strengthen	18	Complete the Passage
3	Must Be True	19	Paradox
4	Flaw	20	Most Strongly Supported
5	Method (Argument) – Except	21	Strengthen
6	Weaken	22	Paradox
7	Method (Argument)	23	Cannot Be True – Except
8	Flaw	24	Weaken
9	Necessary Assumption		
10	Main Conclusion		
11	Paradox		
12	Method (Argument)		
13	Parallel (Reasoning)		
14	Flaw		
15	Necessary Assumption		
16	Strengthen		

Section 3: Reading Comprehension

1	Law	3	Social Sciences
2	Natural Sciences	4	Humanities

Section 4: Logical Reasoning B

1	Principle (Identify)	14	Weaken
2	Main Conclusion	15	Paradox
3	Parallel (Flaw)	16	Principle (Identify)
4	Complete the Passage	17	Flaw
5	Method (Statement)	18	Necessary Assumption
6	Must Be True	19	Principle (Apply)
7	Weaken	20	Parallel (Reasoning)
8	Necessary Assumption	21	Method (Argument)
9	Flaw	22	Necessary Assumption
10	Must Be True	23	Weaken – Except
11	Flaw	24	Most Strongly Supported
12	Sufficient Assumption	25	Flaw
13	Paradox		

PrepTest 19 (June 1996)

Section 1: Logic Games

1	Simple Ordering	3	Grouping (Distribution)
2	Determined Assignment – Limited Scenarios	4	Grouping (Distribution)

Section 2: Logical Reasoning A

1	Flaw	13	Necessary Assumption
2	Necessary Assumption	14	Flaw
3	Most Strongly Supported	15	Necessary Assumption
4	Weaken	16	Point
5	Paradox	17	Must Be True
6	Method (Argument)	18	Sufficient Assumption
7	Flaw	19	Complete the Passage
8	Method (Argument)	20	Parallel (Reasoning)
9	Necessary Assumption	21	Strengthen
10	Principle (Identify)	22	Parallel (Flaw)
11	Method (Argument)	23	Flaw
12	Weaken	24	Most Strongly Supported

Section 3: Reading Comprehension

1	Humanities	3	Natural Sciences
2	Law	4	Social Sciences

Section 4: Logical Reasoning B

1	Flaw	6	Flaw
2	Method (Argument)	7	Strengthen
3	Flaw	8	Necessary Assumption
4	Necessary Assumption	9	Weaken
5	Flaw	10	Weaken

11	Sufficient Assumption		19	Most Strongly Supported
12	Most Strongly Supported		20	Paradox
13	Cannot Be True		21	Parallel (Flaw)
14	Necessary Assumption		22	Evaluate
15	Strengthen		23	Paradox
16	Point		24	Parallel (Reasoning)
17	Method (Statement)		25	Method (Argument)
18	Method (Argument)		26	Weaken

PrepTest 20 (October 1996)

Section 1: Logical Reasoning A

1	Most Strongly Supported		14	Flaw
2	Weaken		15	Flaw
3	Necessary Assumption		16	Necessary Assumption
4	Weaken		17	Parallel (Flaw)
5	Principle (Identify)		18	Paradox
6	Most Strongly Supported		19	Parallel (Reasoning)
7	Must Be True – Except		20	Necessary Assumption – Except
8	Method (Argument)		21	Method (Argument)
9	Strengthen		22	Flaw
10	Flaw		23	Most Strongly Supported
11	Necessary Assumption		24	Must Be True
12	Weaken		25	Method (Argument)
13	Point			

Section 2: Reading Comprehension

1	Humanities		3	Natural Sciences
2	Law		4	Social Sciences

Section 3: Logic Games

1	Determined Assignment		3	Miscellaneous
2	In/Out Grouping		4	Complex Ordering

Section 4: Logical Reasoning B

1	Necessary Assumption		19	Must Be True
2	Flaw		20	Parallel (Flaw)
3	Weaken		21	Point
4	Method (Argument)		22	Flaw
5	Strengthen – Except		23	Weaken – Except
6	Must Be True		24	Principle (Identify)
7	Evaluate		25	Weaken
8	Necessary Assumption		26	Paradox – Except
9	Method (Statement)			
10	Most Strongly Supported			
11	Necessary Assumption			
12	Principle (Identify)			
13	Complete the Passage			
14	Flaw			
15	Parallel (Reasoning)			
16	Necessary Assumption			
17	Weaken			
18	Flaw			

PrepTest 21 (December 1996)

Section 1: Logic Games

1	Determined Assignment – Limited Scenarios	3	Determined Assignment – Limited Scenarios
2	Miscellaneous	4	Undetermined Assignment

Section 2: Logical Reasoning A

1	Main Conclusion	14	Main Conclusion
2	Paradox	15	Parallel (Flaw)
3	Necessary Assumption	16	Principle (Identify)
4	Paradox	17	Weaken
5	Flaw	18	Must Be True
6	Necessary Assumption	19	Necessary Assumption
7	Weaken	20	Sufficient Assumption
8	Must Be True	21	Parallel (Flaw)
9	Method (Argument)	22	Flaw
10	Must Be True	23	Strengthen
11	Necessary Assumption	24	Method (Argument)
12	Method (Argument)	25	Flaw
13	Most Strongly Supported		

Section 3: Logical Reasoning B

1	Must Be True	14	Method (Argument)
2	Main Conclusion	15	Principle (Identify)
3	Paradox	16	Most Strongly Supported
4	Necessary Assumption	17	Principle (Identify)
5	Flaw	18	Most Strongly Supported
6	Necessary Assumption	19	Flaw
7	Paradox	20	Method (Argument)
8	Necessary Assumption	21	Weaken
9	Strengthen	22	Parallel (Reasoning)
10	Main Conclusion	23	Weaken
11	Evaluate	24	Must Be True
12	Most Strongly Supported	25	Parallel (Flaw)
13	Necessary Assumption		

Section 4: Reading Comprehension

1	Humanities	3	Natural Sciences
2	Law	4	Social Sciences

PrepTest 22 (June 1997)

Section 1: Reading Comprehension

1	Humanities	3	Social Sciences
2	Law	4	Natural Sciences

Section 2: Logical Reasoning A

1	Necessary Assumption	3	Method (Argument)
2	Main Conclusion	4	Weaken

5	Most Strongly Supported		16	Parallel (Reasoning)
6	Flaw		17	Most Strongly Supported
7	Flaw		18	Principle (Apply)
8	Weaken – Except		19	Necessary Assumption – Except
9	Strengthen		20	Flaw
10	Flaw		21	Paradox
11	Method (Argument)		22	Most Strongly Supported
12	Flaw		23	Parallel (Flaw)
13	Method (Argument)		24	Flaw
14	Necessary Assumption		25	Flaw
15	Most Strongly Supported			

Section 3: Logic Games

1	Grouping (Distribution)		3	Undetermined Assignment
2	Complex Ordering – Limited Scenarios		4	Undetermined Assignment

Section 4: Logical Reasoning B

1	Flaw		14	Most Strongly Supported
2	Sufficient Assumption		15	Principle (Identify) – Except
3	Point		16	Necessary Assumption
4	Must Be True		17	Paradox
5	Sufficient Assumption		18	Flaw
6	Parallel (Flaw)		19	Weaken
7	Principle (Apply)		20	Parallel (Reasoning)
8	Strengthen		21	Flaw
9	Flaw		22	Necessary Assumption
10	Point		23	Method (Argument)
11	Necessary Assumption		24	Weaken
12	Most Strongly Supported		25	Must Be True
13	Sufficient Assumption		26	Weaken

PrepTest 23 (October 1997)

Section 1: Logic Games

1	Simple Ordering		3	Grouping (Distribution)
2	In/Out Grouping		4	Complex Ordering

Section 2: Logical Reasoning A

1	Method (Argument)		16	Strengthen
2	Main Conclusion		17	Necessary Assumption
3	Method (Argument)		18	Strengthen
4	Flaw		19	Flaw
5	Sufficient Assumption		20	Must Be True
6	Necessary Assumption		21	Flaw
7	Most Strongly Supported		22	Paradox
8	Weaken		23	Parallel (Flaw)
9	Necessary Assumption		24	Most Strongly Supported
10	Must Be True		25	Parallel (Reasoning)
11	Method (Statement)		26	Weaken – Except
12	Must Be True			
13	Principle (Identify)			
14	Strengthen			
15	Method (Argument)			

Section 3: Logical Reasoning B

1	Removed	14	Sufficient Assumption
2	Paradox	15	Strengthen – Except
3	Necessary Assumption	16	Flaw
4	Most Strongly Supported	17	Flaw
5	Principle (Identify)	18	Parallel (Reasoning)
6	Most Strongly Supported	19	Weaken
7	Flaw	20	Most Strongly Supported
8	Method (Argument)	21	Main Conclusion
9	Necessary Assumption	22	Flaw
10	Strengthen	23	Parallel (Flaw)
11	Necessary Assumption	24	Principle (Apply)
12	Most Strongly Supported	25	Main Conclusion
13	Strengthen		

Section 4: Reading Comprehension

1	Humanities	3	Natural Sciences
2	Law	4	Social Sciences

PrepTest 24 (December 1997)

Section 1: Reading Comprehension

1	Natural Sciences	3	Law
2	Social Sciences	4	Humanities

Section 2: Logical Reasoning A

1	Flaw	14	Point
2	Most Strongly Supported	15	Main Conclusion
3	Method (Argument)	16	Evaluate
4	Strengthen – Except	17	Necessary Assumption
5	Parallel (Flaw)	18	Paradox
6	Flaw	19	Weaken – Except
7	Weaken – Except	20	Weaken – Except
8	Flaw	21	Sufficient Assumption
9	Principle (Identify)	22	Principle (Identify)
10	Method (Statement)	23	Flaw
11	Must Be True	24	Sufficient Assumption
12	Main Conclusion	25	Principle (Identify)
13	Parallel (Reasoning)		

Section 3: Logical Reasoning B

1	Point	11	Must Be True
2	Flaw	12	Flaw
3	Method (Argument)	13	Necessary Assumption
4	Flaw	14	Paradox – Except
5	Necessary Assumption	15	Must Be True
6	Weaken	16	Parallel (Flaw)
7	Most Strongly Supported	17	Method (Argument)
8	Must Be True	18	Necessary Assumption
9	Weaken	19	Sufficient Assumption
10	Sufficient Assumption	20	Principle (Identify)

21	Parallel (Reasoning)	24	Principle (Apply)
22	Weaken – Except	25	Flaw
23	Strengthen	26	Principle (Identify)

Section 4: Logic Games

1	Grouping (Distribution) – Limited Solutions	3	Complex Ordering – Limited Scenarios
2	Simple Ordering	4	In/Out Grouping – Limited Solutions

PrepTest 25 (June 1998)

Section 1: Reading Comprehension

1	Law	3	Social Sciences
2	Humanities	4	Natural Sciences

Section 2: Logical Reasoning A

1	Main Conclusion	14	Paradox
2	Parallel (Flaw)	15	Weaken
3	Complete the Passage	16	Necessary Assumption
4	Strengthen	17	Paradox – Except
5	Weaken	18	Flaw
6	Necessary Assumption	19	Most Strongly Supported – Except
7	Main Conclusion	20	Flaw
8	Principle (Identify)	21	Must Be True
9	Flaw	22	Parallel (Reasoning)
10	Strengthen	23	Principle (Identify)
11	Principle (Identify)	24	Principle (Identify)
12	Necessary Assumption	25	Principle (Identify)
13	Most Strongly Supported		

Section 3: Logic Games

1	Undetermined Assignment	3	In/Out Grouping – Limited Scenarios
2	Determined Assignment – Limited Scenarios	4	Complex Ordering

Section 4: Logical Reasoning B

1	Main Conclusion	18	Sufficient Assumption
2	Must Be True	19	Method (Argument)
3	Weaken	20	Parallel (Reasoning)
4	Flaw	21	Method (Argument)
5	Principle (Identify)	22	Point
6	Strengthen	23	Flaw
7	Strengthen	24	Weaken
8	Flaw	25	Necessary Assumption
9	Necessary Assumption	26	Cannot Be True
10	Weaken		
11	Weaken – Except		
12	Parallel (Flaw)		
13	Paradox		
14	Principle (Identify)		
15	Cannot Be True – Except		
16	Cannot Be True – Except		
17	Flaw		

PrepTest 26 (October 1998)

Section 1: Logic Games

1	Complex Ordering		3	Grouping (Distribution) – Limited Scenarios
2	Simple Ordering		4	Undetermined Assignment – Limited Solutions

Section 2: Logical Reasoning A

1	Flaw		14	Paradox
2	Principle (Identify)		15	Flaw
3	Point		16	Parallel (Reasoning)
4	Flaw		17	Flaw – Except
5	Weaken		18	Paradox
6	Must Be True		19	Must Be True – Except
7	Necessary Assumption		20	Parallel (Flaw)
8	Main Conclusion		21	Flaw
9	Most Strongly Supported		22	Necessary Assumption – Except
10	Necessary Assumption		23	Principle (Identify)
11	Strengthen		24	Point
12	Weaken		25	Necessary Assumption
13	Necessary Assumption			

Section 3: Logical Reasoning B

1	Paradox		14	Weaken
2	Method (Argument)		15	Most Strongly Supported
3	Strengthen		16	Method (Argument)
4	Method (Statement)		17	Flaw
5	Flaw		18	Paradox
6	Weaken		19	Flaw
7	Complete the Passage		20	Most Strongly Supported – Except
8	Flaw		21	Sufficient Assumption
9	Necessary Assumption		22	Must Be True
10	Flaw		23	Principle (Apply)
11	Necessary Assumption		24	Weaken
12	Cannot Be True		25	Principle (Apply)
13	Parallel (Flaw)			

Section 4: Reading Comprehension

1	Social Sciences		3	Natural Sciences
2	Humanities		4	Law

PrepTest 27 (December 1998)

Section 1: Logical Reasoning A

1	Point		9	Must Be True
2	Flaw		10	Weaken
3	Most Strongly Supported		11	Parallel (Flaw)
4	Weaken		12	Most Strongly Supported
5	Strengthen		13	Necessary Assumption
6	Method (Argument)		14	Method (Statement)
7	Paradox		15	Method (Argument)
8	Weaken		16	Sufficient Assumption

17	Method (Statement)	22	Must Be True
18	Strengthen	23	Flaw
19	Must Be True	24	Principle (Identify)
20	Most Strongly Supported	25	Flaw – Except
21	Necessary Assumption	26	Parallel (Reasoning)

Section 2: Logic Games

| 1 | Simple Ordering | 3 | Grouping (Distribution) – Limited Scenarios |
| 2 | Determined Assignment – Limited Scenarios | 4 | Simple Ordering – Limited Solutions |

Section 3: Reading Comprehension

| 1 | Law | 3 | Natural Sciences |
| 2 | Social Sciences | 4 | Humanities |

Section 4: Logical Reasoning B

1	Principle (Apply)	14	Must Be True
2	Strengthen	15	Weaken
3	Principle (Apply)	16	Strengthen – Except
4	Necessary Assumption	17	Must Be True
5	Must Be True	18	Weaken
6	Evaluate	19	Necessary Assumption
7	Flaw	20	Necessary Assumption
8	Paradox	21	Method (Argument)
9	Necessary Assumption	22	Must Be True
10	Flaw	23	Most Strongly Supported
11	Point	24	Method (Statement)
12	Method (Argument)	25	Flaw
13	Parallel (Flaw)		

PrepTest 28 (June 1999)

Section 1: Logical Reasoning A

1	Strengthen – Except	14	Must Be True
2	Necessary Assumption	15	Strengthen
3	Parallel (Flaw)	16	Most Strongly Supported
4	Principle (Identify)	17	Paradox
5	Weaken	18	Main Conclusion
6	Point	19	Flaw
7	Method (Argument)	20	Cannot Be True
8	Paradox	21	Necessary Assumption
9	Flaw	22	Most Strongly Supported
10	Principle (Apply)	23	Weaken – Except
11	Cannot Be True – Except	24	Sufficient Assumption
12	Necessary Assumption	25	Flaw
13	Parallel (Reasoning)	26	Strengthen – Except

Section 2: Logic Games

1	Simple Ordering – Limited Scenarios
2	Undetermined Assignment
3	Determined Assignment
4	Determined Assignment – Limited Solutions

Section 3: Logical Reasoning B

1	Must Be True		14	Main Conclusion
2	Flaw		15	Weaken
3	Paradox		16	Necessary Assumption
4	Most Strongly Supported – Except		17	Weaken
5	Flaw		18	Principle (Identify)
6	Strengthen		19	Necessary Assumption
7	Method (Argument)		20	Flaw – Except
8	Must Be True		21	Parallel (Flaw)
9	Strengthen		22	Necessary Assumption
10	Method (Argument)		23	Principle (Apply)
11	Weaken		24	Strengthen
12	Cannot Be True – Except		25	Weaken
13	Strengthen		26	Parallel (Reasoning)

Section 4: Reading Comprehension

1	Law		3	Social Sciences
2	Natural Sciences		4	Humanities

PrepTest 29 (October 1999)

Section 1: Logical Reasoning A

1	Point		14	Flaw
2	Method (Argument)		15	Necessary Assumption
3	Strengthen – Except		16	Weaken
4	Paradox		17	Flaw
5	Necessary Assumption		18	Must Be True
6	Must Be True		19	Principle (Identify)
7	Flaw		20	Sufficient Assumption
8	Most Strongly Supported		21	Must Be True
9	Point		22	Principle (Identify)
10	Paradox		23	Parallel (Flaw)
11	Main Conclusion		24	Weaken
12	Method (Argument)		25	Paradox – Except
13	Parallel (Reasoning) – Except			

Section 2: Reading Comprehension

1	Humanities		3	Natural Sciences
2	Social Sciences		4	Law

Section 3: Logic Games

1	Grouping (Distribution) – Limited Scenarios		3	Simple Ordering
2	Undetermined Assignment – Limited Scenarios		4	Determined Assignment – Limited Allocations

Section 4: Logical Reasoning B

1	Strengthen		5	Necessary Assumption
2	Method (Statement)		6	Main Conclusion
3	Most Strongly Supported		7	Principle (Identify)
4	Necessary Assumption		8	Necessary Assumption

9	Weaken	18	Flaw
10	Principle (Apply)	19	Paradox – Except
11	Strengthen	20	Strengthen – Except
12	Most Strongly Supported	21	Parallel (Flaw)
13	Point	22	Cannot Be True
14	Flaw	23	Must Be True
15	Method (Statement)	24	Weaken
16	Point	25	Flaw
17	Principle (Identify)		

PrepTest 30 (December 1999)

Section 1: Logic Games

1	Miscellaneous	3	Complex Ordering – Limited Scenarios
2	Simple Ordering – Limited Allocations	4	Simple Ordering

Section 2: Logical Reasoning A

1	Weaken	14	Parallel (Reasoning)
2	Flaw	15	Necessary Assumption
3	Strengthen	16	Most Strongly Supported
4	Strengthen	17	Flaw
5	Principle (Identify)	18	Must Be True
6	Parallel (Flaw)	19	Principle (Identify) – Except
7	Method (Argument)	20	Must Be True
8	Weaken	21	Strengthen
9	Weaken	22	Necessary Assumption
10	Point	23	Must Be True
11	Necessary Assumption	24	Strengthen
12	Paradox – Except	25	Flaw
13	Flaw	26	Flaw

Section 3: Reading Comprehension

1	Natural Sciences	3	Law
2	Humanities	4	Social Sciences

Section 4: Logical Reasoning B

1	Sufficient Assumption	18	Strengthen
2	Main Conclusion	19	Necessary Assumption
3	Method (Statement)	20	Strengthen
4	Must Be True	21	Point
5	Paradox – Except	22	Most Strongly Supported
6	Flaw	23	Principle (Identify)
7	Cannot Be True – Except	24	Weaken
8	Flaw	25	Parallel (Flaw)
9	Parallel (Reasoning)		
10	Most Strongly Supported		
11	Weaken		
12	Strengthen		
13	Method (Statement)		
14	Flaw		
15	Strengthen		
16	Method (Argument)		
17	Weaken		

PrepTest 31 (June 2000)

Section 1: Logic Games

Section 2: Logical Reasoning A

Section 3: Logical Reasoning B

Section 4: Reading Comprehension

PrepTest 32 (October 2000)

Section 1: Logical Reasoning A

19	Flaw	23	Necessary Assumption
20	Strengthen – Except	24	Most Strongly Supported
21	Necessary Assumption	25	Necessary Assumption
22	Parallel (Flaw)		

Section 2: Reading Comprehension

1	Law	3	Humanities
2	Social Sciences	4	Natural Sciences

Section 3: Logic Games

1	Undetermined Assignment	3	Simple Ordering
2	Undetermined Assignment	4	Complex Ordering – Limited Scenarios

Section 4: Logical Reasoning B

1	Method (Argument)	14	Most Strongly Supported
2	Weaken	15	Flaw – Except
3	Principle (Apply)	16	Necessary Assumption
4	Sufficient Assumption	17	Paradox
5	Paradox	18	Principle (Apply)
6	Flaw	19	Necessary Assumption
7	Necessary Assumption	20	Point
8	Principle (Identify)	21	Parallel (Flaw)
9	Strengthen	22	Removed
10	Most Strongly Supported	23	Method (Statement)
11	Strengthen	24	Must Be True
12	Main Conclusion	25	Flaw
13	Flaw		

PrepTest 33 (December 2000)

Section 1: Logical Reasoning A

1	Strengthen	14	Paradox
2	Method (Argument)	15	Parallel (Flaw)
3	Point	16	Principle (Apply) – Except
4	Weaken	17	Weaken
5	Main Conclusion	18	Principle (Identify)
6	Strengthen	19	Necessary Assumption
7	Most Strongly Supported	20	Weaken – Except
8	Paradox – Except	21	Principle (Identify)
9	Most Strongly Supported	22	Flaw – Except
10	Necessary Assumption	23	Parallel (Reasoning)
11	Must Be True	24	Flaw
12	Flaw	25	Weaken
13	Necessary Assumption		

Section 2: Reading Comprehension

1	Social Sciences
2	Humanities
3	Natural Sciences
4	Law

Section 3: Logical Reasoning B

1	Paradox	14	Method (Statement)
2	Flaw	15	Flaw
3	Paradox – Except	16	Necessary Assumption
4	Strengthen	17	Flaw
5	Flaw	18	Parallel (Flaw)
6	Principle (Identify)	19	Point
7	Weaken	20	Strengthen
8	Must Be True	21	Sufficient Assumption
9	Strengthen	22	Parallel (Reasoning)
10	Most Strongly Supported	23	Sufficient Assumption
11	Necessary Assumption	24	Weaken
12	Method (Argument)	25	Necessary Assumption
13	Most Strongly Supported		

Section 4: Logic Games

1	Relative Ordering	3	In/Out Grouping – Limited Allocations
2	In/Out Grouping	4	Undetermined Assignment

PrepTest 34 (June 2001)

Section 1: Reading Comprehension

1	Social Sciences	3	Natural Sciences
2	Humanities	4	Social Sciences

Section 2: Logical Reasoning A

1	Flaw	14	Strengthen
2	Sufficient Assumption	15	Main Conclusion
3	Flaw	16	Necessary Assumption
4	Most Strongly Supported	17	Weaken
5	Paradox	18	Main Conclusion
6	Parallel (Reasoning)	19	Most Strongly Supported
7	Paradox	20	Principle (Identify)
8	Method (Argument)	21	Necessary Assumption
9	Flaw	22	Method (Statement)
10	Sufficient Assumption	23	Must Be True
11	Flaw	24	Parallel (Flaw)
12	Weaken	25	Weaken
13	Necessary Assumption		

Section 3: Logical Reasoning B

1	Principle (Identify)	11	Necessary Assumption
2	Paradox – Except	12	Complete the Passage
3	Necessary Assumption	13	Must Be True
4	Flaw	14	Method (Statement)
5	Necessary Assumption	15	Point
6	Weaken	16	Principle (Identify)
7	Point	17	Necessary Assumption
8	Method (Argument)	18	Weaken
9	Necessary Assumption	19	Most Strongly Supported
10	Flaw	20	Weaken

21	Strengthen	24	Strengthen
22	Cannot Be True – Except	25	Parallel (Reasoning)
23	Parallel (Flaw)	26	Method (Statement)

Section 4: Logic Games

1	Simple Ordering – Limited Scenarios	3	Simple Ordering – Limited Scenarios
2	Simple Ordering – Limited Solutions	4	In/Out Grouping

PrepTest 35 (October 2001)

Section 1: Logical Reasoning A

1	Method (Statement)	14	Necessary Assumption
2	Principle (Identify)	15	Strengthen – Except
3	Main Conclusion	16	Main Conclusion
4	Weaken	17	Flaw
5	Method (Argument)	18	Necessary Assumption
6	Flaw	19	Most Strongly Supported
7	Principle (Apply)	20	Sufficient Assumption
8	Weaken	21	Paradox
9	Method (Statement)	22	Sufficient Assumption
10	Paradox – Except	23	Flaw
11	Method (Argument)	24	Parallel (Flaw)
12	Most Strongly Supported	25	Paradox
13	Weaken	26	Point

Section 2: Reading Comprehension

1	Social Sciences	3	Natural Sciences
2	Humanities	4	Law

Section 3: Logic Games

1	Undetermined Assignment	3	Determined Assignment – Limited Scenarios
2	Undetermined Assignment – Limited Allocations	4	Determined Assignment – Limited Solutions

Section 4: Logical Reasoning B

1	Most Strongly Supported – Except	18	Flaw
2	Method (Statement)	19	Sufficient Assumption
3	Most Strongly Supported	20	Weaken
4	Paradox	21	Most Strongly Supported
5	Weaken	22	Cannot Be True – Except
6	Parallel (Flaw)	23	Parallel (Reasoning)
7	Flaw	24	Flaw
8	Flaw	25	Method (Argument)
9	Main Conclusion	26	Most Strongly Supported
10	Strengthen		
11	Principle (Identify)		
12	Paradox		
13	Flaw		
14	Sufficient Assumption		
15	Method (Statement)		
16	Necessary Assumption		
17	Weaken – Except		

PrepTest 36 (December 2001)

Section 1: Logical Reasoning A

1	Method (Argument)		14	Must Be True
2	Weaken		15	Principle (Identify)
3	Necessary Assumption		16	Most Strongly Supported
4	Most Strongly Supported		17	Principle (Apply)
5	Principle (Apply)		18	Sufficient Assumption
6	Main Conclusion		19	Flaw
7	Method (Argument)		20	Necessary Assumption
8	Weaken		21	Parallel (Flaw)
9	Paradox		22	Sufficient Assumption
10	Flaw		23	Paradox – Except
11	Must Be True		24	Evaluate
12	Flaw		25	Weaken
13	Paradox		26	Sufficient Assumption

Section 2: Reading Comprehension

1	Social Sciences		3	Natural Sciences
2	Humanities		4	Law

Section 3: Logical Reasoning B

1	Paradox		14	Necessary Assumption
2	Weaken		15	Principle (Apply)
3	Main Conclusion		16	Necessary Assumption
4	Point		17	Most Strongly Supported
5	Weaken		18	Necessary Assumption
6	Method (Statement)		19	Parallel (Flaw)
7	Strengthen		20	Principle (Identify)
8	Method (Argument)		21	Flaw
9	Main Conclusion		22	Necessary Assumption
10	Method (Argument)		23	Main Conclusion
11	Strengthen		24	Method (Argument)
12	Sufficient Assumption		25	Flaw
13	Flaw		26	Strengthen

Section 4: Logic Games

1	In/Out Grouping		3	Determined Assignment
2	Complex Ordering – Limited Scenarios		4	Complex Ordering – Limited Scenarios

PrepTest 37 (June 2002)

Section 1: Reading Comprehension

1	Law		3	Humanities
2	Natural Sciences		4	Social Sciences

Section 2: Logical Reasoning A

1	Strengthen		3	Flaw
2	Must Be True		4	Weaken

5	Sufficient Assumption	16	Flaw
6	Strengthen	17	Paradox – Except
7	Must Be True	18	Principle (Identify)
8	Paradox – Except	19	Necessary Assumption
9	Complete the Passage	20	Strengthen – Except
10	Method (Argument)	21	Parallel (Flaw)
11	Point	22	Principle (Identify)
12	Must Be True	23	Point
13	Method (Argument)	24	Principle (Identify)
14	Weaken	25	Flaw
15	Necessary Assumption	26	Parallel (Reasoning)

Section 3: Logic Games

| 1 | Determined Assignment | 3 | Grouping (Distribution) – Limited Scenarios |
| 2 | Complex Ordering | 4 | Complex Ordering – Limited Scenarios |

Section 4: Logical Reasoning B

1	Complete the Passage	14	Parallel (Reasoning)
2	Weaken	15	Necessary Assumption
3	Most Strongly Supported	16	Flaw
4	Parallel (Flaw)	17	Flaw
5	Paradox	18	Weaken
6	Most Strongly Supported	19	Necessary Assumption
7	Point	20	Sufficient Assumption
8	Complete the Passage	21	Principle (Identify)
9	Sufficient Assumption	22	Flaw
10	Method (Argument)	23	Necessary Assumption
11	Weaken	24	Method (Argument)
12	Flaw	25	Strengthen
13	Strengthen – Except		

PrepTest 38 (October 2002)

Section 1: Logical Reasoning A

1	Sufficient Assumption	13	Most Strongly Supported
2	Main Conclusion	14	Necessary Assumption
3	Principle (Identify)	15	Most Strongly Supported
4	Strengthen	16	Parallel (Flaw)
5	Point	17	Weaken
6	Flaw	18	Method (Statement)
7	Principle (Apply)	19	Complete the Passage
8	Flaw	20	Most Strongly Supported
9	Paradox	21	Most Strongly Supported
10	Weaken	22	Parallel (Reasoning)
11	Flaw	23	Flaw
12	Necessary Assumption	24	Necessary Assumption

Section 2: Logic Games

1	Relative Ordering
2	Complex Ordering
3	Grouping (Distribution) – Limited Scenarios
4	Complex Ordering – Limited Scenarios

Section 3: Reading Comprehension

Section 4: Logical Reasoning B

PrepTest 39 (December 2002)

Section 1: Logic Games

Section 2: Logical Reasoning A

Section 3: Reading Comprehension

Section 4: Logical Reasoning B

11	Flaw	19	Necessary Assumption
12	Paradox	20	Flaw
13	Strengthen – Except	21	Flaw
14	Principle (Identify)	22	Weaken – Except
15	Flaw	23	Flaw
16	Most Strongly Supported	24	Principle (Apply)
17	Sufficient Assumption	25	Necessary Assumption
18	Strengthen	26	Parallel (Flaw)

PrepTest 40 (June 2003)

Section 1: Logical Reasoning A

1	Paradox	14	Flaw
2	Method (Argument)	15	Flaw
3	Must Be True	16	Necessary Assumption
4	Method (Argument)	17	Weaken
5	Necessary Assumption	18	Principle (Identify)
6	Strengthen	19	Sufficient Assumption
7	Complete the Passage	20	Parallel (Flaw)
8	Sufficient Assumption	21	Sufficient Assumption
9	Main Conclusion	22	Must Be True
10	Flaw	23	Parallel (Reasoning)
11	Strengthen	24	Must Be True
12	Flaw	25	Method (Statement)
13	Strengthen		

Section 2: Logic Games

1	Simple Ordering	3	Miscellaneous
2	Simple Ordering	4	In/Out Grouping

Section 3: Logical Reasoning B

1	Paradox	14	Flaw
2	Strengthen – Except	15	Sufficient Assumption
3	Most Strongly Supported	16	Point
4	Main Conclusion	17	Parallel (Flaw)
5	Weaken	18	Strengthen
6	Method (Statement)	19	Flaw – Except
7	Paradox – Except	20	Necessary Assumption
8	Strengthen	21	Flaw
9	Principle (Identify)	22	Necessary Assumption
10	Flaw	23	Flaw
11	Must Be True	24	Strengthen
12	Flaw	25	Parallel (Reasoning)
13	Method (Argument)	26	Weaken – Except

Section 4: Reading Comprehension

1	Social Sciences
2	Humanities
3	Natural Sciences
4	Law

PrepTest 41 (October 2003)

Section 1: Logical Reasoning A

1	Flaw	14	Principle (Apply)
2	Paradox	15	Parallel (Reasoning)
3	Method (Argument)	16	Weaken
4	Paradox	17	Principle (Identify)
5	Main Conclusion	18	Flaw
6	Necessary Assumption	19	Principle (Identify)
7	Cannot Be True	20	Flaw
8	Paradox	21	Must Be True
9	Most Strongly Supported	22	Flaw
10	Necessary Assumption	23	Parallel (Flaw)
11	Most Strongly Supported	24	Necessary Assumption
12	Strengthen	25	Flaw
13	Weaken		

Section 2: Logic Games

1	Simple Ordering – Limited Scenarios	3	In/Out Grouping – Limited Allocations
2	Complex Ordering – Limited Scenarios	4	Miscellaneous

Section 3: Logical Reasoning B

1	Paradox	14	Principle (Identify)
2	Cannot Be True – Except	15	Strengthen – Except
3	Most Strongly Supported	16	Weaken – Except
4	Flaw	17	Necessary Assumption
5	Paradox – Except	18	Main Conclusion
6	Most Strongly Supported	19	Strengthen – Except
7	Necessary Assumption	20	Flaw
8	Parallel (Flaw)	21	Paradox
9	Method (Argument)	22	Sufficient Assumption
10	Cannot Be True – Except	23	Flaw
11	Flaw	24	Parallel (Reasoning)
12	Method (Argument)	25	Must Be True
13	Flaw	26	Weaken

Section 4: Reading Comprehension

1	Law	3	Social Sciences
2	Humanities	4	Social Sciences

PrepTest 42 (December 2003)

Section 1: Logic Games

1	In/Out Grouping	3	Determined Assignment – Limited Scenarios
2	Relative Ordering	4	Undetermined Assignment – Limited Allocations

Section 2: Logical Reasoning A

1	Weaken	3	Flaw
2	Method (Statement)	4	Weaken

5	Paradox		16	Must Be True
6	Weaken		17	Flaw
7	Most Strongly Supported		18	Strengthen
8	Point		19	Sufficient Assumption
9	Principle (Apply)		20	Weaken
10	Strengthen		21	Principle (Apply)
11	Most Strongly Supported		22	Parallel (Reasoning)
12	Flaw		23	Sufficient Assumption
13	Point		24	Parallel (Flaw)
14	Necessary Assumption		25	Weaken
15	Flaw		26	Flaw

Section 3: Reading Comprehension

1	Law		3	Social Sciences
2	Humanities		4	Natural Sciences

Section 4: Logical Reasoning B

1	Strengthen		14	Flaw
2	Necessary Assumption		15	Principle (Identify)
3	Method (Statement)		16	Method (Statement)
4	Flaw		17	Must Be True
5	Paradox		18	Method (Statement)
6	Weaken		19	Necessary Assumption
7	Most Strongly Supported		20	Flaw
8	Principle (Apply)		21	Method (Statement)
9	Strengthen – Except		22	Parallel (Flaw)
10	Main Conclusion		23	Strengthen
11	Paradox		24	Paradox
12	Flaw		25	Cannot Be True
13	Necessary Assumption		26	Must Be True

PrepTest 43 (June 2004)

Section 1: Reading Comprehension

1	Social Sciences		3	Humanities
2	Social Sciences		4	Law

Section 2: Logical Reasoning A

1	Point		16	Necessary Assumption
2	Method (Statement)		17	Must Be True
3	Paradox		18	Sufficient Assumption
4	Most Strongly Supported		19	Point
5	Flaw		20	Flaw
6	Weaken		21	Principle (Identify)
7	Must Be True		22	Must Be True
8	Strengthen – Except		23	Method (Statement)
9	Flaw		24	Parallel (Flaw)
10	Necessary Assumption		25	Paradox
11	Parallel (Reasoning)			
12	Flaw			
13	Point			
14	Strengthen			
15	Paradox			

Section 3: Logical Reasoning B

1 Necessary Assumption
2 Strengthen – Except
3 Principle (Identify)
4 Flaw
5 Principle (Apply)
6 Point
7 Principle (Identify)
8 Weaken
9 Must Be True
10 Strengthen
11 Principle (Identify)
12 Necessary Assumption
13 Paradox

14 Main Conclusion
15 Paradox – Except
16 Necessary Assumption
17 Cannot Be True – Except
18 Flaw
19 Weaken
20 Flaw
21 Must Be True
22 Parallel (Flaw)
23 Main Conclusion
24 Must Be True
25 Parallel (Reasoning)
26 Principle (Identify)

Section 4: Logic Games

1 Simple Ordering – Limited Scenarios
2 Relative Ordering

3 Determined Assignment
4 Undetermined Assignment – Limited Allocations

PrepTest 44 (October 2004)

Section 1: Reading Comprehension

1 Law
2 Social Sciences

3 Natural Sciences
4 Humanities

Section 2: Logical Reasoning A

1 Flaw
2 Most Strongly Supported
3 Paradox
4 Weaken
5 Necessary Assumption
6 Point
7 Strengthen
8 Weaken – Except
9 Necessary Assumption
10 Paradox
11 Most Strongly Supported
12 Principle (Apply)
13 Sufficient Assumption

14 Most Strongly Supported
15 Strengthen
16 Main Conclusion
17 Principle (Identify)
18 Necessary Assumption
19 Method (Statement)
20 Weaken
21 Flaw
22 Parallel (Flaw)
23 Necessary Assumption
24 Method (Statement)
25 Flaw

Section 3: Logic Games

1 Simple Ordering – Limited Allocations
2 Grouping (Distribution) – Limited Scenarios

3 Complex Ordering
4 Complex Ordering – Limited Allocations

Section 4: Logical Reasoning B

1 Weaken
2 Principle (Identify)
3 Most Strongly Supported
4 Principle (Identify)

5 Weaken
6 Method (Statement)
7 Necessary Assumption
8 Complete the Passage

PrepTest 45 (December 2004)

Section 1: Logical Reasoning A

Section 2: Reading Comprehension

Section 3: Logic Games

Section 4: Logical Reasoning B

PrepTest 46 (June 2005)

Section 1: Reading Comprehension

Section 2: Logical Reasoning A

Section 3: Logical Reasoning B

Section 4: Logic Games

PrepTest 47 (October 2005)

Section 1: Logical Reasoning A

17	Necessary Assumption	22	Weaken
18	Must Be True	23	Flaw
19	Weaken	24	Principle (Apply)
20	Necessary Assumption	25	Point
21	Parallel (Flaw)	26	Strengthen

Section 2: Reading Comprehension

1	Social Sciences	3	Law
2	Humanities	4	Natural Sciences

Section 3: Logical Reasoning B

1	Most Strongly Supported	14	Weaken
2	Strengthen	15	Paradox – Except
3	Most Strongly Supported	16	Flaw
4	Weaken	17	Necessary Assumption
5	Point	18	Principle (Apply)
6	Main Conclusion	19	Flaw
7	Weaken	20	Method (Argument)
8	Flaw	21	Sufficient Assumption
9	Point	22	Principle (Apply)
10	Most Strongly Supported	23	Flaw
11	Paradox – Except	24	Weaken
12	Complete the Passage	25	Parallel (Flaw)
13	Necessary Assumption	26	Principle (Identify)

Section 4: Logic Games

1	Simple Ordering	3	Undetermined Assignment – Limited Allocations
2	In/Out Grouping	4	Undetermined Assignment

PrepTest 48 (December 2005)

Section 1: Logical Reasoning A

1	Weaken	14	Must Be True
2	Flaw	15	Necessary Assumption
3	Strengthen	16	Strengthen
4	Principle (Apply)	17	Flaw
5	Main Conclusion	18	Principle (Identify)
6	Complete the Passage	19	Weaken
7	Strengthen	20	Necessary Assumption
8	Main Conclusion	21	Flaw
9	Principle (Identify)	22	Paradox
10	Strengthen	23	Parallel (Flaw)
11	Principle (Identify)	24	Flaw
12	Parallel (Reasoning)	25	Sufficient Assumption
13	Flaw	26	Must Be True

Section 2: Logic Games

1	In/Out Grouping
2	Relative Ordering
3	Undetermined Assignment – Limited Allocations
4	Determined Assignment – Limited Scenarios

Section 3: Reading Comprehension

1   Social Sciences
2   Humanities

3   Law
4   Natural Sciences

Section 4: Logical Reasoning B

1   Main Conclusion
2   Strengthen
3   Most Strongly Supported
4   Parallel (Flaw)
5   Method (Statement)
6   Principle (Identify)
7   Paradox
8   Sufficient Assumption
9   Weaken
10   Necessary Assumption
11   Flaw
12   Main Conclusion
13   Flaw

14   Must Be True
15   Flaw
16   Principle (Apply)
17   Flaw
18   Cannot Be True
19   Paradox
20   Weaken
21   Sufficient Assumption
22   Parallel (Reasoning)
23   Weaken – Except
24   Paradox
25   Flaw
26   Weaken

PrepTest 49 (June 2006)

Section 1: Logic Games

1   Simple Ordering
2   Grouping (Distribution) – Limited Allocations

3   In/Out Grouping
4   Simple Ordering – Limited Scenarios

Section 2: Logical Reasoning A

1   Point
2   Paradox
3   Principle (Apply)
4   Strengthen – Except
5   Flaw
6   Weaken
7   Sufficient Assumption
8   Weaken
9   Most Strongly Supported
10   Point
11   Strengthen – Except
12   Method (Statement)
13   Flaw

14   Weaken
15   Principle (Identify)
16   Cannot Be True – Except
17   Necessary Assumption
18   Flaw
19   Sufficient Assumption
20   Most Strongly Supported
21   Cannot Be True – Except
22   Necessary Assumption
23   Flaw
24   Parallel (Reasoning)
25   Sufficient Assumption
26   Parallel (Flaw)

Section 3: Reading Comprehension

1   Law
2   Humanities

3   Social Sciences
4   Natural Sciences

Section 4: Logical Reasoning B

1   Flaw
2   Evaluate
3   Must Be True
4   Strengthen – Except

5   Cannot Be True
6   Flaw
7   Main Conclusion
8   Weaken

PrepTest 50 (October 2006)

Section 1: Reading Comprehension

Section 2: Logical Reasoning A

Section 3: Logic Games

Section 4: Logical Reasoning B

PrepTest 51 (December 2006)

Section 1: Logical Reasoning A

1	Main Conclusion		14	Method (Statement)
2	Evaluate		15	Flaw
3	Paradox		16	Sufficient Assumption
4	Flaw		17	Principle (Apply)
5	Parallel (Reasoning)		18	Flaw
6	Flaw		19	Sufficient Assumption
7	Necessary Assumption		20	Parallel (Flaw)
8	Weaken		21	Most Strongly Supported
9	Principle (Apply)		22	Paradox
10	Flaw		23	Point
11	Must Be True		24	Strengthen
12	Flaw		25	Weaken
13	Main Conclusion			

Section 2: Reading Comprehension

1	Humanities		3	Social Sciences
2	Natural Sciences		4	Law

Section 3: Logical Reasoning B

1	Weaken		14	Must Be True
2	Necessary Assumption		15	Necessary Assumption
3	Strengthen		16	Main Conclusion
4	Flaw		17	Flaw
5	Principle (Identify)		18	Necessary Assumption
6	Flaw		19	Must Be True
7	Principle (Identify)		20	Sufficient Assumption
8	Paradox		21	Most Strongly Supported
9	Flaw		22	Parallel (Flaw)
10	Paradox		23	Method (Statement)
11	Method (Statement)		24	Parallel (Reasoning)
12	Most Strongly Supported		25	Strengthen
13	Principle (Identify)			

Section 4: Logic Games

1	Undetermined Assignment – Limited Scenarios		3	Complex Ordering
2	Relative Ordering – Limited Scenarios		4	Relative Ordering

PrepTest 52 (June 2007)

Section 1: Logical Reasoning A

1	Main Conclusion		9	Weaken
2	Flaw		10	Necessary Assumption
3	Parallel (Reasoning)		11	Paradox – Except
4	Strengthen		12	Weaken
5	Must Be True		13	Complete the Passage
6	Flaw		14	Paradox
7	Most Strongly Supported		15	Most Strongly Supported
8	Principle (Identify)		16	Parallel (Flaw)

17	Sufficient Assumption	22	Principle (Apply)
18	Cannot Be True – Except	23	Flaw
19	Principle (Identify)	24	Most Strongly Supported
20	Sufficient Assumption	25	Necessary Assumption
21	Weaken		

Section 2: Logic Games

| 1 | Relative Ordering | 3 | Determined Assignment |
| 2 | Grouping (Distribution) | 4 | Relative Ordering – Limited Scenarios |

Section 3: Logical Reasoning B

1	Principle (Identify)	14	Most Strongly Supported
2	Main Conclusion	15	Sufficient Assumption
3	Strengthen	16	Flaw
4	Flaw	17	Method (Statement)
5	Method (Argument)	18	Principle (Identify)
6	Weaken	19	Weaken
7	Necessary Assumption	20	Paradox
8	Flaw	21	Flaw
9	Necessary Assumption	22	Paradox
10	Point	23	Most Strongly Supported
11	Principle (Identify)	24	Parallel (Flaw)
12	Flaw	25	Principle (Apply)
13	Necessary Assumption		

Section 4: Reading Comprehension

| 1 | Humanities | 3 | Natural Sciences |
| 2 | Social Sciences – Comparative | 4 | Law |

PrepTest 53 (October 2007)

Section 1: Logical Reasoning A

1	Strengthen – Except	14	Method (Statement)
2	Point	15	Necessary Assumption
3	Weaken	16	Must Be True
4	Main Conclusion	17	Principle (Apply)
5	Principle (Identify)	18	Flaw
6	Strengthen	19	Parallel (Reasoning)
7	Must Be True	20	Sufficient Assumption
8	Weaken	21	Parallel (Flaw)
9	Necessary Assumption	22	Flaw
10	Strengthen	23	Necessary Assumption
11	Method (Statement)	24	Paradox – Except
12	Flaw	25	Flaw
13	Necessary Assumption		

Section 2: Logic Games

1	Grouping (Distribution) – Limited Scenarios
2	Relative Ordering
3	Complex Ordering
4	Determined Assignment – Limited Scenarios

Section 3: Logical Reasoning B

1   Strengthen
2   Flaw
3   Main Conclusion
4   Weaken
5   Main Conclusion
6   Flaw
7   Complete the Passage
8   Necessary Assumption
9   Weaken
10 Method (Statement)
11 Strengthen
12 Principle (Identify)
13 Parallel (Flaw) – Except

14 Weaken
15 Necessary Assumption
16 Weaken
17 Flaw
18 Principle (Identify)
19 Must Be True
20 Necessary Assumption
21 Most Strongly Supported
22 Paradox – Except
23 Parallel (Reasoning)
24 Method (Argument)
25 Principle (Apply)

Section 4: Reading Comprehension

1   Humanities
2   Law

3   Social Sciences – Comparative
4   Natural Sciences

PrepTest 54 (December 2008)

Section 1: Reading Comprehension

1   Law
2   Natural Sciences – Comparative

3   Humanities
4   Social Sciences

Section 2: Logical Reasoning A

1   Flaw
2   Necessary Assumption
3   Weaken
4   Paradox
5   Flaw
6   Necessary Assumption
7   Complete the Passage
8   Principle (Identify)
9   Necessary Assumption
10 Method (Argument)
11 Main Conclusion
12 Most Strongly Supported
13 Sufficient Assumption

14 Weaken
15 Flaw
16 Must Be True
17 Method (Statement)
18 Principle (Identify)
19 Flaw
20 Most Strongly Supported
21 Parallel (Flaw)
22 Flaw
23 Parallel (Reasoning)
24 Strengthen
25 Must Be True
26 Sufficient Assumption

Section 3: Logic Games

1   In/Out Grouping
2   Determined Assignment – Limited Allocations

3   Simple Ordering
4   Simple Ordering – Limited Scenarios

Section 4: Logical Reasoning B

1   Strengthen
2   Method (Argument)
3   Necessary Assumption
4   Flaw

5   Most Strongly Supported
6   Paradox
7   Necessary Assumption
8   Parallel (Flaw)

9	Principle (Identify)	18	Necessary Assumption
10	Weaken	19	Flaw
11	Main Conclusion	20	Strengthen
12	Most Strongly Supported	21	Paradox
13	Paradox	22	Sufficient Assumption
14	Flaw	23	Must Be True
15	Method (Statement)	24	Necessary Assumption
16	Flaw	25	Parallel (Reasoning)
17	Principle (Apply)		

PrepTest 55 (June 2008)

Section 1: Logical Reasoning A

1	Parallel (Flaw)	14	Flaw
2	Necessary Assumption	15	Must Be True
3	Method (Argument)	16	Principle (Apply)
4	Sufficient Assumption	17	Necessary Assumption
5	Most Strongly Supported	18	Main Conclusion
6	Principle (Identify)	19	Method (Statement)
7	Weaken	20	Flaw
8	Most Strongly Supported	21	Principle (Identify)
9	Weaken	22	Weaken
10	Principle (Identify)	23	Strengthen
11	Principle (Apply)	24	Flaw
12	Necessary Assumption	25	Must Be True – Except
13	Paradox		

Section 2: Reading Comprehension

1	Law	3	Humanities
2	Natural Sciences – Comparative	4	Social Sciences

Section 3: Logical Reasoning B

1	Paradox	14	Strengthen
2	Flaw	15	Parallel (Reasoning)
3	Complete the Passage	16	Most Strongly Supported
4	Weaken	17	Principle (Identify)
5	Most Strongly Supported	18	Flaw
6	Principle (Identify) – Except	19	Necessary Assumption
7	Method (Statement)	20	Main Conclusion
8	Necessary Assumption	21	Sufficient Assumption
9	Weaken	22	Weaken
10	Sufficient Assumption	23	Parallel (Flaw)
11	Flaw	24	Necessary Assumption
12	Most Strongly Supported	25	Flaw
13	Main Conclusion		

Section 4: Logic Games

1	Determined Assignment
2	Simple Ordering – Limited Scenarios
3	Relative Ordering
4	Complex Ordering

PrepTest 56 (October 2008)

Section 1: Logic Games

1   Simple Ordering – Limited Scenarios
2   Undetermined Assignment – Limited Allocations
3   Undetermined Assignment – Limited Solutions
4   Determined Assignment – Limited Allocations

Section 2: Logical Reasoning A

1   Flaw
2   Point
3   Weaken
4   Necessary Assumption
5   Must Be True
6   Necessary Assumption
7   Parallel (Flaw)
8   Weaken
9   Method (Statement)
10 Sufficient Assumption
11 Method (Argument)
12 Flaw
13 Paradox
14 Strengthen
15 Flaw
16 Principle (Identify)
17 Point
18 Principle (Apply)
19 Must Be True
20 Principle (Identify)
21 Point
22 Paradox
23 Must Be True
24 Strengthen
25 Method (Statement)

Section 3: Logical Reasoning B

1   Flaw
2   Most Strongly Supported
3   Principle (Identify)
4   Flaw
5   Main Conclusion
6   Method (Argument)
7   Paradox
8   Strengthen
9   Necessary Assumption
10 Flaw
11 Most Strongly Supported
12 Principle (Identify)
13 Strengthen
14 Parallel (Flaw)
15 Most Strongly Supported
16 Sufficient Assumption
17 Flaw
18 Necessary Assumption
19 Main Conclusion
20 Weaken
21 Flaw
22 Cannot Be True – Except
23 Principle (Apply)
24 Parallel (Reasoning)
25 Necessary Assumption

Section 4: Reading Comprehension

1   Humanities
2   Natural Sciences
3   Social Sciences – Comparative
4   Social Sciences

PrepTest 57 (December 2009)

Section 1: Logic Games

1   Simple Ordering
2   Determined Assignment – Limited Allocations
3   Undetermined Assignment
4   Undetermined Assignment – Limited Scenarios

Section 2: Logical Reasoning A

1   Principle (Identify)
2   Complete the Passage
3   Paradox
4   Flaw

5	Strengthen		16	Method (Statement)
6	Flaw		17	Weaken
7	Sufficient Assumption		18	Complete the Passage
8	Parallel (Flaw)		19	Parallel (Reasoning)
9	Weaken		20	Weaken
10	Principle (Identify)		21	Method (Statement)
11	Point		22	Strengthen
12	Sufficient Assumption		23	Cannot Be True
13	Method (Statement)		24	Necessary Assumption
14	Weaken		25	Must Be True
15	Flaw		26	Flaw

Section 3: Logical Reasoning B

1	Paradox		14	Principle (Apply)
2	Flaw		15	Parallel (Flaw)
3	Main Conclusion		16	Principle (Identify)
4	Paradox		17	Necessary Assumption
5	Method (Argument)		18	Flaw
6	Weaken		19	Principle (Identify)
7	Paradox		20	Parallel (Reasoning)
8	Flaw		21	Method (Statement)
9	Strengthen		22	Flaw
10	Flaw		23	Most Strongly Supported
11	Weaken		24	Sufficient Assumption
12	Necessary Assumption		25	Most Strongly Supported
13	Most Strongly Supported			

Section 4: Reading Comprehension

1	Law		3	Humanities – Comparative
2	Social Sciences		4	Natural Sciences

PrepTest 58 (June 2009)

Section 1: Logical Reasoning A

1	Necessary Assumption		14	Necessary Assumption
2	Principle (Apply)		15	Must Be True
3	Strengthen		16	Necessary Assumption
4	Principle (Identify)		17	Paradox
5	Weaken		18	Flaw
6	Method (Argument)		19	Necessary Assumption
7	Parallel (Flaw)		20	Must Be True
8	Paradox – Except		21	Principle (Apply)
9	Flaw		22	Necessary Assumption
10	Most Strongly Supported		23	Principle (Identify)
11	Flaw		24	Weaken
12	Sufficient Assumption		25	Sufficient Assumption
13	Main Conclusion		26	Method (Argument)

Section 2: Reading Comprehension

1	Social Sciences
2	Natural Sciences
3	Law
4	Humanities – Comparative

Section 3: Logic Games

1	Determined Assignment		3	Complex Ordering
2	In/Out Grouping		4	In/Out Grouping

Section 4: Logical Reasoning B

1	Paradox		14	Flaw
2	Weaken		15	Most Strongly Supported
3	Main Conclusion		16	Principle (Identify)
4	Principle (Apply)		17	Necessary Assumption
5	Flaw		18	Flaw
6	Most Strongly Supported		19	Sufficient Assumption
7	Paradox		20	Paradox
8	Flaw		21	Necessary Assumption
9	Must Be True		22	Parallel (Flaw)
10	Weaken		23	Strengthen
11	Necessary Assumption		24	Sufficient Assumption
12	Method (Argument)		25	Principle (Identify)
13	Most Strongly Supported			

PrepTest 59 (October 2009)

Section 1: Logic Games

1	Determined Assignment – Limited Scenarios		3	In/Out Grouping
2	Simple Ordering		4	Simple Ordering – Limited Scenarios

Section 2: Logical Reasoning A

1	Strengthen		14	Necessary Assumption
2	Point		15	Flaw
3	Strengthen		16	Parallel (Reasoning)
4	Flaw		17	Sufficient Assumption
5	Strengthen		18	Method (Statement)
6	Flaw		19	Must Be True
7	Method (Statement)		20	Flaw
8	Flaw		21	Weaken
9	Parallel (Flaw)		22	Strengthen
10	Main Conclusion		23	Principle (Identify)
11	Paradox		24	Complete the Passage
12	Complete the Passage		25	Weaken
13	Principle (Identify)		26	Sufficient Assumption

Section 3: Logical Reasoning B

1	Paradox		11	Strengthen
2	Weaken		12	Necessary Assumption
3	Most Strongly Supported		13	Weaken
4	Paradox		14	Method (Argument)
5	Flaw		15	Parallel (Flaw)
6	Principle (Apply)		16	Necessary Assumption
7	Most Strongly Supported		17	Paradox – Except
8	Flaw		18	Principle (Identify)
9	Main Conclusion		19	Must Be True
10	Sufficient Assumption		20	Flaw

21	Most Strongly Supported	24	Flaw
22	Flaw	25	Necessary Assumption
23	Method (Argument)		

Section 4: Reading Comprehension

1	Natural Sciences – Comparative	3	Humanities
2	Law	4	Social Sciences

PrepTest 60 (December 2010)

Section 1: Logical Reasoning A

1	Flaw	14	Necessary Assumption
2	Method (Argument)	15	Flaw
3	Must Be True	16	Weaken
4	Method (Statement)	17	Parallel (Reasoning)
5	Paradox	18	Principle (Identify)
6	Weaken	19	Removed
7	Necessary Assumption	20	Necessary Assumption
8	Main Conclusion	21	Parallel (Flaw)
9	Paradox	22	Sufficient Assumption
10	Flaw	23	Principle (Identify)
11	Strengthen	24	Most Strongly Supported
12	Flaw	25	Method (Argument)
13	Weaken		

Section 2: Logic Games

1	Determined Assignment	3	Simple Ordering – Limited Solutions
2	Relative Ordering	4	Determined Assignment – Limited Scenarios

Section 3: Logical Reasoning B

1	Paradox	14	Complete the Passage
2	Strengthen	15	Main Conclusion
3	Sufficient Assumption	16	Flaw
4	Weaken	17	Must Be True
5	Method (Statement)	18	Principle (Apply)
6	Parallel (Reasoning)	19	Flaw
7	Method (Statement)	20	Principle (Apply)
8	Flaw	21	Strengthen
9	Principle (Identify)	22	Necessary Assumption
10	Most Strongly Supported	23	Parallel (Flaw)
11	Necessary Assumption	24	Principle (Identify)
12	Must Be True	25	Point
13	Weaken		

Section 4: Reading Comprehension

1	Social Sciences
2	Natural Sciences – Comparative
3	Humanities
4	Law

PrepTest 61 (June 2010)

Section 1: Reading Comprehension

1	Law		3	Natural Sciences – Comparative
2	Humanities		4	Social Sciences

Section 2: Logical Reasoning A

1	Flaw		14	Weaken
2	Principle (Apply)		15	Complete the Passage
3	Must Be True		16	Necessary Assumption
4	Method (Argument)		17	Must Be True
5	Principle (Identify)		18	Flaw
6	Strengthen		19	Paradox – Except
7	Point		20	Weaken
8	Flaw		21	Principle (Identify)
9	Main Conclusion		22	Strengthen – Except
10	Must Be True		23	Parallel (Flaw)
11	Weaken		24	Sufficient Assumption
12	Paradox		25	Paradox
13	Sufficient Assumption			

Section 3: Logic Games

1	Determined Assignment – Limited Scenarios		3	Simple Ordering – Limited Scenarios
2	Relative Ordering – Limited Scenarios		4	Simple Ordering

Section 4: Logical Reasoning B

1	Principle (Identify)		14	Paradox
2	Evaluate		15	Flaw
3	Most Strongly Supported – Except		16	Main Conclusion
4	Strengthen		17	Method (Statement)
5	Most Strongly Supported		18	Point
6	Main Conclusion		19	Principle (Apply)
7	Most Strongly Supported		20	Necessary Assumption
8	Weaken		21	Weaken
9	Parallel (Reasoning)		22	Method (Statement)
10	Most Strongly Supported		23	Principle (Identify)
11	Flaw		24	Flaw
12	Paradox		25	Sufficient Assumption
13	Sufficient Assumption		26	Parallel (Flaw)

PrepTest 62 (October 2010)

Section 1: Reading Comprehension

1	Natural Sciences		3	Natural Sciences – Comparative
2	Law		4	Humanities

Section 2: Logical Reasoning A

1	Principle (Identify)		3	Strengthen
2	Strengthen		4	Strengthen

5	Flaw		16	Strengthen
6	Must Be True		17	Sufficient Assumption
7	Parallel (Flaw)		18	Principle (Apply) – Except
8	Flaw		19	Must Be True
9	Sufficient Assumption		20	Paradox
10	Main Conclusion		21	Most Strongly Supported
11	Flaw		22	Weaken
12	Necessary Assumption		23	Principle (Identify)
13	Principle (Apply)		24	Cannot Be True
14	Method (Argument)		25	Necessary Assumption
15	Sufficient Assumption		26	Principle (Identify)

Section 3: Logic Games

1	Simple Ordering – Limited Scenarios		3	Determined Assignment – Limited Scenarios
2	Undetermined Assignment – Limited Scenarios		4	Simple Ordering

Section 4: Logical Reasoning B

1	Main Conclusion		14	Weaken
2	Principle (Identify)		15	Principle (Identify)
3	Strengthen		16	Sufficient Assumption
4	Method (Statement)		17	Paradox – Except
5	Weaken		18	Sufficient Assumption
6	Must Be True		19	Flaw
7	Paradox		20	Strengthen
8	Most Strongly Supported		21	Method (Argument)
9	Parallel (Flaw)		22	Strengthen
10	Flaw		23	Necessary Assumption
11	Most Strongly Supported		24	Complete the Passage
12	Main Conclusion		25	Parallel (Reasoning)
13	Flaw		26	Paradox – Except

PrepTest 63 (December 2011)

Section 1: Logical Reasoning A

1	Complete the Passage		14	Point
2	Weaken		15	Strengthen
3	Flaw		16	Strengthen
4	Paradox		17	Method (Argument)
5	Necessary Assumption		18	Principle (Apply)
6	Must Be True		19	Necessary Assumption
7	Weaken – Except		20	Must Be True
8	Main Conclusion		21	Parallel (Reasoning)
9	Must Be True		22	Strengthen
10	Sufficient Assumption		23	Flaw
11	Strengthen		24	Parallel (Flaw)
12	Most Strongly Supported		25	Flaw
13	Main Conclusion			

Section 2: Logic Games

1	Grouping (Distribution) – Limited Allocations
2	Simple Ordering
3	Relative Ordering – Limited Scenarios
4	Simple Ordering – Limited Allocations

Section 3: Logical Reasoning B

Section 4: Reading Comprehension

PrepTest 64 (June 2011)

Section 1: Logical Reasoning A

Section 2: Logic Games

Section 3: Logical Reasoning B

21	Sufficient Assumption	24	Strengthen
22	Most Strongly Supported	25	Parallel (Reasoning)
23	Parallel (Flaw)	26	Sufficient Assumption

Section 4: Reading Comprehension

1	Law	3	Natural Sciences – Comparative
2	Social Sciences	4	Humanities

PrepTest 65 (October 2011)

Section 1: Logical Reasoning A

1	Strengthen	14	Principle (Apply)
2	Main Conclusion	15	Flaw
3	Evaluate – Except	16	Sufficient Assumption
4	Complete the Passage	17	Flaw
5	Weaken	18	Necessary Assumption
6	Principle (Apply)	19	Strengthen
7	Complete the Passage	20	Flaw
8	Flaw	21	Necessary Assumption
9	Main Conclusion	22	Method (Statement)
10	Method (Statement)	23	Point
11	Parallel (Flaw)	24	Principle (Identify)
12	Paradox	25	Must Be True
13	Strengthen		

Section 2: Logic Games

1	Relative Ordering	3	In/Out Grouping
2	Complex Ordering – Limited Scenarios	4	Simple Ordering – Limited Scenarios

Section 3: Reading Comprehension

1	Humanities	3	Law – Comparative
2	Social Sciences	4	Natural Sciences

Section 4: Logical Reasoning B

1	Paradox	18	Principle (Identify)
2	Necessary Assumption	19	Weaken – Except
3	Weaken	20	Necessary Assumption
4	Point	21	Method (Statement)
5	Principle (Identify)	22	Strengthen
6	Must Be True	23	Principle (Identify)
7	Evaluate	24	Parallel (Flaw)
8	Flaw	25	Point
9	Most Strongly Supported	26	Flaw
10	Paradox		
11	Flaw		
12	Method (Statement)		
13	Necessary Assumption		
14	Main Conclusion		
15	Complete the Passage		
16	Method (Argument)		
17	Parallel (Reasoning)		

PrepTest 66 (June 2012)

Section 1: Reading Comprehension

1 Social Sciences
2 Law – Comparative

3 Humanities
4 Natural Sciences

Section 2: Logical Reasoning A

1 Flaw
2 Necessary Assumption
3 Strengthen – Except
4 Necessary Assumption
5 Weaken
6 Sufficient Assumption
7 Principle (Identify)
8 Flaw
9 Principle (Identify)
10 Necessary Assumption
11 Flaw
12 Principle (Identify)
13 Flaw

14 Must Be True
15 Flaw
16 Parallel (Reasoning)
17 Strengthen
18 Main Conclusion
19 Sufficient Assumption
20 Point
21 Flaw
22 Most Strongly Supported
23 Paradox
24 Parallel (Flaw)
25 Method (Argument)

Section 3: Logic Games

1 Determined Assignment – Limited Scenarios
2 Simple Ordering – Limited Scenarios

3 Grouping (Distribution) – Limited Scenarios
4 Complex Ordering – Limited Scenarios

Section 4: Logical Reasoning B

1 Flaw
2 Principle (Identify)
3 Necessary Assumption
4 Weaken
5 Main Conclusion
6 Weaken
7 Necessary Assumption
8 Weaken
9 Main Conclusion
10 Paradox
11 Principle (Identify)
12 Strengthen
13 Parallel (Reasoning)

14 Principle (Apply)
15 Paradox
16 Principle (Apply)
17 Sufficient Assumption
18 Paradox
19 Point
20 Sufficient Assumption
21 Must Be True
22 Flaw
23 Point
24 Parallel (Flaw)
25 Flaw
26 Main Conclusion

PrepTest 67 (October 2012)

Section 1: Reading Comprehension

1 Humanities
2 Humanities

3 Natural Sciences – Comparative
4 Law

Section 2: Logical Reasoning A

1 Weaken
2 Paradox

3 Strengthen
4 Paradox – Except

Section 3: Logic Games

Section 4: Logical Reasoning B

PrepTest 68 (December 2012)

Section 1: Reading Comprehension

Section 2: Logical Reasoning A

Section 3: Logical Reasoning B

Section 4: Logic Games

PrepTest 69 (June 2013)

Section 1: Logical Reasoning A

Section 2: Logic Games

Section 3: Reading Comprehension

Section 4: Logical Reasoning B

9	Most Strongly Supported	18	Flaw
10	Parallel (Reasoning)	19	Weaken
11	Flaw	20	Must Be True
12	Method (Statement)	21	Sufficient Assumption
13	Sufficient Assumption	22	Flaw
14	Parallel (Flaw)	23	Strengthen
15	Weaken	24	Main Conclusion
16	Flaw	25	Point
17	Principle (Identify)		

PrepTest 70 (October 2013)

Section 1: Logical Reasoning A

1	Complete the Passage	14	Principle (Identify)
2	Flaw	15	Flaw
3	Strengthen	16	Weaken
4	Point	17	Method (Statement)
5	Paradox	18	Main Conclusion
6	Principle (Apply)	19	Parallel (Reasoning)
7	Sufficient Assumption	20	Flaw
8	Must Be True	21	Necessary Assumption
9	Flaw	22	Must Be True
10	Parallel (Flaw)	23	Principle (Identify)
11	Evaluate – Except	24	Must Be True
12	Paradox	25	Strengthen
13	Necessary Assumption		

Section 2: Reading Comprehension

1	Natural Sciences	3	Social Sciences – Comparative
2	Humanities	4	Law

Section 3: Logic Games

1	Simple Ordering	3	Determined Assignment
2	In/Out Grouping	4	Complex Ordering

Section 4: Logical Reasoning B

1	Principle (Identify)	18	Most Strongly Supported
2	Most Strongly Supported	19	Weaken
3	Flaw	20	Necessary Assumption
4	Strengthen	21	Must Be True
5	Point	22	Sufficient Assumption
6	Necessary Assumption	23	Parallel (Flaw)
7	Paradox	24	Method (Statement)
8	Method (Argument)	25	Necessary Assumption
9	Flaw	26	Method (Argument)
10	Necessary Assumption		
11	Flaw		
12	Weaken		
13	Paradox		
14	Must Be True		
15	Principle (Identify)		
16	Main Conclusion		
17	Parallel (Reasoning)		

PrepTest 71 (December 2013)

Section 1: Logical Reasoning A

Section 2: Logic Games

Section 3: Logical Reasoning B

Section 4: Reading Comprehension

PrepTest 72 (June 2014)

Section 1: Reading Comprehension

Section 2: Logical Reasoning A

5	Flaw	16	Flaw
6	Principle (Identify)	17	Most Strongly Supported
7	Strengthen	18	Flaw
8	Sufficient Assumption	19	Point
9	Paradox	20	Flaw
10	Weaken	21	Necessary Assumption
11	Paradox	22	Parallel (Flaw)
12	Necessary Assumption	23	Strengthen
13	Method (Statement)	24	Must Be True
14	Flaw	25	Strengthen
15	Necessary Assumption	26	Parallel (Reasoning)

Section 3: Logical Reasoning B

1	Paradox	14	Flaw
2	Weaken	15	Method (Statement)
3	Main Conclusion	16	Complete the Passage
4	Necessary Assumption	17	Principle (Identify)
5	Paradox	18	Necessary Assumption
6	Strengthen	19	Principle (Apply)
7	Flaw	20	Most Strongly Supported
8	Strengthen	21	Principle (Identify)
9	Main Conclusion	22	Flaw
10	Weaken	23	Parallel (Reasoning)
11	Flaw	24	Must Be True
12	Strengthen	25	Parallel (Flaw)
13	Principle (Identify)		

Section 4: Logic Games

1	Determined Assignment	3	Grouping (Distribution)
2	Simple Ordering – Limited Scenarios	4	Miscellaneous – Limited Scenarios

PrepTest 73 (September 2014)

Section 1: Reading Comprehension

1	Natural Sciences	3	Social Sciences
2	Humanities	4	Law – Comparative

Section 2: Logical Reasoning A

1	Necessary Assumption	16	Method (Argument)
2	Paradox	17	Parallel (Reasoning)
3	Flaw	18	Flaw
4	Principle (Apply)	19	Weaken
5	Flaw	20	Necessary Assumption
6	Principle (Identify)	21	Must Be True
7	Parallel (Flaw)	22	Strengthen
8	Necessary Assumption	23	Most Strongly Supported
9	Weaken	24	Paradox
10	Sufficient Assumption	25	Complete the Passage
11	Main Conclusion		
12	Sufficient Assumption		
13	Flaw		
14	Method (Argument)		
15	Flaw		

Section 3: Logic Games

1   Relative Ordering – Limited Scenarios
2   Determined Assignment
3   Grouping (Distribution) – Limited Scenarios
4   Undetermined Assignment

Section 4: Logical Reasoning B

1   Weaken
2   Principle (Identify)
3   Flaw
4   Method (Argument)
5   Main Conclusion
6   Evaluate
7   Principle (Identify)
8   Most Strongly Supported
9   Method (Statement)
10 Flaw
11 Main Conclusion
12 Most Strongly Supported
13 Necessary Assumption
14 Most Strongly Supported
15 Paradox
16 Most Strongly Supported
17 Weaken
18 Parallel (Flaw)
19 Necessary Assumption
20 Strengthen
21 Parallel (Reasoning)
22 Paradox
23 Principle (Apply)
24 Sufficient Assumption
25 Flaw
26 Necessary Assumption

PrepTest 74 (December 2014)

Section 1: Logical Reasoning A

1   Complete the Passage
2   Strengthen
3   Principle (Identify)
4   Strengthen
5   Flaw
6   Weaken
7   Principle (Identify)
8   Necessary Assumption
9   Paradox
10 Principle (Apply)
11 Most Strongly Supported
12 Sufficient Assumption
13 Main Conclusion
14 Method (Statement)
15 Paradox
16 Flaw
17 Strengthen
18 Flaw
19 Parallel (Reasoning)
20 Sufficient Assumption
21 Evaluate
22 Most Strongly Supported
23 Weaken
24 Must Be True
25 Parallel (Flaw)

Section 2: Logic Games

1   Relative Ordering – Limited Scenarios
2   Complex Ordering – Limited Scenarios
3   Undetermined Assignment – Limited Allocations
4   Grouping (Distribution)

Section 3: Reading Comprehension

1   Humanities
2   Law
3   Natural Sciences – Comparative
4   Social Sciences

Section 4: Logical Reasoning B

1   Most Strongly Supported
2   Main Conclusion
3   Strengthen
4   Necessary Assumption
5   Principle (Identify)
6   Necessary Assumption
7   Complete the Passage
8   Flaw

PrepTest 75 (June 2015)

Section 1: Logical Reasoning A

Section 2: Reading Comprehension

Section 3: Logical Reasoning B

Section 4: Logic Games

PrepTest 76 (October 2015)

Section 1: Reading Comprehension

1   Humanities
2   Law
3   Social Sciences
4   Natural Sciences – Comparative

Section 2: Logical Reasoning A

1   Flaw
2   Complete the Passage
3   Point
4   Flaw
5   Necessary Assumption
6   Principle (Identify)
7   Paradox
8   Method (Argument)
9   Weaken
10 Sufficient Assumption
11 Paradox
12 Weaken
13 Must Be True
14 Principle (Apply)
15 Complete the Passage
16 Flaw
17 Most Strongly Supported
18 Necessary Assumption
19 Flaw
20 Paradox
21 Parallel (Flaw)
22 Sufficient Assumption
23 Principle (Identify)
24 Necessary Assumption
25 Strengthen
26 Principle (Apply)

Section 3: Logic Games

1   Simple Ordering – Limited Scenarios
2   Undetermined Assignment – Limited Scenarios
3   Determined Assignment – Limited Scenarios
4   In/Out Grouping

Section 4: Logical Reasoning B

1   Sufficient Assumption
2   Principle (Identify)
3   Paradox
4   Point
5   Flaw
6   Parallel (Flaw)
7   Method (Statement)
8   Strengthen
9   Principle (Identify)
10 Point
11 Principle (Apply)
12 Necessary Assumption
13 Flaw
14 Sufficient Assumption
15 Flaw
16 Necessary Assumption
17 Most Strongly Supported
18 Necessary Assumption
19 Must Be True
20 Necessary Assumption
21 Weaken
22 Parallel (Reasoning)
23 Weaken
24 Necessary Assumption
25 Paradox

PrepTest 77 (December 2015)

Section 1: Reading Comprehension

1   Humanities
2   Law
3   Social Sciences – Comparative
4   Natural Sciences

Section 2: Logical Reasoning A

1   Strengthen
2   Strengthen
3   Necessary Assumption
4   Weaken

5	Parallel (Flaw)	16	Principle (Identify)
6	Necessary Assumption	17	Method (Argument)
7	Strengthen	18	Flaw
8	Principle (Identify)	19	Paradox
9	Sufficient Assumption	20	Method (Statement)
10	Evaluate	21	Principle (Apply)
11	Main Conclusion	22	Flaw
12	Principle (Apply)	23	Must Be True
13	Complete the Passage	24	Necessary Assumption
14	Flaw	25	Cannot Be True – Except
15	Sufficient Assumption		

Section 3: Logic Games

1	Simple Ordering – Limited Solutions	3	Miscellaneous
2	Simple Ordering	4	Undetermined Assignment – Limited Allocations

Section 4: Logical Reasoning B

1	Principle (Identify)
2	Point
3	Paradox
4	Strengthen
5	Complete the Passage
6	Flaw
7	Method (Statement)
8	Main Conclusion
9	Flaw
10	Cannot Be True
11	Weaken
12	Flaw
13	Must Be True
14	Method (Statement)
15	Most Strongly Supported
16	Method (Statement)
17	Principle (Apply)
18	Must Be True
19	Weaken
20	Sufficient Assumption
21	Paradox – Except
22	Method (Statement)
23	Parallel (Reasoning)
24	Sufficient Assumption
25	Parallel (Flaw)
26	Necessary Assumption

Appendix A: Logic Games Conversions

Cambridge LSAT	Manhattan (MLG)	PowerScore (LGB)
Relative Ordering	Relative Ordering	Pure Sequencing
Simple Ordering	Basic Ordering	Basic Linear: Balanced
	Mismatch Ordering	Basic Linear: Unbalanced
Complex Ordering	3D Ordering	Advanced Linear
In/Out Grouping	Open Conditional Grouping	Grouping: Partially Defined
		Grouping: Undefined
	Closed Conditional Grouping	Grouping: Defined
Grouping (Distribution)	Basic Grouping	Grouping: Defined-Fixed
	3D Grouping	
Determined Assignment	Hybrid	Grouping/Linear Combination
Undetermined Assignment	Open Grouping	Grouping: Partially Defined-Moving
Miscellaneous	Other	Pattern
		Circular Linearity
		Mapping

Keep in mind that these are rough approximations, as the types don't always line up perfectly.

Cambridge LSAT	Blueprint Prep (BPLG)
Relative Ordering	Basic Ordering
Simple Ordering	1:1 Ordering
	Under/Overbooked Ordering
Complex Ordering	Tiered Ordering
In/Out Grouping	In and Out Grouping
Grouping (Distribution)	Two Groups
	Two or More Groups
Determined Assignment	Combo
Undetermined Assignment	Profiling
Miscellaneous	Neither
Limited Allocations	Play the Numbers
Limited Scenarios	Scenarios

Keep in mind that these are rough approximations, as the types don't always line up perfectly.

Appendix B: Logical Reasoning Conversions

Cambridge LSAT	Manhattan (MLR)	PowerScore (LRB)
Must Be True	Inference	Must Be True/Most Supported
Most Strongly Supported		
Complete the Passage		Main Point—Fill in the Blank
Cannot Be True		Cannot Be True
Main Conclusion	Identify the Conclusion	Main Point
Principle (Identify)	Principle Support	Principle*
Principle (Apply)	Principle Example	
Necessary Assumption	Necessary Assumptions	Assumption
Sufficient Assumption	Sufficient Assumptions	Justify the Conclusion
Method (Argument)	Procedure	Method of Reasoning
Method (Statement)	Determine the Function	Method of Reasoning—Argument Part
Strengthen	Strengthen and Weaken	Strengthen/Support
Weaken		Weaken
Evaluate		Evaluate the Argument
Parallel (Reasoning)	Match the Reasoning	Parallel Reasoning
Parallel (Flaw)	Match the Flaw	Parallel Flaw
Point	Identify the Disagreement	Point at Issue
Flaw	Identify a Flaw	Flaw in the Reasoning
Paradox	Explain a Result	Resolve the Paradox

* Note that PowerScore considers Principle to be an overlay of other question types as opposed to its own question type.

Appendix C: PrepTest Usage

With this chart, you can plan out your usage of the various PrepTests. In the usage column, write "drilling," "sections," or "full-length," depending on your plan for that particular test.

PT	Month/Year	Book	Usage
J07	June 2007	June 2007 LSAT PrepTest	
A	February 1996	The Official LSAT SuperPrep	
B	February 1999	The Official LSAT SuperPrep	
C	February 2000	The Official LSAT SuperPrep	
C2	Unknown	The Official LSAT SuperPrep II	
1	June 1991		
2	October 1991		
3	December 1991		
4	June 1992		
5	October 1992		
6	December 1992		
7	June 1993	10 Actual, Official LSAT PrepTests	
8	October 1993		
9	December 1993	10 Actual, Official LSAT PrepTests	
10	June 1994	10 Actual, Official LSAT PrepTests	
11	October 1994	10 Actual, Official LSAT PrepTests	
12	December 1994	10 Actual, Official LSAT PrepTests	
13	June 1994	10 Actual, Official LSAT PrepTests	
14	October 1995	10 Actual, Official LSAT PrepTests	
15	December 1995	10 Actual, Official LSAT PrepTests	
16	June 1995	10 Actual, Official LSAT PrepTests	
17	October 1995		
18	December 1992	10 Actual, Official LSAT PrepTests	
19	June 1996	10 More Actual, Official LSAT PrepTests	
20	October 1996	10 More Actual, Official LSAT PrepTests	
21	December 1996	10 More Actual, Official LSAT PrepTests	

PT	Month/Year	Book	Usage
22	June 1997	10 More Actual, Official LSAT PrepTests	
23	October 1997	10 More Actual, Official LSAT PrepTests	
24	December 1997	10 More Actual, Official LSAT PrepTests	
25	June 1998	10 More Actual, Official LSAT PrepTests	
26	October 1998	10 More Actual, Official LSAT PrepTests	
27	December 1998	10 More Actual, Official LSAT PrepTests	
28	June 1999	10 More Actual, Official LSAT PrepTests	
29	October 1999	The Next 10 Actual, Official LSAT PrepTests	
30	December 1999	The Next 10 Actual, Official LSAT PrepTests	
31	June 2000	The Next 10 Actual, Official LSAT PrepTests	
32	October 2000	The Next 10 Actual, Official LSAT PrepTests	
33	December 2000	The Next 10 Actual, Official LSAT PrepTests	
34	June 2001	The Next 10 Actual, Official LSAT PrepTests	
35	October 2001	The Next 10 Actual, Official LSAT PrepTests	
36	December 2001	The Next 10 Actual, Official LSAT PrepTests	
37	June 2002	The Next 10 Actual, Official LSAT PrepTests	
38	October 2002	The Next 10 Actual, Official LSAT PrepTests	
39	December 2002		
40	June 2003		
41	October 2003		
42	December 2003		
43	June 2004		
44	October 2004		
45	December 2004		
46	June 2005		
47	October 2005		
48	December 2005		
49	June 2006		
50	October 2006		
51	December 2006		

PT	Month/Year	Book	Usage
52	June 2007	10 New Actual, Official LSAT PrepTests	
53	October 2007	10 New Actual, Official LSAT PrepTests	
54	December 2008	10 New Actual, Official LSAT PrepTests	
55	June 2008	10 New Actual, Official LSAT PrepTests	
56	October 2008	10 New Actual, Official LSAT PrepTests	
57	December 2009	10 New Actual, Official LSAT PrepTests	
58	June 2009	10 New Actual, Official LSAT PrepTests	
59	October 2009	10 New Actual, Official LSAT PrepTests	
60	December 2010	10 New Actual, Official LSAT PrepTests	
61	June 2010	10 New Actual, Official LSAT PrepTests	
62	October 2010	10 Actual, Official LSAT PrepTests Volume V	
63	December 2011	10 Actual, Official LSAT PrepTests Volume V	
64	June 2011	10 Actual, Official LSAT PrepTests Volume V	
65	October 2011	10 Actual, Official LSAT PrepTests Volume V	
66	June 2012	10 Actual, Official LSAT PrepTests Volume V	
67	October 2012	10 Actual, Official LSAT PrepTests Volume V	
68	December 2012	10 Actual, Official LSAT PrepTests Volume V	
69	June 2013	10 Actual, Official LSAT PrepTests Volume V	
70	October 2013	10 Actual, Official LSAT PrepTests Volume V	
71	December 2013	10 Actual, Official LSAT PrepTests Volume V	
72	June 2014	The Official LSAT PrepTest 72 (June 2014)	
73	September 2014	The Official LSAT PrepTest 73 (September 2014)	
74	December 2014	The Official LSAT PrepTest 74 (December 2014)	
75	June 2015	The Official LSAT PrepTest 75 (June 2015)	
76	October 2015	The Official LSAT PrepTest 76 (October 2015)	
77	December 2015	The Official LSAT PrepTest 77 (December 2015)	

Made in the USA
Columbia, SC
26 March 2019